# WORD
# BIBLICAL
# COMMENTARY

*General Editors*
**David A. Hubbard**
**Glenn W. Barker †**

*Old Testament Editor*
**John D. W. Watts**

*New Testament Editor*
**Ralph P. Martin**

# WORD
# BIBLICAL
# COMMENTARY

VOLUME 6A

# Deuteronomy 1-11

# DUANE L. CHRISTENSEN

WORD BOOKS, PUBLISHER • DALLAS, TEXAS

Word Biblical Commentary
DEUTERONOMY 1–11
Copyright © 1991 by Word, Incorporated

**Library of Congress Cataloging-in-Publication Data**
Main entry under title:

Word biblical commentary.

  Includes bibliographies.
    1. Bible—Commentaries—Collected works.
BS491.2.W67    220.7'7    81–71768
ISBN  0–8499–0205–3 (v. 6a)  AACR2

*Printed in the United States of America*

99 00 01 02 QPV 9 8 7 6 5 4

To
Georg Braulik, O. S. B.
and
Norbert Lohfink, S. J.

*Kollegen im Deuteronomiumstudien*

# Contents

viii

# Editorial Preface

The launching of the *Word Biblical Commentary* brings to fulfillment an enterprise of several years' planning. The publishers and the members of the editorial board met in 1977 to explore the possibility of a new commentary on the books of the Bible that would incorporate several distinctive features. Prospective readers of these volumes are entitled to know what such features were intended to be; whether the aims of the commentary have been fully achieved time alone will tell.

First, we have tried to cast a wide net to include as contributors a number of scholars from around the world who not only share our aims, but are in the main engaged in the ministry of teaching in university, college, and seminary. They represent a rich diversity of denominational allegiance. The broad stance of our contributors can rightly be called evangelical, and this term is to be understood in its positive, historic sense of a commitment to Scripture as divine revelation, and to the truth and power of the Christian gospel.

Then, the commentaries in our series are all commissioned and written for the purpose of inclusion in the *Word Biblical Commentary.* Unlike several of our distinguished counterparts in the field of commentary writing, there are no translated works, originally written in a non-English language. Also, our commentators were asked to prepare their own rendering of the original biblical text and to use those languages as the basis of their own comments and exegesis. What may be claimed as distinctive with this series is that it is based on the biblical languages, yet it seeks to make the technical and scholarly approach to a theological understanding of Scripture understandable by—and useful to—the fledgling student, the working minister, and colleagues in the guild of professional scholars and teachers as well.

Finally, a word must be said about the format of the series. The layout, in clearly defined sections, has been consciously devised to assist readers at different levels. Those wishing to learn about the textual witnesses on which the translation is offered are invited to consult the section headed *Notes.* If the readers' concern is with the state of modern scholarship on any given portion of Scripture, they should turn to the sections of *Bibliography* and *Form/Structure/Setting.* For a clear exposition of the passage's meaning and its relevance to the ongoing biblical revelation, the *Comment* and concluding *Explanation* are designed expressly to meet that need. There is therefore something for everyone who may pick up and use these volumes.

If these aims come anywhere near realization, the intention of the editors will have been met, and the labor of our team of contributors rewarded.

General Editors: *David A. Hubbard*
*Glenn W.Barker* †
Old Testament: *John D. W. Watts*
New Testament: *Ralph P. Martin*

# Author's Preface

When I agreed to write this commentary some years ago, I knew it was a major task which would probably shape the course of my academic life for some time. I had no idea, however, that it would cause me to rethink my whole approach to the Bible, both in terms of my teaching experience as a seminary professor preparing pastors for ministry in the church and in my own personal use of the biblical text in reflection, meditation, and prayer. The Bible is much more than I had thought, and concepts like the "Word of God" and "inerrancy" have taken on new meaning because of my personal journey in the Hebrew text of Deuteronomy these several years.

The journey began with a trip to Vienna in August 1980 to present an academic paper at the meeting of the International Organization for the Study of the Old Testament (IOSOT) and to meet a Benedictine monk at the University of Vienna by the name of Georg Braulik, who was secretary of that congress. Norbert Lohfink, a Jesuit scholar, had suggested by mail that I might find it useful to consult with Prof. Braulik in my work on Deuteronomy. The simple fact that Braulik had treated the Hebrew text of Deuteronomy 4 as though it were poetry in the published version of his doctoral dissertation opened whole new worlds of possibilities for inquiry. The first major phase of that journey ended with another trip to Vienna in August 1990 to present an academic paper at an international academic conference— this time at the International SBL (Society of Biblical Literature) meeting—and to work with Georg Braulik once again. It was there that the manuscript for this volume of the commentary reached final form.

This book is dedicated to Professors Georg Braulik, O.S.B., and Norbert Lohfink, S.J., without whose generous assistance, in terms of the sharing of their research, it could not have been written. The format of the Word Biblical Commentary series provides for extensive bibliography at all levels of analysis. The bibliography contained here, though by no means complete, is surely the most extensive yet published on the book of Deuteronomy. For the most part that bibliographical detail is simply copied from the catalogue of entries in the voluminous files of such entries gathered over the course of the past twenty years or so by these two scholars. That bibliography is the basis of their work on the forthcoming volume on Deuteronomy in the Hermeneia series (Fortress Press). In no way, however, should these two scholars be held accountable for the method of analysis adopted in this commentary. That method, with all its limitations, is completely my own.

This particular commentary has two features which separate it from other such works. First, it contains the most extensive bibliography on Deuteronomy yet published. Though only a relatively small portion of this material is actually incorporated into the discussion of specific passages, the references provide an opportunity for the student to enter the world of the secondary literature with relative ease at any specific point of inquiry. The second feature of worth is that of a completely fresh reading and translation of the Hebrew text of Deuteronomy based on the

author's structural and rhythmic analysis of that text. The method of analysis utilized will surely be controversial within the academic community, particularly
because of the implications it may have in relation to some of the established
presuppositions in the field. However the validity of that method may be assessed
by my academic colleagues in the months and years ahead, it has already proved
its heuristic worth for me personally, in that it has provided a new "set of eyeglasses"
through which I am beginning to see what Leonard Thompson once described
as "a more fantastic country" (see L. L. Thompson, *Introducing Biblical Literature:
A More Fantastic Country* [Englewood Cliffs, NJ: Prentice-Hall, 1978]).

I would take this opportunity to offer a public word of thanks to some of my
students at the American Baptist Seminary of the West and the Graduate Theological Union in Berkeley who assisted me in the laborious detail of checking
and completing the bibliographical entries to conform with the form selected
for the Word Biblical Commentary and in the tedious task of proofreading. These
students include Wayne Santos, Virgil Turner, Tom Riley, Penny Schoyer, Bill
McCready, and Eric Thompson. Without their able assistance this long overdue
publication would have been delayed still further.

I am also deeply grateful to the staff of the Flora Lamson Hewlett Library of
the Graduate Theological Union for assistance far beyond the call of duty. I would
single out Oscar Burdick in particular who helped me appreciate the surprising
depth and breadth of that library's holdings in the major European languages so
far as biblical studies are concerned. I expected to find the resources to complete
my bibliographical work. I did not expect to find the vast bulk of those materials
literally at my fingertips. Berkeley is indeed an ideal location for biblical studies.

*Berkeley, California*                                            DUANE L. CHRISTENSEN

# Abbreviations

| | |
|---|---|
| *AAAS* | *Annales archéologiques arabes de Syrie* |
| AASOR | Annual of the American Schools of Oriental Research |
| AB | Anchor Bible |
| *AbLA* | M. Noth, *Aufsätze zur biblischen Landes- und Altertumskunde* |
| *AcOr* | *Acta orientalia*, Leiden |
| ActOr | Acta Orientalia, Copenhagen |
| *AfO* | *Archiv für Orientforschung* |
| AfOBei | Beihefte zur Archiv für Orientforschung |
| ÄgAT | Ägypten und Altes Testament |
| *AHDO* | *Archiv d'histoire du droit oriental* |
| AION | Annali del'istituto universitario orientale di Napoli |
| AJBI | Annual of the Japanese Biblical Institute |
| *AJP* | *American Journal of Philology* |
| *AJSL* | *American Journal of Semitic Languages and Literature* |
| ALGHJ | Arbeiten zur Literatur und Geschichte des hellenistischen Judentums |
| ALUOS | Annual of Leeds University Oriental Society |
| AnBib | Analecta Biblica |
| *ANEP* | J. B. Pritchard (ed.), *Ancient Near East in Pictures* |
| *ANET* | J. B. Pritchard (ed.), *Ancient Near Eastern Texts* |
| AnOr | Analecta orientalia |
| *ANQ* | *Andover Newton Quarterly* |
| *AnSt* | *Anatolian Studies* |
| AOAT | Alter Orient und Altes Testament |
| *AOT* | H. Gressman (ed.), *Altorientalische Texte und Bilder* |
| *ArOr* | *Archiv orientální* |
| *ARW* | *Archiv für Religionswissenschaft* |
| *ASeign* | *Assemblées du Seigneur* |
| ASOR | American Schools of Oriental Research |
| *ASTI* | *Annual of the Swedish Theological Institute* |
| *AsTJ* | *Asbury Theological Journal* |
| ATA | Alttestamentliche Abhandlungen (Münster) |
| ATANT | Abhandlungen zur Theologie des Alten und Neuen Testaments |
| ATD | Das Alte Testament Deutsch |
| *AThD* | *Acta theologica Danica* |
| ATSAT | Arbeiten zu Text und Sprache im Alten Testament |
| *Aug* | *Augustinianum* (Rome) |
| *AUSS* | *Andrews University Seminary Studies* |
| AVTRW | Aufsätze und Vorträge zur Theologie und Religionswissenschaft |

| | |
|---|---|
| AzTh | Arbeiten zur Theologie |
| *BA* | *Biblical Archaeologist* |
| *BARev* | *Biblical Archaeology Review* |
| *BASOR* | *Bulletin of the American Schools of Oriental Research* |
| BAT | Die Botschaft des Alten Testaments |
| BB | Biblische Beiträge, (Fribourg) |
| BBB | Bonner biblische Beiträge |
| *BBC* | *Broadman Bible Commentary* |
| *BCPE* | *Bulletin du Centre protestant d'etudes* |
| BDB | F. Brown, S. R. Driver, and C. A. Briggs, *Hebrew and English Lexicon of the Old Testament* |
| BDBAT | Beiheft Dielheimer Blätter zum Alten Testament |
| *BeO* | *Bibbia e oriente* |
| BETL | Bibliotheca ephemeridum theologicarum lovaniensium |
| BEvT | Beiträge zur evangelischen Theologie |
| BFCT | Beiträge zur Förderung christlicher Theologie |
| BGBE | Beiträge zur Geschichte der biblischen Exegese |
| *BHH* | *Biblisch-historisches Handwörterbuch* |
| *BHK* | R. Kittel (ed.), *Biblia hebraica.* |
| *BHS* | K. Elliger and W. Rudolph (eds.), *Biblia hebraica stuttgartensia* |
| BHTh | Beiträge zur historischen Theologie |
| *Bib* | *Biblica* |
| *BibBh* | *Bible Bhashyam* |
| *BibIll* | *Biblical Illustrator* |
| BibOr | Biblica et orientalia |
| *BibRes* | *Biblical Research* |
| *BIES* | *Bulletin of the Israel Exploration Society* |
| *BiKi* | *Bibel und Kirche* (Stuttgart) |
| *BiOr* | *Bibliotheca Orientalis* (Leiden) |
| *BJRL* | *Bulletin of the John Rylands University Library of Manchester* |
| BJS | Brown Judaic Studies |
| *BLit* | *Bibel und Liturgie* |
| BMS | BIBAL Monograph Series |
| *BMik* | *Beth Mikra* |
| *BN* | *Biblische Notizen* |
| *BO* | *Beiträge zur Orientalistik* |
| *BRev* | *Bible Review* |
| *BSac* | *Bibliotheca Sacra* |
| *BTB* | *Biblical Theology Bulletin* |
| *BThW* | *Bibeltheologisches Wörterbuch* |
| BWANT | Beiträge zur Wissenschaft vom Alten und Neuen Testament |
| *BZ* | *Biblische Zeitschrift* |
| BZAW | Beihefte zur ZAW |
| CahRB | Cahiers de la *Revue biblique* |
| CBC | Cambridge Biblical Commentary |
| CBib | The Cambridge Bible |

| | |
|---|---|
| *CBQ* | *Catholic Biblical Quarterly* |
| *ChrJRel* | *Christian and Jewish Relations* |
| *ChW* | *Christliche Welt* |
| *CJ* | *Concordia Journal* |
| *CMHE* | F. M. Cross, Jr., *Canaanite Myth and Hebrew Epic* |
| *ColT* | *Collectanea Theologica* |
| ConB | Coniectanea biblica |
| *ConBas* | *Concilium Baseliense* |
| *Conc* | *Concilium* |
| *ConsJud* | *Conservative Judaism* |
| CSCO | Corpus scriptorum christianorum orientalium |
| *CT* | *Christianity Today* |
| *CTA* | A. Herdner, *Corpus des tablettes en cunéiformes alphabétiques* |
| CThM | Calwer theologische Monographien |
| *CTQ* | *Concordia Theological Quarterly* |
| *CV* | *Communio viatorum* |
| *Das Deut* | N. Lohfink (ed.), *Das Deuteronomium.* BETL 68 (Leuven UP, 1985). |
| *Das Land* | G. Strecker (ed.), *Das Land in biblischer Zeit.* GTA 25 (Göttingen: Vandenhoeck & Ruprecht, 1983) |
| *DD* | *Dor le Dor* |
| DJD | Discoveries in the Judean Desert |
| DNEB | Die Neue Echter Bibel |
| EB | Echter Bibel |
| Ecout Bib | Écouter la Bible |
| *EglT* | *Eglise et Théologie* |
| *EI* | *Ereṣ Israel* |
| *EncBib* | *Encyclopedia Biblica* (Jerusalem, 1954–75 [Heb.]) |
| *EncJud* | *Encyclopedia Judaica* |
| *EphC* | *Ephemerides Carmeliticae* |
| *EstBib* | *Estudios bíblicos* |
| *EstEcl* | *Estudios Eclesiásticos* |
| *ETL* | *Ephemerides theologicae lovanienses* |
| *ETR* | *Études théologiques et religieuses* |
| ETS | Erfurter theologische Studien |
| *EvQ* | *Evangelical Quarterly* |
| *EvT* | *Evangelische Theologie* |
| *ExpTim* | *Expository Times* |
| FBB | Forschung zur Bibel Band (Echter Verlag) |
| *FolOr* | *Folia Orientalia* |
| FRLANT | Forschungen zur Religion und Literatur des Alten und Neuen Testaments |
| *FZPhTh* | *Freiburger Zeitschrift für Philosophie und Theologie* |
| *GeistLeb* | *Geist und Leben* (Würzburg) |
| *GesStAT* | *Gesammelte Studien zum Alten Testament.* G. von Rad, BT 8 (1965) and 48 (1973); M. Noth, BT 6 (1966) and 39 (1969) (Munich: Kaiser) |
| GKC | Gesenius' Hebrew Grammar, ed. E. Kautzsch; tr. A. E. Cowley |

| | |
|---|---|
| *GLECS* | *Comptes rendus du groupe linguistique d'etudes chamito-sémitiques* |
| *GOST* | *Glasgow Oriental Society Transactions* |
| GTA | Göttinger theologischen Arbeiten |
| HAR | Hebrew Annual Review |
| HAT | Handbuch zum Alten Testament |
| *HBT* | *Horizons in Biblical Theology* |
| HDR | Harvard Dissertations in Religion |
| *Hen* | *Henoch* |
| *Herm* | *Hermathena* |
| HKAT | Handkommentar zum Alten Testament |
| *HOTTP* | *Preliminary and Interim Report on the Hebrew Old Testament Text Project*, vol. 1, Pentateuch. 2nd rev. ed. Eds. D. Barthélemy et al. (New York: United Bible Societies, 1979) |
| HSM | Harvard Semitic Monographs |
| HSS | Harvard Semitic Studies |
| *HTR* | *Harvard Theological Review* |
| *HUCA* | *Hebrew Union College Annual* |
| *IB* | *Interpreter's Bible* |
| *IBHS* | B. K. Waltke and M. O'Connor, *An Introduction to Biblical Hebrew Syntax* (Winona Lake, IN: Eisenbrauns, 1990) |
| *IBS* | *Irish Biblical Studies* |
| ICC | International Critical Commentary |
| *IDB* | G. A. Butrick (ed.), *Interpreter's Dictionary of the Bible* |
| *IDBSup* | Supplementary volume to *IDB* |
| *IEJ* | *Israel Exploration Journal* |
| *IKZ* | *Internationale kirchliche Zeitschrift* |
| *Int* | *Interpretation* |
| *IntDialZ* | *Internationale Dialog Zeitschrift* |
| IOSOT | International Organization for the Study of the Old Testament |
| *ISBE* | G. W. Bromiley (ed.), *International Standard Bible Encyclopedia*, 4 vols. (Grand Rapids: Eerdmans, 1979–1988) |
| IsrOrSt | Israel Oriental Studies, Tel Aviv University |
| *JAAR* | *Journal of the American Academy of Religion* |
| *JANESCU* | *The Journal of the Ancient Near Eastern Society of Columbia University* |
| *JAOS* | *Journal of the American Oriental Society* |
| JAOSSup | Supplement to *JAOS* |
| *JBC* | R. E. Brown et al. (eds.), *The Jerome Biblical Commentary* |
| *JBL* | *Journal of Biblical Literature* |
| JBLMonSer | Journal of Biblical Literature Monograph Series |
| *JBR* | *Journal of Bible and Religion* |
| JBTh | Jahrbuch für Biblische Theologie (Neukirchener Verlag) |
| *JEA* | *Journal of Egyptian Archaeology* |
| *JESHO* | *Journal of the Economic and Social History of the Orient* |
| *JETS* | *Journal of the Evangelical Theological Society* |

| | |
|---|---|
| *JHS* | *Journal of Hellenic Studies* |
| *JJS* | *Journal of Jewish Studies* |
| JLH | Jahrbuch für Liturgik und Hymnologie |
| *JNES* | *Journal of Near Eastern Studies* |
| *JNSL* | *Journal of Northwest Semitic Languages* |
| *JQR* | *Jewish Quarterly Review* |
| *JRAS* | *Journal of the Royal Asiatic Society* |
| *JSJ* | *Journal for the Study of Judaism* |
| *JSOT* | *Journal for the Study of the Old Testament* |
| JSOTSup | *JSOT* Supplement Series |
| *JSS* | *Journal of Semitic Studies* |
| *JThS* | *Journal of Theological Studies* |
| *JTSoA* | *Journal of Theology for Southern Africa* |
| *Jud* | *Judaica* (Zürich) |
| KAT | Kommentar zum Alten Testament |
| *KatBl* | *Katechetische Blätter* |
| KB | L. Koehler and W. Baumgartner, *Lexicon in Veteris Testamenti libros* |
| *KD* | *Kerygma und Dogma* |
| KeH | Kurzgefasstes exegetisches Handbuch zum Alten Testament |
| KHC | Kurzer Hand-Commentar zum Alten Testament |
| *KlSchr* | *Kleine Schriften zur Geschichte des Volkes Israel.* A. Alt, 3 vols. (Munich: Beck, 1953–59); O. Eissfeldt, 6 vols. (Tübingen: Mohr, 1962–79). |
| KT | Kaiser Traktate |
| *Lat* | *Lateranum* |
| LBC | The Layman's Bible Commentary |
| LD | Lectio divina |
| *Leš* | *Lešonénu* |
| *LingBib* | *Linguistica Biblica* |
| *LQ* | *Lutheran Quarterly* |
| *LS* | *Lebendiger Seelsorge* |
| LSSt | Leipziger semitistische Studien |
| *LTJ* | *Lutheran Theological Journal* |
| MANE | Monographs on the Ancient Near East (Leiden: Brill) |
| MBPR | Münchener Beiträge zur Papyrusforschung und antiken Rechtsgeschichte |
| *MDB* | *Le Monde de la Bible* |
| *MGWJ* | *Monatsschrift für Geschichte und Wissenschaft des Judentums* |
| MHUC | Monographs of the Hebrew Union College |
| MThS | Münchener theologische Studien |
| MThSt | Marburger theologische Studien |
| *MThZ* | *Münchener theologische Zeitschrift* |
| MVÄG | Mitteilungen der vorderasiatisch-ägyptischen Gesellschaft |
| NCBC | New Century Bible Commentary |
| *NedTTs* | *Nederlands theologisch tijdschrift* |
| NGAW | Nachrichten der Akademie der Wissenschaften in Göttingen |

| | |
|---|---|
| *NGTT* | *Nederduitse gereformeerde teologiese tydskrif* |
| NICOT | New International Commentary on the Old Testament |
| *NKZ* | *Neue kirchliche Zeitschrift* |
| *NorTT* | *Norsk Teologisk Tidsskrift* |
| *NRT* | *La nouvelle revue théologique* |
| *NThS* | *Nieuwe theologische Studien* |
| *NTS* | *New Testament Studies* (London) |
| OBO | Orbis biblicus et orientalis |
| OLP | Orientalia lovaniensia periodica |
| *OLZ* | *Orientalische Literaturzeitung* |
| *Or* | *Orientalia* |
| *OrAnt* | *Oriens antiquus* |
| OTL | Old Testament Library |
| OTS | Oudtestamentische Studiën |
| *OTWSA* | *Die Ou Testamentiese Werkgemeenskap in Suid-Afrika* (Pretoria) |
| *PalCl* | *Palestra del Clero* |
| *ParVi* | *Parole di Vita* |
| *PEQ* | *Palestine Exploration Quarterly* |
| PG | J. Migne, Patrologiae Cursus Completus, series graeca |
| *PIBA* | *Proceedings of the Irish Biblical Association* |
| *PJ* | *Palästina-Jahrbuch* |
| PL | J. Migne, Patrologiae Cursus Completus, series latina |
| POS | Pretoria Oriental Series |
| *POTT* | D. J. Wiseman (ed.), *People of Old Testament Times* |
| *PRU* | *Le Palais royal d'Ugarit* |
| *PSB* | *Princeton Seminary Bulletin* |
| *PSBA* | *Proceedings of the Society of Biblical Archaeology* |
| QD | Quaestiones disputatae |
| *RA* | *Revue d'assyriologie et d'archéologie orientale* |
| *RB* | *Revue biblique* |
| *RBibIt* | *Rivista Biblica Italiana* (Brescia) |
| RechBib | Recherches bibliques |
| *ResQ* | *Restoration Quarterly* |
| *RevExp* | *Review and Expositor* |
| *RevistBib* | *Revista bíblica* |
| *RevQ* | *Revue de Qumran* |
| *RGG* | *Religion in Geschichte und Gegenwart* |
| *RHPR* | *Revue d'histoire et de philosophie religieuses* |
| *RHR* | *Revue de l'histoire des religions* |
| *RivB* | *Rivista biblica* |
| *RMP* | *Rheinisches Museum für Philologie* |
| *RRel* | *Review for Religious* |
| *RSEHA* | *Revue Sémitique d'epigraphie et d'histoire ancienne* |
| *RSJB* | *Recueils de la société Jean Bodin pour l'histoire comparative des institutions* |
| *RSO* | *Revista degli studi orientali* |
| *RSP* | L. R. Fisher and S. Rummel (eds.), *Ras Shamra Parallels*, AnOr 49–51 |

| | |
|---|---|
| *RSPhTh* | *Revue des sciences philosophiques et théologiques* |
| *RSR* | *Recherches de science religieuse* |
| *RThQR* | *Revue de Théologie et de Questions Religieuses* |
| *Salm* | *Salmaticensis* (Salamanca) |
| SB | Studia Biblica |
| SBAB | Stuttgarter Biblische Aufsatzbände Altes Testament |
| SBEsp | Semana bíblica española |
| *SBFLA* | *Studii biblici Franciscani liber annuus* |
| SBL | Society of Biblical Literature |
| SBLASP | SBL Abstracts and Seminar Papers |
| SBLDS | SBL Dissertation Series |
| SBLMS | SBL Monograph Series |
| SBS | Stuttgarter Bibelstudien |
| SBT | Studies in Biblical Theology |
| SBM | Stuttgarter biblische Monographien |
| *ScEccl* | *Sciences ecclésiastiques* |
| *ScEs* | *Science et esprit* |
| *Schol* | *Scholastik*, Freiburg |
| ScrHier | Scripta hierosolymitana |
| *SDHI* | *Studi et Documenta Historiae et Iuris* |
| *SEÅ* | *Svensk exegetisk årsbok* |
| *SEAJT* | *South East Asia Journal of Theology* |
| *Sem* | *Semitica* |
| SGKA | Studien zur Geschichte und Kultur des Altertums |
| SGKAO | Schriften zur Geschichte und Kultur des Alten Orients |
| SHR | Studies in the History of Religions |
| SJLA | Studies in Judaism in Late Antiquity |
| *SJOT* | *Scandinavian Journal of the Old Testament* |
| *SJT* | *Scottish Journal of Theology* |
| SKGG | Schriften der Königsberger Gelehrten Gesellschaft |
| *SR* | *Studies in Religion / Sciences religieuses* |
| *ST* | *Studia theologica* |
| StANT | Studien zum Alten und Neuen Testament |
| *StMor* | *Studia moralia* |
| *StudBT* | *Studia Biblica et Theologica* |
| *StZ* | *Stimme der Zeit* |
| SUNT | Studien zur Umwelt des Neuen Testaments |
| SWBA | Social World of Biblical Antiquity |
| *SWDS* | *Scrolls from the Wilderness of the Dead Sea* (British Museum, 1965) |
| TBC | Torch Bible Commentaries |
| *TBT* | *The Bible Today* |
| TBü | Theologische Bücherei |
| *TD* | *Theology Digest* |
| TDOT | G. J. Botterweck and H. Ringgren (eds.), *Theological Dictionary of the Old Testament* |
| TEH | Theologische Existenz heute |
| TGUOS | Transactions of the Glasgow University Oriental Society |
| ThA | Theologische Arbeiten |

| | |
|---|---|
| *THAT* | *Theologisches Handwörterbuch zum Alten Testament* |
| *ThBl* | *Theologische Blätter* |
| *ThPh* | *Theologie und Philosophie* |
| *ThQ* | *Theologische Quartalschrift* (Tübingen) |
| ThSt | Theologische Studiën (Utrecht) |
| *ThVers* | *Theologische Versuche* |
| ThViat | Theologia Viatorum |
| ThZ | Theologische Zeitschrift (Basel) |
| *TLZ* | *Theologische Literaturzeitung* |
| TOTC | Tyndale Old Testament Commentaries |
| TRE | Theologische Realenzyklopädie |
| *TRev* | *Theologische Revue* |
| *TRu* | *Theologische Rundschau* |
| *TS* | *Theological Studies* |
| TSJTSA | Texts and Studies of the Jewish Theological Seminary of America |
| *TSK* | *Theologische Studien und Kritiken* |
| TsTNijm | Tijdschrift voor Theologie (Nijmegen) |
| *TT* | *Teologisk Tidsskrift* |
| TThSt | Trierer theologische Studien |
| *TThZ* | *Trierer theologische Zeitschrift* |
| TWAT | G. J. Botterweck, and H. Ringgren (eds.), *Theologisches Wörterbuch zum Alten Testament* |
| TWNT | G. Kittel and G. Friedrich (eds.), *Theologisches Wörterbuch zum Neuen Testament* |
| *TynBul* | *Tyndale Bulletin* |
| UCPNES | University of California Publications in Near Eastern Studies |
| *UF* | *Ugarit-Forschungen* |
| *UT* | C. H. Gordon, *Ugaritic Textbook* |
| *VC* | *Vigilae christianae* |
| *VD* | *Verbum domini* |
| *VetChr* | *Vetera Christianorum* |
| *VT* | *Vetus Testamentum* |
| VTSup | *VT* Supplements |
| WBT | Wiener Beiträge zur Theologie |
| *WD* | *Wort und Dienst* |
| WF | Wege der Forschung |
| WMANT | Wissenschaftliche Monographien zum Alten und Neuen Testament |
| *WO* | *Die Welt des Orients* |
| *WoWa* | *Wort und Wahrheit* |
| *Wor* | *Worship* |
| *WTJ* | *Westminster Theological Journal* |
| WUNT | Wissenschaftliche Untersuchungen zum Neuen Testament |
| YJS | Yale Judaica Series |
| *ZA* | *Zeitschrift für Assyriologie* |
| *ZAW* | *Zeitschrift für die alttestamentliche Wissenschaft* |
| *ZDMG* | *Zeitschrift der deutsche morgenländischen Gesellschaft* |

| ZDPV | *Zeitschrift der deutschen Palästina-Vereins* |
| ZEE | *Zeitschrift für evangelische Ethik* |
| ZTK | *Zeitschrift für Theologie und Kirche* |
| ZVS | *Zeitschrift für Völkerpsychologie und Sprachwissenschaft* |
| ZWT | *Zeitschrift für wissenschaftliche Theologie* |
| ZZ | *Die Zeichen der Zeit* |

## TEXTS, VERSIONS, AND ANCIENT WORKS

| | | | |
|---|---|---|---|
| Akk | Akkadian | LXX<sup>A</sup> | LXX Ms, Alexandrian Codex |
| Arab | Arabic | | |
| Aram | Aramaic | LXX<sup>B</sup> | LXX Ms, Vatican Codex |
| B | MT Ms, edited by Jacob ben Chayim, Venice (1524/25) | LXX<sup>S*</sup> | LXX Ms, Sinai Codex, original reading |
| | | LXX<sup>Sc</sup> | LXX Ms, Sinai Codex, corrector |
| Copt | Coptic | | |
| DSS | Dead Sea Scrolls | MT | Masoretic Text |
| Egy | Egyptian | Q | Qere |
| Eng. | English | SP | Samaritan Pentateuch |
| Eth | Ethiopic | Syh | Syrohexaplaris |
| Fr. | French | Syr | Syriac |
| Ger. | German | Tg | Targum |
| Gr. | Greek | Tg<sup>J</sup> | Targum Jonathan |
| Heb. | Hebrew | Ug/Ugar | Ugaritic |
| K | Kethibh | Vg | Vulgate |
| L | MT Ms, Leningrad Codex | Vss | ancient versions |
| | | α' | Aquila |
| LXX | Septuagint | Θ' | Theodotion |
| | | σ' | Symmachus |

## HEBREW GRAMMAR

| | | | |
|---|---|---|---|
| abs | absolute | hoph | hophal |
| acc | accusative | impf | imperfect |
| act | active | impv | imperative |
| adv acc | adverbial accusative | ind | indicative |
| c | common | inf | infinitive |
| conj | conjunction, conjunctive | juss | jussive |
| | | masc | masculine |
| consec | consecutive | niph | niphal |
| constr | construct | pass | passive |
| def art | definite article | pf | perfect |
| disj | disjunctive | pilp | pilpel |
| du | dual | pl | plural |
| fem | feminine | prep | preposition |
| fut | future | ptcp | participle |
| hiph | hiphil | sg | singular |
| hithp | hithpael | suff | suffix(es) |

## BIBLICAL AND APROCRYPHAL BOOKS

| | | | |
|---|---|---|---|
| Gen | Genesis | Hos | Hosea |
| Exod | Exodus | Joel | Joel |
| Lev | Leviticus | Amos | Amos |
| Num | Numbers | Obad | Obadiah |
| Deut | Deuteronomy | Jonah | Jonah |
| Josh | Joshua | Mic | Micah |
| Judg | Judges | Nah | Nahum |
| Ruth | Ruth | Hab | Habakkuk |
| 1–2 Sam | 1–2 Samuel | Zeph | Zephaniah |
| 1–2 Kgs | 1–2 Kings | Hag | Haggai |
| 1–2 Chr | 1–2 Chronicles | Zech | Zechariah |
| Ezra | Ezra | Mal | Malachi |
| Neh | Nehemiah | Sir | Ecclesiasticus or The |
| Esth | Esther | | Wisdom of Jesus Son |
| Job | Job | | of Sirach |
| Ps(s) | Psalm(s) | Matt | Matthew |
| Prov | Proverbs | Mark | Mark |
| Eccl | Ecclesiastes | Luke | Luke |
| Cant | Canticles, Song of Songs | Rom | Romans |
| Isa | Isaiah | Phil | Philippians |
| Jer | Jeremiah | Gal | Galatians |
| Lam | Lamentations | Heb | Hebrews |
| Ezek | Ezekiel | Rev | Revelation |
| Dan | Daniel | | |

## MISCELLANEOUS

| | | | |
|---|---|---|---|
| ANE | Ancient Near East | KJV | King James Version |
| B.C.E. | Before Common Era, Before Christ | lit. | literally |
| | | Ms(s) | manuscript(s) |
| c. | century | n. | note |
| ca. | circa | n.d. | no date |
| C.E. | Common Era (A.D.) | NEB | New English Bible |
| chap(s). | chapter(s) | NIV | New International Version |
| col(s). | column(s) | n.s. | new series |
| conj | conjunction; conjunctive | NT | New Testament |
| diss. | dissertation | OT | Old Testament |
| ed(s). | edition; edited by; editor(s) | p(p). | page(s) |
| | | repr. | reprint |
| esp. | especially | RSV | Revised Standard Version |
| ET | English translation | tr. | translated; translator |
| EV(V) | English verse(s) | UP | University Press |
| FS | Festschrift | v(v) | verse(s) |
| *hap. leg.* | *hapax legomenon* | § | section/paragraph |

# Main Bibliography

A Chronological Bibliography of Commentaries on Deuteronomy
(cited in the *Commentary* by author and date)

For a survey of works on Deuteronomy, see: **Cross, L. B.** "Commentaries on Deuteronomy." *Theology* 64 (1961) 184–89. **Preuss, H. D.** *Deuteronomium.* Erträge der Forschung 164. Darmstadt: Wissenschaftliche Buchgesellschaft, 1982. 203–43.

Commentaries by the *church fathers* are listed here chronologically, with the date of the book or a date pertaining to the author in parentheses after the author's name: **Origen** (ca. 250). *Selecta.* PG 12, 805–18.————. Adnotationes. PG 17, 23–36. **Hieronymus** (Jerome) (410). PG 28, 451–504. **Augustine** (354–430). *Locutiones.* PL 34, 531–38.————. *Opus Quaestionum.* PL 34, 747–76. **Cyril of Alexandria** (441). PG 69, 643–78. **Theodoretus of Cyrrhus** (457). PG 80, 401–56. **Procopius of Gaza** (538). PG 87, 891–992. **Paterius** (ca. 600). PL 79, 773–84. **Isidore of Seville** (636). PL 83, 359–70. **Bede** (673–735). PL 91, 189–394. **Pseudo–Bede** (ca. 800). PL 93, 409–16. **Walafrid Strabo** (849). PL 93, 67–506. **Rabanus Maurus** (856). PL 108, 839–998. Only fragments remain of the commentary by **Diodorus of Tarsus** (394). PG 33, 1585–86; PL 50, 781–82.

In recent years there has been renewed interest in the study of *early Jewish commentary* on Deuteronomy. See in particular: **Hammer, R.** (ed.). *Sifre: A Tannaitic Commentary on the Book of Deuteronomy.* YJS 24. New Haven: Yale, 1986. **Neusner, J.** *Sifre to Deuteronomy; An Analytical Translation,* I, II. BJS 98, 101. Atlanta: Scholars, 1987.————. *Sifre to Deuteronomy: An Introduction to the Rhetorical, Logical, and Topical Program,* III. BJS 124. Atlanta: Scholars, 1987.

Commentaries by *medieval Jewish scholars* primarily in France, Spain, and North Africa who wrote in Hebrew include: **Saadia ben Joseph** (882–942). **Ibn Janah (Jonah)** (ca. 1000–1050). **Rashi (Solomon ben Isaac)** (1040–1105). **Rashbam (Shemuel ben Meir)** (1080–1174). **Ibn Ezra (Abraham ben Meir)** (1089–1164). **Bekhor Shor (Joseph ben Isaac)** (12th c.). **Judah ben Samuel he-Hasid** (1150–1217, Regensburg). **Radak (David Kimchi)** (1160–1235). **Ramban (Moshe ben Nahman** or **Nahmanides)** (1194–1270). **Bahya ben Asher** (1291). **Hizkuni (Hezekiah ben Manoah)** (13th c.). **Aaron ben Joseph ha-Rofe (Aaron the Elder)** (1250–1320). **Ralbag (Levi ben Gershon or Gersonides)** (1288–1344). **Aaron ben Elijah (Aaron the Younger)** (1328–1369). **Abravanel (Isaac ben Judah)** (1437–1508). **Sforno (Obadiah ben Jacob)** (15th-c. Italy).

Renewed scholarly interest is making some of this material more readily available for detailed study in such works as: *Ibn Ezra's Commentary on the Pentateuch.* Tr. H. N. Strickmann and A. M. Silver. New York: Menorah, 1988. **Bechor-Schor, J**. *Der Pentateuch-Kommentar des Joseph Bechor-Schor zum fünften Buche Moses.* Breslau: Koebnersche, 1914 [Heb.]. **Rashi**. *Sefer Debarim.* Wilna, 1886. **Silbermann, A. M.** (tr.). *Pentateuch Rashi's Commentary.* London, 1933. **Lehmann, M. R.** (ed.). *The Commentary of Rashi on the Pentateuch by R. Shlomo Yitzhaki* (1040–1105). Berliners Edition and Sefer ha-Zikkaron, based on the first printed edition (Reggio de Calabria, 1475). New York: Manfred and Anne Lehmann Foundation, 1981. **Ramban (Nachmanides)**. *Commentary to the Pentateuch.* Jerusalem: Makor Publishing Ltd., n.d. [facsimile copy of 1470? ed.]. *Commentary on the Torah: Deuteronomy.* Tr. C. B. Chavel. New York: Shilo Publishing House, 1976. **Rosin, D.** (ed.). *Der Pentateuch-Commentar des R. Samuel ben*

*Meir* (Rashbam). Breslau, 1881. **Sforno, O.** *Sforno Commentary on the Torah.* Tr. R. Pelcovitz. The ArtScroll Mesora Series, vol. 2. Brooklyn: Mesora Publications, 1989. See also the commentary by **S. Fisch** (1947).

Commentaries by *Christian scholars in the Middle Ages* include: **Peter Damian** (1007–72). PL 145, 1063–1070. **Bruno of Astensis** (1032–1101). PL 164, 505–50. **Rupert of Deutz** (1070–1129). PL 167, 917–1000. **Hugh of St. Victor** (1096–1141). PL 175, 29–86. **Peter the Chanter** (1197) [See Dahan, G. "Les interprétations juives dans les commentaires du pentateuque de Pierre le Chantre." In *The Bible in the Medieval World: Essays in Memory of Beryl Smalley.* Ed. K. Walsh and D. Wood. Studies in Church History, Subsidia 4. Oxford: Basil Blackwell, 1985. 131–55]. **Nicholas of Lyra** (1270–1349). Postilla Super Totam Bibliam, I. Frankfurt/Main: Minerva GmbH., 1971 [rep. of Strassburg 1492 ed.]. **Denis le Chartreux** (Dionysius the Carthusian) (1402–71). In *Opera Omnia.* Montreuil, 1896 II. 519–721.

Among *Protestant Reformers* who returned the Church to an emphasis on the Bible, see: **Luther, M.** *Vorlesung über das Deuteronomium.* 1523/24.————. *Deuteronomion Mose cum Annotationibus.* Wittenberg: Hans Luft, 1525 [See *Lectures on Deuteronomy.* Luther's Works, vol. 9. Saint Louis: Concordia, 1960]. **Calvin, J.** *Commentarii Ioannis Calvini in Quinque Libros Mosis.* Geneva: Gaspar, 1573.————. *Sermons upon Deuteronomie.* Tr. by A. Golding. Folio, 1583.————. *Commentaries on the Four Last Books of Moses Arranged in the Form of a Harmony,* 2 vols. Grand Rapids, MI: Baker Book House, 1981.

Commentaries on the part of *Roman Catholic scholars* in the century after the Council of Trent include: **Sanctis Pagnini** (1470–1541) [See *Commentario in Mosi Pentateuchum.* Ed. Hieronymus ab Oleastro. Antwerp, 1568]. **Cornelius a Lapide** (Antwerp, 1623) [See "Commentaria in Deuteronomium." In *Commentarii in Scripturam Sacram,* Tomus I. Paris: J. P. Pelagaud et Socios, 1854. 959–1147. See also "In Deuteronomium Commentarium." In *Scripturae Sacrae Cursus Completus,* Tomus VII. Paris: J.-P Migne Ed., 1861. 125–498]. **Bonfrère, J.** (Antwerp, 1625). **Menochius, G. S.** (Lyon, 1627). **Tirin, J.** (Lyon, 1632) [see *Universam S. Scripturam Commentarius.* Ed. P. Zachariae and P. J. Brunengo. Taurini: Eq. Petri Marietti, 1882. I, 676–752]. **Jansenius, C.** (Leuven, 1641). **Malvenda, T.** (Lyon, 1650). **Calmet, A.** (Paris, 1707) [See *Commentarius Literalis in omnes Libros Veteris Testamenti.* Ed. J. D. Mansi. Wirceburgi Sumtibus Publicis, 1789. II, 524–839]. **Mansi, I. D.** (Venice, 1754).

*Other commentaries before 1800* include: **Bar Hebraeus, G. A.** (1226–85). *A Commentary to Deuteronomy.* Ed. G. Kerber. Chicago: Univ. of Chicago Press, 1897. **Bugenhagen, J.** *Annotationes ab ipso iam emissae: In Deuteronomium.* Basil: Petri, 1524. **Rabani Mavri.** *Commentaria, antehac nunquam typis excusa.* Mense Martio, 1532. **Pellicanus, C.** (1478–1556). *In Pentateuchum, sive Quinque libros Mosis . . . commentarii.* Tigvri: Christophorvs Froschovervs, 1582. **Spangenberg, C.** *In sacri Mosis Pentateuchum.* Basil, 1564. **Pelargi, C.** *In Deuteronomium Sacrum; sive, Quintum librum Mosis commentarius.* Leipzig: Lambergi, 1608. **Piscator, J.** *Commentarius in Deuteronomium.* Herbornae Nassov, 1615. **Drusius, J.** *Ad loca difficiliora Pentateuchi, Quinque liborum Mosis commentarius Conscriptus.* Franekerae Frisiorum, 1617. **Marius, L.** *Commentariorum . . . in universam S. Scripturam.* Dvsseldorpffii: Coloniae Agrippinae, 1621. **Lorini, J.** *Commentarii in Deuteronomium.* Lugduni: Cardon, 1629. **Ainsworth, H.** *Annotations upon the Five Bookes of Moses.* London: M. Parsons, 1639. **Gerhard, J.** (1634). *Commentarius super Deuteronomium.* Jena, 1657. **Henry, M.** (1662–1714). *An Exposition of the Five Books of Moses.* Edinburgh: Lunisden & Robertson, 1757. **Le Maistre, I. L.** *Le Deuteronome.* Paris: G. Desprez, 1685. **Kidder, R.** *A Commentary on the Five Books of Moses.* London: J. Heptinstall, 1694. **Leclerc, J.** *Mosis prophetae libri quatuor: Exodus, Leviticus, Numeri, et Deuteronomium.* Amstelodami: Wetstenium, 1696. **Frassen, C.** *Disquisitiones Biblicae in universum Pentateuchum.* Paris: P. Witte, 1705. **Parker, S.** (ed.). *Bibliotheca biblica: Being a Commentary upon . . . the Old and New Testament.* Oxford, 1720. **Guillemin, P.** *Commentaire*

*littéral abrégé sur les livres de l'ancien et du Nouveau Testament.* Paris: Emery, 1721. **Patrick, S.**
*Commentary on the Pentateuch.* London, 1727?. **[Anonymous]** *Explication de cinq chapitres du*
*Deutéronome; et des prophéties d'Habacuc, et de Jonas.* Paris: Babuty, 1734 [Deut 29–33]. **Jameson,**
**R.** *A Critical and Practical Exposition of the Pentateuch.* London: Knapton, 1748 [rep. in
Philadelphia: Martien, 1860]. **Teller, R.** *Die Heilige Schrift des Alten und Neuen Testaments,*
*nebst einer vollständigen Erklärung derselben.* Leipzig: Bernhard Christoph Breitkopf, 1750. II,
659–1013. **Wesley, J.** (1765–66). See *Wesley's Notes on the Bible.* Grand Rapids: Zondervan,
1987. 134–51. **Arguiti, Y. B.** (1773), *Debarim,* 3 vols. In *MeAm Lóez.* The Torah Anthology,
vols. 15–17 [Deut 1:1–21:9]. Tr. A. Kaplan and S. Yerushalmi. New York and Jerusalem:
Maznaim, 1984–85. **Michaelis, J. H.** (1717–91). See *Commentaries on the Laws of Moses.* Tr. A.
Smith. London: Rivington, 1814.

For purposes of convenience the writing of commentaries on Deuteronomy in
the *nineteenth and twentieth centuries* may be divided into four phases: 1805–1894;
1894–1943; 1943–1963; and 1963–present, each of which is introduced by a major
breakthrough in critical study: namely, W. L. de Wette's 1805 dissertation on
Deuteronomy, which laid the cornerstone for the edifice of pentateuchal literary
criticism; the simultaneous, but independent, publications of C. Steuernagel and
W. Staerk in 1894, which introduced redaction critical study of Deuteronomy based
primarily on the so-called *Numeruswechsel* (see *Excursus* below); the publication of
M. Noth's theory that ties the study of Deuteronomy to the so-called deuteronomic
(or deuteronomistic) history (Joshua through 2 Kings), which eventually led to
what is today called canonical criticism; and N. Lohfink's "stylistic" analysis of
Deut 5–11 in 1963, which suggests unity of authorship and opens the door to
new models for understanding the canonical process in ancient Israel.

PHASE ONE (1805–94): **Vater, J. S.** *Commentar über den Pentateuch. III: Deuteronomium.* Halle:
Verlag der Waisenhaus-Buchhandlung, 1805. **Clarke, A.** (1811–16). "The Fifth Book of
Moses Called Deuteronomy." In *The Holy Bible: with a Commentary and Critical Notes.* Nash-
ville: Abingdon, n.d. I, 734–848. **Benson, J.** (1815). "Critical, Explanatory, and Practical
Notes." In *The Holy Bible.* New York: G. Lane & C. B. Tippett, 1846. 483–587. **Bellamy, J.**
*The Holy Bible, newly translated . . . with notes, critical and explanatory.* London: Longman, 1818
[includes Pentateuch only]. **Rosenmüller, E. F. K.** *Scholia in Vetus Testamentum,* vol. 2:
Leviticus, Numeri, Deuteronomion. Leipzig: J. A. Bartius, 1821. **Scott, T.** *The Holy Bible*
*Containing the Old and New Testaments,* 5 vols. Boston: Samuel T. Armstrong, 1823. I, 488–
585. **Amat, D. F.** "Libro del Deuteronomio." In *La Sagrada Biblia Nuevamente Traducida de*
*la Vulgata al Español.* Madrid: Don Leon Amarita, 1824. II, 3–102. **Felipe, D. scio de San**
**Miguel.** "El Deuteronomio." In *La Biblia Vulgata Latina Traducida en Español, y Anotada*
*Confrome al sentido de los Santos Padres y Espositores Católicos.* Mégico: En Casa de Cornelio C.
Sebring, 1831. II, 323–478. **Brentano, D. von.** *Die Heilige Schrift des Alten Testament.* 1. Theils
dritter Band, welcher das 5. Buch Mosis entahalt. Frankfurt am Main: Varrentrapp, 1832.
**Maurer, F. J. V. D.** "Deuteronomium." In *Commentarius Grammaticus Criticus in Vetus*
*Testamentum.* Leipzig: Fridericus Volckmar, 1835. I, 74–97. **Baumgarten, M.** *Theologischer*
*Commentar zum Pentateuch. Erste Hälfte: Vom Anfang bis zum Gesetz.* 1843. *Zweite Hälfte:*
*Gesetzgebung.* Kiel: Universitätsbuchhandlung, 1843, 1844. **Kalisch, M.** *A Historical and*
*Critical Commentary on the Old Testament.* London: Longman, 1855. **Schultz, Fr. W.** *Das*
*Deuteronomium erklärt.* Berlin: Schlawitz, 1859. **Knobel, A. W.** *Die Bücher Numeri, Deuteronomium*
*und Josua. Nebst einer Kritik des Pentateuchs und Josua.* KeH 13. Leipzig: S. Hirzel, 1861. **Keil,**
**C. F.** *Biblischer Commentar über das Alte Testament,* 2 vols. Leipzig: Dörffling und Franke, 1865
[²1870; ET, *Biblical Commentary on the Old Testament.* Edinburgh: Clark, 1864–65].
**Feilchenfeld, W.** *Die zwei letzten Abschnitte des Pentateuch's übersetzt und erklärt.* Düsseldorf: W.
de Haen, 1866. **Schroeder, F. W. J.** *Das Deuteronomium.* Theologisch-homiletisches Bibelwerk.

Bielefeld: Velhagen & Klasing, 1866 [ET enlarged by A. Gosman. New York: Scribner's Sons, 1879]. **Jamieson, R.** "The Fifth Book of Moses, Called Deuteronomy."In *The Critical and Explanatory Pocket Bible.* Glasgow: William Collins, 1870. I, 131–58. **Lees, R. L.** and **Burns, D.** "The Book of Deuteronomy." In *The Temperance Bible-Commentary.* London: S. W. Partridge & Co., ³1872 [²1868]. **Du Clot, M.** "Notes sur le Deutéronome." In *La Sainte Bible Vengée des Attaques de l'Incrédulité.* Paris: Librairie de Louis Vivès, 1875. II, 352–71. **Jamieson, R., Faussett, A. R.** and **Brown, D.** (ca. 1875). "The Fifth Book of Moses, Called Deuteronomy." In *A Commentary: Critical, Experimental and Practical on the Old and New Testaments.* Grand Rapids: Eerdmans, 1948. I, 620–715. **M[ackintosh], C. H.** *Notes on the Book of Deuteronomy.* 2 vols. Chicago: Revell, 1880. **Dillman, A.** *Die Bücher Numeri, Deuteronomium und Josua.* KeH 13. 2nd ed. rev. Leipzig: S. Hirzel, 1886. **Fillion, L.** *Biblia Sacra, juxta Vulgatae exemplaria et correctoria romana.* Paris, 1887. **Trochon, C.** *Introduction a l'étude de l'Écriture Sainte d'aprés "La Sainte Bible avec commentaires."* Paris: P. Lethielleux, 1889. **Waller, C. H.** *The Fifth Book of Moses, Called Deuteronomy.* Ed. C. J. Ellicott. The Handy Commentary on the Old Testament, 5. New York, n.d. [188–?]. **Anonymous.** "Deuteronomy." In *The Sermon Bible.* New York: Funk & Wagnalls, [189–?]. I/1, 303–56. **Weill, A.** *Le cinq livres de Moïse.* Paris, 1890–91. **Lindsay, J. W.** *Deuteronomy.* Commentary on the Old Testament. Ed. D. D. Whedon. New York: Eaton, 1891. **Montet, F.** *Le Deutéronome et la Question de l'Hexateuque. Étude critique et exégétique sous form de'introduction et de commentaire du Deutéronome considéré dans ses rapports avec les quatre premiers livres Pentateuque et Josué.* Paris, 1891. **Westphal, A.** *Le Deutéronome.* Toulouse, 1891. **Oettli, S.** *Das Deuteronomium und die Bücher Josua und Richter.* Kurzgefasster Kommentar zu den heiligen Schriften Alten und Neuen Testaments. Ed. H. Strack and O. Zöckler. Munich, 1893.

PHASE TWO (1894–1943): **Driver, S. R.** *A Critical and Exegetical Commentary on Deuteronomy.* ICC. Edinburgh: T & T Clark, 1895. **Espin, T. E.** "Deuteronomy." In *The Holy Bible with an Explanatory and Critical Commentary.* Ed F. C. Cook. New York: Charles Scribner's Sons, 1895. I/1, 790–928. **Harper, A.** *The Book of Deuteronomy.* The Expositor's Bible. London: Hodder & Stoughton, 1895. **Moulton, R. G.** *Deuteronomy.* The Modern Reader's Bible. New York: Macmillan, 1896. **Steuernagel, C.** *Das Deuteronomium.* HAT I/3. Göttingen: Vandenhoeck & Ruprecht, 1898 [²1923]. **Bertholet, A.** *Deuteronomium.* KHC 5. Ed. K. Marti. Tübingen: Mohr, 1899. **Girdlestone, R. B.** *The Student's Deuteronomy.* London, New York: Eyre and Spottiswoode, 1899. **Steuernagel, C.** *Übersetzung und Erklärung der Bücher Deuteronomium und Josua und allgemeine Einleitung in den Hexateuch.* HKAT I/3. Göttingen: Vandenhoeck & Ruprecht, 1900 [²1923]. **Hummelauer, F. von.** *Commentarius in Deuteronomium.* Cursus Scripturae Sacrae III, 2. Paris: Sumptibus P. Lethielleux, 1901. **Schroeder, W. J.** *Das Deuteronomium oder das Fünfte Buch Mose.* Theologisch-homiletisches Bibelwerk. Ed. J. P. Lange. Teil 3. Zweite verbesserte Auflage. Ed. G. Stosch. Bielefeld and Leipzig, 1902. **Wilkins, G.** *The Fifth Book of Moses, Called Deuteronomy.* The Temple Bible, 5. London, Philadelphia: J. B. Lippincott, 1902. **Gray, J. C.** and **Adams, G. M.** "The Book of Deuteronomy." In *The Biblical Encyclopedia.* Cleveland: F. M. Barton, 1903. I, 457–553. **Robinson, H. W.** *Deuteronomy and Joshua.* New Century Bible. Oxford UP, 1907. **Hoberg, G.** *Exegetisches Handbuch zum Pentateuch mit hebräischem Text und lateinischem Text.* Freiburg: Herder, 1908. **Dummelow, J. R.** (ed). "Deuteronomy." In *A Commentary on the Holy Bible.* New York: Macmillan, 1909. 121–40. **Gressmann, H.** *Die Schriften des Alten Testament.* Göttingen, 1910. **Jordan, W. G.** *Commentary on the Book of Deuteronomy.* New York: Macmillan, 1911. **Hoffmann, D.** *Das Buch Deuteronomium. Erster Halbband: Deut. I-XX, 9.* Berlin, 1913; *Zweiter Halbband: Deut. XXI, 16–XXXI.* Berlin: Poppelauer, 1922. **Maclagan, H.** *The Book of Deuteronomy Intepreted and Explained.* Paisley: Gardner, 1914. **Betteridge, W. R.** *The Book of Deuteronomy.* An American Commentary on the OT, 2. Philadelphia: American Baptist Publication Society, 1915. **König, E.** *Das Deuteronomium.* KAT 3. Leipzig: A Deichert, 1917. **Smith, G. A.** *The Book of Deuteronomy.* CBib. Cambridge: Cambridge UP, 1918. **Witton, D. T.** "Deuteronomy." In *Peake's Commentary on the Bible.* London, 1920. 231–43. **Gressmann, H.**

*Die Schriften des Alten Testament.* Göttingen, [2]1922. **Marti, K.** *Das fünfte Buch Moses oder Deuteronomium.* In E. F. Kautzsch, Die Heilige Schrift des Alten Testament. Ed. A. Bertholet. Tübingen: J. C. B. Mohr, [4]1922. **Kretzmann, P. E.** "The Book of Deuteronomy." In *Popular Commentary of the Bible.* St. Louis, MO: Concordia Publishing House, 1923. I, 303–62. **Halley, H. H.** "Deuteronomy." In *Pocket Bible Handbook.* Chicago: Henry H. Halley, 1924 [[20]1955 as *Bible Handbook*]. 142–47. **Hastings, J.** (ed.). "The Book of Deuteronomy." In *The Speaker's Bible.* Aberdeen, Scotland: The *'Speakers' Bible'* Offices, 1924. III, 1–192. **Eerdmans, B. D.** *Deuteronomy.* Ed. D. C. Simpson. London: Griffin & Co., 1927. **Harford, J. B.** *Deuteronomy.* A New Commentary on the Holy Scripture. Eds. Gore, Goudge, Guillaume. London, 1928. **Irwin, C. H.** "The Book of Deuteronomy." In *Irwin's Bible Commentary.* Chicago: John C. Winston Co., 1928. 59–68. **Scott, D. R.** "Deuteronomy." In *The Abingdon Bible Commentary.* Ed. F. C. Eiselen, E. Lewis, and D. G. Downey. New York: Abingdon, 1929. 318–44. **Junker, H.** *Das Buch Deuteronomium.* Die Heilige Schrift des Alten Testament. Bonn: P. Hanstein, 1933. **André, M. T.** "Le Deutéronome." In *La Bible du Centenaire: La Sainte Bible: traduction nouvelle d'aprés les meilleurs textes avec introduction et notes.* Paris: Société Biblique de Paris, 1936. 237–90. **Hertz, J. H.** (ed.). *Deuteronomy.* The Pentateuch and the Haftorahs 5. London: Oxford UP, 1936. **Reider, J.** *Deuteronomy. The Holy Scriptures with Commentary.* Philadelphia: Jewish Publication Society, 1937. **Maclaren, A.** "The Book of Deuteronomy." In *Expositions of Holy Scripture.* Grand Rapids: Eerdmans, 1938. II, 1–86. **Clamer, A.** (ed.). *Lévitiqué, Nombres, Deutéronome.* La Sainte Bible 2. Paris: Letouzey et Ané, 1940.

PHASE THREE (1943–63): **Cohen, A.** (ed.). *The Soncino Chumash: The Five Books of Moses with Haphtaroath.* Hindhead: Soncino Press, 1947. **Cooper, C. M.** "The Book of Deuteronomy." In *Old Testament Commentary.* Ed. H. C. Alleman and E. E. Flack. Philadelphia: Muhlenberg Press, 1948. 300–328. **Cazelles, H.** *Le Deutéronome.* La Sainte Bible. Paris: du Cerf, 1950 [[3]1966]. **Ridderbos, J.** *Het boek Deuteronomium, opnieuw uit den grondtekst vertaald en verklaard.* Kampen: J. H. Kok, 1950. **Crichton, T. S.** *Deuteronomy.* Books of the Bible Series 5. Edinburgh: The Church of Scotland Youth Committee, 1951. **Cunliffe-Jones, H.** "Deuteronomy." TBC. London: SCM Press, 1951. **Clarke, W. K. L.** "Deuteronomy." In *Concise Bible Commentary.* London: SPCK, 1952. 383–93. **Junker, H.** *Das Buch Deuteronomium.* Das Alte Testament. Zweites bis fünftes Buch Moses. Echter Bibel. Würzburg: Echter Verlag, 1952. **Erdman, C. R.** *The Book of Deuteronomy: An Exposition.* Westwood, NJ: Revell, 1953. **Manley, G. T.** "Deuteronomy." In *The New Bible Commentary.* Ed. F. Davidson. Grand Rapids: Eerdmans, 1953 [[2]1954]. 195–222. **Nichol, F. D.** (ed.). "The Fifth Book of Moses Called Deuteronomy." In *The Seventh-Day Adventist Bible Commentary.* Washington, DC: Review and Herald Publishing Assoc., 1953. I, 951–1077. **MacKenzie, R. A. F.** "Deuteronomy." In *A Catholic Commentary on Holy Scripture.* Ed. B. Orchard et al. London: Thomas Nelson, 1953. 261–72. **Shires, H. H.** and **Parker, P.** "Deuteronomy. Exposition." *IB*, II. Nashville: Abingdon, 1953. **Wright, G. E.** "The Book of Deuteronomy." *IB*, II. Nashville: Abingdon, 1953. **Cunliffe-Jones, H.** "The Book of Deuteronomy." In *The Twentieth Century Bible Commentary.* Ed. G. H. Davies, A. Richardson, and C. L. Wallis. New York: Harper, 1955. 150–57. **Krämer, K. F.** *Numeri und Deuteronomium.* Herders Bibelkommentar II/1. Freiburg: Herder, 1955. **Dhorme, E.** *La Bible.* Paris: Gillimard, 1956. **Haratom, E. S.** *Sefer Debarim.* Tel Aviv: Yavneh, 1956 [Heb.]. **Holwerda, B.** *Oudtestamentische voordrachten: Deel III. Exegese Oude Testament (Deuteronomium) (gehouden in de collegejaren 1946–1952).* Kampen: Copiëerinrichtin v.d. Berg, n.d. [1957]. **Rabinowitz, C. D.** *Da'at Sofrim.* Jerusalem, 1957 [Heb.]. **Morgan, G. C.** "Deuteronomy." In *An Exposition of the Whole Bible.* Westwood, NJ: Fleming H. Revell Co., 1959. 77–91. **Rabinowitz, C.D.** *Sefer Debarim.* In Samaritan characters. Tel Aviv: Nezach, 1959 [Heb. tr. from German]. **Colunga, A.** and **Garcia Cordero, M.** *Biblia Comentada. I. Pentateuco. Deuteronomio.* Madrid: Editorial Catolica, 1960. 908–1057. **Glanzman, G. S.** *The Book of Deuteronomy.* Pamphlet Bible Series 9. New York: Paulist Press, 1960. **Kuhn, H. B.** "Deuteronomy." In *The Biblical Expositor.* Ed. C. F. H. Henry. Philadelphia: A. J. Holman, 1960. I, 184–208. **Moraldi, L.** "Deuteronomio." In *La Sacra Bibbia.* Garofalo I. Turin, 1960.

395–467. **Steinmann, J.** *Deutéronome. Texte français par Jean Steinmann. Introduction et commentaires par une équipe biblique du centre d'études Notre-Dame.* Connaître la Bible. Brussels, 1961. **Davies, G. H.** "Deuteronomy." In *Peake's Commentary on the Bible.* Ed. M. Black. London: Thomas Nelson, 1962. 269–88. **Hirsch, S. R.** *The Pentateuch,* V. London, 1962. **Neil, W.** "Deuteronomy." In *Harper's Bible Commentary.* London: Hodder & Stoughton, 1962. 131–41.

PHASE FOUR(1963–present): **Buis, P.** and **Leclerq, J.** *Le Deutéronome.* Sources bibliques. Paris: J. Gabalda & Cie, 1963. **Drubbel, A.** *Numeri uit de grondtekst vertaald en uitgelegd.* De Boeken van het Oude Testament II/2. Romen & Zonen: Roermonden Maaseik, 1963. **Kline, M. G.** *Treaty of the Great King. The Covenant Structure of Deuteronomy: Studies and Commentary.* Grand Rapids: Eerdmans, 1963. **Ridderbos, J.** *Het Boek Deuteronomium. Opnieuw uit de grontekst vertaald en verklaard.* Kampen: J. H. Kak, 1963–64. **Blair, E. P.** *The Book of Deuteronomy. The Book of Joshua.* LBC 5. Richmond: John Knox Press, 1964. **Cunliffe-Jones, H.** *Deuteronomy.* TBC. London: SCM Press, 1964. **Francisco, C. T.** *The Book of Deuteronomy.* Shield Bible Study Series. Grand Rapids, 1964. **Lamsa, G. M.** *Old Testament Light: A Scriptural Commentary Based on the Aramaic of the Ancient Peshitta Text.* Englewood Cliffs: Prentice-Hall, 1964. **Moraldi, L.** *Introduzione alla Bibbia; corso sistematico di studi biblici.* Turin: Marietti, 1964. **Rad, G. von.** *Das fünfte Buch Mose.* ATD 8. Göttingen: Vandenhoeck & Ruprecht, 1964. **Brown, R. E.** *The Book of Deuteronomy.* OT Reading Guide 10. Collegeville: Liturgical Press, 1965. **Hirsch, S. R.** *Deuteronomy.* In *The Pentateuch,* V. 2nd ed., tr. I. Levy (completely revised). London: Bloch Publishing Co., 1966. **Rad, G. von.** *Deuteronomy.* Tr. D. Barton. OTL. Philadelphia: Westminster Press, 1966. **Criado, R.** *Deuteronomio.* La Sagrada Biblia, I. Madrid: Editorial Catolica, 1967. **Hanke, H. A.** "The Book of Deuteronomy." In *The Wesleyen Bible Commentary.* Ed. C. W. Carter and W. R. Thompson. Grand Rapids: Eerdmans, 1967. I/1, 467–50. **Rennes, J.** *Le Deutéronome: traduction et commentaire.* Geneva: Ed. Labor et Fides, 1967. **Blenkinsopp, J.** "Deuteronomy." In *Jerome Biblical Commentary.* New Jersey: Prentice-Hall, 1968. 101–22. **Buis, P.** *Le Deutéronome.* Verbum Salutis: Ancien Testament 4. Paris: Beauchesne, 1969. **Laconi, M.** *Deuteronomio.* Nuovissima Versione della Bibbia dai Testi Originali, 5. Rome: Edizione Paoline, 1969. **Moran, W. L.** "Deuteronomy." In *A New Catholic Commentary on Holy Scripture.* Ed. R. C. Fuller, L. Johnston, and C. Kearns. New and fully rev. ed. London: Nelson, 1969. **Munk, E.** קול התורה: *La Voix de la Thora,* V. Paris: Fondation Samuel et Odette Levy, 1969 [²1978]. **Alonso Schökel, L.** *Deuteronomio.* Los Libros Sagrados I/2. Madrid: Ediciones Cristianidad, 1970. 257–404. **Laconi, M.** *Deuteronomio.* Nuovissima Versione della Bibbia dai Test Originale, 5. Rome: Edizioni Paoline, 1970. **Manley, G. T.** and **Harrison, R. K.** "Deuteronomy." In *New Bible Commentary,* rev. 3rd ed. Ed. D. Guthrie and J. A. Motyer. Grand Rapids: Eerdmans, 1970. 201–29. **Watts, J. D. W.** "Deuteronomy." In *BBC* 2. Ed. C. J. Allen, 2. Nashville: Broadman, 1970. 175–296. **Gottwald, N. K.** "The Book of Deuteronomy." In *The Interpreter's One-Volume Commentary on the Bible.* Ed. C. M. Laymon. Nashville: Abingdon, 1971. 100–121. **Schultz, S. J.** *Deuteronomy: The Gospel of Love.* Everyman's Bible Commentary. Chicago: Moody, 1971. **Wijngaards, J.** *Deuteronomium.* Die Boeken van het Oude Testament II/III. Roermond: J. J. Romen & Zonen, 1971. **Ackland, D. F.** "Deuteronomy." In *The Teacher's Bible Commentary.* Ed. H. F. Paschall. Nashville: Broadman, 1972. 115–36. **Phillips, A.** *Deuteronomy.* CBC. Cambridge: Cambridge UP, 1973. **Chouraqui, A.** *Deuteronomie.* La Bible traduite et présentée, vol. 5. Paris: Desclée, De Brouer, 1974. **Plaut, W. G.** *Deuteronomy.* The Torah: A Modern Commentary 5. New York: Union of American Hebrew Congregations, 1974. **Thompson, J. A.** *Deuteronomy.* TOTC. London: Inter-Varsity, 1974. **Braulik, G.** *Das Testament des Mose. Das Buch Deuteronomium.* Stuttgarter Kleiner Kommentar Altes Testament 4. Stuttgart: Katholisches Bibelwerk, 1976. **Craigie, P. C.** *The Book of Deuteronomy.* NICOT. Grand Rapids: Eerdmans, 1976. **Penna, A.** *Deuteronomio.* La Sacra Bibbia. Turin: Marietti, 1976. **Lamparter, H.** *Der Aufruf zum Gehorsam. Das 5. Buch Mose.* BAT 9. Stuttgart: Calwer, 1977. **Malbim, M. L.** *Rabbenu Meir Leibush ben Yechiel Michel: Commentary on the Torah.* Tr. with notes by Z. Faier. Jerusalem: Hillel Press,

1978. **Achtemeier, E.** *Deuteronomy, Jeremiah.* Proclamation Commentaries. Philadelphia: Fortress, 1979. **Mayes, A. D. H.** *Deuteronomy.* NCBC. Grand Rapids: Eerdmans, 1979. **Kaplan, A.** "Deuteronomy: Translation with Notes." In *The Living Torah.* New York: Moznaim, 1981. **Unger, M. F.** "Deuteronomy." In *Unger's Commentary on the Old Testament.* Chicago: Moody Press, 1981. I, 233–78. **Clifford, R.** *Deuteronomy, with an Excursus on Covenant and Law.* OT Message, A Biblical-Theological Commentary 4. Wilmington: Glazier, 1982. **Hamilton, V. P.** *Handbook on the Pentateuch.* Grand Rapids: Baker Book House, 1982. 375–474. **Chouraqui, A.** *L'Univers de la Bible,* II. Paris: Éditions Lidis, 1983. **Plaut, W. G.** *Deuteronomy.* In *The Torah: A Modern Commentary.* New York: Union of American Hebrew Congregations, 1983. **Payne, D. F.** *Deuteronomy.* The Daily Study Bible. Philadelphia: Westminster, 1985. **Braulik, G.** *Deuteronomium 1–16, 7.* DNEB. Würzburg, 1986. **Cousins, P. E.** "Deuteronomy." In *The International Bible Commentary,* rev. Ed. F. F. Bruce. Grand Rapids: Zondervan, 1986 [1st ed. 1979]. 256–82. **Labuschagne, C. J.** *Deuteronomium,* Deel IA and IB. De Prediking van het Oude Testament. Nijkerk: Uitgeverij Callenbach, 1987. **Polzin, R.** "Deuteronomy." In *The Literary Guide to the Bible.* Ed. R. Alter and F. Kermode. Cambridge, MA: Harvard UP, 1987. 92–101. **Garcia Lopez, F.** *Le Deuteronome. Une loi prêchée.* Cahiers Evangile 63. Paris: Editions du Cerf, [1988]. **Nelson, R. D.** "Deuteronomy." In *Harper's Bible Commentary.* Ed. J. L. Mays et al. San Francisco: Harper & Row, 1988. 209–34. **Clements, R. E.** *Deuteronomy.* Old Testament Guides. Ed. R. N. Whybray. Sheffield: JSOT Press, 1989. **Gilchrist, P. R.** "Deuteronomy." In *The Evangelical Commentary on the Bible.* Ed. W. A. Elwell. Grand Rapids: Baker, 1989. 107–30. **Hoppe, L.** "Deuteronomy." In *The Collegeville Bible Commentary.* Ed. D. Bergant and R. J. Karris. Collegeville: Liturgical Press, 1989. 196–228. **Sanders, J. A.** "Deuteronomy." In *The Books of the Bible.* Ed. B. W. Anderson. New York: Charles Scribner's Sons, 1989. I, 89–102. **Blenkinsopp, J.** "Deuteronomy." In *The New Jerome Biblical Commentary.* Ed. R. E. Brown, J. Fitzmyer, and R. Murphy. Englewood Cliffs, NJ: Prentice-Hall, 1990. 94–109. **Labuschagne, C. J.** *Deuteronomium,* Deel II. De Prediking van het Oude Testament. Nijkerk: Uitgeverij Callenbach, 1990. **Miller, P. D.** *Deuteronomy.* Interpretation: A Bible Commentary for Teaching and Preaching. Louisville: John Knox Press, 1990.

CHRONOLOGICAL LIST OF SELECTED BOOKS AND MONOGRAPHS ON DEUTERONOMY

The list that follows is given in chronological order beginning with the seminal work of W. M. L. de Wette in 1805, which marked the beginning of the modern critical era in the study of Deuteronomy. Monographs on specific passages or portions are noted in the chapter bibliographies.

1805–89: **Wette, W. M. L. de.** *Dissertatio critica qua Deuteronomium a prioribus Pentateuchi libris diversum alius cuiusdam recentioris auctoris opus esse monstratur.* Jena, 1805.————. *Beiträge zur Einleitung in das Alte Testament,* 2 vols. Halle, 1806/7 [rep. Darmstadt, 1971]. **Bertheau, E.** *Die sieben Gruppen mosaischer Gesetz in den drei mittleren büchern des Pentateuchs. Ein Beitrag zur Kritik des Pentateuchs.* Göttingen: Vandenhoeck & Ruprecht, 1840. **Stähelin, J. J.** *Kritische Untersuchungen über den Pentateuch, die Bücher Josua, Richter, Samuels und der Könige.* Berlin: G. Reimers, 1843. **Saalschütz, J. L.** *Das Mosaische Recht.* 2 Theile. Berlin: Cotteymann, 1853f. **Riehm, E.** *Die Gesetzgebung Mosis im Lande Moab. Ein Beitrag zur Einleitung in's alte Testament.* Gotha, 1854. **Schultz, F. W.** *Das Deuteronomium erklärt.* Berlin, 1859. **Colenso, J.W.** *The Pentateuch and the Book of Joshua Critically Examined,* Part III: *The Book of Deuteronomy.* London: Longman, 1863. **Schroeder, F. W. J.** *Das Deuteronomium oder das Fünfte Buch Mose theologisch-homiletsich bearbeitet.* Theologisch-homiletisches Bibelwerk des Alten Testament 3. Ed. J. P. Lange. Bielefeld, 1866. **Kübel, R.** *Das alttestamentliche Gesetz und seine Urkunde.* Stuttgart, 1867. **Schoebel, C.** *Demonstration critique de l'Authenticité Mosaique du Deutéronome.* Paris, 1868. **Maine, H.** *Ancient Law.* London: Murray, 1870. **Dahler, J.** *Jérémie et le Deutéronome.*

Strasbourg, 1872. **Kleinert, P.** *Das Deuteronomium und der Deuteronomiker. Untersuchungen zur alttestamentliche Rechts- und Literaturgeschichte.* Bielefeld and Leipzig, 1872. **Kayser, A.** *Das vorexilische Buch der Urgeschichte Israels und seine Erweiterungen: Ein Beitrag zur Pentateuchkritik.* Strassburg, 1874. **Sime, J.** *Deuteronomy, the People's Book, Its Origin and Nature.* London, 1877.

1890–99: **Zahn, A.** *Das Deuteronomium: Eine Schutzschrift wider modernkritisches Unwesen.* Gütersloh: Vlg. C. Bertesmann, 1890. **Montet, F.** *Le Deutéronome et la Question de l'Hexateuque. Étude critique et exégétique sous form d'introduction et de commentaire du Deutéronome considéré dans ses rapports avec les quatre premiers livres Pentateuque et Josué.* Paris, 1891. **Moor, F. de.** *La Date de la Composition du Deutéronome.* Amien, 1891. **Weill, A.** *Les cinq Livres (Mosaïstes) de Moïse. Cinquième Livre: Deutéronome.* Paris, 1891. **Preiss, H.** *Zum Deuteronomium.* Schulprogramme Progress Nr. 55. Berlin, 1892. **Hartmann, A. T.** *Historisch-kritische Forschungen über die Bildung, das Zeitalter und den Plan der fünf Bücher Moses.* Rostock-Gustrow, 1893. **Klostermann, A.** *Der Pentateuch. Beiträge zu seinem Verständnis und seiner Entstehungsgeschichte,* 2 vols. Leipzig: A. Deichert, 1893, 1907. **König, J. L.** *Alttestamentliche Studien. Zweites Heft: Das Deuteronomium und der Prophet Jeremiah, gegen Bohlen, nebst anderen Beiträgen zur Authentie des Deuteronomiums.* Berlin: G. Reimer, 1893. **Reuss, E.** *Das Alte Testament, III. Die Heilige Geschichte und das Gesetz. Der Pentateuch und Josua.* Braunschweig, 1893 [French ed., 1879]. **Montet, F.** *La Composition de l'Hexateuque, de Juges, de Samuel et des Tois. Étude critique biblique.* Basel, 1894. **Staerk. W.** *Das Deuteronomium. Sein Inhalt und seine literarische Form. Eine kritische Studie.* Leipzig: Hinrich, 1894.————. *Beiträge zur Kritik des Deuteronomiums.* Leipzig, 1894. **Steuernagel, C.** *Der Rahmen des Deuteronomiums. Literarcritische Untersuchung über seine Zusammensetzung und Entstehung.* Halle: J. Krause, 1894. **Wellhausen, J.** *Die Composition des Hexateuchs und der historischen Bücher des Alten Testament.* Berlin: W. de Gruyter, 1894 [³1899]. **Kraetzschmar, R.** *Die Bundesvorstellung im Alten Testament in ihrer geschichtlichen Entwickelung untersucht und dargestellt.* Marburg: Elwert, 1896. **MacDill, D.** *Mosaic Authorship of the Book of Deuteronomy.* Dayton: W. J. Shuey, 1896. **Muir, W.** *Die Abfassung des Deuteronomiums.* Leipzig: E. Ungleich; *The Authorship of Deuteronomy.* Tr. G. J. Metzger. London, 1896. **Steuernagel, C.** *Die Entstehung des deuteronomischen Gesetzes.* Halle: J. Krause, 1896. **Naumann, O.** *Das Deuteronomium: Das prophetische Staatsgesetz des theokratischen Königtums mit seinen Eingangs- und Schlussworten, aus der prophetischen Geschichte und Theologie erläutert.* Gütersloh, 1897. **Addis, W. E.** *The Documents of the Hexateuch Translated and Arranged in Chronological Order with Introduction and Notes.* London: Putnam, 1898. **Girdlestone, R. B.** *The Student's Deuteronomy.* London, 1899.

1900–1909: **Halévy, J.** "Recherches bibliques: le Deutéronome." *RSEHA* 7 (1899) 313–32; 8 (1900) 1–8, 97–114, 193–216. **Harper, A.** *The Book of Deuteronomy.* New York: Armstrong, 1901. **Carpenter, J. E.** *The Composition of the Hexateuch. An Introduction with Select Lists of Words and Phrases and an Appendix on Laws and Institutions by G. Harford.* London: Longmans, 1902. **McGarvey, J. W.** *The Authorship of the Book of Deuteronomy.* Cincinnati: Standard Publishing Co., 1902. **Schroeder, W. J.** *Das Deuteronomium oder das fünfte Buch Mose.* Theologisch-homiletisches Bibelwerk. Ed. J. P. Lange, part 3. 2nd improved ed. Ed. G. Stosch. Bielefeld and Leipzig, 1902. **Cullen, J.** *The Book of the Covenant in Moab: A Critical Inquiry into the Original Form of Deuteronomy.* Glasgow, 1903. **Erbt, W.** *Die Sicherstellung des Monotheismus durch die Gesetzgebung im vorexilischen Juda.* Göttingen: Vandenhoeck & Ruprecht, 1903. **Fries, D. S. A.** *Die Gesetzesschrift des Königs Josia. Eine kritische Untersuchung.* Leipzig: A. Deichert'sche Verlagsbuchh., 1903. **Grimme, H.** *Das Gesetz Hammurabis und Moses.* Cologne, 1903 [ET, London 1907]. **Müller, D. H.** *Die Gesetze Hammurabis und ihr Verhältnis zur mosaischen Gesetzgebung sowie zu den XII Tafeln.* Vienna: A. Hölder, 1903. **Bruston, C.** *L'Histoire sacerdotale et le Deutéronome primitif.* Paris, 1906. **Merx, A.** *Die Bücher Moses und Josua.* Tübingen: Mohr, 1907. **Sternberg, G.** *Die Ethik des Deuteronomiums: Inaugural-Dissertation.* Berlin: Trowitzsch, 1908. **Wiener, H.** *Essays in Pentateuchal Criticism.* Oberlin: Bibliotheca Sacra Co., 1909.

1910–19: **Naville, E.** *La découverte de la loi sous le roi Josias.* Mémoires del'académie des inscriptions et belles lettres 38,2. Paris, 1910. **Pope, H.** *The Date of the Composition of Deuteronomy: A Critical Study.* Holy Apostolic See and the Sacred Congregation of Rites. Rome: Frederick Pustet, 1910. **Puukko, A. F.** *Das Deuteronomium. Eine literarkritische Untersuchung.* BWANT 5. Leipzig: Hinrichs, 1910. **Euringer, S.** *Der Streit um das Deuteronomium.* Biblische Zeitfragen 4,8. Münster, 1911. **Griffiths, J. S.** *The Problem of Deuteronomy.* London, 1911. **Jordan, W. G.** *Deuteronomy.* New York: Macmillan, 1911. **Naville, E.** *The Discovery of the Book of the Law under King Josiah.* London: SPCK, 1911. **Oestreicher, T.** *Die josianische Reform.* Das Reich Christi 12. Berlin, 1911. **McNeile, A. H.** *Deuteronomy. Its Place in Revelation.* London: Longmans, 1912. **Smend, R.** *Die Erzählung des Hexateuch: Auf ihre Quellen untersucht.* Berlin: Verlag Ge. Reimer, 1912. **Wiener, H. M.** *Pentateuchal Studies.* London: E. Stock, 1912. **Hempel, J.** *Die Schichten des Deuteronomiums. Ein Beitrag zur israelitischen Literatur- und Rechtsgeschichte.* Leipzig: R. Voigtländer, 1914.

1920–29: **Kennett, R. H.** *Deuteronomy and the Decalogue.* Cambridge UP, 1920. **Wiener, H. M.** *Das Hauptproblem des Deuteronomiums.* Tr. M. Kegel. Gütersloh: Bertelsman, 1924. **Kittel, G.** *Sifre zu Deuteronomium.* Stuttgart, 1922. **Kugler, F. X.** *Von Moses zu Paulus.* Münster: Aschendorf, 1922. **Oestreicher, T.** *Das deuteronomische Grundgesetz.* BFCT 27/4. Gütersloh, 1923. **Löhr, M.** *Untersuchungen zum Hexateuchsproblem.* BZAW 38. Giessen: A. Töpelmann, 1924. **Longacre, L. B.** *Deuteronomy, a Prophetic Lawbook.* New York: Methodist Book Concern, 1924. **Naville, E.** *Le Deutéronome, un Livre Mosaïque.* Fontenay-sous-Bois, 1924. **Šanda, A.** *Moses und der Pentateuch.* ATA 9. Münster: W. Aschendorff, 1924. **Staerk, W.** *Das Problem des Deuteronomiums. Ein Beitrag zur neuesten Pentateuchkritik.* BFCT 29/2. Gütersloh, 1924. **Löhr, M.** *Das Deuteronomium: Untersuchungen zum Hexateuchproblem II.* SKGG I/6. Berlin: Deutsche Verlagsgesellschaft, 1925. **Möller, W.** *Rückbeziehungen des 5. Buches Moses auf die vier ersten Bücher. Ein Beitrag zur Einleitung in den Pentateuch im Sinne seiner Einheit und Echtheit.* Lütjenburg, 1925. **Welch, A. C.** *The Code of Deuteronomy: A New Theory of Its Origin.* London, 1924; New York, 1925. **Bentzen, A.** *Die josianische Reform und ihre Voraussetzungen.* Copenhagen: Haas & Söhne, 1926. **Ring, E.** *Israels Rechtsleben in Lichte der neuentdeckten assyrischen und hethitischen Gesetzeurkunden.* Stockholm: V. Petterson/Leipzig: G. Fock, 1926. **Jirku, A.** *Das weltliche Recht im Alten Testament. Stilgeschichtliche und rechtsvergleichende Studien in den juristischen Gesetzen des Pentateuch.* Gütersloh, 1927. **Bewer, J. A., Paton, L. B.,** and **Dahl, G.** "The Problem of Deuteronomy: A Symposium." *JBL* 47 (1928) 305–79. **Menes, A.** *Die vorexilschen Gesetze Israels.* BZAW 50. Berlin, 1928. **Mowinckel, S.** *Femte Mosebok. Det Gamle Testament. I: Loven eller de Fem Mosebøker.* Oslo, 1929. **Rad, G. von.** *Das Gottesvolk im Deuteronomium.* BWANT 47. Stuttgart: W. Kohlhammer, 1929. **Siebens, A.-R.** *L'origine du code deutéronomique: Examen historique et littéraire du sujet à la lumiére de la critique contemporaine.* Paris: Leroux, 1929.

1930–39: **Horst, F.** *Das privilegrecht Jahves: Rechtsgeschichtliche untersuchungen zum Deuteronomium.* FRLANT 45. Göttingen: Vandenhoeck & Ruprecht, 1930. **Noth, M.** *Reichstempel und Ortsheiligtümer in Israel.* BFCT 33. Gütersloh, 1930. **Krause, H.-H.** *Das Deuteronomium in der wissenschaftlichen Bearbeitung des 19. und 20. Jahrhunderts.* Diss., Breslau, 1931. **Cadoux, C. J.** *The Book of Deuteronomy: Introduction and Translation.* London, 1932. **Welch, A. C.** *Deuteronomy: The Framework to the Code.* London: Oxford UP, 1932. **Breit, H.** *Die Predigt des Deuteronomisten.* Munich: Kaiser, 1933. **Stoderl, W.** *Das Gesetz Israels nach Inhalt und Ursprung. I. Beiträge zur Einleitung ins Alte Testament.* Marienbad, 1933. **Alt, A.** *Die Ursprunge des Israelitischen Rechts.* Berichte über die Verhandlungen der Sächsischen Akademie der Wissenschaften zu Leipzig, Philologisch-historische Klasse 86/1. Leipzig, 1934 [ET: "The Origins of Israelite Law." In *Essays on Old Testament History and Religion* (1966) 79–132]. **Mackintosh, C. H.** *Deuteronomium I. Vestaling.* The Haag, 1935. **Auerbach, E.** *Wüste und Gelobtes Land II.* Berlin: Schocken, 1936. **Rad, G. von.** *Das Formgeschichtliche Problem des Hexateuch.* BWANT IV 26. Stuttgart: Kohlhammer, 1936 [ET, 1966]. **Hertz, J. H.**

The Pentateuch and Haftorahs. V. Deuteronomy. Berlin, 1937. **Hulst, A. R.** *Het Karakter van den Cultus in Deuteronomium.* Diss., Groningen, 1938. **Rudolph, W.** *Der "Elohist" von Exodus bis Jusua.* BZAW 68. Berlin: Töpelmann, 1938.

1940–49: **Noth, M.** *Die Gesetze im Pentateuch.* Ihre Voraussetzungen und ihr Sinn. SKGG, Geisteswissenschaft-liche Klasse 17, 2. Halle, 1940. **Pedersen J.** *Israel—Its Life and Culture,* vol. III/IV. Copenhagen, 1940. 580ff. **Allis, O. T.** *The Five Books of Moses.* Phillipsburg, NJ: Presbyterian and Reformed Publishing Co., 1943. **Noth, M.** *Überlieferungsgeschichtliche Studien I. Die sammelnden und bearbeitenden Geschichtswerke im Alten Testament.* Tübingen: Halle, 1943. **Leroy, J.** *Introduction a l'étude des anciens codes orientaux.* Paris: Maisonneuve, 1944. **Östborn, G.** *Tōrā in the Old Testament. A Semantic Study.* Lund: Ohlssons Bookstore, 1945. **Brinker, R.** *The Influence of Sanctuaries in Early Israel.* Manchester UP, 1946. **Cazelles, H.** *Études sur le Code de l'Alliance.* Paris: Letouzey, 1946. **Daube, D.** *Studies in Biblical Law.* Cambridge UP, 1947. **Hospers, J. H.** *De Numeruswisseling in het Boek Deuteronomium.* Utrecht: Kemink, 1947. **Rad, G. von.** *Deuteronomium-Studien.* FRLANT 40. Göttingen: Vandenhoeck & Ruprecht, 1947 [ET, SBT 9. 1956] **Rabast, K.** *Das apodiktische Recht im Deuteronomium und im Heiligkeitsgesetz.* Berlin: Heimatdienstverlag, 1948. **Winnet, F. V.** *The Mosaic Tradition.* Near and Middle East Series 1. Toronto UP, 1949.

1950–59: **Diamond, A. S.** *The Evolution of Law and Order.* London, 1951. **Robinson, D. W. B.** *Josiah's Reform and the Book of the Law.* London: Tyndale, 1951. **Althaus, P.** *Gebot und Gesetz. Zum Thema "Gesetz und Evangelium."* BFCT 46, 2. Gütersloh, 1952. **Kuyper, L. J.** "The Book of Deuteronomy." *Int* 6 (July 1952) 321–40. **Rad, G. von.** *Studies in Deuteronomy.* ET, SBT I/ 9. Chicago: Henry Regnery Co., 1953 [German ²1948]. **Wilson, J. A.** et al. *Authority and Law in the Ancient Orient.* JAOSSup 17. New Haven: American Oriental Society, 1954. **Lewy, I.** *The Growth of the Pentateuch: A Literary, Sociological and Biographical Approach.* New York: Bookman Associates, 1955. **Mendenhall, G. E.** *Law and Covenant in Israel and the Ancient Near East.* Pittsburgh: Biblical Colloquium, 1955. **Gray, J.** *The Legacy of Canaan.* VTSup 5. Leiden: Brill, 1957. **Kraus, H.-J.** *Die Prophetische Verkündigung des Rechts in Israel.* Theologische Studien 51. Zollikon: Evangelischer Verlag, 1957. **Manley, G. T.** *The Book of the Law: Studies in the Date of Deuteronomy.* London: Tyndale, 1957. **Teeple, H. M.** *The Mosaic Eschatological Prophet.* JBLMonSer 10. Philadelphia: Society of Biblical Literature, 1957. **Cazelles, H.** *Le Deutéronomie.* La Sainte Bible. Paris: du Cerf, 1958. **Smend, R.** *W. M. Leberecht de Wettes Arbeit zum Alten und am Neuen Testament.* Basel: Helbirg & Lichtenhahn, 1958. **Hempel, J.** *Der textkritische Wert des Konsonantentextes von Kairener Genizafragmenten in Cambridge und Oxford zum Deuteronomium.* NGAW I. Phil.-Hist. Kl. Nr. 10, 1959.

1960–64: **Baltzer, K.** *Das Bundesformular.* WMANT 4. Neukirchen: Verlag der Buchhandlung des Erziehungsvereins, 1960 [ET, 1971]. **Ellul, J.** *The Theological Foundation of Law.* New York: Doubleday, 1960. *Interpretation* 15 (January 1961). **Maarsingh, B.** *Onderzoek naar de Ethiek van de Wetten in Deuteronomium.* [Diss., Utrecht, 1961.] Winterswijk, 1961. **Bächli, O.** *Israel und die Völker. Eine Studie zum Deuteronomoium.* Zürich: Zwingli Verlag, 1962. **Peucker, H.** *Deuteronomium Kapitel 12–26 form- und rechtsgeschichtlich Untersucht.* Diss., Greifswald, 1962. **Cazelles, H.** (ed.). *Moses in Schrift und Uberlieferung.* Düsseldorf: Patmos, 1963. **Lohfink, N.** *Das Hauptgebot: Eine Untersuchung literarischer Einleitungsfragen zu Deuteronomium 5–11.* AnBib 20. Rome: Pontifical Biblical Institute, 1963. **McCarthy, D. J.** *Treaty and Covenant: A Study in Form in the Ancient Oriental Documents and in the Old Testament.* AnBib 21. Rome: Biblical Institute Press, 1963. **Porter, J. R.** *Moses and Monarchy.* Oxford: Blackwell, 1963. **Smend, R.** *Die Bundesformel.* Theologische Studien 68. Zürich: EVZ-Verlag, 1963. **Wijngaards, J.** *The Formulas of the Deuteronomic Creed.* Tilburg: A. Reijnen, 1963. *Review and Expositor* (Fall 1964). *Southwestern Journal of Theology* (Fall 1964). **Boecker, H. J.** *Redeformen des Rechtslebens im Alten Testament.* WMANT 14. Neukirchen-Vluyn: Neukirchener Verlag, 1964 [2nd ed. 1984]. **Falk, Z. W.** *Hebrew Law in Biblical Times.* Jerusalem: Wahrmann Books, 1964. **Fenz, A. K.** *Auf Jahwes*

*Stimme Hören.* WBT 6. Vienna: Herder, 1964. **Thompson, J. A.** *The Ancient Near Eastern Treaties and the Old Testament.* Tyndale Lecture in Biblical Archaeology 1963. London: Tyndale, 1964.

1965–69: **Becker, J.** *Gottesfurcht im Alten Testament.* Rome, 1965. **Clements, R. E.** *Prophecy and Tradition.* London: SCM, 1965. **Gerstenberger, E.** *Wesen und Herkunft des apodiktischen Rechts.* WMANT 20. Neukirchen-Vluyn: Neukirchener Verlag, 1965. **Gunneweg, A. H. J.** *Leviten und Priester.* FRLANT 89. Göttingen: Vandenhoeck & Ruprecht, 1965. **Lohfink, N.** *Höre Israel! Auslegung von Texten aus dem Buch Deuteronomium.* Die Welt der Bibel 18. Düsseldorf: Patmos, 1965. **Alt, A.** *Essays on Old Testament Religion.* Tr. R. A. Wilson. Oxford: Blackwell, 1966. **Kitchen, K. A.** *Ancient Orient and the Old Testament.* London: Tyndale Press, 1966. **L'Hour, J.** *La Morale de l'Alliance.* Paris: J. Gabalda, 1966. **McCarthy, D. J.** *Der Gottesbund im Alten Testament.* SBS 13. Stuttgart: Katholisches Bibelwerk, 1966. **McKay, J. W.** *Josiah's Reformation: Its Antecedents, Nature and Significance.* Diss., Cambridge, 1966/67. **Noth, M.** *The Laws of the Pentateuch and Other Studies.* Tr. D. R. Ap-Thomas. Philadelphia: Fortress, 1966 [Ger. ed., *GesStAT,* 1960]. **Rad, G. von.** *The Problem of the Hexateuch and Other Essays.* Tr. E. W. T. Dicken. New York: McGraw-Hill, 1966 [Ger. ed., *GesStAT,* 1958]. **Richter, W.** *Recht und Ethos. Versuch einer Ortung des weisheitlichen* Mahnspruchs. StANT 15. München, 1966. **Aharoni, J.** *The Land of the Bible: A Historical Geography.* London: Burns & Oates, 1967. **LaBonnardiére, A. M.** *Biblia Augustiniana Ancien Testament: la Deutéronome.* Paris: Études Augstiennes, 1967. **Loersch, S.** *Das Deuteronomium und seine Deutungen. Ein forschungsgeschichtlicher Überblick.* SBS 22. Stuttgart: Katholische Bibelwerk, 1967. **Lohfink, N.** *Die Landverheissung als Eid.* SBS 28. Stuttgart: Katholisches Bibelwerk, 1967.————. *Bibelauslegung im Wandel.* Frankfurt a.M.: Knecht, 1967. **Nicholson, E. W.** *Deuteronomy and Tradition.* Oxford: Blackwell, 1967. **Plöger, J. G.** *Literarkritische, formgeschichtliche und stilkritische Untersuchungen zum Deuteronomium.* BBB 26. Bonn: Hanstein, 1967. **Poulsen, N.** *König und Tempel im Glaubenszeugnis des Alten Testament.* SBM 3. Stuttgart, 1967. **Segal, M. H.** *The Pentateuch: Its Composition and Authorship and Other Biblical Studies.* Jerusalem: Magnes, 1967. **Albright, W. F.** *Yahweh and the Gods of Canaan.* London: Athlone, 1968. **Barkun, M.** *Law without Sanctions.* New Haven: Yale UP, 1968. **Claburn, W. E.** *Deuteronomy and Collective Behavior.* Diss., Princeton Univ., 1968. **Clements, R. E.** *God's Chosen People: A Theological Interpretation of the Book of Deuteronomy.* London: SCM Press, 1968. **Coulton, P. E.** *Geographical Aspects in the Deuteronomistic History.* Diss., Trinity College, Dublin, 1968/69. **Jocz, J.** *The Covenant: A Theology of Human Destiny.* Grand Rapids: Eerdmans, 1968. **Lohfink, N.** "Lectures in Deuteronomy." Rome, 1968 [Graduate Theological Union Library, Berkeley, CA]. **Preuss, H. D.** *Jahweglaube und Zukunftserwartung.* BWANT 5,7. Stuttgart: Kohlhammer, 1968. **Schmid, H.** *Moses. Überlieferung und Geschichte.* BZAW 110. 1968. **Finkelstein, L.** (ed.). *Sifre on Deuteronomy.* New York: Jewish Theological Seminary of America, 1969. **Hillers, D. R.** *Covenant: The History of a Biblical Idea.* Baltimore: Johns Hopkins, 1969. **McBride, S. D.** *The Deuteronomic Name Theology.* Diss, Harvard Univ., 1969. **Merendino, R. P.** *Das deuteronomische Gesetz. Eine literarkritische, gattungs- und überlieferungsgeschichtliche Untersuchung zu Dt. 12–26.* BBB 31. Bonn: Hanstein, 1969. **Ottoson, M.** *Gilead: Tradition and History.* ConB 3. Lund: Gleerup, 1969. **Walkenhorst, K. H.** *Der Sinai im liturgischen Verständnis der deuternomistischen und priesterlichen Tradition.* BBB 33. Bonn: Hanstein, 1969. **Welten, P.** *Die Königstempel. Ein Beitrag zur Militärpolitik unter Hiskia und Josia.* Wiesbaden: Harrassowitz, 1969. **Wenham, G. J.** *The Structure and Date of Deuteronomy.* Diss., King's College, London, 1969. **Wijngaards, J. N. M.** *The Dramatization of Salvific History in the Deuteronomic Schools.* OTS 16. Leiden: Brill, 1969.

1970–74: **Broide, I.** *The Speeches in Deuteronomy.* Diss., Univ. of Tel Aviv, 1970 [Heb., Eng. abstract]. **Nebeling, G.** *Die Schichten des deuteronomischen Gesetzeskorpus.* Diss., Münster, 1970. **Paul, S. M.** *Studies in the Book of the Covenant in the Light of Cuneiform and Biblical Law.* VTSup 18. Leiden: Brill, 1970. **Perlitt, L.** *Bundestheologie im Alten Testament.* WMANT 36. Neukirchen-Vluyn: Neukirchener Verlag, 1970. **Phillips, A.** *Ancient Israel's Criminal Law: A New Approach to the*

*Decalogue.* Oxford: Blackwell, 1970. **Schmitt, G.** *Du sollst keinen Frieden schliessen mit den Bewohnern des Landes. Die Wegweisung gegen die Kanaanäer in Israels Geschichte und Geschichtsschreibung.* BWANT 91. Stuttgart: Kohlhammer, 1970. **Schneider, B. N.** *Deuteronomy: A Favored Book of Jesus.* Grand Rapids, 1970. **Speyer, W.** *Bucherfunde in der Glaubenswerbung der Antike.* Göttingen: Vandenhoeck & Ruprecht, 1970. **Thompson, R. J.** *Moses and the Law in a Century of Criticism since Graf.* VTSup 19. Leiden: Brill, 1970. **Baltzer, K.** *The Covenant Formulary.* Tr. D. Green. Philadelphia: Fortress, 1971 [from Ger. ²1964; BWANT 4, 1960]. **Liedke, G.** *Gestalt und Bezeichnung alttestamentlicher Rechtssätze. Eine formgeschichtlich-terminologische Studie.* WMANT 39. Neukirchen-Vluyn: Neukirchener Verlag, 1971. **Lindblom, J.** *Erwägungen zur Herkunft der josianischen Tempelurkunde.* Lund, 1971. **Seitz, G.** *Redaktionsgeschichtliche Studien zum Deuteronomium.* BWANT 93. Stuttgart: Kohlhammer, 1971. **Beegle, D. M.** *Moses, the Servant of Yahweh.* Grand Rapids: Eerdmans, 1972. **Diepold, P.** *Israels Land.* BWANT 95. Stuttgart/Berlin/Köln/Mainz, 1972. **Kline, M. G.** *The Structure of Biblical Authority.* Grand Rapids: Eerdmans, 1972. **McCarthy, D. J.** *Old Testament Covenant. A Survey of Current Opinion.* Richmond: John Knox, 1972. **Wagner, V.** *Rechtssätze in gebundener Sprache und Rechtssatzreihen im israelitischen Recht.* BZAW 127. Berlin: de Gruyter, 1972. **Weinfeld, M.** *Deuteronomy and the Deuteronomic School.* Oxford: Clarendon, 1972. **Wittstruck, T. K.** *The Greek Translation of Deuteronomy.* Diss., Yale Univ., 1972. **Barthélemy, D., Hulst, A. R., Lohfink, N., McHardy, W. D., Ruger, H. P.,** and **Sanders, J. A.** *Preliminary and Interim Report on the Hebrew Old Testament Text Project. I. The Pentateuch.* London: United Bible Societies, 1973. **Bellefontaine, M. E.** *A Study of Ancient Israelite Laws and Their Function as Covenant Stipulations.* Indiana, 1973. **Kane, T. F.** *God Who Gives: A verbal study of the actions attributed to God in the "deuteronomic school," with special attention to the concept of God's giving.* Universidad de Navarro Coleccion Teologica 7. Pamplona: Ediciones Universidad de Navarra, 1973. **Kutsch, E.** *Verheissung und Gesetz. Untersuchungen zum Sogenannten 'Bund' im Alten Testament.* BZAW 131. Berlin: de Gruyter, 1973. **Rücker, H.** *Die Begründungen der Weisungen Jahwes im Pentateuch.* ETS 30. Leipzig: St. Benno, 1973. **Bergren, R. V.** *The Prophets and the Law.* MHUC 4. Cincinnati: HUC-Jewish Institute of Religion, 1974. **Carmichael, C. M.** *The Laws of Deuteronomy.* Ithaca: Cornell UP, 1974. **Cogan, M.** *Imperialism and Religion: Assyria, Judah and Israel in the Eighth and Seventh Centuries* B.C.E. Missoula: Society of Biblical Literature, 1974. **Kutsch, E.** *Gottes Zuspruch und Anspruch.* BETL 33. Gembloux: Ed. Duculut, 1974. **Levine, B. A.** *In the Presence of the Lord.* Leiden: Brill, 1974. **Schedl, C.** *Baupläne des Wortes.* Vienna: Herder, 1974. **Whybray, R. N.** *The Intellectual Tradition in the Old Testament.* BZAW 135. Berlin: de Gruyter, 1974.

1975–79: **Floss, J. P.** *Jahwe dienen—Göttern dienen. Terminologische, literarische und semantische Untersuchung einer theologischen Aussage zum Gottesverhältnis im Alten Testament.* BBB 45. Cologne: Hanstein, 1975. **Gilmer, H. W.** *The If-You Form in Israelite Law.* SBLDS 15. Missoula: Scholars, 1975. **Jackson, B. S.** *Essays in Jewish and Comparative Legal History.* SJLA 10. Leiden: Brill, 1975. **Jüngling, H.-W.** *Das Gesetz der Wiedervergeltung und das Ideal der Versöhnung im Alten Testament.* Augsburg: Blasaditsch, 1975. **Mittmann, S.** *Deuteronomium 1,1–6,3. Literarkritisch und traditionsgeschichtlich untersucht.* BZAW 139. Berlin: de Gruyter, 1975 [see G. Braulik, *Bib* 59 (1978) 351–83]. **Morris, P. M. K.** and **James, E.** *A Critical Word Book of Leviticus, Numbers, Deuteronomy.* The Computer Bible 8. Missoula: Scholars, 1975. **Neumann, P. K.** *Hört das Wort Jahwäs. Ein Beitrag zur Komposition alttestamentlicher Schriften.* Schriften zur Stiftung Europa-Kolleg 30. Hamburg: Fundament-Verlag Sasse, 1975. **Otto, E.** *Das Mazzotfest in Gilgal.* BWANT 107. Stuttgart, 1975. **Rofé, A.** *Introduction to the Book of Deuteronomy I. Cult-Unity and Anti-Idolatry Laws* Jerusalem: Aqademon, 1975 (Heb.). **Rose, M.** *Der Ausschliesslichkeitsanspruch Jahwes. Deuteronomische Schultheologie und die Volksfrömmigkeit in der späten Königszeit.* BWANT 106. Stuttgart: Kohlhammer, 1975. **Weinfeld, M.** *Introduction to Deuteronomy, Part I.* Jerusalem, 1975 (Heb.). **Bright, J.** *Covenant and Promise.* Philadelphia: Westminster, 1976. **Buis, P.** *La Notion d'Alliance dans l'Ancien Testament.* LD 88. Paris, 1976. **Cholewinski, A.** *Heiligkeitsgesetz und Deuteronomium.* AnBib 66. Rome: Biblical Institute,

1976. **Rupprecht, K.** *Der Temple von Jerusalem.* Ed. G. Fohrer. BZAW 144. Berlin: de Gruyter, 1976.
**Siwiec, St.** *La guerre de conquête de Canaan dans le Deutéronome.* Rome, 1976. **Blenkinsopp, J.**
*Prophecy and Canon.* Notre Dame UP, 1977. **Brueggemann, W.** *The Land: Place as Gift, Promise,
and Challenge in Biblical Faith.* Philadelphia: Fortress, 1977. **Cohen, A.** *L'entrée en Terre
promise: Deutéronome, Josué, Juges, une lecture de la Bible.* EcoutBib 3. Paris: Desclée De Br., 1977.
**Gutman, J.** (ed.). *The Image and the Word: Confrontations in Judaism, Christianity and Islam.*
Religion and the Arts 4. Missoula, MT: Scholars Press, 1977. **Lohfink, N.** *Unsere grossen Wörter.*
*Das Alte Testament zum Thema dieser Jahre.* Freiburg i.B., 1977 [³1985; ET 1981]. **Mann, T. W.**
*Divine Presence and Guidance in Israelite Tradition.* Baltimore: Johns Hopkins, 1977. **Weimar,
P.** *Untersuchungen zur Redaktionsgeschichte des Pentateuch.* BZAW 146. Berlin: de Gruyter, 1977.
**Begg, C. T.** *Contributions to the Elucidation of the Composition of Deuteronomy with Special Atten-
tion to the Significance of the Numeruswechsel,* 5 vols. Diss., Univ. of Leuven, 1978. **Braulik, G.**
*Die Mittel Deuteronomischer Rhetorik. Erhoben aus Deuteronomium 4,1–40.* AnBib 68. Rome:
Biblical Institute Press, 1978. **Hoppe, L.** *The Origins of Deuteronomy.* Diss., Northwestern Univ.,
1978. **McCarthy, D. J.** *Treaty and Covenant* (new ed., completely rewritten). AnBib 21A.
Rome: Biblical Institute Press, 1978. **Terrien, S.** *The Elusive Presence: Toward a New Biblical
Theology.* Religious Perspectives 26. New York: Harper and Row, 1978. **Tiffany, F. C.** *Parenesis
and Deuteronomy 5–11 (Deut. 4:45; 5:2–11:29): A Form Critical Study.* Diss., School of Theology
at Claremont, 1978. **Valentin, H.** *Aaron: Eine Studie zur vorpriesterschriftlichen Aaron-
Überlieferung.* OBO 18. Göttingen: Vandenhoeck & Ruprecht, 1978. **Wevers, J. W.** *Text
History of the Greek Deuteronomy.* Göttingen: Vandenhoeck & Ruprecht, 1978. **Davies, G. I.**
*The Way of the Wilderness.* Cambridge: Cambridge UP, 1979. **Dietrich, W.** *Israel und Kanaan:
Vom Ringen zweier Gesellschaftssysteme.* SBS 94. Stuttgart: Katholisches Bibelwerk, 1979. **Fritz,
V.** *Israel in der Wüste: Traditionsgeschichtliche Untersuchung der Wüstenüberlieferung des Jahwisten.*
MThSt 7. Marburg: Elwert, 1979. **Köppel, U.** *Das deuteronomistiche Geschichtswerk und seine
Quellen. Der Absicht der deuteronomistischen Geschichtsdarstellung aufgrund des Vergleichs zwischen
Num 21,21–35 und Dtn 2,26–3,3.* Europäische Hochschulschriften, Reihe 23, Theologie 122.
Bern: Lang, 1979. **Schmidt, W. H.** *Einführung in das Alte Testament: Das Deuteronomium.*
Berlin: de Gruyter, 1979. **Skweres, D. E.** *Die Rückverweise im Buch Deuteronomium.* AnBib 79.
Rome: Biblical Institute, 1979.

1980–84: **Auld, A. G.** *Joshua, Moses and the Land: Tetrateuch—Pentateuch—Hexateuch in a
Generation since 1938.* Edinburgh: T. & T. Clark, 1980. **Hoffmann, H.-D.** *Reform und Reformen.
Untersuchungen zu einem Grundthema der deuteronomischen Geschichtsschreibung.* ATANT 66.
Zürich: Theologischer Verlag, 1980. **Leibowitz, N.** *Studies in Devarim.* Tr. A. Newman.
Jerusalem: World Zionist Organization, 1980. **McGonville, J. G.** *Cultic Laws in Deuteronomy.*
Diss, Queen's Univ., Belfast, 1980. **Polzin, R.** *Moses and the Deuteronomist: A Literary Study of
the Deuteronomic History:* Part One: *Deuteronomy, Joshua, Judges.* New York: Seabury Press, 1980.
**Rifat, S.** *Motive Clauses in Hebrew Law: Biblical Forms and Near Eastern Parallels.* Missoula:
Scholars, 1980. **Friedman, R. E.** *The Exile and Biblical Narrative: The Formation of the
Deuteronomistic and Priestly Works.* HSM 22. Chico: Scholars, 1981. **Giesen, G.** Die Wurzel שבע
*"schwören": Eine semasiologische Studie zum Eid im Alten Testament.* BBB 56. Bonn: Hanstein,
1981. **Lang, B.** *Der einzige Gott: Die Geburt des biblischen Monotheismus.* Munich: Kösel, 1981.
**Lemaire, A.** *Les Écoles et la formation de la Bible dans l'Ancien Israel.* OBO 39. Göttingen:
Vandenhoeck & Ruprecht, 1981. **Lohfink, N.** *Great Themes from the Old Testament.* Tr. R. Walls.
Franciscan Herald Press, 1981 [Ger. ed. 1977]. **Nelson, R. D.** *The Double Redaction of the
Deuteronomistic History.* JSOTSup 18. Sheffield: JSOT, 1981. **Noth, M.** *The Deuteronomistic
History.* JSOTSup 15. Sheffield: JSOT, 1981 [Ger. ed. 1943]. **Rose, M.** *Deuteronomist und
Jahwist. Untersuchung zu den Berührungspunkten beider Literaturwerke.* ATANT 67. Zürich:
Theologische Verlag, 1981. **Wilms, F.-E.** *Freude vor Gott: Kult und Fest in Israel.* Schlüssel zur
Bibel. Regensburg: Pustet, 1981. **Ginsberg, L. H.** *The Israelian Heritage of Judaism.* Texts and
Studies of the Jewish Theological Seminary of America 24. New York: Jewish Theological
Seminary of America, 1982. **Mettinger, T. N. D.** *The Dethronement of Sabaoth: Studies in the*

*Shem and Kabod Theologies.* ConB OT Series 18. Lund: CWK Gleerup, 1982. **Preuss, H. D.** *Deuteronomium.* Erträge der Forschung 164. Darmstadt: Wissenschaftliche Buchgesellschaft, 1982. **Rofé, A.** *Introduction to Deuteronomy: Further Chapters.* Jerusalem: Akademon Publishing House, 1982 (Heb.). **Sanmartin Ascaso, J.** *Las guerras de Josué: Estudio de Semiótica narrativa.* Institución San Jerónimo 14. Valencia, 1982. **Benjamin, D. C.** *Deuteronomy and City Life: A Form Criticism of Texts with the Word CITY (ᶜîr) in Deuteronomy 4:41–26:19.* Lanham, MD: University Press of America, 1983. **Epsztein, L.** *La justice sociale dans le Proche-Orient ancien et le peuple de la Bible.* Études annexes de la Bible de Jérusalem. Paris: du Cerf, 1983. **Nielsen, E.** *Law, History and Tradition: Selected Essays Issued by Friends and Colleagues.* Ed. N. Holm-Nielsen and O. Benedikt. Copenhagen: Gad, 1983. **Ries, G.** *Prolog und Epilog in Gesetzen des Altertums.* MBPR 76. Munich: Beck, 1983. **Schuman, N. A.** *Deuteronomium; op weg naar hat land Utopia.* Kampen: VBG ed., 1983. **Strecker, G.** (ed.). *Das Land Israel in biblischer Zeit: Jerusalem Symposium 1981 der Hebräischen Universität und der Georg-August-Universität.* GTA 25. Göttingen: Vandenhoeck & Ruprecht, 1983. **Tan, Chew Weng.** *A Comparative Study of the Concept of Election in the Book of Deuteronomy and the Book of Jonah and Its Implications for Bible Study in the Chinese Churches in South-East Asia Today.* Diss., School of Theology at Claremont, 1983. **McConville, J. G.** *Law and Theology in Deuteronomy.* JSOTSup 33. Sheffield: JSOT Press, 1984.

1985–90: **Carmichael, C. M.** *Law and Narrative in the Bible: The Evidence of the Deuteronomic Laws and the Decalogue.* Ithaca: Cornell University Press, 1985. **Fishbane, M.** *Biblical Interpretation in Ancient Israel.* Oxford: Oxford UP, 1985. **Gottfriedsen, C.** *Die Fruchtbarkeit von Israels Land.* Europäische Hochschulschriften 23. Frankfurt: Peter Lang, 1985. **Haag, E.** (ed.). *Gott der Einzige. Zur Entstehung des Monotheismus in Israel.* QD 104. Vienna: Freiburg, Basel/Vienna: Herder, 1985. **Lohfink, N.** (ed.). *Das Deuteronomium. Entstehung, Gestalt und Botschaft.* BETL 68. Leuven: UP, 1985. **Patrick, D.** *Old Testament Law.* Atlanta: Knox, 1985. **Weinfeld, M.** *Justice and Righteousness in Israel and the Nations: Equality and Freedom in Ancient Israel in Light of Social Justice in the Ancient Near East.* Jerusalem: Magnes Press, 1985. **Wesel, U.** *Frühformen des Rechts in vorstaatlichen Gesellschaften.* Frankfurt, 1985. **Bovati, P.** *Ristabilire la Giustizia. Procedure, Vocabulario, Orientamenti.* AnBib 110. Rome: Biblical Institute Press, 1986. **Koch, D.-A.** *Die Schrift als Zeuge des Evangeliums.* BHTh 69. Tübingen: Mohr, 1986. **Tigay, J. J.** *You Shall Have No Other Gods: Israelite Religion in the Light of Hebrew Inscriptions.* HSS 31. Atlanta: Scholars, 1986. **Knapp, D.** *Deuteronomium 4. Literarische Analysen und theologische Interpretation.* GTA 35. Göttingen: Vandenhoeck & Ruprecht, 1987. Issue on"The Book of Deuteronomy." *Int* 41 (July 1987) 229–440. **Niehr, H.** *Rechtsprechung in Israel.* Ed. H. Merklein and E. Zenger. SBS 130. Stuttgart: Katholisches Bibelwerk, 1987. **Rüterswörden, U.** *Von der politischen Gemeinschaft zur Gemeinde. Studien zu Dt 16,18–18,22.* BBB 65. Frankfurt: Athenaum, 1987. **Schulz, H.** *Leviten im vorstaatlichen Israel und im Mittleren Osten.* Munich: Kaiser, 1987. **Sitarz, E.** (ed.). *Höre, Israel! Jahwe ist einzig. Bausteine für eine Theologie des Alten Testament.* BBB 5. Stuttgart: Katholisches Bibelwerk, 1987. **Whybray, R. N.** *The Making of the Pentateuch: A Methodological Study.* JSOTSup 53. Sheffield: Sheffield Academic Press, 1987. **Aurelius, E.** *Der Fürbitter Israels. Eine Studie zum Mosebild im Alten Testament.* Ed. T. N. D. Mettinger and M. Y. Ottoson. ConB OT 27. Lund: Almqvist & Wiksell, 1988. **Boling, R. G.** *The Early Biblical Community in Transjordan.* SWBA 6. Sheffield: Almond Press, 1988. **Braulik, G.** *Studien zur Theologie des Deuteronomiums.* SBAB 2. Stuttgart: Verlag Katholisches Bibelwerk, 1988. **Buchholz, J.** *Die Ältesten Israels im Deuteronomium.* GTA 36. Göttingen: Vandenhoeck & Ruprecht, 1988. **Coats, G. W.** *Moses: Heroic Man, Man of God.* JSOTSup 57. Sheffield: Sheffield Academic Press, 1988. **Garcia Lopez, F.** *Le Deutéronome une Loi Prêchée.* Cahiers Evangile 63. Paris: du Cerf, 1988. **Lohfink, N.** *Studien zum Pentateuch.* SBAB 4. Stuttgart: Verlag Katholisches Bibelwerk, 1988. **Mulder, M. J.** (ed.). *Mikra: Text, Translation, Reading and Interpretation of the Hebrew Bible in Ancient Judaism and Early Christianity.* Assan/Maastricht: Van Gorcum, 1988. **Otto, E.** *Wandel der Rechtsbegründungen in der Gesellschaftsgeschichte des antiken Israel. Eine Rechtsgeschichte des*

"Bundesbuches" Ex XX 22—XXIII 13. SB 3. Leiden: Brill, 1988. **Regt, L. J. De.** *A Parametric Model for Syntactic Studies of a Textual Corpus, Demonstrated on the Hebrew of Deuteronomy 1–30.* Studia Semitica Neerlandica. Assen-Maastricht: Van Gorcum, 1988. **Rofé, A.** *Introduction to Deuteronomy: Part I and Further Chapters.* Jerusalem: Akademon Publishing House, 1988 (Heb.). **Westbrook, R.** *Studies in Biblical and Cuneiform Law.* CahRB 26. Paris: Gabalda, 1988. **White, S.** *The Critical Edition of Seven Manuscripts of Deuteronomy.* Diss., Harvard University, 1988. *"Gesetz" als Thema Biblischer Theologie.* JBTh 4. Neukirchen-Vluyn: Neukirchener Verlag, 1989. Issue on "The Decalogue." Interpretation 43/3 (July 1989). **Duncan, J.** *A Critical Edition of Deuteronomy Manuscripts from Qumran Cave 4.* Diss., Harvard University, 1989. **Eslinger, L.** *Into the Hands of the Living God.* JSOTSup 84. Bible and Literature Series 24. Sheffield: Almond Press, 1989. **Ha, J.** *Genesis 15: A Theological Compendium of Pentateuchal History.* Ed. O. Kaiser. BZAW 181. Berlin: de Gruyter, 1989. **Hossfeld, F.-L.** (ed.). *Vom Sinai zum Horeb. Stationen alttestamentlicher Glaubensgeschichte.* Würzburg: Echter, 1989. **Lohfink, N.** *Unsere neuen Fragen und das Alte Testament. Wiederendeckte Lebensweisung.* Frieburg: Herder, 1989. **Firmage, E. B., Weiss, B. G.,** and **Welch, J. W.** *Religion and Law: Biblical-Judaic and Islamic Perspectives.* Winona Lake, IN: Eisenbrauns, 1990. Issue on "The Figure of Moses." *Interpretation* 44/3 (July 1990). **Lohfink, N.** *Studien zum Deuteronomium und zur deuteronomistischen Literatur I.* SBAB 8. Stuttgart: Verlag Katholisches Bibelwerk, 1990.————.*Studien zum Deuteronomium und zur deuteronomistischen Literatur II.* SBAB 12. Stuttgart: Verlag Katholisches Bibelwerk, 1990. **Merwe, C. H. J. van der.** *The Old Hebrew particle gam: A syntactic-semantic description of gam in Gn–2Kg.* ATSAT 34. St. Ottilien: EOS Verlag, 1990. **Christensen, D. L.** (ed.). *A Song of Power and the Power of Song: Essays in Deuteronomy.* Winona Lake, IN: Eisenbrauns, 1991. **Haïk-Vantoura, S.** *The Music of the Bible Revealed.* Tr. D. Weber, ed. J. Wheeler. Berkeley: BIBAL Press, 1991.

## FESTSCHRIFTEN
(WITH SIGNIFICANT ARTICLES ON DEUTERONOMY)

A number of important articles on Deuteronomy appear in collections of essays presented in honor of various scholars. Since these entries tend to take up considerable space when cited in full, and are referred to numerous times throughout the commentary, they are listed here for reference in chronological order. Citations of these works in the commentary will include both the name of the person honored and the date of publication.

1897–1949: *Semitic Studies in Memory of Rev. Dr. Alexander Kohut.* Ed. G. A. Kohut. Berlin, 1897. *Abhandlungen zur Semitischen Religionskunde und Sprachwissenschaft: FS Baudissin.* Ed. W. Frankenberg. Giessen: Töpelmann, 1918. Εὐχαριστήριον. *FS H. Gunkel.* Ed. H. Schmidt. FRLANT 36. Göttingen: Vandenhoeck & Ruprecht, 1923. *Vom Alten Testament: FS K. Marti.* Ed. K. Budde. Giessen: Töpelmann, 1925. *Beiträge zur Religionsgeschichte und Archäologie Palästinas: FS Ernst Sellin.* Leipzig: A. Deichertsche Verlagsbuchhandlung, 1927. *FS für Georg Beer zum 70. Geburtstag.* Ed. A. Weiser. Stuttgart: Kohlhammer, 1935. *Jewish Studies in Memory of G. A. Kohut.* Ed. S. W. Baron and A. Marx. New York, 1935. *Theologische Aufsätze K. Barth zum 50. Geburstag.* Munich: Kaiser, 1936.

1950–59: *FS A. Bertholet.* Tübingen: Mohr, 1950. *Alexander Marx Jubilee Volume on the Occasion of His 70th Birthday.* New York: Jewish Theological Seminary of America, 1950. *Studies in Old Testament Prophecy, Presented to Th. H. Robinson.* Ed. H. H. Rowley. Edinburgh: T & T Clark, 1950. *Antwort: FS K. Barth.* Zollikon-Zürich: Evangelischer Verlag, 1956. *Von Ugarit nach Qumran. Beiträge zur alttestamentlichen und altorientalischen Forschung: FS O. Eissfeldt.* BZAW 77. Berlin: de Gruyter, 1958.

1960–64: *Kirche und Überlieferung: FS J. R. Geiselmann.* Ed. J. Betz. Freiburg: Herder, 1960. *Studies in Bible and Jewish Religion: FS Y. Kaufmann.* Ed. M. Haran. Jerusalem, 1960. *The Bible and the Ancient Near East: Essays in Honor of W. F. Albright.* Garden City, NY: Doubleday, 1961 [Anchor Book Edition, 1965]. *A la Rencontre Dieu: FS A. Gelin.* Bibliothèque de la Faculté Catholique de Théologie de Lyon 8. Le Puy: Mappus, 1961. *Lex Tua Veritas: FS H. Junker.* Trier: Paulinus, 1961. *Verbannung und Heimkehr: FS W. Rudolph.* Tübingen: Mohr, 1961. *Israel's Prophetic Heritage: FS J. Muilenburg.* Ed. B. W. Anderson and W. Harrelson. London: SCM, 1962. *Hebrew and Semitic Studies: FS G. R. Driver.* Ed. D. W. Thomas and W. D. McHardy. Oxford: Clarendon Press, 1963. *Abraham Unser Vater: FS O. Michel.* Arbeiten zur Geschichte des Spätjudentums und Urchristentums 5. Leiden: Brill, 1963. *Gattung und Herkunft des Rahmens im Richterbuch: FS A. Weiser.* Ed. E. Würthwein and O. Kaiser. Göttingen, 1963. *Mullus: FS T. Klauser.* Jahrbuch für Antike und Christentum 1. Münster: Aschendorffsche Verlagsbuchhandlung, 1964. *Gott in Welt: Festgabe für Karl Rahner,* Band I. Ed. J. B. Metz et al. Freiburg: Herder, 1964.

1965–69: *Gottes Wort und Gottes Land: FS H. W. Hertzberg.* Göttingen: Vandenhoeck & Ruprecht, 1965. *Parrhesia: K. Barth zum 80. Geburtstag.* Zürich: EVZ-Verlag, 1966. *Freude am Evangelium, A. de Quervain zum 70. Geburtstag.* Ed. J. J. Stamm and E. Wolf. BEvT 44. Munich: Kaiser, 1966. *Studie Biblica et Semitica: Th. C. Vriezen Dedicata.* Ed. W. van Unnik and A. van der Woude. Wageningen, 1966. *Hebräische Wortforschung: FS W. Baumgartner.* VTSup 16. Leiden: Brill, 1967. *Studi sull' oriente e la Bibbia: FS G. Rinaldi.* Ed. G. Buccellati. Gênes: Editrice Studio e Vita, 1967. *Das ferne und das nahe Wort: FS L. Rost.* Ed. F. Maass. BZAW 105. Berlin: Töpelmann, 1967. *Religions in Antiquity: FS E. R. Goodenough.* Ed. J. Neusner. Leiden: Brill, 1968. *Leben Angesichts des Todes: FS H. Thielicke.* Tübingen: Mohr, 1968. *Words and Meanings: FS D. W. Thomas.* Ed. P. Ackroyd and B. Lindars. Cambridge: Cambridge UP, 1968. *FS W. F. Albright.* Ed. A. Malamat. *EI* 9. Jerusalem: Israel Exploration Society, 1969. *Studi in Onore de Edoardo Volterra,* vol. 6. Ed. A. Giuffré. Milan, 1969.

1970–74: *Proclamation and Presence: FS G. H. Davies.* Ed. J. I. Durham and J. R. Porter. Richmond-London, 1970 [rep. Macon, GA: Mercer UP, 1983]. *Fides et Communicatio: FS M. Doerne.* Ed. D. Rössler et al. Göttingen: Vandenhoeck & Ruprecht, 1970. *Near Eastern Archaeology in the Twentieth Century: FS N. Glueck.* Ed. J. A. Sanders. New York: Doubleday, 1970. *Die Zeit Jesu. FS für Heinrich Schlier.* Ed. G. Bornkamm and K. Rahner. Freiburg: Herder, 1970. *Near Eastern Studies in Honor of W. F. Albright.* Ed. H. Goedicke. Baltimore: Johns Hopkins UP, 1971. *Mélanges A. Dupont-Sommer.* Paris, 1971. *Die Kirche im Wandel der Zeit: Festgabe für Kardinal Joseph Höffner.* Ed. F. Groner. Cologne: Bachem, 1971. *Schalom. Studien zu Glaube und Geschichte Israels. Alfred Jepsen zum 70. Geburtstag.* Ed. K. Bernhardt. Arbeiten zur Theologie 1. Stuttgart: Calwer, 1971. *Testimonium Veritati, FS für Bischof Wilhelm Kempf.* Ed. H. Wolter. Frankfurter Theologische Studien 7. Frankfurt, 1971. *Probleme Biblischer Theology: FS G. von Rad.* Ed. H. W. Wolff. Munich: Kaiser, 1971. *De Fructu Oris Sui: Essays in Honour of A. van Selms.* POS 9. Leiden: Brill, 1971. *Wort, Lied und Gottesspruch: Beiträge zu Psalmen und Propheten: FS J. Ziegler.* Ed. J. Schreiner. Würzburg: Echter, 1972. *Wort und Geschichte: FS K. Elliger.* Ed. H. Gese and H. Rüger. AOAT 18. Neukirken: Kevealer, Butzon & Berker, 1973. *Das Wort und die Wörter: FS G. Friedrich.* Stuttgart: Kohlhammer, 1973. *FS Theodor Herzel Gaster.* Ed. M. David. JANESCU 5. New York: Columbia University, 1973. *Orient and Occident: FS C. H. Gordon.* Ed. H. A. Hoffner. AOAT 22. Neukirken: Kevealer, Butzon & Berker, 1973. *Symbolae Biblicae et Mesopotamicae F. M. T. de Liagre Böhl Dedicatae.* Leiden: Brill, 1973. *Wort Gottes in der Zeit: FS K. H. Schelkle.* Ed. H. Feld and S. Nolte. Düsseldorf: Patmos, 1973. *Daube Noster: Essays in Legal History for D. Daube.* Ed. A. Watson. Edinburgh-London, 1974. *Essays in Old Testament Ethics: J. Philip Hyatt in Memoriam.* Ed. J. L. Crenshaw and J. T. Willis. New York: Ktav, 1974. *A Light unto My Path: FS J. M. Myers.* Ed. H. Bream. Philadelphia: Temple UP, 1974.

1975–79: *Grace upon Grace: Essays in Honor of Lester J. Kuyper.* Ed. J. I. Cook. Grand Rapids: Eerdmans, 1975. *No Famine in the Land: Studies in Honor of J. L. McKenzie.* Ed. J. W. Flanagan and A. W. Robinson. Missoula: Scholars, 1975. *Word and Spirit: Essays in Honor of David Michael Stanley SJ on his 60th Birthday.* Ed. J. Plevnik. Willowdale, Ontario: Regis College Press, 1975. *Jews, Greeks and Christians: Religious Cultures in Late Antiquity: FS W. D. Davies.* Ed. R. Hammerton-Kelly and R. Scroggs. Leiden: Brill, 1976. *Magnalia Dei: The Mighty Acts of God. Essays on the Bible and Archaeology in Memory of G. E. Wright.* Ed. F. M. Cross. Garden City, NY: Doubleday, 1976. *Bausteine Biblischer Theologie: FS G. J. Botterweck zum 60. Geburtstag.* Ed. H.-J. Fabry. BBB 50. Cologne: Hanstein, 1977. *Essays on the Ancient Near East in Memory of Jacob Joel Finkelstein.* Memoirs of the Connecticut Academy of Arts and Sciences 19. Hamden, CT: Archon Books, 1977. *Studien zum Pentateuch: FS W. Kornfeld zum 60. Geburtstag.* Ed. G. Braulik. Vienna: Herder, 1977. *Beiträge zur Alttestamentlichen Theologie: FS W. Zimmerli.* Ed. H. Donner et al. Göttingen: Vandenhoeck & Ruprecht, 1977. *Gabe für Friedrich Lang zum 65. Geburtstag.* Tübingen, 1978. *Biblical and Near Eastern Studies: FS W. S. LaSor.* Ed. G. A. Tuttle. Grand Rapids: Eerdmans, 1978. *Studies in Bible and Ancient Near East: FS E. Loewenstamm.* Ed. Y. Avishur and J. Blaub. Jerusalem: Rubenstein, 1978.

1980–84: *Kirche: FS G. Bornkamm zum 75. Geburtstag.* Ed. D. Lührmann and G. Strecker. Tübingen, 1980. *The Bible World: FS C. H. Gordon.* Ed. G. Rendsburg et al. New York: Ktav, 1980. *Études d'histoire et de pensée juives: FS G. Vajda.* Ed. G. Nahon and C. Touati. Louvain-la-Neuve, 1980. *Werden und Wirken des Alten Testament: FS C. Westermann.* Ed. R. Albertz et al. Göttingen: Vandenhoeck & Ruprecht, 1980. *Mélanges D. Barthélemy. Études Bibliques Offertes a l'Occasion de son 60ᵉ Anniversaire.* Ed. P. Casetti, O. Keel, A. Schenker. OBO 38. Fribourg, 1981. *Mélanges Bibliques et Orientaux en l'Honneur de M. Henri Cazelles.* Ed. A. Caquot and M. Delcor. AOAT 212. Kevelaer/Neukirchen-Vluyn: Butzon & Bercker/Neukirchener, 1981. *De la Torah an Messie: FS H. Cazelles.* Ed. M. Carrez, J. Doré, and P. Grelot. Paris: Desclee, 1981. *Tradition and Transformation: Turning Points in Biblical Faith: FS F. M. Cross.* Ed. B. Halpern and J. Levenson. Winona Lake: Eisenbrauns, 1981. *Im Gespräch: der Mensch: FS J. Möller.* Ed. H. Gauly et al. Düsseldorf: Patmos, 1981. *Studies Presented to Hans Jakob Polotsky.* Ed. D. W. Young. East Gloucester, MA: Pirtle & Polson, 1981. *Die Botschaft und die Boten: FS H. W. Wolff.* Ed. J. Jeremias and L. Perlitt. Neukirchen-Vluyn: Neukirchener Verlag, 1981. *FS A. Brelich.* Ed. V. Lanternari and M. Massenzio. Religioni e Civiltà 3. Bari: Dedalolibri, 1982. *Societies and Languages of the Ancient Near East: Studies in Honor of I. M. Diakonoff.* Ed. M. A. Dandamayev. Warminster: Aris & Phillips, 1982. *Vom Amt des Laien in Kirche und Theologie: FS G. Krause.* Ed. H. Schröer and G. Müller. Theologische Bibliothek Töpelmann 39. Berlin: de Gruyter, 1982. *Vonn Kanaan bis Kerala: FS J. P. M. van der Ploeg.* Ed. W. C. Delsman et al. AOAT 211. Kevelaer: Butzon & Bercker, 1982. *Interpreting the Hebrew Bible: Essays in Honour of E. I. J. Rosenthal.* Ed. J. A. Emerton and S. C. Reif. University of Cambridge Oriental Publications 32. Cambridge: Press Syndicate of the University of Cambridge, 1982. *Das Lebendige Wort: Beiträge zur kirchlichen Verkündigung. FS F. G. Voigt.* Ed. H. Seidel and K.-H. Bieritz. Berlin: Evangelische Verlagsanstalt, 1982. *FS Y. Yadin. JJS* 33 (1982). *El Misterio de la Palabra: Homenaje de sus alumnos al profesor D. Luis Alonso Schökel al cumplir veinticinco años de magisterio en el Biblico Pontificio.* Ed. V. Collado and E. Zurro. Madrid: Edicines Cristiandad, 1983. *Fontes agque Pontes: FS Helmut Brunner.* Ed. M. Görg. ÄgAT 5. Wurtemburg: Harrassowitz, 1983. *The Word of the Lord Shall Go Forth: Essays in Honor of David Noel Freedman in Celebration of His Sixtieth Birthday.* Ed. C. Meyers and M. O'Connor. ASOR: Special Volume Series 1. Winona Lake: Eisenbrauns, 1983. *"Wenn Nicht Jetzt, Wann Dann?": Aufsätze für Hans-Joachim Kraus zum 65. Geburtstag.* Ed. H.-G. Geyer et al. Neukirchen-Vluyn: Neukirchener Verlag, 1983. *The Quest for the Kingdom of God: Studies in Honor of George E. Mendenhall.* Ed. H. Huffmon, F. Spina, and A. Green. Winona Lake: Eisenbrauns, 1983. *Meqor Ḥajjim: FS für Georg Molin zu seinem 75. Geburtstag.* Ed. I. Seybold. Graz: Akademische

Druck; und Verlagsanstalt, 1983. *Freude am Gottesdienst: Aspekte ursprünglicher Liturgie: FS J.G. Plöger.* Ed. J. Schreiner. Stuttgart: Katholisches Bibelwerk, 1983. *Essays on the Bible and the Ancient World: Isaac Leo Seeligmann Volume.* Ed. A. Rofé and Y. Zakovitch. Jerusalem, 1983. *Essays in Honor of Yigael Yadin.* Ed. G. Vermes and J. Neusner. Totowa, NJ: Allanheld, Osmun & Co., 1983. *In the Shelter of Elyon: Essays on Ancient Palestinian Life and Literature in Honor of G. W. Ahlström.* Ed. W. B. Barrick and J. R. Spencer. JSOTSup 31. Sheffield: JSOT Press, 1984. *Palabra y Vida: FS José Alonso Díaz.* Ed. A. Vargas-Machuca and G. Ruiz. Publicaciones de la Universidad Pontificia Comillas de Madrid, Serie I, 28. Madrid: Universidad Comillas, 1984. *Diener in Eurer Mitte: FS für Dr. Anonius Hofmann Bischof von Passau zum 75. Geburtstag.* Ed. R. Beer et al. Schriften der Universität Passau, Reihe Katholische Theologie 5. Passau: Passavia Universitätsverlag, 1984. *Hommage à Robert Martin-Achard.* Ed. M. Faessler. Bulletin du Centre Protestant d'Études. Geneva, 1984. *The New Testament Age: Essays in Honor of Bo Reiche,* vol. 2. Ed. W. C. Weinrich. Macon, GA: Mercer UP, 1984. *De Septuaginta: Studies in Honor of John William Wevers on his Sixty-fifth Birthday.* Ed. A. Pietersma and C. Cox. Mississauga, Ontario: Benben, 1984.

1985–90: *Mélanges Biblique Orientaux: FS Matthias Delcor.* AOAT 215. Kevelaer: Butzon & Berker, 1985. *The Bible in the Medieval World: Essays in Memory of Beryl Smalley.* Ed. K. Walsh and D. Wood. Studies in Church History, Subsidia 4. Oxford: Blackwell, 1985. *Theologische Brosamen für Lothar Steiger zu seinem 50. Geburtstag.* Ed. E. Stegemann. BDBAT 5. Heidelberg, 1985. *Scripta Signa Vocis: FS J. H. Hospers.* Groningen: Egbert Forsten, 1986. Ancient Israelite Religion: *FS F. M. Cross.* Ed. P. Miller, P. Hanson, and S. McBride. Philadelphia: Fortress, 1987. *Love and Death in the Ancient Near East: Essays in Honor of Marvin H. Pope.* Ed. J. H. Marks and R. M. Good. Guilford, CT: Four Quarters Publishing Co., 1987. *Ascribe to the Lord: Biblical & Other Studies in Memory of Peter C. Craigie.* Ed. L. Eslinger and G. Taylor. JSOTSup 67. Sheffield: JSOT Press, 1988. *Israel's Apostasy and Restoration: Essays in Honor of Roland K. Harrison.* Ed. A. Gileadi. Grand Rapids, MI: Baker, 1988. *FS N. Lohfink.* BN 43 (1988). *Justice and the Holy: Essays in Honor of Walter Harrelson.* Ed. D. A. Knight and P. J. Paris. Atlanta: Scholars Press, 1989. *Prophet und Prophetenbuch: FS Otto Kaiser zum 65. Geburtstag.* Ed. V. Fritz. BZAW 185. Berlin: de Gruyter, 1989. *Die Väter Israels: Beiträge zur Theologie der Patriarchenüberlieferungen im Alten Testament: FS für Josef Scharbert zum 70. Geburtstag.* Ed. M. Görg. Stuttgart: Katholisches Bibelwerk, 1989. *Neues Testament und Ethik: Für Rudolf Schnackenburg.* Ed. H. Merklein. Freiberg: Herder, 1989. *Die alttestamentliche Botshaft als Wegweisung: FS für Heinz Reinelt.* Ed. J. Zmijewski. Stuttgart: Katholisches Bibelwerk, 1990. *Ein Gott eine Offenbarung: Beiträge zur biblischen Exegese, Theologie und Spiritualität: FS für Notker Füglister OSB zum 60. Geburtstag.* Ed. V. Reiterer. Würzburg: Ecther Verlag, 1991.

# Introduction

Deuteronomy is the last of the five books of the Pentateuch, which in Jewish tradition are commonly called the Torah or the books of Moses. The name Deuteronomy comes from a mistranslation by the Septuagint translators of a clause in Deuteronomy 17:18, which refers to a *repetition* (δευτερονόμιον) *of this law.* The Hebrew actually instructs the king to make "a copy of this law." The error on which the English title rests, however, is not serious, for Deuteronomy is in fact a repetition of the law of Moses as delivered at Mount Sinai (Horeb) in the books of Exodus, Leviticus, and Numbers. It is also the literary bridge connecting the first two major segments of the canon in the Hebrew Bible: the Torah and the Former Prophets (Joshua, Judges, Samuel, and Kings—sometimes called the Deuteronomic History).

As with the other books of the Pentateuch, the Hebrew title is taken from the opening words of the book, אלה הדברים, sometimes cited in English as simply "Devarim." Since the root דבר, in its various derived forms, cannot be translated consistently by a single English term, its presence will be noted in the English translation of the Hebrew text throughout the commentary. The significance of the Hebrew title of the book will become readily apparent to the careful reader.

As a legal document, Deuteronomy is essentially a national "constitution," or what S. D. McBride has called the "Polity of the Covenant People" (*Int* 41 [1987] 229–44). Though it contains a series of laws, it is not a law code as such, but rather a work intended for religious instruction and education in ancient Israel. As such, it is a work of extraordinary literary coherence, poetic beauty, and political sophistication. In short, Deuteronomy represents a very early, and a remarkably comprehensive, attempt to reform and transmit religion by means of a program of religious education in which every person was to be included, from the king as the head of the nation to each child in every home (cf. Deut 4:9, 10; 6:7, 20; 11:19; 31:13; 32:7, 46).

The book expounds the implications of the historic agreement at Mount Sinai between God and Israel by which the latter became the chosen people. The author's purpose was to maintain the loyalty toward God which Israel professed when the Sinai covenant was ratified, so that the people would never be in doubt as to the high moral and spiritual standards demanded by God of His people. The book is essentially an exposition of the great commandment: "You shall love the Lord your God with all your heart, and with all your soul, and with all your might" (Deut 6:5). It was from Deuteronomy that Jesus summarized the entire old covenant in a single sentence (Matt 22:37; cf. Deut 6:5); and from the same he quoted God's revelation in response to each of Satan's temptations (Matt 4:4, 7, 10; cf. Deut 8:3; 6:16, 13).

Deuteronomy is often outlined as a series of three discourses, followed by three short appendices: 1:1–4:43, an historical review of God's dealings with Israel recounting the chief events in the nation's experience from Horeb to Moab, concluding with an earnest appeal to be faithful and obedient, and in particular to keep clear of all forms of idolatry; 4:44–26:19, a hortatory résumé of Israel's moral and civil statutory rulings; and 27:1–31:30, a predictive and minatory section, which begins with a ritual of covenant blessings and curses and concludes with Moses' farewell charge to Israel and his formal commission of Joshua as his successor, following the renewal of the covenant in Moab. Three appendices close the book: the "Song of Moses" (Deut 32), which the great lawgiver taught the people; the "Blessing of Moses" (Deut 33), which forecasts the future of the various tribes; and an account of Moses' death and burial (Deut 34).

The structure of the book may also be described in terms of a five-part concentric design, as follows:

A    THE OUTER FRAME: A Look Backwards (Deut 1–3)
  B    THE INNER FRAME: The Great Peroration (Deut 4–11)
    C    THE CENTRAL CORE: Covenant Stipulations (Deut 12–26)
  B'   THE INNER FRAME: The Covenant Ceremony (Deut 27–30)
A'   THE OUTER FRAME: A Look Forwards (Deut 31–34)

The two parts of the Outer Frame (Deut 1–3 and 31–34) may be read as a single document, tied together by the figure of Joshua who appears only in Deut 3, 31, and 34. The two parts of the Inner Frame (Deut 4–11 and 27–30) may also be read as a single document, joined together by the reference to blessings and curses connected with a cultic ceremony on Mount Gerizim and Mount Ebal (Deut 11:26–32 and 27:1–14), which are mentioned only in these two contexts within the book of Deuteronomy. At the center of this construction lies the Central Core (Deut 12–26), which is the primary body of instruction in the culture of ancient Israel, sometimes called the deuteronomic law code. This block of material is in turn arranged in "a remarkably coherent five-part structure" (McBride, *Int* 41 [1987] 239), which is also organized concentrically. In fact, it will be shown in this commentary that each of these five major parts of the book of Deuteronomy may in turn be analyzed into somewhat similar concentric structures.

The presence of carefully balanced structures at virtually all levels of analysis within the book of Deuteronomy suggests a rather different model for explaining the form and function of the book from what is often assumed. Such structures are common in works of art, both from antiquity and in the present, particularly in the fields of epic poetry and music. The reason for the similarity is apparently the simple fact that in its essential nature the book of Deuteronomy is itself a work of literary art in poetic form, subject to the restraints of the musical media to which it was originally composed in ancient Israel.

## Text and Versions of Deuteronomy

BIBLIOGRAPHY: TEXT AND VERSIONS OF DEUTERONOMY

**Aly, Z.** *Three Rolls of the Early Septuagint: Genesis and Deuteronomy.* Papyrologische Texte und Abhandlungen 27. Bonn: Rudolf Habelt, 1980. **Baars, W.** *New Syro Hexaplaric Texts edited, commented upon and compared with the Septuagint.* Leiden, 1968. **Barr, J.** "Vocalization and the Analysis of Hebrew among the Ancient Translators." VTSup 16. Leiden: Brill, 1967. 1–11. **Ben Hayyim, Z**. *The Literary and Oral Tradition of Hebrew and Aramaic amongst the Samaritans* (Heb.), 5 vols. Jerusalem, 1957–77 [contains phonetic transcription of Samaritan tradition]. **Berliner, A**. *Targum Onkelos*, 1–2. Berlin, 1884. **Billen, A. V**. *The Old Latin Text of the Heptateuch.* Cambridge, 1928. **Bowker, J**. *The Targums and Rabbinic Literature: An Introduction to Jewish Interpretation of Scripture.* Cambridge UP, 1969. **Boyarin, D**. (ed.). *Targum Onkelos to the Pentateuch: A Collection of Fragments in the Library of the Jewish Theological Seminary of America, New York.* First Series: Mss. New York 152–153, 2 vols. Jerusalem, 1976. **Brock, S. P., Fritsch, C. T., and Jellicoe, S**. *A Classified Bibliography of the Septuagint.* ALGHJ 6; 1973 [literature to 1969]. **Brooke, A. E**. and **McLean, N**. *The Old Testament in Greek.* Vol. 1, Part 3. *Numbers and Deuteronomy.* Cambridge UP, 1911. **Ceriani, A. M**. *Translatio Syra Pescitto Veterus Testamenti ex codice Ambrosiano,* vol. 1. Milan, 1876. **Clarke, E. G**. *Targum Pseudo-Jonathan of the Pentateuch: Text and Concordance.* Hoboken: Ktav, 1984. **Cox, C. E**. *The Armenian Translation of Deuteronomy.* University of Pennsylvania Armenian Texts and Studies 2. Chico: Scholars, 1981. ————. *Hexaplaric Materials Preserved in the Armenian Version.* SBL: Septuagint and Cognate Studies 21. Atlanta: Scholars, 1986. **Cross, F. M**. and **Talmon, S**. *Qumran and the History of the Biblical Text.* Cambridge: Harvard UP, 1975. **Diez Macho, A**. *The Pentateuch with the Masorah Parva and the Masorah Magna and with the Targum Onkelos,* Ms. Vat. Heb. 448, 2 vols. Jerusalem, 1977. ————. *Neofyti I: Targum Palestinense MS. de la Biblioteca Vaticana. V: Deuteronomio.* Madrid: Consejo Superior de Investigaciones Científicas, 1978. ————. *Deuteronomium.* Biblia Polyglotta Matritensia. Series 4, Targum Palaestinense in Pentateuchum; L. 5. Ed. A. Díez Macho. Madrid: Matriti, 1965. **Drazin, I**. *Targum Onkelos to Deuteronomy: An English Translation to the Text with Analysis and Commentary.* (Based on A. Sperber's ed.). New York: Ktav, 1982. **Dunand, F**. *Papyrus grecs bibliques (Papyrus F. Inv 266), Volumina de la Genèse et du Deutéronome.* Cairo: l'Institut français d'archéologie orientale, 1966. **Esh, S**. "Variant Readings in Medieval Hebrew Commentaries: R. Samuel Ben Meir (Rashbam)." *Textus* 5 (1966) 84–92. **Gall, A. F. von**. *Der hebräische Pentateuch der Samaritaner.* Giessen: Töpelmann, 1914–18. **Ginsburg, C. D**. *Introduction to the Massoretical-Critical Edition of the Hebrew Bible.* London, 1897 [rep. Ktav, 1966]. ————. *Jacob Ben Chayim Ibn Adoniajah's Introduction to the Rabbinic Bible . . . and the Massoreth of the Massoreth of Elias Levita.* Library of Biblical Studies. NY: Ktav, [1968]. **Ginsburger, M**. *Das Fragmententhargum (Thargum jeruschalmi zum Pentateuch).* Berlin, 1899. ————. *Pseudo-Jonathan (Thargum Jonathan ben Uziel zum Pentateuch).* Berlin: Calvary, 1903 [rep. Hildesheim: Olms, 1971]. **Goshen-Gottstein, M. H**. and **Shirin, H**. (eds.). *The Bible in the Syropalestinian Version: Part I Pentateuch and Prophets.* Hebrew University Bible Project. Ed. Goshen-Gottstein, M., Rabin, C. and Talmon, S. Jerusalem: Magnes, 1973. ————. *The Aleppo-Codex I. Plates.* Jerusalem, 1976. **Grossfeld, B**. *A Bibliography of Targum Literature.* 2 vols. Bibliographica Judaica, 2 and 8. Cincinnati/New York: HUC Press/Ktav, 1972 and 1977. ————. *The Targum Onqelos to Deuteronomy.* The Aramaic Bible 9. Wilmington, DE: Michael Glazier, 1988. **Hempel, J**. *Librum Deuteronomii: Biblia Hebraica,* 3rd ed. Stuttgart: Privileg. Württembergische Bibelanstalt, 1935. ————. *Der textkritische Wert des Konsonantentextes von Kairener Genizafragmenten in Cambridge und Oxford zum Deuteronomium. Nach Kollationen von H. P. Rüger.* NGAW 2, Philologisch-Historisch Klasse. Göttingen: Vandenhoeck and Ruprecht, 1959. 207–36. ————. *Libum Deuteronomii: Biblia Hebraica Stuttgartensia.* Stuttgart: Deutsche Bibelgesellschaft, 1972. [**Jellicoe**]. *Studies in the Septuagint: Origins, Recensions, and Interpretations: Selected Essays with a Prolegomenon.* Ed. S. Jellicoe. Library of Biblical Studies. NY: Ktav, 1974 ————. *The Septuagint and Modern Study.* Oxford, 1968 [repr. Winona Lake, IN: Eisenbrauns, 1978]. **Kahle, P**. *Masoreten des Westens.* 2 vols. Stuttgart: 1927, 1930 [repr. Hildesheim, 1967]. ————. *The Cairo Geniza,* 2nd ed. New York: Praeger, 1959. ————. *Masoreten des Ostens: Die ältesten punktierten Handschriften des Alten Testaments und der Targums.* Leipzig: Hinrichs, 1963. **Kasser, R**. (ed.). *Deutéronome i–x en sahidique.* Cologny-Genève: Bibliotheca Bodmeriana, 1962. **Klein,**

**M. L.** *The Fragment-Targums of the Pentateuch, according to the Extant Sources,* 2 vols. AnBib 76. Rome: Biblical Institute Press, 1980. ————. *Geniza Manuscripts of Palestinian Targum to the Pentateuch,* 1–2. Cincinnati, 1986. **Lamsa, G. M.** *Old Testament Light: A Scriptural Commentary Based on the Aramaic of the Ancient Peshitta Text.* Englewood Cliffs: Prentice-Hall, 1964. **Le Déaut, R.** and **Robert, J.** *Targum du Pentateuque: Traductions des deux recensions palestiniens complètes.* Vol. 4: *Deutéronome. Bibliographie générale, glossaire et index des quatre tomes.* Sources Chrétiennes 271. Paris: du Cerf, 1980. **Lee, J. A. L.** *A Lexical Study of the Septuagint Version of the Pentateuch.* SBL Septuagint and Cognate Studies 14. Chico: Scholars, 1983. **Peters, M. K. H.** *An Analysis of the Textual Character of the Bohairic of Deuteronomy.* SBL Septuagint and Cognate Studies 9. Missoula: Scholars, 1979. ————. *A Critical Edition of the Coptic (Bohairic) Pentateuch: Vol. V: Deuteronomy.* SBL Septuagint and Cognate Studies 15. Chico: Scholars, 1983. **Reider, D.** *Pseudo-Jonathan: Targum Jonathan ben Uziel on the Pentateuch Copied from the London MS. (British Museum add. 27031).* Jerusalem: Salomon, 1974. **Robert, U.** *Pentateuchi versio latina antiquissima e Codice Lugdunensi.* Paris, 1881. ————. *Heptateuchi partis posterior versio latina antiquissima e Codice Lugdunensi.* Lyon, 1900. **Sabatier, P.** *Biblorum Sacrorum Latinae Versiones antiquae seu Vetus Italica,* 3 vols. Rheims, 1743–49. **Sadaka, A.** *Samaritan Version of the Pentateuch.* Tel Aviv, 1959 [Heb.]. **Sanders, H. A.** (ed.). *The Old Testament Manuscripts in the Freer Collection.* Part I. *The Washington Manuscripts of Deuteronomy and Joshua.* New York, 1917. **Schultz, S. J.** *The Difference between the Masoretic and Septuagint Texts of Deuteronomy.* Diss., Harvard Univ., 1948 [microfilm]. **Sibinga, J. S.** *The Old Testament Text of Justin Martyr. I. The Pentateuch.* Leiden: Brill, 1963. **Skehan, P. W.** "Texts and Versions." *JBC* 2:561–67. **Sperber, A.** *The Bible in Aramaic. I: The Pentateuch according to Targum Onkelos.* Leiden: Brill, 1959. **Tal, A.** *The Samaritan Targum of the Pentateuch: A Critical Edition: Part II: Leviticus, Numeri, Deuteronomium.* Texts and Studies in the Hebrew Language and Related Subjects 5. Tel Aviv: Univ. of Tel Aviv Press, 1981. ————. *The Samaritan Targum of the Pentateuch: A Critical Edition: Part III. Introduction.* Texts and Studies in the Hebrew Language and Related Subjects 6. Tel Aviv: Tel Aviv UP, 1983. **Tov, E.** *The Text-Critical Use of the Septuagint in Biblical Research.* Jerusalem Biblical Studies 3. Jerusalem: Simor, 1981. **Vercellone, C.** *Variae Lectiones Vulgatae Latinae Bibliorum.* Rome: Iospehum Spithöver, 1860. I, 479–584. **Vööbus, A.** *The Pentateuch in the Version of the Syro Hexapla: A Facsimile Edition of a Midyat MS. Discovered in 1964.* CSCO Subsidia, Tomus 45. Louvain, 1975. **Waltke, B. K.** "The Samaritan Pentateuch and the Text of the Old Testament." In *New Perspectives of the Old Testament.* Ed. J. B. Payne. Waco: Word, 1970. 212–39. **Weber, R.** *Biblia Sacra iuxta Vulgatam Versionem I.* Stuttgart: Württembergische Bibelanstalt, 1969. **Wevers, J. W.** (ed.). *Septuaginta: Vetus Testamentum Graecum Auctoritate Academiae Scientiarum Gottingensis editum, III 2: Deuteronomium.* Göttingen: Vandenhoeck & Ruprecht, 1977. **Wittstruck, T. K.** *The Greek Translations of Deuteronomy.* Diss., Yale Univ., 1972.

The text on which this commentary is based is the traditional Masoretic Text (MT), as published in *Biblia Hebraica Stuttgartensia (BHS),* which reproduces the Leningrad manuscript B19ᵃ dating from the eleventh century C.E. A second Hebrew tradition, the Samaritan Pentateuch (SP), is available for study in the critical edition of A. von Gall (1914–18). The most important of the early versions is that of the Greek translation known as the Septuagint (LXX), which for the Pentateuch was made in the third century B.C.E. and is preserved in many Christian Mss from the fourth century C.E. onwards. For Deuteronomy two critical editions are available, that of A. E. Brooke and N. McLean (1911) and, more recently, J. W. Wevers (1977). Through this latter work we also have access to the important Old Latin textual tradition, which is preserved in a few medieval witnesses (see discussion of Deut 4:1 and 27:4 below).

Careful study of the Qumran scrolls discovered since 1947 have led to renewed confidence in the relative antiquity and general superiority of the MT over other available textual traditions and versions. My own study of the Masoretic accentual system within Deuteronomy adds confirmation to the veracity of details preserved within that tradition. Waltke (1970) has shown that the Samaritan Pentateuch (SP) represents a revision of the MT, in which Hebrew grammar was modernized and linguistic, historical, and theological problems "normalized" within sectarian ideology. Though the MT remains the de facto canonical text of Deuteronomy, the commentator must examine each variant reading on its own merits. Usually the MT offers the most trustworthy text; but the SP, the Qumran Mss, LXX, and even the Old Latin at times offer superior readings.

As Craigie has argued (NICOT [1976] 66–67), the Hebrew text of Deuteronomy is a "palimpsest" of sorts, in that it reflects various "layers" of orthographic practice in the history of the transmission of the written text. The most obvious example of this phenomenon is the vocalization of the text in terms of a system of "vowel points," since the original written form contained the consonants only. Careful study of the system of vowel points suggests that there was apparently a leveling in the pronunciation of the text according to the so-called "Judahite" dialect common in Jerusalem. The appearance of final *kaph* and final *nun* with *qāmeṣ* [ךָ and ךָ] in the received textual tradition suggests that these consonants closed the final syllable in the original text, since the "Judahite" pronunciation *-kā* and *-nā* is indicated by כה and נה in Mss from Qumran. The system of scansion employed in this commentary corrects for this dialectal leveling throughout the text of Deuteronomy. Later "layers" in the received tradition are represented by the Masoretic accentual system, including the so-called "*pāsēq* list"; division of the text into the *sᵉtûmaʾ* and *pᵉtûḥāʾ* "paragraphs" and *sᵉdārîm*; and the still later division into chapters and verses in the Christian tradition.

In the latter part of the nineteenth century a manuscript discovery was made that may yet prove to be relevant to the study of Deuteronomy. A Jerusalem antiquities dealer by the name of Moses Wilhelm Shapira tried to sell an ancient manuscript, which he claimed was discovered in a cave near the Dead Sea. The manuscript contained extensive sections of Deuteronomy in a text form somewhat similar to that of the Moabite Stone (ninth century B.C.E.). When the manuscript was declared a forgery by the French scholar C. Clermont-Ganneau and by C. D. Ginsburg as well, the unfortunate Shapira committed suicide (see J. Allegro, *The Shapira Affair* [Garden City, NY: Doubleday, 1965]). Some scholars think that the manuscript, now apparently lost, was indeed an ancient one though not as old as Shapira thought. Though the evidence from the translations and transcriptions of the Shapira manuscript has not been used in this commentary, except for the alternate numbering of the Ten Commandments in Deuteronomy 5, that evidence may prove useful if and when the debate on its authenticity is resolved.

Important evidence for the Hebrew text of Deuteronomy has emerged from the discovery of the Dead Sea Scrolls in the vicinity of Qumran since 1947. The evidence consists of many fragments of Deuteronomy, which apparently was a popular book within that particular community. Besides these fragments, sections of Deuteronomy are quoted in other religious texts from Qumran. 4QTestimonia brings together several prophecies, including three quotations from Deuteronomy. Portions of Deuteronomy are also preserved in three *phylacteries* and one *mezuzah*, which are discussed more fully in the commentary on Deuteronomy 6:6–9 and 11:18–21.

Craigie (NICOT [1976] 84–86) has assembled a useful list of the Qumran materials relating to Deuteronomy, which is reproduced below in modified form, with additions for the forthcoming volume in the series Discoveries in the Judean Desert (DJD X). I am grateful to Eugene Ulrich, Sidnie White, and Julie Duncan for their assistance in updating this list. Though the list appears to be rather extensive, it should be noted that most of these fragments are very small, often preserving only one or two words in any given verse. Thus the textual evidence from Qumran will never replace the much later texts, such as that of the Leningrad manuscript B19ᵃ, upon which this commentary is based.

LIST OF QUMRAN EVIDENCE RELATING TO DEUTERONOMY

| Deut | Published source | Identification of text |
|------|------------------|------------------------|
| 1:1–17 | DJD X | 4QDt8 |
| 1:7–9 | DJD III, 60 | 2Q10.1 |
| 1:9–13 | DJD I, 58 | 1Q5.1 |
| 1:22 | DJD I, 54 | 1Q4.1 |
| 1:22–23 | DJD X | 4QDt8 |
| 1:29–39 | DJD X | 4QDt8 |
| 1:40–41 | DJD X | 4QDt8 |
| 1:43–2:5 | DJD X | 4QDt8 |
| 2:24–36 | DJD X | 4QDtd |
| 2:28–30 | DJD X | 4QDt8 |
| 3:14–4:1 | DJD X | 4QDtd |
| 3:18–21 | DJD X | 4QDtm |
| 3:24 | DJD X | 4QDte |
| 3:25–26 | DJD X | 4QDtc |
| 4:13–17 | DJD X | 4QDtc |
| 4:23–27 | DJD X | 4QDtf |
| 4:31–32 | DJD X | 4QDtc |
| 4:31–34 | DJD X | 4QDto |
| 4:32–33 | DJD X | 4QDtm |
| 4:47–49 | DJD I, 54 | 1Q4.2 |
| 5:1–3 | DJD X | 4QDto |
| 5:1–11 | DJD X | 4QDtj |
| 5:1–14 | DJD III, 149–57 | 8Q3.20–25 (phylactery) |
| 5:1–22 | DJD I, 73–74 | 1Q13.1–18 |
| 5:1–6:1 | *SWDS* (1965) 31–32 | 4QDeut |
| 5:1–6:1 | DJD X | 4QDtn |
| 5:8–9 | DJD X | 4QDto |
| 5:13–15 | DJD X | 4QDtj |
| 5:21 | DJD X | 4QDtj |
| 5:22–27 | DJD X | 4QDtj |
| 5:23–27 | DJD I, 74 | 1Q13.19 (phylactery) |
| 5:28 | DJD X | 4QDtj |
| 5:28–29 | DJD V, 57–60 | 4QTestimonia (quotation) |
| | Cf. *JBL* 75 (1956) 182–87 | |
| 5:28 | DJD X | 4Qtk1 |

| | | |
|---|---|---|
| 5:29 | DJD V, 3 | 4Q158.6 (paraphrase) |
| 5:29–33 | DJD X | 4QDtj |
| 5:30–31 | DJD V. 3 | 4Q158.7–8 (paraphrase) |
| 6:1–3 | DJD III, 149–57 | 8Q3.12–16 (phylactery) |
| 6:1–3 | DJD X | 4QDtj |
| 6:4–6 | DJD X | 4Dtp |
| 6:4–9 | DJD II, 83–84 | Mur. Phyl. (phylactery) |
| | Cf. *RB* 60 (1953) 268–75 | |
| 6:4–9 | DJD III, 149–57 | 8Q3.4–6, 8 (phylactery) |
| 6:8–10 | DJD X | 4QDtp |
| 7:3–4 | DJD X | 4QDtc |
| 7:12–16 | DJD X | 4QDte |
| 7:15–24 | DJD III, 174 | 5Q1.1.i |
| 7:19–22 | DJD X | 4Qdtm |
| 7:21–26 | DJD X | 4QDtf |
| 7:21–8:4 | DJD X | 4QDte |
| 8:1–5 | DJD X | 4QDtc |
| 8:2–14 | DJD X | 4QDtf |
| 8:5–10 | *SWDS* (1965) 31 | 4QDeut |
| 8:5–10 | DJD X | 4QDtj |
| 8:5–10 | DJD X | 4QDtn |
| 8:5–16 | DJD X | 4QDte |
| 8:5–9:2 | DJD III, 171 | 5Q1.1.ii |
| 8:8–9 | DJD I, 58 | 1Q5.2 |
| 8:18–19 | DJD I, 54 | 1Q4.3–4 |
| 9:6–7 | DJD X | 4QDtf |
| 9:10 | DJD I, 58 | 1Q5.3 |
| 9:11–12 | DJD X | 4QDtc |
| 9:12–14 | DJD X | 4QDtg |
| 9:17–19 | DJD X | 4QDtc |
| 9:27–28 | DJD I, 54 | 1Q4.5 |
| 9:29–10:2 | DJD X | 4QDtc |
| 10:1–3 | DJD II, 79 | Mur. Deut. |
| 10:5–8 | DJD X | 4QDtc |
| 10:8–12 | DJD III, 61–62 | 2Q12.1 |
| 10:12 | DJD X | 4QDtl |
| 10:12–17 | DJD III, 149–57 | 8Q3.17–19, 21 (phylactery) |
| 10:12–11:21 | DJD III, 158–61 | 8Q4.1 (mezuzah) |
| 10:13 (?) | DJD III, 149–57 | 8Q3.26–27 (phylactery) |
| 10:14 | DJD X | 4QDtl |
| 10:17–18 | DJD I, 74 | 1Q13.20 (phylactery) |
| 10:19 | DJD III, 149–57 | 8Q3.21 (phylactery) |
| 10:20–22 | DJD III, 149–57 | 8Q3.12, 15–16 (phylactery) |
| 10:21–11:1 | DJD I, 74 | 1Q13.21–22 (phylactery) |
| | DJD III, 149–57 | 8Q3.26–29 (phylactery) |
| 11:2 | DJD III, 149–57 | 8Q3.26–27 |
| 11:2–3 | DJD II, 79 | Mur. Deut. |
| 11:2–4 | DJD X | 4QDtc |
| 11:3 (?) | DJD III, 149–57 | 8Q3.26–27 |
| 11:6–10 | DJD X | 4QDtj |
| 11:6–12 | DJD III, 149–57 | 8q3.27–29 |
| 11:6–13 | DJD X | 4QDtk1 |
| 11:8–11 | DJD I, 74 | 1Q13.23–25 (phylactery) |

| | | |
|---|---|---|
| 11:9–13 | DJD X | 4QDtc |
| 11:12 | DJD 1, 75 | 1Q13.26–27 (phylactery) |
| 11:12–13 | DJD X | 4QDtj |
| 11:13–21 | DJD II, 83–84 | Mur. Phyl. (phylactery) |
| | DJD III, 149–57 | 8Q3.4, 7–11 (phylactery) |
| | Cf. *RB* 60 (1953) 268–75 | |
| 11:18–19 | DJD X | 4QDtc |
| 11:27–30 | DJD I, 55 | 1Q4.6 |
| 11:30–33 | DJD I, 58 | 1Q5.4 |
| 12:18–19 | DJD X | 4QDtc |
| 12:25–26 | DJD II, 79 | Mur. Deut. |
| 12:26 | DJD X | 4QDtc |
| 12:30–31 | DJD X | 4QDtc |
| 13.1–4 | DJD I, 55 | 1Q4.7–8 |
| 13:4–6 | DJD I, 55 | 1Q4.9 |
| 13:5–7 | DJD X | 4QDtc |
| 13:11–12 | DJD X | 4QDtc |
| 13:13–14 | DJD I, 55 | 1Q4.10 |
| 13:16 | DJD X | 4QDtc |
| 14:21 | DJD I, 55 | 1Q4.11 |
| 14:24–25 | DJD I, 56 | 1Q4.12 |
| 15:1–5 | DJD X | 4QDtc |
| 15:14–15 | DJD I, 58 | 1Q5.5 |
| 15:15–19 | DJD X | 4QDtc |
| 16:2–3 | DJD X | 4QDtc |
| 16:4 | DJD I, 56 | 1Q4.13 |
| 16:5–11 | DJD X | 4QDtc |
| 16:6–7 | DJD I, 56 | 1Q4.14 |
| 16:20–17:7 | DJD X | 4QDtc |
| 17:12–15 | DJD III, 60–61 | 2Q11.1 |
| 17:15–18:1 | DJD X | 4QDtc |
| 17:16 | DJD I, 58 | 1Q5.6 |
| 17:17–18 | DJD X | 4QDtf |
| 18:6–10 | DJD X | 4QDtf |
| 18:18–19 | DJD V, 57–60 | 4QTestimonia (quotation) |
| | Cf. *JBL* 75 (1956) 182–87 | |
| 18:18–22 | DJD X | 4QDtf |
| 18:18–20, 22 | DJD V, 3 | 4Q158.6 |
| 19:8–16 | DJD X | 4QDtk2 |
| 19:17–20:3 | DJD X | 4QDtf |
| 20:4–6 | DJD X | 4QDtf |
| 20:6–19 | DJD X | 4QDtk2 |
| 20:9–13 | DJD X | 4QDti |
| 21:4–12 | DJD X | 4QDtf |
| 21:8–9 | DJD I, 58 | 1Q5.7 |
| 21:23–22:9 | DJD X | 4QDti |
| 22:12–19 | DJD X | 4QDtf |
| 23:6–17 | DJD X | 4QDti |
| 23:18–20 | DJD X | 4QDtg |
| 23:21–26 | DJD X | 4QDtf |
| 23:22–24:1 | DJD X | 4QDti |
| 23:22–24:3 | DJD X | 4QDtk2 |
| 23:26–24:8 | DJD X | 4QDta |

| | | |
|---|---|---|
| 24:2–7 | DJD X | 4QDtf |
| 24:10–16 | DJD I, 58 | 1Q5.8 |
| 24:16–22 | DJD X | 4QDtg |
| 25:1–5 | DJD X | 4QDtg |
| 25:3–9 | DJD X | 4QDtf |
| 25:13–18 | DJD I, 59 | 1Q5.9 |
| 25:14–26:5 | DJD X | 4QDtg |
| 25:19–26:4 | DJD X | 4QDtk2 |
| 26:18–19 | DJD X | 4QDtk2 |
| 26:18–27:10 | DJD X | 4QDtf |
| 26:19 (?) | DJD III, 106–07 | 6Q3.1 |
| 26:19–27:2 | DJD X | 4QDtc |
| 27:24—28:14 | DJD X | 4QDtc |
| 28:15–18 | DJD X | 4QDto |
| 28:18–20 | DJD X | 4QDtc |
| 28:21–24 | DJD X | 4QDtg |
| 28:22–25 | DJD X | 4QDtc |
| 28:27–29 | DJD X | 4QDtg |
| 28:29–30 | DJD X | 4QDtc |
| 28:33–35 | DJD X | 4QDto |
| 28:44–48 | DJD I, 59 | 1Q5.10 |
| 28:47–49 | DJD X | 4QDto |
| 28:48–50 | DJD X | 4QDtc |
| 28:51–52 | DJD X | 4QDto |
| 28:58–62 | DJD X | 4QDto |
| 28:61 | DJD X | 4QDtc |
| 28:67–68 | DJD X | 4QDtl |
| 29:2–5 | DJD X | 4QDtl |
| 29:9–11 | DJD I, 59 | 1Q5.11 |
| 29:12–20 | DJD I, 59 | 1Q5.12–13 |
| 29:17–19 | DJD X | 4QDtc |
| 29:20 (?) | DJD I, 61 | 1Q5.28 |
| 29:24–27 | DJD X | 4QDtb |
| 30:3–14 | DJD X | 4QDtb |
| 30:19–31:6 D | DJD I, 59 | 1Q5.13 |
| 31:7–10 | DJD I, 60 | 1Q5.14 |
| 31:9–11 | DJD X | 4QDt8 |
| 31:9–14 | DJD X | 4QDtb |
| 31:12 | DJD X | 4QDtl |
| 31:12–13 | DJD I, 60 | 1Q5.15 |
| 31:15–17 | DJD X | 4QDtb |
| 31:16–19 | DJD X | 4QDtc |
| 31:24–32:3 | DJD X | 4QDtb |
| 32:3 | DJD X | 4QDtc |
| 32:7–8 | DJD X | 4QDtj |
| 32:8 | *BASOR* 136 (1954) 12–15 | |
| 32:17–18 | DJD X | 4QDtk1 |
| 32:17–21 | DJD I, 60 | 1Q5.16 |
| 32:20–21(?) | DJD III, 171 | 5Q1.2–3 |
| 32:21–22 | DJD I, 60 | 1Q5.17 |
| 32:22–23 | DJD X | 4QDtkl |
| 32:22–29 | DJD I, 60 | 1Q5.18–19 |
| 32:25-27 | DJD X | 4QDtkl |

| | | |
|---|---|---|
| 32:37–43 | *BASOR* 136 (1954) 12–15 | |
| | VTSup 4 (1957). 120 | |
| | *JBL* 78 (1959) 21–22 | |
| 33:1–2(?) | DJD III, 171 | 5Q1.4–5 |
| 33:1–2 | DJD X | 4QDtl |
| 33:8–11 | DJD V, 56 | 4QFlorilegium (quotation) |
| | DJD V, 57–60 | 4QTestimonia (quotation) |
| | Cf. *JBL* 75 (1956) 182–87 | |
| 33:9–20 | DJD X | 4QDt8 |
| 33:12(?) | DJD V, 56 | 4QFlorilegium (quotation) |
| 33:12–17 | DJD I, 61 | 1Q5.20 |
| 33:18–19 | DJD I, 61 | 1Q5.21 |
| 33:19–21 | DJD V, 56 | 4QFlorilegium (quotation) |
| 33:21–23 | DJD I, 61 | 1Q5.22 |
| 33:24 | DJD I, 61 | 1Q5.23 |
| 34:4–6 | DJD X | 4QDtl |
| 34:8 | DJD X | 4QDtl |

## *Review of Critical Research*

The secondary literature on Deuteronomy is overwhelming, since any serious study of literary, theological, and social issues in ancient Israel must deal with this text. In spite of the voluminous nature of the material, it is possible to discern a series of impulses that divide modern study of the book into four phases: 1) from de Wette to Steuernagel (1900); 2) from Steuernagel to Noth's theory on the relationship between Deuteronomy and the so-called Deuteronomistic History (1943); 3) from Noth to Lohfink's "stylistic" approach to the study of Deuteronomy 5–11 (1963); and 4) the current methodological quandary, which in some respects appears to be a merging of the older impulse from "form criticism" with more recent reflection on the canonical process in ancient Israel.

W. M. L. de Wette's 1805 dissertation laid the cornerstone for the edifice of pentateuchal literary criticism of the nineteenth century. The book of Deuteronomy was identified with the scroll found in the Temple in Jerusalem under the reign of King Josiah. Starting from this one fixed point of departure, the familiar JEDP documentary theory of pentateuchal criticism took shape within the mainstream of European scholarship. The Jahwist (J), Elohist (E), and Priestly (P) sources of the "Tetrateuch" (Genesis through Numbers) were set over against Deuteronomy (D).

The history of pentateuchal criticism has been recounted many times and will not be repeated in detail here. Though there were numerous precursors to the nineteeth-century movement, it was the dating of Deuteronomy to the seventh century B.C.E. that enabled the so-called Reuss-Graf-Kuenen-Wellhausen hypothesis to emerge triumphant by the last quarter of the nineteeth century. In particular, Julius Wellhausen's *Prolegomena to the History of Ancient Israel* (Cleveland: Meridian Books, 1957), which appeared in its first German edition in 1878, summed up the scholarly contributions of previous generations with the "assured results" of literary criticism in a compact and persuasive fashion, which is often summarized by the scholarly tetragrammaton JEDP. J and E were narrative sources, dating to the ninth and eighth centuries B.C.E. respectively. The combination of these two sources into JE took place by the the seventh century. D (Deuteronomy) was composed in the seventh century, while P was written after the exile. The final editing of the Pentateuch took place ca. 400 B.C.E. For a stimulating modern restatement of the matter, which takes into account the research of the century since Wellhausen as well, see R. E. Friedman, *Who Wrote the Bible?* (New York: Summit Books, 1987).

Though analysis from the point of view of source documents had produced a consensus regarding the formation of the Pentateuch as a whole by the turn of the century, that approach had not succeeded in drawing a convincing picture of the literary structure of the source D. Working independently of each other in the last decade of the nineteenth century, C. Steuernagel and W. Staerk posited a "redactional" model to explain the growth of Deuteronomy, on the basis of the so-called *Numeruswechsel*—the frequent change in the form of address in terms of second person singular and plural forms. They posited an older stratum which used the singular pronoun and a later one which used the plural (see *Excursus:* "The *Numeruswechsel* in Deuteronomy" below). There are a number of places in Deuteronomy where one can say with some certainty that the plural passage was apparently inserted into the singular context, and, consequently, many critical scholars still continue this line of research. On the other hand, the detailed analysis presented by Steuernagel in his *Kommentar* (2nd ed., 1923) has found relatively few followers. His assumption of several parallel "editions" of the original Deuteronomy, each with its own parenetic introduction, seems improbable, and the "plural edition" he extracted probably never existed by itself.

G. von Rad's important study, *Das Gottesvolk in Deuteronomium* (BWANT 47 [Stuttgart: Kohlhammer, 1929]), may well mark the beginning of the end for the "stratigraphical" approach of traditional literary criticism to the study of Deuteronomy as exemplified by Steuernagel and Staerk. For von Rad theological issues replaced most of the questions raised by the established historical critical method. Though source and redaction criticism will remain useful, if not essential in critical analysis, the time had come for new directions in pentateuchal studies, and Deuteronomy in particular.

The third major impulse into the study of Deuteronomy in the modern era flows from the theory of M. Noth (1943) that Deuteronomy 1–3 (4) and 31–34 are the introduction to the deuteronomic historical work (Joshua through 2 Kings). Steuernagel had regarded Deuteronomy 1–3 as the introductory address of one edition of Deuteronomy. Noth's theory undermines the basic assumptions of that earlier one and carries subsequent discussion in new directions. The implications of Noth's theory will be worked out in some detail in this commentary.

At the same time that Minette de Tillesse championed the basic redactional theory of Steuernagel in a brilliant essay on the so-called *Numeruswechsel* (1962), another major impulse in modern study of Deuteronomy was taking shape in the work of W. L. Moran and his student N. Lohfink. Lohfink's doctoral dissertation, *Das Hauptgebot* (1963), turned to "stylistics" as the primary focus of attention. The new approach tended to find unity in the text, in spite of the apparent diversity in surface form, which led Steuernagel, and others after him, to posit complex theories of redactional growth.

Meanwhile another lesson from the history of research in Deuteronomy was making its mark as well. Contrary to what de Wette and others had said, the search for the original Deuteronomy must ignore the account of 2 Kgs 22–23 almost completely. Even if Deuteronomy did influence history at the time of Josiah, it is not to be assumed that it had its full effect at that time. It can be argued that Josiah may have gone well beyond Deuteronomy in his measures. Moreover, the assumption that the original Deuteronomy is to be found only within chaps. 12–26 must be rejected; that section cannot be designated as the real "codex" as opposed to the "introduction" (chaps. 6–11), since both of these sections share the same characteristic signs (*Numeruswechsel,* parenetic style, etc.).

The zeal for literary analysis along lines suggested by the so-called documentary hypothesis has flagged now for a good many years. The realization is growing that the method of purely literary critical analysis in the traditional sense will unveil the complexity of Deuteronomy only to a limited degree, because the strata which are present do not point to literary processes but rather to a preliterate process of slow enrichment of the original mass of tradition. The time seems right for a new model of analysis, or at least a significant modification of the prevailing one, which will account for the unity of the text within the context of diversity of traditions. That model will build on the work of M. Noth, who saw the canonical function of Deuteronomy within the context of what D. N. Freedman has called the "primary history" (Genesis through 2 Kings in the Hebrew Bible; see *IDBSup* [1976] 131–32). It will also build on the older impulse of form criticism as it entertains new possibilities for understanding the genre of Deuteronomy within the canonical process in ancient Israel. It will take as its starting point the seminal work of N. Lohfink, with primary focus on the artistic design and function of the received textual tradition, particularly as preserved in the MT. But its primary motive force will come from areas of interdisciplinary concern, especially from the fields of epic and narrative poetry within the context of musical performance of texts in antiquity (see D. Christensen, "Form and Structure in Deuteronomy 1–11," BETL 68 [Leuven UP, 1985] 135–44).

## Deuteronomy and the Canonical Process

The central event in the shaping of the epic story of the Hebrew Bible is the deliverance of the people of Israel from slavery in Egypt. Regardless of how one chooses to reconstruct the historical details of this event, the Exodus itself constitutes the starting point in our model for explaining the canonical process in ancient Israel. The event of the Exodus calls for its counterpart in the "Eisodus." The people who came out of Egypt under Moses began an epic journey, one which eventually brought them "home" to the promised land under the leadership of Joshua. The Exodus is balanced by the Conquest. The linking of these two events in a single lexical item, the "Exodus-Conquest," by F. M. Cross in his discussion of the "Ritual Conquest" in pre-monarchic Israel (*CMHE* [1973] 99–111), bears witness to the fact that these two events are so closely connected that they constitute a single category from a cultic point of view. The phrase "Book of the Wars of Yahweh" seems to be a descriptive title of this block of material on the lips of the people of ancient Israel (cf. Num 21:14–15 and my discussion in *CBQ* 36 [1974] 359–60). The "Wars of YHWH" were divided into two phases: namely, the Exodus under Moses and the Eisodus (the Conquest) under Joshua.

In each of its two halves the primary epic story takes on a threefold structure within the canonical process in ancient Israel by the insertion of theophanic visitations, first to Moses and subsequently to Elijah—on the same mountain (Exod 33–34; 1 Kgs 19). The Exodus involves a journey from *Yam Suf* ("Sea of Reeds" or "Red Sea") to the Jordan River in three stages. The great theophany at Sinai in which the presence of the Divine Warrior is made known to Israel through Moses is framed, on the one hand, by the wilderness journey from Egypt to Sinai and, on the other, by the wilderness journey from Sinai to Mount Nebo and the transfer of leadership from Moses to Joshua. E. Newing has shown that the "Promised Presence," as depicted in Exod 33:1–17, is situated at the center of the first major section of the canon of the Hebrew Bible. Though his analysis is based on the final form of the biblical text, it seems to reflect the earliest stages of the actual canonical process, which eventually produced the Pentateuch as we now know it. The structure is ternary in nature. As Newing put it, the journey "From Egypt to Canaan" is in three stages: 1) "From Slavery/Promise," to 2) the great theophany ("Promised Presence") on the Mountain of God at Sinai/Horeb, and from there 3) "To Freedom/Fulfillment" ("A Rhetorical and Theological Analysis of the Hexateuch," *SEAJT* 22 [1981] 1–15).

A parallel structure can be seen within the so-called Deuteronomic History (Joshua through 2 Kings). Here the journey is from 1) the desert to the promised land symbolized as a mountain, to 2) central theophanies on Mount Carmel (1 Kgs 18) and Mount Horeb (1 Kgs 19), which depict the rule of God through both prophet and king; and 3) the journey to Mount Zion as the city of God, particularly as seen in the climactic reforms of Hezekiah (2 Kgs 18–20) and Josiah (2 Kgs 22–23).

Wholeness in Jungian thought is normally expressed in quaternary, or four-part, structures. Within these structures the four elements in any given structure tend to be arranged in a chiasm; at the same time, three of the four are generally set over against the fourth. The final arrangement of the canon of the Hebrew Bible still reflects an earlier "three plus one" structuring of the tradition within the developing canonical process.

| Exodus | Numbers | | *Joshua* | Samuel |
| Leviticus | *Deuteronomy* | | Judges | Kings |

Here the three "wilderness books" (Exodus, Leviticus, and Numbers) are supplemented by a "second recitation of the law" (Deuteronomy) on the part of Moses, immediately prior to his death. Joshua in turn stands over against the story of the possession of the promised land—under a series of twelve judges, followed by the united kingship under David and Solomon (with the building of the Temple), and the subsequent divided monarchy in the land. The chiastic relationship within this pair of pairs should be noted. As R. D. Nelson has shown, Joshua and Josiah were paired as an envelope, or inclusion, around what eventually came to be known as the Former Prophets within the canonical process ("Josiah in the Book of Joshua," *JBL* 100 [1977] 531–40).

The Torah and the Former Prophets were subsequently framed by two new blocks of material, which ultimately become the book of Genesis and the Latter Prophets of the Masoretic tradition.

|  | Exodus | Numbers |  | *Joshua* | Samuel |  |  |
|---|---|---|---|---|---|---|---|
| "Fathers" |  |  |  |  |  |  | "Prophets" |
|  | Leviticus | *Deuteronomy* |  | Judges | Kings |  |  |

Once again it is easy to see the "three plus one" structuring within these categories in terms of the final canonical shape of the tradition:

"Fathers" = Abraham, Isaac, Jacob + Jacob's 12 sons

"Prophets" = Isaiah, Jeremiah, Ezekiel + "Book of the 12"

J. Blenkinsopp was apparently the first person to comment on this phenomenon (*Prophecy and Canon: A Contribution to the Study of Jewish Origins* [Notre Dame: Univ. of Notre Dame, 1977] 227–36, 422–28).

The center in the developing canonical process then shifted to the book of Deuteronomy, which functions as a bridge.

| Genesis | Leviticus |  |  | Joshua | Samuel |
|---|---|---|---|---|---|
|  |  | Deuteronomy |  |  |  |
| Exodus | Numbers |  |  | Judges | Kings |

Deuteronomy is thus the completion (and the center) of the Pentateuch and the beginning of the Former Prophets (Joshua through 2 Kings) as canonical categories. It can be argued that Deuteronomy also plays a similar role as a bridge between the Former Prophets and the Latter Prophets, as follows:

| Joshua | Samuel |  |  | Isaiah | Ezekiel |
|---|---|---|---|---|---|
|  |  | Deuteronomy |  |  |  |
| Judges | Kings |  |  | Jeremiah | "The 12" |

Though the relation of Deuteronomy to the individual books within the Latter Prophets is more subtle, it can be demonstrated in various ways. Note in particular the literature on the deuteronomic prose sermons in the book of Jeremiah, the so-called deuteronomic redaction of the book of Amos, and the close relationship between Hosea and Deuteronomy. B. Dahlberg has argued for the placing of Malachi within the deuteronomic corpus as well (*Studies in the Book of Malachi*, [Diss. Columbia Univ., 1963]). In one sense, then, S. Herrmann was correct when he suggested that Deuteronomy be declared the "centre" of biblical theology (see J. Høgenhaven, *Problems and Prospects of Old Testament Theology* [Sheffield: JSOT, 1988] 40). The only problem with his observation is that it fails to take into account the dynamic nature of the canonical process as a whole and the fact that Deuteronomy does not remain the center.

Within the developing canonical process, apparently from the time of Hezekiah and Josiah, Deuteronomy was the center of what eventually became a hypothetical seventeen-book canon of the Hebrew Bible, which may be reconstructed as follows (see D. Christensen, "Josephus and the Twenty-two-book Canon of Sacred Scripture," *JETS* 29 [1986] 37–46).

| Genesis | Leviticus | | Joshua | Samuel |
|---------|-----------|------|--------|--------|
| Exodus | Numbers | | Judges | Kings |
| | | Deuteronomy | | |
| Isaiah | Ezekiel | | Psalms | Job |
| Jeremiah | "The 12" | | Proverbs | "Meg" |

"Meg" here stands for the "Megilloth" or Festal Scrolls, which ultimately will be in five parts: i.e., Song of Songs, Ruth, Lamentations, Ecclesiastes, and Esther.

The four sections of the above structure represent the four primary canonical divisions, which are arranged in a chiasm, with Deuteronomy functioning as a bridge between them.

| Torah | Former Prophets |
|-------|-----------------|
| Latter Prophets | "Hagiographa" |

It should be noted, however, that the fourth category did not yet include Daniel, Ezra, Nehemiah, and Chronicles. The canon was thus "open" in the sense that additions could be made within this fourth category, which eventually became the "Writings." I would date the formation of this seventeen-book canon of the Hebrew Bible to ca. 500 B.C.E., and would connect it with the rebuilding and dedication of the Second Temple in Jerusalem. At this point in time, Esther and Ecclesiastes were not yet among the Megilloth (Festal Scrolls) as a canonical entity.

In the canonical shaping of the Festal Scrolls, the book of Lamentations was apparently the initial center around which the Song of Songs and Ruth were added as the festal scrolls for Passover and Shavuoth (Feast of Weeks or Pentecost) respectively, in a ternary structure. Ecclesiastes was subsequently added as the scroll of Succoth (Feast of Tabernacles) to form a quaternary pattern as follows:

| Song of Songs | Lamentations |
|---------------|--------------|
| Ruth | Ecclesiastes |

Within this structure, the pair / Song of Songs // Ecclesiastes / is associated with Solomon, and / Ruth // Lamentations / with David. Ruth is David's great-grand-mother whereas Lamentations commemorates the destruction of the Davidic dynasty/temple in Jerusalem at the hands of Nebuchadnezzar of Babylon. Josephus is the first clear witness to the next stage in the developing canonical process—the arrangement of the canon of the Hebrew Bible into twenty-two books, which seems to be reflected in the received tradition within the Jewish community, at least in the Masoretic text. Note that a dual center seems to emerge with Daniel and Deuteronomy as bridges of some sort, around which are arranged five "pairs of pairs" as follows:

| Genesis | Leviticus | | | Joshua | Samuel |
|---------|-----------|------|------|--------|--------|
| | | Deuteronomy | | | |
| Exodus | Numbers | | | Judges | Kings |
| | | Isaiah | Ezekiel | | |
| | | Jeremiah | "The 12" | | |
| Ezra | 1 Chr | | | Psalms | Job |
| | | Daniel | | | |
| Nehemiah | 2 Chr | | | Proverbs | "Meg" |

The total number of twenty-two books in this canon was subsequently legitimated by Origen (ca. 250 C.E.) in terms of the number of letters in the Hebrew alphabet (see M. Stuart, *Critical History and Defense of the Old Testament Canon.* [Andover: Warren F. Draper, 1872] 404). This fact would suggest that this canon was theoretically closed (or complete) from a psychological point of view. It is the inclusion of Esther into this "closed" canon within Jewish tradition that ultimately "exploded" the canon in a transformation from twenty-two to the twenty-four-book structure of Talmudic tradition. The inclusion of Esther resulted in the breaking up of the Megilloth (Festal Scrolls) as a canonical unit within Jewish tradition, and the redistribution of these five scrolls so as to come up with twenty-four books. Ruth was attached to Judges in some instances, elsewhere with Psalms. Lamentations was attached to Jeremiah. The resultant loss of discernible canonical structure produced the fluidity of canonical reflection within the early Jewish and Christian communities. As Stuart has noted, no two of these early lists are identical, even among those that insist on a total of twenty-two books (M. Stuart, 258).

Within the Christian tradition it would appear that the addition of Esther somehow resulted in a twenty-seven-book canon of the Hebrew Bible, which was subsequently legitimated by Epiphanius (ca. 368 C.E.) with the argument that the Hebrew alphabet does in fact have twenty-seven letters, since five of the letters appear in two forms (see Stuart, 415). It is interesting to note that the NT itself eventually emerged in a twenty-seven-book canon, perhaps patterned (consciously or unconsciously) on a twenty-seven-book canon of the OT. If the structure of the two testaments is in fact parallel, the resultant structure of the Bible as a whole within Christian tradition is most revealing (see my article, "The Center of the First Testament within the Canonical Process," *BTB* [forthcoming]). The center of the Hebrew Bible, as read through Christian eyes, shifted from Deuteronomy to Daniel and the world of apocalyptic thought.

## Law, Poetry and Music in Ancient Israel

As Bishop Robert Lowth noted 200 years ago (*Lectures on the Sacred Poetry of the Hebrews,* tr. G. Gregory [London, 1815] 54–55), the law codes throughout the Mediterranean world were sung at the festivals in antiquity.

It is evident that Greece for several successive ages was possessed of no records but the poetic: for the first who published a prose oration was Pherecydes, a man of the Isle of Syrus, and the contemporary with king Cyrus, who lived some ages posterior to that of Homer and Hesiod: somewhat after the time Cadmus the Milesian began to compose history. The laws themselves were metrical, and adapted to certain musical notes: such were the laws of Charondas, which were sung at the banquets of the Athenians: such were those which were delivered by the Cretans to the ingenuous youth to be learned by rote, with the accompaniments of musical melody, in order that by the enchantment of harmony, the sentiments might be forcibly impressed upon their memories. Hence certain poems were denominated νόμοι (nomoi) which implied convivial or banqueting songs, as is remarked by Aristotle; who adds, that the same custom of chanting the laws to music, existed even in his own time among the Agathyrsi.

The law book we call Deuteronomy was in the hands of the Levites (Deuteronomy 17:18), who were commanded by Moses to proclaim it at the Feast of Booths (Deut 31:9). Though we do not know the precise nature of this proclamation of the law, which was handed down within levitical circles, it is likely that it was sung and that this greater "Song of Moses" (i.e., the entire book of Deuteronomy) was taught to the people.

When J. van Goudoever commented that Deuteronomy is "the most liturgical book of the Bible" (*Das Deut* [1985] 148), he described the function of the book within a larger cultic pattern in ancient Israel. The book of Deuteronomy is presented as the Testament of Moses, to be read in preparation for the Passover in Joshua 5. In short, the Torah itself is a Passover-story, which is made up of three Passovers: in Egypt (Exod 12), in the wilderness at Sinai (Num 9), and in the promised land (Josh 5). This tradition of three Passovers is the basis of the "Poem of the Four Passovers," known within both the Jewish and Samaritan traditions. This observation bears witness to the memory of the original form and function of the book of Deuteronomy, which is captured in the descriptive phrase "A Song of Power and the Power of Song" in ancient Israel. J. Lundbom apparently intuited at least part of the picture in his suggestion that it was the "Song of Moses" (Deut 32), rather than the entire book of Deuteronomy, which was found in the Temple in Jerusalem during the reign of King Josiah (*CBQ* 38 [1976] 293). As the most archaic material in the book of Deuteronomy, this official "Song of Moses" dates from the premonarchic era of ancient Israel in essentially its present form. But that song was imbedded in a much larger "Song of Moses," which we now call the book of Deuteronomy. For generations that song was recited in levitical circles as a primary means of religious education. Eventually it was put in written form and promulgated in Jerusalem as part of a reform movement in the days of King Josiah. Within that movement, Deuteronomy became the center of a canonical process which eventually produced the Hebrew Bible as we now know it. That canonical text was recited within the musical tradition of the Second Temple in Jerusalem. The memory of that tradition is still reflected in the Masoretic accentual system of the Hebrew Bible, which is examined in detail throughout this commentary.

For centuries now the main stream of the scholarly community has virtually ignored the Masoretic accentual system so far as detailed analysis and commentary on the text of the Hebrew Bible are concerned. Though there has been fairly widespread agreement that the system is essentially a form of musical notation of some sort, the consensus has been that, whatever the system represents, it is medieval in origin and imposed on the Hebrew text—perhaps as a form of chant to recite the text in a liturgical setting. After all, the so-called tropes of this Masoretic system are still used to instruct those who cant the text within synagogal traditions. Recently the French musicologist Suzanne Haïk-Vantoura has championed the idea that these cantillation signs represent an ancient tradition of musical interpretation, which predates the Masoretes by a millennium, or more (see the American edition of her book, *The Music of the Bible Revealed*, tr. D. Weber and ed. J. Wheeler [Berkeley, CA: BIBAL Press, 1991]).

Haïk-Vantoura argues convincingly that the Masoretes did not invent the musical tradition reflected in their sophisticated system of notation. They merely fixed a once living tradition on paper so as to preserve it for all time. The source of their knowledge was apparently the "Elders of Bathyra," certain sages among the predecessors of the Karaite community during the first century C.E. (see Paul Kahle, *The Cairo Geniza*, 2nd ed. [New York: Praeger, 1959] 82–86, 103).

Haïk-Vantoura attempts to recover the actual melodies of what she believes were part of the text of the Hebrew Bible in the period of the Second Temple in ancient Israel, which the Masoretes themselves only partially understood. Though they were aware of the fact that the system represented a rich musical heritage, they themselves were apparently not musicians. Consequently, they focused their attention primarily on the linguistic features of that system and used it to work out elaborate grammatical treatises on the accentual system they had inherited.

The analysis which is presented in detail in this commentary does not presuppose the work of Suzanne Haïk-Vantoura. The method of prosodic analysis used here was worked out independently of the work of Haïk-Vantoura. It is essentially a form of rhythmic analysis which combines the two dominant methods of Hebrew metrical study currently practiced within the field of OT studies: a quantitative assessment of the length of individual lines, in terms of mora-count; and the careful study of the distribution of accentual stress units, as marked by the so-called disjunctive accents, following the system of the Polish linguist Jerzy Kurylowicz (see his *Studies in Semitic Grammar and Metrics*. [London: Curzon Press, 1973]).

The traditional approach to Hebrew meter remains that of the Ley-Sievers method which focuses on patterns of word stress within given poetic lines (see W. H. Cobbs, *A Criticism of Systems of Hebrew Metre: An Elementary Treatise* [Oxford: Clarendon, 1905] 83–107, 169–184). Recently Jerzy Kurylowicz suggested an important modification to this approach, which is followed here. As he put it: "Parallelism of members etc. are adornments proper to poetic style, but must be left out of consideration in the analysis of metre" (*Studies in Semitic Grammar and Metrics* [1973] 176). This statement needs qualification, since it is only with meter in the sense of rhythm in terms of accentual "beats" within a given line that "parallelism of members" is not significant. Some aspects of parallelism itself can be described quantitatively through a second metrical approach to be described below. By paying careful attention to the diacritical marks of the Masoretic accentual system, Kurylowicz has devised a system of "Syntactic Accentual Meter" (the term is that of Tremper Longman III, *Bib* 63 [1982] 238). In short, he counts syntactic units rather than individual words.

A second approach to the study of Hebrew meter in vogue at the present time focuses on the actual length of poetic lines in terms of counting syllables. Though this particular approach does produce interesting, and often persuasive, insights into the prosodic structure of some texts, the method itself is in need of refinement. Since counting syllables is essentially a means of assessing the length of poetic lines rather than the rhythmical manner in which those same lines were spoken or sung, there is no inherent reason to see the method of syllable counting as in opposition to that of stress counting. The presence of "parallelism of members" in Hebrew poetry does produce quantitative parallelism which can often be shown by counting syllables, regardless of how the rhythmic stresses of that particular line were read. But since the Hebrew language makes a distinction between long and short vowels, there is a need to modify such an approach if one hopes to assign meaningful numbers to the relative length of particular lines, especially if such numbers are to represent a measure of the length of time used in speaking or singing those lines in the manner intended by the author.

The most useful approach to measuring the length of lines in Hebrew poetry is that of counting morae, i.e., the length of time utilized in saying or singing the simplest syllable from a phonetic point of view. Though this particular approach to scanning Hebrew poetry has been around a long time, it has not been the subject of serious discussion in recent years. It was a dominant approach in German scholarship from the middle of the seventeenth century to the early nineteeth century (see B. Pick, "The Study of Hebrew among Jews and Christians," *BSac* 42 [1885] 490–93). The most prevalent of the early advocates were such scholars as J. Alting (1608–79) and J. A. Danz (1654–1727) who gave their names to this approach, namely the "Alting-Danzian System," which survived into the nineteeth century. B. Spinoza (1677) was an advocate of this approach, as were such scholars as H. B. Starke (1705), J. W. Meiner (1748, 1757), and J. F. Hirt (1771). Nineteenth-century "Metriks" who counted morae included J. Bellermann (1813), J. Saalschütz (1825), and H. Grimme (1896–97, 1903). The basic problem with these early approaches to counting morae is that the system was applied to the wrong ends and became much too complex and overly refined. There is no need to take into account the consonants; nor is there any reason to break down the possibilities into the four categories commonly listed. As with similar scanning devices in other modern languages where the vowel length is significant, it is sufficient to ascribe individual vowels to one of two categories—either phonetically short or long, assigning a count of one for the former and two for the latter.

The system of counting morae is foundational to the present analysis of the Hebrew text of Deuteronomy. It is by this means that the essential prosodic units were determined and the boundaries between the larger groupings of what are largely binary units were ascertained. It is at this point that the syntactic accentual method of Kurylowicz was introduced to determine the rhythmic structure. The two approaches were found to complement each other. Together they comprise a system which is the basis of a structural analysis of the entire book of Deuteronomy. The end result is remarkable in that the structural patterns which emerge also provide a fresh glimpse into some of the theological concerns of the author(s) of the book of Deuteronomy as reflected in the architectural design of the "poetic composition" taken as a whole.

In the translation and prosodic analysis presented in this commentary the presence of a disjunctive accent in the Masoretic system of accentation is marked with a single slash (/). A double slash (//) is used to mark the presence of both ʾ*atnāḥ* and *sillûq* (the two strongest disjunctive accents). A reverse slash (\) is used to indicate where an apparent disjunctive accent is read as a conjunctive accent for reasons cited in the notes to the translation. The *setûmāʾ* and *petûḥāʾ* paragraph markers of the Masoretic system are indicated in the translation with the appearance of ס or פ, as in the Heb. Mss and printed editions of the Hebrew Bible. For the most part these marks correspond with major structural divisions in the text (cf. Deut 3:22, 29).

The rules for counting both morae and syntactic-accentual stress units may be summarized as follows:

## RULES FOR COUNTING MORAE

1. Short vowels which are counted as one mora include the standard short vowels *i e a o u* and the reduced vowels, i.e., the vocal shewa and the composite shewas.

2. Long vowels which are counted as two morae include the unchangeable long vowels *î ê ô û* and normally the changeable long vowels *ē ā ō* as well.
3. The furtive *pataḥ* is counted as one morae; ie., *šămōă<sup>c</sup>* (Deut 1:16—five morae).
4. In propretonic position the changeable long *ō* is considered short when followed by a long vowel and is counted as one mora; ie., *šoptêkem* (Deut 1:16—four morae).
5. Postaccentual *qāmeṣ* in nonverbal situations is considered short and counted as one mora; i.e., *láylah* (two morae) or *midbārah* (four morae).
6. The shewa under the labial consonants (b m p) following the conjunction is considered vocal and is counted as one mora. Elsewhere such shewas are considered silent (no count).
7. Vowels within a final *kaph* or *nun* are not counted. A preceding silent shewa is opened (counted as one mora).
8. The final *qāmeṣ* in the 2nd sg of verbal forms in the perfect tense is counted as long (two morae) when the form in question has a disjunctive accent mark. Elsewhere it is considered short (one mora).

RULES FOR COUNTING SYNTACTIC-ACCENTUAL STRESS UNITS

1. The boundaries of the syntactic-accentual units are normally marked by the appearance of one of the eighteen disjunctive accents (*distinctive vel domini*) as listed on the insert to *BHS*.
2. At times the versification of the MT may be in error. In such cases the *ṭipḥāh* governed by the *sillûq* (or *ʾatnāḥ*) may not be disjunctive.
3. Textual problems almost inevitably result in a disturbance of the distribution of the disjunctive accents.
4. There is apparently some inconsistency in the use of *yetîb* in monosyllabic particles when followed by the *zāqēp qāṭôn*. In some cases it is to be taken as the conjunctive accent *mahpāk* which shares the same sign, though in a different position.

There is a rather fluid line between poetry and prose in the Hebrew Bible, as I have argued elsewhere (see "Prose and Poetry in the Bible: The Narrative Poetics of Deuteronomy 1, 9–18," *ZAW* 97 [1985] 179–89). Such features as inclusion, concentric framing devices, and inversion throughout the book of Deuteronomy illustrate more familiar poetic features. At the same time, the text is clearly written in rhythmic form which displays studied parallelism at higher levels of analysis. And yet, having said all this, it remains clear that we have in Deuteronomy a "prose" text in relation to the lyric poetry of the Psalter. Or should we say that "prose" in this context is but a lower form of "heightened language" which might be more adequately described as didactic poetry?

It should be noted that music and poetry are a common medium for transmitting cultural tradition among virtually all so-called preliterate peoples. In light of this fact some missionaries and administrators of mission agencies are beginning to ask new questions about the translation of the Bible into previously unwritten languages. The model of the Wycliffe Bible translator has been seriously challenged in recent years, from within the very ranks of those translators themselves, as the most effective means of communicating the "Word of God" in such situations. Should an individual scholar give virtually a lifetime to the tedious task of reducing such a language to written form in order to translate the Bible into one more of the 2000 such languages which exist to the present time? Where this has been done, the Bible sometimes remains as an external artifact which never really becomes a vital part of the cultural tradition of such tribal groups. Would it not be better to translate the Bible into media already present in such societies for the transmission of culture, namely into their own forms of music? Recent experiments with the oral communication of the Scripture in sub-Sahara Africa, as reported by Herbert Klem (*Oral Communication of the Scriptures: Insights from African Oral Art* [Pasadena: W. Carey Library, 1982]), suggest a positive answer to this question. Moreover, it may well be that these very experiments provide a closer analogue to the actual historical situation in ancient Israel than the several models advanced in recent years within the mainstream of the academic study of the Bible.

In short, Deuteronomy is best explained as a didactic poem, composed to be recited publicly to music in ancient Israel within a liturgical setting. The book is primarily a work of literary art designed to transmit a canonical body of tradition as effectively as possible to a given people. It was composed for oral recitation and, as the models in the field of ethnomusicology suggest, was no doubt composed with music as an essential aspect of the tradition itself. Moreover, as a work of literary art, the book of Deuteronomy was consciously composed in what some would call an "epic style," which is similar in its structural features to other epic texts in the world of ancient Near Eastern and classical literatures. Thus we ought not to be surprised to find concentric structural features which are also the subject of investigation on the part of students of such classics as Homer's *Iliad* and Virgil's *Aeneid*. And indeed such features are present in the biblical text, as witnessed by the spate of such observations emerging in our discipline in recent years.

It should also be noted that concentric structural features are not only characteristic of liturgical expression, from so-called primitive peoples to the celebration of the Roman Catholic Mass; they are also common to both musical composition and epic literature in general. A particularly striking example of such concentric structures in music is illustrated by a recent symphony by A. Panufnik, which was commissioned by the Boston Symphony Orchestra as part of its centennial celebration (see D. Christensen, "Andrzej Panufnik and the Structure of the Book of Jonah: Icons, Music and Literary Art," *JETS* 28 [1985] 133–40). The composer explained in detail in the program for that occasion an intricate concentric design based on the number eight—since this was his eighth symphony. Such structuring devices are one of the means of achieving that feeling of balance and symmetry which are essential aspects of making art appear beautiful to both the ear and the eye. The astute observer of modern cinematography will be struck with how well some of our modern film makers have mastered this same technique in the composition of another art form for popular consumption.

When one realizes the essential "musical" quality in the rhythmic structure of the Hebrew text of Deuteronomy, it is useful to think through the implications this has for the traditional question of Mosaic authorship (see D. Christensen and M. Narucki, "The Mosaic Authorship of the Pentateuch," *JETS* 32 [1989] 465–71). Since Deuteronomy was probably performed and sung in liturgical settings in ancient Israel, its form is essentially poetic. This fact suggests something about the very nature of Scripture and points to a hermeneutic whose comprehension supports Mosaic authorship. Poetry is the ideal tool for theology. It is a way of seeing that is not just a system for interpretation but a way of life, a way of making present that which lies beyond the bounds of human experience and understanding.

When it comes to ascribing authorship of sacred tradition, within a worshiping community of faith, we should be careful that we do not say more than we mean. When Robert Robinson wrote the words of the hymn, "Come, Thou Fount of Every Blessing," almost two hundred years ago, the second stanza began with "Here I raise mine Ebenezer." In the hymnal used in the First Baptist Church of Richmond, California, the words are "Here I raise to Thee an altar" (*Praise—Our Songs and Hymns* [Grand Rapids: Zondervan, 1983 (1979)] 35). We can understand why the editors of this particular hymnal made the change. The reference to the story of Ebenezer in 1 Sam 7 is not as familiar to the average worshiper today as it was two hundred years ago. But at the top of the page the author of the hymn is still Robert Robinson. Did he write the hymn as it stands in this popular hymnal? Well, yes and no. He is the author of the hymn, though all the individual words we sing are not his—at least not in the manner in which he originally composed them.

My research in Deuteronomy suggests that the Hebrew text in its present form, as preserved by the Masoretes, is a musical composition. The canting tradition of the synagogues preserves accurate memory of the original performance of the text during the period of the Second Temple in Jerusalem, and perhaps earlier, if Suzanne Haïk-Vantoura is correct. In short, though details in her decipherment of the musical information preserved in the accentual system of the Hebrew Bible may change with further research, much of Haïk-Vantoura's work is likely to stand the test of time. The Bible as we have it is not a collection of independent books, which certain scribes in antiquity gathered together into a library. It is a single book, by a single author—if we are to give credence to the common affirmation in public worship that it is the Word of God. That being the case, we can now say much more about the canonical process that brought the book to us than did our predecessors.

An important aspect of the earlier stages of that canonical process was suggested by the work of Milman Parry and Albert Lord in their oral-formulaic theory, which is based on field work among Yugoslavian poet/musicians (see A. B. Lord, *The Singer of Tales* [Cambridge: Harvard UP, 1960]). The idea of "oral composition-in-performance," for instance, provides a useful model to explain the transmission of the *Iliad* from the time of Homer to the fixing of that text in written form centuries later in ancient Greece. A somewhat parallel phenomenon has been posited by F. M. Cross and some of his students for the presumed "Hebrew Epic" that lies behind the Pentateuch as we now know it (see F. M. Cross, *Canaanite Myth and Hebrew Epic* [Cambridge: Harvard UP, 1973]). The recent study of Richard P. Martin, *The Language of Heroes: Speech and Performance in the Iliad* (Ithaca: Cornell UP, 1989), opens perhaps another chapter in this fascinating story. Though Martin is aware of the musical dimension of the text of the *Iliad*, he builds his investigation primarily on the basis of the disciplines of text linguistics and classical rhetoric, which include careful attention to the new performance-centered approach to verbal art that takes into account the audience for which the speech-act in question was composed (see E. Fine, *The Folklore Text: From Performance to Print* [Bloomington: Indiana UP, 1984]). He notes at the outset of his study that, in the final analysis, it does not really matter whether or not Homer's *Iliad* is a piece of oral poetry. We simply do not have an oral *Iliad*, "because the poem has somehow become a text; and that has made all the difference. To put it another way, our *Iliad* is no longer an action, as it must have been if it was ever an oral composition-in-performance. Instead, it is an artifact" (1). The same is true of the book of Deuteronomy.

The book of Deuteronomy was the center of a complex process of canonical activity, from at least the time of Josiah to the dedication of the Second Temple in Jerusalem at the end of the sixth century B.C.E. In my own opinion, the book of Deuteronomy enjoyed generations of use within public worship in ancient Israel, in the hands of levitical singers in ancient Israel, *before* its use at the center of canonical activity in the time of Josiah. That canonical process included much more than the mere compilation of the Pentateuch. It also included the Former Prophets, or what some would call the Deuteronomic History, within a larger canonical entirety that D. N. Freedman has called the "primary history" (*IDBSup* [1976] 131–32). It may have included both the Latter Prophets and Writings as canonical categories as well, though perhaps not in the form we now know.

T. Georgiades, a music historian, has shown convincingly, at least for ancient Greek literature, that the distinct concepts of music and poetry as we understand them were not known in antiquity: "The ancient Greek verse line was a singular formation for which there is no analogy in Western Christian civilization. It was, if you will, music and poetry in one, and precisely because of this it could not be separated into music and poetry as two tangibly distinct components. For this particular vehicle of meaning the Greeks, however, had a special term "μουσική" (*Music and Language: The Rise of Western Music as Exemplified in Settings of the Mass* [Cambridge: Cambridge UP, 1982] 6). The work of S. Haïk-Vantoura is essentially built on the same observation (see her book, *The Music of the Bible Revealed* [BIBAL Press, 1991]). As with ancient Greek literature, the Hebrew Bible emerged in the form of μουσική—a combination of music and language. What is unique about the situation in ancient Israel is the fact that the canonical form of the musical performance of the biblical text is apparently recoverable, at least in part. Aspects of that speech-act, which is in the form of a musical performance of considerable sophistication, opens the door to a whole new set of questions we may now address in the study of the biblical text.

In a fundamental sense, then, the book of Deuteronomy in its entirety may be described as "poetry" in the broadest sense. Though it contains a lyric "Song of Moses" (chap. 32), most of the book is in the form of didactic poetry of a lesser nature so far as heightened speech goes. The composer of the original was Moses, but the text as we have it enjoyed a life of its own for generations within the public worship of ancient Israel. Like Robert Robinson's hymn, individual words no doubt changed in usage through time. Indeed, the very structure of the greater "Song of Moses," which we now call the book of Deuteronomy, may have changed as it developed in public performance by a long line of singers in the festivals and in levitical circles of ancient Israel through hundreds of years. The concentric structural patterns, found at virtually all levels of analysis, bear witness to its tightly woven composition. That structure points to an author. On one level of observation that author is Moses, who composed the original Torah in musical form. But on another level the author is God himself, at work through that long chain of poet-prophets, like Moses, in ancient Israel who recited this text in public worship and who made it the center of an elaborate canonical process that gave us the Bible itself as the Word of God.

# I. The Outer Frame:
## Part 1—A Look Backwards (1:1–3:29)

Like the structure of the book of Deuteronomy as a whole, chaps. 1–3 are shaped concentrically, a bit like a Jewish candelabrum (Menorah), as follows:

A    Summons to Enter the Promised Land (1:6b–8)
  B    Organization of the People for Life in the Land (1:9–18)
    C    Israel's Unholy War (1:19–2:1)
      D    The March of Conquest (2:2–25)
    C'    YHWH's Holy War (2:26–3:11)
  B'    Distribution of the Land in Transjordan (3:12–17)
A'    Summons to Take the Promised Land (3:18–22)

Each of these sections is in turn organized along similar lines, with the structure highlighting the theological meaning. Thus, it is useful to take note of the center of each structure, which is often closely related to the most external units (i.e., the "A" sections).

Part 1 of the Outer Frame of Deuteronomy (chaps. 1–3) focuses on "The March of Conquest," or what may be called the first phase of YHWH's "Holy War" (i.e., the Exodus-Conquest as celebrated event in ancient Israel). Under Moses the children of Israel defeated the two Amorite kings in Transjordan to set the stage for the second phase of YHWH's "Holy War"—the conquest of Cisjordan under Joshua. Within the canonical process in ancient Israel, these two phases of the "Wars of YHWH" evolved to eventually form the Torah, on the one hand, and the Former Prophets, on the other (see D. Christensen, "The Center of the First Testament within the Canonical Process," *BTB* [forthcoming]). The first has Moses as its "author" and the second Joshua.

The seven-part structure in 1:6b–3:22 is in turn framed by two transitional elements: 1:1–6a, the Superscription, which links Deuteronomy to the book of Numbers and anticipates the structure and content of what follows; and 3:23–29, "From Moses to Joshua," which also functions as an introduction to chap. 31 and part 2 of the Outer Frame of Deuteronomy (chaps. 31–34).

### Bibliography for Deut 1–3

(See also the Main Bibliography and Bibliographies under *Excursus:* "The *Numeruswechsel* in Deuteronomy" and *Excursus:* "Holy War as Celebrated Event in Ancient Israel" below.)

**Andersen, F. I.** "The Socio-Juridical Background of the Naboth Incident." JBL 85 (1966) 46–57. **Astour, M. C.** "Political and Cosmic Symbolism in Genesis 14 and Its Babylonian Sources." In *Biblical Motifs: Origins and Transformations.* Ed. A. Altmann. Cambridge: Harvard UP, 1966. 65–112. **Baltzer, K.** *The Covenant Formulary* (ET 1971; BWANT 4, 1960). **Bartlett, J. R.** "The Land of Seir and the Brotherhood of Edom." *JThS* 20 (1969) 1–20. **Beltz, W.** *Die Kaleb-Traditionen im Alten Testament.* BWANT 98. Stuttgart, 1972. **Ben-Barak, Z.** "Meribaal and the System of Land Grants in Ancient Israel." *Bib* 62 (1981) 73–91. **Ben-Shem, I.** *The Conquest of Trans-Jordan.* Tel Aviv, 1972. **Boling, R. G.** *The Early Biblical Community in Transjordan.* SWBA 6. Sheffield: Almond Press, 1988. **Buis, P.** "Les Conflicts entre Moïse et Israel dans Exode et Nombres." *VT* 28 (1978) 257–70. **Carroll, R. P.** "Rebellion and Dissent in Ancient Israelite Society." *ZAW* 89 (1977) 176–204. **Christensen, D. L.** "Form and Structure in Deuteronomy 1–11." BETL 68. Leuven UP, 1985. 135–44. **Coats, G.** "The Wilderness Itinerary." *CBQ* 34 (1972) 135–52. **Davies, G. I.** "The Wilderness Itineraries: A Comparative Study." *TynBul* 25 (1974) 46–81. ————. *The Way of the Wilderness* (1979). ————. "The Wilderness Itineraries and the Composition of the Pentateuch." *VT* 33 (1983) 1–13. ————. "The Wilderness Itineraries and Recent Archaeological Research." In VTSup 41. Leiden: Brill, 1990. 161–75. **Fritz, V.** *Israel in der Wüste* (MThSt 7, 1979). **Greenfield, J. C.** "*našu-nadānu* and Its Congeners." In *FS J. J. Finkelstein* (1977). 87–91. **Grintz, Y.** *Studies in Early Biblical Ethnology and History.* Jerusalem: Hakibbutz Hameuchad, 1969 (Heb. with Eng. summary). **Hempel, J.** *Die Schichten des Deuteronomiums* (1914). **Herion, G. A.** "The Role of Historical Narrative in Biblical Thought: The Tendencies Underlying Old Testament Historiography." *JSOT* 212 (1981) 25–57. **Hoonacker, A. van.** "L'origine des quatre chapitres du Deutéronome." *Le Muséon* 7 (1888) 464–82; 8 (1889) 67–85, 141–49. **Horbury, W.** "Exterpation and Excommunication." *VT* 35 (1985) 13–38. **Kallai, Z.** "The Wandering-Traditions from Kadesh-Barnea to Canaan: A Study in Biblical Historiography." *JJS* 33 (1982) 175–83. **Laberge, L.** "La Septante de Dt 1–11: Pour une Étude du 'Text'." *Das Deut* (1985). 129–34. **Levenson, J. D.** "Who Inserted the Book of the Torah?" *HTR* 68 (1975) 203–33. **Lipinski, E.** "Sale, Transfer and Delivery in Ancient Semitic Terminology." In *Gesellshaft und Kultur im alten Vorderasien.* SGKAO 15. Berlin: Akademie-Verlag, 1982. 173–85. **Loewenstamm, S. E.** "The Formula בעת ההיא in Deuteronomy." *Tarbiz* 38 (1968/69) 99–104 (Heb. with Eng. summary). **Lohfink, N.** "Darstellungskunst und Theologie in Dtn 1,6–3, 29." *Bib* 41 (1960) 105–34. ————. "Wie stellt sich das Problem Individuum und Gemeinschaft in Deuteronomium 1, 6–3, 29?" *Schol* 35 (1960) 403–7. ————. "Die deuteronomistische Darstellung des Übergangs der Führung Israels von Mose auf Josue." *Schol* 37 (1962) 32–44. **Malamat, A.** "The Danite Migration and the Pan-Israelite Exodus-Conquest: A Biblical Narrative Pattern." *Bib* 51 (1970) 1–16. ————. "Die Wanderung der Daniten und die panisraelitische Exodus-Landnahme: Ein biblisches Erzählmuster." In *FS G. Molin* (1983). 259–65. **Mann, T.** "Theological Reflections on the Denial of Moses." *JBL* 98 (1979) 481–94. **McCarthy, D.** "An Installation Genre?" *JBL* 90 (1971) 31–41. ————. "The Wrath of Yahweh and the Structural Unity of the Deuteronomistic History." In *FS J. P. Hyatt* (1974). 97–110. ————. *Treaty and Covenant* (AnBib 21A, 1978). **McKenzie, J.** "The Historical Prologue of Deuteronomy." In *Proceedings of the Fourth World Congress of Jewish Studies,* vol. 1. Jerusalem, 1967. 95–101. **Milgrom, J.** "The Levitic Town: An Exercise in Realistic Planning." *JJS* 33 (1982) 185–88. **Mittmann, S.** *Deuteronomium 1, 1–6, 3* (1975). **Nelson, R.** "Josiah in the Book of Joshua." *JBL* 100 (1981) 531–40. **Nielsen, E.** "Historical Perspectives and Geographical Horizons: On the Question of North-Israelite Elements in Deuteronomy." In *Law, History and Tradition* (1983). 82–92. **Noth, M.** "Der Wallfahrtsweg zum Sinai (Nu 33)." *PJ* 36 (1940) 5–28 (=AbLA I [1971] 55–74). ————. *The Deuteronomistic History* (ET, JSOTSup 15, 1981; Ger. ed. 1943). ————. "Zur Geschichtsauffassung des Deuteronomisten." In *Proceedings of the 22nd Congress of Orientalists, Istanbul 1953.* Leiden: E. J. Brill, 1957. 558–67. **Ottoson, M.** *Gilead.* ConB OT 3. Lund: Gleerup, 1969. **Perlitt, L.** "Deuteronomium 1–3 im Streit der exegetischen Methoden." *Das Deut* (1985). 149–63. **Plöger, J.** *Deuteronomium* (BBB 26, 1967). **Polzin, R.** "Reporting Speech in the Book of Deuteronomy: Towards a Compositional Analysis of the Deuteronomic History." In *FS F. M. Cross* (1981). 194–211. **Porter, J.** "The Succession of Joshua." In *FS G. Davies* (1970). 102–32. **Radjawane, A. N.** *Israel zwischen Wüste und Land. Studien zur Theologie von Deuteronomium 1–3.* Diss., Univ. Mainz, 1972. **Rose, M.** *Der Ausschliesslichkeitsanspruch Jahwes* (BWANT 106, 1975). ————. *Deuteronomist und Jahwist* (ATANT 67, 1981). **Sanmartin Ascaso, J.** *Las guerras de Josué* (1981). **Schultz, W.** *Stilkritische*

*Untersuchungen zur deuteronomischen Literatur.* Diss., Tübingen, 1974. **Schwertner, S.** *"Das verheissene Land": Bedeutung und Verständnis des Landes nach den frühen Zeugnissen des Alten Testaments.* Diss., Heidelberg, 1966. **Seters, J. Van** "Histories and Historians of the Ancient Near East: The Israelites." *Or* 50 (1981) 137–85. ————. *In Search of History: Historiography in the Ancient World and the Origins of Biblical History.* New Haven: Yale UP, 1983. **Spencer, J. R.** *The Levitical Cities: A Study of the Role and Function of the Levites in the History of Israel.* Diss., Univ. of Chicago, 1980. **Steinthal, H.** "Die erzählenden Stücke im fünften Buche Mose." *ZVS* 12 (1880) 253–89. **Veijola, R.** "Principal Observations on the Basic Story in Deuteronomy 1–3." In *Wünschet Jerusalem Frieden: Collected Communications to the XIIth Congress of the International Organization for the Study of the Old Testament,* ed. M. Augustin and K.-D. Schunck. Frankfurt: Peter Lang, 1988. 249–59. **Vorländer, H.** *Die Entstehungszeit des jehowistischen Geschichtswerkes.* Frankfurt a.M.: P. Lang, 1978. **Wagner, S.** "Die Kundschaftergeschichten im Alten Testament." *ZAW* 76 (1964) 255–69. **Weeks, N. K.** "Causality in the Assyrian Royal Inscriptions." In *OLP* 14. Leuven: Instituut voor Orientalistiek, 1983. 115–27. **Weinfeld, M.** "The Period of the Conquest and of the Judges as Seen by the Earlier and the Later Sources." *VT* 17 (1967) 93–113. **Welch, A.** *Framework to the Code* (1932). ————. "The Sources of Nehemia IX," *ZAW* 47 (1929) 130–37. **Wuest, M.** *Untersuchungen zu den Siedlungsgeographischen Texten des Alten Testaments.* Tübinger Atlas des Vorderen Orient. Reihe B, Geisteswissenschaften 9. Wiesbaden: Reichert, 1975. **Zevit, Z.** "Converging Lines of Evidence Bearing on the Date of P." *ZAW* 94 (1982) 481–511. **Zuber, B.** *Das Tempussystem des biblischen Hebräisch: Eine Untersuchung am Text.* BZAW 164. Berlin: de Gruyter, 1986.

# Superscription: Deuteronomy in a Nutshell (1:1–6a)

## Bibliography

**Aharoni, Y.** *The Land of the Bible.* London, 1966. **Albright, W. F.** "The Land of Damascus Between 1850 and 1750 B.C." *BASOR* 83 (1941) 30–36. **Bartlett, J. R.** "The Land of Seir and the Brotherhood of Edom." *JThS* 20 (1969) 1–20. ———. "Sihon and Og, Kings of the Amorites." *VT* 20 (1970) 257–77. ———. "The Conquest of Sihon's Kingdom: A Literary Re-examination." *JBL* 97 (1978) 347–51. **Batto, B. F.** "The Reed Sea: *Requiescat in Pace.*" *JBL* 102 (1983) 27–35. ———. "Red Sea or Reed Sea?" *BAR* 10 (1984) 57–63. **Beecher, W. J.** "*Torah:* A Word Study in the Old Testament." *JBL* 24 (1905) 1–16. **Ben Hayyim, A.** "Observations on the Hebrew and Aramaic Lexicon from the Samarian Tradition." In *FS W. Baumgartner* (1967). 12–24. **Braulik G.** "Die Ausdrücke für '*Gesetz*'im Buch Deuteronomium." *Bib* 51 (1970) 39–66 (=SBAB 2, 11–38). **Cazelles, H.** "Tophel (Deut. 1:1)." *VT* 9 (1959) 412–15. ———. "Torah et loi. Préalables àl étude historique d' une notion Juive." In *FS G. Vajda* (1987). 1–12. **Davies, G. I.** "The Significance of Deuteronomy 1:2 for the Location of Mount Horeb." *PEQ* 111 (1979) 87–101. **Davis, J. J.** *Biblical Numerology.* Grand Rapids: Baker, 1968. 51–54, 122. **Eissfeldt, O.** "Gilgal or Shechem?" In *FS G. H. Davies* (1970). 90–101. **Fichtner, J.** *Die altorientalische Weisheit in ihrer israelitisch-jüdischen Ausprägung.* BZAW 62. Giessen, 1933. **Flanagan, J. W.** "The Deuteronomic Meaning of the Phrase '*kol yiśrāʾēl*'." *SR* 6 (1976/77) 159–68. **Foresti, F.** "Characteristic Literary Expressions in the Arad Inscriptions Compared with the Language of the Hebrew Bible." *EphC* 32 (1981) 327–41. **Gemser, B.** "*Beʿ ēber Hajjardēn:* In Jordan's Borderland." *VT* 2 (1952) 349–55. **Haldar, A.** *Who Were the Amorites?* MANE 1. Leiden: Brill, 1971. **Haran, M.** "Book-Scrolls in Israel in Pre-Exilic Times." *JJS* 33 (1982) 161–73. **Hill, R.** "Aetheria XII 9 and the Site of Biblical Edrei." *VT* 16 (1966) 412–20. **Hulst, A. R.** "Der Name '*Israel*'im Deuteronomium." *OTS* 9 (1951) 65–106. **Kellermann, D.** "'*Aśtārōt—ʿAśtārōt Qarnayim—Qarnayim:* Erwägungen zu Orten im nördlichen Ostjordanland." *ZDPV* 97 (1981) 45–61. **Koenig, J.** "La localisation du Sinaï et les traditions des scribes." *RHPR* 43 (1963) 2–31. **Kraeling, E. J.** "Two Place Names in Hellenistic Palestine." *JNES* 7 (1948) 201. **Kutsch, E.** "Menschliche Weisung—Gesetz Gottes: Beobachtungen zu einem aktuellen Thema." In *Gott ohne Eigenschaften?* Ed. S. Heinne and E. Heintel. Vienna: Evangelisher Presseverband, 1983. 77–106. **Lindars, B.** "*Torah* in Deuteronomy." In *FS D. W. Thomas* (1968). 117–36. **Lohfink, N.** "Der Bundesschluss im Lande Moab. Redaktionsgeschichtliches zu Dt 28, 69–32, 47." *BZ* n.s. 6 (1962) 32–56. **Moran, W. L.** "Deuteronomy." In "Nelson Commentary" (1969). 260. **Mussner, F.** "Das Toraleben im jüdischen Verständnis." In *Die Kraft der Wurzel-Judentum-Jesus-Kirche.* Freiburg/Basel/Vienna: Herder, 1987. 13–26. **Nielsen, E.** "Historical Perspectives and Geographical Horizons: On the Question of North-Israelite Elements in Deuteronomy." *ASTI* 11 (1978) 77–89. ———. "Moses and the Law." *VT* 32 (1982) 87–98. **Noth, M.** "Der Wallfahrtsweg zum Sinai (Nu 33)." *PJ* 36 (1940) 5–28 (=AbLA I [1971] 55–74). **Perlitt, L.** "Sinai und Horeb." In *FS W. Zimmerli* (1977). 302–22. ———. "Priesterschrift im Deuteronomium?" *ZAW* 100 (1988) 65–88. **Rinaldi, G.** "Nota (ʾēlleh)." *BeO* 11 (1969) 124. **Roscher, W. H.** "Die Zahl 40 im Glauben, Brauch und Schrifttum der Semiten." *Abhandlungen der Phil.-Histor. Klasse der Königlich Sächsischen Gesellschaft der Wissenschaften* 27 (1909) 93–138. **Sánchez Caro, J. M.** "Las recensiones targúmicas. Estudio de Tg Dt 1, 1." *Salm* 19 (1972) 605–34. ———. "Tradiciones del Targum palestinense a Dt 1, 1." *Salm* 26 (1979) 109–24. **Sauer, G.** "Die chronologischen Angaben in den Büchern Deuteronomium bis 2 Könige." *ThZ* 24 (1968) 1–14. **Segal, M. H.** "The Composition of the Pentateuch—A Fresh Examination." ScrHier 8. Jerusalem: Magnes

Press, 1961. 90. **Seters, J. Van** "The Conquest of Sihon's Kingdom: A Literary Examination." *JBL* 91 (1972) 182–97. ————. "The Terms 'Amorite' and 'Hittite' in the Old Testament." *VT* 22 (1972) 64–81. **Snaith, N. H.** "סוּף יָם: The Sea of Reeds." *VT* 15 (1965) 395–98. **Tsumura, D. T.** "Hab 2, 2 in the Light of Akkadian Legal Practice." *ZAW* 94 (1982) 294–95. **Van Goudoever, J.** "The Liturgical Significance of the Date in Dt 1, 3." In *Das Deut* (1985). 145–48. **Weinfeld, M.** "The Tribal League at Sinai." In *FS F. M. Cross* (1987). 303–14.

*Translation and Prosodic Analysis\**

1:1–6a  [6:8:(6:6):8:6]

| | | | |
|---|---|---:|---:|
| 1 | These[a] are the words (הדברים)[b] / | 9 | 1 |
| | Which Moses spoke (דבר)[b] / unto all Israel / | ⌐ 15 | 2 |
| | In the vicinity of \\[c] the Jordan // | └ 8 | 1 |
| | In the wilderness / in the Arabah opposite Suph / | ⌐ <u>15</u> | 2_ |
| | Between Paran and Tophel / | └ 13 | 1 |
| | And Laban and Hazeroth / and Dizahab // | ⌐ 18 | 2 |
| 2 | It is eleven days / from Horeb / | └ 14 | 2 |
| | By way \\[a] of Mount Seir // to / Kadesh-barnea // | ⌐ <u>16</u> | 3_ |
| 3 | [a][And it was / in the fortieth year / | └ 14 | 2 |
| | In the eleventh month / on the first of the month[a] // | 19 | 2][a] |
| | Moses spoke (דבר) / unto[b] the children of Israel / | 15 | 2 |
| | According to all / | ⌐ 3 | 1 |
| | that Yahweh commanded / him / unto them // | ⌐ 16 ⌐ | 3 |
| | | └ 15 ┘ | 3 |
| 4 | After he had smitten / both / Sihon / | ⌐ <u>19</u> | 3_ |
| | King of the Amorites / who ruled / in Heshbon // | └ 12 | 3 |
| | And / Og / king of Bashan / | ⌐ 12 | 1 |
| | Who ruled in Ashtaroth / | └ 5 | 1 |
| | in Edrei[a] // | | |
| 5 | In the vicinity of the Jordan / in the land of Moab // | 15 | 2 |
| | Moses began / | ⌐ <u>8</u> | 1_ |
| | to expound / this Torah / (saying) [a] // | └ 17 | 3 |
| 6 | "Yahweh our God / spoke (דבר) unto us / | <u>18</u> | 2 |
| | in Horeb (saying) // | 9 | 1_ |

## Notes

\* The numbers in the first column indicate the mora-count in the Hebrew text for that line. These numbers tend to fall into parallel groups, which are usually binary in nature and occasionally separated by a bridging element ( i.e., "pivot pattern"—see vv 4b–5a). This phenomenon may be described as quantitative parallelism. The brackets in that column are to show such parallelism. The numbers in the second column indicate the syntactic-accentual stress units, which are delineated by the disjunctive accents in that line (as indicated by single slash / and double slash //in the translation). See Introduction (pp. lviii, lix) for a discussion of the rules for counting morae and syntactic-accentual stress units.

1.a. The reading ואלה is attested in some Heb. Mss, LXX[A], and Syr[w], both here and in 12:1. The prosodic analysis supports MT.

1.b. The term דבר, in its various forms, is noted throughout this commentary, since, הדברים is the title of the book of Deuteronomy and the term appears to be used for rhetorical effect. There is no single English equivalent for this important Heb. term, which is roughly equivalent to the Gr. λογος (cf. John 1:1).

1.c. The reverse slash (\) is used to indicate the substitution of a conj accent for the disj *ṭiphā'*, when the corresponding *'atnāḥ* or *sillûq* does not fall at a major rhythmic break in the prosodic analysis.

2.a. See note 1.c. above.

3.a-a. The first half of v 3 is commonly assigned to P in older Pentateuchal criticism, along with 32:48–52 (see S. R. Driver, ICC [1895], 7). The prosodic analysis supports the conclusion that this is a secondary insertion. In content the lines continue the focus on time by placing the words which Moses spoke at the end of the wilderness era. In terms of mora-count, the insertion matches its immediate context, forming a triplet [14+19=33] [15+3+16=34] [15+19=34]. Such triplets are relatively uncommon in Deut, and the insertion destroys the larger metrical configuration of the passage as a whole, which appears to be concentric in its rhythmic structure (i.e., the distribution of accentual-stress units) [6:8:(6:6):8:6].

3.b. Two Heb. Mss and some Gr. witnesses (LXX^L, *a' σ' θ'*) insert כל , which is possible in terms of mora-count.

4.a. Mss in LXX, Syr, and Vg read ובאדרעי with Josh 12:4, which is possible in terms of mora-count. The fact that the term occupies a pivot position in terms of prosodic structure ([24:5:23] in mora-count) helps to explain why the term was sometimes read with what follows, contrary to MT.

5.a. The term לאמר is often roughly equivalent to use of quotation marks in English and best left untranslated. Nonetheless, the term is often significant from a rhythmic perspective, as is the case here.

## Form/Structure/Setting

That some have taken this as a conclusion to Numbers rather than an introduction to Deuteronomy (see discussion of Buis and Leclercq, *Le Deutéronome* [1963] 31) indicates that vv 1–3 are transitional in nature. W. Moran was perhaps the first, among modern scholars, to comment on the concentric structure of the passage as a whole ("Deuteronomy" [1969] 260), which may be outlined as follows (cf. N. Lohfink, *BZ* n.s. 6 [1962] 32, n. 2):

A    These Words (דברים) Moses spoke (דבר)
  B    Place: In the vicinity of the Jordan
    C    Time: It is eleven days from Horeb to Kadesh-barnea
      D    Moses spoke (דבר) what Yahweh commanded
    C'   Time: After he had smitten the Amorite kings
  B'   Place: In the vicinity of the Jordan
A'   Moses expounded this Torah which Yahweh spoke (דבר)

In form and content 1:1–6a serves as an introduction to the book of Deuteronomy as a whole. Its concentric nature, in terms of both content and original prosodic structure, foreshadows the larger structure and content of what follows:

A    THE OUTER FRAME: Part 1—A Look Backward (chaps. 1–3)
  B    THE INNER FRAME: Part 1—The Great Peroration (chaps. 4–11)
    C    THE CENTRAL CORE: Covenant Stipulations (chaps. 12–26)
  B'   THE INNER FRAME: Part 2—The Covenant Ceremony (chaps. 27–30)
A'   THE OUTER FRAME: Part 2—A Look Forward (chaps. 31–34)

Each of these five major sections of the book is in turn structured in similar concentric patterns. In short, the book is composed along lines most clearly paralleled in the work of musicians and epic poets, past and present (see D. Christensen, "Andrzej Panufnik and the Structure of the Book of Jonah: Icons, Music and Literary Art," *JETS* 28 [1985] 133–40).

The structure of 1:1–6a focuses attention on what Moses spoke to Israel before his death, namely the words of the Torah as given to him by Yahweh. The verbal root דבר appears three times after the opening phrase, "These are the words (דברים)." In the first instance it is Moses who spoke (v 1). Moses spoke what Yahweh commanded him to say (v 3). And finally it is Yahweh who spoke; Moses is merely quoting his words (v 6).

Deut 1:1–6a functions as a bridge joining together the ending of the book of Numbers with what follows. Taken together with the rest of the Outer Frame (chaps. 1–3 and 31–34), it serves as an introduction to the Deuteronomic History as well. In short, like the book of Deuteronomy taken as a whole, these opening verses serve as a bridge connecting major segments of the canonical Hebrew Bible. J. Lundbom argues that 1:1–5 forms an inclusion with 28:69, which leads him to the conclusion that chaps. 1–28 make up "the first identifiable *book* of Deuteronomy" (*CBQ* 38 [1976] 293, n. 5). He identifies Deut 1–28 as the reform document from King Hezekiah's time and Deut 32 as the lawbook found in the Temple under King Josiah (295).

The long sojourn in the wilderness has ended. The conquest of the two Amorite kings in the Jordan Valley has set the stage for a new phase in the journey of faith. Moses is about to pass the torch of leadership to his successor, Joshua, who will bring them into the promised land (see also 3:23–28; 31:1–8; 34:5–9). This moment of transition forms an inclusion around each section of the Outer Frame (chaps. 1–3 and 31–34) of Deuteronomy. The Exodus is now past history. The Conquest is both a present reality and the hope of the future.

## Comment

1    The phrase כל־ישראל, "all Israel," serves as an inclusion around Deuteronomy as a whole, as Craigie has noted (NICOT [1976] 89–90). In 1:1 it is the *words* of Moses that are addressed to *all Israel;* whereas, in 34:12 it is the mighty deeds of Moses, which he did in the sight of *all Israel,* that set him apart as a prophet without peer.

1–2    In this introductory speech Moses is clearly located "In the vicinity of the Jordan in Moab" (vv 1, 5); thus we are in a position to speak more directly of the meaning of the various place names mentioned. Though some of these terms appear as stopping points on the Exodus trek, from Sinai (Horeb) to Kadesh-barnea (cf. Num 10:12; 11:35; 12:16; 13:3, 26; and 33:17, 20), it is also possible to locate some of them in the vicinity of Mount Nebo: Suf (*Khirbet Sufe*), Laban (*Khirbet el-Libben*), Hazeroth ("encampments"), and Dizahab (*ed-Dhebe*), as N. Lohfink has noted (see his "Lectures in Deuteronomy" [1968] 11–12; cf. M. Noth, *JSOTSup* 15 [1981], 108–9, n. 6). It seems best to see double entendre here, particularly as we turn our attention to the "C" elements in the outline of 1:1–6a, which focus on the matter of time. The setting of Moses expounding the Torah is clearly at the end of the wilderness era in the land of Moab, after the defeat of the two Amorite kings in the Jordan Valley (1:4). But this verse is set over against a reference to a march of eleven days from Horeb to Kadesh-barnea (1:2), which may refer to some cultic pilgrimage in early Israel (see Y. Aharoni and M. Avi-Yonah, *The Macmillan Bible Atlas* [1977] 17, map 10). The events at the end of the journey through the wilderness are connected with those of the beginning of that era.

הר־שעיר, "Mount Seir," is usually taken as the mountainous region east of the Arabah. Bartlett (*JThS* 20 [1969] 1–20) argues for its location west of the Arabah in the highlands of Beersheba, later connected with the east through Esau and Edom.

**3** The date here is the only exact date given in Deuteronomy and is probably part of a complex system of dating that was edited into the biblical record at the time Deuteronomy was placed in its present canonical context. As G. Braulik (DNEB [1986] 22) and J. Van Goudoever (*Das Deut* [1985] 145) have noted, Moses died two and a half months before Passover (Deut 32:48; cf. Deut 1:3), and Aaron died two and a half months before Sukkoth (Num 33:38), both being opposite days within the liturgical year-cycle. Van Goudoever concludes that "the book of Deuteronomy is presented as the Testament of Moses, to be read as a preparation for the Passover" in Josh 5—the Passover in the land which is reflected in Deut 26. For him, Deuteronomy and Joshua are a single composition. Cf. also the dates given in Exod 12:41; Num 10:11; Josh 4:19.

**4** The term עשתרת does not appear in the parallel passage in 3:1–22. On its probable location in Bashan, see W. F. Albright (*BASOR* 83 [1941] 33). For a detailed discussion of the literature on the location of Edrei, see R. Hill (*VT* 16 [1966] 412–20). The identification of Edrei with Dera is at least as old as Eusebius. For a map of this region see S. R. Driver's article "Trachonitis" (*Encyclopaedia Biblica* 4 [New York, 1903] cols. 5142–46).

**5** The phrase בעבר הירדן has sometimes been taken as displaying a point of view from within the promised land, long after the death of Moses. It should be noted, however, that it appears occasionally as a geographical expression, like the term Mesopotamia ("between the rivers"), and thus may sometimes be rendered simply as Transjordan (or east of the Jordan). As Gemser has shown, the noun עֵבֶר does not necessarily indicate the idea of "beyond" but rather "in the region of" or "alongside" (*VT* 2 [1952] 349–55); hence the rendering here: "in the vicinity of."

בֵּאֵר, "to expound," appears also in 27:8 and Hab 2:2, with the sense of making a written statement plain or distinct. In post-biblical Heb. the term בִּיאוּר denotes an exposition, or commentary. Tsumura has argued for parallels in Akkadian *burru*, the D-stem of *bâru*, meaning "to establish the true legal situation (ownership, liability, etc.) by a legal procedure involving ordeal, oath, or testimony" (*ZAW* 94 [1982] 294–95).

1:1–6a should be compared with 4:44–49, which forms the introduction to 5:1–6:3, the section on the Ten Commandments. It is sometimes argued that 4:44–49 was the original introduction to Deuteronomy, before the Outer Frame was added to the book.

*Explanation*

The book of Deuteronomy forms a bridge between the Tetrateuch (Genesis through Numbers) and the Former Prophets (Joshua through 2 Kings in the Hebrew canon), which are sometimes called the Deuteronomic (or Deuteronomistic) History. One of the ways of constructing such a "bridge" in the literary world of ancient Israel was what some have described as "ring composition." At the center stands the central concern: the word of God, which in this case is mediated through his servant Moses. What follows is much more than the mere words of Moses. Moses spoke what Yahweh commanded him to say. In fact, as vv 5–6a make clear, Moses is quoting and expounding the very words of Yahweh himself, which he has received. The author "nests" this primary revelation in both time (vv 2–3a, 4) and space (vv 1, 5) in a carefully balanced structure. Though it is certainly possible to separate two distinct narrative voices in the material that follows, as Polzin has shown (*Moses and the Deuteronomist* [1980] and "Deuteronomy" [1987]), one should never lose sight of the fact that this book is the word of Yahweh. To claim, as some have in recent years, that the Bible nowhere claims to be the "Word of God" is to fail to hear a central claim of Deuteronomy.

# Summons to Enter the Promised Land (1:6b–8)

## Bibliography

**Aharoni, Y.** *The Land of the Bible.* London, 1966. **Anbar, M.** "Genesis 15: A Conflation of Two Deuteronomic Narratives." *JBL* 101 (1982) 39–55. **Bückmann, O.** "Leben und Gesetz nach dem Deuteronomium: Eine Meditation." *In Freudlan am Evangelium.* Ed. J. J. Stamm and E. Wolf. München, 1966. 7–18. **Carpenter, E. E.** "Literary Structure and Unbelief: A Study of Deuteronomy 1:6–46." *AsTJ* 42 (1987) 77–84. **Clements, R. E.** "Deuteronomy and the Jerusalem Cult Tradition." *VT* 15 (1965) 300–312. **Cross, F. M.** and **Freedman, D. N.** "The Song of Miriam." *JNES* 14 (1955) 249–50. **Daube, D.** "A Reform in Acts and Its Models." In *FS W. D. Davies* (1976). 151–63. **Dhorme, P.** "Les Amorrhéens." *RB* 37 (1928) 63–79, 161–80. **Emerton, J. A.** "The Origin of the Promises to the Patriarchs in the Older Sources of the Book of Genesis." *VT* 32 (1982) 14–32. **Fohrer, G.** "Israel's Haltung gegenüber den Kanaanäern und anderen Völkern." In *Studien zu Alttestamentlichen Texten und Themen, 1966–1972.* Ed. G. Fohrer. BZAW 155. Berlin, 1981. 107–116. **Gibson, J. C. L.** "Observations on Some Important Ethnic Terms in the Pentateuch." *JNES* 20 (1961) 217–38. **Giesen, G.** *Die Wurzel* שבע *"Schwören": Eine semasiologische Studie zum Eid im Alten Testament.* BBB 56 Bonn: Hanstein, 1981. **Gross, W.** "Syntaktische Erscheinungen am Anfang althebräischer Erzählungen: Hintergrund und Vordergrund." In VTSup 32. Leiden: Brill, 1981. 131–45. **Halévy, J.** "Recherches bibliques: le Deutéronome." *RSEHA* 7 (1899) 313–32. **Heltzer, M.** "Mortgage of Land Property and Freeing from It in Ugarit." *JESHO* 19 (1976) 89–95. **Hoffmann, Y.** "The Root *QRB* as a Legal Term." *JNSL* 10 (1982) 67–73. **Japhet, S.** "People and Land in the Restoration Period." In *Das Land* (1983). 103–25. **Kallai, Z.** "The Boundaries of the Land of Canaan and the Land of Israel in the Bible." *EI* 12 (1975) 27–34 (Heb). —————. "The Reality of the Land and the Bible." In *Das Land* (1983). 76–90. **Koenig, J.** "La localisation du Sinai et les Traditions des Scribes." *RHPR* 43 (1963) 2–31. **Labuschagne, C.** "Some Significant Compositional Techniques in Deuteronomy." In *FS J. H. Hospers* (1986). 121–31. **Liverani, M.** "The Amorites." In *Peoples of Old Testament Times.* Ed. D. J. Wiseman. Oxford, 1973. 100–133. **Lohfink, N.** "Darstellungskunst und Theologie in Dtn. 1:6–3:29." *Bib* 41 (1960) 105–34. —————. "ירש." *TWAT* 3 (1982) 953–85. —————. "Dtn 12, 1 und Gen 15, 18: Das dem Samen Abrahams geschenkte Land als der Geltungsbereich der deuteronomischen Gesetze." In *FS J. Scharbert* (1989). 183–210. **Menezes, R. de.** "The Pentateuchal Theology of Land." *BibBh* 12 (1986) 5–28. **Pearson, R.** "Long Enough at the Mountain: Deut 1:3, 5–8; 4:9." *ANQ* 16 (1975) 210–15. **Perlitt, L.** "Motive und Schichten der Landtheologie im Deuteronomium." In *Das Land* (1983). 46–58. **Rad, G. von.** "The Promised Land and Yahweh's Land in the Hexateuch." In *The Problem of the Hexateuch and Other Essays* (1966). 79–93 (Ger. ed., *ZDPV* 66 [1943] 191–204 [=*GesStAT* I (1958) 87–100]). **Rendtorff, R.** "Genesis 15 im Rahmen der theologischen Bearbeitung." In *FS C. Westermann* (1980). 74–81. **Saebø, M.** "Grenzbeschreibung und Landideal im Alten Testament mit besonderer Berucksichtigung der *min 'ad*-Formel." *ZDPV* 90 (1974) 14–37. **Safrai, S.** "The Land of Israel in Tannaitic *Halacha.*" In *Das Land* (1983). 201–15. **Schiffmann, I.** "Die Grundeigentumsverhältnisse in Palästina in der ersten Hälfte des 1. Jahrtausends v.u.Z." *Wirtschaft im alten Vorderasien.* Ed. J. Harmatta and G. Komoróczy. Budapest, 1976. 457–71. **Schmidt, L.** "Israel ein Segen für die Volker?" *TV* 12 (1973/74 [1975]) 135–51. **Seters, J. Van** "Confessional Reformulations in the Exilic Period." *VT* 22 (1972) 448–59. **Smend, R.** "Das uneroberte Land." In *Das Land* (1983). 91–102. **Sperber, A.** "Der Personenwechsel in der Bibel." *ZA* 32 (1918) 23–33. **Veijola, T.** "Davidverheissung und Staatsvertrag: Beobachtungen auf die biblische Sprache am Beispiel von Ps 89." *ZAW* 95 (1983) 22–29. **Weinfeld, M.** "Zion and Jerusalem as Religious and Political Capital: Ideology and Utopia." In

*The Poet and the Historian.* Ed. R. E. Friedmann. HSS 26. Chico: Scholars, 1983. 75–115.
————. "The Extent of the Promised Land—the Status of Transjordan." In *Das Land* (1983). 59–75.

## Translation and Prosodic Analysis

1:6b–8  [7:7]  [6:6]

| | | |
|---|---|---|
| 6bᵃ " 'You have tarried long enough / on this mountain // | ⌐ 13 | 2 |
| 7  Turnᵃ / and break camp / | ∟ 10 | 2 |
| And come Iᵇ to the hill country of the Amorites / | ⌐ 14 | 2 |
| and unto all their neighbors / | ∟ 8 | 1_ |
| In the Arabah, in the hill country / | ⌐ 11 | 1 |
| Andᶜ in the Shephelah andᵈ in the Negeb / | [ 13⌐ | 1 |
| and by the coast of the sea // | ∟ 8⌐ | 1 |
| The land of the Canaanites / and the Lebanon / | ⌐ 15 | 2 |
| as far as the great river / the river Euphrates' // | ∟ 16 | 2_ |
| | | |
| 8"ᵃ*See* / *I have set before*ᵃ you / the land // | ⌐ 18 | 3 |
| Come in / and possess Iᵇ the land / | ∟ 14 | 3_ |
| Which Yahweh swore ᶜ / to your fathers / | ⌐ 14 | 2 |
| to Abraham, to Isaac, and to Jacob / | ∟ 17 | 1 |
| To give ᵈ to them / | 7 | 1 |
| And to their descendants ᵈ / | 6 | 1 |
| after them" //ᵉ | 5 | 1_ |

## Notes

6b.a. The boldface type is used in vv 6b–7 to indicate that this is part of a series of Travel Notices in the Outer Frame of Deuteronomy, which are distributed throughout the Outer Frame (chaps. 1–3, 31–34) in a discernible pattern. The phrase רב־לכם, which appears again in 2:3, is used to introduce the series, which includes 1:6, 19; 2:1, 3, 8, 13, 24, 34; 3:1, 4, 29; 31:1; 32:44; 34:1. See *Excursus* below.

7.a. The term סעה is to be taken in the sense of the rush of the storm wind; i.e., "go quickly, run; be energetic" (cf. Ps 55:9). The pl impv וסעו לכם may point to two different verbal roots: נסע, "to set out (on a journey)," and סעה, "go quickly" (from rushing wind [סער]). Both meanings are probably intended.

7.b. The vertical mark (I) is used to mark the addition of a disj accent. The sequence here of *ʾazlaʾ* followed by *mêrekaʾ* may well be disj, though it is not listed as such in the standard tables.

7.c. Some Heb. Mss and Tgᴶ omit the *waw*-conj.

7.d. SP and Vg omit *waw*-conj.

8.a-a. DSS, SP, LXX, Syr, and Tg read pl. The abrupt change from 2nd pl to 2nd sg in MT is probably intentional and part of the so-called problem of the *Numeruswechsel* (see *Excursus:* "The *Numeruswechsel* in Deuteronomy" below). The change marks the boundary of a new rhythmic unit. Sections in 2nd sg are indicated here by italic type and 2nd pl by roman type.

8.b. The *ʾatnāḥ* should have been placed at the end of this verset, which would call for a *ṭiphāʾ* here rather than the *mûnaḥ*. Line-halves or line-thirds are here disignated "versets," following Robert Alter, who borrows the term from Benjamin Hrushovsky ("Prosody, Hebrew," *Encyclopedia Judaica* [New York, 1971] 1200–02). As Alter has noted, "the older scholarly term 'hemistich' and the current 'colon' (plural 'cola') both have misleading links with Greek versification" (*The Art of Biblical Poetry* [New York: Basic Books, 1985] 9).

8.c. SP and LXX (except for LXXᴸᴼ) read נשבעתי (as does Craigie, NICOT [1976] 93). The emendation is not necessary.

8.d-d. SP and one Heb. Ms read לזרעם for להם ולזרעם The prosodic analysis supports MT.
8.e. The boundary is indicated in both *BHK* and *BHS* by extra space.

## Form/Structure/Setting

The parallel structural unit in 3:18–22 is concentric in design. Here the pattern appears to be linear, in two parts. In the initial [7:7] unit, which may also be read [4:3:3:4], Yahweh is the speaker commanding the people to enter the promised land. The following [6:6] unit repeats the same message on the lips of Moses. Failure to distinguish the two parts has led interpreters, ancient and modern, to emend the text.

## Comment

**6b–7** Moses begins his address by quoting the words of YHWH, commanding the people to enter the promised land. The dimensions given for that land are enormous, an area far larger than Israel ever possessed, even during the Davidic empire. The terms used indicate the principal geographical divisions of the land (see Y. Aharoni, *The Land of the Bible*, rev. ed. [1979] 41–42): namely, the *hill country of the Amorites* (i.e., the central mountainous regions of Judah and Ephraim); the *Arabah,* that is, the great rift valley extending from the Sea of Galilee in the north to the Gulf of Aqaba in the south; the *Shephelah,* a range of low hills situated west of the Judean mountains; the *Negeb,* which is the dry land in southern Palestine extending from Kadesh-barnea to the Judean mountains; and *the coast of the sea,* that is, the plain in western Palestine bordering the Mediterranean Sea. These areas together can be placed under the general term, *the land of the Canaanites,* as Gibson has noted (*JNES* 20 [1961] 217–38). *The Lebanon* is the land north of the Canaanites, and still further to the northeast lie the upper reaches of the *river Euphrates.* This extended vision of the land reflects the promise made to Abraham that YHWH would give to him and to his descendants the land from "the river of Egypt to the great river, the river Euphrates" (Gen 15:18). On some of the implications of this description of the promised land, see Gordon, *UT* 19 (1899) 459.

**8** The term ראה, "see!" (2 m sg impv), appears six times in the Outer Frame of Deut (1:8, 21; 2:24, 31; 3:27; 32:49) and three times in the Inner Frame (Deut 4:5; 11:26; 30:15). The first four occurrences are accompanied by the root ירש, the sense of which is to possess by dispossessing (see N. Lohfink, *TDOT,* "ירש"). In contrast to the first three occurrences, the fourth in 3:27 concludes a sentence, making what appears to be the end of a sequence, at least for part one of the Outer Frame (chaps. 1–3). Here the root ירש is not present (particularly in the form of the masculine singular imperative רֵשׁ); and the term ראשׁ, "head," has taken its place. Moses pled for permission to cross over the Jordan that he might *see* the land in the sense of possessing it (the root ירש being absent). Yahweh's response is a pun on the previous two occurrences of the root ירש in this series of passages introduced by the term ראשׁ (2:24, 31). He is told to go up on the ראשׁ, "top," of Mount Pisgah and "see" (ראה). The sixth and final occurrence of ראה in the singular imperative within the Inner Frame appears in 32:49, which repeats the scene of Moses "seeing" the land of Canaan from the top of Mount Nebo. Two further occurrences of the root ראה, "to see," complete the sequence: namely, the prophecy (32:52) and the fulfillment of Moses' actual ascent of Nebo (34:1) to "see all the land" which he was not permitted to enter. In 34:1 the term ראש appears once again, but not ראה. From the top of Mount Nebo Moses is permitted to "see" the land in terms of a glorious vision, but he is not permitted to "see" it by way of actual possession, as he had requested.

## Explanation

One of the most memorable student sermons I have heard in my seminary teaching experience was titled "You Have Dwelt Long Enough on This Mountain." Taking the opening words of Yahweh in this "Summons to Enter the Promised Land," Paul Perkins made them come alive in the black Baptist preaching tradition. It is not enough to enjoy the presence of God in the wilderness; we must "turn and take (our) journey . . . unto all (our) neighbors in the Arabah, in the hill country and in the Shephelah and in the Negeb and by the coast of the sea." Ours is not a task of dispossessing them as enemies, but rather of including them within the people of God by showing them how "to possess the land" along with us. Years later that message still rings in my ears.

The extended vision of the promised land in this passage reflects the patriarchal covenant to Abraham, in which God promised to give his descendants the land from "the river of Egypt to the great river, the river Euphrates" (Gen 15:18). This text, and others like it, should never be used to justify continued expansion on the part of modern Israel at the expense of her Arab neighbors. The Deuteronomic vision of the promised land is theological in nature. Through the descendants of Abraham all peoples will be blessed (Gen 12:3). In fact, Abraham is to be "the father of a multitude of nations" (Gen 17:5). From a canonical point of view, the people of God in the OT were never limited to the political state of Israel. See D. Christensen, "A New Israel: The Righteous from among All Nations," in *FS R. K. Harrison* (1988) 251–59.

## EXCURSUS: *Travel Notices in the Outer Frame of Deuteronomy*

One of the rhetorical features used to structure the Outer Frame of Deuteronomy (chaps. 1–3 and 31–34) is a series of imperatives in the second person plural followed by responses in the first person plural. The latter, in particular, stand out markedly when the text is read in Hebrew. The content of these verses tends to focus on specific geographical places in terms of a journey. Moreover, these Travel Notices seem to be arranged according to a discernible pattern.

The beginning of the series is probably to be found in 1:2, which anticipates the journey from Horeb, by way of Mount Seir, to Kadesh-barnea: "It is eleven days from Horeb, by way of Mount Seir, to Kadesh-barnea." Though this reference to a journey of eleven days may actually refer to a pilgrimage route of later times, it functions here as an outline of sorts for the first phase of the journey from Sinai to the promised land.

The Travel Notices are arranged in four groups: 1:6b–2:8; 2:13–24; 2:34–3:29; and 31:1–34:4. The first group consists of two parts (1:6b–2:1 and 2:3–8), each of which is introduced by the phrase רב־לכם, which is difficult to translate. In 1:6b the people are told to depart from Mount Horeb and to go to the hill country of the Amorites. That journey took them to Kadesh-barnea (1:19). From there they turned back toward the Red Sea and journeyed about Mount Seir (2:1). After "many days," they were told that they had circled that mountain long enough (רב־לכם). They were commanded to turn northward (2:3) to a new phase of their journey, going by way of the Arabah, to the wilderness of Moab (2:8) in two stages.

This brings us to the second group of Travel Notices (2:13 and 2:24), which is introduced by the term עתה, "now." This group focuses on the journey across the wadi Zared (2:13), from Edom into Moab, and finally across the wadi Arnon (2:24), from Moab into the promised land. Each phase is introduced by the phrase ק(ו)מו ועברו. In the second case (2:24) the verb סעו is inserted in the middle of this phrase, which is the verb used in the initial departure from Horeb (1:19), where it is followed by the ונלך and ונבא—two verbs which are not used again in the series of Travel Notices until the final group in 31:1–34:4, where Moses וילך ("went," 31:1) and ויבא ("came," 32:44) before he spoke (וידבר) all the words of the song, after which he went up (ויעל) from the plains of Moab to Mount Nebo (34:1) in anticipation of his own death.

The climax of the journey is the crossing of the wadi Arnon in the third two-part group of Travel Notices (2:34–3:1 and 3:4–29), which led to two battles, each introduced by the verb ונלכד, "and we destroyed," against the cities of Sihon (2:34) and Og (3:4), the kings of the Amorites. The conclusion of these two battles introduces three verbs which tie the whole series together: ונפן, "and we turned," and ונעל, "and we went up," in 3:1 and ונשב, "and we dwelt," in 3:29. The first of these echoes פנו in 1:7 and 2:3 and ונפן in 2:8. The second anticipates the final verb in the series, where Moses "went up" (ויעל) Mount Nebo. The verb ונשב ("to remain," 3:29) forms an inclusion with the opening verb of the entire series in the phrase רב־לכם שבת ("you have tarried long enough," 1:6b). The verbal root ישב in 1:6b and 3:29 brackets part 1 of the Outer Frame (chaps. 1-3) and appears nowhere else in the series of Travel Notices.

The arrangement of these four groups of Travel Notices displays both a chiastic structure and the curious "three plus one" pattern of Jungian psychology, which appears at virtually all levels within the developing canonical process (see D. Christensen, "The Center of the First Testament within the Canonical Process, *BTB* [forthcoming]). The first three groups have second person plural imperatives followed by descriptive responses in the first person plural. The fourth group, on the other hand, is in the third person singular, with Moses as the subject of four verbs; three of these verbs belong to the series of verbs introduced in the previous three groups of Travel Notices, while the fourth in 32:44 (את־כל־הדברים האלה . . . וידבר) echoes the opening words of the book of Deuteronomy (1:1–6a).

The chiastic relation between the four groups of Travel Notices is shown by the repetition of two verbal roots, which appear only in these two contexts within the series: ונלך (1:19) / וילך (31:1) and ונבא (1:19) / ויבא (32:44). In narrative content the first and fourth groups are closely connected. The initial command to journey from Mount Horeb takes them to Kadesh-barnea and the aborted command to enter the promised land (1:19–2:1—"Israel's Unholy War"). The fourth group of Travel Notices anticipates another entry into the promised land, under Joshua's leadership, which is clearly the focus of Yahweh's "Holy War" (31:1–34:12) in the Exodus-Conquest tradition.

The second and third groups of Travel Notices are also closely related as witnessed by both narrative content and the repetition of the key verb ועברו (2:13 and 2:24). The second group takes the people northward (2:3) from the Arabah to the wilderness of Moab (2:8), while the third takes them across Moab (2:13) and then across the wadi Arnon (2:24) to the edge of the promised land, and the conquest of the two Amorite kings (2:34–3:4).

# Organization of the People for Life in the Land (1:9–18)

## Bibliography

**Albright, W. F.** "The Judicial Reform of Jehoshaphat." In *FS A. Marx* (1950). 61–82. **Amusin, J. D.** "Die Gerim in der sozialen Legislatur des Alten Testaments." *Klio* 63 (1981) 15–23. **Bartlett, J. R.** "The Use of the Word ראש as a Title in the Old Testament." *VT* 19 (1969) 1–10. **Bellefontaine, E.** "Customary Law and Chieftainship: Judicial Aspects of 2 Sam 14, 4–21." *JSOT* 38 (1987) 47–72. **Bernhardt, K.-H.** "Verwaltungspraxis im spätbronzezeitlichen Palästina." In *Beiträge zur sozialen Struktur des alten Vorderasien*. Ed. H. Klengel. SGKAO 1. Berlin: Akademie-Verlag, 1971. 133–47. **Carpenter, E. E.** "Literary Structure and Unbelief: A Study of Deuteronomy 1:6–46." *AsTJ* 42 (1987) 77–84. **Causse, A.** "L'ideal politique et social du Deutéronome. La fraternité d'Israel." *RHPR* 13 (1933) 289–323. **Cazelles, H.** "Institutions et terminologie en Deutéronome 1, 6–17." In VTSup 15. Leiden: E. J. Brill, 1966. 97–112. ———. "*SMᶜ QÔL* et *SMᶜ B QÔL*." *Comptes rendus de linguistiques d'études Chamito-Sémitiques* 10 (1966) 148–50. ———. "De l'idologie royale." In *FS T. H. Gaster* (1973). 59–73. ———. "Tradition israélite et culture orientale: le Deutéronome." *Annuaire de l'École Pratique des Hautes Études. Section: Sciences Religieuses* 83 (1975/76) 153–58. **Childs, B. S.** *Isaiah and the Assyrian Crisis.* SBT, 2nd Series. London, 1967. 70–71. **Christensen, D. L.** "Prose and Poetry in the Bible: The Narrative Poetics of Deuteronomy 1, 9–18." *ZAW* 97 (1985) 179–89. **Dandamayev, M. A.** "The Social Position of Neo-Babylonian Scribes." In *Gesellschaft und Kultur im alten Vorderasien*. Ed. H. Klengel. SGKAO 15. Berlin: Akademie-Verlag, 1982. 35–39. **Daube, D.** "A Reform in Acts and Its Models." In *FS W. D. Davies* (1976). 151–63. **Deller, K.** "Die Rolle des Richters im neobabylonischen Prozessrecht." In *FS E. Volterra*, vol. 6 (1971). 639–53. **Dus, J.** "Die 'Sufeten' Israels." *ArOr* 31 (1963) 444–69. **Ellul, J.** *The Theological Foundation of Law.* New York: Seabury Press, 1969. **Emerton, J.** "A Consideration of Some Alleged Meanings of *ydᶜ* in Hebrew." *JSS* 15 (1970) 145–80. **Eybers, I. H.** "Some Examples of Hyperbole in Biblical Hebrew." *Semitics* 1 (1970) 38–49. **Falk, Z. W.** "שופט ושבט." *Leš* 30 (1965/66) 243–47 (Heb). **Fendler, M.** "Zur Sozialkritik des Amos." *EvT* 33 (1973) 32–53. **Fensham, F. C.** "The Judges and Ancient Israelite Jurisprudence." *OTWSA* 2 (1959) 15–22. **Geus, C. H. J. de.** "De richteren van Israel." *NedTTs* 20 (1965/66) 81–100. **Gross, W.** "Das nicht substantivierte Partizip als Prädikat im Relativsatz hebräischer Prosa." *JNSL* 4 (1974) 23–47. **Halévy, J.** "Recherches bibliques: le Deutéronome." *RSEHA* 8 (1900) 216–17. **Hoppe, L.** "Elders and Deuteronomy: A Proposal." *EglT* 14 (1983) 259–72. *HOTTP* I, 267. **Knierim, R.** "Exodus 18 und die Neuordnung der mosaischen Gerichtsbarkeit." *ZAW* 73 (1961) 146–71. **Lemaire, A.** "Notes d'épigraphie nord-ouest sémitique." *Sem* 30 (1980) 17–32. **Loewenstamm, S.** "The Formula *bᶜt hhwᵓ* in Deuteronomy." *Tarbiz* 38 (1968/69) 99–104. **Loretz, O.** "Neues Verständnis einiger Schriftstellen mit Hilfe des Ugaritischen." *BZ* 2 (1958) 287–91. **Lurje, M.** "Die Agrarverhältnisse." *Studien zur Geschichte der wirtschaftlichen und sozialen Verhältnisse im Israelitisch-Jüdischen Reiche.* Giessen: Töpelmann, 1927. 1–19. **Milgrom, J.** "The Ideological and Historical Importance of the Office of the Judge in Deuteronomy." In *FS I. A. Seeligmann* (1983). 129–39. **Neufeld, E.** "The Prohibitions against Loans at Interest in Ancient Hebrew Laws." *HUCA* 26 (1955) 404–6. **Niehaus, J.** "*PAᶜAM ᵓEHĀT* and the Israelite Conquest." *VT* 30 (1980) 236–38. **Perlitt, L.** "'Ein einzig Volk von Brüdern.' Zur deuteronomischen Herkunft der biblischen Bezeichnung 'Brüder.'" In *FS G. Bornkamm* (1980). 27–52. **Ploeg, J. van der.** "*Shapat* et *Mishpat*." In OTS 2 (1943). 144–55. ———.

"Les ṣōṭerîm d'Israel." In OTS 10 (1954). 185–96. **Rad, G. von.** "Bruder und Nächster im Alten Testament." In *Gottes Wirken in Israel. Vorträge zum Alten Testament.* Ed. O. H. Steck. Neukirchen-Vluyn: Neukirchener Verlag, 1974. 238–49. **Reviv, H.** "Leadership in the Period of the Judges—Central Points and Resolutions." *Beersheba Annual: Studies in Bible, Ancient Israel and the Ancient Near East* 1 (1973) 204–21 (Heb). ————. "Elders and 'Saviors'." *OrAnt* 16 (1977) 201–4. ————. "The Traditions Concerning the Inception of the Legal System in Israel: Significance and Dating." *ZAW* 94 (1982) 566–75. ————. *The Elders in Ancient Israel: A Study of a Biblical Institution.* Tr. L. Plitmann. Jerusalem: Magnes, 1989 (Heb. ed. 1983). **Richter, W.** "Zu den 'Richtern Israels'." *ZAW* 77 (1965) 40–72. **Rösel, H.** "Die 'Richter Israels': Rückblick und neuer Ansatz." *BZ* 25 (1981) 180–203. **Rozenberg, M. S.** "The Šofeṭîm in the Bible." *EI* 12 (1975) 77–86. **Rüterswörden, U.** *Die Beamten der israelitischen Königszeit.* BWANT 117. Stuttgart: Kohlhammer, 1985. 23–30, 109–111. **Salmon, J. M.** *Judicial Authority in Early Israel: An Historical Investigation of Old Testament Institutions.* Diss., Princeton, Univ., 1968. **Schedl, K.** "Prosa und Dichtung in der Bibel. Logotechnische Analyse von Dtn 1, 9–18." *ZAW* 98 (1986) 271–77. **Schunck, K.-D.** "Die Richter Israels und ihr Amt." In VTSup 15. Leiden: E. J. Brill, 1966. 252–62. **Seeligmann, I. L.** "Zur Terminologie für das Gerichtsverfahren im Wortschatz des biblischen Hebräisch." In *FS W. Baumgartner.* VTSup 16. Leiden: Brill, 1967. 251–78. **Selms, A. van.** "The Title 'Judge'." *OTWSA* 2 (1959) 41–50. **Sole, F.** "Potere e Procedura giudiziaria presso gli Israeliti." *PalCl* 44 (1965) 703–14. **Tadmor, H.** and **Cogan, M.** "Ahaz and Tiglath-Pileser in the Book of Kings: Historiographic Considerations." *Bib* 60 (1979) 491–508. **Thomson, H. C.** "Shopet and Mishpat in the Book of Judges." *GOST* 19 (1961/62) 74–85. **Weinfeld, M.** "Judge and Officer in Ancient Israel and in the Ancient Near East." In IsrOrSt 7. Tel Aviv Univ., 1977. 65–88. **Whitelam, K. W.** *The Just King: Monarchical Judicial Authority in Ancient Israel.* JSOTSup 12. Sheffield: Sheffield University, 1979. **Wolff, H. J.** *Justizwesen. Das Justizwesen der Ptolemäer.* MBPR 44. Munich, 1970.

### *Translation and Prosodic Analysis*

1:9–18　[5:5:5:5] [5:4:4:5] [3:3] [8:4:4:8]

| | | |
|---|---|---|
| [9] And I said unto you / AT THAT TIME [a] / saying // | 20 | 3 |
| "I am not able alone / to bear you // | 14 | 2_ |
| [10] YHWH your God / has multiplied you // | 14 | 2 |
| And behold you are TODAY / | 7 | 1 |
| as the stars of the heavens / in number // | 15 | 2_ |
| [11] YHWH / God of your fathers / | 14 | 2 |
| may he increase you / as you are / a thousand times // | 18 | 2 |
| And may he bless you / just as \a he spoke (דבר) to you // | 16 | 2 |
| [12] How can I bear \a alone // your burdens [b] / | 15 | 2 |
| your problems and your disputes? // | 8 | 1_ |

| | | |
|---|---|---|
| [13] Choose from among you [a] / men who are wise and understanding / | 23 | 2 |
| And who are known [b] \c in your tribes // | 11 | 1 |
| and I will appoint them / as your heads" // | 12 | 2_ |
| [14] And you answered / me // and you said / | 15 | 3 |
| "Good is the word (הדבר) |a | 7 | 1_ |
| which you said / we should do" // | 9 | 2 |
| [15] And I took / [a]the heads of your tribes[a] / | 13 | 2_ |
| Men (who were) wise / and known[b] / | 16 | 2 |
| And I established them / (as) heads / over you // | 17 | 3_ |

| | | |
|---|---|---|
| Commanders of thousands / | 9 | 1 |
| and commanders of hundreds / | 9 | 1 |
| and [c] commanders of fifties / | 9 | 1_ |
| and commanders of tens / | 10 | 1 |
| and officers / throughout your tribes [d] // | 11 | 2_ |

|  |  |  |
|---|---|---|
| [16] And I commanded / | 6 | 1 |
| your judges / AT THAT TIME / saying // | ⌈ 16 | 3 |
| "Hear (the disputes) between your brothers / | ⌊ 11 | 1 |
| And judge righteously / between a man and his brother / | ⌈ 18 | 2 |
| and an alien // | ⌊ 8 | 1_ |
| [17] Do not show partiality / in judgment / | 15 | 2 |
| Both the small and the great / hear (alike)! / | 15 | 2_ |
| Do not be afraid / of anyone / | 14 | 2 |
| For the judgment / it (belongs) to God // | 14 | 2_ |
| And the case (והדבר) / which is too hard for you / | 12 | 2 |
| Bring to me / and I will hear it" // | 13 | 2 |
| [18] And I commanded you AT THAT TIME // | 14 | 2 |
| All the things (הדברים) / which you are to do //[a] | 15 | 2_ |

## Notes

9.a. The phrase AT THAT TIME is in capital letters here and elsewhere, as is the word TODAY in v 10, to suggest that these terms play a rhetorical function in the larger structure of the book of Deuteronomy as a whole. It seems best to highlight in a visual sense what surely was an important aural signal to those who recited and heard this text in ancient Israel. For a historical interpretation of this phrase (which appears fifteen times in Deut 1–5 and 9:1–10) as a scribal marker for enlargements, or expansions, of the original text, see Loewenstamm, *Tarbiz* 38 (1968/69) 99–104.

11.a. See note on 1:1.c.

12.a. See note 1:1.c.

12.b. This verse is one of the few places in Deuteronomy where there appears to be a textual problem. As it stands, the MT would scan as follows:

| | | |
|---|---|---|
| May YHWH / God of your fathers / | 14 | 2 |
| increase you / as you are / a thousand times // | 18 | 3 |
| And may he bless you / as / he said (he would) to you // | 16 | 3 |
| How can I bear / alone // | 11 | 2 |
| your problems and your burdens / and your disputes? // | 14 | 2 |

Such a reading is difficult to fit into any larger pattern. It would appear that the verse division is incorrect and has resulted in a series of unfortunate adjustments. It is better to see a single verse here and thus to remove both the *sillûq* at the end of v 11 and the *ʾatnāh* in v 12. This enables us to remove the two occurrences of *ṭiphāʾ*, replacing them with conj accents. Exchanging the order of the terms טרחכם and משאכם not only improves the metrical balance in terms of mora-count; it also sharpens the parallelism with the corresponding line in v 9 and improves the assonance here as well.

*lōʾ ʾûkal lᵉbaddî śᵉʾēt ʾetkem* (v 9)
*ʾêkâ ʾeśśāʾ lᵉbaddî maśśᵃkem* (v 12)

The fact that paired words are frequently exchanged in transmission of poetic texts is well illustrated in the recent publication of a popular record by the singer Jack Jones. In his rendition of the song, "Everything Is Beautiful," he sang the following two lines:

We shouldn't care about the *color* of his hair,
Or the *length* of his skin.

Here the exchange took place even when the end result was nonsense. When the sense is not affected, exchange of parallel words is much more likely. The absence of the conjunction before משאכם in SP offers at least minimal support for a variant textual tradition to that of the MT at this point.

13.a. The grammatical construction here is the so-called *dativus commodi,* as Craigie has noted (NICOT [1976] 97; cf. GKC § 119s).

13.b. Qal pass ptcp of ידע. See the discussion of J. Emerton, *JSS* 15 (1970) 175–78, who argues that the term means "experienced," as M. Luther suggested more than 450 years earlier (*Luther's Works,* vol. 9 [Saint Louis: Concordia, 1960] 18).

13.c. See note 1:1.c.

14.a. A disj accent is added to achieve rhythmic balance in vv 13–15. If a [5:5:5:5] rhythmic unit is read here in parallel to vv 9–12, followed by a [2:2] unit read as a coda, this would have been at the very center of a strophe in a situation somewhat parallel to that between stanzas three and four of Martin Luther's hymn, "A Mighty Fortress Is Our God," which curiously turns on a similar lexical item: "One little *word* shall fell him. // That *word* above all . . ." The resultant mora count between vv 9–12 (70+71=141) and vv 13–15b (68+73=141) is almost exact (see D. Christensen, *ZAW* 97 [1985] 188).

15.a-a. LXX reads ἐξ ὑμῶν (מכם). The prosodic analysis supports MT.

15.b. See note 13.b. above.

15.c. Numerous Heb. Mss, SP, and some LXX and Tg witnesses omit *waw.* The variant is probably caused by the pressure to read vv 13–15 as though they were a [5:5:5:5] unit in parallel to vv 9–12 (see note 14.a. above). Such a reading would make this word the beginning of the coda.

15.d. LXX reads τοῖς κριταῖς ὑμῶν (לשפטיכם).

18.a. The boundary is indicated in both *BHK* and *BHS* by extra space.

## Form/Structure/Setting

The opening rubric in v 9 functions as an inclusion with the first half of v 18 to frame the pericope as a whole:

> And I said to you, AT THAT TIME (v 9)
> And I commanded you, AT THAT TIME (v 18)

The second half of v 18 begins with the phrase כל־הדברים, which parallels the opening phrase of the book of Deuteronomy (אלה הדברים). Each of the three major sections of Deut 1:9–18 is framed by similar inclusions. After the opening rubric in v 9 the passage begins with the sentence, "I am not able alone to bear you (לבדי שאת אתכם)." In v 12 we find the phrase, "How can I bear alone your burdens (משאכם . . . לבדי אשא)?" The third section (vv 16–18) is framed by a repetition of the phrase, "And I commanded . . . AT THAT TIME." In the center section (vv 13–15) Moses instructs the people to choose "men who are wise and . . . known" (v 13), whereas in v 15 Moses took "men who were wise and known" and established them in leadership roles. The text then expands the list of leaders in the second half of v 15 in terminology that is clearly military rather than the judicial usage elsewhere in this passage.

A good example of "nesting" of terms within a larger concentric design appears in vv 16–18 as follows:

> A    "And I commanded (ואצוה) your judges AT THAT TIME"
>    B    "Hear (שמע) the disputes"
>      C    "Do not show partiality in judgment (במשפט)"
>      C'    For judgment (המשפט) belongs to God"
>    B'    "And I will hear it (ושמעתיו)"
> A'    "And I commanded (ואצוה) you AT THAT TIME"

Up to the appearance of the "tacked-on" element in v 15b there is no explicit reference to military matters. The leaders whom Moses is choosing (vv 9–13) and instructing (vv 16–17) clearly have a judicial function. But in v 15b the leaders are to be "heads over you—commanders of thousands, and commanders of hundreds, and commanders of fifties, and commanders of tens; . . . officers throughout your tribes." In light of the subsequent discussion of "Israel's Unholy War" (Deut 2:26–3:11), this focus on military language is significant. Continued life in the promised land is dependent on prior conquest of that land, and Moses' successors must exercise both a judicial and a military role in the life of YHWH's people. The inherent tension between the demand for both justice and power on the part of Moses' successors will be a dominant theme in the Deuteronomic History.

*Comment*

**9–10**   This time Moses' complaint is addressed to the people and not to God (cf. Num 11:11–15). Before leaving Horeb, Moses had found it necessary to organize the Israelites for judicial purposes, because of their great number. Now, on the eve of their entry into the promised land, they had become even more numerous, for YHWH had fulfilled his promise to Abraham that his descendants would become as numerous as the stars in the heavens (Gen 15:5; 22:17). It was his father-in-law, Jethro, who earlier advised Moses to delegate responsibility to carefully selected men who would be placed over thousands, hundreds, fifties, and tens (Exod 18:13–23).

**11–12**   In Moses' request that the people be further increased and blessed, an occasion for complaint is transformed into one of blessing, in the pattern of psalms of lament. The repetition of Moses' need for help to bear the Israelites' *burdens, problems,* and *disputes* forms an inclusion with v 9. The term for *problems* here (טרחכם) occurs elsewhere only in Isa 1:14, where Israel's festivals and cultic activities are described as a weight YHWH is weary of bearing. The term *disputes* (ריבכם) implies legal cases (see also the commentary on Deut 17:8).

**13–15**   The qualifications of the leaders whom the people are to provide for themselves differs somewhat from those given earlier in Exod 18:21. There the emphasis is on their moral qualities ("able men" who "fear God" and "are trustworthy and who hate a bribe"). Here it is on the basis of their wisdom that they are to be chosen. They are to be *wise, understanding,* and *known* (in the sense of being publicly experienced).

The reference to the appointment of these men as *your heads* is the first suggestion that the qualifications for leadership include military abilities as well as judicial (see Bartlett's discussion, *VT* 19 [1969] 1–10 along with that of Knierim, *ZAW* 32 [1961] 146–71). The term *heads* (ראשׁי(ם) is repeated twice in v 15a, perhaps to set the stage for the explicit military organization that follows. The *commanders* (שׂרים) were military figures. The divisions (*thousands, hundreds, fifties, tens*) may refer to military units of different sizes, rather than to specific numbers (cf. R. de Vaux, *Ancient Israel: Its Life and Institutions* [New York: McGraw-Hill, 1961] 216–17). The precise meaning of the term *officers* (שׁטרים) is difficult to ascertain. Weinfeld argued that they "fulfilled secretarial functions," based on the meaning of the verb *šṭr* in Akk "to write" and the translation "scribe" in the ancient versions (IsrOrSt 7 [Tel Aviv Univ., 1977] 83–86). At the same time he concludes that the term is comprehensive in biblical usage and "includes all the subordinate personnel" to the judges (86). Mayes has suggested that the conjunction here be taken as emphatic such that the term *officers* is "a summary reference to all the commanders of the various divisions" (NCBC [1979] 124).

**16–18** As quickly as the attention shifted to military matters, so it returns to judicial matters in Moses' appointment of *judges* (שפטים), who are to judge righteously without showing partiality—whether *between a man and his brother* (i.e., full Israelites) or involving the *resident alien* (גר), a landless foreigner residing with the Israelites under their protection. The Israelites knew by bitter experience the plight of an alien in a foreign land (see Deut 10:19). Their own resident aliens were not to be treated as the Egyptians had treated the people of Israel. The concept that judgment belongs to God (v 17) is of enormous importance, as Craigie has noted (NICOT [1976] 98; cf. J. Ellul, *The Theological Foundation of Law* [New York: Seabury Press, 1969] 37–45), for it removed the authority of the law from the human realm. The judge administers the law on behalf of God, which is no easy task as the reference to cases *too hard* for the judges bears witness. Those difficult cases are to be referred to Moses himself. The concluding summary statement in v 18 forms an inclusion with 1:16, 1:9, and 1:1.

*Explanation*

Among the many possible readings of the Pentateuch, one of the most interesting is that of Aaron Wildavsky, who takes the figure of Moses as a paradigm for the study of political leadership. As he put it, "Moses' experience reveals the dilemmas of leadership under the major types of rule, from slavery in Egypt to anarchy before the Golden Calf episode to equity (association without authority) in the desert, until his final effort to institutionalize hierarchy" (*The Nursing Father: Moses as a Political Leader* [University of Alabama Press, 1984] 1). One of the central issues in political leadership is the tension between justice and power. As Lord Acton once wrote, "Power corrupts; and absolute power corrupts absolutely."

The juxtaposition of judicial and military roles introduced here is explored more explicitly in subsequent narrative contexts within the Deuteronomic History, particularly in the Jephthah story (Judg 11). Here in Deuteronomy the term ראש is the first hint that the judges Moses is appointing to share the burdens of leadership are to be much more than wise and understanding persons, experienced in judicial responsibility. They are to be military commanders as well. The military aspects of leadership in the Mosaic era will take center stage in the following chapters of Deuteronomy.

In Judg 11 Jephthah is introduced as "a mighty warrior, [who] was the son of a harlot" (v 1). In the face of the Ammonite threat, the elders of Gilead approached Jephthah and asked him to be both their קָצִין, "leader," and ראש, "head," over all the inhabitants of Gilead (vv 6–8). Jephthah agrees only to be their ראש, "head," in spite of the fact that the elders and the people of Gilead made him both head and leader over them (vv 9–11). The story that unfolds, with the sacrificial death of Jephthah's daughter as a result of his rash vow, presents perhaps the most unjust deed on the pages of Scripture. A careful study of the word קָצִין, "leader," reveals that its primary meaning is that of judicial leader, in the sense of one who dispenses justice. The term ראש, "head," on the other hand, refers primarily to a military figure. The point is clear. The people want a leader who exercises both justice and power, but these two attributes seldom appear "under the same hat." Power is necessary for effective leadership, but political power is constantly in tension with the more fundamental demand for justice. Moses anticipates a major problem in the matter of political leadership as he appoints judges who also have military authority. That problem remains for all who would be leaders, whether in the public political sphere or within our church structures. Those who would be the "heads" of our institutions will all too often, like Jephthah, fail in the matter of dispensing justice, and justice is the primary matter, so far as leadership in the Deuteronomic sense is concerned.

In his lectures on Deuteronomy, Luther noted that the question of persons and government precedes the exposition of Law, for laws are of no effect without persons to administer and enforce them. Those who are given the responsibility of magistracy are to endure the burdens and disputes of the people as servants, not as masters (*Collected Words,* vol. 9 [1960] 17). He also noted that no account is taken here of the rich, powerful, noble, or strong for handling public office, as is the usual custom. It is the wise, understanding, and experienced who are to be selected, even if they are poor, lowly, and weak. Moreover, if one must choose between a leader who is good but not prudent and one who is prudent but not good, the latter is the proper choice so far as this text is concerned. In Luther's words, such a "good man would actually rule nothing but would be ruled only by others, and at that only by the worst people. Even if the prudent man harms good people, yet at the same time he governs the evil ones, which is the most necessary . . . since the world is nothing else than a crowd of evil people" (19).

# Israel's Unholy War (1:19–2:1)

## Bibliography

**Aejmelaeus, A.** "Participium Coniunctum as a Criterion of Translation Technique." *VT* 32 (1982) 385–93. **Aharoni, J.** "Arad." *BA* 31 (1968) 2–32. **Albrektson, B.** *History and the Gods.* Lund, 1967. 39. **Ararat, N.** "The Biblical War at *RMH*." *BMik* 26/84 (1980) 67–78. **Barth, C.** "Mose, Knecht Gottes." In *FS K. Barth* (1966). 76–78. **Batto, B.** "The Reed Sea: *requiescat in pace*." *JBL* 102 (1983) 27–35. ————. "Red Sea or Reed Sea?" *BARev* 10 (1984) 57–63. **Begg, C.** "The Function of Josh 7, 1–8, 29 in the Deuteronomistic History." *Bib* 67 (1986) 324–26. **Buis, P.** "Qadesh, un lieu maudit?" *VT* 24 (1974) 268–85. **Buber, M.** *Two Types of Faith.* Tr. N. P. Goldhawk. London: Routledge & Paul, 1951 [*Zwei Glaubensweisen.* Zürich: Manesse Verlag, 1950]. **Carpenter, E. E.** "Literary Structure and Unbelief: A Study of Deuteronomy 1:6–46." *AsTJ* 42 (1987) 77–84. **Cazelles, H.** "Tradition israélite et culture orientale: le Dt." *École Pratique des Hautes Études. Section: Sciences Religieuses. Annuaire* 83 (1974) 153. **Coats, G. W.** *Rebellion in the Wilderness: The Murmuring Motif in the Wilderness Traditions of the Old Testament.* Nashville: Abingdon, 1968. ————. "Conquest Traditions in the Wilderness Theme." *JBL* 95 (1976) 177–90. **Coppens, J.** "La doctrine biblique sur l'amour de Dieu et du prochain." *ETL* 40 (1964) 252–99. **Craigie, P. C.** "Yahweh is a Man of Wars." *SJT* 22 (1969) 183–88. **Dahood, M.** "Besprechungen von R. Mayer, Gegensinn und Mehrdeutigkeit in der althebräischen Wort- und Begriffsbildung, 1979." *BO* 38 (1981) 671–73. **Davies, G. I.** "The Significance of Deuteronomy 1:2 for the Location of Mount Horeb." *PEQ* 111 (1979) 87–101. **Fensham, F. C.** "Father and Son as Terminology for Treaty and Covenant." In *FS W. F. Albright* (1971). 121–35. **Fonseca, L. G.** "Filios Enacim vidimus ibe (Dt 1,28)." *VD* 8 (1928) 145–47. **Funck, B.** "Studien zur sozialökonomischen Situation Babyloniens im 7. und 6. Jahrhundert vor unsere Ziet." *Gesellschaft und Kultur im alten Vorderasien.* Ed. H. Klengel. SGKAO 15. Berlin: Akademie-Verlag, 1982. 47–67. **Giesen, G.** *Die Wurzel* שבע *"Schwören": Eine semasiologische Studie zum Eid im Alten Testament.* BBB 56. Bonn: Hanstein, 1981. 261. **Gowan, D. E.** "The Use of *yaᶜan* in Biblical Hebrew." *VT* 21 (1971) 168–85. **Grelot, P.** "La racine *hwn* en Dt 1, 41." *VT* 12 (1962) 198–201. **Ha, J.** *Genesis 15: A Theological Compendium of Pentateuchal History.* Ed. O. Kaiser. BZAW 181. Berlin: de Gruyter, 1989. **Halévy, J.** "Recherches bibliques: le Deutèronome." *RSEHA* 8 (1900) 317–21. *HOTTP* I, 267. **Heller, J.** "Die Entmythisierung des ugaritischen Pantheons." *TLZ* 101 (1976) 1–10. **Horst, F.** "Zwei Begriffe für Eigentum (Besitz)." In *FS W. Rudolph* (1961). 135–56. **Hulst, A. R.** "Opmerkingen over de *ka'aser*-zinnen in Dt." *NedTTs* 18 (1963) 337–61. **Kuschke, A.** "Arm und reich im Alten Testament." *ZAW* 57 (1939) 31–57. **Lohfink, N.** "Dtn 12, 1 und Gen 15, 18: Das dem Samen Abrahams geschenkte Land als der Geltungsbereich der deuteronomischen Gesetze." In *FS J. Scharbert* (1989). 183–210. ————. "Darstellungskunst und Theologie in Dtn 1, 6–3, 29." *Bib* 41 (1960) 119–20. **Loretz, O.** "Neues Verständnis einiger Schriftstellen mit Hilfe des Ugaritischen." *BZ* 2 (1958) 287–91. **Malamat, A.** "Israelite Conduct of War in the Conquest of Canaan according to the Biblical Tradition." In *Symposia 75th Anniversary of the American Schools of Oriental Research.* Ed. F. M. Cross. Cambridge, MA: AASOR, 1979. 35–55. "A Forerunner of Biblical Prophecy: The Mari Documents." In *FS F. M. Cross* (1987). 33–52. **McCarthy, D.** "An Installation Genre?" *JBL* 90 (1971) 31–41. **McCarthy, D. J.** "Notes on the Love of God in Deuteronomy and the Father-Son Relationship between Yahweh and Israel." *CBQ* 27 (1965) 144–47. ————. "Some Holy War Vocabulary in Joshua 2." *CBQ* 33 (1971) 228–30. **Miller, P. D.** "God the Warrior." *Int* 19 (1965) 39–46. **Mittmann, S.** "Ri 1, 16f. und das Siedlungsgebiet der kenitischen Sippe Hobab." *ZDPV* 93 (1977) 213–35. **Moran, W.** "The End of the Unholy War and the Anti-Exodus." *Bib* 44 (1963) 333–42. **Perlitt, L.** "Jesaja und Deuteronomisten."

In *FS O. Kaiser* (1989). 133–49. **Pfeiffer, E.** "Der alttestamentliche Hintergrund der liturgischen Formel 'Amen'." *KD* 4 (1958) 129–41. ————. "Glaube im Alten Testament." *ZAW* 71 (1959) 151–64. **Porter, J. R.** "The Succession of Joshua." In *FS G. H. Davies* (1970). 102–32. **Rendtorff, R.** "Genesis 15 im Rahmen der theologischen Bearbeitung der Vätergeschichten." In *FS C. Westermann* (1980). 74–81. **Schnutenhaus, F.** "Das Kommen und Erscheinen Gottes im Alten Testament." *ZAW* 76 (1964) 1–22. **Sklba, R. J.** "The Redeemer of Israel." *CBQ* 34 (1972) 1–18. **Smend, R.** "Zur Geschichte von הֶאֱמִין." In *FS W. Baumgartner* (1967). 285–90. **Snaith, N.** "יָם סוּף: The Sea of Reeds: The Red Sea." *VT* 15 (1965) 395–98. **Tomes, R.** "Exodus 14: The Mighty Acts of God. An Essay in Theological Criticism." *SJT* 22 (1969) 455–78. **Toperoff, S. P.** "The Bee in the Bible and Midrash." *DD* 13 (1985) 246–50. **Vanhoye, A.** "Longue marche on accès tout proche? Le context biblique de Hébréux 3, 7–4, 11." *Bib* 49 (1968) 9–26. **Vervenne, M.** "The Protest Motif in the Sea Narrative (Ex 14, 11–12)." *ETL* 63 (1987) 257–71. **Vorläuder, H.** *Die Entstehungszeit des jehowistischen Geschichtswerkes.* Frankfurt a.M.: Lang, 1978. **Walkenhorst, K.-H.** "Neueste Deuteronomiumforschung in Japan." *BZ* n.s. 33 (1989) 81–92. **Weinfeld, M.** "The Covenant of Grant in the Old Testament and in the Ancient Near East." *JAOS* 90 (1970) 184–203. **Weiser, A.** "Glauben im Alten Testament." In *FS G. Beer* (1935). 88–99. **Wildberger, H.** "'Glauben': Erwägungen zu הֶאֱמִין." In *FS W. Baumgartner* (1967). 372–86. **Williams, R. J.** *Hebrew Syntax: An Outline,* 2nd ed. Toronto: Univ. of Toronto Press, 1976. 58 No. 341.

### Translation and Prosodic Analysis

1:19–33    [5:7:6] [6:4] [(8:6):(6:6)] [6:4:4:6] [(6:6):(6:8)] [4:6] [6:5:7]
1:34–2:1   [8:9:9:8] [(5:5):(8:9):(6:6:6):(9:8):(5:5)]

| | | |
|---|---:|---:|
| [19] **And we set out from Horeb / and we went /** | 13 | 2 |
| **through all that great and fearful desert /** | 21 ⎤ | 1 |
| **which you saw / on the way /** | 8 ⎦ | 2_ |
| **(To) the hill country of the Amorites /** | 8 ⎤ | 1 |
| **just as YHWH our God / commanded / us //** | 22 ⎦ | 3 |
| **And we came / as far as / Kadesh-barnea[a] //** | 14 | 3_ |
| [20] And I said / unto you / | 9 | 2 |
| "You have come / to the hill country of the Amorites / | 12 | 2 |
| Which YHWH our God / is giving to us // | 20 | 2_ |
| [21] *Look![a] / YHWH your God has put (it) / before you* | 19 | 3 |
| *The land //* | 6 | 1 |
| *go up, take possession / just as YHWH spoke (דבר) /* | 13 | 2_ |
| *The God of your fathers / (spoke) to you /* | 12 | 2 |
| *Do not fear / and do not be dismayed!" //* | 11 | 2_ |
| [22] And you came near unto me / all of you / and you said / | 17 | 3 |
| "Let us send men / before us / | 16 | 2 |
| And they may explore for us \[a] the land // | 15 | 1 |
| and they may bring back to us / | 13 | 1 |
| a report (דבר) / | 4 | 1_ |
| (Namely) the way / by which we shall go up in it / | 11 | 2 |
| and / the cities / by which we shall come / unto them"[b] // | 18 | 4_ |
| [23] And it was good in my eyes / the matter (הדבר) // | 13 | 2 |
| and I took from you[a] / | 6 | 1 |
| Twelve men / one man / for each tribe // | 20 | 3_ |

²⁴ And they turned / and they went up into the hill country /    14  2
And they came / as far as the valley of Eshkol //    <u>13</u>  2
And they spied / it out<sup>a</sup> //    5+4  2_

²⁵ And they took in their hands /    9  1
    from the fruit of the land /    <u>9</u>  1
And they brought (it) down / to us //    13  2
And they brought back to us |<sup>a</sup> a report (דבר) /    17  2_
    and they said /    6  1
"The land is good / which YHWH our God / is giving to us" //    <u>29</u>  3_
²⁶ And you were not willing \\<sup>a</sup> to go up //    11  1
    and you rebelled /    4  1
    against the mouth of YHWH / your God<sup>b</sup> //    <u>12</u>  2_
²⁷ And you murmured in your tents / and you said /    20  2
"In YHWH's hatred / toward us / he brought us forth /    <u>20</u>  3
    from the land of Egypt //    8  1_

To give us / into the hand of the Amorites /    19  2
    <and><sup>a</sup> to destroy us //    10  1
²⁸ Where / are we to go up? /    11  2
    Our brothers<sup>a</sup> have disquieted our hearts /    <u>18</u>  1_
Saying / "The people are greater and taller<sup>b</sup> / than we<sup>c</sup> /    17  3
    (with) cities<sup>d</sup> /    4  1
    great and fortified / to the heavens //    <u>18</u>  2_
And also the children of the Anakim / we saw there" //    18  2
²⁹    and I said / unto you //    9  2
"Do not be in dread and do not be afraid / of them //    <u>17</u>  2_
³⁰YHWH [your God]<sup>a</sup> / the One who goes before you /    12  2
    he / will fight for you //    10  2
According to all / that he did for you /    12  2
    in Egypt / before your eyes //    <u>10</u>  2_

³¹ And in the wilderness / where <sup>a</sup>*you saw* /    13  2
*How he bore you / YHWH your God /*    <u>14</u>  2_
*Just as a man bears / his son // in all the way /*    17  3
*That<sup>a</sup> you went / until you come / to this place" //*    <u>18</u>  3_

³² And in this / matter (ובדבר) //    9  2
    You did not / believe /    10  2
    in YHWH / your God<sup>a</sup> //    <u>10</u>  2_
³³ The One going before you<sup>a</sup> / in the way /    12  2
    to seek you out / a place / to pitch your tents<sup>b</sup> //    21  3_
In fire / by night / to show you /    11  3
    the way / in which you should go in it /    12  2
And in a cloud / by day //<sup>c</sup>    <u>11</u>  2_

³⁴ And YHWH heard / the sound of your words (דבריכם) //    13  2
And he was angry / and he swore saying //    13  2

35 "Not a single person will see / from among these men /    17   2
     ᵃthis / evil generation ᵃ //               9   2_
The / ᵇ good land / which I have sworn /            18   3
     to give ᶜ / to your fathers ᵈ //             11   2
36 Except / Caleb son of Jephunneh /             14   2
     he will see it / and to him I will give the land /    17   2_
Upon which he has trodden in it / and to his sons //    14   2
Because / he has wholeheartedly followed / ᵃafter YHWH" ᵃ //    14   3
37 Even with me / YHWH was angry /            9   2
     on account of you / saying //              8   2_
"You also / will not come thither ᵃ //          13   2
38     Joshua son of Nun / the one standing before you /    20   2
He himself \ᵃ will come in thither // strengthen him ᵇ /    16   2
For (it is) he / who will cause Israel to inherit it //    16   2_

39a     And your little ones of whom you said /          9   1
     'They will be as spoil' ᵃ / yea, your children ᵇ /    12   2
     who do not know TODAY / good and evil /       18   2
They themselves / will come thither //           12   2
And to them I shall give it /                 8   1
     and they themselves / will possess it" //       10   2_
40 And (as for) you / **turn yourselves around** //       9   2
     **and journey into the wilderness** / **by way of Yam Suf** //    15   2
41 And you answered / and you said unto me /       14   2
     "We have sinned / against YHWH ᵃ /           10   2_
We ourselves shall go up / and we shall make war /    12   2
     according to all that he has commanded us / YHWH our God" //    20   2
And you put on / each one / his instruments of war /    15   3
     and you deemed it easy / to go up to the hill country //    16   2_
42 And YHWH said / unto me / "Say to them /       16   3
Do not / go up / and do not make war /          15   3_
For I am not / in your midst //              11   2
Lest / you be struck down / before / your enemies" //    18   4_
43 And I spoke (ואדבר) unto you / and you would not listen //    16   2
And you rebelled / against the mouth of YHWH ᵃ /    10   2
And you were presumptuous /                7   1
And you went up to the hill country //          10   1_
44 And the Amorites ᵃ came forth /             12   1
The ones living in that hill country /          12   1
Against you / and they chased you /           11   2
Just as the bees (הדברים) / do //             15   2
And they smote you / in Seir / as far as Hormah //    16   3_
45 And you returned ᵃ and you wept / before YHWH ᵇ //    16   2
     and YHWH did not listen / to your voice /       14   2
And he did not give ear / unto you //          11   2
46 And you remained in Kadesh /              11   1
     many days ᵃ //                      7   1_

Like the days / that you remained (there) // [b]

**2:1 and we turned /**

**And we journeyed toward the wilderness /**

   **by way of Yam Suf /**

**Just as / YHWH spoke (דבר) / unto me //**

**And we went about Mount Seir / many days //** ס [a]

$$\begin{array}{cc} 10 & 2 \\ 4 & 1 \\ 13 & 2 \\ 11 & 3 \\ \underline{17} & \underline{2} \end{array}$$

## Notes

19.a. The boldface type indicates a continuation of the series of Travel Notices in the Outer Frame of Deuteronomy. See note 1:6b.a.

21.a. See note 1:8.a-a. The usage of ראה here introduces the first extended instance of the *Numeruswechsel*, the sudden change from 2nd pl to 2nd sg forms. It is interesting to note that the first two instances of the *Numeruswechsel*, the [6:4] metrical unit in 1:21 and the [4:6] unit in 1:31, balance each other structurally.

22.a. See note 1:1.c.

22.b. SP reads עליהן, "against them."

23.a. Q reads מכמה שני.

24.a. DSS, Syr, and Vg read הארץ for אתה. Either is possible from a prosodic point of view. MT is preferred as the more difficult reading.

25.a. A *ṭiphā'* is substituted for the *mahpāk* with relocation of *'atnāḥ* (see note 1:7.b.). It is also possible to see the sequence of *'azlā'* followed by *mahpāk* as disj.

26.a. The *ṭiphā'* is removed because of misplaced *'atnāḥ* (see note 1:1.c.).

26.b. LXX, Syr, and Vg 1st pl אלהינו.

27.a. The text is emended with some LXX witnesses and Vg to achieve closer mora-count between the two versets (for discussion of versets, see note 1:8.b.).

28.a. SP adds *waw*-conj; some LXX witnesses read 2nd pl (אחיכם).

28.b. SP, LXX, and some Heb. Mss read ורב, perhaps influenced by 2:21.

28.c. Some LXX witnesses read 2nd pl (ממכם).

28.d. SP, LXX, and Syr add *waw*-conj, which is possible in terms of mora-count.

30.a. אלהיכם deleted *metri causa*. Some LXX witnesses read אלהים.

31.a-a. Italic type indicate 2nd sg context. See note 1:21.

32.a. Some LXX witnesses read אלהינו.

33.a. Some LXX witnesses read לפנינו.

33.b. Some LXX witnesses read לחנתנו.

33.c. Both *BHK* and *BHS* have extra space here to mark the boundary.

35.a-a. Missing in some LXX witnesses; cf. Num 14:22–23.

35.b. The *yᵉtîb* is read as conj.

35.c. The term לתת is missing in SP, LXX, Vg, and some Heb. Mss.

35.d. LXX, Syr, and Tg read 3rd pl (לאבתיהם).

36.a-a. Some scholars emend to read אחרי, "after me"; cf. 1:8.

37.a. Reading שמה with a number of Heb. Mss, SP, Syr, Tg, and Vg.

38.a. Removing *ṭiphā'* with misplaced *'atnāḥ* (see note 1:1.c.).

38.b. SP reads ק (י) החז.

39.a-a. Missing in some LXX witnesses; cf. Num 14:31.

39.b. LXX reads καὶ πᾶν παιδίον νέον (וכל טף).

41.a. SP, LXX, Syr, and two Heb. Mss add אלהינו. The prosodic analysis suggests that the addition is influenced by the length of the following two versets (for versets, see note 1:8.b.).

43.a. SP adds אליכם (cf. 1:26).

44.a. SP adds העמלקי והכנעני, "the Amalakites and the Canaanites."

45.a. SP, LXX, and Syr read ותשבו as in v 46.

45.b. LXX adds τοῦ θεοῦ ἡμῶν (ὑμῶν).

46.a. From a prosodic perspective, the phrase ימים רבים functions in a pivot pattern. Thus it is possible to scan 1:44–2:1 as [9:8:10], with the phrase "many waters" ending each of the last two units.

46.b. The boundary is marked in MT by a new chapter division.

*Form/Structure/Setting*

In terms of content and overall prosodic structure, Deut 1:19–2:1 may be outlined as follows:

A      Travel Notice: We went from Horeb to Kadesh-barnea (1:19)
  B      Report: You have reached the promised land (1:20)
    C      Summons to Possess the Land (1:21)
      D      Israel's Sin: They Request Spies (1:22)
        E      Report: I sent the spies (1:23–24)
          F      Report of the Spies and Israel's Rebellion (1:25–28)
            1)      Spies: It is a good land
            2)      Israel's Murmuring and Rebellion
            3)      Spies: The people are too strong for us
              G      Summons Not to Fear (1:29–31)
          F'  Israel's Rebellion and Yahweh's Judgment (1:32–36)
            1)      Report of Moses: Israel's Lack of Trust
            2)      Yahweh's Judgment: Postponement of Conquest
            3)      Report of Moses: The Exception of Caleb
        E'      Report: Yahweh was angry with me (1:37–39)
          1)      Joshua is to lead the Conquest
          2)      The land is to be possessed by your children
      D'      Israel's Sin: They Confess but Act Presumptuously (1:40–41)
    C'      Summons Not to Fight for the Land (1:42)
  B'      Report: You failed to enter the land (1:43–44)
A'      Travel Notice: We went from Kadesh to Mount Seir (1:45–2:1)

It should be noted that some of the elements in this outline, and those to follow, are part of still other structures, some of which are not concentric in nature. As is the case in other works of art in both music and literature, no single analysis can possibly uncover all that is there. Works of art can seldom be reduced to a single structure. And even when dominant structural patterns are observed, one is still a long way from describing what makes the resultant work aesthetically appealing. When the composer Panufnik described the intricate mathematical conceptual design of his eighth symphony, he also cautioned the reader about taking the design too seriously. His advice was to simply enjoy the music, for too much attention on the structure may detract from that experience. For me personally, however, my first encounter with his symphony in 1982 was substantially enhanced by an awareness of the structure utilized by the artist in the composition of a truly beautiful work of art—conceived, incidentally, in terms of concentric structures not unlike both Deuteronomy and the book of Jonah (see D. Christensen, "The Song of Jonah: A Metrical Analysis," *JBL* 104 [1985] 217–31; and "Andrzej Panufnik and the Structure of the Book of Jonah: Icons, Music and Literary Art," *JETS* 28 [1985] 133–40).

From a prosodic point of view, Deut 1:19–2:1 is in two parts of unequal length. An elaborate concentric design is present in the first section (1:19–33), as follows:

| [(5:7):6] | [6:4] | [(8:6):(6:6)] | [6:4:4:6] | [(6:6):(6:8)] | [4:6] | [6:(5:7)] |
|-----------|-------|---------------|-----------|---------------|-------|-----------|
| 1:19–20   | 21    | 22            | 23–24     | 25–27         | 28    | 29–30     |

Though the opening prosodic unit in vv 19–20 forms an inclusion with vv 32–33, it also forms an inclusion with 1:45–2:1 (which can be scanned [6:7:5]), in its use of 1st pl forms within the series of Travel Notices (see *Excursus:* "Travel Notices" under discussion of 1:6b–8 above). Taken in that latter context, the units scan respectively [12:6] and [6:12] in terms of the distribution of accentual stress units.

The fact that v 21 and v 31 are a structural pair is evident from the use of 2nd sg forms in both contexts, as the first two instances of the so-called *Numeruswechsel* in Deuteronomy. This rhetorical device frames the initial account of Israel's rebellion (vv 22–30), which may be outlined as follows:

[8:6] A   Israel's Sin: They Request Spies (v 22)
[6:6]   B   Report: I sent the spies (23–24).
[6:4:4:6]   C   Israel's Sin: Murmuring and Rebellion (25–27a)
[6:6]   B'   Report: "Our brothers have disquieted our hearts" (27b–28).
[6:8] A'   Summons Not to Fear (29–30)

The opening part (vv 34–38) of the second section (1:34–2:1) scans [8:9:9:8], with the "Exception of Caleb" (v 36) at its center. Yahweh's anger extends to Moses as well, who is commanded to strengthen Joshua (v 38), "who will cause Israel to inherit" the land. This unit anticipates 3:23–28 and 31:1–8, and the transfer of leadership from Moses to Joshua. The concentric design of 1:39–2:1 may be outlined as follows:

[5:5] A   The land is to be possessed by your children (v 39)
[8:9]   B   Israel's Sin: They Confess but Act Presumptuously (vv 40–41)
[6:6:6]   C   Summons Not to Fight for the Land (v 42)
      C'   Israel's Sin: "You would not listen" (v 43)
[9:8]   B'   Consequences: Israel Defeated by the Amorites (v 44–46a)
[5:5] A'   The people journey away from the promised land (1:46b–2:1)

## Comment

**19–20**   The opening verse of this section serves as both a connecting link between the previous Travel Notice concerning Mount Horeb in 1:6–7 and the next one in 2:1. In relation to the latter it functions as a frame around the episode of Israel's "Unholy War." The journey took the Israelites more than a hundred miles through an arid and barren wilderness, *that great and fearful desert,* in response to Yahweh's command to enter the promised land, *the hill country of the Amorites.*

**21**   The abrupt change from second person plural (and first person plural) forms to second person singular here introduces the phenomenon of the *Numeruswechsel* (see *Excursus* below). Kadesh-barnea itself was not the promised land, but the border of that land. The call to vision expressed in the term ראה, "Look!" draws attention to the previous use of this term in 1:8 where the "fathers" Abraham, Isaac, and Jacob are named. The verbal root ירש carries the sense of possessing by dispossessing. The promised land was already inhabited by the Canaanites. To possess it, the Israelites must wage a war of conquest, which required strength and courage. The summons not to fear, which concludes this rhythmic unit, belongs to the language of "Holy War" (see *Excursus* below).

**22–24** The sudden shift back to a second person plural verbal form in the opening word of this verse (ותקרבון) marks the boundary of a new rhythmic unit which continues through v 30. Moses begins by quoting the people who decide to send spies to explore the land. Moses approved the plan and appointed twelve men, one for each tribe (v 23), who set out to spy out the land (v 24). In the parallel account (Num 13:1–2), Yahweh commanded Moses to send the spies. Here the people initiate the action, which becomes part of their sin. The spies went as far as the valley of Eshkol in the vicinity of Hebron. The exact location of this ancient site in not known (see D. Baly, *Geographical Companion to the Bible* [New York: McGraw-Hill, 1963] 171).

**25–27** The spies returned with their report and samples of the remarkable fruit of the land. It was indeed a good land, but the people were afraid and rebelled against the commandment to go up and possess it. As Craigie has noted (NICOT [1976] 102), the "facts" were the same for both Moses and the people. Moses, the man of vision and faith, chose to minimize the difficulties, whereas the people, with little vision, could not see past those difficulties. Their rebellion perverted their understanding of God as they murmured, complaining that Yahweh hated them (v 27). In their eyes Yahweh had brought them out of Egypt to deliver them into the hands of the Amorites who would exterminate them. Their perception was precisely the opposite of the truth.

**28** The report of the spies terrified the Israelites. Their enemies became even bigger than they were, as is usually the case when a person is afraid. The cities of the enemy were *great and fortified to the heavens*. Moreover, among the enemy were Anakim who were traditionally giants (cf. LXX which renders the term γιγάντων).

**29–30** Moses encouraged them by repeating words from the tradition of "Holy War" (see *Excursus* below), urging them not to be afraid. What Yahweh did for them in Egypt in times past will be repeated in the future as he continues to wage "Holy War" in their behalf (v 30). According to R. J. Williams [*Hebrew Syntax* (1967) 61 (no. 341)], the particle את here, with the pronominal suffix, is used to express "advantage."

**31** The *waw*-conjunction before the first word is disjunctive and sets the stage for the shift to second person singular forms. Together with v 21, this verse forms a frame around the account of Israel's rebellion (vv 20–30). On the father/son imagery here see D. J. McCarthy (*CBQ* 27 [1965] 144–47). This imagery is an important aspect of the theme of the love of God in Deuteronomy, which is much more than a mere reflection of treaty terminology.

**32–33** The shift back to 2nd pl forms at the end of v 31 marks the rhythmic or metrical boundary of this concluding segment of 1:19–33. The people do not place their trust in Yahweh. In this matter (בדבר) they have not followed Yahweh's "words" (הדברים) as set forth in Deuteronomy. To experience God in their history is not sufficient, for the people must be constantly reminded that God's provisions of times past continue in the present and in the future. The use of the verb "to seek out" (לתור) in v 33 is ironic, as Craigie has noted (NICOT [1976] 103–4). The people sent spies to explore the land and bring back a report (דבר, v 22), while simultaneously God was already seeking out a place for them to pitch their tents in that very land, if they would only obey his words (דברים, cf. 1:1).

**34–36** Moses continues his report by recounting once more the words of Yahweh, who *heard the sound of your words* (דברים), though whispered in secrecy in the tents (v 27). Yahweh knew their rebellion and in anger swore an oath. The niph form of the verb is the same as that used both in Yahweh's earlier promise to the patriarchal fathers (Gen 50:24; Exod 33:1) and to the Israelites (Num 14:16) to give them the land, but the content is reversed. One generation is to be excluded, for *this evil generation* (v 35) would not see the promised land—except for Caleb and his family (v 36). According to the account in Num 13, Caleb was one of the twelve spies sent out from Kadesh and the only one who advocated immediate attack. According to Josh 15:13 his family subsequently received land in the vicinity of Hebron, presumably the valley of Eshkol through which the spies journeyed. The Hebrew term יַעַן is used to introduce words spoken either by God or a representative of God (see D. Gowan, "The Use of *yaʿan* in Biblical Hebrew," *VT* 21 [1971] 168–85).

**37–38** The meaning of the initial phrase here approaches indignation: *Even with me* (see Craigie, NICOT [1976] 105). In Num 20:10–12 Moses is excluded because of his presumptuous sin in striking the rock, an incident which took place some time after the events at Kadesh-barnea (see S. Driver, ICC [1895] 26–27). The reason presented here seems to be related to the people (i.e., *on account of you*). Though Moses himself was not to blame for their failure, as their leader he suffered the consequences, and Joshua was selected to take his place. In Num 27:15–18 the appointment of Joshua took place some years after the events at Kadesh-barnea.

**39–40** The *waw*-conjunction before the initial word in v 39 is disjunctive to mark the beginning of a new rhythmic subunit (1:39–2:1). Children below the age of discernment (*who do not know today good and evil*, v 39) would be permitted to enter the promised land. It is that generation, assembled at Mount Nebo, to whom the words of this book are addressed. It would appear that the adults had used these children (*They will be as spoil*) as an excuse in their rebellion. Though their concern for the children was valid, it is to be contrasted with Yahweh's past concern (*How he bore you . . . as a man bears his son*, v 31) in light of his present demands. Moses then commands the people to turn around and journey in the direction of *Yam Suf*. It seems best not to translate the Hebrew by either Red Sea or Reed Sea so as to remind the reader of the inherent ambiguity and mythic overtones in this phrase (see B. Batto, "The Reed Sea: *Requiescat in Pace*," *JBL* 102 [1983] 27–35; and "Red Sea or Reed Sea?" *BARev* 10 [1984] 57–63).

**41** The people acknowledge their sin but act presumptuously in their decision to wage war rather than return to the wilderness. They *deemed it easy to go up to the hill country*, and in so doing failed to see the seriousness of their task. Though they had missed their one chance to fight Yahweh's war, they decided to advance under their own power.

**42–44** Yahweh responded by uttering a summons not to fight, for Yahweh was no longer in their midst (v 42). Without Yahweh's presence the war could not be a "Holy War." In spite of the warning they continued in their rebellion against Yahweh and set out to fight an "Unholy War" (v 43). The result was inevitable; the Amorites smote them as far as Hormah, a town to the northeast of Kadesh-barnea.

**45–46** Though the children of Israel returned to weep before Yahweh at Kadesh-barnea, it was now too late: *Yahweh did not listen to your voice; and he did not give ear unto you* (v 45). And so they tarried in Kadesh *many days* (v 46).

**2:1**    The concluding Travel Notice is a sad note as the people set out in a southeasterly direction retracing their steps toward the Gulf of Aqaba. On route they journeyed *many days* in the vicinity of Mount Seir, a mountain range of Edom to the south of the Dead Sea that extends down the eastern side of the Arabah. This verse forms the second half of a frame around this section of Deuteronomy (1:19–2:1), which began in 1:19 with the notice taking the people from Mount Horeb to Kadesh-barnea.

### Explanation

The concept of "Holy War" is offensive to the modern reader because it suggests the barbarism of the Crusades of medieval times, or the *jihad* of Islamic fundamentalists who would "drive the nation of Israel into the Sea." War is inherently evil. Nonetheless, imagery from warfare remains closely linked to the idea of the holy from the days of ancient Israel to the present, no doubt primarily because of what lies behind the text of Deuteronomy and related literature in the Hebrew Bible. On "Holy War" as a celebrated event in ancient Israel see the *Excursus* below. Here we are interested in the theological and psychological principles implied in this text.

At the structural center of Deut 1:19–2:1 stands a summons not to fear (vv 29–31). Yahweh, as Divine Warrior, protects his people and wages war in their behalf. As we become aware of the reality of evil in the spiritual realm, we also become aware of our need for God's power to cope with forces of darkness. The human response is that of fear. Like the spies, we conclude that the enemy is too strong for us, and that is precisely the point. If we are to prevail over the forces of evil, we must wage battle with a power greater than our own. Therefore, in the words of Paul, we must "Put on the whole armor of God. . . . For we are not contending against flesh and blood, but against . . . spiritual hosts of wickedness in the heavenly places" (Eph 6:10–12). It is this spiritual battle to which this text speaks.

To enter the promised land one must trust God to defeat the forces of evil. If we fear the enemy, that very foe will increase in stature before our eyes to become "giants in the land." As we engage the foe in spiritual battle, we must constantly be aware of the fact that it is God who fights in our behalf. The moment we step forth in our own strength alone, we will be smitten "as far as Hormah" (i.e., back to the very outskirts of our own camp from which we set out to engage the enemy in combat).

Failure to engage the enemy at the time of God's choosing will result in a reluctant return to "that great and fearful desert" through which we have already come. Even Moses is not immune from God's judgment when the people fail to place their trust in God's power against evil. The example of Caleb should be constantly before our eyes. If we "wholeheartedly follow after Yahweh," we will truly possess the land "upon which we have trodden in it."

There is certainly historical memory behind these events of the Exodus-Conquest, but to read the text only as mere historical account is to rob it of its power to motivate meaningful change and growth. To wage an "Unholy War" is dangerous business, for us today as well as for ancient Israel.

# EXCURSUS: *The* Numeruswechsel *in Deuteronomy*

## Bibliography

**Airoldi, N.** "Le 'sezioni noi' in Deuteronomio." *RivB* 16 (1968) 143–57. ————. "A proposito dei passi al singolare in Dtn 1, 6–3, 29." *Aug* 11 (1971) 355–87. **Begg, C. T.** *Contributions to the Elucidation of the Composition of Deuteronomy with Special Attention to the Significance of the* Numeruswechsel, 5 vols. Diss., Univ. of Leuven, 1978. ————. "The Significance of the *Numeruswechsel* in Deuteronomy: The 'Prehistory' of the Question." *ETL* 55 (1979) 116–124. **Braulik, G.** *Die Mittel Deuteronomischer Rhetorik.* AnBib 68. Rome: Biblical Institute Press, 1978. **Cazelles, H.** "Passages in the Singular within Discourse in the Plural of Dt 1–4." *CBQ* 29 (1967) 207–19. **Christensen, D. L.** "The *Numeruswechsel* in Deuteronomy 12." In *Proceedings of the Ninth World Congress of Jewish Studies.* Division A: The Period of the Bible. Jerusalem: World Union of Jewish Studies, 1986. 61–68. **Fitzmyer, J. A.** "The Phoenician Inscription from Pyrgi." *JAOS* 86 (1966) 285–97. **Garbini, G.** "Nuovo materiale per la grammatica dell'Aramaico antico." *RSO* 34 (1959) 41–54. **Georgiades, T.** *Music and Language.* Trans. M. L. Göllner. Cambridge: Cambridge University Press, 1982. **Higgs, W. R.** *A Stylistic Analysis of the* Numeruswechsel *Sections of Deuteronomy.* Diss., The Southern Baptist Theological Seminary, Louisville, 1982. **Knapp, D.** *Deuteronomium 4: Literarische Analyse und theologische Interpretation.* Göttingen: Vandenhoeck & Ruprecht, 1987. **Lohfink, N.** *Das Hauptgebot.* AnBib 20. Rome Biblical Institute Press, 1963. ————. "Zum 'Numeruswechsel' in Dtn 3, 21f." *BN* 49 (1989) 39–52. **Sperber, A.** "Der Personenwechsel in der Bibel." *ZA* 32 (1918) 23–33. **Suzuki, Y.** *The 'Numeruswechsel' in Deuteronomy.* Diss., Claremont School of Theology, 1982. **Tillesse, G. M. de.** "Sections 'Tu' et Sections 'Vous' dans le Deutéronome." *VT* 12 (1962) 29–87. **Veijola, T.** "Principal Observations on the Basic Story in Deuteronomy 1–3." In *Wünschet Jerusalem Frieden.* Ed. M. Augustin and K.-D. Schunck. Collected Communications to the XIIth Congress of the International Organization for the Study of the Old Testament, Jerusalem 1986. Frankfurt: Lang, 1988. 249–59.

One of the more perplexing problems in the study of the Hebrew text of Deuteronomy is the frequent change in the use of second person singular and plural forms in verbs and pronominal suffixes, which is generally designated as the *Numeruswechsel.* Since modern English makes no distinction between the singular and plural in the second person, there is no simple way to mark the changes in translation. Moreover, since the changes have no obvious effect on the meaning of the text in question, the matter is often ignored by commentators.

Modern discussion of the *Numeruswechsel* is oriented around the work of G. Minette de Tillese (1962) and N. Lohfink (1963). Minette de Tillesse explained the phenomenon in terms of a redactional process in a detailed study of Deut 5–12. H. Cazelles (1967) subsequently included Deut 1–4 in a somewhat similar analysis. Lohfink, on the other hand, chose to explain the phenomenon on stylistic grounds in his study of Deut 5–11. The attempt of his student G. Braulik (1978) to explain the same phenomenon in Deut 4 on stylistic grounds has precipitated a lively debate in recent years. D. Knapp's recent study of Deut 4 (1987), which stands in the tradition of G. M. de Tillesse, represents what continues to be a majority opinion in current German scholarship.

The larger problem has led to at least three doctoral dissertations in recent years: an enormous work by C. Begg (1978); one by Y. Suzuki (1982); and another by W. R. Higgs (1982). Begg presents a masterful survey of pertinent literature from the time of de Wette (1805) to the present and suggests what appears to be a combination of the two perspectives in his focus on the use of the second person singular in the quotation of earlier material. Suzuki offers an elaboration of the redactional point of view, arguing for several levels of scribal activity marked by changes in both person and number beyond that of the *Numeruswechsel.* Higgs affirms the use of the *Numeruswechsel* for purposes of redactional literary analysis on statistical grounds.

My own work on the rhythmic structure of the Hebrew text of Deuteronomy had its starting point in the work of Braulik (1978), in which the text of Deut 4 was scanned using the familiar word-stress system of the Ley-Sievers approach to poetic scansion. Finding Braulik's discussion provocative, but not entirely persuasive, I sought to find a more sensitive system of metrical scansion. That search led to the combination of perhaps the oldest approach in the field of OT studies, the so-called Alting-Danzian system (1654–1771 C.E.), with the recent work of the Polish linguist J. Kurylowicz (1972), which Longman has described as the system of "Syntactic-Accentual Meter" (*Bib* 63 [1982] 230–54; see Bibliography under "Law, Poetry, and Music in Ancient Israel" in the *Introduction* to this commentary).

Books in antiquity were written for the ear and not the eye. Deuteronomy is perhaps the most liturgical book in the Hebrew Bible, as J. van Goudoever has noted (*Das Deut* [1985] 148). Thus we ought not to be surprised to find in it an elaborate set of aural signals to facilitate its transmission in recitation. If the text was composed to be recited, and if that text still retains its ancient rythmic form, it follows that it may also have been composed with music as an essential aspect of the tradition itself. In this regard we would do well to look more closely at what T. Georgiades has shown for the ancient Greeks. As he put it, "For the ancient Greeks, music existed primarily as verse. The Greek verse line was a linguistic and simultaneously a musical reality. The connecting element, common to both language and music, was rhythm" (*Music and Language,* trans. M. L. Göllner [Cambridge: Cambridge UP, 1982] 4). Georgiades went on to argue that it is quite inaccurate to translate the term $\mu o \upsilon \sigma \iota \kappa \acute{\eta}$ as music. The two terms designate quite different things. The term $\mu o \upsilon \sigma \iota \kappa \acute{\eta}$ represents a form of musically determined verse from which our familiar concepts of both music and prose and ultimately poetry come. For him, "The ancient Greek line was a singular formation for which there is no analogy in Western Christian civilization. It was, if you will, music and poetry in one, and precisely because of this it could not be separated into music and poetry in two tangibly distinct components" (6). It is my personal belief that a somewhat analogous situation existed in ancient Israel. The book of Deuteronomy is thus a peculiarly useful text in our quest to redefine the terms "prose" and "poetry" in biblical studies.

The first two instances of the *Numeruswechsel* in Deuteronomy are found in 1:21 and 1:31, which form a structural frame around the account of Israel's rebellion (vv 22–30). This frame probably represents some kind of parallel musical structures in the original composition and performance of the text. In the commentary below it will be shown that most of the instances of the *Numeruswechsel,* like the first two occurrences here in chap. 1, appear to be structural markers, particularly of boundaries between rhythmic units of the text, and sometimes the center, or turning point, within specific structures.

# The March of Conquest (2:2–25)

## Bibliography

**Alt, A.** "Emiter und Moabiter." *PJ* 36 (1940) 29–43 [=*KlSchr* III, 203–15]. **Bartlett, J. R.** "The Land of Seir and the Brotherhood of Edom." *JTS* 20 (1969) 5–8. ————. "Sihon and Og Kings of the Amorites." *VT* 20 (1970) 257–77. ————. "The Moabites and the Edomites." In *Old Testament Times*. Ed. D. J. Wiseman. Oxford, 1973. 229–58. ————. "Yahweh and Qaus: A Response to Martin Rose." *JSOT* 5 (1978) 29–38. **Boling, R. G.** *The Early Biblical Community in Transjordan*. SWBA 6. Sheffield: Almond Press, 1988. **Bordreuil, P.** "Textes alphabétiques inédits de Ras Shamra. Nouveaux textes alphabétiques de Ras Ibn Hani." *AAAS* 29/30 (1979/80) 11–15 [*repaʾim*, 13]. **Briend, J.** "La Marche des tribes d'Israel en Transjordanie." *MDB* 46 (1986) 41–42. **Caquot, A.** "Les rephaim ougaritiques." *Syria* 37 (1960) 75–93. ————. "La tablette RS 24.252 et la question des Rephaim ougaritiques." *Syria* 53 (1976) 295–304. ————. "Héros, mânes et géants à Ougarit." *RHR* 193 (1978) 141–42. ————. "Remarques sur la tablette alphabétique." In *FS S. E. Loewenstamm* (1978). 1–6. **Childs, B. S.** "A Study of the Formula 'Until this Day.'" *JBL* 82 (1963) 279–92. **Coats, G.** "The Song of the Sea." *CBQ* 31 (1969) 1–17. ————. "Conquest Traditions in the Wilderness Theme." *JBL* 95 (1976) 185–90. **Cross, F. M.** and **Freedman, D. N.** "The Song of Miriam." *JNES* 14 (1955) 237–50. **Dearman, J. A.** "The Levitical Cities of Reuben and Moabite Toponymy." *BASOR* 276 (1989) 55–66. **Dietrich, M., Loretz, O.,** and **Sanmartin, J.** "Die ugaritischen Totengeister PRU(M) und die biblischen Rephaim." *UF* 8 (1976) 45–52. **Foresti, F.** "Composizione e redazione deuteronomistica in Ex 15,1–18." *Lat* 48 (1982) 41–69. **Giesen, G.** *Die Wurzel* שבע (1981). 336–37. **Ginsberg, H. L.** "Judah and the Transjordan States." In *FS A. Marx* (1950). 347–68. **Glueck, N.** "The Topography and History of Ezion Geber and Elath." *BASOR* 72 (1938) 2–13. **Gray, J.** "The Rephaim." *PEQ* 81 (1949) 127–39. ————. "*DTN* and *RPʾUM* in Ancient Ugarit." *PEQ* 84 (1952) 39–41. **Grintz, Y. M.** *Studies in Early Biblical Ethnology and History*. Jerusalem: Hakibbutz hameuchad, 1969. 91–129, 201–57 (Heb.). **Halkin, A. S.** "The Scholia to Numbers and Deuteronomy in the Samaritan-Arabic Pentateuch." *JQR* 34 (1943–44) 41–59. **Heltzer, M.** *The Suteans*. Istituto Universitario Orientale. Seminario di Studi Asiatiche. Series minor 13. Naples, 1981. 51–55 [Rephaim]. *HOTTP* I, 268–69. **Hulst, A. R.** *Old Testament Translation Problems*. Helps for Translators 1. Leiden: Brill, 1960. ————. "Opmerkingen over de *kaʾaser*-zinnen in Dt." *NedTTs* 18 (1963) 337–61. **Jirku, A.** "*Rapaʾu* der Fürst der *Rapaʾuma*-Rephaim." *ZAW* 77 (1965) 82–83. **Köppel, U.** *Das deuteronomistische Geschichtswerke* (1979). **Kuntzmann, R.** *Le symbolisme des jumeaux au Proche-Orient ancien. Naissance, fonction et évolution d'un symbole*. Beauchesne Religions 12. Paris: Beauchesne, 1983. **Labuschagne, C. J.** "The Emphasizing Particle *Gam* and Its Connotations." In *Studia Biblica et Semitica*. Wageningen: H. Veenman and Sons, 1966. 193–203. **L'Heureux, C.** "The Ugaritic and Biblical Rephaim." *HTR* 67 (1974) 265–74. ————. *Rank Among the Canaanite Gods: El, Baʿal, and the Rephaim*. HSM 21. Scholars Press, 1979. **McEvenue, S.** "A Source Critical Problem in Num 14, 26–38." *Bib* 50 (1969) 454–56. **Miller, P. D.** "Aspects of the Religion of Ugarit." In *FS F. M. Cross* (1987). 53–66. **Moor, J. D. de.** "*Rāpiʾūma*—Rephaim." *ZAW* 88 (1976) 223–45. **Moran, W. L.** "The End of the Unholy War and the Anti-Exodus." *Bib* 44 (1963) 333–42. **Nelson, R. D.** "Josiah in the Book of Joshua." *JBL* 100 (1981) 531–40. **Noth, M.** "Num 21 als Glied der 'Hexateuch'-Erzählung," *ZAW* 58 (1940/41) 161–89 [=*AbLA* I, 75–101]. ————. "Das Land Gilead als Siedlungsgebiet israelitischer Sippen." *PJ* 37 (1941) 50–101 [=*AbLA* I, 347–90]. ————. "Israelitische Stämme zwischen Ammon und Moab." *ZAW* 60 (1944) 11–57 [=*AbLA* I, 391–433]. ————. "Emiter und Moabiter." In *Die Welt des Alten Testaments. Einführung in die Grenzgebiete der alttestamentlichen Wissenschaft*. Berlin: Topelmann, 1940. 203–15. ————.

"Die Nachbarn der israelitischen Stämme im Ostjordanland." *ZDPV* 68 (1946–51) 1–50 [=*AbLA* I, 434–75]. ————. "Der Jordan in der alten Geschichte Palästinas." *ZDPV* 72 (1956) 123–48. ————. "Gilead und Gad." *ZDPV* 75 (1959) 14–73 [=*AbLA* I. 489–543]. **Obed, B.** "A Note on Joshua 13:25." *VT* 21 (1971) 239–41. **Prignaud, J.** "Caftorim et Keretim." *RB* 71 (1964) 215–29. **Rose, M.** "Yahweh in Israel—Qaus in Edom?" *JSOT* 2 (1977) 28–34. **Sauer, G.** "Die chronologischen Angaben in den Büchern Deuteronomium bis 2 Könige." *ThZ* 24 (1968) 1–14. **Seters, J. Van** "The Conquest of Sihon's Kingdom: A Literary Examination." *JBL* 91 (1972) 182–97. ————. "The Terms 'Amorite' and 'Hittite' in the Old Testament." *VT* 22 (1972) 64–81. ————. "Once Again—the Conquest of Sihon's Kingdom." *JBL* 99 (1980) 117–24. **Simian, H.** *Die theologische Nachgeschichte der Prophetie Ezekiels: Form- und traditionskritische Untersuchung zu Ez 6; 35; 36.* FBB 14. Würzburg: Echter Verlag, 1974. 282–84. **Strange, J.** *Caphtor / Keftiu: A New Investigation.* Acta Theologica Danica 14. Leiden: Brill, 1980. **Strobel, A.** *Der spätbronzezeitiche Seevölkersturm.* BZAW 145. Berlin: Töpelmann, 1976. **Summer, W. A.** "Israel's Encounters with Edom, Moab, Ammon, Sihon, and Og according to the Deuteronomist." *VT* 18 (1968) 216–28. **Tadmor, H.** and **Cogan, M.** "Ahaz and Tiglath-Pileser in the Book of Kings: Historiographic Considerations." *Bib* 60 (1979) 491–508. **Talmon, S.** "Biblical *REPĀʾÎM* and Ugaritic *RPU/I(M)*." *HUCA* 7 (1983) 235–49. **Ullendorff, E.** "The Knowledge of Languages in the Old Testament." *BJRL* 44 (1962) 455–65. **Vaux, R. de.** "Notes d'histoire et de topographie transjordaniennes." *RB* 50 (1941) 16–47 [=*Bible et Orient.* Paris: du Cerf, 1967. 115–37]. ————. "Les Hurrites de l'histoire et les Horites de la Bible." *RB* 74 (1967) 481–503. ————. "L'itinéraire des israélites de cadès aux plaines de moab." In *FS A. Dupont-Sommer* (1971). 331–42. **Walsh, J. T.** "From Egypt to Moab: A Source Critical Analysis of the Wilderness Itinerary." *CBQ* 39 (1977) 20–33. **Weippert, M.** "The Israelite 'Conquest' and the Evidence from Transjordan." In *Symposium Celebrating the 75th Anniversary of the Founding of ASOR (1900–1975).* Ed. F. M. Cross. Cambridge, 1979. 15–34. **Zenger, E.** "Tradition und Interpretation in Exodus xv 1–21." In VTSup 32. Leiden: Brill, 1981. 452–83.

### *Translation and Prosodic Analysis*

2:2–12    [5:4] [(5+4):8:7] [5:8] [8][5] [7:8:(5+4):4:5]
2:13–25    [4:7:(4+6):(4:3)] [8:6:6:6:6:8] [3:4] [(4+6):7:4]

| | | |
|---|---:|---|
| [2] And YHWH said / unto me (saying) // | 14 | 2 |
| [3] **"It is enough / your going round / this mountain //** | 13 | 3_ |
| **Turn yourselves / northward**[a] // | 11 | 2 |
| [4] And the people / command saying / | 11 | 2_ |
| 'You are about to cross over / into the territory / | 10 | 2 |
| Of your brothers the children of Esau / | 11 | 1 |
| Those living / in Seir // | 11 | 2_ |
| And they will fear you / | 8 | 1 |
| And you shall be careful / exceedingly // | 7 | 2 |
| [5] Do not contend with them [a] / | 8 | 1_ |
| For / I will not give to you / any of their land [b] / | ⌈ 15 | 3 |
| not so much as / what your foot treads on // | ⌊ 7 | 2 |
| For as a possession to Esau / I have given / Mount Seir // | 22 | 3_ |
| [6] Food you may purchase from them / for money / | ⌈ 15 | 2 |
| that you may eat // | ⌊ 4 | 1 |
| And also water / you may buy from them / for money / | ⌈ 15 | 3 |
| that you may drink'" // | ⌊ 5 | 1_ |

7 For YHWH *your God / has blessed you /*      14   2
  *In all / the work of your hand(s)* [a]*/ he has known your going /*      15   3_
  *Through this / great wilderness* [b] *// this / forty year (period) /*      22   4
  *YHWH your God / is with you /*      ⌈ 11   2
    *you have not lacked / a thing* (דבר)[c] *//*      ⌊ 10   2_

8 **And we crossed over /**      5   1
    **away from our brothers the children of Esau /**      16   1
    **who live / in Seir /**      ⌈ 11   2
  **By the way / of the Arabah /**      10   2
    **from Elath / and from Ezion-geber //** ס      ⌊ 15   2_

  **And we turned / and we crossed over /**      9   2
  **by way \\**[a] **of the wilderness of Moab //**      8   1
9 *And YHWH said / unto me /*      10   2_
  *"Do not hassle* [a]*/ Moab / and do not contend* [b] *with them /*      16   3
  *in battle* [b]*//*      5   1
  *For / I will not give you any of his land / as a possession /*      17   3_
  *For to the children of Lot / I gave Ar / as a possession /*      19   3
10 *The Emim formerly / lived in it //*      18   2
  *A people great and numerous / and tall / as the Anakim" //*      18   3_
11 [a]*Rephaim / they too are called \\*[b] *like the Anakim //*      ⌈ 22   2
  *but the Moabites / call them /*      ⌊ 15   2
  *Emim //*      4   1_
12 *And in Seir / the Horites lived / formerly /*      ⌈ 22   3
  *and the children of Esau dispossessed them /*      ⌊ 15   1_
  [a]*And they destroyed them / from before them* [a]*/*      11   2
  *And they dwelt / in their stead //*      10   2_
  *Just as Israel did /*      12   1
    *to the land / of their possession /*      9   2
    *which YHWH gave / to them //*      11   2_

13 Now [a] / rise up! [b]/      7   2
    and cross over for yourselves /      7   1
    the Zered Valley /      6   1_
  **And we crossed over / the Zered Valley //**      ⌈ 11   2
14     **And the days / which we went /**      ⌊ 13   2
  **From Kadesh-barnea / until we crossed over /**      ⌈ 17   2
    **the Zered Valley /**      ⌊ 6   1_
  **(They were) thirty-eight / years //**      ⌈ 15   2
    until the whole generation perished / the men of war[a] /      ⌊ 16   2
  From the midst of the camp /      ⌈ 7   1
    just as / YHWH [b] swore / to them //      11   3
15 and so also the hand of YHWH / was against them /      ⌊ 13   2_
  To destroy them / from the midst of the camp //      11   2
  until \\[a] they had perished //[b]      4   1
16 And it happened just as they had perished /      10   1
    all the men of war /      10   1
    by dying / from among the people // ס      11   2_

<sup>17</sup> And YHWH spoke (וידבר) / unto me saying //      ⌈ 15   2
                                                 ⌊ 10   1

<sup>18</sup> *"You are about to cross over TODAY /*      ⌈ 11   2
     *the boundary of Moab / at Ar //*      ⌊ <u>14</u>   3_

<sup>19</sup> *And you will approach / the frontier / of the Ammonites /*      ⌈ 6   1
     *Do not hassle them! /*
     *and do not contend with them* |ª *<in battle>* ª//      ⌊ 11   2

     *For I will not give /*      7   1
     *you any of the land of the Ammonites / as a possession /*      <u>16</u>   2_
     *For to the children of Lot /*      ⌈ 7   1
     *I have given it as a possession" //*      ⌊ 9   1

<sup>20</sup> *The land of the Rephaim it was considered / that also //*      16   2
     *Rephaim dwelt in it / formerly /*      <u>17</u>   2_
     *And the Ammonites / they called them / Zamzummim //*      19   3

<sup>21</sup> *A people great and numerous / and tall / as the Anakim //*      <u>18</u>   3_
     *And YHWH destroyed them / from before them /*      ⌈ 14   2
     *and they dispossessed them /*      ⌊ 7   1

     *And they dwelt in their stead //*      ⌈ 9   1
<sup>22</sup>    *just as he did / to the children of Esau /*      ⌊ <u>14</u>   2_
     *Those who dwell / in Seir // who destroyed the Horites /*      22   3
     *from before them /*      5   1
     *And they dispossessed them /*      ⌈ 7   1
     *and they dwelt in their stead / UNTIL / THIS DAY //*      ⌊ <u>15</u>   3_

<sup>23</sup> *And (as for) the Avvim /*      ⌈ 6   1
     *the ones who dwell in villages* ª/ *as far as Gaza //*      ⌊ 16   2_
     *Caphtorim /*      5   1
     *the ones who went forth from Caphtor /*      ⌈ 10   1
     *They destroyed them / and they dwelt in their stead //*      ⌊ <u>14</u>   2_

<sup>24</sup> **"Rise up (and) break camp /**      <u>7</u>   1
     **And cross over / the Arnon Valley /**      ⌈ 10   2
     *See* ª *I have given into your hand* ᵇ/      ⌊ 13   1_
     *Sihon, king of Heshbon the Amorite /*      ⌈ 17   1
     *and his land /*      ⌊ 5   1
     *Begin to take possession // and wage against him / war //*      ⌈ 17   3
<sup>25</sup>    *THIS VERY DAY /*      ⌊ <u>5</u>   1_
     *I will begin* ª/ *to put the dread of you /*      ⌈ 8   2
     *And the fear of you / upon / <all>ᵇ the peoples /*      ⌊ 16   3
     *(that are) under / the whole* ᶜ *heaven //*      9   2_
     *Who shall hear* ᵈ / *the report of you /*      ⌈ 8   2
     *And they shall tremble and be in anguish / because of you"* ᵉ//ᶠ      ⌊ <u>16</u>   2_

### Notes

3.a. The change to boldface type indicates a resumption of the series of Travel Notices (see Deut 1:6b; 2:8, 14).

5.a. LXX adds מלחמה with vv 9 and 24 (cf. v 19). The prosodic analysis supports MT.

5.b. SP and Syr add ירשה. The prosodic analysis supports MT.

7.a. Reading the dual ידיך with a number of Heb. Mss, SP, LXX, Vg, and Tg.

7.b. LXX adds καὶ τὴν φοβεράν (והנורא). Prosodic analysis supports MT.

7.c. SP adds material from Num 20:14, 17.

8.a. The *ṭiphāʾ* is removed because of misplaced *ʾatnāḥ* (see note 1:1.c).

9.a. Reading אֶל with a number of Heb. Mss.

9.b-b. SP reads בוֹ, in place of מלחמה בם which is certainly possible from a prosodic point of view, since it would eliminate the pivot pattern.

11.a. The sequence of verbal forms here departs somewhat from normal usage. יקרחו and יחשבו impf are read with a frequentative force, of a custom, with Driver (ICC [1895] 37). יירשום impf is more difficult, since the parallel in v 20 has the *waw*-conversive, which may be restored here by the principle of shared consonants. If MT is retained, it may reflect an archaic verbal usage preserved in a quotation from already ancient folklore. On the problems of the verbal system in Hebrew see *IBHS* (1990) 33 29–33; B. Zuber, *Das Tempussystem des biblischen Hebräisch: Eine Untersuchung am Text*, BZAW 164 (Berlin: Töpelmann, 1986); and Leslie McFall, *The Enigma of the Hebrew Verbal System* (Sheffield: Almond Press, 1982). The use of the pf forms עשׂה and נתן at the end of this sequence reflects a perspective subsequent to the time of Moses, when the conquest of the land was already complete.

11.b. See note 1:1.c.

12.a-a. SP reads דם יהוה מפניהם ויירשום (י)וישמ. Prosodic analysis supports MT.

13.a. A few Heb. Mss, SP, and Tg add *waw*-consec. Prosodic analysis supports MT.

13.b. SP and most LXX witnesses add סעו (with v 24 below).

14.a. Some LXX witnesses add לָמוּת with v 16 below.

14.b. Some LXX witnesses read אלהים. Prosodic analysis supports MT.

15.a. See note 1:1.c.

15.b. *BHK* and *BHS* have added space after this verse, which is not supported by the prosodic analysis.

19.a. Adding מלחמה with LXX (cf. vv 9 and 24) and an additional disj accent to improve the prosodic balance.

23.a. LXX^B reads *Aσηδωθ* (= אשׂדוד).

24.a. On the use of this term in the Outer Frame of Deuteronomy see the *Comment* on 1:8.

24.b. LXX and Syr read du בידיך, which is possible from a prosodic point of view.

25.a. One Heb. Ms, SP, and LXX read החל with v 24 above.

25.b. Adding כל with one Heb. Ms, Cairo Geniza fragments, and LXX.

25.c. The כל־ is omitted in some Heb. Mss, LXX, and Syr, which is possible from a prosodic perspective.

25.d. SP adds את.

25.e. The pointing of מִפָּנֶיךָ in *BHS* is in error; cf. *BHK*, which shows מִפָּנֶיךָ

25.f. BHK and BHS add extra space and indent the following verse on a new line.

## Form/Structure/Setting

As the structural center of part 1 of the Outer Frame of Deuteronomy (chaps. 1–3), 2:2–25 may be outlined as follows:

| | | |
|---|---|---|
| [5:4] | A | Travel Notice: Summons to Journey Northward (vv 2–4a) |
| [9:8:7] | B | Summons Not to Contend with the "Children of Esau" (vv 4b–6) |
| [5:8] | C | A Look Backward: Provision 40 Years in the Wilderness (v 7) |
| [8:5] | D | Travel Notice: From Seir to the Wilderness of Moab (v 8) |
| [7:8:9] | | Summons Not to Contend with Moab (v 9ab) |
| | | Emim dispossessed by "Children of Lot" (vv 9c–10) |
| | | Horites dispossessed by "Children of Esau" (vv 11–12a) |
| [4:5] | | They dispossessed them the same as Israel did (v 12bc) |
| [4:7] | D' | Travel Notice: Crossing the Zered Valley (vv 13–14a) |
| [(4+6):7] | C' | YHWH's Judgment: A Generation of Warriors Dead (vv 14b–16) |
| [8:6] | | A Look Forward: Beginning of the Conquest (vv 17–19) |
| [6:6:6] | B' | Summons Not to Contend with the "Children of Lot" (vv 20–21) |
| [8:7] | | YHWH Gave the "Children of Esau" Their Land (vv 22–23) |
| [4+6] | A' | Travel Notice: Summons to Cross the Arnon to battle Sihon (v 24) |
| [7:4] | | Yahweh to spread the fear of Israel in the land (v 25) |

The center of this structure (vv 9–12) is framed by a pair of Travel Notices (see *Excursus:* "Travel Notices"), which take the people of Israel from Seir, across the Zered Valley (Wadi Hasa), into the land of Moab—as far as the Arnon Valley (Wadi Mujib). The promised land is on the other side of the "Grand Canyon" of the Arnon, to the north. The second phase of Yahweh's "Holy War," the Conquest, was about to begin (see *Excursus:* "Holy War as Celebrated Event"). From a prosodic point of view, 2:2–25 is in two parts, each of which is arranged in an elaborate concentric design. The respective units of the parallel structures are carefully marked by a series of rhetorical features.

The first half (2:2–12) has at its center vv 7–8, which focus on God's provision during the forty years of wandering in the wilderness (v 7), and the journey through Edom (v 8). This center (vv 7–8) is framed by two parallel units, which summon the Israelites not to contend with Edom (vv 4–6) and Moab (v 9), who dispossessed the Emim (vv 10–11) and the Horites (v 12) in an earlier era. The opening summons to journey northward (vv 2–3) is set against the summary travel notice of v 8, which takes the Israelites from Elath, on the Red Sea, through Edom to the wilderness of Moab. At the same time it anticipates the pair of travel notices in vv 14 and 24, which frame the central part of the second major subunit of this section (2:13–25)

The structural center of 2:13–25 is an elaborate [8:6:6:6:6:8] rhythmic unit, which is curiously similar to the [6:8:(6:6):8:6] unit in 1:1–6a, at the beginning of Deuteronomy. This is not surprising in that the principle of concentricity calls for a close connection between external elements and the center of prosodic structures; 2:2–25 is the center of the larger structure of 1:1–3:29, which is introduced by 1:1–6a.

*Comment*

**2–4a**   Yahweh addressed Moses again, for the people had spent long enough in the vicinity of Mount Seir. The command to *Turn yourselves northward* marks the beginning of "The March of Conquest," which ultimately brought Israel into the promised land. The resumption of the series of Travel Notices (see *Excursus: "Travel Notices"*) in v 3 is framed by two versets, each of which ends with the word לֵאמֹר, "saying," the second of which is preceded by a singular usage of the 2nd impv צֵא within a context of plural imperatives. Though this is probably not an instance of the *Numeruswechsel,* it does fall on the boundary of a new rhythmic unit.

**4b–6**   Though the exact route the Israelites took through or around Edom is not clear (cf. G. A. Smith, *Deuteronomy* [1918] 30–32), the relationship between Israel and their *brothers the children of Esau* appears to be positive. For the occupation of this land by Esau, the brother of Jacob, see Gen 36:1–8. There is little evidence here of the "Damn Edom" theology of a later era (cf. Jer 49:7–22 and Obad 8–21). Nonetheless, the Israelites are told to proceed with caution because *they will fear you* (cf. Exod 15:15, "now are the chiefs of Edom dismayed").

Israel is not to engage Edom in battle, since their land is not part of Israel's promised land; *for as a possession to Esau* [Yahweh has] *given Mount Seir* (v 5). On the parallel passage, "*udm* is the gift of El," in the Ugaritic Keret Legend, see the discussion of Craigie (NICOT [1976] 108, n. 4, and the literature cited there).

The near perfect poetic parallelism in v 6 is notable. Craigie, and others, have assumed that the words of Yahweh end with v 5. The prosodic analysis here suggests that these words are the conclusion of the speech which Yahweh commanded Moses to make to the people (vv 4–6).

**7** The *Numeruswechsel* here marks this brief addition as the words of Moses, for Yahweh is referred to in the third person. Israel can afford to treat Edom with equanimity because *Yahweh has blessed you in all the work of your hands.* Despite their failures at Kadesh-barnea, Yahweh has faithfully provided for his people these forty years. The reference to the fact that they *have not lacked a thing* (דבר) may also be taken as a subtle allusion to the fact that "these words" (דברים, i.e., the book of Deuteronomy) were not lacking, even before the people of Israel reached Mount Nebo where they were recited afresh.

**8** The 1st c pl verbal forms of the travel notice are resumed, which is clearly an extension of the *Numeruswechsel,* as Suzuki has noted (see his disseration). The details of the trek through Edom are not given. On the identification of Elath and Ezion-Geber, see N. Glueck, "The Topography and History of Ezion Geber and Elath," *BASOR* 72 (1938) 2–13. The journey continued northward past Edom to the *wilderness of Moab.*

**9** The *Numeruswechsel* again marks the boundary of a new rhythmic unit, in which the Israelites are commanded not to do battle with Moab. Though Moab was the incestuous son of Lot (Gen 19:37), the land was given *as a possession* to his descendants by Yahweh. ער, "Ar," appears to be used as a synonym for Moab here, though elsewhere it apparently refers to one of the principle cities in Moab near the edge of the Arnon Valley (cf. Num 21:28). Weippert argues from Num 21:15 "that Ar is a designation for (the?) territory possessed by the Moabites" ("The Israelite 'Conquest'," [1979], 18, n. 7). More recently, Boling has rejected the location of Ar at el-Misnaᶜ by geographers, arguing that both Deut 2:18 and Num 21:14–15 "suggest a location much nearer the Arnon" (*The Early Biblical Community in Transjordan* [1988] 48).

**10–12** These verses are the first of a series of explanatory notes inserted into the text of Deuteronomy, that provide comments of historical interest regarding legendary matters of the distant past. The prosodic analysis suggests that these notes are not secondary additions to the text, but essential parts of the original poetic (musical?) composition. In epic poetry blocks of traditional material are sometimes inserted for various reasons.

האמים, "the Emim," were apparently the traditional predecessors of the Moabites, who were apparently assumed to have been giants, like the הענקים, "Anakim" (see the *Comment* on 1:28). The presence of mysterious stone structures, somewhat like Stonehenge in England, involving huge stones known as dolmens may have given rise to these legends (see A. J. Birkey, *ISBE* I [1979] 982–83).

רפאים, "Rephaim," appear to have been the aboriginal inhabitants of the Bashan, the region now known as the Golan Heights. They were apparently the Transjordanian equivalent of the Anakim in Cisjordan (see P. K. McCarter, *ISBE,* IV [1988] 137). Though they have been the subject of much study (see Craigie, NICOT [1976] 111, n. 3 and literature cited there, to which add the work of C. L'Heureux, "The Ugaritic and Biblical Rephaim." *HTR* 67 [1974] 265–74; idem, *Rank among the Canaanite Gods: El, Baᶜal, and the Rephaim,* HSMS 21 [Scholars Press, 1979], they remain an enigma.

החרים, "Horites," are commonly identified with the Hurrians, a non-Semitic people located in various places in Syria, Palestine, and Mesopotamia, but this identification poses serious difficulties (see F. W. Bush, *ISBE*, II [1982] 756–57). Here they are the traditional aboriginal inhabitants of Edom, whose displacement by *the children of Esau* is analogous to Israel's conquest of the Canaanites: *Just as Israel did to the land of their possession which Yahweh gave to them* (v 12). This latter clause is a clear indication that the final composition of Deuteronomy, as we know it, is much later than Moses' actual address on the plains of Moab.

**13–16**    The speaker in v 13 is not certain, whether the words of Moses or the words of Yahweh to Moses. The presence of the *Numeruswechsel* marks the beginning of a new rhythmic unit, which in this instance turns out to be a major structural break. Consequently, I take these words to be Moses addressing the people. It is also not clear exactly where the Travel Notice actually ends in v 14. The command to *rise up and cross over . . . the Zered Valley*, followed by a Travel Notice with 1st c pl verbal forms (vv 13–14), is balanced by the command to *rise up . . . and cross over the Arnon Valley* (v 24), followed by a "Holy War" section introduced by the term ראה ("see"; see the *Comment* on 1:8), forming a frame around this rhythmic unit (2:13–25).

נחל זרד, "Zered Valley,"—Wadi el-Hasa, at the southeast end of the Dead Sea, apparently formed the southern boundary of Moab. Unlike the rebellion at Kadesh-barnea (1:25–36), the command this time was followed by obedience: we *crossed over the Zered Valley* (v 14). The crossing of the Zered marks the beginning of the end of the wilderness wanderings. It was now thirty-eight years since Israel's departure from Kadesh-barnea, and the rebellious generation had *perished . . . from the midst of the camp, just as Yahweh swore to them*. They are called *the men of war*, which of course is what they should have been. The crossing of the Zered, like the crossing of *Yam Suf* in the Exodus from Egypt, marked the beginning of a new era. The subsequent crossing of the Arnon Valley anticipates the crossing of the Jordan River, which marks the beginning of another new era—the Conquest of Canaan. Paul made use of the death of these "men of war" as a warning in his instruction (1 Cor 10:5–6), which curiously includes reference to both the supernatural "Rock" (cf. Deut 32:4, 15, 30–31) and the tradition of a "wandering well" (see J. Milgrom, "Moses Sweetens the 'Bitter Waters' of the 'Portable Well': An Interpretation of a Panel at Dura-Europos Synagogue," in *Experiencing the Exodus from Egypt*, ed. D. Christensen [Berkeley: BIBAL Press, 1988] 81–87; cf. also 3–36). The Letter of Jude (v 5) singles out the death of this rebellious generation as a warning comparable to that of Sodom and Gomorrah (v 7), for those who would "reject authority" (v 8).

**17–22**    The *Numeruswechsel* again marks the boundary of a new rhythmic unit in which Yahweh warns the people of Israel not to wage war against the Ammonites. The unit is framed by the use of the temporal expression היום, "today" and עד היום הזה, "unto this day." On the rhetorical use of such temporal expressions see the *Comment* on 1:9–10. The focus is probably on liturgical time, perhaps in conj with "Holy War as Celebrated Event" in ancient Israel (see *Excursus* below).

On the location of Ar (v 18) near the Arnon Valley, see the *Comment* on 2:9 above. Crossing the Arnon commences the Conquest of the promised land. Israel is not to wage war against the Ammonites; for, like Moab, they are *the children of Lot* (v 19). Yahweh has given them their land *as a possession*. The translation in v 18 is problematic because גבול can mean either "territory" or "boundary"; the verb עבר can mean either "travel through" or "cross over"; and ער may be a synonym for

Moab, or the name of a city in Moab (see the discussion of A. R. Hulst, *Old Testament Translation Problems* [1960] 12).

רפאים, "Rephaim"—aboriginal giants in Bashan (see the *Comment* on 1:10–12). The Ammonites called their predecessors זמזמים, "Zamzummim," another foreign word. On the use of foreign words in Hebrew, here and in 2:10–12 and 3:9, see E. Ullendorff, "The Knowledge of Languages in the OT," *BJRL* 44 (1962) 455–65. On החרי, "Horites," see the *Comment* on 2:10–12.

**23** העוים, "the Avvim"—aboriginal village dwellers of southwestern Palestine in the vicinity of Gaza, who were displaced by the כפתרים, "Caphtorim," which is apparently an early name for the Philistines who came from *Caphtor* (probably Crete). For a discussion of the identity and origin of the Caphtorim, see the literature cited by Craigie (NICOT [1976] 113, n. 10; to which add Strange, *Caphtor/Keftiu: A New Investigation* [Leiden: Brill, 1980]).

**24–25** The rhythmic boundary is marked by the insertion of a brief Travel Notice, which forms an inclusion with the previous one in vv 13–14, and a return to the citation of Yahweh's words, which broke off at the end of v 19.

On the series of passages in the Outer Frame of Deuteronomy, which are introduced by the term ראה, "See!" see the *Comment* on 1:8. The command to *cross over the Arnon Valley* (v 24) was also a command to begin the Conquest of the promised land, the first phase of which was a battle with Sihon, an Amorite king who ruled in Heshbon. The kingdom of Sihon extended from the Jabbok River (Wadi Zarqa) in the north to the Arnon Valley (Wadi Mujib) in the south, between the Dead Sea and the Jordan River on the west and the kingdom of the Ammonites on the east. This region was subsequently allotted to the Israelite tribes of Gad and Reuben (Josh 13:8–28).

Because of their rebellion, the previous generation was given "into the hand of the Amorites" (1:27), in the reversal of Yahweh's "Holy War." To the new and obedient generation Yahweh has delivered the Amorite king Sihon into their hand. The prosodic analysis suggests that the phrase *this very day* should be taken as the conclusion of v 24 rather than the beginning of v 25. On the liturgical use of such temporal language see the *Comment* on 1:9–10. The language of v 25 belongs to the tradition of "Holy War" in ancient Israel: Yahweh will put the dread/fear of Israel upon all peoples.

*Explanation*

In Deut 2:2–25 Travel Notices are central from a structural point of view, since the unit as a whole is framed by such notices, which take the Israelites from the wilderness of Mount Seir (Edom) to the Arnon Valley (Wadi Mujib) and the edge of the promised land. A similar pair of Travel Notices frame the center of the larger construction (vv 9–12), with the journey from Elath to the southern border of Moab (v 8), set over against the crossing of the Zered Valley (Wadi el-Hasa) into Moab (vv 13–14).

Since "The March to Conquest" (2:2–25) stands at the structural center of chaps. 1–3, it is interesting to note what is in its center. The central section of this passage is in two parts, focusing on Moab (vv 9–11) and Edom (v 12), each of whom displaced former inhabitants to take possession of land Yahweh gave them, "just as Israel did to the land of their possession which Yahweh gave to them" (v 12).

This positive concern for Moab and Edom is in tension with a superficial reading of subsequent legislation regarding the nations of Egypt, Edom, Moab, and Ammon (see the *Comment* on 23:3–8). As I have argued elsewhere, the concepts embodied in the structure of this text "are a literary and canonical challenge to a simplistic reading of the Book of Deuteronomy" ("A New Israel: The Righteous from among All Nations," in *FS R. K. Harrison* [1988] 258).

The metaphor of life as a journey is worth pursuing in greater depth in light of both the structural use of Travel Notices here and the larger context of the journey which takes the people out of bondage, through the wilderness, on route "home" to the promised land. Though C. L'Heureux has not chosen to explore the text of Deuteronomy in his recent book, *Life Journey and the Old Testament: An Experiential Approach to the Bible and Personal Transformation* (Paulist Press, 1986), the title suggests that he understands the power of this metaphor. Recent experience with Jo Milgrom's method of "Handmade Midrash," as developed in relation to the going out from Egypt and the entrance into the land of promise, has opened new personal vistas of possibility for Bible study, in which the "wild power" of the biblical text is set free. As I put it on another occasion (*Experiencing the Exodus from Egypt* [BIBAL Press, 1988] 32–33):

> Bible study through "handmade midrash" is much more than an intellectual exercise. Symbols help the individual get in touch with feelings; and feelings in turn lead to personal meaning, perhaps in an ultimate sense. Too much of our academic experience deals only with the cognitive element in the strictly rational sense. It is essential that we continue to develop facility with left-brain, analytical study of ancient texts if we would understand them in any depth; but to get those texts deeply inside our own psyche involves another process altogether, a process which apparently focuses on right-brain activity. The rabbis of ancient Israel knew this in their use of midrash as an exegetical method. Jo Milgrom's adaptation of their approach provides a useful tool to liberate the power of the Scripture in our time. As C. G. Jung might have put it, in this approach, we, as human beings, liberate God by setting Him free to accomplish His own purposes through the biblical text.

Life is a journey—for us today, as well as for those in ancient Israel who organized the text of Deuteronomy in terms of the several stages of a faith journey, which took them through the land of apparent enemies who somehow were at the same time also their "brothers" whom Yahweh himself had chosen to bless and to use for his own purposes.

# EXCURSUS: *Holy War as Celebrated Event in Ancient Israel*

*Bibliography*

**Aharoni, Y.** "The Battle on the Waters of Merom and the Battle with Sisera." In *The Military History of the Land of Israel in Biblical Times.* Ed. J. Liver. Tel Aviv: Maarachoth, 1965 (Heb.). 91–109. **Albrektson, B.** *History and the Gods: An Essay on the Idea of Historical Events as Divine Manifestations in the Ancient Near East and in Israel.* ConB 1. Lund, 1967. **Arnold, W. R.** *Ephod and Ark.* HTR 3. Cambridge/London, 1917. **Bach, R.** *Die Aufforderungen zur Flucht und zum Kampf im alttestamentlichen Prophetenspruch.* Neukirchen-Vluyn, 1962. **Bächlie, O.** *Amphiktyonie im Alten Testament.* ThZ 6. Basel: Friedrich Reinhardt, 1977. **Boling, R. G.** "Holy Warfare and the Rule of Ethic: Every Inspired Scripture Has Its Use." In *Witness of Faith in Life and Worship.* Yearbook Tantur. Jerusalem: Ecumenical Institute for Theological Research, 1981. 187–200. **Brekelmans, C. H.** W. *De Herem in het Oude Testament.* Nijmegen, 1950. ————. "Le *herem* chez les prophètes du royaume du nord et dans le Deutéronome." BETL 12–13. Leuven UP, 1959. 377–83. **Christensen, D. L.** "Num 21:14–15 and the Book of the Wars of Yahweh." *CBQ* 36 (1974) 359–60. ————. *Prophecy and War in Ancient Israel.* BMS 3. Berkeley: BIBAL Press, 1989 (rep. of HDR 3. Missoula: Scholars Press, 1975). **Collins, J.** "The Mythology of Holy War in Daniel and the Qumran War Scroll: A Point of Transition in Jewish Apocalyptic." *VT* 25 (1975) 596–612. **Craigie, P.C.** "Yahweh Is a Man of Wars." *SJT* 22 (1969) 183–88. ————. *The Problem of War in the Old Testament.* Grand Rapids: Eerdmans, 1978. **Cross, F. M.** "The Divine Warrior in Israel's Early Cult." In *Studies and Text III: Biblical Motifs.* Ed. A. Altmann. Cambridge, MA: Harvard UP, 1966. 11–30. ————. "The 'Ritual Conquest'." In *CMHE* (1973) 91–111. **Dion, P. E.** "The 'fear not' Formula and Holy War." *CBQ* 32 (1970) 565–70. **Eissfeldt, O.** "Jahwe Zebaoth." In *KlSchr.* III, 103–23. **Eph'al, I.** "On Warfare and Military Control in the Ancient Near Eastern Empires: A Research Outline." In *History, Historiography and Interpretation: Studies in Biblical and Cuneiform Literatures.* Ed. H. Tadmor and W. Weinfeld. Jerusalem: Magnes Press, 1983. 88–106. **Fredriksson, H.** *Jahwe als Krieger. Studien zum altestamentlichen Gottesbild.* Lund: C.W.K. Gleerup, 1945. **Gevirtz, S.** "Jericho and Shechem: A Religio-Literary Aspect of City Destruction." *VT* 13 (1963) 52–62. **Gottwald, N. K.** "Holy War in Deuteronomy: Analysis and Critique." *RevExp* 61 (1964) 296–310. **Gressmann, H.** *Der Ursprung der israelitisch-jüdischen Eschatologie.* FRLANT 6. Göttingen: Vandenhoeck & Ruprecht, 1905. **Grønback, H. G.** "Juda und Amalek: Überlieferungsgeschichtliche Erwägunen zu Exodus 17:8–16." *ST* 18 (1964) 26–45. **Gunn, D.** "The 'Battle Report': Oral or Scribal Convention?" *JBL* 93 (1974) 513–18. **Holladay, J. S.** "The Day(s) the Moon Stood Still." *JBL* 87 (1968) 166–78. **Humbert, P.** *La "Terou'a". Analyse d'un rite biblique.* Neuchatel: Secrétariat de l'Université, 1946. **Jacobsen, T.** "Religious Drama in Ancient Mesopotamia." In *Unity and Diversity.* Ed. H. Goedicke and J. J. M. Roberts. Baltimore: Johns Hopkins UP, 1975. 65–97. **Jones, G. H.** "Holy War or YHWH War?" *VT* 25 (1975) 642–58. **Kaiser, O.** *Die Mythische Bedeutung des Meeres in Ägypten, Ugarit und Israel.* BZAW 78. Berlin, 1959. **Kang, S.-M.** *Divine War in the Old Testament and in the Ancient Near East.* BZAW 177. Berlin/New York: de Gruyter, 1989. **Kuhnert, G.** "Das Gilgalpassah: Literarische, überlieferungsgeschichtliche und geschichtliche Untersuchungen zu Josua 3–6." *TLZ* 109 (1984) 77–78. **Langlamet, F.** *Gilgal et les Récits de la Traversée du Jourdain (Jos. III–IV).* CahRB 11. Paris: J. Gabalda, 1969. ————. "La traversée du Jourdain et les documents de l'Hexateuque." *RB* 79 (1972) 7–38. **Lind, M.** "Paradigm of Holy War in the Old Testament." *BR* 16 (1971) 16–31. ————. *Yahweh Is a Warrior: The Theology of Warfare in Ancient Israel.* Pennsylvania/Ontario, 1980. **Lohfink, N.** "Der 'heilige Krieg' und der 'Bann' in der Bibel." *IKZ* 18 (1989) 104–12. **Malamat, A.** "The Ban in Mari and in the Bible." In *Biblical Essays 1966: Proceedings of the 9th Meeting of Ou testamentiese werkgemeenskap in Suid-Afrika.* 40–49. ————. "The War of Gideon and

Midian." In *The Military History of the Land of Israel in Biblical Times.* Ed. J. Liver (1973) (Heb.)
110–23. **McCarthy, D. J.** "Some Holy War Vocabulary in Joshua 2." *CBQ* 33 (1971) 228–30.
**Medico, H. E. del.** "Le Rite de la Guerre dans l'Ancien Testament." *L'Ethnographie* n.s. 45
(1947–1950) 127–70. **Miller, P. D.** "God the Warrior: A Problem in Biblical Interpretation
and Apologetics." *Int* 19 (1965) 39–46. ———. *The Divine Warrior in Early Israel.* HSM 5.
Cambridge: Harvard UP, 1973. **Nielsen, E.** "La Guerre considérée comme une religion et
la Religion comme une guerre." *ST* 15 (1961) 93–112. **Norin, S. I. L.** *Er Spaltete das Meer.
Die Auszügsuberlieferung in Psalmen und Kult des alten Israels.* ConB 9. Lund, 1977. **Ottoson, J.**
*Gilead: Tradition and History.* ConB 3. Lund, 1969. **Paul, S. M.** "Book of the Wars of the Lord."
*EncJud* 4 (Jerusalem, 1971) 1218–19. **Porter, J. R.** "The Background of Joshua III–IV." *SEÅ*
36 (1971) 5–23. **Pury, A. de.** "La Guerre Sainte Israélite: Réalité Historique ou Fiction
Litéraire?" *ETR* 56 (1981) 5–38. **Rad, G. von.** *Der Heilige Krieg im alten Israel,* 4. Auflage.
Göttingen: Vandenhoeck & Ruprecht, 1965. **Roberts, J. J. M.** "Myth versus History." *CBQ*
38 (1976) 1–13. Sanmartin Ascaso, J. *Las Guerras de Josué: Estudio de Semiótica Narrativa.*
Institución San Jerónimo 14. Valencia, 1982. **Schwally, F.** *Semitische Kriegsaltertümer, I. Der
heilige Krieg im Alten Israel.* Leipzig: Dietrich, 1901. **Smend, R.** *Jahwekriege und Stämmebund,* 2nd
ed. FRLANT 84. Göttingen: Vandenhoeck & Ruprecht, 1966. [Trans. M. G. Rogers as
*Yahweh War & Tribal Confederation: Reflections upon Israel's Earliest History.* Nashville: Abingdon,
1970.] **Soggin, J. A.** "The Conquest of Jericho through Battle." *EI* 19 (1982) 215–17. **Stolz,
F.** *Jahwes und Israels Kriege. Kriegstheorien und Kriegsfahrungen im Glaube des alten Israels.* ATANT
60. Zürich: Theologischer Verlag, 1972. **Talmon, S.** "YHWH War." *EncBib* 4. (Jerusalem,
1963). 1064–65. **Tur-Sinai, N. H.** "Was there a Book of the Wars of YHWH in the Bible?"
*BIES* 24 (1959/60) 146–48. **Wambacq, B. N.** *L'epithéte divine Jahvé Ṣeba'ôt.* Brouwer, 1947.
**Weimar, R.** "Die Jahwekriegserzahlungen in Ex 14, Jos 10, Richter 4 und 1 Sam 7." *BMik*
12 (1967) 121–27. **Weinfeld, M.** "Divine War in Ancient Israel and in the Ancient Near
East." In *FS S. E. Loewenstamm* (1978). 171–81. ———. "Divine Intervention in War in
Ancient Israel and in the Ancient Near East." In *History, Historiography and Interpretation:
Studies in Biblical and Cuneiform Literatures.* Ed. H. Tadmor and M. Weinfeld. Jerusalam:
Magnes Press, 1983. 121–47. **Weippert, M.** "Jahwekrieg und Bundesfluch in Jer 21,1–7."
*ZAW* 82 (1970) 396–409. ———. "Heiliger Krieg in Israel und Assyrien. Kritische
Anmerkungen zu Gerhard von Rads Konzept des 'Heiligien Krieges in Israel'." *ZAW* 84
(1972) 460–93. **Wijngaards, J. N. M.** *The Dramatization of Salvific History in the Deuteronomic
Schools.* OTS 16. Leiden: Brill, 1969. **Wilcoxen, J. A.** "Narrative Structure and Cult Legend:
A Study of Joshua 1–6." In *Transitions in Biblical Scholarship.* Ed. J. C. Rylaarsdam. Chicago:
Univ. of Chicago Press, 1958. 43–70.

The institution of holy war during the period of the Tribal League in ancient Israel
should be distinguished from Yahweh's Holy War as celebrated in the cultus of the
Ritual Conquest. Yahweh's Holy War was the ritual fusing of the events of the Exodus-
Conquest into one great cultic celebration, in which the Divine Warrior marched with
his hosts from Sinai to Shittim and then across the Jordan River to Gilgal, the battle
camp for the Conquest of Canaan. The nature of the institution of holy war as reflected in the Song of Deborah (Judg 5) can be reconstructed, at least in part, from
an analysis of Yahweh's Holy War as celebrated in the Ritual Conquest tradition. The
ark of the covenant was a battle palladium. The tribal groups had designated positions
within the battle camp under priestly supervision. Moses and Joshua, as "Judges" over
Israel, filled the role later assumed by the prophets in delivering war oracles to inspire
the troops in battle.

The quotation from the "Book of the Wars of the Lord" in Num 21:14 presents the
Divine Warrior as poised on the edge of the promised land, before the most celebrated
battles of the Exodus-Conquest. Yahweh has come in the whirlwind with his hosts to
the sources of the River Arnon in Transjordan. He marches westward through the wadis,

turning aside to settle affairs with Moab before marching against the two Amorite kings to the north, and then across the Jordan to Gilgal and the conquest of Canaan.

The actual conquest of Canaan was apparently reenacted as part of the annual festival traditions within ancient Israel, from the period of the judges down into the monarchic era—and perhaps beyond, as suggested by the so-called War Scroll from the Dead Sea community at Qumran. The tribal units of Israel took up their designated positions around the ark of the covenant at Gilgal. From there they set out to conquer Jericho in ritual tradition, as part of the spring festival of Passover each year.

The crossing of the Jordan River in the tradition of Ritual Conquest was set over against the crossing of the Red Sea or "Sea of Reeds" (ים סוף), in which the people of Israel were delivered from their traditional foe, the Egyptians (cf. Exod 15, the "Song of the Sea," and Ps 114:5). After the crossing of the Sea, Israel's first military encounter was against the Amalekites (Exod 17:8–15). Amalek was defeated and cursed in the name of Yahweh, who pledged "war with Amalek from generation to generation" (Exod 17:16; cf. Deut 25:17–19). Though not much is known about Amalek, so far as history is concerned, her traditional enmity with Israel surfaces in the story of Saul's demise because of his refusal to slay Agag, king of Amalek, and again in the story of Esther, whose archenemy Haman is identified as the Agagite (Esth 3:1, 10; 8:3, 5; 9:25).

The war with Amalek is the first in a series of wars which, together with the defeat of the Egyptians at the Red Sea, constitute Yahweh's Holy War par excellence. Further battles in this series include the war with the Canaanite king of Arad (Num 21:1–3), the wars with the Amorite kings Sihon and Og (Num 21:21–35; cf. Deut 1:4; 2:24–3:11; 4:46; 29:6), and the war against Midian (Num 31:1–54)—all under the leadership of Moses. After Moses' death, Joshua led the people across the Jordan River to the second phase of Yahweh's Holy War against Jericho, Ai, and the Canaanite inhabitants of the promised land.

# Yahweh's Holy War (2:26–3:11)

## Bibliography

**Albright, W. F.** "The Land of Damascus between 1850 and 1750 B.C.," *BASOR* 83 (1941) 31–36. **Alt, A.** "Herren und Herrensitze Palästinas im Anfang des zweiten Jahrtausends v. Chr." *ZDPV* 64 (1941) 21–39 [Sirjon, 31–32, =*KlSchr* III, 67]. **Bartlett, J. R.** "Sihon and Og, Kings of the Amorites." *VT* 20 (1970) 257–77. —————. "The Conquest of Sihon's Kingdom: A Literary Reexamination." *JBL* 97 (1978) 347–51. **Cazelles, H.** "Argob biblique, Ugarit et les mouvements hurrites." In *FS G. Rinaldi* (1967). 21–27. **Coats, G.** "The Conquest Traditions in the Wilderness Theme." *JBL* (1976) 184–90. **Dearman, J. A.** "The Levitical Cities of Reuben and Moabite Toponymy." *BASOR* 276 (1989) 55–66. **Driver, G. R.** "Mistranslations." *PEQ* 80 (1948) 64–65. —————. "On ʾlh 'went up country' and yrd 'went down country'." *ZAW* 69 (1957) 74–77. **Ehlich, K.** *Verwendung der Deixis beim sprachlichen Handeln.* Frankfurt a. M.: Lang, 1979. 571–82. **Floss, J. P.** "Verbfunktionen der Basis *HYY*." *BN* 30 (1986) 35–101. **Foresti, F.** "Composizione e redazione deuteronomistica in Ex 15,1–18." *Lat* 48 (1982) 41–69. **Gibson, J. C. L.** "Some Observations on Some Important Ethnic Terms in the Pentateuch." *JNES* 20 (1961) 217–38. **Hill, R.** "Aetheria XII 9 and the Site of Biblical Edrei." *VT* 16 (1966) 412–19. *HOTTP* I, 268–69. **Hurd, H. P.** *A Forgotten Ammonite War.* Newark, NJ: Hurd, 1967. **Köppel, U.** *Das deuteronomistische Geschichtswerk* (1979). **Labuschagne, C.** "On the Structural Use of Numbers as a Composition Technique." *JNSL* 12 (1984) 87–99. **Langlamet, F.** "Gilgal et les récits de la traversée du Jourdain (Jos III–IV)." CahRB 11. Paris, 1969. 72–83. **Lohfink, N.** "Textkritisches zu *jrš* im Alten Testament." In *FS D. Barthélemy* (1981). 273–88. **Millard, A. R.** "King Og's Bed and Other Ancient Ironmongery." In *FS P. C. Craigie* (1988). 481–92. —————. "King Og's Iron Bed—Fact or Fancy?" *BRev* 6,2 (April 1990) 16–21, 44. **Noth, M.** "Nu 21 als Glied der 'Hexateuch'-Erzählung." *ZAW* 58 (1940/41) 161–89 [=*AbLA* I, 75–101. —————. *The Deuteronomistic History* (1981). 31–33. **Ottosson, M.** *Gilead: Tradition and History.* ConB 3. Lund: Gleerup, 1969. **Pohl, A.** "Mons Hermon quem Sidonii Sarion vocant (Dt 3,9)." *VD* 21 (1941) 190. **Rabin, C.** "Og." *EI* 8 (1967) 251–54. **Stoebe, H. J.** "Raub und Beute." In *FS W. Baumgartner* (1967). 340–54. **Sumner, W. A.** "Israel's Encounters with Edom, Moab, Ammon, Sihon and Og according to the Deuteronomist." *VT* 18 (1968) 216–28. **Seters, J. Van** "The Conquest of Sihon's Kingdom: A Literary Examination." *JBL* 91 (1972) 182–97. —————. "Once again—the Conquest of Sihon's Kingdom." *JBL* 99 (1980) 117–24. **Ullendorff, E.** "The Knowledge of Languages in the Old Testament." *BJRL* 44 (1961/62) 455–65. **Wagner, M.** "Beiträge zur Aramaismenfrage im alttestamentlichen Hebräisch." In *FS W. Baumgartner* (1967). 355–71. **Weippert, M.** "The Israelite 'Conquest' and the Evidence from Transjordan." In *Symposia Celebrating the Seventy-fifth Anniversary of the Founding of the American Schools of Oriental Research (1900–1975).* Ed. F. M. Cross. Cambridge, MA: ASOR, 1979. 15–34. **Wilcoxen, J. A.** "Narrative Structure and Cult Legend: A Study of Joshua 1–6." In *Transitions in Biblical Scholarship.* Ed. J. C. Rylaarsdam. Chicago: Univ. of Chicago Press, 1958. 43–70. **Wilson, R. R.** "The Hardening of Pharaoh's Heart." *CBQ* 41 (1979) 18–36. **Wiseman, D. J.** "'Is It Peace?'—Covenant and Diplomacy." *VT* 32 (1982) 311–26. **Zenger, E.** "Tradition und Interpretation in Exodus xv 1–21." In *VTSup* 32. Leiden: Brill, 1981. 475.

## Translation and Prosodic Analysis

2:26–3:1   [5:(6+5):8:5] [5:7] [6:4] [4:6:7:5:5:8] [(6+5):5]
3:2–11    [7:6] [5:4:8:6:5:5] [6:8:4:5] [6:7]

26 *And I sent messengers* / *from the wilderness of Kedemoth* /    17   2
*To Sihon* / *king of Heshbon* // *words* (דברי) *of peace* /    17   3_
*Saying* // 27 *"Let me pass through your land* /    11   2
*only by the road* ª/ *will I go* //    10   2
*I will not turn aside* / *to the left or to the right* //    15   2_
28 *Food for money you shall sell me* / *and I shall eat* /    19   2
*And water* / *for money you shall give to me* /    11   2
*and I shall drink* //    7   1_
*Only* \ª *let me pass through on foot* //    8   1
29    *just as they did to me* /    9   1
*The children of Esau* / *the ones dwelling* / *in Seir* /    18   3
*And the Moabites* / *the ones dwelling* / *in Ar* //    17   3_
*Until I have crossed over* / *the Jordan* / *to the land* /    12+6   3
*Which YHWH* **our God** / *is giving to us"* //    12+7   2_
30 **And he was not willing** / **Sihon** / **king of Heshbon** /    16   3
**(to let) us pass through** / **it** //    10   2_
*For YHWH your*ª *God hardened* / *his spirit* /    18   2
*And he made obstinate* / *his heart* /    10   2
*in order* / *to give him into your hand<s>* ᵇ/    11   2
*as*ᶜ *AT THIS DAY* // ס    5   1_
31 *And YHWH said* / *unto me* / *"See!* / *I have begun* /    19   4
*to give over to you* / *Sihon* /    12   2_
*<king of Heshbon the Amorite>*ª *and his land* //    17   1
*begin to take* / *possession* / *of his land"* //    14   3_
32 *And Sihon came forth* **against us** /    16   1
**He and all his people** / **to battle** / **at Jahaz** //    16   3_
33 **And YHWH our God** / **delivered him** /    17   2
**over to us** //    7   1
34 **And we smote him** / **and his sons**ª / **and all his people** //    18   3_
**And we captured all his cities** / **at that time** /    17   2
**and we devoted to destruction** /    5   1
**All <his>**ª **cities** |ª**men** / **and**ᵇ **women** / **and children** //    17   4_
**We did not leave** \ᶜ **a survivor** // 35**Only the cattle** /    17   2
**we took spoil for ourselves** /    9   1
**Yea, the booty of the cities** / **which we captured** //    17   2_
36 **From Aroer** / **which is on the edge of the Arnon Valley** /    17   2
**Yea, the city which** |ª **is in the valley** /    10   2
**indeed as far as Gilead** /    6   1_
**There was not** / **a town** /    10   2
**which was not inaccessibly high** / **for us** //    11   2
**the whole of it** /    4   1
**YHWH our God** / **gave** / **over to us**ᵇ //    20   3_

37 *Only* / *unto the land of the children of Ammon* /    10   2
*you*ª *did not draw near* //    7   1
*(To) both bank(s)* / *of the*ᵇ *Jabbok Valley* /    7   2
*and the cities of the* ᵇ *hill country* /    9   1_

| | | |
|---|---|---|
| *<According to>* c *all that he commanded* d / *YHWH our God* // | ⌐ 18 | 2 |
| 3:1    we turned and we went up / by way of / the Bashan // | └ 14 | 3_ |
| And Og king of the Bashan came forth against us / | 21 | 1 |
| He and all his people / <with him> a ǀa to battle / at Edrei // | 21 | 4_ |

| | | |
|---|---|---|
| 2 *And YHWH said* ǀa *to me* / *"Do not fear him!* / | ⌐ 19 | 3 |
| *For into your hand* b / *I have given him* / *and all his people* / | └ 20 | 3 |
| *and his land* / | 5 | 1_ |
| *And you shall do to him* / *just as you did* / *to Sihon* / | ⌐ 21 | 3 |
| *king of the Amorites* / *who rules* / *in Heshbon"* // | └ 19 | 3_ |

| | | |
|---|---|---|
| 3 And YHWH our God gave / into our hand a / | ⌐ 20 | 2 |
| also / Og king of the Bashan / and all his people // | └ 17 | 3_ |
| We smote him b / until there were no \c survivors // | ⌐ 19 | 2 |
| 4    and we captured all his cities / AT THAT TIME / | └ 17 | 2_ |
| There was not / a town / which we did not take / from them // | 24 | 4 |
| Sixty cities / the whole region a of <the> a Argob / | ⌐ 14 | 2 |
| the kingdom of Og / in the Bashan // | └ 10 | 2_ |
| 5 All [these] a \a <the> fortified cities b / (with) high walls / | 19 | 2 |
| (with) gates and bars // | 11 | 1 |
| Besides / the unwalled cities / very many // | 20 | 3_ |
| 6 And we devoted them to destruction / just as we did / | 18 | 2 |
| To Sihon \a king of Heshbon // | ⌐ 10 | 1 |
| devoting to destruction / every inhabited city / | └ 9 | 2_ |
| <Yea>, b the women / and children // 7and all the cattle / | 17 | 3 |
| And the spoil of the cities / | ⌐ 9 | 1 |
| we took as booty a for ourselves // b | └ 9 | 1_ |

| | | |
|---|---|---|
| 8 And we took / AT THAT TIME / the land / | 16 | 3 |
| From the hand / of the two / kings of the Amorites / | 15 | 3_ |
| Who \a were beyond the Jordan // | 10 | 1 |
| From the Arnon Valley / as far as b Mount Hermon // | 11 | 2 |
| 9 The Sidonians / they call Hermon \a Sirion // | 17 | 2 |
| And the Amorites / they call it / Senir // | 17 | 3_ |
| 10 (We took) all / the cities of the tableland / | ⌐ 11 | 2 |
| and all Gilead / and all the Bashan / | └ 13 | 2_ |
| As far as Salecah / and Edrei // | ⌐ 10 | 2 |
| cities / of the kingdom of Og / in the Bashan // | └ 14 | 3_ |

| | | |
|---|---|---|
| 11 For only Og / king of Bashan / | 12 | 2 |
| was left / of the remnant of the Rephaim / | 12 | 2 |
| <And> a behold his bedstead (is) / a bedstead b of iron / | 11 | 2_ |
| Is it not c / in Rabbah / of the Ammonites? // | 14 | 3 |
| nine cubits (is) its height / | 9 | 1 |
| And four cubits / its breadth / | ⌐ 9 | 2 |
| according to the cubit of a man // | └ 5 | 1_ |

## Notes

27.a. The second בדרך is frequently omitted with LXX or emended to הַמֶּלֶךְ, "the king's high-way." Prosodic analysis supports MT. On the use of repetition to express an exceptional aspect, or to intensify the expression in the highest degree, see GKC § 123e.

28.a. See note 1:1.c..

30.a. LXX reads 2nd pl and Syr 1st pl. The change to 1st c pl forms at the end of v 29 and back to 2nd m sg forms in the middle of v 30 marks a rhythmic boundary.

30.b. Reading the du form ביד<'> with LXX and Vg.

30.c. Some LXX witnesses read ἐν τῇ ἡμέρᾳ = ביום.

31.a. Adding with SP and LXX to achieve closer prosodic balance.

33.a. Reading the pl form בניו with Qere and numerous witnesses.

34.a. Reading עריו with SP and replacing *mûnaḥ* with a disj accent to achieve closer rhythmic balance over against v 31.

34.b. Some Heb. Mss, SP, and Syr omit *waw*-conj, which is possible from a prosodic point of view.

34.c. See note 1:1.c.

36.a. The combination of *'azlā'* followed by *mahpāk* is here taken as disj to achieve closer rhythmic balance over against v 30.

36.b. SP and LXX read ביד(י)נו, which may be interpretive.

37.a. LXX, Syr, and Vg read 1 pl. The change here, and the reverse change in v 32 above, is probably to be taken as a further instance of the *Numeruswechsel*, which once again marks significant rhythmic boundaries. In the case of v 32, that boundary is also the precise center of the larger structure, which extends from 2:26 through 3:1.

37.b. SP adds the def art. Prosodic analysis supports MT.

37.c. Reading ככל with LXX and Tg. From a prosodic perspective the chapter division is incorrect.

37.d. Sp, Syr, Vg, and most LXX witnesses add 1 c pl suff here. The change back to 1 c pl forms at the end of the verse marks a major rhythmic boundary.

3:1.a. Adding עמו with LXX (μετ' αὐτοῦ) and an additional disj accent, to achieve closer balance in mora-count and rhythmic structure.

2.a. Reading the sequence of the accents *'azlā'* followed by *mahpāk* as disj (see 2.36.a. above).

2.b. Reading du בידיך with LXX, and Syr.

3.a. Reading du בידינו with several Heb. Mss, Cairo geniza fragments, LXX, and Vg.

3.b. SP reads ונכנו.

3.c. See note 1:1.c.

4.a. Reading חֶבֶל <הָ>ארגב with some Heb. Mss, to achieve closer balance in mora-count.

5.a. Omitting אלה with one Heb. Ms, LXX, and Vg. The omission necessitates the removal of the disj accent *gereš*.

5.b. Reading הערים with some Heb. Mss and Syr^Mss.

6.a. See note 1:1.c.

6.b. Adding the conj *waw*, read emphatically, with a few Heb. Mss, Cairo geniza fragments, and Tg^J.

7.a. SP reads בזזנו; cf. 2:35.

7.b. *BHS* and *BHK* both leave a space between vv 7 and 8.

8.a. See note 1:1.c.

8.b. A few Heb. Mss, SP, LXX, and Syr read ועד. Prosodic analysis supports MT.

9.a. See note 1:1.c.

11.a. Adding the *waw*-conj with a few Heb. Mss.

11.b. The translation "bedstead" is probably a euphemism for sarcophagus, a place of permanent sleep (cf. the term "slumber room" in the modern funeral business).

11.c. Reading הֲלֹא with numerous Heb. Mss, Cairo geniza fragments, SP, and Tg (cf. LXX, Syr, and Tg^J).

## Form/Structure/Setting

Yahweh's "Holy War," as celebrated event in ancient Israel, had two foci: the Exodus under Moses and the Eisodus under Joshua. Around these two major themes, the first two parts of the canon of the Hebrew Bible eventually took shape; namely, the Pentateuch and the Former Prophets (see D. Christensen, "The Center of the First Testament within the Canonical Process," BTB [forthcoming]). It should be noted that it is not correct to limit discussion of the "Conquest of Canaan" to Joshua and his successors, through the establishment of the Davidic empire, as a growing number of recent historians do. According to the biblical story, Moses not only brought the people out of Egypt, he led the conquest of Transjordan. It is this first phase of Yahweh's "Holy War" which is in focus here, namely, the defeat of the two Amorite kings, Sihon and Og, which sets the stage for the death of Moses and the transfer of leadership to Joshua, who led the conquest of Cisjordan. Though Joshua appears in both parts of the Outer Frame of Deuteronomy (chaps. 1, 3, 31, and 34), he is a subordinate figure in Deuteronomy and assumes leadership in the midst of Yahweh's "Holy War."

The rhythmic unit in 2:26–3:11 is in two parts, which are framed by anecdotes about Sihon (2:26–30) and Og (3:11). The central part of this structure presents the battles in Transjordan: the conquest of Heshbon (2:31–36) and the conquest of Bashan (2:37–3:1). The larger structure of the passage as a whole may be outlined as follows:

| | | |
|---|---|---|
| A | Anecdote about Sihon, king of Heshbon (vv 26–31) | |
| | Moses requests safe conduct from Sihon (vv 26–29). | [5:(6+5):8:5] |
| | Sihon refuses Israel's request (v 30) | [5:7] |
| | Summons to possess Sihon's land (v 31). | [6:4] |
| B | The Conquest of Heshbon AT THAT TIME (vv 32–36) | [4:6:7:5:5:8] |
| C | Travel Notice: We went up to Bashan (2:37–3:1) | [(6+5):5] |
| C' | Summons Not to Fear Og, king of Bashan (v 2) | [7:6] |
| B' | The Conquest of Bashan AT THAT TIME (vv 3–7) | [(5:4):8:6:5:5] |
| A' | Anecdote about Og, king of Bashan (vv 8–11) | |
| | Conquest of Transjordan AT THAT TIME (vv 8–10) | [6:8:(4:5)] |
| | Og was the Last of the Rephaim (v 11) | [6:7] |

The subunits in this concentric structure are, for the most part, carefully marked by a complex system of rhetorical features. Moreover, from a rhythmic point of view, each half of this larger structure is in turn arranged concentrically. The structure of 2:26–3:1 may be outlined as follows:

| | | |
|---|---|---|
| A | The request to pass through Sihon's kingdom (2:26–29) | [5:11:8:5] |
| B | Sihon's refusal (2:30) | [5:7] |
| C | Yahweh's conquest of Sihon, king of Heshbon (2:31–33) | [6:4:4:6] |
| B' | Sihon's kingdom despoiled (2:34) | [7:5] |
| A' | From the Arnon Valley to the Bashan (2:37–3:1) | [5:8:11:5] |

The structure of this section focuses on the conquest of Sihon's kingdom, from the Arnon to the Jabbok, which is presented as Yahweh's war of conquest. In the center of this unit (2:31–33), it is clearly Yahweh who both promised victory (v 31) and "delivered" on that promise (v 32), in the defeat of Sihon.

The second half (3:2–11) has a somewhat similar structure, which may be outlined as follows:

| A | Summons not to fear Og, king of Bashan (3:2) | [7:6] |
|---|---|---|
| B | Yahweh's conquest of Bashan AT THAT TIME (3:3–5) | [9:8:6] |
| C | Og's kingdom devoted to destruction (3:6–7) | [5:5] |
| B' | Conquest of the whole of Transjordan AT THAT TIME (3:8–10) | [6:8:9] |
| A' | Og was the last of the Rephaim (3:11) | [6:7] |

Once again the structure focuses on Yahweh's "Holy War," this time on the חרם, "devotion to destruction" as applied to Og and his kingdom. The conquest of Bashan (3:3–5) is set over against the summary of the conquest of Transjordan as a whole (3:8–10), "from the Arnon Valley as far as Mount Hermon . . . all Gilead and all the Bashan." The Outer Frame of this unit focuses on the person of Og, who was not to be feared (3:2), even though he was the last of the "giants" of yore (3:11). This was Yahweh's "Holy War," and all Israel, past and future, would share the experience of participation in it.

*Comment*

**26–29** In the previous rhythmic unit (2:24–25) the speaker was Yahweh, quoted by Moses. Here the speaker is Moses himself who *sent messengers from the wilderness of Kedemoth to Sihon king of Heshbon* (v 26) requesting permission to purchase provisions for a journey through his land (vv 28–29). The unit is separated from what follows by the sudden shift from 1st c sg forms to 1 c pl at the end of v 29.

The capital of Sihon's kingdom was Heshbon (modern *Tell Ḥesbân*), which guards the northern edge of the Moabite plain about fifteen miles east of where the Jordan River enters the Dead Sea. The kingdom extended from the Arnon Valley in the south to the Jabbok Valley in the north, with the Jordan River and the Dead Sea as its western border. Some of this territory was taken from the Moabites in an event celebrated in the "Song of Heshbon" (Num 21:27–30). In the story of Jephthah, this land was claimed by the king of the Ammonites (Judg 11:13). Jephthah's response (Judg 11:15–23) confirms the summary of events recounted here in Deuteronomy. According to Aharoni (*The Land of the Bible* [1967] 86, map 14), the wilderness of Kedemoth was located a few miles inside Sihon's territory, north of the Arnon, near the border of the Ammonite kingdom to the east of the Amorite state.

It would appear that Sihon's kingdom was not part of the promised land, at least as Moses envisioned it. Up to this point the Israelites had passed peacefully through Edom and Moab, though the account in Numbers makes it clear that their journey was not without incident.

**30** It was Sihon's refusal that led to war and the possession of his land by the Israelites. The continued use of the 1st c pl verbal form marks the initial boundary of this brief rhythmic unit, which ends with the liturgical phrase *at this day* and the *setûmā'* paragraph marker of the Masoretic tradition. The statement that Yahweh *hardened [Sihon's] spirit and made obstinate his heart* is "Holy War" language, to be compared with the hardening of Pharaoh's heart in the book of Exodus. This was Yahweh's war. Though human beings are free and responsible for their actions, all human response is subject to the larger domain of God's activity in history.

**31** On the use of ראה, "see," as a rhetorical device within the Outer Frame of Deuteronomy, see the *Comment* on 1:8–10. The verbal root חלל, "begin," is used as a frame in the quotation of Yahweh's words here. Since Yahweh has begun (הַחִלֹּתִי) to give Sihon into their hands, the Israelites are to begin (הָחֵל) to possess his land.

**32–36** The resumption of 1st c pl forms marks the beginning of a new rhythmic unit in which Moses is speaking. The battle against Sihon took place at יַהְצָה, "Jahaz," the precise location of which is not certain though it was in the southeastern part of the Amorite state, which was given to the tribe of Reuben by Moses. According to Mesha, on the so-called Moabite Stone (lines 18–21), the king of Israel fought against Moab at Jahaz. At that time the city passed into Moabite hands (cf. Isa 15:4 and Jer 48:21, 34, where it is referred to as a city of Moab).

Once again the language which recounts the battle (vv 33–36) is that of "Holy War." It begins and ends with reference to that fact: Yahweh *delivered him over to us* (v 33); *and Yahweh gave [him] over to us* (v 36). Within this frame, it is the people of Israel who *smote him and his sons and all his people* (v 33); and who *captured all his cities at that time* (v 34). The cities with all their inhabitants were *devoted to destruction* (חרם), a practice which is referred to on the Moabite Stone (line 17) as well as here and elsewhere within the Hebrew Bible. For further discussion of this practice see the *Comment* on Deut 20:10–18, in the laws on warfare (in vol 6B).

At this point the conquest extended *from Aroer which is on the edge of the Arnon Valley . . . as far as Gilead* (v 36). The unnamed *city which is in the [Arnon] Valley* may have been a suburb, or perhaps even part of the city of Aroer, as suggested by the poetic parallelism here. Gilead is located north of Sihon's territory. The fact that none of the towns were *inaccessibly high for us* (v 36) is to be contrasted with the response of the rebellious generation at Kadesh-barnea to the report of the spies who described the cities of Canaan as "fortified to the heavens" (1:28). In fear the people refused to obey Yahweh at Kadesh-barnea, but this time they were obedient and consequently victorious.

**2:37–3:1** The theme of obedience is expanded here with a note that Israel did not carry the battle into the land of the Ammonites in the upper reaches of the Jabbok Valley (2:37). The Travel Notice here (see *Excursus:* "Travel Notices") marks the conclusion of the first half of Yahweh's "Holy War" under Moses against the Amorites and sets the stage for the battle at Edrei against Og, king of the Bashan. Though the borders of Bashan are not precisely defined in the Hebrew Bible, it included the Golan Heights east of the Sea of Galilee on the border of modern Israel and Syria, and extended south beyond the river Yarmuk, which enters the Jordan just south of the Sea of Galilee. The region of Gilead, to the south of the Bashan, includes both sides of the river Jabbok. Gilead and the Bashan are closely associated in most historical periods and are noted for their fertility as the "breadbasket" of Transjordan.

**3:2** The second part of the presentation of Yahweh's "Holy War" in 3:2–11 begins with a summons not to fear Og. Though the conquest of the Bashan took Israel a bit off their route, so far as their subsequent battle camp at Gilgal is concerned, the campaign was wise from a military point of view. G. A. Smith has noted that the Roman general Pompey used much the same tactic, as did the first Muslim invaders, to secure their flank before crossing over into Cisjordan.

**3–5** The return to 1st c pl forms marks the boundary of a new rhythmic unit in which, once more, the language of "Holy War" is dominant. It is *Yahweh our God who gave [him] into our hands* (v 3). Though the verbal root חרם is not used here, the description of total destruction is similar to that of the parallel conquest of

Sihon's kingdom in 2:33–36. Israel left no survivors as they destroyed *sixty cities, the whole region of the Argob, the kingdom of Og in the Bashan* (v 4). The term אַרְגֹּב(ה), "[the] Argob," appears to be used here in poetic parallelism to הַבָּשָׁן, "the Bashan," perhaps as the term עַר is used earlier with respect to Moab (cf. the discussion of W. LaSor in *ISBE* 1:288–89). The term אַרְגֹּב(ה) appears only four times in the Hebrew Bible, each time preceded by the term חֶבֶל, "region." Some of the cities conquered were *fortified cities with high walls, gates, and bars*, while many others were apparently small agricultural villages (v 5).

**6–7** The language here is that of "Holy War" with repetition of the root חרם, "devoted to destruction." The prosodic analysis suggests that the phrase מְתִם (ו) הַנָּשִׁים וְהַטָּף may be a poetic expression with a rather different meaning from that assumed in most handbooks and translations. The *zāqēp parvum* over the term מְתִם is a strong disjunctive accent, so that the phrase is distributed between the two parallel rhythmic units. It is thus the male population who are slaughtered, with the women and children being treated like the cattle, as *the spoil of the cities.*

**8–10** Though this unit continues the use of 1st c pl forms, it is not clear at what point this rhetorical feature actually ends. The summary statement of the conquest of Transjordan in v 8 concludes with a reference to Mount Herman, part of the Anti-Lebanon mountain range, which, at its highest point reaches an altitude of more than 9000 feet. The well-known site prompts an explanatory note in the form of a carefully balanced bicolon (v 9). The Phoenicians to the north called the mountain שִׂרְין, "Sirion," whereas the Amorites called it שְׂנִיר, "Senir." The note is a parenthesis, with v 10 picking up where v 8 left off.

שִׂרְין, "Sirion," is now known from the Ugaritic texts (see *CTA* 4.VI.19,21 (=*UT* 51. VI. 19, 21; cf. C. Gordon, *UT* [1965] 495).

שְׂנִיר, "Senir," is found in an Assyrian historical account from the time of Shalmaneser (cf. I. M. Price, *The Monuments and the Old Testament* (1909) 154.

סַלְכָה, "Salecah," has been identified with Salkhad, a citadel in Jebel ed-Druze (the mountain of Bashan). Craigie has noted a later Nabatean reference to Ṣalhad on the southern heights of Mount Hauran (NICOT [1976] 120).

אֶדְרֶעִי, "Edrei," has been located on one of the eastern tributaries of the river Yarmuk, north of Ramoth-gilead and slightly south of the Sea of Galilee, with Salecah still further to the east.

**11** This section concludes with an anecdote about Og as the last *of the remnant of the Rephaim,* whose עֶרֶשׂ, "bedstead" in Rabbah, capital of the Ammonite kingdom, remained a tourist attraction of note. The term may be translated "sarcophagus" with Craigie and others. On the other hand, the dimensions (13.5 x 6 feet [4.1 x 1.8 m.]), along with the term בַּרְזֶל, "iron," have thrown this interpretation in doubt for some scholars (cf. Boling's translation, "iron bedframe," in *The Early Biblical Community in Transjordan* [1988] 43; A. R. Millard, "King Og's Bed and Other Ancient Ironmongery," in *FS P. C. Craigie* [1988] 481–92; and *Bible Review* [April 1990] 16–21). My own experience with the basalt sarcophagus in the great pyramid of Cheops at Giza lends support to interpreting the term as sarcophagus. When struck with a sharp object such basalt structures ring out with a metallic sound, which explains the reference to iron (in sound rather than substance).

רַבַּת בְּנֵי עַמּוֹן, "Rabbah of the Ammonites," is modern Amman in Jordan.

## Explanation

Much has been said about the inadequacy of the ancient Hebrew reflection on the relationship between human freedom and divine sovereignty. If God is responsible for "hardening Sihon's [and Og's] spirit" and "making obstinate his heart," how can Sihon (or Og) be held accountable for his actions? One way to cope with this problem is to insist, with Craigie (NICOT [1976] 116), that human beings "are free and responsible in action, but the(ir) actions. . . are set within the sphere of history, and God (is) the Lord of history." On a rational level this position is no doubt correct, at least in principle, but it fails to recognize the profound depth of intuitive understanding the ancient Hebrews knew.

One of the primary lessons in the first half of the book of Jonah is the simple fact that human freedom is not what it appears to be. Jonah thought he was free to "flee from the presence of Yahweh" (Jonah 1:3), and in one sense he achieved that goal, when he took the great plunge into the depths, away "from [God's] presence" (Jonah 2:4). But the moment he "went down" to the depths of the nether world, whom did he meet? It was Yahweh himself who brought him up out of the Pit alive (Jonah 2:6). He was not really free to disobey Yahweh, as he thought he was. Like the proverbial "hound of heaven," Yahweh continued in his pursuit until Jonah eventually was brought to inner awareness of that Presence. As I have argued elsewhere, "the story of Jonah [is] a powerful metaphor for the exodus story, which in turn is a metaphor for the life journey of an individual today" (see *Experiencing the Exodus* [1988] 32).

There are profound limits to the freedom of human beings to do what they choose to do. In pathological instances, like that of the "Son of Sam" murders, we are reminded of this fact. When the killer said, "The Devil made me do it," he was speaking the truth, so far as he knew it. There are often internal forces, or what some would call "complexes" which do more to shape our responses and actions than most of us realize. We are seldom truly free to do or to be what we choose. Paul spoke of these inner forces when he said "that when I want to do right, evil lies close at hand. For I delight in the law of God, in my inmost self, but I see in my members another law at war with the law of my mind and making me captive to the law of sin which dwells in my members" (Rom 7:21–23).

God works in history, but he also works in and through the unconscious mind—what the ancient Hebrews called the "heart." When the text insists that Yahweh "hardened [Sihon's] spirit" and "made obstinate his heart" (2:30), the author is describing profound spiritual truth. Like the pharaoh of the Exodus from Egypt, Sihon was not free to act on simple logic so as to do what was in his own best interests. Instead he impulsively, with reckless abandon, acted in a manner that was certain to further his own demise. If we have eyes to see, most of us would see ourselves in the person of Sihon. All too often we are our own worst enemies, because we are not in fact free to act on our conscious desires.

The ancient Greeks explored this phenomenon in depth within their literature and mythology. For example, Oedipus was not free to choose not to kill his own mother as the gods had foretold. The forces of "history" worked relentlessly to bring about what had been determined to be his destiny. Is the case any different with Sihon? Or with any of us who glory in our apparent freedom? We are never truly free until our conscious minds are brought into alignment with our "hearts" (the unconscious mind), where God is to be found. Like the little train, of children's literature, who wanted so much to be free that it "jumped the tracks" to achieve that freedom, our pursuit of freedom is often self-destructive.

# Distribution of the Land in Transjordan (3:12–17)

## Bibliography

**Cazelles, H.** "Argob biblique, Ugarit et les mouvements hurrites." In *FS G. Rinaldi* (1967) 21–27. **Childs, B. S.** "A Study of the Formula 'Until this Day'." *JBL* 82 (1963) 279–92. **Cross, F. M.** "Reuben, First-Born of Jacob." *ZAW* 100 (1988) 46–65. **Curtis, J. B.** "Some Suggestions Concerning the History of the Tribe of Reuben." *JBR* 33 (1965) 247–49. Driver, G. R. "Mistranslations." *PEQ* 80 (1948) 64–65. **Halévy, J.** "Recherches bibliques: le Deutéronome." *RSEHA* 7 (1899) 323. *HOTTP* I, 270–71. **Labuschagne, C.** "On the Structural Use of Numbers as a Composition Technique." *JNSL* 12 (1984) 87–99. **Lohfink, N.** "ירשׁ." *TWAT* 3. Stuttgart, 1982. 953–85. **Mazar, B.** "Geshur and Maacah." *JBL* 80 (1961) 16–28. **Simons, J.** "Two Connected Problems Relating to the Israelite Settlements. I. The Meaning מִן + a Proper Name in Dt III 16 and Some Other Geographical Texts." II. 'From Arnon unto Yabboq.'" *PEQ* 79 (1947) 27–39, 87–102 [and G. R. Driver's response in 80 (1948) 64–65].

## Translation and Prosodic Analysis

3:12–17   [6:6:5] [5:5] [5:6:6]

| | | |
|---|---:|---:|
| [12] And this (is) the land / we possessed / AT THAT TIME // | 2 | 3 |
| From Aroer / which is <on the edge of>[a] the Arnon Valley / | 17 | 2 |
| yea,[b] half the hill country of Gilead / | 9 | 1_ |
| and its cities / I gave / | 10 | 2 |
| to the Reubenites \[c] and to the Gadites // | 14 | 1 |
| [13] And the rest of Gilead and all of the Bashan / | 14 | 1 |
| the kingdom of Og / I gave / | 10 | 2_ |
| To the half \[a] tribe of Manasseh // | 12 | 2 |
| all the region of the Argob[b] / | 9 | 1 |
| Yea, [c]all of the Bashan / | 7 | 1 |
| that is called / the land of the Rephaim // | 15 | 2_ |
| [14] Jair[a] son of Manasseh / took / all the region of Argob[b] / | 18 | 3 |
| As far as the border of the Geshurites / | 10 | 1 |
| and the Maacathites // | 8 | 1_ |
| And he called them after his own name (that is) Bashan / | 18 | 1 |
| (is called) Havvoth-Jair / | 7 | 1 |
| to this day// | 7 | 1 |
| [15] Yea, to Machir / I gave the Gilead // | 17 | 2_ |
| [16] And to the Reubenites and to the Gadites / | 16 | 1 |
| I gave (the territory) from Gilead / | 10 | 1 |
| [Yea][a] as far as the Arnon Valley / | 7 | 1 |
| (with) the middle of the valley / indeed[b] as border // | 10 | 2_ |
| And as far as[a] / (the)[c] Jabbok Valley / | 8 | 2 |
| border / of the Ammonites // | 9 | 2 |
| [17] And the Arabah / and the Jordan indeed[a] as border // | 18 | 2_ |

| | | |
|---|---|---|
| **From Chinnereth / yea, as far as the sea of the Arabah /** | 15 | 2 |
| **the Salt Sea /** | 5 | 1 |
| **beneath / the slopes of the Pisgah / on the east //** | 14 | 3 |

## Notes

12.a. Adding שָׂפַת, "edge, bank," with some Heb. Mss and the versions, as in 2:36 and 4:48. Aroer was apparently situated on the northern rim of the "Grand Canyon" of the Arnon.

12.b. The *waw*-conj is read as emphatic because of its position at the end of a rhythmic subunit.

12.c. See note 1:1.c.

13.a. See note 1:1.c.

13.b. Both here and in the parallel passages (3:4, 14) variant texts provide for alternate possibilities in pointing and use of the definite article. The prosodic analysis supports MT in both cases.

13.c. See note 12.b. above.

14.a. LXX, SP, and Syr add *waw*-conj.

14.b. See note 13.b. above.

16.a. The *waw*-conj is omitted in the first instance with some Heb. Mss and LXX.

16.b. The *waw* is read as emphatic.

16.c. The def art appears in some Mss of Syr (cf. 2:37).

17.a.. The *waw* is read as emphatic

## Form/Structure/Setting

In the larger structure of the first half of the Outer Frame in Deuteronomy (chaps. 1–3), this brief section (3:12–17) stands over against 1:9–18, where Moses organized the judicial (and military) aspects of life in ancient Israel. In that earlier setting political power was dispersed among selected leaders of the people, in anticipation of the actual possession of the promised land. Here the focus is on the allotment of land to the tribal groups, following the initial phase of Yahweh's war of conquest. From a prosodic point of view the section is arranged in simple chiastic fashion as follows:

| | | |
|---|---|---|
| A | Distribution of land to Reuben, Gad, and Manasseh (vv 12–13) | [6:6:5] |
| B | Jair's possession of the Argob in Bashan (v 14) | |
| B' | Machir's possession of Gilead (v 15) | [5:5] |
| A' | Distribution of land to Reuben and Gad (vv 16–17) | [5:6:6] |

## Comment

**12–13** The land taken from Sihon, from the Arnon Valley to the hill country of Gilead, was given to the tribes of Reuben and Gad, whereas the land taken from Og in Bashan was given to the half-tribe of Manasseh. On the Rephaim see the *Comment* at 2:10–12.

**14–15** The allotment to the half-tribe of Manasseh in Bashan is given in detail, namely the region of the Argob (see the *Comment* at 3:3–5), which was taken by Jair, a son of Manasseh. The borders of this region extend northward to Maacah and westward to Geshur. Maacah was a small kingdom in the Golan Heights, south of Mount Herman, north of Gilead, and west of Bashan. The kingdom of Geshur adjoined it to the south, on the eastern shore of Chinnereth (Sea of Galilee). Jair was responsible for capturing the villages of the region (Num 32:41), which he named after himself. Though Machir is listed as another son of Manasseh who was responsible for dispossessing the Amorites in Gilead (Num 32:39–40), the term appears to be used here as a synonym for Manasseh.

**16–17** These verses are set over against 3:12–13a, marking out the boundaries of the territory given to Reuben and Gad more explicitly, from the Arnon in the south to the Jabbok in the north, and from the border with the Ammonites in the east to the Jordan and the Dead Sea in the west.

הערבה, "the Arabah" (the Jordan rift valley), here defines the western border of the territory taken by the two and one-half tribes in Transjordan, which sets off their land from that of their "brothers" in Cisjordan.

ים המלח, "the Salt Sea," is, of course, the Dead Sea, which lies beneath the slopes of הפסגה, "the Pisgah." D. Baly understood the latter term to be similar to the modern Arab. *neqb*, meaning the high precipitous slope which marks the edge of a plateau (*Geographical Companion to the Bible*. [New York: McGraw-Hill, 1963]. 53–54). Others have identified Pisgah with the mountain range of which Mount Nebo was the summit (J. Gray, *Joshua, Judges and Ruth*. CBC [1967] 125; K. Elliger, *BHH*, col. 1475). If it is to be identified with a specific peak, *Jebel Siâghah*, slightly lower and to the northwest of Mount Nebo, is perhaps the best candidate. See the *Comment* on 34:1.

### Explanation

Though the Hebrew root ירשׁ carries the meaning of possession by dispossession, those two aspects are in tension. The land of the two Amorite kings was taken by force in an act of conquest. But for that same land to be incorporated into the emerging political state of ancient Israel, something more was required.

Jair and Machir took the initiative in the violence of dispossessing the Amorites of Bashan and Gilead. For their obedience they were awarded the opportunity to integrate that land into the larger promised land of Israel as a whole, along with the tribes of Reuben and Gad. But first they must cross over the Jordan with their brothers to complete the conquest on the other side in Cisjordan.

# Summons to Take the Promised Land (3:18–22)

### Bibliography

**Braulik, G.** "Zur deuteronomistischen Konzeption von Freiheit und Frieden." In VTSup 36. Leiden: Brill, 1985. 29–39. **Halévy, J.** "Recherches bibliques: le Deutéronome." *RSEHA* 7 (1899) 323–25. **Lohfink, N.** "Zum 'Numeruswechsel' in Dtn 3,21f." *BN* 49 (1989) 39–52. **Roth, W.** "The Deuteronomic Rest Theology: A Redactional Critical Study." *BibRes* 21 (1976) 5–14. **Schäfer-Lichtenberger, C.** "Joschua und Elischa. Ideal-Typen von Führerschaft in Israel." In *"Wünschet Jerusalem Frieden": Collected Communications to the XIIth Congress of the IOSOT, Jerusalem 1986.* Ed. M. Augustin and K.-D. Schunck. Frankfurt: Lang, 1988. **Seebass, W.** "Josua." *BN* 28 (1985) 53–65. **Ska, J.-L.** *Le passage de la mer.* Diss., Pontifical Biblical Institute, Rome, 1984. **Ziegler, J.** "Zur Septuaginta-Vorlage im Deuteronomium." *ZAW* 72 (1960) 255.

### Translation and Prosodic Analsysis

3:18–22   [6:4] [(5:4):(5:3:5)] [(4:5):(4:6)]

| | | |
|---|---|---|
| [18] And I commanded you / AT THAT TIME \a saying // | 18 | 2 |
| "YHWH (is) your God / | 9 | 1 |
| He has given to you / this land / to possess it / | 19 | 3_ |
| Equipped for war you shall pass over / | 9 | 1 |
| before \b your brothers Ib | 7 | 1 |
| The children of Israel / all the 'sons of valor' // | 15 | 2_ |
| | | |
| [19] Only \a your wives [and] b your little ones / | 8 | 1 |
| and your cattle / | 6 | 1 |
| I know / that you have / many cattle // | 13 | 3_ |
| They shall remain / in your cities / | 11 | 2 |
| Which I have given / to you // | 10 | 2_ |
| [20] Until / YHWH grants rest \a to your brothers / | 16 | 2 |
| as to you / | 3 | 1 |
| And they also shall possess / the land / | 15 | 2_ |
| Which [YHWH]b your God / is giving to themc / | 15 | 2 |
| in the vicinity of the Jordan // | 8 | 1 |
| And you shall return / each one / to his possession / | 12 | 3 |
| which I have given / to you // | 10 | 2_ |
| | | |
| [21] And Joshua I commanded / AT THAT TIME / | 20 | 2 |
| saying // *"Your eyes*a *are the ones seeing* / | 14 | 2 |
| *All*b Ib *the things which he has done* / *YHWH your God* / | 19 | 3 |
| *to these* / *two kings* / | 14 | 2_ |
| Thus will YHWHc do / to all the kingdoms / | 16 | 2 |
| to which *you*c / *are crossing over thither* // | 12 | 2_ |
| [22] You shall not / fear thema // for / YHWH (is) your God / | 19 | 4 |
| he / (is) the one fighting for you" // ᴐ | 9 | 2_ |

## Notes

18.a. See note 1:1.c.

18.b. This is one of the few places where the prosodic analysis necessitates relocating a disj accent to achieve poetic balance.

19.a. The *tᵉlîšāʾ magnum*, a relatively weak disj, has been changed to a conj accent to achieve closer balance with the corresponding element in v 21a.

19.b. The *waw*-conj is omitted with Heb. Ms[Ken 80.232] and SP.

20.a. The sequence of *mêrᵉkāʾ* plus *pāseq* is read as conj. The *pāseq* was apparently introduced into the Masoretic system at a later date than the original accentual system and is usually ignored in the prosodic analysis.

20.b. The Vg omits אלהיכם יהוה. The term YHWH is omitted to achieve balance in mora-count with the following colon.

20.c. More than fifty Heb. Mss, Vg, and the Seberin read לכם for להם.

21.a. The use of the 2nd m sg pronominal suffix is taken as an occurrence of the *Numeruswechsel* here, though 2nd pl, 1st pl, and 3rd pl variants appear with the several LXX traditions.

21.b. כל־אשר of MT is read כל אשר with the addition of a disj accent to achieve better balance in both mora-count and accentual stress units.

21.c. Some LXX witnesses apparently read יהוה אלהיכם.

22.a. A few Heb. Mss and SP read אם־ in place of אום־.

## Form/Structure/Setting

The summons to take the promised land in Cisjordan, presented here in 3:18–22, is balanced in the larger structure of the Outer Frame in Deuteronomy (chaps. 1–3) by the summons to enter the promised land, uttered by both Yahweh and Moses, in 1:6b–8. From the prosodic perspective the structure here is in the form of simple chiasm, which may be outlined as follows:

A   Moses summons all Israel to "holy war" AT THAT TIME (v 18)          [6:4]
  B   Only wives and children to remain in Transjordan (v 19)          [5:4]
  B'  When "Yahweh grants rest," the men will return (v 20)          [5:3:5]
A'  Moses commands Joshua AT THAT TIME not to fear (vv 21–22)   [(5:4):(4:6)]

In the "A" elements of this structure, Moses summons all Israel to battle, including the warriors of the transjordanian tribes, against the Canaanites in Cisjordan (v 18); and commands Joshua not to fear as he leads the people in battle (vv 21–22). This is "Holy War," for Yahweh is fighting for them. The two references to Yahweh as Divine Warrior frame the unit as a whole:

Yahweh is your God; he has given to you this land to possess it (v 18).
For Yahweh is your God; he is the one fighting for you (v 22).

Both the beginning and ending of this unit (3:18–22) are marked by the appearance of the *Numeruswechsel*. BHS has extra space before v 18 and the *sᵉtûmāʾ* paragraph marker after v 22.

The "B" elements in this structure focus on the wives and children of the transjordanian tribes, who are left behind (v 19), and the return of the transjordanian warriors, after "Yahweh grants rest to [their] brothers" in Cisjordan (v 20).

## Comment

**18**  The *Numeruswechsel*, in the form of a sudden shift to 2nd m pl forms, marks the beginning of a new rhythmic unit. The transjordanian tribes are commanded to participate in the conquest of Cisjordan: Your men *equipped for war . . . shall pass over before your brothers, the children of Israel.* In later periods the eastern tribes sometimes failed their brothers in times of war, as witnessed by the Song of Deborah (Judg 5:15–17) and the story of Jephthah (Judg 11).

**19–20** The rebellious generation at Kadesh-barnea had used their children as an excuse for their disobedience (Deut 1:39). Here the obedient generation is able to leave their families in security, as they cross over the Jordan to further battles. The parenthetical reference to their *many cattle* (v 19), refers to the spoil taken in the wars with Sihon and Og (2:35 and 3:7). The emphasis here is on the newly acquired wealth of the eastern tribes. At times the phrase בעבר הירדן, "in the vicinity of the Jordan," refers to Transjordan (see the *Comment* at 1:5). Here it clearly refers to Cisjordan from the perspective of someone in Transjordan (as it does also in 3:25 and 11:30).

**21–22** The repetition of the *Numeruswechsel* at the beginning and end of v 21 anticipates a major rhythmic boundary, which is also indicated by the *setûmāʾ* paragraph marker at the end of v 22. Now that the first phase of Yahweh's "Holy War" is completed, it is time for Moses to turn his attention to Joshua as his successor. Moses elicits courage for the future on the basis of what Yahweh has already done in Israel's behalf. As Yahweh has done in the past, *Thus will Yahweh do to all the kingdoms to which you are crossing over thither* (v 21). Joshua receives a summons not to fear, for this is Yahweh's war.

### Explanation

It is important to remember that this account of Israel's conquest of Transjordan, as well as the subsequent summons to take Cisjordan (3:18–22), is presented in the language of "Holy War." It is difficult to move from these pages directly into history per se. This is schematized history, presented as theology to encourage obedience and trust on the part of each new generation who celebrated these events. Yahweh, the God of Israel, is a God of might and power who will deliver those who place their trust in him. In terms of Deuteronomic theology we are to face the future in confidence, with full awareness of what God has already done for us in the past.

The Deuteronomic "Rest Theology" has been explored by W. Roth, who traced the redactional history of the notion that Yahweh grants rest to Israel. Roth found two stages in the development within the eleven relevant texts. In the first group, which includes Deut 3:20, rest was given to all of Israel once and for all in the conquest of the promised land. It was "rest *from* the enemy *in* the land." The situation shifts with the subsequent loss of the land in the Babylonian Exile. The idea of rest was reinterpreted to become "rest *for* obedience *wherever* Israel finds itself." In short, the "'rest' was now despatialized and seen as periodically available to Israel, even in the restless period of the Exile" (*BibRes* 21 [1976] 5).

There is an important principle here. Yahweh grants rest from time to time to give his people a chance to respond. Rest is a relational term, which concerns the mutuality with which Yahweh and his people are bound to each other through the law. Limited neither by space nor time, as appears to be the case in Solomon's dedicatory prayer in 1 Kgs 8:56–61, the people of God are granted rest whenever and wherever they turn to Yahweh. The blessing of "rest" can be a spiritual reality even within the most adverse circumstances, for those who trust Yahweh and obey his commandments.

# Transition: From Moses to Joshua (3:23–29)

## Bibliography

**Anbar,** "Genesis 15: A Conflation of Two Deuteronomic Narratives." *JBL* 101 (1982) 42. **Barth, C.** "Moses, Knecht Gottes." In *FS K. Barth* (1966). 68–81. **Braulik, G.** "Das Deuteronomium und die Geburt des Monotheismus in Israel." In *Gott, der Einzige. Zur Entstehung des Monotheismus in Israel.* QD 104. Ed. E. Haag. Freibug/Basel/Vienna: Herder, 1985. 115–59. **Bruston, C.** "Le Deutéronome primitif et ce qu'il suppose." *RThQR* 5 (1896) 247–57. **Fischer, G.** and **Lohfink, N.** "'Diese worte sollst du summen': Dtn 6,7 *wᵉdibbarta bam*—ein verlorener Schüssel zur meditativen Kultur in Israel." *ThPh* 62 (1987) 59–72. **Foresti, F.** "Composizione e redazione deuteronomistica in Ex 15,1–18." *Lat* 48 (1982) 41–69. **Fraade, D.** "Sifre Deuteronomium 26 (ad Deut 3,23): How Conscious the Composition?" *HUCA* 54 (1983) 245–301. **Greenfield, J. C.** "Some Aspects of Treaty Terminology in the Bible." In *Fourth World Congress of Jewish Studies.* Jerusalem, 1967. I, 117–19. **Henke, O.** "Zur Lage von Beth Peor." *ZDPV* 75 (1959) 155–63. **Labuschagne, C.** *The Incomparability of Yahweh in the Old Testament.* POS 5. Leiden: Brill, 1966. 22–24. **Lohfink, N.** "Wie stellt sich das Problem Individuum—Gemeinschaft in Deuteronomium 1,6–3, 29?" *Schol* 35 (1960) 405–6. **Riesener, I.** *Der Stamm* עבד *im Alten Testament. Eine Wortuntersuchung unter Berücksichtigung neuerer sprachwissenschaftlicher Methoden.* BZAW 149. Berlin, 1979. 186. **Vernes, M.** "Le sanctuaire moabite de Beth-Péor: Moise et la promulgation de la loi du Deutéronomie." *RHR* 75 (1917) 240–61. **Zenger, E.** "Tradition und Interpretation in Exodus xv 1–21." In *VTSup* 32. Leiden: Brill, 1981. 472.

## Translation and Prosodic Analysis

3:23–29  [(3:4):6:8] [5:5] [8:6:4] [3]

| | | |
|---|---|---|
| [23] And I sought the favor[a] \b of YHWH // AT THAT TIME / saying // | 20 | 3 |
| [24] "O Lord YHWH / | 8 | 1 |
| *You have (only) begun / to show your servant / your greatness /* | 20 | 3_ |
| *And your mighty[a] / hand // (for) what God (is there) /* | 18 | 3 |
| *in heaven and earth /* | 12 | 1 |
| *Who can do such works / and mighty acts as yours? //* | 18 | 2_ |
| [25] *Let me cross over[a] I pray / that I may see /* | 10 | 2 |
| *th<is>[b] good land /* | 14 | 1 |
| *Which / is beyond the Jordan //* | 10 | 2 |
| *the [ ][c] goodly / hill country / and the Lebanon" //* | 14 | 3_ |
| | | |
| [26] *And YHWH was cross[a] with me / on your account /* | 14 | 2 |
| *and he did not listen / unto me //* | 10 | 2 |
| *and YHWH said unto me /* | 10 | 1_ |
| *"Enough of you! / Do not continue / speaking* (דבר) *unto me /* | 13 | 3 |
| *further / concerning this matter* (בדבר) *//* | 9 | 2_ |
| | | |
| [27] *Go up / (to the)[a] top of Pisgah / and lift up your eyes /* | 16 | 3 |
| *westward and northward /* | 9 | 1 |
| *and southward and eastward /* | 12 | 1 |
| *And see with your eyes //* | 10 | 1 |
| *for you shall not cross over / this Jordan //* | 15 | 2_ |

| | | |
|---|---|---|
| <sup></sup>28 *So command Joshua / and strengthen him* \|ᵃ | 16 | 2 |
| *and encourage him //* | 7 | 1 |
| *For he shall cross over / before / this people /* | <u>17</u> | 3_ |
| *And he himself / shall make them possess / the land /* | 16 | 3 |
| *which you shall see" //* | 4 | 1_ |
| <sup></sup>29 **And we remained in the valley / opposite / Beth-peor //** פ | <u>15</u> | 3_ |

### Notes

23.a. Some Mss read וָאֶתְחַנָּן, which is possible in terms of mora count.

23.b. See 1:1.c. above.

24.a. LXX and Syr add וְאֶת־זְרוֹעֲךָ הַנְּטוּיָה, "and your outstretched arm"; cf. 4:34). The prosodic analysis supports MT.

25.a. The translation here attempts to communicate the pun in the Hebrew use of ויתעבר in v 26 (אעברה in v 25), where the Heb. root עבר normally means "to cross over."

25.b. הזאת, "this," is added with LXX and Vg.

25.c. הזה is omitted in with some LXX witnesses.

26.a. See note 25.a. above.

27.a. SP adds אל, which is possible in terms of mora-count.

28.a. A disj accent is added to achieve prosodic balance within this verse and with its parallel rhythmic element in v 24b.

### Form/Structure/Setting

The structure of 3:23–29 may be outlined in the form of a simple chiasm as follows:

| | | |
|---|---|---|
| A | Moses requests permission to cross over (vv 23–25) | [(3:4):6:8] |
| B | Yahweh is "cross" with Moses (v 26) | [5:5] |
| B' | Moses is permitted to "see" the land (v 27) | [8] |
| A' | Moses is told to command Joshua to cross over (v 28) | [6:4] |
| | Travel Notice: "We remained opposite Beth-Peor" (v 29) | [3] |

Moses' solemn request for permission to cross over into Cisjordan (vv 23–25) is set over against Yahweh's command that Moses encourage Joshua, who will "cross over before this people" (v 28). The center of the structure is marked by a whimsical sense of humor. Yahweh is "cross" with Moses in response to his request to "cross over" into Cisjordan (v 26), and Yahweh, at the same time, both denies and grants Moses' request to "see this good land which is beyond the Jordan" (v 25). Yahweh "did not listen" to Moses (v 26); and yet he did, for he commanded him to "go up to the top of Pisgah . . . and see with your eyes" (v 27). Moses will subsequently see from the top of Mt. Nebo what no tourist today can see: namely, "all the land, the Gilead as far as Dan, and all of Naphtali, and all the land of Ephraim and Manasseh, and all the land of Judah as far as the Western Sea, the Negev, and the Plain, that is, the valley of Jericho the city of palms, as far as Zoar" (34:1–3). In short, Moses "saw" the land, but he never set foot on it.

The Travel Notice in v 29, with its shift to 1st c pl forms, is sharply disj to signal a major structural break before the first half of the Inner Frame of Deuteronomy (chaps. 4–11), which begins in 4:1.

## Comment

**23–25** Up to this point in Deuteronomy, when Moses has spoken with Yahweh he has functioned as an intermediary between the people and their God, speaking in their behalf. Here he makes a personal request (vv 24–25).

ואתחנן, "and I sought the favor of" (hithp of חנן), indicates that this is a solemn request (cf. Ps 30:7–8 [EVV] for a similar usage).

אדני יהוה, "O Lord Yahweh," appears in Deut only here and in 9:26, on both occasions in a prayer of Moses. On similar occurrences in contexts of prayer, see Gen 15:2, 8 (Abraham) and Josh 7:7–9 (Joshua). On the use of אדני in direct speech to a superior, see I. Lange, *Formelhafte Wendungen der Umgangssprache im Alten Testament* (Leiden: Brill, 1949) 28–35, 81.

עבדך, "your servant," stresses Moses' position before Yahweh. He is keenly aware of Yahweh's earlier prohibition in regards his entry into the promised land (Deut 1:37). Yahweh has already revealed (להראות) himself through his mighty acts (v 24). Moses now asks that he might be permitted to *see* (ואראה) *the good land* (v 25), in the sense of experiencing the possession of it. Yahweh displays a whimsical sense of humor as he does in fact honor Moses' request, but not in the manner Moses wished. Yahweh tells Moses to *go up to the top of Pisgah . . . and see* [וראה] *with your eyes* (v 27). At a later point Moses indeed "saw" the entire land in a remarkable vision from the top of Mount Nebo (Deut 34:1–6); but he never set foot in Cisjordan. On the rhetorical use of ראה in the Outer Frame of Deuteronomy (chaps. 1–3 and 31–34), see the *Comment* at 1:8 .

מי־אל , "What God (is there)?" is reminiscent of מי־כמכה in Exod 15:11—"Who is like You, O Yahweh, among the gods? Who is like You, majestic in holiness, terrible in glorious deeds, doing wonders?" On further links between the language of the "Song of Moses" in Exod 15 and the Outer Frame of Deuteronomy (chaps. 1–3 and 31–34) see W. Moran, "Some Remarks on the Song of Moses," *Bib* 43 (1962) 317–27; idem, "The End of the Unholy War and the Anti-Exodus." *Bib* 44 (1963) 333–42.

בעבר הירדן, "beyond the Jordan"— see the *Comment* at 3:20 and 1:5. The repetitive parallelism in the Hebrew text of v 25 is worthy of comment:

Let me cross over [אעברה] . . . [to] see this good [טובה] land;
Which is beyond [בעבר] the Jordan, the goodly [הטוב] hill country.

With such careful parallelism in terms of repetition of specific words, as well as in mora-count, it is easy to see how textual variants were introduced to pair הזאת, "this," and הזה, "this," as well within this bicolon.

**26** The *Numeruswechsel* marks the beginning and end of this brief rhythmic unit, which occupies the center of the concentric rhythmic structure in 2:23–29. The use of the term ויתעבר, "to become furious," is a pun on the use of the verbal root עבר in Moses' prayer (v 25—איברה "Let me cross over"). The reason given for the denial of Moses' request is the same here as in 1:37. Though he himself was blameless, Moses had to accept responsibility for the rebellious generation at Kadesh-barnea: it was *on your account* that Yahweh *did not listen unto me.*

רב־לך "Enough of you!" On other uses of this construction see the *Comment* at 1:6 and the *Excursus*: "Travel Notices in the Outer Frame of Deuteronomy." The command אל־תוסף דבר אלי, "Do not continue speaking unto me" implies that Moses had been persistent in regards this prayer.

**27–28** On *Pisgah* see the *Comment* at 3:17 and 34:1. The command to strengthen and encourage Joshua picks up a major theme of the Outer Frame of Deuteronomy, namely the succession of leadership from Moses to Joshua. The book of Deuteronomy itself is evidence of the fact that Moses was obedient to Yahweh's command to encourage Joshua.

**29** This Travel Notice marks the end of the journey, so far as Moses is concerned (see *Excursus:* "Travel Notices in the Outer Frame of Deuteronomy"). All that remains for Moses, so far as travel is concerned, is the journey to the summit of Mount Nebo (Deut 32:48–52 and 34:1–3) to "see" the promised land, followed by the mysterious journey to his own grave (Deut 34:4–6), which no other human eyes were privileged to see.

בית פעור, "Beth-peor," located in the vicinity of Mount Nebo, was used to identify both where Moses renewed the covenant of Sinai in Moab and where Moses was buried ("opposite Beth-peor"; 34:6). It was located within the tribal allotment of Reuben (Josh 13:20), near the mountain where Balaam built seven altars and where Israel later "began to play the harlot with the daughters of Moab" and "yoked themselves to Baal of Peor" (Num 25:1–5, 18; cf. Deut 4:3; 31:16; Josh 22:17; Ps 106:28; Hos 9:10).

## Explanation

This transitional passage could easily be titled "Crossing Over" because of the pun on the root עבר, "to cross over," in vv 25, 26, and 28. A number of rhetorical features here establish a close connection with 31:1–6; 32:48–52; and 34:1–6. In short, this is a transitional passage, designed to help the reader (hearer) "cross over" to the second half of the Outer Frame of Deuteronomy in chaps. 31–34. The connection with its prosodic counterpart in 1:1–6a is highlighted by repetition of the root דבר at the structural center of this rhythmic unit in v 26, which carries the reader (hearer) back to the opening words of the book: אלה הדברים, "these are the words," and by the conclusion of the series of Travel Notices in v 29, which calls attention back to the beginning of that series in 1:1–7 (esp. vv 6b–7).

The whimsical sense of humor displayed in the language of this text is often missed by commentators and readers alike, perhaps due to a mind set we tend to bring to our experience with the biblical text. Because we are not looking for humor, we fail to see it when it is there, even when it may highlight the central message of the text, as it does here. The rabbis within ancient Judaism were more open to this dimension than most modern scholars of the biblical tradition.

To blaze the trail in the journey of faith is almost always a lonely task. Like Moses, most people who travel very far in their religious quest get a glimpse of the "promised land" and desire deeply to "see" it more clearly in actual personal experience. But because the process of change is often slow, particularly regarding institutions, that experience is often denied to those who would be leaders—or, at least, so it seems to the person involved. Evil is present with us, and all who take up the task of leadership are tainted with the consequences of evil, whether personally culpable or not. When the actual experience of our vision seems to be denied, we need to open our eyes. Perhaps God will permit us to "see the promised land" in unanticipated ways and times.

Moses was apparently persistent in his request to "see" the land. Jesus once commended a widow for importunity in her requests of the unjust judge: "yet because this widow bothers me, I will vindicate her, or she will wear me out by her continual coming" (Luke 18:5). Jesus went on to say, "will not God vindicate his elect, who cry to him day and night?" (Luke 18:7). God does hear us when we pray, but sometimes we need to "open our eyes," if we would "see" what he disposes in response to our requests. According to this text, God apparently enjoys surprising us—by granting our requests in ways we least expect.

# II. THE INNER FRAME:
## Part 1—The Great Peroration (4:1–11:25)

Though the structure of each half of the Inner Frame (Deut 4–11 and 27–30) is concentric in nature, the form is quite different from that noted in Deut 1–3. Key words and phrases are used here to mark the beginning of corresponding sections, rather than mere content. The major structural units themselves are also more complex in nature and less easy to capture in an apt summary statement. The menora-structure for Deut 4–11 is in ten parts, as follows:

A    "And now, O Israel, obey Yahweh's commandments" (4:1–40)
  B    "Then Moses set apart three cities" (4:41–43)
    C    "This is the Torah"—the Ten Words (4:44–6:3)
      D    "Hear, O Israel, Yahweh is our God, Yahweh alone" (6:4–7:11)
        E    When you obey you will be blessed (7:12–26)
        E'    When you disobey, you will perish (8:1–20)
      D'    "Hear, O Israel, you are about to cross the Jordan" (9:1–29)
    C'    At that time Yahweh spoke the Ten Words (10:1–7)
  B'    "At that time Yahweh set apart the tribe of Levi" (10:8–11)
A'    "And now, O Israel, what does Yahweh ask of you?" (10:12–11:25)

The fully complementary nature of 4:1–40 over against 10:12–11:25 was noted by A. D. H. Mayes in "Deuteronomy 4 and the Literary Criticism of Deuteronomy" (*JBL* 100 [1981] 41).

The familiar deuteronomic concept of God's blessing on those who keep his commandments stands at the center of this construction and anticipates the presentation of blessing and curse in Deut 11:26–32 at the very end of the Inner Frame: Part 1 (Deut 4–11). The corresponding discussion of curses on those who fail to keep Yahweh's commandments is central in the Inner Frame: Part 2 (Deut 27–30). Note in particular the curses from Mount Ebal in Deut 27, which sets the stage for the lengthy recitation of curses in Deut 28. The focus of attention in Deut 4–11 is on the ideal Israel, those who are called to obey Yahweh's commandments as they set forth to conquer the land. The focus of attention in Deut 27–30 is already directed to a more distant future in its call to a renewal of the covenant and subsequent prosperity after their dispersal "among the nations" (Deut 30:1).

### Bibliography for Deut 4–11

**Benjamin, D**. *Deuteronomy and City Life* (1983). **Cullen, J**. "Das Deuteronomium: Eine Erwiderung." *ZWT* 48 (1905) 181–93 (190–93). **Garcia Lopez, F**. "Analyse Littéraire de Dt V-XI." *RB* 84 (1977) 481–522; 85 (1978) 5–49, 161–200; 86 (1979) 59–91. **Gerhardsson, B**. *The Testing of God's Son (Matt 4:1–11 & Par): An Analysis of an Early Christian Midrash*. ConB NTSer 2. Lund: Gleerup, 1966. 36–70. **Goshen-Gottstein, M. H**. "A Recovered Part of the Aleppo Codex." *Textus* 5 (1966) 53–59. **Haran, M**. "Book-Scrolls at the Beginning of the Second Temple Period: The Transition from Papyrus to Skins." *HUCA* 54 (1983) 111–22. ———. "Book-Scrolls in Israel in Pre-Exilic Times." *JJS* 33 (1982) 161–73 (117). **Hempel, J**. *Die*

*Schichten des Deuteronomiums* (1914). 103–4. **Kuschke, A.** "Arm und Reich im Alten Testament." *ZAW* 57 (1939) 31–57. **Laberge**, L. "La Septante de Dt 1–11: Pour une étude de 'texte'." In *Das Deut* (1985). 129–34. **Labuschagne, C. J.** "Some Significant Compositional Techniques in Deuteronomy." In *FS J. H. Hospers* (1986). 121–31 (127–29). **L'Hour, J.** "Formes Littérraires, Structure et Unité de Dt 5–11." *Bib* 45 (1964) 551–55. **Lohfink, N.** *Das Hauptgebot* (1963). ————. "Mandatum Magnum in Dtn 5–11." *VD* 41 (1963) 73–77. ————. "Das Hautgebot im Alten Testament." *GeistLeb* 36 (1963) 271–81. ————. *Höre Israel!* (1965). **McCarthy, D. J.** *Treaty and Covenant* ($^2$1978). 159–70. **Mello, A.** "L'ascolto della Parola nel Dt." In *Ascolta Israele.* Ed. S. Panimolle. Parola, Spiritu e Vita 1. Rome, 1980. 27–41. **Merendino, R. P.** "Zu Dt V–VI: eine Klärung." *VT* 31 (1981) 80–83. **Peckham, B.** "The Composition of Deuteronomy 9:1–10:11." In *FS D. M. Stanley* (1975).3–59. ————. "The Composition of Deuteronomy 5–11." In *FS D. N. Freedman* (1983). 217–40. **Ruprecht, E.** "Exodus 24,9–11 als Beispiel lebendiger Erzähltradition aus der Zeit des babylonischen Exils." In *FS C. Westermann* (1980). 138–73 (159–60). **Seitz, G.** *Studien zum Deuteronomium* (1971). 45–91. **Tiffany, F. C.** *Parenesis and Deuteronomy 5–11 (Deut. 4:45; 5:2–11:29): A Form Critical Study.* Diss., Claremont School of Theology, 1978. **Vermeylen, J.** "Les sections narratives de Deut 5–11 et leur relation à Ex 19–34." In *Das Deut* (1985). 174–207.

# "And Now, O Israel, Obey Yahweh's Commandments" (4:1–40)

In recent years few chapters of Deuteronomy have received as much attention as this one, or have been the focus of such sharp scholarly disagreement. Earlier commentators were uncertain as to whether chap. 4 belonged with chaps. 1–3 as a conclusion, or with chaps. 5–11 as an introduction. G. E. Wright, for instance, took it as the final section of Moses' "First Address: The Acts of God" (1:1–4:43) (*IB* [1953] 2, 329). In somewhat similar fashion Noth included Deut 4 in his analysis of the Outer Frame as an introduction to what he called the Deuteronomistic History (Joshua through Kings), which he considered to be a unified and self-contained literary whole by a single author, writing during the exilic period, whom he called Dtr (for "Deuteronomistic author"). The introduction to this larger historical work was understood to be Deut 1–3(4) and 31–34. By putting the 4 in parentheses Noth was indicating that Deut 4:1–40 is "a special case" (*The Deuteronomistic History*, JSOTSup 18 [1981] 14). The references to exile from the land in this section persuaded Noth, and most critical scholars after him, that it belongs to the latest strata in the redactional history of the book, along with chaps. 31 and 34.

Lohfink's study of Deut 4 (*BiKi* 19 [1964] 247–56) opened a new chapter of scholarly debate on the question of unity of authorship, one which is yet to be resolved. The study of the *Numeruswechsel* by de Tillesse (*VT* 12 [1962] 29–87) was based primarily on Deut 5–11. Cazelles extended that study to include Deut 1–4 (*CBQ* 29 [1967] 207–19). The redactional model, however, was least convincing for this particular chapter, and Mittmann's "stratigraphical" interpretation of the composition of Deut 4 (BZAW 139 [1975]) was sharply challenged by Braulik (*Die Mittel Deuteronomischer Rhetorik* [1978]), who argued for the unity of the chapter. A number of recent critics who have taken up the problem have taken a stand against the unity of authorship, in favor of a redactional model which discerns various strata in the literary history of this chapter, the most notable of which is the recent monograph of Knapp (*Deuteronomium 4* [1987]). Nonetheless, Lohfink and Braulik continue to champion unity of authorship for this chapter, though at the same time seeing it as belonging to the latest material included in the book of Deuteronomy.

The prosodic analysis presented here supports the argument for unity of authorship in Deut 4. In fact, the use of the *Numeruswechsel* turns out to be evidence for unity of authorship, rather than the reverse as so many scholars have assumed since the epochal study of de Tillesse. In terms of prosodic structure, Deut 4 consists of three sections (4:1–10; 11–24; 25–40), each of which is arranged concentrically. These three sections in turn constitute a single literary whole, which also displays a concentric design as follows:

A     Keep YHWH's commandments that you may live in the land (4:1–4)
  B      Uniqueness of Israel as shown in her Torah (4:5–8)
    C     Be careful not to forget what happened at Horeb (4:9–10)
      D       Covenant stipulation issued at Horeb (the ten words) (4:11–14)
        E       No images or astral deities (allotted to other peoples) (4:15–19)
          F       The Exodus made the people YHWH's "family property" (4:20)
          F'      The Conquest makes the land Israel's "family property" (4:21)
        E'      No images: YHWH is a jealous God (4:22–24)
      D'      Covenant curses in effect in the land (4:25–28)
    C'     YHWH will not forget his covenant with your fathers (4:29–31)
  B'      Uniqueness of YHWH shown in the Exodus-Conquest (4:32–38)
A'     Keep YHWH's commandments that you may live in the land (4:39–40)

The above structure highlights the necessity of keeping YHWH's Torah and
the Exodus-Conquest tradition in relation to the Hebrew term נחלה, "family
property."

Though the parallel structure of respective elements in the above outline cannot be demonstrated with equal certainty in all cases, there is sufficient evidence
to suggest that the structural design as a whole was a conscious "authorial" decision on the part of the composer of this text. This conclusion does not rule out
the possibility of different ages and provenance for individual segments of this
tradition, but it does suggest the need for a different model for explaining the
redactional process than that commonly assumed by most critical scholars. This
new model is to be found in terms of musical composition and the transmission
of epic and legal texts in antiquity (see the section "Law, Poetry, and Music in
Ancient Israel" in the *Introduction*).

Within this larger concentric design of 4:1–40 as a whole, each of the three
major subunits (1–10; 11–24 and 25–40) is also arranged in concentric fashion. A
similar conceptual design of "circles within circles" has been shown to be present
in the book of Jonah. (See my articles: "The Song of Jonah: A Metrical Analysis,"
*JBL* 104 [1985] 217–31; "Andrzej Panufnik and the Structure of the Book of Jonah:
Icons, Music and Literary Art," *JETS* 28 [1985] 133–40; "Narrative Poetics and the
Interpretation of the Book of Jonah," in *Directions in Biblical Hebrew Poetry*, ed. E. R.
Follis, JSOTSup 40 [Sheffield, 1987] 29–82.)

The parallel nature of vv 1–4 and 39–40 is not difficult to show. The opening
command to "listen to the statutes and to the judgments" (v 1) and "to keep the
commandments of Yahweh your God" (v 2) is echoed in the parallel command
to "keep his statutes and his commandments" (v 40). The motivation for this
command in v 1 is "that you may live and you shall come in and you shall possess
the land." In v 40 the motivation is "that you may prolong your days upon the
ground which Yahweh your God is giving you."

In somewhat similar fashion vv 5–8 and 32–38 are parallel in form, with contrasting content. In both cases rhetorical questions are used to demonstrate the
incomparability of Yahweh in giving Israel "all this Torah which I am setting before you today" (v 8), on the one hand, and in taking "for himself a nation from
the midst of a nation" (v 34), on the other hand, in order "to drive out nations
greater and mightier than yourselves from before you to bring you in to give you
their land as family property" (v 38). In short, Israel's uniqueness (vv 5–8) is set
over against Yahweh's uniqueness (vv 32–38).

The Hebrew verb שׁכח, "to forget," is used to tie together vv 9–11 and 29–31. On the one hand, the people are told "to take heed to yourself . . . lest you forget [פֶּן־תִּשְׁכַּח] all the things [הַדְּבָרִים] which your eyes have seen" (v 9). On the other, the people are reminded that "all these things [הַדְּבָרִים] shall come upon you" (v 30) and Yahweh "will not forget [וְלֹא יִשְׁכַּח] the covenant with your fathers which he swore to them" (v 31).

The relation between vv 11–14 and 25–28 is more subtle, and consequently more difficult to demonstrate in a convincing manner. In vv 11–14 the covenant at Mount Sinai is in view, where Yahweh spoke from the mysterious fire (v 12) and declared "his covenant which he commanded you to do, the ten words [הַדְּבָרִים] and he wrote them upon two tablets of stone" (v 13). Yahweh then commanded Moses to teach these "statutes and judgments for you to do them in the land which you are crossing over thither to possess" (v 14). A very different situation is envisioned in vv 25–28, where the people have broken the covenant by making a graven image (v 25), thus bringing upon themselves the covenant curses: "you shall surely perish quickly from the land which you are crossing over the Jordan thither to possess" (v 26); "and Yahweh will scatter you among the peoples" (v 27), where "you will serve gods made by human hands of wood and stone who do not see and do not hear and do not eat and do not smell" (v 28). The impotence of these non-gods stands in sharp contrast to the "real" God who revealed himself on Mount Sinai (vv 11–13).

The sections in vv 15–19 and 22–24 have much in common. The opening phrase in v 15 וְנִשְׁמַרְתֶּם מְאֹד, "You shall take good heed," is paralleled by הִשָּׁמְרוּ לָכֶם, "take heed to yourselves." The people are told in vv 16–18 not to make any sort of "graven image." In v 23 they are also commanded not to "make for yourselves a graven image in the form of anything." In v 19 the heavenly bodies are allotted by Yahweh "to all the people under the whole heaven," whereas in v 24 "Yahweh your God is a consuming fire, he is a jealous God." The implication is clear: Yahweh has singled out Israel as a peculiar people from among the nations.

The central two verses in this structure present differing usages of the Hebrew word נַחֲלָה, "family property." In v 20 Yahweh used the Exodus experience to make of Israel "a people (who are) family property [נַחֲלָה] as at this day." In v 21 Moses is denied entry into the promised land "which Yahweh your God is giving to you as family property [נַחֲלָה]."

The parallelism in structure within 4:1–40 as a whole is too detailed to be happenstance. A careful study of the parallel usages in individual terms and phases throughout these verses reveals that they run roughshod over any division of the text into strata suggested by the usual interpretation of the *Numeruswechsel.* This text is a carefully constructed literary whole, from the hand of a single literary artist.

### Bibliography for Deut 4:1–40

**Baltzer, K.** *The Covenant Formulary* (1971). 31–34. **Beauchamp, P**. "Pour un théologie de la lettre." *RSR* 67 (1979) 481–94. **Bee, R. E**. "A Study of Deuteronomy based on Statistical Properties of the Text." *VT* 29 (1979) 1–22. **Begg, C**. "The Literary Criticism of Deut 4, 1–40. Contributions to a Continuing Discussion." *ETL* 56 (1980) 10–55. **Bernhardt, K. H**. *Gott und Bild. Ein Beitrag zur Begründung und Bedeutung des Bilderverbotes im Alten Testament.*" ThA

2. Berlin, 1956. **Braulik, G**. "Aufbrechen von geprägten Wortverbindungen und Zusammenfassen von stereotypen Ausdrücken in der Alttestamentlichen Kunstprosa (Dt 4, 1–40)." *Semitics* 1 (1970) 7–11. ————. *Die Mittel Deuteronomischer Rhetorik* (1978). ————. "Literarkritik und archäologische Stratigraphie. Zu S. Mittmann's Analyse von Dtn 4,1– 40." *Bib* 59 (1978) 351–83. **Brueggemann, W**. "Trajectories in Old Testament Literature." *JBL* 98 (1979) 175–77. ————. "Old Testament Theology as a Particular Conversation: Adjudication of Israel's Socio-Theological Alternatives." *TD* 32 (1985) 303–25. **Budde, K.** "Imageless Worship in Antiquity." *ExpTim* 9 (1897/98) 396–99. **Carroll, R. P.** "The Aniconic God and the Cult of Images." *ST* 31 (1977) 51–64. **Cholewinski, A.** "Zur theologischen Deutung des Moabbundes." *Bib* 66 (1985) 104. **Curtis, E. M.** "The Theological Basis for the Prohibition of Images in the Old Testament." *JETS* 28 (1985) 277–87. **Davies, P. R.** "The Ideology of the Temple in the Damascus Document." In *FS Y. Yadin* (1983). 287–301. **Dohmen, C.** "Die Statue von Tell Fecherije und die Gottebenbildlichkeit des Menschen." *BN* 20 (1983) 91–106. ————. *Das Bildervorbot. Seine Entstehung und seine Entwicklung im Alten Testament.* BBB 62. Bonn, 1985. ————. "Religion gegen Kunst?" In . . . *kein Bildnis machen. Kunst und Theologie im Gespräche.* Ed. C. Dohmen and T. Sternberg; Würzburg: Thomas Sternberg. 1987. 11–23. **Dus, J.** "Das Zweite Gebot (Zum Sieg der heiligen Lade über das Schnitzbild in Bethel)." *CV* 4 (1961) 37–50. **Fishbane, M.** "Varia Deuteronomica." ZAW 84 (1972) 349–52. ————. "Torah and Tradition." In *Tradition and Theology in the Old Testament.* Ed. D. A. Knight. Philadelphia: Fortress, 1977. 275–300. **Frey, J. B.** "La question des images chez les Juifs à la lumière des récouvertes." *Bib* 15 (1934) 265–300. **Friedman, R. E.** "From Egypt to Egypt: Dtr¹ and Dtr²." In *FSF. M. Cross* (1981). 167–92 (180– 82). **Giesen, G.** *Die Wurzel* שבע (1981). 296–98. **Goudoever, J. van.** "Tora und Galut." In *Jüdisches Volk -Gelobtes Land.* Ed. W. Eckert. Munich: Kaiser, 1970. 197–202. **Gunneweg, A. H. J.** "Bildlosigkeit Gottes im Alten Israel." *Hen* 6 (1984) 257–70. **Gutmann, J.** "The 'Second Commandment' and the Images in Judaism." *HUCA* 32 (1961) 161–74. **Habel, N. C.** "Appeal to Ancient Tradition as a Literary Form." *ZAW* 88 (1976) 253–72. **Hallo, W. W.** "Cult Statue and Divine Image: A Preliminary Study." In *Scripture in Context* II: *More Essays on the Comparative Method.* Ed. W. W. Hallo, J. C. Moyer, and L. G. Perdue. Winona Lake, IN: Eisenbrauns, 1983. 1–17. **Hempel, J.** *Die Schichten des Deuteronomium* (1914). 61– 65. ————. *Das Bild in Bibel und Gattesdienst.* Tübingen: Mohr, 1957. **Hossfeld, F.-L.** *Der Dekalog: Seine späten Fassungen, die originale Komposition und seine Vorstufen.* OBO 45. Göttingen: Vandenhoeck & Ruprecht, 1982. **Hyldahl, N.** "A Reminiscence of the Old Testament (Dt 4,15– 18) at Rom 1,23." *NTS* 2 (1956) 285–88. **Knapp, D.** *Deuteronomium 4. Literarische Analyse und theologische Interpretation.* Göttingen: Vandenhoeck & Ruprecht, 1987. **Konikoff, D.** *The Second Commandment and Its Interpretation in the Art of Ancient Israel.* Geneva: Imprimerie du Journal de Genève, 1973. **Küchler, M.** *Frühjüdische Weisheitstradition.* OBO 26. Freibourg/ Göttingen: Universitätsverlag, 1979. **Levenson, J. D.** "Who Inserted the Book of the To-rah?" *HTR* 68 (1975) 203–33. **Link, C.** "Das Bilderverbot als Kriterium theologischen Redens." *ZTK* 74 (1977) 58–85. **Lohfink, N.** "Review of K. Baltzer, *Das Bundesformular*." *Schol* 36 (1961) 419–23. ————. "Auslegung deuteronomischer Texte. IV. Verkündigung des Hauptgebots in der jüngsten Schicht des Deuteronomiums (Dt 4,1–40)." *BiKi* 19 (1964) 247–56. ————. *Höre Israel!* (1965). 87–120. **Mayes, A. D. H.** "King and Covenant: A Study of 2 Kings chs 22–23." *Herm* 125 (1978) 34–47. ————. "Exposition of Deuteronomy 4:25– 31." *IBS* 2 (1980) 67–83. ————. "Deuteronomy: Law of Moses or Law of God?" *PIBA* 5 (1981) 36–54. ————. "Deuteronomy 4 and the Literary Criticism of Deuteronomy." *JBL* 100 (1981) 23–51. **McCarthy, D. J.** *Treaty and Covenant,* 2nd ed. (1978). 190–94. **Merendino, R. P.** *Das deuteronomische Gesetz* (1969). 57–60. **Mittmann, S.** *Deuteronomium 1, 1– 6, 3* (1978). 1–6. **Moore, B. R.** *The Scribal Contribution to Deut 4,1–40.* Diss., Notre Dame, 1976. **Mørstad, E.** "Dt 4,25–28 og 29–40." *NorTT* 60 (1955) 34–45. **Mowinckel, S.** "Wann wurde der Jahwekultus in Jerusalem offiziell bildlos?" *AcOr* 8 (1930) 257–79. **North, C. R.** "The Essence of Idolatry." In *FS O. Eissfeldt* (1958). 151–60. **Noth, M.** *The Deuteronomistic History.* JSOTSup 15 (1981). 33–34. **Obbink, H. T.** "Jahwebilder." *ZAW* 47 (1929) 264–74.

**Oberholzer, J. P.** "The Text of Ex. 20:22, 23." *JNSL* 12 (1984) 101–105. **Otto, E.** "Monotheistische Tendenzen in der ägyptischen Religion." *WO* 2 (1955) 99–110. **Ouelette, J.** "Le deuxième commandement et le rôle de l'image dans la symbolique religieuse de l'Ancien Testament. Essai d'interpretation." *RB* 74 (1967) 504–16. **Pfeiffer, R. H.** "The Polemic against Idolatry in the Old Testament." *JBL* 43 (1924) 229–40. ———. "Images of Yahweh." *JBL* 45 (1926) 211–22. **Quervain, A. de.** "Das zweite Gebot in der dogmatischen Arbeit." In *FS K. Barth* (1936). 191–201. **Rad, G. von.** "εἰκών. The Prohibition of Images in the OT." *TDNT* II (1964) 381–83. ———. "Some Aspects of the Old Testament World-View." In *The Problem of the Hexateuch* (1966). 144–65. **Roux, J. H. le.** "A Holy Nation Was Elected (The Election Theology of Exodus 19:5–6)." *OTWSA* 25/26 (1982/83) 59–78. **Schenker, A.** "Unwiderrufliche Umkehr und neurer Band. Vergleich zwischen der Wiederherstellung Israels in Dt 4,25–31; 30,1–14 und dem neuen Bund in Jer 31,31–34." *FZPhTh* 27 (1980) 93–106. **Schmid, H.** "Gottesbild, Gottesschau und Theophanie." *Jud* 23 (1967) 241–54. **Schmidt, W. H.** "Bilderverbot und Gottesebenbildlichkeit. Exegetische Notizen zur Selbstmanipulation des Menschen." *WoWa* 23 (1968) 209–16. ———. "Ausbrägungen des Bilderverbots? Zur Sichtbarkeit und Vorstellbarkeit Gottes im Alten Testament." In *FS G. Friedrich* (1973). 25–34. **Schroer, S.** *In Israel gab es Bilder. Nachrichten von darstellender Kunst in Israel.* OBO 74. Göttingen: Vandenhoeck & Ruprecht, 1987. **Schultz, S. J.** "Interpreting the Pentateuch. Deuteronomy 4, 1–24." In *The Literature and Meaning of Scripture.* Ed. M. A. Inch. Grand Rapids: Baker Book House, 1981. 21–38. **Shafer, B. E.** "The Root *bhr* in Pre-Exilic Concepts of Closeness in the Hebrew Bible." *ZAW* 89 (1977) 20–42. **Stahl, R.** *Aspekte der Geschichte deuteronomistischer Theologie: Zur Traditionsgeschichte der Terminologie und zur Redaktionsgeschichte der Redekompositionen.* Diss., Jena, 1982. **Talstra, E.** "Towards a Distributional Definition of Clauses in Classical Hebrew: A Computer-Assisted Description of Clauses and Clause Types in Deut 4:3–8." *ETL* 63 (1987) 95–105. **Vischer, W.** "Du sollst dir kein Bildnis machen." In *FS K. Barth* (1956). 764–62. **Welch, A. C.** "The Purpose of Deuteronomy . . . " *ExpTim* 42 (1930/31) 227–31. **Williams. W. H.** "A Look within the Deuteronomic History." *SJT* 25 (1972) 337–45. **Zimmerli, W.** "Das zweite Gebot." In *FS A. Bertholet* (1950). 550–63 [= *Gottes Offenbaarung. Gesammelte Aufsätze.* ThB 19. Munich: Kaiser, 1963. 234–48]. ———. "Das Bilderverbot in der Geschichte des alten Israel." In *FS A. Jepsen* (1971). 86–96.

*Bibliography for Deut 4:1–10*

**Becker, J.** *Gottesfurcht im Alten Testament.* AnBib 25. Rome: Biblical Institute Press, 1965 **Braulik, G.** "Weisheit, Gottesnähe und Gesetz—Zum Kerygma von Dt 4, 5–8." In *FS. W. Kornfeld* (1977). 165–95. **Brongers, H. A.** "Bemerkungen zum Gebrauch des adverbialen wĕ ʿattāh im Alten Testament." *VT* 15 (1965) 289–99. **Cancik, H.** *Mythische und historische Wahrheit: Interpetationen zu Texten der hethitischen, biblischen und friechischen Historiographyie.* SBS 48. Stuttgart: Katholische Bibelwerk, 1970. 86, 100–102. **Couturier, G.** "Sagesse Babylonienne et Saggesse Israelite." *ScEc* 14 (1962) 293–309 (305). **Daube, D.** "The Culture of Deuteronomy." *Orita* 3 (1969) 27–52. **Donner, H.** "Gesichtspunkte zur Auflösung des klassischen Kanonbegriffes bei Johann Salomo Semler." In *FS M. Doerne* (1970). 56–68 (61). ———. "Hier sind deine Götter, Israel!" In *FS K. Ellinger* (1973). 45–50. **Dummermuth, F.** "Biblische Offenbarungsphänomene." ThZ 21. Basel: T. Reinhardt, 1965. 1–21. **Dus, J.** "Der ferne Gott und das nahe Gebot (Eine Studie zum Deuteronomium)." *CV* 7 (1964) 193–200. ———. "Die Herabfaurung Jahwes auf die Lade und Entziehung der Feuerwolke." *VT* 19 (1969) 290–311. **Emerton, J. A.** "New Light on Israelite Religion: The Implications of the Inscriptions of Kuntillet ʿAjrud." *ZAW* 94 (1982) 2–20 (11–12). **Fishbane, M.** "Varia Deuteronomica." *ZAW* 84 (1972) 349–52. ———. "Ancient Wisdom and Modern Man—With Special Reference to the Hebrew Bible." *ChrJRel* 20 (1987) 37–48. **Foresti, F.** "Composizione e redazione deuteronomistica in Ex 15,1–18." *Lat* 48

(1982) 46. **Frankena, R**. "The Vassal-Treaties of Esarhaddon and the Dating of Deuteronomy."
In *OTS* 14 (1965). 122–54 (141–42). **Geiger, A**. *Urschrift und Übersetzungen der Bibel in ihrer
Abhängigkeit von der inneren Entwicklung des Judentums.* Frankfurt a.M., ²1928. 286–87.
**Greenberg, M**. "נשה in Exodus 20:20 and the Purpose of the Sinaitic Theophanie." *JBL* 79
(1960) 273–76. **Gross, W**. "Syntaktische Erscheinungen am Anfang althebräischer
Erzählungen: Hintergrund und Vordergrund." In *Congress Volume Vienna.* Ed. J. Emerton.
VTSup 32. Leiden: Brill, 1981. 131–45 (133). **Halévy, J**. "Recherches biblique: le
Deutéronome." *RSEHA* 7 (1899) 326. **Hartmann, B**. "Es gibt keiner Gott ausser Jahwe." *ZDMG*
110 (1961) 229–35 (232). **Hermann, J**. "Ägyptische Analogien zum Funde des Dt." *ZAW* 11
(1908) 291–302. **Herrmann, W**. "Jeremia 23,23f als Zeugnis der Gotteserfahrung im
babylonischen Zeitalter." BZ 27 (1983) 155–66. **Hulst, A. R**. Het Woord *kahal* in Deuteronomium." *NThS* 22 (1939) 159–66. ———. "Der Name 'Israel' im Deuteronomium." IN
*OTS* 9 (1951). 65–106. ———. "Opmerkingen over de *kaᵓăšer*-zinnen in Dt." *NedTTs* 18
(1963) 337–61. **Jackson, B. S**. *Essays in Jewish and Comparative Legal History.* SJLA 10. Leiden:
Brill, 1975. 171. **Johannes, G**. *Unvergleichlichkeitsformulierungen im Alten Testament.* Diss., Mainz,
1968. **Johnson, M. D**. "The Paralysis of Torah in Habakkuk I 4." *VT* 35 (1985) 257–66. **Kalugila,
L**. *The Wise King: Studies in Royal Wisdom as Divine Revelation in the Old Testament and Its
Environment.* ConB OT 15. Lund: CWK Gleerup, 1980. **Kegler, J**. *Politisches Geschehen und
theologisches Verstehen: Zum Geschichtsverständnis in der frühen israelitischen Königszeit.* CThM 8.
Stuttgart: Calwer, 1977. 14–15. **Koch, K**. "Wesen und Ursprung der 'Gemeinschaftstreue' im
Israel der Königszeit." *ZEE* 5 (1961) 72–90. **Krašovec, J**. *La Justice (Sdq) de Dieu dans la Bible
Hébraïque et l'Interpétation Juive et Chrétienne.* OBO 76. Freiburg-Göttingen: Vandenhoeck &
Ruprecht, 1988. 182–84. **Kritzinger, J. D. W**. *Qehal Jahwe, Wat dit is en wie daaraan mag behoort.*
Kampen, 1957. **Leipoldt, J**. and **Morenz, S**. *Heilige Schriften. Betrachtungen zur Religionsgeschichte
der antiken Mittelmeerwelt.* Leipzig: Harrassowitz, 1953. 56–57. **Lemke, W. E**. "The Near and the
Distant God: A Study of Jer 23:23–24 in Its Theological Biblical Context." *JBL* 100 (1981) 541–
55. **Lindars, B**. "Torah in Deuteronomy." In *FS D. W. Thomas* (1968). 117–36 (128).
**Loewenstamm, S. E**. "The Address 'Listen' in the Ugaritic Epic and the Bible." In *FS C. H.
Gordon* (1980). 123–31. **Lohfink, N**. *Option for the Poor.* Berkeley: BIBAL Press, 1987. 45–46.
———. "Dtn 12,1 und Gen 15, 18: Das dem Samen Abrahams geschenkte Land als der Gel-
tungsbereich der deuteronomischen Gesetze." In *FS J. Scharbert* (1989). 183–210. ———. Das
deuteronomische Gesetz in der Endgestalt—Entwurf einer Gesellschaft ohne marginale
Gruppen. BN 51 (1990) 25–40. **Luzarraga, J**. *Las Tradiciones de la Nube en la Biblia en el Judaismo
Primitivo.* AnBib 54. Rome: Pontificio Instituto Biblico, 1973. **Mayer, W. R**. "'Ich rufe dich von
ferne, höre mich von nahe!' Zu einer babylonischen Gebetsformel." In *FS C. Westermann*
(1980). 302–17. **McEvenue, S. E**. "The Political Structure in Judah from Cyrus to Nehemiah."
*CBQ* 43 (1981) 364. **Merwe, C. H. J. van der**. "Old Hebrew Particles and the Interpretation
of Old Testament Texts." Paper presented at SBL International, Vienna in Aug. 1990 (ועתה/
עתה). **Müller, H.-P**. "Die kultische Darstellung der Theophanie." *VT* 14 (1964) 183–91.
**Neumann, P. K**. *Hört das Wort Jawäs* (1975). 67–74. **Pax, E**. *EPIPHANIA. Ein religionsgeschichtlicher
Beitrag zur biblischen Theologie.* MThS 10. Munich, 1955. **Ringgren, H**. *Word and Wisdom: Studies
in the Hypostatization of Divine Qualities and Functions in the Ancient Near East.* Lund: Gleerup,
1947. **Ruprecht, E**. "Exodus 24,9–11 als Beispiel lebendiger Erzähltradition aus der Zeit des
babylonischen Exils." In *FS C. Westermann* (1980). 138–73 (158–59). **Schawe, E**. *Gott als Lehrer
im Alten Testament: Eine semantisch-theologische Studie.* Diss., Freibourg, 1979. **Seitz, G**. *Studien zum
Deuteronomium* (1971). 104–5. **Sheppard, G. T**. *Wisdom as a Hermeneutical Construct: A Study in
Sapientializing of the Old Testament.* BZAW 151. Berlin: de Gruyter, 1980. 62–71. **Soebagjo, M**. *The
"Fear" of Yahweh in the Old Testament.* Diss., Edinburgh, 1980. **Talstra, E**. "Towards a Distributional Definition of Clauses in Classical Hebrew: A Computer-Assisted Description of Clauses
and Clause Types in Deut 4, 3–8." *ETL* 63 (1987) 95–105. **Unnik, W. D. van**. "De la règle Μήτε
προσθεῖναι μήτε ἀφελεῖν dans l'histoire du canon." *VC* 3 (1949) 1–36. **Weinfeld, M**. "Erra-
Epos." *UF* 3 (1971) 256. ———. *Deuteronomy and the Deuteronomic School* (1972). 150–51;
261–65. ———. "'Justice and Righteousness' in Ancient Israel against the Background

of 'Social Reforms' in the Ancient Near East." In *Mesopotamien und Seine Nachbarn*. Ed. H.-J. Nissen and J. Renger. Berlin: D. Reimer, 1982. Part 2, 491–519. **Whybray, R. N.** *The Intellectual Tradition in the Old Testament*. BZAW 135. Berlin: de Gruyter, 1974. 87–88. **Xella, P.** "Il Culto dei Morto nell'Antico Testamento: tra Teologica e Storia della Religioni." In *FS A. Brelich* (1982). 645–66. **Yaron, R.** "Semitic Elements in Early Rome." In *FS D. Daube* (1974). 343–57.

## Translation and Prosodic Analysis

4:1–10   [8:8:6:(5:5:5)] [(6:5):9] [(5:6):(5:5)] [(5:6):8:8]

| | | |
|---|---|---|
| [1] **And now, O Israel** / listen to the statutes / | 16 | 2 |
| and the judgments / | 8 | 1 |
| Which I / am teaching you[a] / to do / | 14 | 3 |
| so that you may live / and you shall come in / | 11 | 2_ |
| And you shall possess the land / | 10 | 1 |
| which YHWH / God of your fathers / | 16 | 2 |
| <has given>[b] to you // | 6 | 1 |
| [2] You shall not add / to the word (הדבר) / | 14 | 2 |
| which I / am commanding you[a] / | 13 | 2_ |
| And you shall not detract \[b] from it // (that you may) keep / | 14 | 2 |
| the commandments / of YHWH your God / | 13 | 2 |
| which I / am commanding you[c] // | 13 | 2_ |
| [3] Your eyes / (are the ones) seeing / <all>[a] ǀ [a] | 15 | 3 |
| that YHWH did / in[b] Baal-peor // | 15 | 2_ |
| For each one / who walked / after Baal of Peor / | 21 | 3 |
| He [YHWH *your God*][c] destroyed him / *from your[c] midst* // | 8 | 2_ |
| [4] But you / the ones holding fast / to YHWH \[a] your God // | 20 | 3 |
| all of you are alive / TODAY // | 9 | 2_ |
| [5] *See!*[a] / I have taught you / statutes / and judgments / | 19 | 4 |
| just as he commanded me / YHWH [my God][b] // | 10 | 2_ |
| To do thus / in the midst of the land / | 14 | 2 |
| Which you / are coming thither / to possess it // | 15 | 3_ |
| [6] And you shall keep (them) / and you shall do (them) / | 9 | 2 |
| for that will be your wisdom / | 7 | 1 |
| And your understanding / in the eyes / of [a]the peoples // | 16 | 3 |
| Who will hear / all / these statutes / | 16 | 3_ |
| And they will say / | 6 | 1 |
| "Surely / (it is) a wise and understanding people / | 11 | 2 |
| this / great nation" // | 11 | 2_ |
| [7] For \[a] what great nation (is there) / | 10 | 1 |
| Who has a God / so near to it // | 18 | 2 |
| As YHWH our God (is to us) / | 11 | 1 |
| Whenever we call / unto him? // | 11 | 2_ |
| [8] And what / great nation (is there) / | 10 | 2 |
| that has / statutes and judgments / (so) righteous // | 19 | 3_ |

| | | |
|---|---|---|
| As all / this Torah / | 11 | 2 |
|     which I / am setting before you / TODAY // | <u>19</u> | 3_ |
| [9] *Only[a] / take heed to yourself and keep your soul-life /* | 15 | 2 |
|     *diligently /* | 3 | 1 |
| *Lest you forget <all>[b] the things (הדברים) /* | 12 | 1 |
|     *which your eyes have seen /* | 10 | 1_ |
| *And lest they depart / from your hearts /* | 15 | 2 |
|     *all / the days of your life //* | 8 | 2 |
| *And make them known to your children /* | 11 | 1 |
|     *and to your children's children //* | <u>8</u> | 1_ |
| [10] *(There was) a day / when you[a] stood / before YHWH your[a] God /* | 19 | 3 |
|     *in Horeb /* | 5 | 1 |
| *When YHWH said / to me / "Gather to me / the people /* | <u>19</u> | 4_ |
| *And I will cause them to hear \[b] my words (דברי) //* | 12 | 1 |
|     *that they may learn / to fear me /* | 14 | 2 |
| *All the days /* | 6 | 1 |
|     *which they are alive / on the earth /* | 15 | 2 |
| *And their children / may they teach (them)" //* | <u>12</u> | 2_ |

### Notes

1.a. LXX (σήμερον) and Syr add היום. Prosodic analysis supports MT.

1.b. Reading נתן with Old Latin (cf. Deut 12:1). I am grateful to Norbert Lohfink for this observation (private communication).

2.a. Some LXX witnesses (σήμερον) and Arabic add היום. Prosodic analysis supports MT.

2.b. LXX (σήμερον) adds היום. Prosodic analysis supports MT.

2.c. Most LXX witnessess add σήμερον = היום. Prosodic analysis supports MT.

3.a. Adding כל with some Heb. Mss, LXX, Syr, and Vg. A disj accent is read after this addition to achieve better balance in the distribution of syntactic accentual stress units.

3.b. A few Heb. Mss, LXX, and Syr read לבעל instead of בבעל.

3.c. Omitting יהוה אלהיך with Vg; LXX and Syr read 2nd m pl suffix here and in the following word, מקרבך:

4.a. See note 1:1c.

5.a. On the rhetorical use of ראה in the Outer Frame of Deuteronomy see the *Comment* at 1:8.

5.b. Omitting אלהי with one Heb. Ms and LXX[Bmin].

6.a. LXX and one Heb. Ms add כל, which is possible in terms of mora-count.

7.a. Replacing disj *y[e]tîb* with conj *mahpāk* to achieve closer balance in distribution of syntactic accentual stress units.

9.a. LXX omits. Prosodic analysis supports MT.

9.b. Adding כל with one Heb. Ms, LXX, and Syr.

10.a. LXX, Syr, and Tg[J] read 2 pl.

10.b. See note 1:1c.

### Form/Structure/Setting

In terms of the *Numeruswechsel* (vv 1, 3, and 9) and the occurrences of the temporal marker היום, "today" in vv 4 and 8, Deut 4:1–10 is divided into three sections: vv 1–4, 5–8, and 9–10. The second of these units may be subdivided in terms of content, to give the following outline:

| A | Keep Yahweh's commandments and live (v 1–4) | [8:8:6:(5:5:5)] |
|---|---|---|
| B | Keep these statutes (vv 5–6a) | [6:5:9] |
| B' | What great nation has such a Torah (vv 6b–8) | [5:6:(5:5)] |
| A' | Do not forget the "words" you have seen (vv 9–10) | [(5:6):8:8] |

Within this structure the focus is clearly on the necessity of observing Yahweh's commandments as recorded in the Torah. The verbal root שׁמר, "to keep, observe," appears in each of the three major sections, in vv 2, 6, and 9 (twice), along with the root שׁמע, "to hear, listen, obey," in vv 1, 6, and 10. The rhetorical question posed in vv 6b–8 is part of a larger structure which ties vv 5–8 to its parallel prosodic unit in vv 32–38.

In Deut 1–3 the focus of attention was on the past in terms of a review of the "mighty acts" of God as celebrated in Yahweh's "Holy War" (see *Excursus:* "Holy War as Celebrated Event"). Here in chap. 4 the recollection of Yahweh's action in history continues, but the focus of attention shifts to the future. Within the larger rhetorical structure of Deut 4–11 this chapter is set over against 10:12–11:25, which sets the stage for a detailed presentation of Yahweh's commandments in the Central Core (Deut 12–26). The function of Deut 4 is similar in that it sets the stage for the presentation of the עשׂרת הדברים, "ten words," which are mentioned explicitly, for the first time, in 4:13 (and again later in 10:4).

## Comment

**1** The *waw* in ועתה, "And now," is disjunctive to underscore the transition to a major new section of the book of Deuteronomy, which was already signaled by the concluding Travel Notice in 3:29. The opening clause here introduces a series of rhetorical markers involving the terms ועתה ישׂראל and שׁמע ישׂראל (4:1; 5:1; 6:4; 9:1; and 10:12), which foreshadows the change in character of the Inner Frame of Deuteronomy (chaps. 4–11) with its focus on the present demands on the worshiping community as they anticipate life in the land. The opening words ועתה ישׂראל appear again to introduce the corresponding rhythmic structure of 10:12–11:25 which parallels 4:1–40 in the larger architectural design of the Inner Frame. The phrase שׁמע ישׂראל anticipates the rhetorical use of the phrase שׁמע ישׂראל in 5:1; 6:4; and 9:1.

*The statutes* (החקים) and *the judgments* (המשׁפטים) mentioned here constitute the "laws" as recorded in Deut 5–26. For a detailed study of these and related words in the legal vocabulary of ancient Israel, see Braulik ("Die Ausdrücke für Gesetz im Buch Deuteronomium," *Bib* 51 [1970] 39–66).

אשׁר אנכי מלמד אתכם, "which I am teaching you"—these words suggest the didactic purpose of the book of Deuteronomy within the formal structures of religious education in ancient Israel (see the section on "Deuteronomy and the Canonical Process" in the *Introduction*. The motivation for learning this Torah is *that you may live*. The term תחיו forms an inclusion with חיים, "life," in v 4.

**2** The term הדבר, "the word," here refers to the whole of *the commandments of Yahweh*. It also is to be understood in relation to the title of the book of Deuteronomy אלה הדברים, "These are the words," in 1:1. The "canonical formula" not to add or detract anything from the word of Yahweh has parallels in other ancient texts, such as the warning against altering the text in the treaty of Esarhaddon (see M.

G. Kline, *Treaty of the Great King* [1963] 43). On earlier parallels in texts from the ancient Near East, see M. Fishbane, "Varia Deuteronomica," *ZAW* 84 (1972) 349–52.

**3–4** The incident at Baal Peor, as recorded in Num 25:1–5, involved sexual acts with Moabite women, probably in the context of worshiping Baal, the Canaanite god of fertility. On that occasion the guilty parties were executed. Here, *the ones holding fast to Yahweh* are the ones who *are alive today* (v 4).

**5–6a** On the use of the term ראה, "see!" (2 m sg impv), within the Outer Frame (Deut 1–3, 31–34), see 1:8 above. The term appears three times in the Inner Frame (4:5; 11:26; 30:15) to introduce rhetorical units which form an inclusion, of sorts, around both the first half of the Inner Frame (chaps. 4–11), and the Inner Frame as a whole (chaps. 4–11 and 27–30).

The term (ה)חקים, "statutes," forms an inclusion around this rhythmic subunit and functions within the phrase חקים ומשפטים, "statutes and judgments," as well, which forms an inclusion around vv 5–8. The term למדתי, "I have taught you," is a further reminder of the didactic function of the text of this book, for Israel will demonstrate her wisdom . . . *in the eyes of the peoples* by means of her fidelity to Yahweh's commandments.

**6b–8** הגוי הגדול הזה, "this great nation"—Israel's greatness lies in her special relationship to Yahweh, as the following rhetorical questions make explicitly clear: *What great nation is there who has a God so near to it as Yahweh our God?* (v 7); *And what great nation is there that has statutes and judgments so righteous as all this Torah?* (v 8). It is ready access to God through his "righteous" Torah that makes Israel unique among the nations.

**9** השמר לך ושמר נפשך, *take heed to yourself and keep your soul-life*—the verbal root שמר appears also in vv 2 and 6. Israel is to take great care not to *forget all the things* (הדברים) they have seen. The term נפש, "soul-life" is sometimes rendered "soul," "self," or "desire." The translation of נפש as "soul-life" is borrowed from my student Patricia Dutcher-Walls in an attempt to capture the unusual breadth of meaning in this term. The word "soul" alone tends to convey a Greek concept in which soul and body are considered to be separate entities, in a manner quite foreign to ancient Hebrew. See the discussion of H. W. Wolff, *Anthropology of the Old Testament* (Philadelphia: Westminster, 1974). 10–25. The attempt here is to capture some of the intuitive psychological insight on the part of the ancient Hebrews. The "soul" is not to be understood as distinct from the "body." It is a recognition of profound depth in the human psyche. The term מלבבך, "from your heart" is also to be understood psychologically (cf. H. W. Wolff, 40–58). The "heart" here is not the physical organ, but the "mind" in the sense of conscious (or perhaps even unconscious) "memory."

The command to make *all the[se] things* [הדברים] . . . *known to your children and your children's children* points once again to the theme of religious education in ancient Israel (cf. Deut 6:7, 20; 11:19; 31:13; 32:46). The future of Israel is dependent on the transmission of the experience of God's mighty acts in history, and his demands, to each successive generation.

**10** The abruptness in style in the Hebrew expression here is eased somewhat by supplying the understood form of the verb "to be." It is also possible to see the verse as continuing the admonition of v 9, with Craigie (NICOT [1976] 133), in the sense "(lest you forget) the day," but this interpretation involves the addition of the definite article as well. Horeb (Sinai) was where the Torah was given through Moses to the people of Israel. As such it constitutes a major aspect of what the people are to remember and to transmit to their children after them. The verb ואשמעם, "and I will cause them to hear," forms an inclusion with שמע, "hear," at the beginning of this unit in 4:1. On the meaning of ליראה, "to fear," see the discussion below at 6:2 and 10:12. The reference to *their children* at the end of v 10 anticipates vv 25 and 40 below, which form a frame around 4:15–40—the third major segment of this chapter.

### *Explanation*

The presentation of law was a matter of public education in ancient Israel. The motivation for obedience to the law was based on cultic remembering, in which the past was made present. Within that context real limits were placed on matters of interpretation. The people were not free to "add to the word" or to "detract from it" in any way. They were to know the commandments and to keep them faithfully.

In the history of the Christian community Deut 4:2 has been used (along with 12:32 and Rev 22:18–19) as a commandment with reference to the canonical writings of both Testaments. Though it is true that mischief has been done by limiting the extent of the canon arbitrarily in this manner, there is an important principle here we need to retain. R. Laurin once insisted "that final canonization was an illegitimate closure of [the canonical] process by the community at one moment in its history" (in *Tradition and Theology in the Old Testament*, ed. D. A. Knight [Philadelphia: Fortress, 1977] 261). Be that as it may, God's revelation is mediated to us primarily through the transmission of a sacred text within a worshiping community of faith. Once that text was fixed in its canonical written form, we would alter it by "adding to the word" or "detracting from it" to our own peril. Our primary task is to find ways to transmit that text effectively within our community and to interpret it responsibly and faithfully, even the most difficult parts of it. It remains the Word of God. We do well not to look beyond the Scriptures as we know them for texts to add to that body, but rather to examine each aspect of that sacred tradition against the whole of it. The canonical process continues, but in a rather different way—once the First Testament is incorporated into the larger Christian Bible in relation to the Second Testament and the ultimate revelation of God's Word in the person of Jesus Christ.

One of the great lessons we can learn from the experience of ancient Israel in the religious life is that memory serves to lead to the continuing experience of the presence and activity of God. It is forgetfulness that opens the door to tragic failure on the part of the community of faith. As Elton Trueblood once put it, ours is unfortunately a "cut-flower civilization," particularly among youth today. We are not interested in the past because we do not feel that it is relevant to our future. We need to remember that cut flowers are beautiful for a brief period of time, but they have no roots—and they have no future! Remembering means making the past present. It suggests much more than a mere recall of data. It is a making present of the past that recreates the present through presence. Remembering signals the transmission of the norming presence from generation to generation.

As M. Narucki has argued (*JETS* 32 [1989] 467–78), Scripture is a symbolic theology in which symbols actually communicate the presence of that which they symbolize. What really happened in history becomes presence through symbol. The power is in the event itself, which becomes a transforming symbol actually making present the event through time. The nature of the symbol is intimately related to the nature of sacred time. Even the material on which the law was written was treated as having presence and power. Only a symbolic consciousness can know presence. The fact that the poem of Scripture was probably sung at a special time set aside suggests a quality of *ekstasis* in worship, in which remembering is acted out by the whole person and by the whole community. It is a remembering that is larger than the individual or even the community. It is a remembering of the prophet Moses, chosen by God to presence this people with himself. We would do well to make the process of remembering a more vital part of our life as a community of faith today.

## Bibliography for Deut 4:11–24

**Barr, J.** "The Image of God in the Book of Genesis—A Study of Terminology." *BJRL* 51 (1968) 11–26 (20). **Born, A. van den.** "Zum Tempelweihspruch (1 Kg VIII 12f)." In OTS 14. Leiden: Brill, 1965. 235–44. **Braulik, G.** "Das Deuteronomium und die Geburt des Monotheismus." In SBAB 2 (1988) 257–300. **Cazelles, H.** *"šmᶜqôl et šmᶜbqôl."* *GLECS* 10 (1963/66) 148–50. ———. "La Rupture de la Berît selon les Prophetes." *JJS* 33 (1982) 133–44 (137). **Curtis, E. M.** "The Theological Basis for the Prohibition of Images in the Old Testament." *JETS* 28 (1985) 277–87. **Daube, D.** *Studies in Biblical Law.* Cambridge UP, 1947. **Delcor, M.** "Les Cultes Étrangeres en Israel au Moment de la Réforme de Josias d'apres 2 Rois 23." In *FS H. Cazelles* (1981). 91–123 (98–99). **Diepold, P.** *Israels Land.* BWANT 95. Stuttgart: Kohlhammer, 1972. 81–84. **Dohmen, C.** "Heisst סֶמֶל 'Bild, Statue?'" *ZAW* 96 (1984) 263–66. ———. *Das Bilderverbot. Seine Entstehung und seine Entwicklung im Alten Testament.* Ed. F. Hossfeld and H. Merklein. BBB 62. Bonn: Hanstein, 1985. **Dummermuth, F.** "Zur deuteronomischen Kulttheologie." *ZAW* 70 (1958) 59–98 (89). **Emerton, J. A.** "The Etymology of *hištaḥăwāh*." In OTS 20. Leiden: Brill, 1977. 41–55. **Fascher, E.** "Abraham φυσιόλογος and φύλος θεοῦ. Eine Studie zur ausserbiblischen Abrahamstradition im Anschluss an Deuteronomium 4,19." In *FS T. Klauser* (1964). 111–24. **Fishbane, M.** "Varia Deuteronomica." *ZAW* 84 (1972) 349–52. ———. "Torah and Tradition." In *Tradition and Theology in the Old Testamant.* Ed. D. A Knight. Philadelphia, 1977. 275–300 (278–79). **Foresti, F.** "Composizione e redazione deuteronomistica in Ex 15,1–18." Lat 48 (1982) 46. **Forshey, H. O.** "The Construct Chain *naḥălat YHWH / ᵓēlōhîm."* *BASOR* 220 (1975) 51–53. **Giesen, G.** *Die Wurzel* שבע (1981). 338–39. **Gilbert, M.** "La Place de la Loi dans la Prière de Néhemie 9." In *FS H. Cazelles,* 2 (1981). 307–16 (311). **Gottstein, M. H.** "Afterthought and the Syntax of Relative Clauses in Biblical Hebrew." JBL 68 (1949) 35–47 (39). **Gerlemann, G.** "Nutzrecht und Wohnrecht. Zur Bedeutung von אחנה und נחלה." *ZAW* 89 (1977) 313–25. **Gressmann, H.** "Josia und das Deuteronomium." *ZAW* 42 (1924) 313–46 (32). **Gunneweg, A. H. J.** "Bildlosigkeit Gottes im Alten Israel." Hen 6 (1984) 257–70. **Holladay, W. L.** "The Identification of the Two Scrolls of Jeremiah." *VT* 30 (1980) 452–67 (463–64). **Horst, F.** "Zwei Begriffe für Eigentum (Besitz)." In *FS W. Rudolph* (1961). 135–56 (140–43). *HOTTP* I, 272. **Hyldahl, N.** "A Reminiscence of the Old Testament (Dt 4,15–18) at Rom 1, 23." *NTS* 2 (1956) 285–88. **Kline M. G.** "The Two Tables of the Covenant." *WTJ* 22 (1960) 133–46. ———. *The Structure of Biblical Authority.* Grand Rapids: Eerdmans, 1972. 113–30. **Kreuzer, S.** "Zur Bedeutung und Etymologie von HIŠTAḤᴬWĀH/YŠTḤWY." *VT* 35 (1985) 39–60. **Lohfink, N.** "Beobachtungen zur Geschichte des Ausdrucks עם יהוה." In *FS G. von Rad*

(1971). 275–305 (304). ————. "Kennt das Alte Testament einen Unterschied von 'Gebot' und 'Gesetz'? In *"Gesetz" als Thema biblischer Theologie.* JBTh 4. Neukirchen-Vluyn: Neukirchener Verlag, 1989. 63–89. **Luzarraga, J.** *Las tradiciones de la nube en la biblia en el judaismo primitivo.* AnBib 54. Rome: Pontificio Instituto Biblico, 1973. **May, H. G.** "Some Aspects of Solar Worship at Jerusalem." *ZAW* 55 (1937) 269–81. **Müller, H.-P.** "Die kultische Darstellung der Theophanie." *VT* 14 (1964) 183–91. **Quervain, A. de.** "Das zweite Gebot in der dogmatische Arbeit." In *FS K. Barth* (1936). 191–201. **Preuss, H. D.** *Verspottung fremder Religionen im alten Testament.* BWANT 92. Stuttgart: Kohlhammer, 1971. 241–43. **Rad, G. von.** "The Promised Land and Yahweh's Land in the Hexateuch." In *The Problem of the Hexateuch and Other Essays* (1966). 79–93 (=*GesStAT* ³1965, 87–100). **Schnutenhaus, F.** "Darstellung der Theophanie in Israels Gottesdienst durch Töne, Rauchwolke und Licht?" In *JLH* 8 (1963). 80–83. **Schützinger, H.** "Bild und Wesen der Gottheit im Alten Mesopotamien." In *Götterbild in Kunst und Schrift.* Ed. H.-J. Joachim. Bonn: Grundmann, 1984. 61–80. **Simonetti, M.** "Note sull'Interpretazione Patristica di Deut. 4,24." *VetChr* 5 (1968) 131–36. **Westphal, G.** *Jahwes Wohnstätten nach den Anschauungen der alten Hebräer: Eine alttestamentliche Untersuchung.* BZAW 15. Giessen: Töpelmann, 1908. **Zenger, E.** "Psalm 87,6 und die Tafeln vom Sinai." In *FS J. Ziegler* (1972). 97–103.

## Translation and Prosodic Analysis

**4:11–24** [(5:4:6:8):6:5:8] [(5+7):5] [5:(5+7)] [8:5:6] [8:6:(4:5)]

| | | |
|---|---|---|
| 11 And you came near and stood / at the foot of the mountain // | 16 | 2 |
| And the mountain / | 5 | 1 |
| (was) burning with fire / to the heart[a] of heaven / | 16 | 2_ |
| (There was) darkness / cloud and dense vapor [b] // | 12 | 2 |
| 12 And YHWH spoke (וידבר) / unto you / | 12 | 2_ |
| From the midst of the fire // | 7 | 1 |
| a voice \[a] of words (דברים) / you were hearing / | ⌈ 14 | 2 |
| And no form / you were seeing / (there was) only a voice // | ⌊ 22 | 3_ |
| 13 And he declared to you / his covenant / | 13 | 2 |
| which he commanded you / | ⌈ 6 | 1 |
| to do / the "ten words" (הדברים) // | ⌊ 13 | 2 |
| And he wrote them / upon two / tablets of stone // | 18 | 3_ |
| 14 And of me / YHWH commanded / AT THAT TIME / | 17 | 3 |
| (That I) teach you / statutes / and judgments // | 16 | 3_ |
| (For) you to do them / in the land / | 15 | 2 |
| Which you / are crossing over thither / to possess it // | 16 | 3_ |
| 15 And you shall take good heed / to your own soul-life // | 14 | 2 |
| For you did not see / any form / | 14 | 2 |
| IN A DAY (when) / YHWH spoke (דבר) unto you / | 12 | 2 |
| In Horeb / from the midst of the fire // | 12 | 2_ |
| 16 (Beware) lest you act corruptly / and you make for yourself / | ⌈ 14 ⌉ | 2 |
| a graven image \[a] (in the) form of any figure // | 10 | 1 |
| the likeness of male / or female // | ⌊ 14 | 2_ |
| 17 The likeness / of any beast / which is on the earth // | ⌈ 16 | 3 |
| The likeness / of any winged bird / | 11 ⌉ | 2 |
| which flies / in the heavens // | ⌊ 12 ⌋ | 2_ |

¹⁸ The likeness / of any creeper / \<creeping\>ᵃ on the ground //   ⌐ 7    2
The likeness /                                                          3 ⌐  1
of any fish that is in the water / under the earth //              ⌐ 18 ⌐ 2_

¹⁹ *And (beware) lest you lift up your eyes /*                      ⌐ 10    1
*heavenward / and you see /*                                          11    2
*The sun and the moon / and the stars /*                             21    2_
*All / the host of the heavens / and you be drawn away /*            15    3
*And you bow down before them / and you serve them //*               15    2_
*What he has allotted / YHWH your God / them /*                      17    3
*To all / the peoples / under / the whole heaven //*                 17    4_

²⁰ And you / YHWHᵃ has taken /                                      ⌐ 9     2
and he brought you forth / from the iron furnace /                   13    2
Out of Egyptᵇ // to be to him /                                    ⌐ 9     2
a people (who are) family property / as AT THIS DAY //             ⌐ 12    2_
²¹ And YHWH was angry with me / because of your words (דבריכם) // 14    2
And he sworeᵃ /                                                       5     1
(that) I should not cross over / \<this\>ᵇ Jordan /                  14    2_
And (that) I should not come / into the goodᶜ land /                19    2
Which / ᵈYHWH yourᵉ Godᵈ / is giving to youᵉ /                    ⌐ 15    3
*(as) family property //*                                          ⌐ 4     1_

²² *For I am about to die / in this land /*                          18    2
*I am not crossing over* \ᵃ *th\<is\>ᵇ Jordan //*                    17    1
But you / are crossing over / and you shall possess /             ⌐ 13    3
this / good land //                                                ⌐ 14    2_
²³ Take heed to yourselves /                                         9     1
lest you forget / the covenant of YHWH / yourᵃ God /             ⌐ 18    3
which he cut / with you //                                         ⌐ 9     2_
And you make for yourselves a graven image /                      ⌐ 10    1
in the form of anything /                                            6 ⌐  1
which *he has commanded you / YHWH [your God]* ᵃ //               ⌐ 8 ⌐ 2_
²⁴ *For / YHWH (is) yourᵃ God /*                                   ⌐ 10    2
*A consuming fire* \ᵇ *(is) he // a jealous / God //* פ          ⌐ 14    3_

## Notes

11.a. Omitted in LXX and Vg; SP reads לבב.

11.b. Some LXX witnesses add φωνὴ μεγάλη (cf. 5:22). Prosodic analysis supports MT.

12.a. Reading disj *yᵉtîb* as conj *mahpāk*.

16.a. See note 1:1c.

18.a. Adding רמש with LXX (ἑρπετοῦ) and Vg. The term apparently dropped out of MT by simple haplography.

20.a. Some LXX witness add ὁ θεός. Prosodic analysis supports MT.

20.b. Prosodic analysis suggests that the ʾatnāḥ should be relocated. The term מִמִּצְרַיִם is repointed מִמְּצָרִים.

21.a. Omitted in one Heb. Ms and SP. Prosodic analysis supports MT.

21.b. Adding הזה with one Heb. Ms, LXX, and Syr (cf. v 22 below).

21.c. Omitted in LXXᴸ. Prosodic analysis supports MT (and the Lucianic tradition of LXX).

21.d-d. Omitted in Vg. Prosodic analsysis supports MT.

21.e. Some LXX witnesses, Syr, Vg, and Tg^J read 2 pl.

22 a. See note 1:1c.

22.b. Adding הזה with LXX (τοῦτον) and Syr (cf. v 21 above).

23.a. Omitted with Vg. Old Latin, Syr, and Tg^J read 2 pl.

24.a. Old Latin, Syr, and Tg^J read 2 pl.

24.b. See note 1:1c.

## *Form/ Structure/ Setting*

Taking the *Numeruswechsel* in vv 11, 19, 21, 22, and 23 as boundary markers, Deut 4:11–24 is divided into four sections, which may be outlined in simple chiastic fashion as follows:

A    At Mount Sinai Yahweh spoke from the fire (vv 11–15),        [(5:4:6:8):(6:5:8)]
        forbidding graven images of any kind (vv 16–18)                      [(5+7):5]
   B        Worship of heavenly bodies is allotted to others (v 19)              [5:(5+7)]
   B'       Israel is Yahweh's "family property" (vv 20–21)                        [8:5:6]
A'    When you cross over, you are to make no graven image (vv 22–23);    [8:6:4]
        for Yahweh is a jealous God (v 24)                                              [5]

The subdivision in the first unit (vv 11–18) is marked by the temporal marker "at that time" in v 14. It is also possible to subdivide section B' (vv 20–21) after the temporal marker "at this day" to obtain a five-part structure in which Israel as Yahweh's נחלה, "family property" in v 20 is separate from the giving of the land to Israel as her נחלה, "family property" in v 21.

The first part of section "A" in this structure (vv 11–13), which recalls the establishment of Yahweh's covenant with Israel at Sinai, is set over against a summary statement in "A'" (v 24), which describes Yahweh's character. The Hebrew word אש, "fire," is used to tie these two sections together. In vv 11–12, "the mountain was burning with fire" (באש), and Yahweh spoke "from the midst of the fire" (מתוך האש). In the concluding note (v 24), Yahweh is described as "a consuming fire" (אש אכלה). There is still further repetition of words and sounds to connect the "A" sections. The term ונשמרתם, "you shall take heed," in v 15 is echoed in v 23 by השמרו לכם, "take heed to yourselves," in v 23. The phrase which follows that verb in v 23, פן־תשכחו . . . ועשיתם "lest you forget . . . and do", recalls פן־תשחתון ועשיתם, "lest you act corruptly and make," of v 16.

The central sections in this structure highlight the unique character of both Yahweh and his people Israel (vv 20–21), which is set over against the non-gods "the host of the heavens" to whom Yahweh has allotted "all the peoples under the whole heaven" (v 19; cf. Deut 32:8–9). Israel is unique among the nations, for she is called to worship the creator himself, not what he has created.

## *Comment*

**11–13**    The opening section in this structure (vv 11–13) recalls the mysterious events at Sinai, when Yahweh *spoke . . . from the midst of the fire* (v 12). At that time Yahweh declared his covenant with Israel and wrote the עשרת הדברים, "ten words" *upon two tablets of stone* (v 13). The delineation of these *ten words* (the Decalogue) follows in the next chapter.

וההר בער באש . . . חשך ענן וערפל, *The mountain was burning with fire . . .
darkness, cloud, and dense vapor*—the language of theophany, which is also the language of mysticism (cf. Deut 33:2; Judg 5:5; Ps 68:8; Hab 3:3; and Pascal's brilliant
essay on "Fire"). Though the original event took place in space and time, within
history, its meaning is to be understood in terms of the profound depths of psy-
chic experience. Out of the fire came *a voice of words* (הדברים); but *no form—only a
voice* (v 12). The use of a series of three active participles here in Hebrew height-
ens the drama of this, the most central moment in the religion of ancient Israel.
On Mount Sinai the voice of Yahweh declared *his covenant* [בריתו] *which he commanded [them] to do*, as summarized in *the ten words* (v 13).

שני לחות אבנים, *two tablets of stone*—the tablets contained two copies of the law,
not several commandments on each, as commonly assumed (see M. Kline, *Treaty
of the Great King* [1963] 13–26). Each party involved in suzerain/vassal treaties in
the ancient Near East had a copy of the covenant agreement.

**14–15** The commandment Moses received *to teach* (ללמד) the *statutes and
judgments* to the people points once again to the essential didactic function of
Deuteronomy, within the context of religious education in ancient Israel. On the
translation of נפש as "soul-life" see *Comment* on of Deut 4:9.

ביום, "in a day." The omission of the definite article here should be compared
to the use of יום in v 10 above. There was a particular day in history when the
event in question happened, but the experience of that moment liturgically is
not restricted to past time (cf. M. Eliade's use of the terms *illud tempus* and *in illo
tempore* in "Sacred Time and Myths," in *The Sacred and the Profane* [New York:
Harcourt, Brace & World, 1959] 68–113).

**16–19** In the larger concentric structural design, vv 16–18 are set over against
v 19 with פן־תשחתון, "lest you act corruptly" (v 16), balanced by ופן־תשא, "lest you
lift up your eyes" (v 19). פסל, "graven image," denotes an image cut from wood
or stone in general, whereas סמל, "figure," represents a specific portrayal of some
entity, a "statue" (cf. *smlt* in a fourth century B.C.E. Phoenician inscription where
it denotes a "statue" of the goddess *ʾAštart;* see G. A. Cooke, *A Textbook of North-
Semitic Inscriptions* [1903] 58). The detailed list of what kinds of images are
forbidden functions as an exegetical interpretation of Deut 5:8–10, the so-called
second commandment.

The warning against images in the form of animals of any kind (vv 17–18)
probably reflects the Israelite memory of their experience in Egypt, where animal deities were commonplace. The Egyptian pantheon was portrayed symbolically
in terms of animal representations of all the important deities. Moreover, mum-
mified remains of bulls, cats, dogs, and other beasts are well known from the
tombs of ancient Egypt. The goddess Hathor was portrayed as a cow; Thoth as a
babboon or an ibis; Horus as a falcon; etc. The symbol of the Egyptian scarab,
which was a representation of the "dung-beetle," may have prompted the inclusion of "creeping things" (v 18) in this list, though the snake was also perhaps in
view. The Proto-Sinaitic inscriptions make reference to a goddess known as the
"Serpent Lady" (see W. F. Albright, *The Proto-Sinaitic Inscriptions and Their Decipherment* [Cambridge: Harvard UP, 1966] nos. 351, 353, 360, 361). Whatever the
significance of רֶמֶשׂ רֹמֵשׂ <רֶמֶשׂ>, "creeping thing" (v 18), may be in the present context, it
should be remembered that the רֶמֶשׂ was part of God's creation (Gen 1:24) and not a
proper object of worship for Israel. The reference to כל־דגה אשר־במים מתחת לארץ,

*any fish that is in the water under the earth,* probably refers to mythic characters from the netherworld in Egyptian and Canaanite thought.

In v 19 attention shifts from the animal world to that of the cosmos. The restriction here is not that of making images, but of worshiping *the sun and the moon and the stars, all the host of the heavens.* In other religions of the ancient Near East the sun, the moon, and the stars were considered deities worthy of worship. For instance, in Egypt, Re was the sun-god (and Aten, the sun-disc), and Thoth originally a moon-god (see H. Frankort, *Ancient Egyptian Religion* [New York: Columbia UP, 1948]. 8–14). In Mesopotamia Shamash was the sun-god, Sin the moon-god, and Ishtar the "star" Venus (see H. W. F. Saggs, *The Greatness That Was Babylon* [New York: Hawthorne Books, 1962]. 314–29). In Canaan Shaphash was the sun-god, Yaraḥ the moon-god, and Athtar the "star" Venus (see W. F. Albright, *Yahweh and the Gods of Canaan* [London: Athlone Press, 1968]. 122–26).

**20–21** If Yahweh has allotted *the host of the heavens* to the other nations (v 19), he has done something extraordinary so far as Israel is concerned. The reference to Egypt as a כּוּר הַבַּרְזֶל, *iron furnace* (v 20), suggests that Israel's time there was seen as a period of testing and purifying (cf. Isa 48:10 and Jer 11:4).

נַחֲלָה, "[family] property"—as Num 36:7 makes clear, only members of the family may receive a נַחֲלָה; non-members such as servants cannot. As Susan Rattray has shown (private communication), even Prov 17:2 is no exception: its whole point is that the intelligent servant will become a full member of the family. Moses recalls the fact that he cannot enter the promised land (cf. 1:37 and 3:26), for he must pay the price for their words (v 21), apparently a reference to what happened at Kadesh-barnea. He will not share in the "inheritance" as Yahweh distributes his *family property* to Israel.

**22–24** Both the beginning and end of this rhythmic unit are marked by the *Numeruswechsel,* the sudden change to 2 pl forms in v 22 and back again to 2 sg at the end of v 23. Moses' disappointment is conveyed in a simple contrast in language within this verse: he announces that he will die *in this land* (Transjordan), whereas the people will cross over to possess *this good land* (Cisjordan). Before the people cross over, Moses reminds them one more time not to make any graven image, an act he equates with forgetting the covenant (v 23).

Yahweh is described as אֵשׁ אֹכְלָה, "a consuming fire," and אֵל קַנָּא, "a jealous God", which is language akin to the theme of love in Deuteronomy, as Buis and Leclerq have noted (*Le Deutéronome* [1963] 59).

### Explanation

The prohibition of images in ancient Israel has led to confusion in some circles, as well as to the obvious dearth of the plastic arts within Jewish (and, indirectly, Moslem) tradition. The text is careful to specify that the voice of God was heard speaking from the midst of the burning fire, but no form was seen. Since no form was seen on the occasion of that awesome theophany, the people were commanded to make no images. The theological reason was expressed well by Craigie: "To attempt to represent and limit God by human form in wood or stone would be to undermine the transcendence of God" (NICOT [1976] 135).

A problem emerges for some in our culture today in light of the intense interest in images and the use of the imagination in Jungian psychology. It should be noted that the use of the term images in this context has virtually nothing to do with the situation in ancient Israel. In fact, the return to language about direct access to spiritual reality through "images" in the inner world of the psyche is, in large measure, a return to the world view of ancient Israel (see M. T. Kelsey, *Encounter With God* [Minneapolis, MN: Bethany Fellowship, ²1975]).

The warning in v 19 against turning to the heavens is more subtle than the mere prohibition of making images in vv 16–18. The tendency among some modern intellectuals is still to replace God with his created order, so far as a practical object of worship is concerned (cf. J. Huxley, *Essays of a Humanist* [New York: Harper & Row, 1964] 113), who rejects what he calls the "god hypothesis" and posits as the proper object of worship a "unitary and evolutionary process").

*Bibliography for Deut 4:25–40*

**Angerstorfer, A**. *Der Schöpfergott des Alten Testaments: herkunft und Entwicklung des hebräischen Terminus.* Regensburger Studien zur Theologie 20. Frankfurt a.M.: P. Lang, 1979. 115–19. **Balscheit, B**. *Alter und Aufkommen des Monotheismus in der Israelitischen Religion.* BZAW 69. Berlin: Töpelmann, 1938. 131. **Begg, C**. "The Significance of the *Numeruswechsel* in Deuteronomy: The 'Prehistory' of the Question." *ETL* 55 (1979) 118. **Bolle, W**. *Das Israelitische Bodenrecht.* Diss., Berlin, 1940. **Braulik, G**. "Gesetz als Evangelium: Rechtfertigung und Begnadigung nach der deuteronomischen Tora." *ZTK* 79 (1982) 152–55 (= SBAB 4 [1988] 123–60). ————. "Das Deuteronomium und die Geburt des Monotheismus." In *Gott, der Einzige. Zur Entstehung des Monotheismus in Israel.* QD 104. Ed. E. Haag. Freiburg/Basel/Vienna: Herder, 1985. 115–59 (= SBAB 2 [1988] 257–300). **Brueggemann, W**. "Isaiah 55 and Deuteronomic Theology." ZAW 80 (1968) 191–203. ————. "Trajectories in Old Testament Literature and the Sociology of Ancient Israel." *JBL* 98 (1979) 161–85 (175–77). **Buchanan, G. W**. "Eschatology and the 'End of Days.'" *JNES* 20 (1961) 188–93. **Buis, P**. "Comment au septième siècle envisagait-on l'Avenir de l'Alliance? Étude de Lv 26, 3–45." In *Questions Disputées d'Ancien Testament. Méthode et Théologie.* Ed. C. Brekelmans. BETL 33. Leuven, 1974. **Carmignac, J**. "La notion d'eschatologie dans la Bible et à Qumrân." *RevQ* 7 (1969) 17–31. **Chiesa, B**. Un Nuovo Frammento del Commento di Samuel ben Hofni a Deut. 4,39–40." In AION 43 (1983) 61–82. **Childs, B. S**. "Deuteronomic Formulae of the Exodus Traditions." In VTSup 16. Leiden: Brill, 1967. 30–39. **Coppens, J**. "La Réforme de Josias." *ETL* 5 (1928) 581–98 (596). **Cross, F. M**. "The Structure of the Deuteronomic History." In *CMHE* (1973). 274–89. **Dahood, M**. "Karatepe Notes." *Bib* 44 (1963) 70–73. ————. "Hebrew-Ugaritic Lexicography I." *Bib* 44 (1963) 289–303 (291). ————. "The Divine Designation *hû'* in Eblaite and the Old Testament." In AION 43 (1983). 193–99 (195). **Delcor, M**. "Les attaches litteraires, l'origine et la signification de l'expression biblique 'Prendre à temoin le ciel et la terre.'" *VT* 16 (1966) 8–25. **Denton, R. C**. "The Literary Affinities of Exodus XXXIV 6f." *VT* 13 (1963) 34–51 (40f). **Diez Merino, L**. "Il vocabulario relativo alle 'ricerca de dio' nell'Antico Testamento." *BiOr* 24 (1982) 81–96, 129–45. **Driver, G. R**. "Colloquialisms in the Old Testament." In *Mélanges Marcel Cohen.* Paris and The Hague: Mouton, 1970. 232–39 (235). **Dus, J**. "Die Herabfahrung Jahwes auf die Lade und Entziehung der Feuerwolke." *VT* 19 (1969) 290–311. **Ebach, J**. "Sozialethische Erwägungen zum alttestamentlichen Bodenrecht." BN 1 (1976) 31–46. **Eerdmans, B. D**. *Deuteronomy.* Ed. D. C. Simpson. London: Griffin & Co., 1927. 77–84. **Fishbane, M**. "Varia Deuteronomica." *ZAW* 84 (1972) 351. **Fisher, L**. (ed.). RSP II (1975). 411–15. **Foresti, F**. "Characteristic Literary Expressions in the Arad Inscriptions Compared with the Language of the Hebrew Bible." *EphC* 332 (1981) 327–41 (338–39). ————. "Composizione e redazione deuteronomistica in Ex 15,1–18." *Lat* 48 (1982) 41–69. **Garcia Cordero, M**. "El Monoteismo en el Antiguo Testamento." *Burgense* 10 (1969) 9–34. **Gelb, I. J**. "Prisoners of

War in Early Mesopotamia." *JNES* 32 (1973) 70–98 (91–92). **Goetschel, R.** "Les traditions juives sur la fin de Moise." *MDB* 44 (1986) 24–26. **Goshen-Gottstein, M. H.** "A Recovered Part of the Aleppo Codex." *Textus* 5 (1966) 53–59. **Gross, W.** "Bundeszeichen und Bundesschluss in der Priesterschrift." *TThZ* 87 (1978) 98–115 (107). **Habel, N. C.** "Appeal to Ancient Tradition as a Literary Form." *ZAW* 88 (1976) 253–72 (258–59). **Hamp, V.** "Montheismus im Alten Testament." In *Sacra Pagina*. BETL 12–13. Gembloux, 1959. I, 516–21. **Hartmann, B.** "Es gibt keinen Gott ausser Jahwe." *ZDMG* 110 (1961) 229–35 (233). ————. "'Es gibt keine Kraft und keine Macht ausser Gott.' Zur Kopula im Hebräischen." In OTS 14. Leiden: Brill, 1965. 115–21. **Hausmann, J.** *Israels Rest. Studien zum Selbstverständnis der nachexilischen Gemeinde.* Ed. S. Herrmann and K. Rengstorf. BWANT 124. Stuttgart: Kohlhammer (1987) 118–20. **Heller, J.** "Die Entmythisierung des ugaritischen Pantheons im AT." *TLZ* 101 (1976) 1–10. **Hermisson, H.-J.** "Zur Erwählung Israels: Alttestamentliche Gedanken zum Amt der Gemeinde." In *FS G. Krause* (1982). 37–66. **Hoffmeier, J. K.** "The Arm of God Versus the Arm of Pharaoh in the Exodus Narratives." *Bib* 67 (1986) 378–87. **Holladay, W. L.** "*subh.*" *HOTTP* I, 272–3. **Jacobsen, T.** "The Graven Image." In *FS F. M. Cross* (1987). 15–32 (20–29). **Johannes, G.** *Unvergleichkeitsformulierungen im Alten Testament.* Diss., Mainz, 1968. **Johnson, A. R.** "Aspects of the Use of the Term אֱנָשִׁים in the Old Testament." In *FS O. Eissfeldt* (1947). 155–59 (159). ————. *The Vitality of the Individual in the Thought of Ancient Israel.* Cardiff: Wales UP, ²1964. 11–22, 75–87. **Katz, P.** "The Meaning of the Root קנה." *JJS* 5 (1954) 126–31. **Kegler, J.** *Politisches Geschehen und theologisches Verstehen: Zum Geschichtsverständnis in der frühen israelitischen Königszeit.* CThM 8. Stuttgart: Calwer, 1977. 14–15. **Kim, J. C.** *Verhältnis Jahwes zu den anderen Göttern in Deuterojesaja.* Diss., Heidelberg, 1964. **Klein, H.** "Der Beweis der Einzigartigkeit Jahwes bei Deuterojesaja." *VT* 35 (1985) 267–73. **Knohl, I.** "The Priestly Torah Versus the Holiness School: Sabbath and the Festivals." *HUCA* 58 (1987) 65–117. **Labuschagne, C. J.** *Incomparability of Jahwe in the Old Testament.* POS 5. Leiden: Brill, 1966. **Lang, B.** *Monotheism and the Prophetic Minority: An Essay in Biblical History and Sociology.* SWBA 1. Sheffield: Almond Press, 1983. 13–59, 158–63. ————. "Zur Entstehung des biblischen Monotheismus." *ThQ* 166 (1986) 135–42. **Lipinski, E.** "*bᵉhryt hymym* dans les textes préexiliques." *VT* 20 (1970) 445–50. **Löwenstamm, S. E.** "*nhltyʾ* The Heritage of Yahweh." In *Studies in Bible* 1986. Ed. S. Japhet. ScrHier 31. Jerusalem: Magnes Press, 1986. 155–92. **Lohfink, N.** *Option for the Poor.* Berkeley: BIBAL Press, 1987. 37–38. **Mayes, A. D. H.** "Exposition of Deuteronomy 4:25–31." *IBS* 2 (1980) 67–83. **Mittmann, S.** *Deuteronomium* 1, 1–6, 3 (1978). 123. **Moran, W. L.** "Some Remarks on the Song of Moses." *Bib* 43 (1962) 317–27 (318–19). **Morstad, E.** "Dt 4, 25–28 og 29–40." *NorTT* 60 (1955) 34–45. **Oden, R. A.** "*Baʿal Šāmēm* and *ʾĒl.*" CBQ 39 (1977) 457–73. **Preuss, H. D.** *Verspottung Fremder Religionen im Alten Testament.* BWANT 92. Stuttgart: Kohlhammer, 1971. 243–47. **Rignell, L. G.** "Isaiah Chapter I. Some exegetical remarks with special reference to the relationship between the text and the book of Deuteronomy." *ST* 11 (1957) 140–58. **Rofé, A.** "The Monotheistic Argumentation in Deuteronomy iv 32–40: Contents, Composition and Text." *VT* 35 (1985) 434–45. **Rosenberg, R. A.** "YAHWEH Becomes King." *JBL* 85 (1966) 297–307 (300). **Sasson, V.** "The Aramaic Text of the Tell Fakhriyah Assyrian-Aramaic Bilingual Inscription." *ZAW* 97 (1985) 86–103. **Sawyer, J. F. A.** "Biblical Alternatives to Monotheism." *Theology* 87 (1984) 172–80. **Schenker, A.** "Unwiderrufliche Unkehr und neuer Bund. Vergleich zwischen der Wiederherstellung Israels in Dt 4, 25–31; 30, 1–14 und dem neuen Bund in Jer 31,31–34." *FZPhTh* 27 (1980) 93–106. **Shafer, B. E.** "The Root *bhr* in Pre-Exilic Concepts of Chosenness in the Hebrew Bible." *ZAW* 89 (1977) 20–42 (27–28). **Sheriffs, D. C. T.** "The Phrases *ina IGI DN* and *lip̄enēj Yhwh* in Treaty and Covenant Contexts." *JNSL* 7 (1979) 55–68. **Ska, J.-L.** "La sortie d'Égypte dans le recit sacerdotal (Pᵍ) et la tradition prophétique." *Bib* 60 (1979) 191–215. **Staerk, W.** "Der Gebrauch der Wendung BᵉHRJT HJMJM im alttestmentische Kanon." *ZAW* 11 (1891) 247–53. **Stolz, F.** Jahwes Unvergleichlichkeit und Unergründlichkeit: Aspekte der Entwicklung zum alttestamentlichen Monotheismus." *WuD* 14 (1977) 9–24. **Untermann, J.** *From Repentance to Redemption: Jeremiah's Thought in Transition.* JSOTSup 54. Sheffield: JSOT Press, 1987. **Veijola,**

**T**. "Zu Ableitung und Bedeutung von hē‘īd im Hebräischen: Ein Beitrag zur Bundesterminologie." *UF* 8 (1976) 343–51. **Wächter, L**. "Erfüllung des Lebens nach dem Alten Testament." *ZZ* 22 (1968) 284–92. **Waldow, H. E. von**. "Israel and Her Land: Some Theological Considerations." In *FS J. M. Myers* (1974). 493–508. **Weil, H. M**. "Gage et cautionnement dans la Bible." *Archiv d'Histoire du Droit International* 2 (1938) 171–241 (220). **Wiéner, C**. *Recherches sur l'Amour pour Dieu dans l'Ancient Testament: Étude d'une Racine.* Paris, 1957. **Wijngaards, J. N. M**. *The Dramatization of Salvific History in the Deuteronomic Schools.* OTS 16. Leiden: Brill, 1969. 68–71. **Williams, W. H**. "A Look within the Deuteronomic History." *SJT* 25 (1972) 337–45. **Wolff, H. W**. "Das Kerygma des deuteronomistischen Geschichtswerks." ZAW 73 (1961) 171–86. **Yahuda, A. S**. *The Language of the Pentateuch in Its Relation to Egyptian.* London: Oxford UP, 1930. (66, 81). **Ziegler, J**. "Zur Septuaginta-Vorlage im Deuteronomium." ZAW 72 (1960) 237–62 (246). **Zimmerli, W**. *Erkenntnis Gottes nach dem Buch Ezekiel. Eine Theologische Studie.* ATANT 27. Zürich, 1954. 28–30, 45.

### *Translation and Prosodic Analysis*

4:25–40    [7+5] [(5:5):9:8] [7:6:(4:6)] [7:7:7:(6:4)] [6:7:8:9] [5:5:(7+5)]

| | | |
|---|---:|---:|
| [25] *When you*[a] *beget children /* | 10 | 1 |
| *and children's children /* | <u>9</u> | 1 |
| And you grow old / in the land // and you act corruptly / | 14 | 3 |
| And you make a graven image / the likeness of anything / | <u>13</u> | 2_ |
| And you do evil / | ⌐ 8 | 1 |
| in the eyes of YHWH *your God* / *to provoke him* // | ∟ 19 | 2 |
| [26] *I call to witness against* you TODAY / | ⌐ 13 | 1 |
| the heavens and the earth / | ∟ <u>13</u> | 1_ |
| | | |
| For you shall surely perish / quickly [a] / from the land / | ⌐ 23 | 3 |
| (to) which you / are crossing over the Jordan / | ∟ 14 | 2_ |
| Thither \[b] to possess it // | ⌐ 7 ⌐ | 1 |
| you will not extend (your) days / upon it // | 17 ∟ | 2 |
| for you will surely / be destroyed // | ∟ <u>14</u> | 2_ |
| [27] And YHWH will scatter / you / among the peoples[a] // | 15 | 3 |
| And you will be left / few in numbers / among the nations[b] / | 15 | 3 |
| Where YHWH will drive / you / thither // | <u>14</u> | 3_ |
| [28] And there you will serve gods[a] / works / of human hands // | 22 | 3 |
| of wood and stone / who do not see / | 13 | 2 |
| And do not hear / and do not eat / and do not smell // | <u>23</u> | 3_ |
| | | |
| [29] And you[a] will seek from there / YHWH *your God* / | ⌐ 17 | 2 |
| *and you will find (him)*[b] // | ∟ 7 | 1 |
| *When you search* / | ⌐ 7 | 1 |
| *with all your heart* / *and with all your soul-life* // | 14 ⌐ | 2 |
| [30] *when you are in trouble*[a] / | ∟ <u>4</u> ∟ | 1_ |
| *And it shall come upon you* / *all* \[b] *these things* (הדברים) // | 21 | 2 |
| *in THE LATTER* / *DAYS* / | ⌐ 10 | 2 |
| *and you shall return* / *unto YHWH your God* / | ∟ <u>12</u> | 2_ |
| *And you shall hear* / *his voice* // | ⌐ 11 | 2 |
| [31] *for a merciful God* / *(is) YHWH your God* / | ∟ 15 | 2_ |

| | | |
|---|---|---|
| He will not fail you / and he will not destroy you // | ⌈ 13 | 2 |
| And he will not forget / the covenant with your fathers / | ⌊ <u>14</u> | 2 |
| which he swore / to them // | 7 | 2_ |

32 *For ask now* [a] *of THE FORMER DAYS* [a] / *which were before you* / — 27 — 2

| | | |
|---|---|---|
| *From* [b] *THE DAY* / *in which God created* \ [c] *human kind* / | ⌈ 20 | 2 |
| *on the earth* / | ⌊ 6 | 1 |
| *From one end of the heavens* / | 10 | 1 |
| *To the other end of the heavens* // | <u>11</u> | 1_ |
| *Has there happened* [d] / *so great a thing* (כדבר) / *as this?* / | ⌈ 17 | 3 |
| *or* / *has anyone ever heard of such (a thing)?* // | ⌊ 11 | 2 |

33 | | |
|---|---|---|
| *Has any people ever heard the voice of God* [a] / | ⌈ 17 | 1 |
| *speaking* (מדבר) *from the midst of the fire* / | ⌊ <u>11</u> | 1_ |
| *Just as you yourselves have heard* / *and still live?* [b] // | 14 | 2 |

34 | | |
|---|---|---|
| *Or* / *has any god ever attempted* [a] / *to come* / | 15 | 3 |
| *To take for himself a nation* / *from the midst of a nation* / | <u>15</u> | 2_ |
| *By trials by signs and by wonders* / | 17 | 1 |
| *And by war* / *and by a mighty hand* / | 18 | 2 |
| *And by an outstretched arm* / *and by great* \ [b] *terrors* // | ⌈ 25 | 2 |
| *according to all* / | ⌊ 3 | 1 |
| *That he has done* for you [c] / YHWH your [d] God / | ⌈ 18 | 2 |
| in Egypt / *before your* [e] *eyes* // | ⌊ 9 | 2_ |

35 | | |
|---|---|---|
| *You yourself* / *were shown so that you might know* / | ⌈ 12 | 2 |
| *that (it is)* YHWH [a] / | ⌊ 5 | 1 |
| *He is the God* // *there is no other* / *beside him* // | <u>17</u> | 3_ |

36 | | |
|---|---|---|
| *From heaven* / | ⌈ 6 | 1 |
| *he caused you to hear his voice* / *to discipline you* // | ⌊ 15 | 2 |
| *And on earth* / *he caused you to see* \ [a] *his great fire* / | 20 | 2 |
| *And his words you heard* / *from the midst of the fire* // | <u>19</u> | 2_ |

37 | | |
|---|---|---|
| *And because* [a] / *he loved* / *your fathers* / | ⌈ 14 | 3 |
| *and he chose* [b] *their descendants* / *after them* [b] // | ⌊ 11 | 2 |
| *And he brought you* [c] *forth in his own presence* / | ⌈ 11 | 1 |
| *in his great power* / *from Egypt* // | ⌊ <u>14</u> | 2_ |

38 | | |
|---|---|---|
| *(In order) to drive out* / *nations* / | ⌈ 9 | 2 |
| *greater and mightier* / *than yourselves* / | ⌊ 14 | 2 |
| *from before you* // | 5 | 1_ |
| *To bring you in* / *to give you their land* / | ⌈ 15 | 2 |
| *as family property* / *as AT THIS DAY* // | ⌊ <u>9</u> | 2_ |

39a | | |
|---|---|---|
| *And you shall know TODAY* [a] / | ⌈ 8 | 1 |
| *and you shall lay it* / *to* [b] *your heart* / | ⌊ 14 | 2 |
| *that YHWH* / *he is the God* / | 14 | 2_ |
| *In the heavens above* / | ⌈ 8 | 1 |
| *and upon the earth* / *beneath* // *there is no* / *other* // | ⌊ <u>15</u> | 4_ |

40 | | |
|---|---|---|
| *And you shall keep* / *his statutes and his commandments* / | 16 | 2 |
| *which I command you* / *TODAY* / | 14 | 2 |
| *That* \ [a] *it may go well with you* / | ⌈ 6 | 1 |
| *and with your children* / *after you* // | ⌊ <u>11</u> | 2_ |

| | | |
|---|---|---|
| *And in order that you may prolong your days /* | ⌐13 | 1 |
| *upon the ground /* | ⌐8 | 1 |
| *Which YHWH your God / is giving you / ALL THE DAYS //* פ | <u>21</u> | 3_ |

### Notes

25.a. SP, Syr, Tg, Tg^J, Old Latin, and Vg read 2 pl.

25.b. LXX, SP, Syr, Tg^J, and Vg read 2 pl.

26.a. Omitted in some LXX witnesses.

26.b. See note 1:1c.

27.a. LXX^-L reads בכל העמים, which is possible in terms of mora-count.

27.b. LXX^AB reads בכל הגוים, which is possible in terms of mora-count.

28.a. Some Heb. Mss and LXX add אחרים, "other." Prosodic analysis supports MT.

29.a. SP, Tg, and Vg read 2 sg.

29.b. SP and Vg read וּמְצָאתוֹ, which is possible in terms of mora-count.

30.a. Reading בצר לך at end of v 29 with SP (some Mss).

30.b. See note 1:1c.

32.a-a. On the use of לְמִן־ as a *terminus a quo*, see S. R. Driver, ICC (1895) 75.

32.b. One Heb. Ms, SP, Syr, and Tg read לְיָמִים הָרִאשֹׁנִים. Prosodic analysis supports MT.

32.c. The *mahpāh* followed by *pāsēq* is read as conj.

32.d. SP reads הן היה; Tg, Tg^J hhwh = הֲהָיָה. Both are possible in terms of mora-count.

33.a. Two Heb. Mss, SP, LXX, Tg add (ה)חיים with Deut 5:26. Prosodic analysis supports MT.

33.b. LXX and Vg read 2 sg ותחי; Syr reads 2 pl; cf. vv 37 and 42 below.

34.a. On Heb. נסה "attempted," "tried," or perhaps "dared," see J. C. L. Gibson (*Textbook of Syrian Semitic Inscriptions*, I [Oxford: Clarendon Press, 1971] 40) and Lachish Ostraca iii.9.

34.b. See note 1:1c.

34.c. Omitted in at least one Heb. Ms, numerous LXX witnesses, and Syr. Prosodic analysis supports MT.

34.d. One Heb. Ms, LXX^-N read אלהינו, "our God."

34.e. One Heb. Ms, SP, Syr and Tg read 2 pl. אלהיכם.

35.a. LXX adds ὁ θεός σου (האלהיך). Prosodic analysis supports MT.

36.a. Replacing paštā᾽ with conj accent to achieve balance in distribution of accentual stress units with parallel element in v 29 above.

37.a. *BHS* suggests reading ותחי האש and attaching this word with the end of v 36 (cf. v 33 above). The prosodic analysis supports MT.

37.b-b. SP, LXX, Syr, Tg, and Vg read 3 pl with Deut 10:15. If MT is retained, it must be interpreted accordingly. LXX adds παρὰ πάντα τὰ ἔθνη with Deut 10:15 (מכל־העמים). Prosodic analysis supports MT.

37.c. Syr and Old Latin read 2 pl suff.

39.a-a. Omitted in some LXX witnesses. Prosodic analysis supports MT.

39.b. SP reads על for אל.

40.a. Replacing paštā᾽ with conj accent to achieve balance in distribution of syntactic accentual stress units with parallel unit in v 25.

### Form/Structure/Setting

According to the system of rhetorical markers observed thus far, 4:25–40 appears to be divided into six subunits, which may be outlined as follows:

| | | | |
|---|---|---|---|
| A | When you make an image, I bear witness against you (vv 25–26a) | | [7:5] |
| | B | You will be scattered and serve other gods (vv 26b–28) | (5:5):9:8] |
| |   C | Future: When you return, Yahweh will forgive (vv 29–31) | [7:6:10] |
| |   C' | Past: Has any god done what Yahweh has done? (vv 32–34) | [7:7:7:10] |
| | B' | Yahweh brought you from Egypt to give you the land (vv 35–38) | [6:7:8:9] |
| A' | Keep Yahweh's commandments to prolong your days (vv 39–40) | | [(5:5):7:5] |

Though the larger concentric design here is not as obvious as in earlier sections of Deuteronomy, it nonetheless can be demonstrated. The reference to "children and children's children" in v 25 forms an inclusion with the wish "that it may go well with you and with your children" in v 40. The concept of forbidden images of God (vv 25–26a) is set over against the reference to the incomparability of Yahweh: "There is no other" (v 39). This conceptual frame around the unit as a whole echoes the reference to the incomparability of Yahweh at the center of this unit (vv 32–34).

The boundaries of each subunit in 4:25–40 are clearly marked by a series of rhetorical features. The *Numeruswechsel* marks three of the five boundaries between these subunits (in vv 26a, 28, and 34). The other boundaries are marked by the use of familiar temporal terms: "the former days" (v 32), "at this day" (v 38), "today" (v 39), and "all the days" (end of v 40). The end of the passage as a whole is also marked by the *p̄etûḥāʾ* paragraph marker. The final rhythmic unit in vv 39–40 is framed by these temporal phrases, with the repetition of the word "today" at the center of that subunit (beginning of v 40). The final verse of this subunit (v 40) also includes repetition of the command to "keep his statutes and his commandments" with which the larger structural unit began in vv 1–2. On the concentric design of 40:1–10 as a whole, see discussion above.

*Comment*

**25–26a** The reference to *children and children's children* (grandchildren) continues the focus on future temptations Israel would face after they had gained possession of Cisjordan. The specific sin in focus is that of making *a graven image* (see *Comment* on vv 16–18 and 22–23).

As numerous scholars have noted, the reference to summoning *the heavens and the earth* as witnesses against the people is characteristic of covenant treaty texts in the ancient Near East. In some of these texts "heaven and earth" are included in the list of deities cited as witnesses to the treaty (see in particular *PRU* IV, 17.365 and 17.338 and Craigie's discussion, NICOT [1976] 139). In terms of the implicit monotheism of the Hebrew Bible, heaven and earth are not considered deities as such, but metaphorical "witnesses." Their permanence in the created order stands in sharp contrast to the fickleness of human beings.

**26b–28** If the Israelites are guilty of making images to represent the invisible Yahweh, they *will surely be destroyed* (v 26) and scattered among the peoples (v 27). In exile the people will serve witless and impotent *gods [made by] human hands* (v 28). Though numerous scholars have taken this prophetic note as a *vaticinium ex eventu*, it should be noted that destruction and dispersion are characteristic punishments for violation of international treaties in the ancient Near East. As a nascent national entity, Israel's greatest danger was the loss of unity among the tribes. Loss of their distinctiveness would result in their being scattered and lost *among the nations where Yahweh will drive you thither* (v 27). Their consequent survival *few in numbers* should be contrasted to the covenant promise as given to both Abraham (Gen 15:15) and Moses (Deut 1:10), in which they were to become "as the stars of the heavens in number."

**29–31** The sudden shift in v 29 from 2nd pl to 2nd sg forms *(Numeruswechsel)* marks the beginning of a new rhythmic unit which continues through v 34, the end of which is marked in similar fashion. The two subdivisions of this larger unit are marked by the reference to "latter days" (v 30), as over against "the former days" (v 32).

The warning against future apostasy continues here with an added note of hope. In exile the Israelites will once again seek Yahweh and they *will find him when [they] search with all [their] heart* (v 29), in spite of their trouble. And when they do *return unto Yahweh* (v 30), they will find him to be *a merciful God who will not forget the covenant with [their] fathers* (v 31). On the meaning of the terms *heart* and *soul-life* here, see *Comment* on Deut 4:9 and Deut 6:5.

**32–34**   The look into the future of "the latter days" in vv 29–31 prompts a corresponding recollection of "the former days" (v 32), in which the God of history acted in behalf of his chosen people. The unit consists of an expanded rhetorical question which knows no chronological or geographical limits: *ask now . . . from the day in which God created human kind on the earth from one end of the heavens to the other end of the heavens* (v 32). The invitation is to examine the whole of human history to see if anything similar to Israel's experience of God is to be found: *Has there happened so great a thing* [הדבר] *as this or has anyone ever heard of such a thing?* The term used here for Yahweh's "great deed" is the singular of the word הדברים, the Hebrew title of the book of Deuteronomy. The rhetorical question continues with reference to Israel's experience at Mount Sinai where *the voice of God* was heard *speaking from the midst of the fire* (v 33). The question continues in reference to Israel's experience of the Exodus from Egypt: *Has any god ever attempted to come to take for himself a nation from the midst of a nation . . . by signs and by wonders* (v 34)? The implied answer to the question is a resounding "No."

**35–38**   In the larger structure, this rhythmic unit is set over against vv 26b–28 which foretold a future time when the Israelites would "serve gods made by human hands" (v 28). The impotence of those "gods" stands in sharp contrast to Yahweh and his mighty acts, as reviewed briefly here.

The knowledge of God in ancient Israel is based on God's action and revelation in history: *his great fire and his words you heard from the midst of the fire* at Mount Sinai (v 36); and his action, when *he brought you forth in his own presence in his great power from Egypt* (v 37). Israel was shown all this in order that they *might know that Yawheh is God; there is no other beside him* (v 35). This is practical monotheism. Though the Israelites were aware of belief in many gods, they were severely warned against serving those gods. Yahweh alone was the true living God. The proof of this reality lay not in any philosophical arguments, but in the historical experience of the Exodus and what was revealed on Mount Sinai. And all this took place in order to bring them into the promised land in the Conquest (v 38).

ליסרך, "to discipline you" (v 36). The root יסר appears also in Deut 8:5 in terms of a man disciplining his son. The covenant, as portrayed in Deuteronomy, is a father/son relationship between Yahweh and his people.

נחלה, "family property"—see the *Comment* at vv 20–21.

**39–40**   The experience of Israel, beginning with the promise made to the *fathers* (v 37) and continuing through the Exodus and the revelation at Mount Sinai to the beginning of the possession of the land (vv 37–38), reached its culmination at one single point and for one purpose: that *you shall know today . . . that Yahweh is God in the heavens above and upon the earth beneath* (v 39).

The recollection of God's mighty acts in history concludes with a restatement of Yahweh's command to *keep his statutes and his commandments which I* [Moses] *command you today* (v 40), which forms an inclusion with the same command as presented at the beginning of this chapter (vv 1–2). The delineation of those statutes and commandments will commence in the following chapter, with the presentation of the Ten Commandments.

## Explanation

The popular view that identifies law with the OT and gospel with the NT will certainly not stand up against a careful reading of the book of Deuteronomy, as G. Braulik has shown ("Law as Gospel: Justification and Pardon according to the Deuteronomic Torah," *Int* 38 [1984] 5–14). To understand Deuteronomy one must recognize God's prior grace to sinners, that is, the priority of gospel over law, in the OT as well as the NT. Though Deuteronomy stresses the fact that obedience to God's Torah is essential, it even more strongly emphasizes the fact that such obedience is dependent upon the grace of God.

Texts like Deut 4:29–31 and 30:1–10 define precisely what constitutes Yahweh's work of grace and Israel's merit in terms of the concept of "conversion," as reflected in the Hebrew word שׁוב. The significance of this theological concept is shown by the position of these two pericopes, which constitute a framework around the Inner Frame of the book (chaps. 4–11 and 27–30). The conversion theme is introduced in the first parenetic passage of the book as its primary intention, and it rounds off the last parenetic text as the decisive message in the last parenetic text of the book. Moreover, the key verb שׁוב is used in its religious sense in Deuteronomy only in these two pericopes (4:30 and 30:1–10).

The larger context of 4:29–31 concerns the structure of the covenant relationship in which these particular verses constitute the section of blessing. As Braulik has noted: "Contrary to the otherwise normal conditional wording, this blessing is historicized. That means that a time of blessing is pledged unconditionally as God's grace. Above and beyond this, the text explicitly promises that Israel will not only search for Yahweh, it will find him" (12). Here Braulik is simply echoing the words of N. Lohfink: "Yahweh will not only let himself be found. He has foretold that he will let himself be found, and these words of prediction are already underway, they are already in search of Israel. It is not Israel which will find Yahweh, but Yahweh's words which will find Israel. Israel must not repent in order that Yahweh once again turns towards it; rather, if Yahweh's words find Israel, then Israel will be granted the grace of repentance" (N. Lohfink, *Höre Israel!* [1965] 113).

"These words" (v 30; cf. 1:1) which will find Israel constitute the covenant's central commandments regarding Israel's relationship with God (v 29; cf. 6:4–5). As such they also constitute the gospel for a guilty people, since even Israel's guilt will not prevail. Yahweh has irrevocably committed himself to Israel by an oath to their fathers (v 31).

According to 4:29–31 Israel's primary quest is to have Yahweh as its God once again. The parallel passage in 30:7–10 develops this theme further in its insistence that the law upon which the fulfillment of Yahweh's blessing depends "is very near to you, in your mouth and in your heart, that you may keep it" (30:14). This is what Paul has in mind in his reference to *"righteousness that comes from faith"* (Rom 10:6). As Braulik put it (Int 38 [1984] 14), "The deuteronomic law, truly interiorized, is the 'word of faith' (Rom 10:8), that is, gospel (Rom 10:16)."

# "Then Moses Set Apart Three Cities" (4:41–43)

## Bibliography

**Auld, A. G.** "Cities of Refuge in Israelite Tradition." *JSOT* 10 (1978) 26–40. **Bartlett, J. R.** "Sihon and Og Kings of the Amorites." *VT* 20 (1970) 257–77 (265). **Benjamin, D.** *Deuteronomy and City Life* (1983). **Boger, H.** "The City of Refuge Bezer." *BIES* 22 (1958) 91–94. **Bruston, C.** "Le Deutéronome primitif et c'est? qu'il suppose." *RThQR* 5 (1896) 247–57. **Delekat, L.** *Asylie und Schutzorakel am Zionsheiligtum: Eine Untersuchung zu den privaten Feindpsalmen. Mit zwei Excursen.* Leiden: Brill, 1967. **Dinur, B.** "The Religious Character of the Cities of Refuge and the Ceremony of Admission into Them" (Heb). EI 3 (1954) 135–46. **Feinberg, M.** "The Cities of Refuge." *BSac* 103 (1946) 411–17; 104 (1947) 36–48. **Fensham, F. C.** "Liability in Case of Negligence in the Old Testament Covenant Code and Ancient Legal Traditions." In *Acta Juridica* 1976. Capetown, South Africa: Juta, 1978. 283–94. **Foresti, F.** "Composizione e redazione deuteronomistica in Ex 15,1–18." *Lat* 48 (1982) 68. **Glueck, N.** "Ramoth-Gilead." *BASOR* 92 (1943) 10–16. **Löhr, M.** *Das Asylwesen im Alten Testament.* SKGG 7,3. Halle: Max Niemeyer, 1930. **Milgrom, J.** "Sancta Contagion and Altar/City Asylum." In VTSup 32 [Congress Vienna 1980]. Leiden: Brill, 1981. 278–310. **Procksch, O.** *Die Blutrache bei den vorislamischen Arabern.* Leipzig: J. C. Hinrichs, 1899. **Rabinowitz, I.** "*ʾāz* Followed by Imperfect Verb-Form in Preterite Contexts: A Redactional Device in Biblical Hebrew." *VT* 34 (1984) 53–62. **Rofé, A.** "Joshua 20: Historico-Literary Criticism Illustrated. "In *Empirical Models for Biblical Criticism.* Ed. J. Tigay. Philadelphia: Univ. of Pennsylvania Press, 1985. 135. **Schlesinger, E.** *Die griechische Asylie.* Diss., Giessen, 1933.

## Translation and Prosodic Analysis

4:41–43    [4:7:7:4]

| | | |
|---|---|---|
| [41] *Then Moses set apart / three cities /* | 16 | 2 |
| *In the vicinity of* \[a] *the Jordan // *[b]*in the\ east*[b] *//* | 15 | 2_ |
| [42] *That he might flee thither /* a[a] *manslayer /* | 12 | 2 |
| *who shall slay his neighbor /* | 11 | 1 |
| *(It was) unintentional /* | 5 | 1 |
| *and he / was not hating him / in time past //* | 18 | 3_ |
| *And he shall flee / unto one / of these*[b] *cities /* | 17 | 3 |
| *and he shall live //* | 4 | 1 |
| [43] *Bezer in the wilderness / in the tableland /* | 15 | 2 |
| *for the Reubenites*[a] *//* | 9 | 1_ |
| *And Ramoth in Gilead / for the Gadites /* | 15 | 2 |
| *And Golan in Bashan / for the Manassites //* | 16 | 2_ |

## Notes

41.a. See note 1:1.c.

41.b-b. Reading מזרח השמש with one Heb. Ms, SP, Tg, Tg[J] (cf. Syr). The disj *ṭipḥāʾ* is replaced with a conj accent to improve the rhythmic balance with the structural counterpart in v 43b.

42.a. LXX and SP (cf. Syr, Tg, Tg^J and 19:4) add the def art, which is possible in terms of mora-count.

42.b. Reading הָאֵלֶּה with the Seberin, one Heb. Ms, SP (cf. 7:22; 19:11).

43.a. Reading לָרֵאוּבֵנִי with a number of Heb. Mss.

## Form/Structure/Setting

Within the larger structure of Deut 4–11, this brief unit stands over against 10:8–11, where Yahweh set apart the tribe of Levi. In content it is related to 19:1–14, which deals with the establishment of three more cities of refuge in Cisjordan. The passage as a whole functions as a disjunctive element, separating the moving challenge on the lips of Moses to obey Yahweh's commandments in 4:1–40 from the beginning of the actual delineation of those commandments (4:44–6:3). The reader (or hearer) cannot help but feel the jarring effect of encountering a totally different type of content as one moves from v 40 to v 41. A narrator suddenly appears, without introduction, to describe the establishment of three cities of refuge for the tribes in Transjordan.

## Comment

**41–43** The reasons for setting aside cities of refuge and laws concerning them are discussed in the *Comment* at 19:1–14. Comments here are limited to geographical notes.

בֶּצֶר, "Bezer," has been identified provisionally by Aharoni with modern Umm el-ʿAmad, eight miles (13 km.) northeast of Medeba (*The Land of the Bible*, rev. ed. [Philadelphia: Westminster, 1979] 339, 433). The name also appears on the Moabite Stone (line 27) as one of the cities fortified by Mesha.

רָאמֹת בַּגִּלְעָד, "Ramoth in Gilead," is identified with Tell-Rāmîth, located between the Yarmuk and the Jabbok near the present border between Syria and Jordan (see N. Glueck, "Ramoth-Gilead," *BASOR* 92 [1943] 10–16).

גּוֹלָן, "Golan," the most northerly of the cities of refuge, identified by Aharoni with Saḥmel-Jōlân, seventeen miles (27 km.) east of the Sea of Galilee (*The Land of the Bible*, rev. ed. [Philadelphia: Westminster, 1979] 435).

## Explanation

One of the problems of legal justice in relation to criminal law in ancient Israel involved the "avenger of blood" (גֹּאֵל הַדָּם; see Deut 19:6), who was apparently the nearest male kinsman of the deceased in instances of violent death. His responsibility was not simply to kill the person responsible for the death of his relative (whether manslayer or murderer), but to bring that person before the established courts of law in his home town, who would determine the case in the proper manner. Nonetheless, the institution was inherently open to abuse on the part of distraught individuals who thought it was their responsibility to take matters into their own hands in terms of revenge. To protect the rights of the manslayer in such circumstances, Moses set apart three "cities of refuge" in Transjordan for the two and a half tribes who settled there (Deut 4:41–43) and made provision for three more in Cisjordan after Israel entered and settled there (Deut 19:8–10).

The rights of the individual need to be protected in our society even against legitimate institutions operating within the law, particularly in matters of capital punishment. Though we do not have "cities of refuge" in a physical sense, we do have courts of appeal, and the person guilty of manslaughter must enjoy the full benefit of protection until murder can be demonstrated. At the same time, we should remember that the "city of refuge" in ancient Israel was not simply a place of safety. It was a place in which the manslayer made atonement for the deed of which he was guilty. Within our present legal system we have often lost sight of this principle. We need to find ways within our legal process to provide means of atonement as well as punishment or mere lengthy delay in reaching appropriate legal decisions within our courts of law.

# "This Is The Torah"—The Ten Words
## (4:44–6:3)

It may well be that the number ten was selected to enumerate the basic commandments because of the simple fact that we have ten digits, five on each hand, which facilitate the process of memorization and recitation, especially within catechetical contexts. And since few texts have been subjected to memory as frequently as the Ten Commandments, it seems a bit peculiar that there has been so little consensus on the actual assignment of the numbers one through ten to each single commandment. Even within specific religious traditions there has been difficulty in this regard. As M. D. Kosters has noted (*VT* 30 [1980] 468–73), the ancient Syrian scribes had difficulty with this task as indicated by the variant colophons in the existing manuscripts. In fourteen attempts to number the commandments, both of the major types of division are represented and some individual efforts "went astray sooner or later, or gave up before reaching the letter *yodh* (ten)" (470). Even the order of the commandments, especially that of the sixth through the eighth (concerning manslaughter, adultery, and stealing) were subject to change. For a detailed discussion of the different ways of numbering the commandments within Judaism and the several Christian traditions, see B. Reicke, *Die zehn Worte in Geschichte und Gegenwart* (Tübingen: Mohr, 1973) 1–49.

Of the several possibilities of numbering the commandments, two main types of divisions can be distinguished. In one of these, which is supported by Augustine and the other Latin Fathers, the Roman Catholics, and the Lutherans, the whole of Deut 5:6–10 is taken as the first commandment, including not only the prohibition against serving other gods (v 7) and that against making idols and bowing down to them (vv 8–9), but in most cases the introductory statement in v 6 as well. By taking so many items together at the beginning, the final sentence concerning coveting in v 21 had to be split into two so as to make up the ninth and tenth commandments. According to Baentsch (*HKAT*, 1903, 179), this is the division that was intended by the MT. It is more likely, however, that both types of division are already reflected in the MT, which in itself represents a conflated tradition.

An interesting variation of this type of division is found in the Shapira manuscript of Deuteronomy, which may reflect an early Jewish sectarian point of view. In that tradition each of the ten commandments is carefully marked off by the repetition of the concluding phrase: "I am God, your God." Here the second commandment (taking the name of Yahweh in vain) is moved to the seventh position, making the sabbath commandment second. Moreover, instead of splitting the final commandment concerning coveting into two parts, an entirely new tenth commandment is added: "You shall not hate your brother in your heart." If J. M. Allegro is correct in his assessment of this document (see his book, *The Shapira Affair* [Garden City, NY: Doubleday, 1965]), this commandment may well be the key to understanding the nature of the sectarian community responsible for this fascinating text.

A second major type of division has been adopted by the mainstream of Jewish tradition, in which v 11, "You shall not take the name of the Lord your God in vain," is already considered the third commandment. In Jewish tradition the introduction in v 6 is considered the first commandment, and the whole of vv 7–10 the second commandment. Philo and Josephus, however, took only vv 8–10 as the second commandment, in which they were followed by the Eastern and Protestant Churches, Calvinists and Socinians alike. For most critical scholars, v 6 ("I am the Lord your God . . . ") is taken as a general introductory remark to the commandments proper with v 7 as the first commandment.

The prosodic analysis adopted in this commentary suggests that Philo and Josephus (and hence the Eastern and Protestant Churches which followed them) were essentially correct. However, it should be noted that even within this tradition there has been little attempt to discern the larger architectural design of the literary context in which the Ten Commandments are presented, or to discern the chiastic literary structure of the commandments themselves.

The central commandment in terms of elaboration and detail is the fourth commandment, "to keep the sabbath" (vv 12–15). Moreover, this commandment contains an elaborate motivation clause (v 15) and is the first commandment in the list to be stated positively, at least initially. The fifth commandment "to honor your parents" (v 16) is also stated positively. These two "positive" commandments stand at the center and are in turn framed by two groups of "negative" commandments which focus on monotheism (vv 6–11), on the one hand, and ethical morality (vv 17–21), on the other.

The first three commandments pertain to Israel's exclusive worship of Yahweh and are set over against the final summary list of five commandments, which focus on ethical morality. Between these two groups are the two central commandments to observe the sabbath and to "honor one's parents." The structure of the Ten Commandments may be outlined as follows:

Monotheism—the First Three Commandments (5:6–11)
    Observe the Sabbath (5:12–15)
    Honor Your Parents (5:16)
Ethical Morality—the Last Five Commandments (5:17–21)

From this structure it is easy to see why the phrase "ethical monotheism" appears so frequently in the secondary literature to describe the unique contribution of the religion of ancient Israel.

As S. Kaufman, G. Braulik, and others have noted, the order of the Ten Commandments here in Deut 5 is the structuring principle for the arrangement of the collection of individual laws in the Central Core (Deut 12–26). The centrality of the command to observe the sabbath is discussed below in the section on Deut 5:12–15. The command to honor one's parents is extended in the Central Core to include all persons in authority, namely judges and officers in general (16:18–20; 17:8–13), the king (17:14–20), the Levites (18:1–8), and the prophet (18:9–22).

The presentation of the Ten Commandments in Deut 5:6–21 is in turn framed by two parallel accounts of Yahweh's covenant and theophany in 5:1–5 and 5:22. The "nesting" of materials continues with a further frame in which an appropriate introduction in 4:44–49 is set over against the conclusion of the matter in 5:23–6:3. The design of the whole may be outlined as follows:

A    Introduction: "This is the Torah" (4:44–49)
  B    Yahweh's Covenant and Theophany (5:1–5)
    C    Monotheism—the First Three Commandments (5:6–11)
      D    Observe the Sabbath (5:12–15
      D'    "Honor your father and your mother" (5:16)
    C'    Ethical Morality—the Last Five Commandments (5:17–21)
  B'    Yahweh's Theophany and Covenant (5:22)
A'    Conclusion of the Matter (5:23–6:3)

Within the Masoretic tradition itself there are two separate traditions so far as division of the text in Deut 5:6–21 is concerned. A system of double accentuation begins with the last two words of v 6, each of which receives two accents. At the outset the situation is peculiar to the careful reader in that there is both an *ʾatnāḥ* and *sillûq* on the same word at the end of v 6, which suggests that vv 6–7 were a single verse in one tradition. The pointing of the final word in v 7 פָּנֶי is also anomalous, not only because the *nun* receives both *rᵉbîaᶜ* and *sillûq* in MT, but also because the use of *pataḥ* in the final syllable is inexplicable.

The enumeration of commandments six through ten introduces further complication in the MT with two systems of versification for the balance of the chapter. In one of these systems the *sᵉtûmāʾ* paragraph markers appear after each of the commands in vv 17–21, dividing the text into six divisions. As will be shown in the *Comment* on v 21, the *sᵉtûmāʾ* marker at the end of the first part of v 21 is probably secondary, reflecting the larger problem of the enumeration of the Ten Commandments as a whole. As done in the system of enumeration adopted later by Augustine (and the Latin Fathers), the Roman Catholic Church, and the Lutherans, the command against coveting in v 21 is split into two commandments.

In one of the traditions reflected in the MT as we now have it, vv 17–20 were numbered together as a single verse—no doubt in four parts. The double enumeration of the verses for the balance of the chapter appears in both *BHS* and *BHK*. The system of double accentuation, which extends from vv 6b–20, and the confusion in the enumeration of the verses in vv 21–30 were sufficient reasons to exclude the Ten Commandments as a possible text for *bar mitsva* readings within Judaism. The situation is simply too confusing for the uninitiated to sort out and remember when reading from an unpointed text.

### Bibliography on the Decalogue

**Albertz, R**. "Exegetische Einleitung zum Dekalog." In *Die Zehn Gebote: Predigten, Auslegungen, Erzählungen.* Ed. H. Nitschke. Gütersloh, 1984. 8–15; 25–26. ————. *Die Zehn Gebote.* Stuttgart: Radius-Verlag, 1985. **Auerbach, E**. "Das Zehngebot—Allgemeine Gesetzesform in der Bibel." *VT* 16 (1966) 255–76. **Barnes, W. E**. "'Ten' Treatises on the 'Ten' Commandments." *The Expositor* 9/2 (July 1924) 7–23. **Beyerlin, W**. *Origins and History of the Oldest Sinaitic Traditions.* Oxford: Blackwell, 1965. 12–14, 59–67 [ET from Ger.: Tübingen, 1961]. **Botterweck, G. J**. "Form- und überlieferungsgeschichtliche Studie zum Dekalog." *ConBas* 1 (1965) 392–401. **Brekelmans, C**. "Deuteronomy 5: Its Place and Function." In *Das Deut* (1985). 164–73. **Bright, J**. "The Apodictic Prohibition: Some Observations." *JBL* 92 (1973) 185–204. **Brooks, R**. *The Spirit of the Ten Commandments: Shattering the Myth of Rabbinic Legalism.* San Francisco: Harper Collins, 1990. **Carmichael, C. M**. *The Ten Commandments: The Ninth Sacks Lecture.* Oxford: Oxford Centre for Postgraduate Hebrew Studies, 1983. **Cazelles, H**. "Les Origines du Décalogue." *EI* 9 (1969)

14–19. **Charles, R. H.** *The Decalogue.* Edinburgh: Clark, 1923. **Crüsemann, F.** *Bewahrung der Freiheit: Das Thema des Dekalogs in Sozialgeschichtlicher Perspektive.* KT 78. Munich: Kaiser, 1983. **Dexinger, F.** "Der Dekalog im Judentum." *BLit* 59 (1986) 86–95. **Diéz Merino, L.** "El Decálogo en el Targum Palestinense." *EstBib* 34 (1975) 23–48. **Eichrodt, W.** The Law and the Gospel: The Meaning of the Ten Commandments in Israel and for Us." *Int* 11 (1957) 23–40. **Eissfeldt, O.** "Lade und Gesetzestafeln." In *KlSchr* III (1966). 526–29. **Freedman, D. N.** "The Nine Commandments: The Secret Progress of Israel's Sin." *BRev* 5 (Dec. 1989) 28–37, 42. **Fretheim, T. E.** "The Ark in Deuteronomy" *CBQ* 30 (1968) 1–14. **Gampert, A.** *Le Décalogue.* Lausanne: La Concorde, 1926. **Gese, H.** "Beobachtungen zum Stil alttestamentlicher Rechtssätze." *TLZ* 85 (1960) 147–50. ————. "The Structure of the Decalogue" In *Fourth World Congress of Jewish Studies.* Jerusalem, 1967. I, 155–59. ————. "Der Dekalog als Ganzheit Betrachtet." *ZTK* 64 (1967) 121–38. **Goldman, S.** *The Ten Commandments.* Ed. M. Samuel. Chicago: Univ. of Chicago Press, 1956. **Graupner, A.** "Zum Verhältnis der beiden Dekalogfassungen Ex 20 und Dtn 5. Ein Gespräch mit F.-L. Hossfeld" *ZAW* 99 (1987) 308–29. **Haag, H.** "Der Dekalog in der Verkündigung." *Anima* 2 (1964) 120–28. **Hamel, E.** *Les dix paroles. Perspectives bibliques.* Bruxelles: Desclée de Brouwer, 1969. **Harrelson, W.** "Karl Barth on the Decalogue." *SR* 6 (1976–77) 229–40. ————. *The Ten Commandments and Human Rights.* Overtures to Biblical Theology 8. Philadelphia: Fortress, 1980. **Heinemann, G.** *Untersuchungen zum apodiktischen Recht.* Diss., Hamburg, 1958. **Hennig, K.** *God's Basic Law: The Ten Commandments for the Man of Today.* Tr. G. Williams. Philadelphia: Fortress, 1969. **Herklots, H. G. G.** *The Ten Commandments and Modern Man.* Fair Lawn, NJ: Essential Books, 1958. **Hölscher, G.** *Geschichte der Israelitischen und Jüdischen Religion.* Giessen: Töpelmann, 1922. 3 57. **Hossfeld, F.-L.** *Der Dekalog* (1982). ————. "Zum synoptischen Vergleich der Dekalogfassungen. Eine Fortführung des begonnenen Gesprächs." In *Vom Sinai zum Horeb.* Ed. F.-L. Hossfeld. Würzburg: Echter, 1989. **Hutter, M.** "Das Ehebruch-Verbot im altorientalischen und alttestamentlichen Zusammenhang." *BLit* 59 (1986) 96–104. **Hyatt, J. P.** "Moses and the Ethical Decalogue." *Encounter* 26 (1965) 199–206. **Jepsen, A.** "Beiträge zur Auslegung und Geschichte des Dekalogs." *ZAW* 79 (1967) 277–304. **Jucci, E.** "Il Decalogo e la Polemica Anticanaanaica." *RevistBib* 28 (1980) 97–109. **Kapelrud, A. S.** "Some Recent Points of View on the Time and Origin of the Decalogue." *ST* 18 (1964) 81–90. **Kaufman, S. A.** "The Second Table of the Decalogue and the Implicit Categories of Ancient Near Eastern Law." In *FS M. H. Pope* (1987). 111–16. **Kennett, R. H.** *Deuteronomy and the Decalogue.* Cambridge: Cambridge UP, 1920. **Kessler, W.** "Die literarische historische und theologische Problematik des Dekalogs." VT 7 (1957) 1–16. **Kilian, R.** "Das Humanum im Ethischen Dekalog Israels." In *FS J. Möller* (1981). 43–52. **Knight, G. A. F.** *Law and Grace: Must a Christian Keep the Law of Moses?* London: SCM Press, 1962. **Köhler, L.** "Der Dekalog." *TRu* 1 (1929) 161–84. **Koster, M. D.** "The Numbering of the Ten Commandments in Some Peschitta Manuscripts." *VT* 30 (1980) 468–73 (473). **Lang, B.** "Neues über den Dekalog." *ThQ* 164 (1984) 58–65. **Lemaire, A.** "Le Décalogue: Essai d'Histoire de la Rédaction." In *FS H. Cazelles.* AOAT 212. (1981). 259–95. **Lestienne, M.** "Les Dix 'Paroles' et le Décalogue." *RB* 79 (1972) 484–510. **Levin, C.** "Der Dekalog am Sinai." *VT* 35 (1985) 165–91. **Lohfink, N.** "Zur Dekalogfassung von Dt 5." *BZ* n.s. 9 (1965) 17–32. ————. *Bibelauslegung im Wandel.* Frankfurt a.M., 1967. ————. *Das Hauptgebot* (1963). 98–101. ————. "Kennt das Alte Testament einen Unterschied von 'Gebot' und 'Gesetz'? Zur bibeltheologischen Einstufung des Dekalogs." In *"Gesetz" als Thema biblischer Theology.* JBTh 4. Neukirchen-Vluyn: Neukirchener Verlag, 1989. 63–89. **Lüthi, W.** *Die Zehn Gebote: Ausgelegt für die Gemeinde.* Basel: Friedrich Reinhardt Verlag, 1950. **Mathes, J.-C.** "Der Dekalog." *ZAW* 24 (1904) 17–41. **Mayes, A. D. H.** "Deuteronomy 5 and the Decalogue." *PIBA* 4 (1980) 68–83. **Meinhold, H.** *Der Dekalog: Rektoratsrede.* Giessen: Töpelmann, 1927. **Meisner, O.** *Der Dekalog.* Halle: Buchdruckerei des Waisenhauses, 1893. **Mittmann, S.** *Deuteronomium 1, 1–6, 3* (1963). 141–44. **Mowinckel, S.** *Le Décalogue.* Études d'Histoire et de Philosophie Religieuses Publiées par la Faculté de Théologie Protestante de l'Université de Strassbourg 16. Paris: Félix Alcan, 1927. ————. "Zur Geschichte der Dekaloge." *ZAW* 55 (1937) 218–35. **Nicholson, E. W.** "The Decalogue as the Direct Address of God." *VT* 27 (1977) 422–33. **Nielsen, E.** "Some Reflections on the History of the Ark." Congress volume 1959. In VTSup 7. Leiden: Brill, 1960. 61–74. ————. *The Ten Commandments in New Perspective.* Tr. D. J. Bourke. SBT 7 (second series). London: SCM Press, 1968. **Nowack, W.** "Der Erste Dekalog." In *FS Baudissin* (1918). 381–97. **Oberforcher, R.** "Der Beitrag der alttestamentliche Forschung zum Verständnis der 10 Gebote." *BLit* 59 (1986) 74–85. **Owens, J. J.** "Law and Love in Deuteronomy." *RevExp* 61 (1964) 274–83. **Oyen, H. van.** *Ethik des Alten Testaments.* Gütersloh: G. Mohn, 1967. 102–32. **Perlitt, L.** *Bundestheologie* (1970). 77–102. ————. "Dekalog I. Altes Testament." *TRE* 8 (1981) 408–13. **Pfeiffer, R. H.** "The Oldest Decalogue." *JBL* 43 (1924) 294–310. **Phillips, A.** *Ancient Israel's Criminal Law: A New Approach to the Decalogue.* Oxford: Blackwell, 1970. ————. "The Decalogue: Ancient Israel's Criminal Law." *JJS* 34 (1983) 1–20. **Reicke, B.** *Die zehn Worte in Geschichte und Gegenwart. Zählung und Bedeutung des Gebote in den verschiedenen Konfessionen.* BGBE 13. Tübingen: J. C. B. Mohr, 1973. **Reventlow, H. G.** *Gebot und Predigt im Dekalog.* Gütersloh, 1962. **Rordorf, W.** "Beobachtungen zum Gebrauch des Dekalogs in der vorkonstantinischen Kirche." In *FS B. Reicke* (1984). 431–42. **Schenker, A.** "Der Monotheismus im ersten Gebot, die Stellung der Frau im Sabbatgebot und zwei andere Sachfragen zum Dekalog." *FZPhTh* 32 (1985) 323–41. **Schmidt, H.** "Moses und der Dekalog." In *FS H. Gunkel* (1923). 78–119. **Schreiner, J.** *Die Zehn Gebote im Leben des Gottesvolkes.* Munich: Kösel, 1988. **Schüngel-Straumann, H.** *Der Dekalog—Gottes Gebot?* SBS 67. Ed. H. Haag, R. Kilian, and W. Pesch. Stuttgart: KBW Verlag, 1973. ————. "Überlegungen zum JAHWE-Namen in den Gottesgeboten des Dekalogs." *ThZ* 38 (1982) 65–78. **Schunck, K. D.** "Luther und der Dekalog." *KD* 32 (1986) 52–68. **Segal, B.** (ed.). *The Ten Commandments: As Reflected in Tradition and Literature throughout the Ages.* Jerusalem: Magnes Press, 1985. **Stamm, J. J.** "DreissigJahre Dekalogforschung." *TRu* n.s.(1961) 189–239, 281–304. ————. *Der Dekalog im Lichte der Neueren Forschungen.* Bern, 1958, ²1962. **Stamm, J. J.** and **Andrew, M. E.** *The Ten Commandments in Recent Research.* London: ²1970. **Stemberger, G.** "Der Dekalog im frühen Judentum." In *"Gesetz" als Thema biblischer Theologie.* JBTh 4. (1989). 91–103. **Wallace, R. S.** *The Ten Commandments: A Study of Ethical Freedom.* Edinburgh: Oliver and Boyd, 1965. **Welch, A. C.** "The Purpose of Deuteronomy, Chapter V." *ExpTim* 41 (1929–30) 396–400. **Welten, P.** "Gott Israels—Gott vom Sinai." *Berliner Theologische Zeitschrift* 1 (1984) 225–39. **White, S. A.** "The All Souls Deuteronomy and the Decalogue." *JBL* 109 (1990) 193–206. **Wright, C. J. H.** "The Israelite Household and the Decalogue: The Social Background and Significance of Some Commandments." *TynBul* 30 (1979) 101–24. **Zenger, E.** "Eine Wende in der Dekalogforschung?" *TRev* 64 (1968) 1889–98. **Zimmerli, W.** *The Law and the Prophets.* Oxford, 1965. ————. "Das Gottesrecht bei den Propheten Amos, Hosea und Jesaja." In *FS C. Westermann* (1980). 216–35 (227–28).

## Bibliography for Deut 4:44–49

**Airoldi, N.** "La funzione giuridica dei cosidetti 'racconti storici' dei IIo discorso di Mosé al popolo (Dt 5. 9s.)." *Aug* 13 (1973) 75–92. **Althaus, P.** *Gebot und Gesetz. Zum Thema "Gesetz und Evangelium."* BFCT 46,2. Gütersloh, 1952. **Braulik, G.** "Die Ausdrücke für Gesetz im Buch Deuteronomium." *Bib* 51 (1970) 39–66. ————. **Cazelles, H.** "La rupture de la *berît* selon les Prophetes." *JJS* 33 (1982) 133–44 (142). **Gross, W.** "Das nicht substantivierte Partizip als Prädikat im Relativsatz hebräischer Prosa." *JNSL* 4 (1974) 23–47 (26). **Hillers, D. R.** *Covenant: The History of a Biblical Idea.* Baltimore: Johns Hopkins, 1969 (160–61). *HOTTP* I, 274. **Levin, C.** *Der Sturz der Königin Atalja: Ein Kapitel zur Geschichte Judas im 9. Jahrhundert v. Chr.* SBS 105. Stuttgart: Katholisches Bibelwerk, 1982. 46–47. **Lindars, B.** "Torah in Deuteronomy." In *FS D. W. Thomas* (1968). 117–36 (127). **Lohfink, N.** "Die ḥuqqîm *ûmišpāṭîm* im Buch Deuteronomium und ihre Neubegrenzung durch 12,1." *Bib* 70 (1989) 1–30. ————. "*ᶜd(w)t* in Deuteronomium und in den Königsbüchern." *BZ* (forthcoming). **Rad, G. von.** "Das jüdaische Königsritual." TLZ 72 (1947) 211–16 [=*GesStAT*, I (1965) 205–13]. **Seitz, G.** *Studien zum Deuteronomium* (1971). 26–27, 45–48. **Volkwein, B.** "Masoretisches *ᶜēdūt, ᶜēdwōt, ᶜēdōt*—'Zeugnis' oder 'Bundesbestimmungen'?" *BZ* 13 (1969) 18–40. **Wiener, H. M.** "Zur Deuteronomiumfrage." *MGWJ* 72 (1928) 24–48.

## Translation and Prosodic Analysis

4:44–49    [ (5:8):(4:5:5:4):(8:6) ]

| | | |
|---|---|---|
| [44] *And*[a] *this / (is) the Torah //* | 8 | 2 |
| *which Moses set / before / the children of Israel //* | 19 | 3_ |
| [45] *These / (are) the testimonies*[a] */* | 9⌉ | 2 |
| *[and]*[b] *the statutes / and the judgments //* | 11⌋ | 2 |
| *which Moses spoke* (rbd) */* | 8 | 1 |
| *Unto the children of Israel*[c] */* | 9 | 1 |
| *When they went forth / from Egypt /* | 10 | 2_ |
| [46] *In the vicinity of the Jordan / in the valley /* | 10 | 2 |
| *opposite / Beth-peor /* | 7 | 2 |
| *in the land / of Sihon /* | 7 | 2 |
| *King of the Amorites / who ruled / in Heshbon /* | 18 | 3_ |
| *Whom Moses smote / and the children of Israel /* | 19 | 2 |
| *When they went forth / from Egypt //* | 10 | 2 |
| [47] *and they took possession of his land /* | 10 | 1_ |
| *And the land / of Og king of the Bashan /* | 13 | 2 |
| *The two / kings of the Amorites /* | 13 | 2_ |
| *Who / (were) beyond the Jordan // *[a]*to the / east*[a] *//* | 15 | 4 |
| [48] *from Aroer /* | 7 | 1 |
| *Which is on the edge of the Arnon Valley /* | 10 | 1 |
| *and as far as Mount Sirion*[a] */ that is Hermon //* | 12 | 2_ |
| [49] *And all the Arabah / beyond the Jordan / to the east /* | 20 | 3 |
| *And as far as \*[a] *the Sea of the Arabah*[b] *//* | 11 | 1 |
| *under / the slopes of the Pisgah //* פ | 9 | 2_ |

## Notes

44.a. Two Heb. Mss, LXX. Syr, and Vg omit *waw*-conj. Prosodic analysis supports MT.

45.a. Reading הע<ד>ת (cf. LXX τὰ μαρτύρια).

45.b. The *waw*-conj is omitted with some Heb. Mss and SP.

45.c. Most LXX witnesses add ἐν τῇ ἐρήμῳ. Prosodic analysis supports MT.

47.a-a. One Heb. Ms reads שמש מזרחה. Other Heb. Mss, SP, Tg, Tg[J] read השמש מזרה. Some SP Mss read השמש מזרחה. Prosodic analysis supports MT.

48.a. Reading שרין for MT שיאן with Craigie (NICOT [1976] 147), based primarily on evidence from Syr.

49.a. See note 1:1c.

49.b. SP adds ים המלה with 3:17. Prosodic analysis supports MT.

## Form/Structure/Setting

These verses are often taken as the introduction to the original scroll of Deuteronomy, prior to its insertion into the so-called Deuteronomic History

(Joshua through 2 Kings), which included the addition of Deut 1–3(4) and 31–34 as a new introduction to the larger work as a whole. It is also possible to see this section, with its introductory formula וזאת התורה, "And this is the Torah," as set over against 29:1 (28:69 in Heb.), which begins אלה דברי הברית, "These are the words of the covenant." The two titles form an envelope around 4:44–11:32 // 27:1–29:1 (28:69 in Heb.), which constitutes the major part of the Inner Frame of Deuteronomy (chaps. 4–11 and 27–30). In terms of prosodic structure 4:44–49 is also similar to 1:1–6a with which it forms an inclusion.

*Comment*

**44–45** התורה, "the Torah," refers to the laws of Deut 5–26, which are further identified as העד<ו>ת והחקים והמשפטים, *the testimonies and the statutes and the judgments,* which Moses proclaimed after the Exodus from Egypt (v 45). On the meaning of the different legal terms, see Braulik (*Bib* 51 [1970] 39–66). Lohfink has made a strong case for the term העדות as the title of the original scroll of Deuteronomy ("*ʿd(w)t* in Deuteronomium und in den Konigsbüchern." *BZ* [forthcoming]). What is proclaimed here is the same law Moses gave the people earlier, but in a new setting—one in which that law is expounded (cf. 1:5).

**46–49** This summary section, like 1:1–6a, gathers together themes explored in greater length in chaps. 1–3. For v 46 see 2:26–37 and 3:29; for v 47 see 3:1–11; for vv 48–49 see 3:8–22.

שׂיאן, "Sirion"—the original text probably read *śrn*, before the *mater lectionis* was introduced around the sixth century B.C.E. This was apparently misread at an early date as *śᵓn*, since *resh* and *ᵓaleph* were easily confused in early Hebrew script (cf. these forms in the Gezer calendar). With further orthographic revisions in the transmission of the text, the *yodh* was put in the wrong place, *śyᵓn*, which should have been *śryn*. As Craigie has noted (NICOT [1976] 147), the initial misreading perhaps lies in the fact that the term שׂרין is not a Hebrew word but probably Sidonian (cf. 3:9).

אשדת הפסגה, "the slopes of Pisgah"—see *Comment* on 32:48–49 and 34:1.

*Bibliography for Deut 5:1–11*

**Albertz, H.** (ed.). *Die Zehn Gebote,* vols. 1–3. Stuttgart: Radius-Verlag, 1985. **Albright, W. F.** "The Hebrew Expression for 'Making a Covenant' in Pre-Israelite Documents." *BASOR* 121 (1951) 21–22. **Anderson, B. W.** "The New Covenant and the Old." *In The Old Testament and Christian Faith.* Ed. B. W. Anderson. London, 1964. 225–41. **André, G.** *Determining the Destiny: PQD in the Old Testament.* Lund: Gleerup, 1980. **Bee, R. E.** "A Study of Deuteronomy Based on Statistical Properties of the Text." *VT* 29 (1979) 18–20. **Bellefontaine, M. E.** *A Study of Ancient Israelite Laws and Their Function as Covenant Stipulations.* Indiana, 1973. **Berg, W.** "Die Eifersucht Gottes—ein Problematischer Zug des Alttestamentlichen Gottesbildes?" *BZ* n.s. 23 (1979) 197–211 (198–202). **Bernhardt, K. H.** *Gott und Bild. Ein Beitrag zur Bergründung und Bedeutung des Bilderverbotes im Alten Testament.* ThA 2. Berlin: Evangelische Verlagsanstalt, 1956. **Berré, M.L.** *The God-List in the Treaty between Hannibal and Philip V of Macedonia: A Study in Light of the Ancient Near Eastern Treaty Tradition.* Baltimore: Johns Hopkins UP, 1983. **Bickerman, E.** "Couper une Alliance." *AHDO* 5 (1950/51) 133–56. ———. "Hannibal's Covenant." *AJP* 73 (1953) 1–23. **Blenkinsopp, J.** "Abraham and the Righteous of Sodom." *JJS* 33 (1982) 119–32. **Boecker, H. J.** "Recht und Gesetz: Der Dekalog." In *Altes Testament*. Ed. H. J. Boecker. Neukirchen-Vluyn, 1983. 209. **Boesche, H.-U**. *Die Polemik gegen die Verehrung anderer Gottheiten neben Jahwe im alten Israel*. Diss., Göttingen, 1961. **Braulik, G**. "Das Deuteronomium und die Geburt des Monotheismus." SBAB 2. Stuttgart: Katholisches Bibelwerk, 1988. 257–300. **Brichto, H. C**. *The Problem of "Curse" in the Hebrew Bible*. JBLMonSer 13. Philadelphia: SBL, 1963. 59–63 **Brueggemann, W**. "Old Testament Theology as a Particular Conversation: Adjudication of Israel's Socio-Theological Alternatives." *TD* 32 (1985) 303–25. **Bückmann, O**. "Leben und Gesetz nach dem Dt. Eine Meditation. In *FS A. de Quervain* (1966). 7–18 (12–15). **Buis, P**. "La Nouvelle Alliance." *VT* 18 (1968) 1–15. ————. "Comment au septième siècle envisagait-on l'avenir de l'Alliance? Étude de Lv 26, 3–45." In *Questions Disputées d'Ancien Testament. Méthode et Théologie*. BETL 33. Leuven, 1974. ————. *La Notion d'Alliance dans l'Ancien Testament*. LD 88. Paris, 1976. ————. "Un Traité d'Assurbanipal." *VT* 28 (1978) 469–72. **Cardascia, G**. "Une justice infallible: Réflexion sur le § 47 des 'lois assyriennes.'" In *FS E. Volterra* (1971). 419–31 (430). **Cazelles, H**. "Theological Bulletin on the Pentateuch." *BTB* 2 (1972) 3–24. ————. "La rupture de la Berît selon les Prophetes." *JJS* 33 (1982) 133–44. ————. "Les structures successives de la 'berît' dans l'Ancien Testament." In *FS R. Martin-Achard* (1984). 2–7, 33–46. **Chiesa, B**. "La 'Nouva Alleanza.'" *BeO* 15 (1973) 173–84. **Childs, B. S**. "Deuteronomic Formulae of the Exodus Traditions." *FS W. Baumgartner*. VTSup 16. Leiden: Brill, 1967. 30–39. **Clements, R. E**. *Prophecy and Covenant* (1965). **Coppens, J**. "La Nouvelle Alliance en Jér 31, 31–34." *CBQ* 25 (1963) 12–21. ————. "La doctrine biblique sur l'amour de Dieu et du prochain." *ETL* 40 (1964) 252–99 (254–56). **Cross, F. M**. "The Cave Inscriptions from Khirbet Beit Lei." In *FS N. Glueck* (1970). 299–306. **Cross, F. M**. and **Saley, R. J**. "Phoenician Incantations on a Plaque of the Seventh Century B.C. from Arslan Tash in Upper Syria." *BASOR* 197 (1970) 42–49 (44–45). **Crüsemann, F**. *Bewahrung der Freiheit. Des Thema des Dekalogs in sozialgeschichtlicher Perspektive*. KT 78. München, 1983. **Daube, D**. "Rechtsgedanken in den Erzählungen des Pentatech." In *FS O. Eissfeldt* (1958). 32–41 (35–37). **Davidsen, O**. "Bund. Ein Religionssemiotischer Beitrag zur Definition der Alttestamentlichen Bundesstructur." *LingBib* 48 (1980) 49–96. **Dequeker, L**. "Noah and Israel: The Everlasting Divine Covenant with Mankind." BETL 33. Leuven UP, 1989 [1st ed. 1974]. 115–29. **Diakonoff, I. M**. "Slaves, Helots and Serfs in Early Antiquity." In *Wirtschaft und Gesellschaft im Alten Vorderasien*. Budapest, 1976. 44–78. **Dion, P.-E**. "Quelques Aspects de l'Interaction entre Religion et Politique dans le Deutéronome." *ScEs* 30 (1978) 39–55. **Dohmen, C**. "פֶּסֶל פָּסִיל: Zwei Nominalbildungen von פסל?" *BN* 16 (1981) 11–12. ————. *Das Bilderverbot. Seine Entstehung und seine Entwicklung im Alten Testament*. Ed. F. Hossfeld and H. Merklein. BBB 62. Bonn: Hanstein, 1985. **Dus, J**. "Das zweite Gebot (Zum Sieg der heiligen Lade über das Schnitzbild in Bethel)." *CV* 4 (1961) 37–50. ————. "Die Herabfahrung Jahwes auf die Lade und Entziehung der Feuerwolke." VT 19 (1969) 290–311. **Eakin, F. E**. "Yahwism and Baalism before the Exile." JBL 84 (1965) 407–14. **Eichrodt, W**. "Bund und Gesetz." In *FS H. W. Hertzberg* (1965). 30–49. ————. "Covenant and Law: Thoughts of Recent Discussion." *Int* 20 (1966) 302–21. ————. "Darf man heute noch von einem Gottesbund mit Israel reden?" *ThZ* 30 (1974) 193–206. **Eissfeldt, O**. "Gott und Götzen im Alten Testament." In *KlSchr* I (1962). 266–73 (267–70). **Elliger, K**. "Ich bin der Herr—euer Gott." In *KlSchr*. TB 32. (1966). 211–31. **Fensham, F. C**. "Covenant, Promise and Expectation in the Bible." *ThZ* 23 (1967) 305–22. ————. "Das Nicht-haftbar-sein im Bundesbuch im Lichte der altorientalischen Rechtstexte." *JNSL* 8 (1980) 17–34. **Fohrer, G**. "Das sogenannte apodiktisch formulierte Recht und der Dekalog." *KuD* 11 (1965) 49–74. ————. "Altes Testament—'Amphiktyonie' und 'Bund?'" In *Studien zur Altestamentliche Theologie und Geschichte*. BZAW 115. Berlin: de Gruyter, 1969. 84–119. **Friedrich, J**. "Der Hethitische Soldateneid." *ZA* 35 (1924) 161–91. **Freedman, D. N**. "Divine Commitment and Human Obligation." *Int* 18 (1964) 419–31. **Gehman, H. S**. "An Insight and a Realization." *Int* 9 (1955) 279–93. **Gerstenberger, E**. "Covenant and Commandment." *JBL* 84 (1965) 38–51. ————. *Wesen und Herkunft des* *"apodiktischen Rechts."* WMANT 20. Neukirchen-Vluyn, 1965. **Gese, H.** "Der Dekalog als Ganzheit betrachtet." *ZTK* 64 (1967) 121–38. **Glueck, N.** *Ḥesed in the Bible.* Tr. A. Gottschalk. Ed. E. L. Epstein. Cincinatti: Hebrew Union College Press, 1967. **Golka, F. W.** "Schwierigkeiten bei der Datierung des Fremdgötterverbots." *VT* 28 (1978) 352–54. **Gonzáles Núnes, A.** "El Rito de la Alianza." *EstBib* 24 (1965) 217–38. **Görg, M.** "Etymologisch-semantische Perspektiven zu ברית." In *FS G. J. Botterweck* (1977). 25–36. ————. "Missrauch des Gottesnamens." *BN* 16 (1981) 16–17. **Graupner, A.** "Zum Verhältnis der beiden Dekalogfassungen Ex 20 und Dtn 5. Ein Gespräch mit Frank-Lothar Hossfeld." *ZAW* 99 (1987) 308–29. **Greenberg, M.** "Some Postulates of Biblical Criminal Law." In *FS Y. Kaufmann* (1960). 21–25. **Greenfield, J. C.** "Some Aspects of Treaty Terminology in the Bible." In *Fourth World Congress of Jewish Studies* I. Jerusalem, 1967. 117–19. **Gross, H.** "Glaube und Bund—Theologische Bemerkungen zu Genesis 15." In *FS W. Kornfeld* (1977). 25–35. **Groves, J. W.** *Actualization and Interpretation in the Old Testament.* Diss., Yale Univ., 1979 (Ann Arbor: Order No. 7926245). **Gunneweg, A. H. J.** "Sinaibund und Davidsbund." *VT* 10 (1960) 335–41. **Haag, H.** "Der Dekalog in der Verkündigung." *Anima* 2 (1964) 120–28. ————. "Das 'Buch des Bundes' (Ex 24,7)." In *FS K. S. Schelkle* (1973). 22–30. **Hartman, L.** "The Enumeration of the Ten Commandments." *CBQ* 7 (1945) 105–8. **Haspecker, J.** "Bund." In *Handbuch theologischer Grundbegriffe,* I. Ed. H. Fries. Munich: Kösel, 1962. 197–204. **Hempel, J.** "Bund im AT." In *RGG*[3] 1 (1957) 1512–16. **Henninger, J.** "Was bedeutet die rituelle Teilung eines Tieres in zwei Hälften?" In *Arabica Sacra: Aufsätze zur Religionsgeschichte Arabiens und seiner Randgebiete.* OBO 40. Freiburg: Universitätsverlag, 1981. 275–85. **Hermisson, H.-J.** "Gottes Freiheit—Spielraum des Menschen." *ZTK* 82 (1985) 129–52. **Herrmann, S.** "'Bund' eine Fehlübersetzung von *bérît*? Zur Auseinandersetzung mit Ernst Kutsch." In *Gesammelte Studien zur Geschichte und Theologie des Alten Testaments.* Munich: Chr. Kaiser, 1986. 210–20. **Hornung, E.** "Zeitliches Jenseits im alten Ägypten." *Eranos* 47 (1978) 269–307. *HOTTP* I, 274–75. **Hunter, A.** "How Many Gods Had Ruth?" *SJT* 34 (1981) 427–36. **Imschoot, P. van.** "L'Alliance dans l'AT." *NRT* 84 (1952) 785–805. ————. "L'Esprit de Yahweh et l'Alliance Nouvelle dans l'AT." *ETL* 13 (1963) 201–20. **Jackson, B.** *Essays in Jewish and Comparative Legal History* (1975). 160. **Jacob, B.** "The First and Second Commandments: An Excerpt from the 'Commentary on Exodus.'" *Judaism* 13 (1964) 3–18. **Jacobsen, T.** "The Graven Image." In *FS F. M. Cross* (1987). 15–32. **Jucci, E.** "Es. 20,7. La Proibizione di un Uso Illegittimo del Nome di Dio nel Decalogo." In *BibOr* 20. Rome, 1978. 245–53. **Kapelrud, A. S.** "The Prophets and the Covenant." In *FS G. W. Ahlström* (1984). 175–83. ————. "The Covenant as Agreement." *SJOT* 1 (1988) 30–38. **Knierim, R.** "Das Erste Gebot." *ZAW* n.s. 36 (1965) 20–39. **Kutsch, E.** "Berit." *THAT* 1 (1971) 339–52. ————. *Verheissung und Gesetz* (1973). ————. *"karat berit*—'Eine Verpflichtung Festsetzen.'" In *FS K. Elliger* (1973). 121–27. ————. "Gottes Zuspruch und Anspruch. *Berit* in der alttestamentliche Theologie." In *Questions Disputées d'Ancien Testament.* Ed. C. Brekelmans. BETL 33. Leuven: University Press, 1974. 71–90. ————. *Neues Testament-Neuer Bund? Eine Fehlübersetzung wird Korrigiert.* Neukirchen-Vluyn: Neukirchener Verlag, 1978. **Lang, B.** "Das Verbot des Meineids im Dekalog." *ThQ* 161 (1981) 97–105. ————. "Neues über den Dekalog." *ThQ* 164 (1984) 58–65 (59). **Lauha, A.** "'Der Bund des Volkes.' Ein Aspekt der deuterojesajanischen Missionstheologie." In *FS W. Zimmerli* (1977). 257–61. **Lemonnyer, A.** "Le Culte des Dieux Étrangers en Israel." *RSPhTh* 4 (1910) 82–103. **Lemp, W.** *Bund und Bundeserneuerung bei Jeremia.* Diss., Tübingen, 1954. **Levin, C.** "Der Dekalog am Sinai." *VT* 35 (1985) 165–91. **Lipinski, E.** "Recherches Ugaritiques. 8. El-Berit (RS 24.278,14–15)." *Syria* 50 (1973) 50–51. **Loewenstamm, S. E.** "The Address 'Listen' in the Ugaritic Epic and the Bible." In *FS C. H. Gordon* (1980). 123–31. **Lofthouse, W. F.** "*Ḥen* and *Ḥesed* in the Old Testament." *ZAW* 51 (1933) 29–35. **Lohfink, N.** *Das Hauptgebot* (1963). 145–52. ————. "Zur Dekalogfassung von Dt 5." *BZ* NS 9 (1965) 17–32. ————. "Die These vom 'deuteronomischen' Dekaloganfang—ein fragwürdiges Ergebnis atomistischer Sprachstatistik." In *FS W. Kornfeld* (1977). 99–109. ————. "Bund." In *Neues Bibel-Lexikon,* 3. Ed. M. Görg and B. Lang. Zürich: Bensiger, 1990. **Loretz, O.** "ברית 'Band-Bund.'" *VT*

108 Deuteronomy 5:1–11

16 (1966) 239–41. **Malamat, A.** "Longevity: Biblical Concepts and Some Ancient Near Eastern Parallels." AfOBei 19. 1982. 215–24. **Martin-Achard, R.** "Quelques remarques sur la nouvelle alliance chez Jérémie (Jer 31, 13–34)." In *Questions disputées d'Ancien Testament.* Ed. C. Brekelmans. BETL 33. Leuven UP, 1974. 141–64. **McComiskey, T. E.** *The Covenants of Promise: A Theology of the Old Testament Covenants.* Nottingham: Inter-Varsity, 1985. **McKeating, H.** "Sanctions against Adultery in Ancient Israelite Society, with Some Reflections on Methodology in the Study of Old Testament Ethics." *JSOT* 11 (1979) 57–72. ————. "A Response to Dr. Phillips." *JSOT* 20 (1981) 25–26. **Meinhold, A.** "Jüdische Stimmen zum Dritten Gebot." *Kirche und Israel* 2 (1987) 159–68. **Michel, D.** "Nur ich bin Jahwe: Erwägungen zur sogenannten Selbstvorstellungsformel." ThViat 11. Berlin, 1973. 145–212. **Minkner, K.** "Die Einwirkungen des Bürgerschaftsrechts auf Leben und Religion Altisraels." *ThVers* 11 (1979) 21–32. **Mittmann, S.** *Deuteronomium 1, 1–6, 3* (1978). 141–43. **Mowinckel, S.** "Wann wurde der Jahwekultus in Jerusalem offiziell bildlos?" In ActOr 8. Copenhagen, 1930. 257–79. **Nelson, R. D.** "Expository Article: Deuteronomy 5:1–15." *Int* 41 (1987) 282–87. **Neumann, P. K.** *Hört das Wort Jahwäs* (1975). 67–74. **Nicholson, E. W.** "Covenant in a Century of Study since Wellhausen." In OTS 24 (1986) 54–69. ————. *God and His People: Covenant and Theology in the Old Testament.* Oxford: UP, 1986. **Oden, R. A.** "The Place of Covenant in the Religion of Israel." In *FS F. M. Cross* (1987). 429–47. **Orthmann, H.** *Der alte und der neue Bund bei Jeremia.* Diss., Berlin, 1940. **Phillips, A.** "Another Look at Adultery." *JSOT* 20 (1981) 3–25. **Quell, G.** "Der alttestamentliche Begriff *bĕrît.*" *TWNT* 2 (1935) 106–27. **Renaud, B.** "L'Alliance Éternelle d'Ez 16,59–63 et l'Alliance Nouvelle de Jér 31,31–34." In *Ezekiel and His Book.* Ed. J. Lust. BETL 74. Leuven UP, 1986. 335–39. **Sakenfeld, K. D.** *The Meaning of Ḥesed in the Hebrew Bible.* HSM 17. Chico: Scholars Press, 1978. **Schenker, A.** "Der Monotheismus im ersten Gebot, die Stellung der Frau im Sabbatgebot und zwei andere Sachfragen zum Dekalog." *FZPhTh* 32 (1985) 323–41 (324–26). ————. "L'origine de l'idée d'une alliance entre Dieu et Israel dans l'Ancien Testament." *RB* 95 (1988) 184–94. **Schildenberger, J.** "Moses als Idealgestalt eines armen Jahwes." In *FS A. Gelin* (1961). 71–84 (75). ————. "Bund." *BThW*³ 1 (1967). 177–86. **Schmidt, W. H.** *Das Erste Gebot. Seine Bedeutung für das Alte Testament.* TEH 165. Munich, 1969. **Schmitt, G.** "El Berit-Mitra." *ZAW* 76 (1964) 325–27. **Segal, A. F.** "Covenant in Rabbinic Writing." In *The Other Judaisms of Late Antiquity.* BJS 127. Atlanta: Scholars, 1987. 147–65. **Segert, S.** "Bis in das dritte und vierte Glied." *CV* 1 (1958) 37–39. **Seitz, G.** *Studien zum Deuteronomium* (1971). 49. **Sekine, M.** "Davidsbund und Sinaibund." *VT* 9 (1959) 47–57. **Sperling, S. D.** "Rethinking Covenant in Late Biblical Books." *Bib* 70 (1989) 50–73. **Staerk, W.** "Berith=diatheke=Bund?" *ThBl* 16 (1937) 291–96. **Stamm, J. J.** and **Andrew, M. E.** *The Ten Commandments in Recent Research.* London: SCM, 1967 [ 1970]. **Staples, W. E.** "The Third Commandment." *JBL* 58 (1939) 325–29. **Swetnam, J.** "Diatheke in the Septuagint Account of Sinai." *Bib* 47 (1966) 438–44. **Testa, E.** "De foedere Patriarcharum." *SBFLA* 15 (1964/65) 5–73. **Valeton, J. J. P.** "Bedeutung und Stellung des Wortes *brjt* im Priestercodex." *ZAW* 12 (1892) 1–22. ————. "Das Wort *bĕrît* in den jehovistischen und deuteronomistischen Stücken des Hexateuchs sowie in den verwandten historischen Büchern." *ZAW* 12 (1892) 224–60. ————. "Das Wort *brjt* bei den Propheten und in den Ketubim." *ZAW* 13 (1893) 245–79. **Vincent, J.** Neuere Aspecte der Dekalogforschung." *BN* 32 (1986) 83–104. **Vriezen, T.** "Exode XX, 2. Introduction au Décalogue: Formule de Loi ou d'Alliance?" In *RechBib* 8 (1967). 35–51. **Waschke, E.-J.** "Das Verhältnis alttestamentlicher Überlieferungen im Schnittpunkt der Dynastiezusage und die Dynastiezusage im Spiegel alttestamentlicher Überlieferungen." *ZAW* 99 (1987) 157–79. **Watson, W. G. E.** "Shared Consonants in Northwest Semitic." *Bib* 50 (1969) 525–33 (Deut 5:5). **Weinfeld, M.** "בְּרִית." *TDOT* 2 (1975). 253–79. **Weingreen, J.** "*ḥwṣᵓtyk* in Genesis 15:7." In *FS D. W. Thomas* (1968). 209–15. **Westermann, C.** "Genesis 17 und die Bedeutung von *bĕrît.*" *TLZ* 101 (1976) 161–70. **Zenger, E.** "Funktion und Sinn der ältesten Herausführungsformel." ZDMG Supplementa 1. Ed. W. Voigt. Wiesbaden: F. Steiner, 1969. 334–42. **Zimmerli, W.** "Sinaibund und Abrahambund. Ein Beitrag zum Verständnis der Priesterschritt." *ThZ* 16 (1960) 268–80.

## Translation and Prosodic Analysis

5:1–11   [8:3] [5:5] [8:6] [6] [8:(5:5):3] [8]

[1] *And Moses proclaimed / unto all Israel /*     ⌐13   2
     *and he said unto them /*    └ 8   1
*"Hear, O Israel / the statutes and the judgments /*    20   2
*Which I / am speaking* (דבר) *in your ears /* TODAY[a] //    <u>20</u>   3_
*You shall learn them /*    9   1
*And you shall keep them / to do them //*    <u>10</u>   2_

[2] **YHWH our God / has cut with us /**    ⌐18   2
**A covenant \\[a] in Horeb //** [3] **(it is) not[a] with our fathers /**    └18   2
     **has YHWH cut (it) /**    6   1_
**This covenant // indeed (is) with us /**    ⌐15   2
**We are the ones here / TODAY / all of us (who are) alive //**    └<u>20</u>   3_

[4] *Face / to face / YHWH spoke* (דבר) *with you / on the mountain[a] /*    ⌐22   4
     *out of the midst of the fire //*    └ 7   1
[5] *I myself[a] / (was) standing between YHWH and you /*    ⌐22   2
     *at THAT TIME /*    └ <u>7</u>   1_
*To declare to you / the word<s>[b] (<ד>דבר) of YHWH //*    14   2
*For you were afraid / from before the fire /*    14   2
*And you did not go up onto the mountain / (saying) //* ס    <u>15</u>   2_

[6] I am \\[a] YHWH *your God / who brought you forth /*    22   2
     *from the land of Egypt* \\[b] *from the house of bondage //*    15   1
[7] *There[a] shall not be to you / other gods / before me //* [b]    <u>21</u>   3_

[8] *You shall not make for yourself a graven image /*    ⌐ 9   1
     *<or>[a] any likeness / of what is in the heavens /* above /    └17   3
*And what is in the earth / beneath //*    ⌐11   2
     *and which is in the waters / under the earth //*    └<u>14</u>   2_
[9] *You shall not bow down to them /*    ⌐ 9⌐   1
     *and you shall not serve them[a] //*    | 7┘   1
*For I / (am) YHWH your God / a jealous God /*    └21   3_
*Visiting / iniquity of the fathers* | [b] *upon the children /*    ⌐16⌐   3
*And[c] upon the third and upon the fourth (generation) /*    |14┘   1
     *to those who hate me //*    └ 6   1_
[10] *And[a] showing steadfast love* \\[b] *to thousands //*    12   1
     *to those who love me /*    5   1
     *and to the ones keeping <my>[c] commandments //* ס    <u>12</u>   1_

[11] *You shall not lift up / the name of YHWH [ ] [a] / in vain //*    15   3
     *for he will not hold guiltless / (that is) YHWH /*    11   2
*The one[b] / [c]who shall lift up his name / in vain[c] //* ס    <u>15</u>   3_

**Notes**

1.a. LXX and DSS add הזה. Prosodic analysis supports MT.
2.a. See note 1:1c.
3.a. DSS adds *waw*-conj.
4.a. The term בהר is omitted in one Heb. Ms, DSS, and LXX^A. Prosodic analysis supports MT.
5.a. SP, LXX, and Syr add *waw*-conj, which is possible in terms of mora-count.
5.b. Emending to read דִּבְרֵי with one Heb. Ms, SP, LXX, Syr, Tg, and Vg.
6.a. The *paśṭāʾ* is replaced with a conj accent to achieve closer rhythmic balance over against v 5. Cf. Exod 20:2 where אנכי has two disj accents, in the double tradition of recitation for the Ten Commandments. In that system both הָיִיתָ and אֱלֹהֶיךָ have *paśṭāʾ* and conj accents in a somewhat analogous situation.
6.b. See note 1:1c.
7.a. DSS reads כי לא, which is possible in terms of mora-count.
7.b. Both *BHK* and *BHS* add extra space between vv 7 and 8.
8.a. Adding *waw*-conj with a number of Heb. Mss, 4QDeut 5:8, Syr, Tg, and Vg.
9.a. DSS reads תעובדם.
9.b. The sequence of *ʾazlāʾ* followed by *dargāʾ* is here read as disj to achieve rhythmic balance over against vv 2–3 above.
9.c. A number of Heb. Mss, LXX, Syr and Tg omit *waw*-conj, which is possible in terms of mora-count.
10.a. DSS reads עושׂי.
10.b. See note 1:1c.
10.c. Reading מצותי with Qere, numerous Heb. Mss, and SP.
11.a. Omitting אלהיך to achieve better balance in terms of mora-count.
11.b. DSS and Tg^J add כ(ו)ל.
11.c-c. DSS omits the entire phrase.

*Form/Structure/Setting*

In terms of the so-called *Numeruswechsel* and the three instances of the *sᵉtûmāʾ* paragraph marker (in vv 5, 10, and 11), 5:1–11 is divided into six subunits as follows:

v 1        "Hear, O Israel, the commandments!"
vv 2–3    Yahweh has made a covenant with us "today."
vv 4–5    Moses recalls Yahweh's theophany on the mountain "at that time."
vv 6–7    First commandment: No other gods.
vv 8–10   Second commandment: No images.
v 11      Third commandment: No misuse of Yahweh's name.

After a lengthy section, which includes no occurrences of 2nd person forms in verbs or pronouns (4:41–5:1a), the *Numeruswechsel* marks the beginning of the formal presentation of the Ten Commandments. The 2nd sg usage of שְׁמַע is followed by the 2nd pl suffix in באזניכם and two 2nd pl verbs. The switch to 1st pl forms in vv 2–3 marks off a second subunit, which displays further evidence of its independent status in the chiastic use of the key words: כרת יהוה // יהוה . . . כרת.

The resumption of 2nd pl forms in vv 4–5 marks the beginning of the third subunit, which recalls the primary theophany to Moses and the people "at that time" on Mount Sinai (Horeb), in which the "words of Yahweh" (דברי יהוה) were revealed. Once again careful chiastic structuring of key words marks the independent status of the section: האשׁ . . . בהר / בהר . . . האשׁ. The formal listing of the Ten Commandments begins in v 6, which is marked by the *Numeruswechsel* with the resumption of 2nd sg forms, which continue through v 21.

## Comment

**1** On כל ישראל see 1:1 above. The proclamation of Moses is binding on all members of the covenant community: past, present, and future. On שמע ישראל see also 4:1; 6:3, 4; 9:1; 20:3; and 27:9. The verb *to hear* appears with the sense of "obey" in treaty texts from the Ancient Near East (see J. A. Thompson, *The Ancient Near Eastern Treaties and the Old Testament* [London: Tyndale, 1964] 36). On the usage of the various terms for "law" in Deuteronomy see G. Braulik, *Bib* 51 (1970) 39–66.

**2–3** The use of 1st c pl forms here highlights the living reality of the covenant relationship between God and his people, which transcends the boundaries of time.

**4–5** As Augustine noted centuries ago, the idiom *face to face* means that God spoke "directly" to the people of Israel while Moses was on the mountain (cited by Buis and Leclerq, *Le Deutéronome* [1963] 36). It obviously cannot be taken literally, since 4:12 states explicitly that the people did not see any form of God at that time. A key passage for studying the meaning of this idiom is Exod 33:7–23, where Yahweh is said to have spoken to Moses "face to face" (Exod 33:11). At the same time, Moses is informed by Yahweh that he "cannot see [God's] face; for human beings shall not see [God] and live" (Exod 33:20).

**6–7** *The first commandment:* the prohibition of gods other than Yahweh. The demand for exclusive loyalty to Yahweh is paralleled in the treaty texts of the ancient Near East by the necessary pledge of fidelity on the part of a vassal to his suzerain. As was often the case in these other texts, the demand for fidelity is based on a summation of the suzerain's benevolent deeds in behalf of the vassal. The fact that Yahweh brought the people forth from bondage in Egypt is sufficient cause for obedience to his commandments. Though the commandment is expressed negatively, it is replete with positive implications. Negatively, Israel is forbidden to acknowledge other gods.

Much has been written about whether to translate the opening clause as "I am Yahweh your God," or "I, Yahweh, am your God." The difference between the two translations is probably not as great as some have made it out to be. The first translation emphasizes God's self-identification as the one who appears under the name Yahweh (cf. Exod 6:2–3). The other translation takes the name Yahweh for granted and puts the emphasis on God's favor extended to his people. He is their God who delivered them from bondage in Egypt. Though the same message of grace is conveyed, there is less emphasis on the special name of God. The disjunctive accent following אנכי suggests that the first of these alternatives is the more likely.

The specific meaning of על-פני, "before Me," has aroused some debate. Knierem has rendered the phrase "before my face," that is, "in my sight," in the sense that no other gods were to be placed in the shrine of Yahweh (ZAW 77 [1965], 20–39). Though this interpretation is possible on a secondary level, it fails to do justice to the primary sense of the commandment, which "is directed rather toward the sphere of relationships and commitments," as Craigie has noted (NICOT [1976] 152). The implications are monotheistic, in spite of the fact that the text makes specific reference to other gods.

**8–10** *The second commandment:* the prohibition of idolatry. Since the first commandment has excluded other gods in general, the command here refers to any physical representation of Yahweh and his domain. This prohibition subsequently had a profound effect in the life of both Judaism and Islam so far as the world of art is concerned. As numerous historians have noted, the command runs contrary to the nearly ubiquitious tendencies elsewhere in the Near East to portray deities in various forms of art. The prohibition is so deeply rooted in the life of ancient Israel that it surely must go back to the time of the very beginning of the religion of ancient Israel, the time of Moses.

Since God was conceived in personal terms in ancient Israel and human beings were made "in the image of God" (Gen 1:27), the human form represented the most obvious means of giving some visual expression of God. Such action was categorically forbidden in ancient Israel, as was the use of any object from the created order, animate or inanimate, to represent the Creator (cf. the discussion above on 4:16–19). The only manner in which God could be represented was through language; and, even here, there are limits. As Craigie has noted, "To construct, by theological propositions, a definition of the nature of God and then to claim adequacy for that definition, would be to construct an image as real as any wooden image" (NICOT [1976] 154).

The danger is that images may become confused with what they are intended to represent. To worship an image of God would detract from the essential relationship of the covenant, namely the commitment of worship as a response of love (cf. Deut 6:5). On Yahweh as "a jealous God" see the *Comment* on 4:24. False forms of worship have profound consequences for future generations, for it means that children and grandchildren would not be properly instructed regarding the covenant relationship (cf. 4:10 above).

On the meaning of חסד as *steadfast love,* see K. D. Sakenfeld, *The Meaning of Hesed in the Hebrew Bible* (HSM 17 [Chico: Scholars Press, 1978]), and the earlier study by N. Glueck, *Hesed in the Bible* (Cincinatti: HUC Press, 1967). The term is difficult to translate with its full implications because it describes essentially the love of God toward his people within the context of the covenant relationship (see Deut 7:9; cf. 1 Kgs 8:23; Neh 1:5; 9:32; Dan 9:4).

**11**  *The third commandment:* the prohibition against the misuse of Yahweh's name. The concern here is the attempt to manipulate God for personal ends. Though the commandment is often taken as a prohibition against blasphemy, that particular interpretation is much too narrow (cf. A. Phillips, *Ancient Israel's Criminal Law* [1970] 53). The commandment is concerned with the name of God, as revealed to Moses (cf. Exod 3:14 and 6:3). What is prohibited is the use of Yahweh's name to harness God's power for personal ends or for a "worthless purpose" (לשוא; which Harrelson translates as "mischief" in *The Ten Commandments and Human Rights* [Philadelphia: Fortress, 1980] 72–74). As Philips has noted, this commandment not only forbad the use of God's name in magic; it also meant that the Israelite, by faith in Yahweh, was free from any influence from the world of magic (55).

## Explanation

The Ten Commandments are presented as the direct address of Yahweh who "spoke with you on the mountain out of the midst of the fire" (5:4). Moses is simply reporting the words that God spoke on that occasion. The first three commandments (5:6–11) focus on God himself in relationship to human beings. Though all three are specifically tied to the revelation of God to Israel on Mount Horeb, the occasion itself is not stressed in the commands themselves (5:6–21). The commandments would no doubt have been understood, even in ancient Israel, as valid for all peoples in all times and places.

The first commandment (5:6–7) calls for a style of life dominated by our relationship to God. The relationship to one God must dominate every sphere of life, whether the life of action, of thought, or of emotion. There can be no area of life in which a person or thing comes before our commitment to the one true God. It should be noted, however, that this commandment is not a summons to monotheism as such in the form of later prophetic announcements about the incomparability of Yahweh, or about the folly of idolatry, like that of Isa 40:18–26; 44:6–8; and 45:5–7. These "other gods" may take on subtle forms. Indeed anything that relegates the relationship with God to second place functions in effect as "another god."

The elimination of visual substitutes for God in the second commandment (5:8–10) means that we are constantly cast back upon our knowledge of God as gained from the experience of God's living reality, especially the experience of the Exodus (5:6). The priestly tradition in the Pentateuch explains more clearly what is behind this prohibition. God made human beings in his own image and likeness (Gen 1:26–27). Human beings themselves are the only valid representation of God on earth, and, as W. Harrelson (*The Ten Commandments,* 1980) put it (64), "they must be such a representation not at the cult center where their representation is set up, but in daily life, demonstrating faithfulness to the commandments of the God who created them."

In the first two commandments we have a double statement of the exclusive claim of God upon his people. In the first place, God will allow for no rival at all, whereas the second commandment insists that there is no adequate representation of God to be found within the created order. There is only one kind of representation that God will permit, and this he requires: namely, a faithful human community committed to doing God's will in this world.

Though the picture of Yahweh as "a jealous God visiting iniquity of the fathers upon the children and upon the third and fourth generation" (v 9) fits the first commandment more directly than the second, it is appropriate to the second as well. As John Calvin saw so clearly in his exposition of the Ten Commandments in his *Institutes* (book 2, chap. 8), Israel is to make no image of God. Israel is to be that image of God in the world. God is jealous of his "family property" (נחלה; cf. Deut 4:20–21). He will shower mercy on those who love him and keep his commandments. When his people are faithful to the demands of the covenant relationship, then God has the kind of representative in the world that he desires.

There is an important principle here. Religious communities understandably seek to find acceptable ways to represent the claims and the power of God. One such way is through the act of worship itself, namely, the identification of specific times and places where we experience the Holy, and the selection of professional leaders skilled in the mediation between God and his community. The danger is that our very worship may neutralize the claims of God upon the very people to be his image in the world God created. The Israelites had various ways to cope with the dangerous power of the Holy, ways in keeping with other ancient peoples in the Near East. They had set rituals, they observed sacred moments in their calendar at carefully chosen cultic sites, and they appointed a specific class of "ordained" leaders. They had an ark of the covenant, which was understood as a representation of Yahweh's presence in their midst. They had cherubim standing alongside that ark within the Holy of Holies of Solomon's temple. But the theologians in ancient Israel insisted that such representations were not to be understood as images of God. No legitimate image of their God was possible. Israel as God's people represented God in the world.

From the very outset limits were imposed on Israel's worship of God: "You shall not make for yourself a graven image or any likeness of what is in the heavens above and what is in the earth beneath and which is in the waters under the earth. You shall not bow down to them and you shall not serve them" (vv 8–9). The only recognized representative of God in the world and among the nations is Yahweh's people. The human being, male and female, is made in God's image and likeness, and living human beings cannot be set up on pedestals in sacred places of worship. People today may not be tempted to actually make representations of God in wood or stone or metal or any other substance, but we are tempted to fail to be adequate representatives of God on earth. As Harrelson has noted (*The Ten Commandments*, 67):

> The second commandment is more violated by what we fail to do than by what we do. We fail to claim our place as human beings, charged to be a representation of the cause and the claim of God on earth, identifiable as God's firstborn child, ready to serve God, committed to let the peoples of earth know what it means to live consciously as those created in God's image and likeness. Our temptation is not to identify the creature with the Creator, to claim a kind of power for our representation of God on earth that should not be claimed for any created thing. Our greater temptation is to miss the corollary of the second commandment: that God will have only one kind of representation on earth, one that is close to his very nature and power— human beings made in his image, and a community called out to embody this vocation before the nations of earth. Every human being is made in God's image and likeness. No images of God can be made for ourselves. Those are the two realities that need to be held together today. When they are, we see what moral force this second commandment actually has.

The implications of the third commandment (5:11), concerning misuse of Yahweh's name, reach far beyond the sphere of magic. Any attempt to manipulate God for personal ends is included. Thus, the name of God may be misused even in prayer when directed toward selfish human ends. In the conduct of war or the undertaking of any human enterprise, the use of God's name may be "in vain." As Craigie has put it, "All such improper uses of God's name have suspended over them a warning, *for the Lord will not leave unpunished him who takes his name in vain*" (NICOT [1976] 156).

The name of Yahweh is full of power and that power must not be abused. We are not to make our religion into a club or weapon with which to assert our way over others. Religion is not be be used as a tool to intimidate individuals or groups to do the bidding of religious authorities. We are all familiar with how those charged with providing religious leadership often find ways to twist words of judgment into instruments of fear and intimidation, by threats uttered in the name of God. But it is not just "TV evangelists" in their concern to meet the high financial costs of their chosen medium who succumb to the temptation to violate the third commandment. At virtually all levels of religious organization the seductive demands of power tempt us to use the name of Yahweh for personal advantage. It is a simple fact that some of the most ruthless examples of raw power politics in which individuals are crushed in the name of God are to be found within our churches and seminaries. It is also a fact that literally thousands of people are struggling for mental health, both in mental institutions and on the streets of our cities, trying to undo, often with professional help, the damage done by those who have driven them to psychosis with their warnings of eternal damnation, as Harrelson has noted (76). When people are unloved by family and friends, they sometimes conclude that God too cannot love them, until they do what the religious leaders demand. In such instances God himself is sometimes identified as a deceiver and destroyer to these unfortunate persons. Some of the more subtle ways of abusing the power of God in our societies today are perhaps more destructive than the situations ancient Israel knew.

The first three commandments focus on God's exclusive claim upon his people. All three have in view the preface which tells of Yahweh's gracious act of deliverance from slavery in Egypt (v 6). No specific penalties are mentioned, for threats would only weaken the force of these basic prohibitions. The concern, however, is not simply with what God will not tolerate of his people. These three commandments, taken together, present a remarkable portrait of God as well. The God who delivered his people from bondage will not be placated by lavish gifts of gold and silver or other bounties. He cannot be bought off. God will not permit the power his people have, through knowing his name, to do harm to their enemies. God's people are his representatives in the world. They are the image of God. As such they are to so live that all peoples will come to know the nature and character of God.

## Bibliography for Deut 5:12–15

**Albertz, R.** "Hintergrund und Bedeutung des Elterngebots im Dekalog." *ZAW* 90 (1978) 348–74. **Andreasen, N.-E.** *The Old Testament Sabbath: A Tradition-Historical Investigation.* SBLDS 7. Missoula: Scholars Press, 1972. ———. "Recent Studies of the Old Testament Sabbath." *ZAW* 86 (1974) 453–69. **Auld, G. A.** "Sabbath, Work and Creation: מלאכה Reconsidered." *Hen* 8 (1986) 273–80. **Beer, G.** *Schabbath: Der Mischnatractat "Sabbat."* Tübingen: J. C. B. Mohr, 1908. **Benjamin, D. C.** *Deuteronomy and City Life* (1983). **Bettenzoli, G.** "Lessemi ebraici di radice SBT." *Hen* 4 (1982) 129–62. ———. "La tradizione del sabbat." *Hen* 4 (1982) 265–93. **Berry, G. R.** "The Hebrew Word נוח." *JBL* 50 (1931) 207–10. **Boecker, H. J.** "'Du sollst dem Ochsen, der da drischt, das Maul nicht verbinden.' Überlegungen zur Wertung der Natur im Alten Testament." In *FS F. Lang* (1978). 72–89. **Bohn, F.** *Der Sabbat im Alten Testament und im altjüdischen religiösen Aberglauben.* Gütersloh: C. Bertelsmann, 1903. **Botterweck, G. J.** "Der Sabbat im Alten Testament." *ThQ* 134 (1954) 134–47, 448–57. **Budde, K.** "The Sabbath and the Week." *JThS* 30 (1928) 1–15. ———. Sabbath und Woche." *ChW* 43 (1929) 202–8, 265–70. ———. "Antwort auf Johannes Meinholds 'Zur Sabbathfrage.'" *ZAW* 48 (1930) 138–45. **Diakonoff, I. M.** "On the Structure of Old Babylonian Society." In *Beiträge zur sozialen Struktur des Alten Vorderasien.* SGKAO

1. Berlin, 1971. 15–31. **Doron, P.** "The Methodology of Targum Onkelos." *EstBib* 43 (1985) 173–87. **Eerdmans, B. D.** "Der Sabbath." In *FS K. Marti* (1925). 79–83. **Fritz, M.** "Rediscovering the Sabbath." *RRel* 41 (1982) 368–72. **Guillén Torralba, J.** "Motivación deuteronómica del descanso sabático." SBEsp 29. Madrid, 1969 (pub. 1971). 121–44. ————. "Motivación deuteronómica del precepto del Sabat." *EstBib* 29 (1970) 73–99. **Hasel, G. F.** *The Sabbath in Scripture and History.* Ed. K. Strand. Washington, DC: Review and Herald Publishing Association, 1982. 21–43. *HOTTP* I, 275–76. **Hehn, J.** *Siebenzahl und Sabbat bei den Babyloniern und im Alten Testament.* Leipzig: J. C. Hinrichs, 1907. ————. "Zur Bedeutung der Siebenzahl." In *FS K. Marti* (1925). **Heschel, A.** "The Sabbath: Its Meaning for Modern Man." In *The Earth is the Lord's and the Sabbath.* Harper Torchbooks. New York: Harper & Row, 1966. **Hulst, A. R.** "Bemerkungen zum Sabbatgebot." In *FS T. C. Vriezen* (1966). 152–64. **Jackson, B.** *Essays in Jewish and Comparatative Legal History* (1975). 31. **Jenni, E.** *Die Theologische Begründung des Sabbatgebotes im Alten Testament.* ThSt 46. Zollikon-Zürich: Evangelischer Verlag, 1956. **Landsberger, B.** *Der kultische Kalender der Babylonier und Assyrer: Erste Hälfte.* LSSt 6. Leipzig: J. C. Hinrichs, 1915. **Lang, B.** "The Social Organization of Peasant Poverty in Biblical Israel." *JSOT* 24 (1982) 47–63. **Lemaire, A.** "Le sabbat á l'époque royale israelite." *RB* 80 (1973) 161–85. **Levin, C.** *Der Sturz der Königin Atalja.* SBS 105. Stuttgart, 1982. 41–42. **Lohfink, N.** "Leisure: The Work Week and the Sabbath in the Old Testament and Especially in the Priestly Chronicle." In *Great Themes from the Old Testament.* Edinburgh: T. & T. Clark, 1982. 203–21. **Mathys, F.** "Sabbatruhe und Sabbatfest. Überlegungen zur Entwicklung und Bedeutung des Sabbat im Alten Testament." *ThZ* 28 (1972) 242–62. **Meinhold, J.** *Sabbat und Woche im Alten Testament.* FRLANT 5. Göttingen, 1905. ————. "Zur Sabbathfrage." *ZAW* 48 (1930) 121–38. **Miller, P. D.** "The Human Sabbath: A Study in Deuteronomic Theology." *PSB* 6 (1985) 81–97 (84, 93). **Palmer, E.** "Living a Rhythmic Life," *Radix* 19/2 (1989) 8–11. **Pons, J.** "La référence au séjour en Egypte et à la sortie d'Egypte dans les codes de loi de l'Ancien Testament." *ETR* 63 (1988) 169–82. **Robinson, G.** *The Origin and Development of the Old Testament Sabbath.* Diss., Hamburg, 1975. **Ruppert, L.** "Symbole im Alten Testament." In *FS J. G. Plöger* (1983). 97–101. **Schottroff, W.** *"Gedenken" im Alten Orient und im Alten Testament: Die Worzel zākar im semitischen Sprachkreis.* WMANT 15. Neukirchen-Vluyn, 1964. 117–26. **Siker-Gieseler, J.** "The Theology of the Sabbath in the Old Testament." *StudBT* 11 (1981) 5–20. **Thiel, W.** "Altorientalische und israelitisch-jüdische Religion." In JLH 28 (1984). 182. **Tigay, J. H.** "Conflation as a Redactional Technique." *Empirical Models for Biblical Criticism.* Ed. J. H. Tigay. Philadelphia: Pennsylvania UP, 1985. 53–89. **Tov, E.** "The Nature and Background of Harmonization in Biblical Manuscripts." *JSOT* 31 (1985) 3–29. **Tsevat, M.** "The Basic Meaning of the Biblical Sabbath." *ZAW* 84 (1972) 447–59. **Veijola, T.** "Die Propheten und das Alter des Sabbatgebots." In *FS O. Kaiser* (1989). 246–64. **Watts, J. D. W.** "Infinitive Absolute as Imperative and the Interpretation of Ex. 20:8." *ZAW* 74 (1962) 141–45. **Zenger, E.** "Die Feier des Sonntags." *LS* 33 (1982) 249–53.

*Translation and Prosodic Analysis*

5:12–15    [7:5:(5:5):5:7]

|  |  |  |
|---|---|---|
| [12] *Keep / the day of the sabbath* \\[a] *to make it holy //* | 16 | 2 |
| *Just as he commanded you / YHWH your God /*[b] | 15 | 2 |
| [13] *Six days* \\[a] *you shall labor /* | 11 | 1 |
| *And you shall do / all*[b] *your work //* | 10 | 2_ |
| [14] *But <in>*[a] *the seventh / day /* | 11 | 2 |
| *(That is a) sabbath / to YHWH* \\[b] *your God //* | 12 | 2 |
| *You shall not do*[c] *any work /* | 11 | 1_ |
| *You and your son and your daughter and your manservant* \|[d] | 16 | 1 |
| *and your maidservant /* | 6 | 1 |

| | | |
|---|---|---|
| [And]ᵉ your ox and your ass / and any of your cattle / | ⌈ 16 | 2 |
| and your alien / | ⌊ <u>5</u> | 1_ |
| Who is in your gates / in order that / he may rest / | 15 | 3 |
| Your manservant and your maidservant / as well as you // | <u>14</u> | 2_ |
| ¹⁵ And you shall remember / that you were a servant / | ⌈ 14 | 2 |
| in the land of Egypt / | ⌊ 6 | 1 |
| And he brought you forth \ᵃ YHWH your God / from there / | <u>19</u> | 2_ |
| With a mighty hand / and an outstretched arm // therefore / | 22 | 3 |
| He commanded you / YHWH your God / | ⌈ 11 | 2 |
| to observe / the sabbath day ᵇ // ס | ⌊ <u>11</u> | 2_ |

## Notes

12.a. Reading conj ᵓazlāᵓ rather than disj *ṭiphāᵓ* in the double accentual system of MT. See also note 1:1.c.

12.b. The *sôph pāsûq* is missing in MT.

13.a. Reading conj *mûnaḥ* rather than disj *pašṭāᵓ* in the double accentual tradition of MT.

13.b. DSS reads אֵת כ(ו)ל, which is possible in terms of mora-count.

14.a. Reading וּבְיוֹם with some Heb. Mss, DSS, and Payrus Nash.

14.b. Reading conj *mûnaḥ* rather than disj *ṭiphāᵓ* in the double accentual system of MT. See also note 1:1.c.

14.c. DSS and Papyrus Nash add ב(ו)ה; SP, LXX, Syr, and Vg add בו. Prosodic analysis supports MT.

14.d. One Heb. Ms, DSS, SP, LXX, and Vg omit *waw*-conj. MT places a *metheg* under this word, which suggests a disj accent should be read in what is otherwise an extremely long accentual-stress unit (i.e., 22 morae).

14.e. Omitting *waw*-conj with one Heb. Ms, DSS, Papyrus Nash, SP, and LXX.

15.a. Reading conj ᵓazlāᵓ rather than disj *gereš* in the double accentual system of MT.

15.b. LXX adds καὶ ἁγιάζειν αὐτήν = וּלְקַדְּשׁוֹ: Prosodic analysis supports MT.

## Form/Structure/Setting

The phrase אֶת־יוֹם הַשַּׁבָּת forms an envelope around the law of the sabbath in Deut 5:12–15. From a rhythmic perspective the section has six subunits which are closely connected. The opening /7:5/ unit (vv 12–14) states the law: "Six days you shall labor . . . but in the seventh day . . . you shall not do any work." The concluding /5:7/ unit (v 15) gives the motivation for observing the sabbath: by keeping the sabbath the people of Israel will remember the Exodus from Egypt. The two sections are introduced by the key verbs שָׁמַר, "keep," and זָכַר, "remember," respectively.

Between these two halves of the sabbath law lies a carefully constructed "filler" in the form of a /5:5/ unit, which emphasizes the seriousness of the law by extending it beyond the people themselves to include their servants, their domestic animals, and even the resident alien in their midst. The phrase עַבְדְּךָ וַאֲמָתֶךָ, "your manservant and your maidservant," forms an envelope around this rythmic unit.

## Comment

**12–14a** *The fourth commandment:* the keeping of the sabbath. Unlike the first three commandments, this one is stated positively, at least initially (vv 12–13).

The concluding clause in v 14a resumes the familiar negative formulation: *You shall not do any work.* As Hasel has noted (*The Sabbath in Scripture and History* [1982] 67), the commandment imposes a double obligation: that of making holy the sabbath day (v 12), and that of working for six days (v 13).

שָׁמוֹר, "keep" or "take care," is used in v 12 in place of the verb זכר, "remember," which appears in the parallel passage in Exod 20:8. On the use of the inf abs here see J. D. W. Watts, "Infinitive Absolute as Imperative and the Interpretation of Ex. 20:8," *ZAW* 74 (1962) 141–45.

The verb שׁבת means "to cease, rest," from which is derived the noun sabbath. Though cognate forms of this verse are found in other Semitic languages, there is no clear evidence of a *sabbath day* or time construed as a seven-day week, apart from the Israelite tradition (see W. Rordorf, *BHH* 3, 1633).

**14b**  A. Phillips has called attention to the fact that there is no mention of wives in this otherwise comprehensive listing of persons within the family setting to whom work is forbidden on the sabbath (*JJS* 34 [1983] 1–20). This omission is probably not to be taken as a further instance of "sexism," so much as a subtle attempt to avoid any suggestion that the law also applied to necessary domestic activities. In other words, the extreme legalism of observance in some Jewish households to the point that even a light switch cannot be turned on during the sabbath is contrary to the spirit of the law itself.

**15**  The reason for the fourth commandment differs substantially here from its parallel in Exod 20:11. In Exodus the doctrine of creation dominates, whereas, in Deuteronomy it is the doctrine of redemption. The two reasons complement each other. To rest on the sabbath is to remember that we are part of God's created order, and to remember that we are totally dependent on the Creator. Our God-given task "to have dominion over" the created order (Gen 1:26) carries with it the privilege of sharing in God's rest. The Exodus from Egypt is the creation of God's people as a nation, as Craigie has noted (NICOT [1976] 157), when he translated the phrase in Exod 15:16 as "your people whom *you have created (qānîtā).*"

*Explanation*

The sabbath principle of ancient Israel is in large measure the root cause of an important social revolution in human history. As Lohfink has noted in his penetrating discussion of leisure in light of the sabbath commandment, the ancient world was clear in its distribution of work and leisure. "Work was for slaves and women; leisure was the substance of a man's life—a free man's life" ("Leisure" [1982] 203). The "Sabbath Commandment" of the people of Israel changed all this, for in this commandment the distribution of work and leisure among those "above" and those "below" was replaced by a new principle based on a temporal cycle. The seventh-day rest is valid for all persons, and even the draft animals as well (v 14). Though the existence of slaves here was assumed, the very foundations of a slave-owning society were seriously undermined in this rejection of the distribution of work and leisure to different classes. In fact, the freeing of slaves is already in sight, at least by implication, in the motivation for this commandment expressed in v 15: "remember that you were a servant in the land of Egypt and Yahweh your God brought you forth from there with a mighty hand and an outstretched arm. Therefore Yahweh your God commanded you to observe the sabbath day." Those who have moved from the harshest exploitation of slavery to the ranks of the fortunate cannot be content with the ancient distribution of work and leisure. They must reach the point where they wish all people to have both work and leisure.

Today it appears, at first glance, that the spirit of this social revolution is almost universal. Work and leisure are no longer distributed simply between those above and those beneath in the social ladder, except in isolated circumstances which appear "as intrusions into our very different world of vestiges from slave-owning and feudal societies" (N. Lohfink, "Leisure" [1982] 207). The Sabbath Commandment has won the day, for everyone works and everyone has leisure. Indeed, many of those at the top of the social ladder work much more than those below them, and many die before their time by literally working themselves to death. As a class, those at the "top" probably work harder than anyone else—sometimes even taking pride in the fact that they are "workaholics."

It is also an established fact that leisure time is increasing. Closing time comes earlier and the four-day work week is already a reality for some. We no longer speak of "Sunday" but "the weekend"—and frequently of the "long weekend" in which holidays are deliberately moved to extend our leisure time. Low-cost tours and recreational vehicles make southern climes and exotic places available to most. It appears that the message of the sabbath has been victorious. Those who refuse to accept the rhythm of working time and leisure time are flying in the face of one of the most sacred laws of modern society.

A closer look, however, suggests that other changes are taking place as well that call for a fresh look at the principle of the sabbath rest in modern society. In many cases increased free time does not bring us time for rest and celebration. In fact there are those who experience dread of free time because it brings with it boredom and loneliness. There are also strong pressures to turn leisure into a new type of activity, often under the guise of a hobby, which in reality sometimes becomes a new type of "servile labor" that stifles communication within families. Excellence in sports, as both participants and spectators, becomes obsession. Some seem to settle for little more than the "dreariness of dragging through the weekend with the help of TV, fast-food meals, a few beers, and 'extra' sleep" (N. Lohfink, "Leisure" [1982] 208).

Leisure itself has become an "industry." We ask ourselves if it has not become a new form of enslavement as well. Through a curious dialectical transformation of leisure into a new type of work, we may be back where we started. If so, it is time to take a closer look at the sabbath commandment which contains words we often fail to hear.

In the commandment to keep the sabbath we are also told "to make it holy" (v 12). What does this mean? As Lohfink reminds us, to make holy "means to remove some thing from the sphere of the normal, the common, the profane; to place it in relation to God through (for example) ritual or prayer or worship" (209). This means that our free time will become truly liberating, in the sense of bringing us rest, only when it culminates in making contact with God through sacred celebration.

Though the fourth commandment does introduce a day of rest for all persons, it also goes a step further. It points the way to genuine rest and celebration, which will only come about when we make that rest a holy rest, one that brings us close to God. It is this aspect of the sabbath commandment that is virtually unknown to our modern society. It may well be that we have here the root cause of the sickness that plagues many of us today when we try to cope with our leisure. The purpose of work for many of us has been reduced to earning the means to utilize our leisure time. If work has no meaning beyond providing us the opportunity of leisure, then leisure must have meaning in itself. Leisure provides time to be with our family, to meet friends, to enjoy the arts and games, to participate in nonutilitarian education—things in which we become more human. In short, leisure provides the occasion for the "pursuit of happiness," which the founding fathers in this country considered a basic human right.

Nonetheless, in all this there remains a danger so far as "meaning" is concerned. Boredom frequently enters the picture even with matters of friendship, art, and entertainment. Almost everything in this life can become empty and meaningless. It is here that the fourth commandment and its demand to keep the sabbath holy provides guidance for us. It is through the ritual of worship in prayer and praise that we experience contact with ultimate meaning. When this becomes a reality, our leisure time becomes a genuine antithesis to work in which we open ourselves to God and consciously shape our lives in reference to him in the very spirit of the sabbath rest.

## Bibliography for Deut 5:16–22

**Albertz, R.** "Hintergrund und Bedeutung des Elterngebots im Dekalog." *ZAW* 90 (1978) 348–74. ————. "Das Überleben der Familie Sichern." *Lutherische Monatshefte* 25 (1986) 401–5. **Alt, A.** "Das Verbot des Diebstahls im Dekalog." In *KlSchr* I (1953). 333–40. **Andrew, M. E.** "Falsehood and Truth." *Int* 16 (1963) 425–38. **Becker, J.** "Das Elterngebot." *IKZ* 8 (1979) 289–99. **Blidstein, G.** *Honor Thy Father and Mother: Filial Responsibility in Jewish Law and Ethics.* New York, 1976. **Boecker, H. J.** "'Du sollst dem Ochsen, der da drischt, das Maul nicht verbinden.' Überlegungen zur Wertung der Natur im Alten Testament." In *FS F. Lang* (1978). 72–89 (77–78). **Bowman, J.** "Samaritan Studies." *BJRL* 40 (1957/58) 298–327. **Buchanan, G. W.** "The 'Spiritual' Commandment." *JAAR* 36 (1968) 126–27. **Buchholz, J.** *Die Ältesten Israels im Deuteronomium.* GTA 36. Göttingen: Vandenhoeck & Ruprecht, 1988. **Bückers, H.** *Die biblische Lehre vom Eigentum.* Bonn, 1947. 23–46. **Casciaro, J. M.** "El concepto de 'Ekklesia' en el AT." *EstBib* 25 (1966) 317–48; 26 (1967) 3–38. **Coates, J. R.** "Thou Shalt Not Covet." *ZAW* 52 (1934) 238–39. **Crüsemann, F.** *Bewahrung der Freiheit: Das Thema des Dekalogs in Sozialgeschichtlicher Perspektive.* KT 78. Munich: Kaiser, 1983. 73. **Dahan, G.** "Les interprétations juives dans les commentaires du pentateuque de Pierre Le Chantre." In *FS B. Smalley* (1985). 131–55. **Dahood, M.** "Review of A. Barucq, *Le Livre des Proverbs.*" *Bib* 46 (1965) 332–34 (332). **Daube, D.** "The Culture of Deuteronomy." *Orita* 3 (1969) 27–52 (39). **Dexinger, F.** "Das Garizimgebot im Dekalog der Semaritaner." In *FS W. Kornfeld* (1977). 111–33. **Diakonoff, I. M.** "On the Structure of Old Babylonian Society." In *Beiträge zür Sozialen Struktur des Alten Vorderasien.* SGKAO 1. Berlin, 1971. 15–31. **Doron, P.** "Motive Clauses in the Law of Deuteronomy: Their Forms, Functions and Contents." In HAR 2 (1978). 61–77. **Fensham, F. C.** "Liability in Case of Negligence in the Old Testament Covenant Code and Ancient Legal Traditions." *Acta Juridica* (1976) 283–94 (285). **Fichtner, J.** "Der Begriff des 'Nächsten' im Alten Testament mit einem Ausblick auf Spätjudentum und Neues Testament." In *Gottes Weisheit: Gesammelte Studien zum Alten Testament.* Ed. K. Fricke. AzTh 2/3. Stuttgart, 1965. 88–114. **Finet, A.** "Hammurapi et l'épouse vertueuse." In *FS F. M. T. de Liagre Böhl* (1973). 137–43. **Fitzmyer, J. A.** "4QTestimonia and the New Testament." *TS* 18 (1957) 513–37 (518). **Flusser, D.** "Do not commit adultery, Do not murder." *Textus* 4 (1964) 220–24.

**Gamberoni, I.** "Das Elterngebot im Alten Testament." *BZ* n.s. 8 (1964) 161–90. **Gese, H.** "Der Dekalog als Ganzheit Betrachtet." *ZTK* 64 (1967) 121–38 (134–36). **Gnuse, R. K.** *You Shall not Steal: Community and Property in the Biblical Tradition.* New York: Orbis Books, 1985. **Görg, M.** "Missbrauch des Gottesnamens." *BN* 16 (1981) 16–17. **Gordon, C. H.** "A Note on the Tenth Commandment." *JBR* 31 (1963) 208–9. ————. "The Ten Commandments." *CT* 8 (1964) 624–28. **Greenberg, M.** "Some Postulates of Biblical Criminal Law." In *FS Y. Kaufmann* (1960). 9–11. **Herrmann, J.** "Das zehnte Gebot." In *FS E. Sellin* (1927). 69–82. **Horst, F.** "Der Diebstahl im Alten Testament." In *Gottes Recht: Studien zum Recht im Alten Testament.* TB 12. Munich: Kaiser, 1961. 167–75. *HOTTP* I, 276. **Hulst, A. R.** "Opmerkingen over de *kaʾaser*-zinnen en Dt." *NedTTs* 18 (1963) 337–61. **Jackson, B.** *Essays in Jewish and Comparative Legal History* (1975). 31–36, 202–34. **Jackson, G. S.** *Theft in Early Jewish Law.* Oxford: Clarendon Press, 1972. **Jacob ben Aaron.** "Mount Gerizim: The One True Sanctuary." *BSac* 64 (1907) 489–518 (507–8). **Klein, H.** "Verbot des Menschendiebstahls im Dekalog?" *VT* 26 (1976) 161–69. **Koch, D.-A.** *Die Schrift als Zeuge des Evangeliums.* BHTh 69. Tübingen: Mohr, 1986. 34. **Koch, R.** "Le siciéme (cinquiéme) commandement (Ex 20, 13; Dt 5, 17)." *StMor* 16 (1978) 9–30. **Kornfeld, W.** "L'adultère dans l'Oriente antique." *RB* 57 (1950) 92–109. **Kremers, H.** "Die Stellung des Elterngebots im Dekalog." *EvT* 21 (1961) 145–61. **Landsberger, B.** *Der Kultische Kalender der Babylonier und Assyrer: Erste Hälfte.* LSSt 6. Leipzig, 1915 (rep. 1968). **Lang, B.** "Altersversorgung, Begräbnis und Elterngebot." In *XIX. Deutscher Orientalistentag 28.9.–4.10.1975 Freiburg i.B.* Ed. W. Voigt. Wiesbaden: Franz Steiner Verlag, 1977. 149–56. ————. "Neues über den Dekalog." *ThQ* 164 (1984) 60–63. ————. "'Du sollst nicht nach der Frau eines anderen verlangen': Eine neue Deutung des 9. und 10. Gebots." *ZAW* 93 (1981) 216–24. **Lemaire, A. Le.** "The Social Organization of Peasant Poverty in Biblical Israel." *JSOT* 24 (1982) 47–63 (48). **Levin, C.** *Der Sturz der Königin Atalja.* SBS 105. Stuttgart, 1982. 41–42. **Loretz, O.** "Vom kanaanäischen Totenkult zur jüdischen Patriarchen- und Elternehrung." *Jahrbuch für Anthropologie und Religionsgeschichte* 3 (1978) 149–204. ————. "Das biblische Elterngebot und die Sohnespflicht in der ugaritsichen Aqht-Legende." *BN* 8 (1979) 14–17. **Lurje, M.** "Die Agrarverhältnisse." In *Studien zur Geschichte der wirtschaftlichen und sozialen Verhältnisse im Israelitisch-jüdischen Reiche.* Giessen: Töpelmann, 1927. 1–19. **Meinhold, A.** "Zum Verständnis des Elterngebotes." *Die Christenlehre* 38 (1985) 248–54. **Moran, W. L.** "The Conclusion of the Decalogue (Ex 20, 17 = Dt 5, 21)." *CBQ* 29 (1967) 543–54. **Mutius, H. G. von.** "Zwei Bibeltextvarianten bei Bachja Ibn Pakuda (Jes XXVI,8; Dt V,21)." *VT* 30 (1980) 234–36. **Nemoy, L.** *Karaite Anthology.* YJS 7. New Haven: Yale UP, 1952. 260–63. **Otto, E.** "Zur Stellung der Frau in den ältesten Rechtstexten des Alten Testamentes (Ex 20,14; 22,15f.)—wider die hermeneutische Naivität im Umgang mit dem Alten Testametnt." *ZEE* 26 (1982) 279–305. **Peri, I.** "*Ecclesia* und *synagoga* in der lateinischen Übersetzung des Alten Testamentes." *BZ* n.s. 33 (1989) 245–51. **Phillips, A.** "Another Look at Murder." *JJS* 28 (1977) 105–26. **Porten, B.** and **Szubin, H. Z.** "'Abandoned Property' in Elephantine." *JNES* 41 (1982) 123–31. **Reviv, H.** "The Pattern of the Pan-Tribal Assembly in the Old Testament." *JNSL* 8 (1980) 85–94. **Ruppert, L.** "Symbole im Alten Testament." In *FS J. G. Plöger* (1983). 93–105 (97–101). **Schenker, A.** "Der Monotheismus im ersten Gebot, die Stellung der Frau im Sabbatgebot und zwei andere Sachfragen zum Dekalog." *FZPhTh* 32 (1985) 330–33. **Schottroff, W.** "*Gedenken*" im *Alten Orient und im Alten Testament: Die Wurzel zākar im Semitischen Sprachkreis.* WMANT 15. Neukirchen-Vluyn, 1964. **Schunck, K.-D.** "Das 9. und 10. Gebot—jüngstes Glied des Dekalogs?" *ZAW* 96 (1984) 104–9. **Stade, B.** "Ein Land, wo Milch und Honig fliesst." *ZAW* 22 (1902) 321–24. **Stamm, J. J.** "Sprachliche Erwägungen zum Gebot 'Du sollst nicht töten.'" *ThZ* 1 (1945) 81–90. **Stoebe, H. J.** "Das achte Gebot." *WD* 3 (1952) 108–26. **Szlechter, E.** "Effets de la captivité en droit assyro-babylonien." *RA* 57 (1963) 181–92; 58 (1964) 23–35. ————. "Effets de l'absence (volontaire) en droit assyro-babylonien." *Or* 34 (1965) 289–311. **Thiel, W.** "Altorientalische und israelitisch-jüdische Religion." In *JLH* 28 (1984). 168–91 (182). **Tigay, J. H.** "Conflation as a Redactional Technique." In *Empirical Models for Biblical Criticism.* Ed. J. H. Tigay. Philadelphia: Pennsylvania UP, 1985. 53–89. **Tov, E.** "The Nature and Background of

Harmonization in Biblical Manuscripts." *JSOT* 31 (1985) 3–29 (10). **Unna, I.** *Die Aguna-Gesetze: Bestimmungen über die Wiederverheiratung der Witwen von Verschollenen.* Frankfurt, 1916. **Usener, H. C.** Milch und Honig." *RMP* n.s. 57 (1902) 177–95. **Vasholz, R. I.** "You Shall Not Covet Your Neighbor's Wife." *WTJ* 49 (1987) 397–403. **Waterhouse, S. D.** "A Land Flowing with Milk and Honey." *AUSS* 1 (1963) 152–66. **Watts, J. D. W.** "Infinitive Absolute as Imperative and the Interpretation of Exodus 20:8." *ZAW* 74 (1962) 141–45. **Wittenberg, G.** "The Tenth Commandment in the Old Testament." *JTSoA* 21 (1978) 3–17.

## Translation and Prosodic Analysis

5:16–22    [4+8] {[2] [2] [2] [2]} [4:4] [4+8]

| | | |
|---|---:|---:|
| [16] *Honor your father / and your mother /* | 13 | 2 |
| [a]*Just as he commanded you / YHWH your God*[a] *//* | 14 | 2_ |
| *In order that / your days may be prolonged /* | ⌈ 14 | 2 |
| *and in order that / it may go well with you /* | ⌊ 9 | 2 |
| *Upon / the ground / which YHWH your God / is giving to you //* ס | 24 | 4_ |
| | | |
| [17] *You shall not / kill //* ס | ⌈ 5 | 2 |
| [18] *[And]*[a] *you shall not / commit adultery //* ס | [ 5 | 2 |
| [19] *[And]*[a] *you shall not / steal //* ס | ⌊ 5 | 2 |
| [20] *And*[a] *you shall not render against your neighbor /* | ⌈ 10 | 1 |
| *a false witness*[b] *//* ס | ⌊ 5 | 1_ |
| | | |
| [21] *[And]*[a] *you shall not covet* \[b] *your neighbor's wife //* ס[b] | ⌈ 12 | 1 |
| *[And]*[c] *you shall not* [d]*desire / your neighbor's house*[d] */* | [ 12 ⌉ | 2 |
| *(or) his field /* | ⌊ 6 ⌋ | 1_ |
| *And*[e] *his manservant and his maidservant /* | ⌈ 10 | 1 |
| *his ox*[f] *and his ass /* | [ 10 | 1 |
| *and anything / that is your neighbor's*[g] *//* ס | ⌊ 10 | 2_ |
| | | |
| [22] *These (are the) words* (דברים) */* | 12 | 1 |
| *YHWH spoke* (דבר) *unto all your assembly /* | 10 | 1 |
| *on the mountain / from the midst of the fire /* | 11 | 2_ |
| *(There was)*[a] *the cloud and the dense vapor / a loud voice /* | ⌈ 18 | 2 |
| *and he added no more //* | ⌊ 7 | 1 |
| *And he wrote them / upon two / tablets of stone*[b] */* | ⌈ 17 | 3 |
| *and he gave them / to me //*[c] | ⌊ 9 | 2_ |

## Notes

16.a-a. This phrase does not appear in Exod 20:12, the parallel passage.

18.a. The *waw*-conj is omitted with some Heb. Mss, SP, LXX, Syr, and Tg[J].

19.a. See note 18.a. above.

20.a. Though the *waw*-conj is omitted in most of the witnesses cited in the previous note, it is here retained for prosodic reasons.

20.b. Some Heb. Mss read שָׁקֶר for שָׁוְא which appears to be an interpretive gloss.

21.a. See note 18.a. above.

21.b. See note 1:1.c. Note that prosodic analysis suggests that the *setûmā* paragraph marker here is in error, and that the command not to covet extends to matters of property as well as to the "neighbor's wife."

21.c. The *waw*-conj is omitted with LXX, Syr, and Vg (cf. Exod 20:17).
21.d-d. SP reads אשׁת תחמד for MT תתאוה בית.
21.e. One Heb. Ms and SP omit *waw*-conj.
21.f. A number of Heb. Mss, Cairo geniza fragments, LXX, and Syr add *waw*-conj.
21.g. SP adds chap. 27:2 here.
22.a. SP and LXX add חשׁך with 4:11. Prosodic analysis supports MT.
22.b. DSS reads האבנים, adding the def art.
22.c. The boundary of this prosodic unit is marked by extra space in both *BHK* and *BHS*.

### Form/Structure/Setting

From a prosodic point of view Deut 5:16–22 is in four parts: v 16, vv 17–20, v 21, and v 22, which scan /(4+8):8:8:(4+8)/. The pairing of vv 16 and 22 is suggestive, with the command to "honor your parents" set over against the summary statement את הדברים האלה, "these words," which recalls the opening phrase and title of Deuteronomy אלה הדברים, "these are the words," in 1:1. The laws in chaps. 12–26 which pertain to the fifth commandment make up the very center of the book (16:18–18:22), which in turn function as a primary text on which the structure of the Deuteronomic History (Joshua through 2 Kings) is based.

The center of the prosodic structure of 5:16–22 has a series of four commandments (vv 17–20) set over against a single commandment, which has been taken as two separate items in alternate listing of the "ten words" within the Masoretic tradition itself (see discussion at the beginning of this section on numbering the Ten Commandments).

### Comment

**16** *The fifth commandment:* parental respect. To some degree this commandment complements the second commandment (5:8–10), as Craigie has noted (NICOT [1976] 158). There the use of images on the part of the parents would have its results "upon the children" and even their great-grandchildren. Here we find the reciprocal side so far as responsibility is concerned. The children are charged to *honor your father and your mother.* The close parallel in language with 4:40 suggests that the basic issue remains the same: parents are responsible to teach their children concerning the covenant, in order that both children and parents may prosper in the land which Yahweh has provided (cf. 4:9–10). If childen refuse to honor their parents, they will also break their covenant with Yahweh, which will bring dire consequences.

The first four commandments (5:6–15) were concerned with the relationship between the people and their God. The final five commandments (5:17–21) deal with human relationships within the covenant community. The fifth commandment falls between these two poles with its focus on the family situation, which is at the very core of the larger covenant community.

**17** *The sixth commandment:* the prohibition of murder. The term תרצח refers to murder (premeditated killing) and manslaughter (accidental killing) and not with the forms of taking life in general. Other laws will follow which involve capital punishment (cf. Deut 17:2–7 and 19:12), and Israelite law does not exclude war (see Deut 20–21). Cases dealing with accidental death require further legislation (see Deut 19:1–13). The sixth commandment prohibits murder by a member of the covenant community for personal and illegitimate reasons.

**18**  *The seventh commandment:* the prohibition of adultery. The verb נאף refers specifically to adultery. Other sexual matters are covered by laws in Deut 22–25. The law here forbids sexual intercourse between two persons, one or both of whom are married to another party or other parties. It is likely that Israelite law considered "betrothed" girls to be the equivalent of married women (cf. Deut 22:23–24).

Marriage is a covenantal relationship and thus the crime of adultery is the moral equivalent of violating the first commandment, that of having "other gods" (5:5). Faithfulness is demanded in every sphere of life, both religious and secular. The theme of fidelity in marriage thus became a primary analogy in ancient Israel to describe the covenant relationship between God and his people (cf. Hos 1–3; Ezek 16).

**19**  *The eighth commandment:* the prohibition of stealing. As A. Alt and others have shown, the primary prohibition of this commandment is against something akin to kidnapping (*KlSchr* I [1953] 333–40). Deut 24:7 presents a more detailed description of the crime in question, which often included the "sale" of the victim for personal gain or profit, such as the capture and sale of Joseph by his brothers (Gen 37:22–28). Such a crime removes the victim from his or her family, and thus the crime, like that of murder, abrogates the covenant relationship between the individual and God. To assume control of the life and fate of another person for one's own personal gain is to play the part of God. In one sense, as Craigie has noted (NICOT [1976] 162), the eighth commandment forms a parallel to the third. Whereas the improper use of God's name was the equivalent of manipulating God for personal gain, "stealing" was the attempt to manipulate a fellow human being for personal gain.

**20**  *The ninth commandment:* the prohibition of false testimony. The language used indicates that the commandment is concerned with the legal process itself. The phrase עד שוא, "false witness," refers to a statement rendered against a רע, "neighbor," a fellow member of the covenant community, in a legal case. More detailed legislation at this point is found in 19:15–21. The principle involved is, once again, faithfulness within the context of the covenant community, particularly as it pertains to personal human relationships.

**21**  *The tenth commandment:* the prohibition of coveting. The last commandment in the list forms a fitting conclusion in that it focuses on the motivation of self-interest, which leads to the violation of commandments 6–9 in matters of ethical morality. A normal person does not kill for the love of killing, but for self-interest. Though the act of adultery involves interest in another person, it too is closely related to self-interest; stealing and false testimony prohibited in commandments eight and nine, likewise, are motivated by self-interest.

חמד, "covet," is sometimes rendered as desire leading to specific action, in contrast with the synonym התאוה, "strongly desire," which does not appear in the parallel text in Exod 20:17. Moreover, unlike the Exodus text, the wife enjoys a place apart in Deuteronomy. From this fact, Moran concluded that this probably reflects the relatively higher status of women in the time of Deuteronomy ("Deuteronomy" [1969] 264). Note that Deut 15:12–18 implies that a woman could own real estate, and 21:19 is clear evidence of legal recognition of a mother's position in the family. Moran also has called attention to a legal text from Ugarit in which the list of "house, field, menservants, maidservants, oxen, asses, and everything else belonging to him" is virtually identical to that of Deut 5:21 (see *CBQ* 29 [1967] 550–51).

**22**  This verse functions as both a summary conclusion to the "ten words" and a bridge to what follows. By way of conclusion, the verse stresses the divine origin of the commandments: *These are the words Yahweh spoke . . . on the mountain from the midst of the fire.* The awesome physical aspects of that theophany are described in symbolic language, familiar to students of mysticism: namely, *the fire, the cloud and the dense vapor* (הערפל; cf. 4:11), *a loud voice.* Awed by this experience the people bring their request to Moses that he serve as mediator between them and this fearful God (5:23–31).

As Craigie has noted (NICOT [1976] 163), the tenth commandment has aroused scholarly debate about its meaning. Unlike the previous nine commandments, this one is concerned primarily with motivation rather than specific action. G. W. Buchanan called it the "spiritual" commandment (*JAAR* 36 [1968] 126–27). The particular emphasis here brings difficulties since these commandments are regulations for life in a community. It is not clear how a breach of this commandment would be known by the community. Some have argued that the verb "covet" (חמד) means desire leading to action. But the same cannot be said for the synonym תתאוה, which appears in the second main clause and clearly expresses strong desire or longing. Consequently it is likely that this final commandment is to be understood as a prohibition of coveting, without any suggestion of an action based on that desire.

## Explanation

The focus of the fifth commandment is on the continuity of the covenant community. The fulfillment of the promise of the covenant God is experienced only as parents teach their children and as the children honor their parents and learn from the faith of their parents. The fifth commandment functions as a bridge connecting the obligations toward God in the first four with those toward fellow human beings in the last five. Like the fourth commandment to keep the sabbath, it is expressed positively and includes a promise rather than a theological reason. The promise speaks of extended life in the promised land, which is based on harmony with the divine order. In this respect the command touches on the relation between authority and order, between God and his representatives in the human sphere. Though no laws in the Central Core (chaps. 12–26) of Deuteronomy deal expressly with parents in relation to children, a group of laws involving positions of leadership correspond to this command, namely the laws of the king, the Levite, and the prophet (Deut 17:14–18:22).

This commandment is frequently interpreted to mean that parents are the visible representatives of God within the human family and hence have the right to bend the will of their children to their own. Elsewhere in Deuteronomy children are encouraged to be obedient and are even subject to severe penalties should they not yield to the wishes of their parents (Deut 21:18–21). Nonetheless, one should not push this line of interpretation too far. As Harrelson has noted (*The Ten Commandments* [1980], 92), parents sometimes "tyrannize their children, crush their spirits, and do damage, the effects of which may continue to the end of life." It is important to bear in mind that the persons addressed here are adults.

Younger members of the covenant community are not excluded, but they are also not the focus of attention. In short, the fifth commandment is not designed primarily to keep young children in line by keeping them dutiful and respectful to their elders.

The central concern of this commandment is to care for aged parents and not to treat them with contempt. But even in this regard it is not easy to translate the substance of this command in contemporary terms. The relation between adult children and their parents is one of the most complex of all human relationships, perhaps even more so than that between husband and wife. Modern depth psychology has produced a vast literature concerning how such relationships can be made more wholesome. One of the major problems in this area is the shift in roles when parents grow old and become increasingly dependent upon their adult children, thus reversing the dependency roles of earlier years.

In this particular instance, as is also the case with most of the commandments to follow, the continuing applicability of this commandment to daily life is not to be seen as direct or literal. To "honor your father and your mother" is to "prize them highly" (Prov 4:8); it carries with it nuances of caring for and showing affection (Ps 91:15). But who is to say that it is a kindness or a curse to keep the elderly in one's own house when they are no longer able to cope with the demands of life in such a home and must appear more and more to those in that household as incompetent? In such instances the very conditions of life in the home may contribute to the feelings of helplessness which make the parents objects of pity, and perhaps even of contempt. What is important to note in this commandment, as Harrelson has put it (100),

> is Israel's insistence that the adult Israelite cannot secure freedom from father or mother at the expense of humiliating, cursing, or doing away with either of them. On the contrary, if the Israelite expects his or own life to flourish, it will be necessary for such a one to bear in mind that in Yahweh's eyes one condition for such flourishing is precisely how the elderly parents are treated.

It was Karl Barth who perhaps best indicated the wide applicability of the sixth commandment to contemporary life (see *Church Dogmatics* [Edinburgh: T & T. Clark, 1957] II/2, 683–86; III/4, 47–564). His treatment of this commandment covers virtually all instances in which human life is taken: murder, capital punishment, war, abortion (and other forms of birth control), euthanasia, and suicide. Using the phrase "reverence for life," but in a manner somewhat different from Albert Schweizer, Barth argued that this commandment rules out the taking of human life under almost any circumstance. Nonetheless, as Harrelson has noted, "if we apply the commandment to all the above aspects of our common life we will enter a thicket of fundamental moral issues facing humankind today, from which there may be no way out!" (109). Though there was no such notion of the sanctity of human life in ancient Israel, at least in the sense Barth has delineated, it is not easy to dismiss the substance of his arguments. Human life has its meaning in relation to God and his purposes. In fact, we must insist that life belongs to God and to God alone. Properly understood, the sixth commandment stakes out God's claim over all life. That claim is to be given priority in all decisions, particularly those involving the termination of human life. In fact, the process leading potentially to the act of murder is also culpable, as Jesus argued in Matt 5:21–22.

In both testaments the path toward obedience and fulfillment of the law is the path of love toward God and our fellow human beings.

The seventh commandment prohibiting adultery, like the law against killing, is stated in general terms, with no definition given and no distinctions drawn. As such the law against adultery was bound to take on an application broader than it probably had in view at the time it was first formulated. In ancient Israel there was a rather sharp distinction made between men and women in regards to adultery. An engaged or married woman committed adultery if she had sexual relations with anyone other than her husband or fiancé. The man, however, committed adultery only if he had sexual relations with the wife or the betrothed of another man. Thus a married man who visited a prostitute was not committing adultery. The apostle Paul marks a significant step away from this situation in his arguments that sexual relations with a prostitute constitute a kind of marriage, regardless of what the partners' intentions may be (1 Cor 6:15–20). The distinction between the meaning of adultery for the man and the woman has now virtually disappeared, as well it should.

It is important to note that there was no notion whatever in ancient Israel that sexual relations were morally ambiguous. That notion rose in other times and places. It was only sex outside the marriage relationship that was prohibited. The commandment against adultery stakes out the claim of the two partners in marriage to a mutual relationship that is not to be compromised or destroyed by the actions of either partner. It is claimed by many today that this law is outmoded. Nonetheless, as Harrelson has argued (131),

> this prohibition can be the guideline for every marriage, expressing the commitment of the partners in marriage to treasure and preserve a unity that has been called into being in marriage and in the sexual relations they have engaged in as marriage partners. And certainly it would seem evident that, if sexual relations do in fact relate persons to one another in ways deeper than might then and there be realized, the wise course is for married persons to have sexual relations with no one other than their spouse, ever.

The remaining three commandments deal with life in community in such a fashion as to assure that human beings can maintain their place and their rights within that social structure. Though the eighth commandment may well have had specific reference to the stealing of a human being rather than the goods of an individual, as numerous scholars have proposed, the traditional reading remains valid. The commandment not to steal means not to claim for one's own the possessions of another.

Taken in the narrower sense of "stealing another person," this commandment takes on peculiar force in today's world. The hijacking of a passenger airplane, or the taking of hostages in general by terrorist groups or nations, constitutes flagrant violation of the eighth commandment. But less obvious forms of manipulation of other human beings for personal gain also fall within the purview of this prohibition as well, such as what frequently takes place in the "rat race" of power politics, even within religious institutions.

Violation of the command against stealing takes place in other, perhaps more pervasive, ways in our society as well. Individuals sometimes accumulate for themselves vast quantities of goods by unjust means. Accumulation of wealth is at the same time accumulation of power, and victims of the rich are often severely mistreated when they dare to demand the smallest compensation for their loss. Wealthy individuals often turn to the eighth commandment as a means of protecting their wealth, when this prohibition has perhaps more to say against those who amass such wealth. As Harrelson put it (138–39):

> When equally applied, the eighth commandment has much more to say to the giver of bribes for political favors, to the manipulator of the economic system for unjust and unearned assets, to the destroyer of businesses for the sake of a favorable tax advantage, to the issuer of stocks who having made his millions then sells out as the vast new enterprise is about to collapse, or to the governmental figure who sets out to make a fortune by compelling the offering of bribes. The stealing with which our society is more familiar lies in such areas as these.

The ninth commandment follows naturally on the eighth. Just as one must not steal the goods of the neighbor by means of false weights and measures, so one must not use false words in public dealings. The false word perverts justice perhaps even more than the false weight. Language forms the very basis of human community. When words cannot be trusted, the very fabric of the community is in jeopardy. A society will maintain its health only when the voices of criticism and protest are plainly heard and not suppressed. This is as true for religious institutions as secular.

The tenth commandment refers to the unnatural desire for the goods of others, not simply to the making of plans to take such goods, which would be included in the eighth commandment. For a particularly insightful discussion of the meaning of the term חמד in this sense, see J. Philip Hyatt in *Exodus,* NCB. (London: Oliphants, 1971), 216–17. The emphasis falls not so much on the deed done as the disposition of the self in the direction of the deed. The term חמד means much more than even longing for something. In Prov 1:22 scoffers are asked how long they will continue "to delight" (חמדו) in their scoffing. In Deut 5:21 the term is used in parallel with the verb אוה, which clearly means to desire, to long for, to lust after.

Some have argued that a law dealing with the attitudes, or the emotions, rather than actual deeds is too subtle and refined for ancient Israel. But love is commanded of both God and our fellow human beings, as we will see in Deut 6:4. To some extent, then, individual feelings, thoughts, and attitudes are legislated, though the test of faithfulness to this command is given only in discernible actions which display those feelings, thoughts, and attitudes. As Harrelson has noted, similar concern for qualities of human motivation as well as action are found in texts from the middle and late kingdoms (ca. 2000–1750 and 1550–1100 B.C.E.) in Egypt (150–51).

We should be careful not to press the meaning of this commandment too far, particularly in relation to peoples in the developing nations who long for the goods and services that constitute the quality of life enjoyed by the more wealthy nations. Such longing is not necessarily a violation of the command not to covet. The tenth commandment must not be used by those who have an abundance of this world's goods to limit the legitimate desires of the poor for a more equitable share of those goods.

The tenth commandment is not as strikingly different from the preceding nine as sometimes claimed. In some respects it forms a fitting inclusion to the Ten

Commandments. The first commandment demands that no other deity or principle count for anything in the life of the Israelite. God's people are bound to him in interior ways. They not only are forbidden to worship other gods; they are to give no place to such powers in their thinking and feeling. In a somewhat similar manner, the Israelite is prohibited by the tenth commandment from lusting for the wife of his neighbor or any other of his neighbor's possessions.

## Bibliography for Deut 5:23–6:3

**Airoldi, N.** "La funzione giuridica dei cosidetti 'raccont storici' del IIo discorso di Mosè al popolo (Dt 5. 9s)." *Aug* 13 (1973) 75–92 (77). **Artzi, P.** "'Vox populi' in the El-Amarna Tablets." *RA* 58 (1964) 159–60. **Bamberger, B. J.** "Fear and Love in the Old Testament." *HUCA* 6 (1929) 39–53 (45). **Buchholz, J.** *Die Ältesten Israels im Deuteronomium.* GTA 36. Göttingen: Vandenhoeck & Ruprecht, 1988. **Buit, F. M.** "Aimer Dieu seul, Dt 6, 2–6." *ASeign* 62 (1970) 40–45. **Cazelles, H.** "Jérémie et le Deutéronome." *RSR* 38 (1951/52) 5–36 (12). **Cholewinski, A.** "Zur theologischen Deutung des Moabbundes." *Bib* 66 (1985) 96–111 (101). **Dahl, N. A.** "La terre où coulent le lait et le miel, selon Barnabé 6, 8–19." In *Aux sources de la tradition Chretienne: FS M. Goguel.* Neuchatel: Delachaux & Niestlé, 1950. 62–70. **Dandamayev, M. A.** "The Neo-Babylonian Elders." In *FS I. M. Diakonoff* (1982). 38–41. **D'Ercole, G.** "La Struttura Giuridica de Israele." *SDHI* 31 (1965) 246–304 (250–55). **Diakonoff, I. M.** "The Rise of the Despotic State in Ancient Mesopotamia." In *Ancient Mesopotamia: Socio-Economic History.* Moscow: Nauka, 1969. 173–203. **Dus, J.** "Die Herabfahrung Jahwes auf die Lade und Entziehung der Feuerwolke." *VT* 19 (1969) 290–311. **Dussaud, R.** "Jahwe, fils de El; Ugaritica; Dt 32, 8." *Syria* 34 (1957) 232–42 (238–39). **Evans, G.** "Ancient Mesopotamian Assemblies." *JAOS* 78 (1958) 1–11. **Fensham, F. C.** "An Ancient Tradition of the Fertility of Palestine." *PEQ* 98 (1966) 166–67. **Fitzmyer, J. A.** "4QTestimonia and the New Testament." *TS* 18 (1957) 513–37 (530–34). **Gammie, J. G.** "The Theology of Retribution in the Book of Deuteronomy." *CBQ* 32 (1970) 1–12 (7–8). **Gottstein, M. H.** "Afterthought and the Syntax of Relative Clauses in Biblical Hebrew." *JBL* 68 (1949) 35–47 (43). **Greenberg, M.** "Some Postulates of Biblical Criminal Law." In *FS Y. Kaufmann* (1960). 9–11. ———. " נסה in Exod 20:20 and the Purpose of the Sinaitic Theophanie." *JBL* 79 (1960) 173–76. **Gross, H.** *Die Idee des ewigen und allgemeinen Weltfriedens im Alten Orient und im Alten Testament.* Trier: Paulinus, 1956. 71–78. **Guidi, I.** "Une terre coulante du lait avec du miel." *RB* 12 (1903) 241–44. **Herrmann, W.** "Götterspeise und Göttertrank in Ugarit und Israel." *ZAW* 72 (1960) 205–16. **Hoppe, L.** "Elders and Deuteronomy: A Proposal." *EglT* 14 (1983) 259–72. *HOTTP* I, 276–77. **Jackson, B.** *Essays in Jewish and Comparative Legal History* (1975). 213. **Jacobsen, T.** "Primitive Democracy in Ancient Mesopotamia." *JNES* 2 (1943) 159–72. **Klengel, H.** "Zu den šībūtum in altbabylonischer Zeit." *Or* 29 (1960) 357–75. ———. "Die Rolle der 'Ältesten' im Kleinasien der Hethiterzeit." *ZA* 57 (1965) 223–36. **Krauss, S.** "Honig in Palästina." *ZDPV* 32 (1909) 151–64. **Kreuzer, S.** *Der Lebendige Gott. Bedeutung, Herkunft und Entwicklung einer alttestamentlichen Gottesbezeichnung.* BWANT VI/16–116. Stuttgart: Kohlhammer, 1983. **Kuhl, C.** "Die 'Wiederaufnahme'—ein literarkritisches Prinzip?" *ZAW* 64 (1952) 1–11. **Lohfink, N.** *Das Hauptgebot* (1963). 67–68. **Malamat, A.** "Kingship and Council in Israel and Sumer: A Parallel." *JNES* 22 (1963) 247–53. **Malfroy, J.** "Sagesse et Loi dans le Deutéronome. Études." *VT* 15 (1965) 49–65 (63). **McKenzie, J. L.** "The Elders in the Old Testament." *Bib* 40 (1959) 522–40. **Mittmann, S.** *Deuteronomium 1, 1–6, 3* (1963). 137–38. **Olivier, H.** "A Land Flowing with Milk and Honey: Some Observations on the Modes of Existence in Ancient Israel." *NGTT* 29 (1988) 2–13. **Ploeg, J. van der.** "Les Anciens dans l'Ancien Testament." In *FS H. Junker* (1961). 175–91. **Power, E.** "Terra lac et mel manans." *VD* 2 (1922) 52–58. **Reviv, H.** "On Urban Representative Institutions and Self-Government in Syria-Palestine in the Second Half of the Second Millenium B.C." *JESHO* 12 (1969) 283–97. ———. "Elders and

'Saviors.'" *OrAnt* 16 (1977) 201–04. ————. *The Elders in Ancient Israel: A Study of a Biblical Institution.* Jerusalem: Magnes, 1983. **Roeroe, W. A.** *Das Ältestenamt im Alten Testament.* Diss., Mainz, 1976. **Rofè, A.** "Deuteronomy 5:28–6:1: Composition and Text in the Light of Deuteronomic Style and Three Tefillin from Qumran (4Q 128, 129, 137)." *Tarbiz* 51 (1982) 177–84 (Heb.), vi (Eng. summary). **Rowley, H. H.** "The Prophet Jeremiah and the Book of Deuteronomy." In *FS T. H. Robinson* (1950). 157–74. **Ruprecht, E.** "Exodus 24, 9–11 als Beispiel lebendiger Erzähltradition aus der Zeit des babylonischen Exils." In *FS C. Westermann* (1980). 138–73 (143). **Schnutenhaus, F.** "Das Kommen und Erscheinen Gottes im Alten Testament." *ZAW* 76 (1964) 1–22 (13). **Stade, B.** "Ein Land, wo Milch und Honig fliesst." *ZAW* 22 (1902) 321–24. **Tov, E.** "The Nature and Background of Harmonizations in Biblical Manuscripts." *JSOT* 31 (1985) 3–29 (14, 17). **Usener, H. C.** "Milch und Honig." *RMP* n.s. 57 (1902) 177–95. **Waterhouse, S. D.** "A Land Flowing with Milk and Honey." *AUSS* 1 (1963) 152–66. **Wilson, G. H.** "'The Words of the Wise': The Intent and Significance of Qohelet 12:9–14." *JBL* 103 (1984) 175–92 (187–88). **Wolf, C. H.** Traces of Primitive Democracy in Ancient Israel." *JNES* 6 (1947) 98–108. **Yeivin, I.** "Composition and Text in the Light of Deuteronomic Style and Three Tefillin from Qumran." *Tarbiz* 49 (1979/80) 177–84 (Heb.). **Ziegler, J.** "Zur Septuaginta-Vorlage im Deuteronomium." *ZAW* 72 (1960) 255.

### *Translation and Prosodic Analysis*

5:23–6:3   [(5+6):7] [(5:5):5] [5:(5:5)] [7:8:8:7] [(5:5):(5:5):5:5] [7:(5+6)]

| | | |
|---|---|---|
| [23] And it was / when you heard the voice / | 12 | 2 |
| from the midst of the darkness[a] / | 7 | 1 |
| And the mountain / (was) burning with fire // | <u>13</u> | 2_ |
| And you came near unto me / | 8 | 1 |
| all the heads of your tribes / and your elders // | 14 | 2 |
| [24] And you said[a] / "Behold he has shown us / YHWH our God / | <u>23</u> | 3_ |
| His glory [b][and his greatness \] and his voice we heard / | 17 | 1 |
| from the midst of the fire // THIS DAY / | 12 | 2 |
| We have seen / that God[c] may speak (ידבר) / | 17 | 2 |
| with a person / and he may (still) live // | <u>11</u> | 2_ |
| | | |
| [25] "AND NOW / why should we die? / | 11 | 2 |
| for it will consume us / this / great fire // | 22 | 3 |
| If we \[a] continue / to hear / | 14 | 2 |
| the voice of YHWH our God / any more / | 15 | 2 |
| then we shall die // | <u>5</u> | 1_ |
| [26] For who (is there) of all flesh / | 9 | 1 |
| who has heard the [a]voice of the living God[a] / | 13 | 1 |
| Speaking (rbdm) from the midst of the fire / as we (have) / | 17 | 1 |
| and has still lived? // | <u>4</u> | 2_ |
| | | |
| [27] *"You go near / and hear /* | 10 | 2 |
| *all / that he will say /* | 8 | 2 |
| *YHWH our God[a] //* | <u>10</u> | 1_ |
| *And you yourself[b] / shall speak (תדבר) unto us /* | 12 | 2 |
| *all that he will speak (ידבר) / YHWH our God / [c]unto you /* | 23 | 3 |

| | | |
|---|--:|--:|
| *And we will hear and we will do (it)* " / / | 13 | 1 |
| [28] *And YHWH heard / the sound of* your words (דבריכם) / | 13 ⌐ | 2 |
| when you spoke (בדברכם) / unto me[c] / / | 8 ⌐ | 2_ |
| | | |
| And YHWH said / unto me / | 10 | 2 |
| "I have heard[d] / | 5 ⌐ | 1 |
| the sound of the words (דברי) \[c] of [this][e] people / | 9 ⌐ | 1 |
| [f]Which they spoke (דברו) unto you / | 10 | 1 |
| they rightly (said) / all that they have spoken[f] (דברו) / / | 14 | 2_ |
| [29] Would that[a] / this were their heart \[b] to them / to fear me / | 26 | 3 |
| and to keep all[c] my commandments / | 10 | 1 |
| All the days / / that it might go well for them / | 15 ⌐ | 2 |
| and for their children / forever / / | 10 | 2_ |
| [30] Go! / Say to them / / 'Return yourselves / to your tents!' / / | 21 | 4 |
| [31] *and (as for) you /* | 4 | 1 |
| *Here / stand with me / and let me speak (ואדברה) unto you /* | 21 | 3_ |
| *All[a] the commandment(s) /* | 7 ⌐ | 1 |
| *[and][b] the statutes and the judgment(s) /* | 11 | 1 |
| *Which you shall teach them / /* | 7 ⌐ | 1 |
| *and they shall do (them) in the land /* | 10 | 1 |
| *Which I / am giving to them / to possess it" /* | 19 | 3_ |
| | | |
| [32] And you shall be careful to do / | 8 ⌐ | 1 |
| just as YHWH your God / commanded / you / / | 17 ⌐ | 3 |
| You shall not turn aside / | 8 ⌐ | 1_ |
| To the right or to the left / / | 8 | 1 |
| [33] In all the way / YHWH [a]your God / commanded / [you /][b] | 19 ⌐ | 3 |
| you shall walk[a] / / | 6 ⌐ | 1_ |
| In order that you may live / and (it might be) well with you / | 12 | 2 |
| and you shall prolong (your) days / in the land / | 14 | 2 |
| which you shall possess / / | 8 | 1_ |
| | | |
| [6:1] And this is the commandment / | 7 ⌐ | 1 |
| <and>[a] the statutes / and the judgments / | 12 ⌐ | 2 |
| which he has commanded / YHWH your God / | 14 ⌐ | 2_ |
| (For me) to teach you / / to do (them) in the land / | 15 | 2 |
| Which you / are crossing over thither / to possess it / / | 16 | 3_ |
| [2] [a]In order that[a] *you may fear / YHWH your God /* | 16 | 2 |
| *By keeping / all his statutes* \[b] *and his commandments /* | 17 | 3_ |
| | | |
| *Which I am commanding you[c] /* | 11 ⌐ | 1 |
| *you / [d]and your children and your children's children[d] /* | 12 | 2 |
| *All / the days of your life / /* | 8 ⌐ | 2 |
| *and in order that / your days may be prolonged / /* | 14 | 2_ |
| [3] *And you shall hear, O Israel /* | 11 ⌐ | 1 |
| *and you shall be careful to do (them) /* | 9 ⌐ | 1 |
| *That[a]* \[b] *it may go well for you /* | 6 ⌐ | 1 |
| *and that you may increase[c] / greatly[d] / /* | 9 ⌐ | 2_ |

*Just as YHWH spoke* (דבר) / *God of your fathers* / *to you*[e] /          ⌈ 20    3
*(It will be) a land* / *flowing with milk* / *and honey* // פ                 ⌊ **14**   3_

### Notes

23.a. One Heb. Ms and LXX read האש for החשך. Two Heb. Mss add האש, which is possible in terms of mora-count. On the other hand, the addition could be an explanatory gloss.

24.a. DSS reads ואתם תאמרו. Prosodic analysis supports MT.

24.b-b. Omitting with LXX[L]. Prosodic analysis would permit the reading of MT, but with a somewhat different interpretation of the expression היום הזה, "this day." The use of 1 c pl forms suggests an interpretation along the lines of 5:2, where the past experience at Horeb is made present for the hearers of this text.

24.c. DSS reads יהוה.

25.a. Reading the conj *mûnaḥ* for disj *mûnaḥ* plus *pāseq* to achieve prosodic balance over against 6:1.

26.a-a. DSS adds את and changes word order. Prosodic analysis supports MT.

27.a. DSS, LXX[A], Syr, and Vg add אליכה.

27.b. A few Heb. Mss and SP read ואתה(ה) for ואת of MT. Prosodic analysis supports MT.

27–28.c-c. Missing in DSS. Prosodic analysis supports MT.

28.d. DSS reads שמעת.

28.e. הזה is omitted with Syr, resulting in the replacement of disj *gereš* on דברי with a conj accent.

28.f-f. DSS omits. Prosodic analysis supports MT.

29.a. DSS reads יתן. Prosodic analysis supports MT.

29.b. Replacing disj *gereš* with a conj accent.

29.c. One Heb. Ms omits את־כל; one Heb. Ms omits את; SP, LXX[L] omit כל. Prosodic analysis tends to support MT.

31.a. Omitted in LXX[L] and Tg[J], which is possible in terms of mora-count.

31.b. The *waw*-conj is omitted in some Heb. Mss and SP (cf. Deut 7:1 and 11:1), which is possible in terms of mora-count.

33.a-a. DSS reads תלכונו.

33.b. With one too many disj accents in v 33a, over against parallel rhythmic structures in 5:25–28a and 5:32–6:2a, the אתכם is deleted (cf. 6:1).

6:1.a. Adding the *waw*-conj with some Heb. Mss, LXX, and Syr, which read והחקים; DSS reads והקים.

2.a-a. Missing in DSS. Prosodic analysis supports MT.

2.b. Reading disj *tipḥā*ʾ here for conj *mûnaḥ*. Prosodic analysis suggests that the ʾ*atnāḥ* should appear under ומצותיו, which would necessitate the correction.

2.c. One Heb. Ms, SP, and LXX add היום. Prosodic analysis supports MT.

2.d-d. Both LXX and Vg read 2nd pl nouns here. Prosodic analysis tends to support MT.

3.a. DSS reads כאשר.

3.b. See note 1:1.c.

3.c. SP, Syr, and Vg read 2nd sg, which would mark the approaching rhythmic boundary.

3.d. DSS reads מאודה.

3.e. LXX adds δοῦναι; Syr adds *dntl lk* = לך נתן, perhaps from 27:3. Prosodic analysis supports MT.

### Form/Structure/Setting

As the concluding subsection of Deut 4:44–6:3 and the "Ten Commandments," 5:23–6:3 is in seven parts arranged in a concentric pattern, from a rhythmic perspective, which may be outlined as follows:

| | | | |
|---|---|---|---|
| A | The theophany on the mountain (5:23–24) | | [(5+6):7] |
| | B | People's complaint to Moses (5:25–26) | [5:5:5] |
| | | C   People's request to Moses: "Be our mediator" (5:27–28a) | [5:5:5] |
| | | D'  Yahweh's response: "Be their mediator" (5:28b–31) | [7:8:8:7] |
| | | C'  Moses's request: "Do as Yahweh has commanded" (5:32–33) | [5:5:5] |
| | B' | "This is the commandment Yahweh has commanded" (6:1–2a) | [5:5:5] |
| A' | Summary: the commandments are for all time (6:2b–3) | | [7:(5+6)] |

In the opening subunit (5:23–24), Moses reminisces about the great theophany at Sinai, when God spoke "from the midst of the darkness and the mountain was burning with fire" (v 23). He recalls the words of the people at that time, when they saw the glory of God and realized "that God may speak with a person and he may still live" (v 24). The content of this unit is closely related to its structural counterpart in 6:2b–3, which focuses on the content of Yahweh's message on that mountain: "you shall hear, O Israel, and you shall be careful to do" God's commandments. What happened in the past at that specific point in time applies for all time: to "your children and your children's children, all the days of your life" (6:2).

Repetition of specific words and phrases set off vv 23–24 as a distinct rhetorical unit: כְּשָׁמְעֲכֶם אֶת־הַקּוֹל מִתּוֹךְ הַחֹשֶׁךְ (v 23) at the beginning is echoed by the words וְאֶת־קֹלוֹ שָׁמַעְנוּ מִתּוֹךְ הָאֵשׁ (v 24). The temporal marker "this day" is used, together with "and now" in v 25 to mark the boundary between the first two subunits.

The "B" elements in the larger structure are also structurally connected, with the complaint of the people about the great danger experienced at the moment of revelation in the past (5:26–27) set over against the grand summary of the content of that revelation: namely, "the commandment, the statutes and the judgments" that God instructed Moses to teach the people (6:1–2a). The boundary between the "B'" and "A'" units is clearly marked by the *Numeruswechsel* and the use of הַמִּצְוָה and וּמִצְוֹתָיו as a rhetorical envelope in 6:1–2a.

The "C" elements contain two requests: on the part of the people to Moses that he stand between them and God as a mediator of his revelation (5:27); and the request of Moses to the people that they should "be careful to do just as YHWH your God commanded" (v 32) "in order that you may live . . . and prolong your days in the land" (v 33; cf. 6:2b–3). Once again the *Numeruswechsel* marks both boundaries of "C" (5:27–28) and the beginning of "C'" (v 32).

The center of the larger rhetorical structure in this section (5:28b–31) contains the words of God, whose desire is that the people would indeed "fear me and keep all my commandments . . . that it might go well for them" (v 29). God then expressly designates Moses as their mediator, to receive "all the commandments, the statutes and judgments" which he is to teach them (v 31). The *Numeruswechsel* here appears to mark the center of the larger rhetorical structure as a rhythmic turning point, rather than a boundary.

## Comment

**23–26** In apprehension evoked by the theophany on the mountain, the people delegate the *heads* (רָאשִׁים; cf. 1:15) of their tribes and the *elders* (זְקֵנִים; cf. 25:7–9) to approach Moses with their request. Their anxiety stems from the simple fact that they have heard God's voice and seen visible signs of his presence, and yet have lived to tell of their experience (v 24). The mediatory role of Moses in the covenant at Sinai (Horeb) parallels that of third parties involved in the making of treaties in the ancient Near East (see Buis and Leclercq, *Le Deutéronome* [1963] 73).

It is possible to render the term תִּקְרְבוּן as "they came near," assuming a 3rd masc pl impf with preformative /t/, as occasionally in Ugaritic (see Craigie,

NICOT [1976] 165), though it should be noted that this is clearly a context of 2nd masc pl forms.

The term כבד, "glory," appears only here in Deuteronomy in describing God, in sharp contrast to its usage elsewhere in the Pentateuch—particularly in the familiar phrase כבוד־יהוה, "glory of Yahweh."

On the use of the word אשׁ, "fire," in the language of theophany in Deuteronomy see the *Comment* on 4:12.

**27–28** Lohfink has shown the palistrophic structuring of verb forms in 5:27–6:3, as follows (*Das Hauptgebot* [1963] 67–68):

| | | |
|---|---|---|
| 5:27 | A | ושמע . . . ושמענו ועשׂינו |
| 5:29 | B | ליראה . . . ולשמר |
| 5:31 | C | תלמדם ועשׂו |
| 5:32f | X | ושמרתם לעשׂות . . . תסרו תלכו |
| 6:1 | C' | ללמד . . . לעשׂות |
| 6:2 | B' | תירא . . . לשמר |
| 6:3 | A' | ושמעת . . . ושמרת לעשׂות |

Though Mayes has insisted that "the presence of this literary form does not in itself guarantee the existence of an original literary unit" (NCBC [1979] 173), his argument seems rather weak in light of both the above prosodic analysis and the larger rhetorical structure of 5:23–6:3 as a whole.

**29** *Would that this were their heart . . . to fear Me* (v 29)—the people's attitude is proper but, unfortunately, not typical. As was the case in an earlier situation, "Yahweh heard the sound of [their] words and he was angry" (Deut 1:34). If the people could make this true reverence a life pattern, then indeed *it might go well for them and for their children forever* (v 29).

**30** The command to *return . . . to your tents* has interesting connotations. Some years ago, Harold Forshey called my attention to the fact that the phrase "To your tents!" in 1 Kgs 12:16, as voiced spontaneously by the people of Judah in response to the demands of Rehoboam, is not a call to arms but rather a dismissal or disavowal of legal obligations (see *Prophecy and War in Ancient Israel* [1989] 44–45; cf. Judg 7:8; 20:8; 1 Sam 13:2; 2 Sam 20:1; and the discussion of A. Alt, "Zelte und Hütten," in *KlSchr* II [1959] 233–42; A. Malamat, "Organs of Statecraft in the Israelite Monarchy," *BA* 27 [1965] 34–65). In that context the people refused to recognize the political authority of Rehoboam, who then assembled the armies of Judah and Benjamin to wage war against Israel, only to be thwarted by the prophet Shemaiah. According to the tradition, Shemaiah delivered an oracle from Yahweh in the form of a summons *not* to fight (1 Kgs 12:24): "Do not go up! Do not wage war against your kinsmen, the children of Israel. Return every man to his home, for this thing is from me." Rehoboam and his hosts returned home and civil war was averted. It would appear that the legal rights of the people, so far as receiving God's revelation is concerned, are abrogated. From this point on Moses alone is the mediator of that revelation.

**31** Yahweh's command to Moses to *stand with me* found an interesting interpretation in early Christianity. Dositheus, as leader of an early Gnostic sect, is referred to as the "standing one," who thus claimed to have knowledge of the true commandments of God (see R. M. Grant, *Gnosticism and Early Christianity* [1966] 92). In sharp contrast, Moses' mediatory role involves no arrogant claims for himself, as Craigie has noted (NICOT [1976] 166). Moses assumed the role of sole mediator in response to the people's request and with the permission of God, who terminated the people's legal rights to that role.

**32–33** The attention now shifts from recollection of past events to present and future obligations. The people are charged to *be careful to do just as Yahweh your God commanded you . . . in order that you may live and . . . prolong your days in the land.* The temptation would be for them to assume that the law was, after all, only the words of Moses, but such is not the case. Moses' role as mediator means that he has communicated the revelation of God himself. The authority of that revelation resides in its source, God—not in the mediator. The focus of the text is once again on the land beyond the Jordan, which Moses will not enter, but the people are soon to possess (see the *Comment* on Deut 4:25–40).

**6:1–3** These three verses function as a bridge, to conclude the larger section on the "ten words" (4:44–6:3) and to introduce the next major section (6:4– 7:11), which contains what some have called the "first and great commandment"—to love God.

המצוה—the singular usage, *this is the commandment,* apparently refers to the principle underlying all the law (cf. 5:31). Thus, *the statutes and the judgments* stand in apposition, describing the general laws based on the first principle.

ללמד אתכם לעשות, *to teach you to do* (them)—as Craigie has noted (NICOT [1976] 167), these words may well refer back to 5:22–23, where Moses' mediatorial role is described, to form an envelope of sorts around the larger subunit 5:23–6:3. They also call attention to the primary function of the book of Deuteronomy in the life of ancient Israel: namely, religious education. For generations the "book" was in the hands of the Levites who sang it in order to teach the people what God required of them. The paradigmatic teacher was Moses, whose primary objective was to instill the *fear [of] Yahweh your God* (v 2). For a discussion of the meaning of the "fear of God" in Deuteronomy as "covenantal loyalty" and its relation to the so-called wisdom literature in ancient Israel, see M. Weinfeld (*Deuteronomy and the Deuteronomic School* [1972] 274–81). See also the discussion below in what is perhaps the classic text on the subject: Deut 10:12– 13—to fear God is "to love him and to serve [him] with all your heart."

On first glance, the phrase *a land flowing with milk and honey* (v 3) seems to be a bit out of place. RSV resolves the matter by adding the preposition "in" a land. On the basis of a prosodic analysis, it seems preferable to take the clause as a nominal sentence (cf. F. I. Andersen, *The Hebrew Verbless Clause in the Pentateuch* [Nashville: Abingdon, 1970]).

## Explanation

In Deut 5:23–6:3 the verbal root דבר is used eleven times to emphasize the fact that both the Ten Commandments, which are now concluded, and the Great Commandment, which follows immediately (Deut 6:5), are indeed the word of God. Though one cannot look on the face of God and live, one can hear God's voice speaking "from the midst of the fire . . . and he may still live" (5:24). It is easy for us to have too small a view of God in mind. The actual experience of God often shatters the inadequacy of our views to impress us with the awesomeness of "the living God" (5:26). That living God has now entrusted to us his commandments in order that we may keep them, and that we may teach them to our children. In so doing we will prosper.

# "Hear O Israel, Yahweh Is Our God, Yahweh Alone" (6:4–7:11)

### Bibliography for Deut 6:4–7:11

**Crump, W.** "Deuteronomy 7: A Covenant Sermon." *RevQ* 17 (1974) 222–35. **Cullen, J.** "Das Deuteronomium: Eine Erwiderung." *ZWT* 48 (1905) 181–93. **Floss, J. P.** *Jahwe dienen—Göttern dienen. Terminologische, literarische und semantische Untersuchung einer theologischen Aussage zum Gottesverhältnis im Alten Testament.* BBB 45. Köln, 1975. 320–23. **Garcia Lopez, F.** *Un Dios, un pueblo, una tierra, una ley. Análisis de crítica literaria, de la forma y del género, de la composición y redacción de Dt 6, 4–9, 7; 10, 12–11, 25.* Diss., Pontifical Biblical Institute (Rome), 1977. ————. "Analysis littéraire de Dt V–XI." *RB* 84 (1977) 481–522; 85 (1978) 5–49. ————. "Deut. VI et la tradition-rédaction du Deutéronome." *RB* 85 (1978) 161–200; 86 (1979) 59–91. ————. "'Un peuple consacré': Analyse critique de Deutéronome VII." *VT* 32 (1982) 438–63. ————. "Election-Vocation d'Israel et de Jérémie: Deutéronome VII et Jérémie I." *VT* 35 (1985) 1–12. **Gerhardsson, B.** *The Testing of God's Son (Matt 4:1–11 & Par): An Analysis of an Early Christian Midrash.* ConB NT 2. Lund: Gleerup, 1966. **Halbe, J.** *Das Privilegrecht Jahwes Ex 34, 10–26.* FRLANT 114. Göttingen: Vandenhoeck & Ruprecht, 1975. 256–69. **Langlamet, F.** "Israël et 'l'habitant du pays'." *RB* 76 (1969) 321–50, 481–507. **Lohfink, N.** *Das Hauptgebot* (1963). 153–87. **Merendino, R. P.** "Die Zeugnisse, die Satzungen und die Rechte. Überlieferungsgeschichtliche Erwägungen zu Deut 6." In *FS G. J. Botterweck* (1977). 161–208. ————. "Zu Dt. v–vi. Eine Klärung. *VT* 31 (1981) 80–83. **Otto, E.** *Das Mazzotfest in Gilgal.* BWANT 107. Stuttgart: W. Kohlhammer, 1975. 25, 203–38. **Perlitt, L.** *Bundestheologie im Alten Testament.* WMANT 36. Neukirchen, 1970. 55–77. **Schmitt, G.** *Du sollst keinen Frieden schliessen mit den Bewohnern des Landes. Die Wegweisung gegen die Kanaanäer in Israels Geschichte und Geschichtsschreibung.* BWANT 91. Stuttgart, 1970. **Seitz, G.** *Studien zum Deuteronomium* (1971). 70–79. **Welch, A. C.** "The Purpose of Deuteronomy . . ." *ExpTim* 41 (1929/30) 548–51; 42 (1930/31) 409–12. **Wilms, F. E.** "Das Jahwistische Bundesbuch in Ex 34." *BZ* 16 (1972) 24–53.

From a structural perspective chaps. 6–9 stand at the center of the Inner Frame in Deut 4–11. The repetition of key phrases is used to frame the four major parts of this section, which display a chiastic architectural design around which the detail unfolds as follows:

A  שמע ישראל—Hear, O Israel, YHWH is our God, YHWH alone (6:4–7:11)
  B  עקב תשמעון—When you obey YHWH, you will be blessed (7:12–26)
  B'  עקב לא תשמעון—When you forget YHWH, you will perish (8:1–20)
A'  שמע ישראל—Hear, O Israel, you are about to cross the Jordan (9:1–29)

The familiar phrase שמע ישראל, "Hear O Israel," introduces each of the outer sections of this structure, which contains some of the most familiar words in the book of Deuteronomy to most readers. The words of 6:4 are in fact the most familiar words of the entire Bible to the observant Jew, since they are repeated daily.

The phrase עקב תשמעון appears only twice in the Hebrew Bible—as a frame in 7:12 and 8:20 around the central section of Deut 4–11. It is interesting to note the use of the verb שמע here, which now comes after the preposition עקב. What is perhaps more interesting is the obvious pun on the word יעקב, "Jacob" (= Israel). In short, the theological message of the book of Deuteronomy as a whole is carried on a pun here at the center of the first half of the Inner Frame (chaps. 4–11). As long as Jacob/Israel "hears" *the words* (הדברים) of Yahweh (cf. Deut 1:1), they will experience God's blessing in the land, but the moment Jacob/Israel refuses to "hear" *these words,* they will "surely perish like the nations which Yahweh makes to perish before you" (8:20).

At the very center of this structure in 8:1 stands the grand summary of God's requirement of his people: "All the commandment which I command you today you shall be careful to do, that you may live, and you may multiply and come in; and you may possess the land which Yahweh swore to your fathers." These words are highlighted in the received MT by the use of the *Numeruswechsel* and the fact that they stand outside the prosodic structure of what precedes and follows. Moreover, as will be shown in detail below, from the perspective of prosodic structure the words of 8:1 are balanced by another summary statement in 8:18, namely: "And you shall remember Yahweh your God, that it is he who gives to you power to get wealth in order to establish his covenant, which he swore to your fathers, as at this day."

Though the internal structure of each of the four major sections of Deut 6:4–9:29 is not developed in the same manner, the first section (6:4–7:11) has an eleborate concentric design as follows:

A    The Great Commandment: Love God (6:4–9)
  B    Remember to fear Yahweh for he is a jealous God (6:10–15)
    C    Be careful to keep the commandments (6:16–19)
      D    Tell your children of the Exodus from Egypt (6:20–22)
    C'    God will preserve us if we keep his commandments (6:23–25)
  B'    "Destroy your enemies" for you are a holy people (7:1–10)
A'    Summary: Keep the commandment (7:11)

In terms of rhythmic structure these seven subsections may be reduced to five in that 6:16–25 is a single concentric structure, as argued below.

### Bibliography for Deut 6:4–9

**Aejmaleus, A.** "Participum Coniunctum as a Criterion of Translation Technique." *VT* 32 (1982) 385–93. **André, G.** "'Walk', 'Stand', and 'Sit' in Psalm I 1–2." *VT* 32 (1982) 327. **Avishur, Y.** "Expressions of the Type *byn ydym* in the Bible and Semitic Languages." *UF* 12 (1980) 125–33. **Badé, W. F.** "Der Monojahwismus des Deuteronomium." *ZAW* 13 (1910) 81–90. **Balscheit, B.** *Alter und Aufkommen des Monotheismus in der israelitischen Religion.* BZAW 69. Berlin: Töpelmann, 1938. **Bamberger, B. J.** "Fear and Love of God in the Old Testament." *HUCA* 6 (1929) 39–53. **Barr, J.** "The Problem of Israelite Monotheism." In TGUOS 17 (1959). 52–62. **Becker, J.** "Feindesliebe—Nachstenliebe—Bruderliebe." *ZEE* 25 (1981) 5–17. **Bee, R. E.** "A Study of Deuteronomy Based on Statistical Properties of the Text." *VT* 29 (1979) 1–22. **Ben-Shammai, H.** "Qirqisānî on the Oneness of God." *JQR* 73 (1982) 105–11. **Beutler, J.** "Das hauptgebot im Johannesevangelium." In *Das Gesetz im Neuen Testament.* Ed. K. Karl. QD 108. Freiburg, 1986. 222–36. **Boer, P. A. H. de.** "Some Observations on VI 4 and 5." In *FS J. P. M. van der Ploeg* (1982). 45–52. **Bornkamm, G.** "Das Doppelgebot der Liebe." In *Geschichte und Glaube.* BEvT 48. Munich: Kaiser, 1969. 37–45. **Braulik, G.** "Das Deuteronomium und die Geburt des Monotheismus." In *Gott, der Einzige* (1985). 115–59

[=SBAB 2 (1988) 257–300]. **Brelich, A.** "Der Polytheismus." *Numen* 7 (1960) 123–36. **Caloz, M.** "Exode XIII, 3–16 et son rapport au Deutéronome." *RB* 75 (1968) 5–62 (51–53). **Causse, A.** "L'ideal politique et social du Deutéronome. La fraternité d'Israel." *RHPR* 13 (1933) 289–323 (290). **Coppens, J.** "La doctrine biblique sur l'amour de Dieu et du prochain." *ETL* 40 (1964) 252–99 (260–70). **Couroyer, B.** "La Tablette du Coeur." *RB* 90 (1983) 416–34. **Couturier, G.** "Sagesse Babylonienne et Sagesse Israelite." *ScEccl* 14 (1962) 293–309 (308). **Crenshaw, J. L.** "Education in Ancient Israel." *JBL* 104 (1985) 601–15. **Cross, F. M.** and **Saley, R. J.** "Phoenician Incantations on a Plaque of the Seventh Century B.C. from Arslan Tash in Upper Syria." *BASOR* 197 (1970) 42–49. **Dahood, M.** *Ugaritic-Hebrew Philology: Marginal Notes to Recent Publications.* BO 17. Rome, 1965. 74. ———. "Hebrew-Ugaritic Lexicography VIII." *Bib* 51 (1970) 391–404 (391). **Delzant, A.** *La Communication de Dieu. Par delà utile et inutile. Essai théologique sur l'ordre symbolique.* Paris: Cerf, 1978. **Demsky, A.** "Education in the Biblical Period." *EncJud* (Jerusalem, 1971) VI, 382–98. **Dietrich, E. L.** "Die Liebe des Einzelnen zu Gott in der jüdischen Frömmigkeit von der Zeit der Gaonen bis zum Auftreten der Kabbala." *Oriens* 17 (1964) 132–60 (135–38). **Dion, P.-E.** "Quelques aspects de l'interaction entre religion et politique dans le Deutéronome." *ScEs* 30 (1978) 39–55 (47). **Donner, H.** "Hier sind deine Götter, Israel!" In *FS K. Elliger* (1973). 45–50. **Donovan, V. J.** "The Mark on the Door." *Wor* 31 (1957) 345–48. **Drazin, N.** *History of Jewish Education from 515 B.C.E. to 220 C.E.* Baltimore: Rams Horn Books, 1940. **Driver, G. R.** "Problems of the Hebrew Text and Languages." In *Fs Nötscher.* BBB 1. Bonn, 1950. 46–61. **Dürr, L.** *Das Erziehungswesen im Alten Testament und im Antiken Orient.* MVÄG 36, 2. Leipzig: J. C. Hinrichs, 1932. **Duschak, M.** *Schulgesetzgebung und -methodik der alten Israeliten.* Vienna: Braumüller, 1872. **Emerton, J. A.** "New Light on Israelite Religion: The Implications of the Inscriptions of Kuntillet ʿAjrud." *ZAW* 94 (1982) 2–20 (12–13). **Evans, G.** "'Coming' and 'Going' at the City Gate: A Discussion of Prof. Speiser's Paper." *BASOR* 150 (1958) 28–35. **Falk, Z. W.** "Forms of Testimony." *VT* 11 (1961) 88–91. **Fensham, F. C.** "The Ugaritic Root *ṭpt*." *JNSL* 12 (1984) 63–69. **Fischer, G.** and **Lohfink, N.** "'Diese Worte sollst du summen': Dtn 6, 7 *wĕdibbarta bam*—ein verlorener Schlüssel zur meditativen Kultur in Israel." *ThPh* 62 (1987) 59–72. **Fishbane, M.** "Torah and Tradition." In *Tradition and Theology in the Old Testament.* Ed. D. A. Knight. Philadelphia: Fortress, 1977. 275–300 (284). **Fisher, L.** *RSP.* I, 158, 361. **Freedman, D. N.** "Yahweh of Samaria and His Asherah." *BA* 49 (1986) 241–49. **Friedman, R. E.** "From Egypt to Egypt: Dtr¹ and Dtr²." In *FS F. M. Cross* (1981). 167–92 (171). **Gerhardsson, B.** *The Testing of God's Son (Matt 4:1–11 & Par): An Analysis of an Early Christian Midrash.* ConB NT 2. Lund: Gleerup, 1966. ———. "The Hermeneutic Program in Matthew 22:37–40." In *FS W. D. Davies* (1976). 129–50. **Golka, F. W.** "Die israelitsiche Weisheitsschule oder 'Des Kaisers neue Kleider.'" *VT* 33 (1983) 257–70. **Gordon, C. H.** "His Name is 'One.'" *JNES* 29 (1970) 198–99. **Görg, M.** "*T(w)ṭpt*—eine fast vergessene Deutung." *BN* 8 (1979) 11–13. ———. "Ein weiteres Beispiel hebraisierter Nominalbildung." *Hen* 3 (1981) 336–39. **Haag, E.** (ed.). *Gott der Einzige. Zur Entstehung des Monotheismus in Israel.* QD 104. Freiburg: Herder, 1985. **Hadley, J. M.** "The Khirbet el-Qom Inscription." *VT* 37 (1987) 50–62. **Hamp, V.** "Monotheismus im Alten Testament." In *Sacra Pagina.* BETL 12–13. Gembloux, 1959. 516–21. **Haran, M.** "On the Diffusion of Literacy and Schools in Ancient Israel." In *VTSup* 40. Leiden: Brill, 1988. 81–95. **Hartmann, B.** "Es gibt keinen Gott ausser Jahwe." *ZDMG* 110 (1961) 229–35. **Henrix, H. H.** (ed.). *Jüdische Liturgie. Geschichte—Struktur—Wesen.* QD 86. Freiburg i. B.: Herder, 1979. **Hermisson, H. J.** *Studien zur israelitischen Spruchweisheit.* WMANT 28. Neukirchen-Vluyn.: Neukirchener Verlag, 1968. 96–136. **Herzog, A., Aharoni, M.** and **Rainey, A.** "Arad: An Ancient Fortress with a Temple to Yahweh." *BARev* 13 (1987) 16–35. **Höffken, P.** "Eine Bemerkung zum religionsgeschichtlichen Hintergrund von Dtn 6, 4." *BZ* n.s. 28 (1984) 88–93. **Holzman, M.** "Zu Deuteronomium 6, 4." *MGWJ* 73 (1929) 263–67. **Horowitz, H. L.** "The Shmaʿ." *Judaism* 24 (1975) 476–81. **Hunter, A.** "How Many Gods Had Ruth?" *SJT* 34 (1981) 427–36. **Jacobs, I.** "Eleazar Ben Yahir's Sanction for Martyrdom." *JSJ* 13 (1982) 184–86. **Janzen, J. G.** "On the Most Important Word in the Shema (Deuteronomy VI 4–5)." *VT* 37 (1987) 280–

300. ————. "An Echo of the Shema in Isaiah 51:1–3." *JSOT* 43 (1989) 69–82. **Kasher, M. M.** *Sefer Shema Yiśrael.* American Bible Encyclopedia Society. New York: Monsey, 1980 (Heb.). **Keel, O.** *Monotheismus im Alten Israel und Seiner Umwelt.* BBB 14. Freiburg/Schweiz, 1980 (168–72—Kuntilat-Ajrud). ————. "Zeichen der Verbundenheit. Zur Vorgeschichte und Bedeutung der Forderungen von Deuteronomium 6, 8f. und Par." In *FS D. Barthélemy* (1981). 159–240. **Kiehl, R. H.** "19th Sunday after Pentecost." *CJ* 10 (1984) 183–84. **Klostermann, A.** "Schulwesen im Alten Israel." In *Theologische Studien Theodor Zahn.* Leipzig, 1908. 193–232. **Knight, G. A. F.** "The Lord is One." *ExpTim* 79 (1967/68) 8–10. **Köckert, M.** "Das nahe Wort: Zum entscheidenden Wandel des Gesetzesverständnis im Alten Testament." *ThPh* 60 (1985) 496–519. **Kooy, V. H.** "The Fear and Love of God in Deuteronomy." In *FS L. J. Kuyper* (1975). 106–16. **Krauss, S.** *Talmudische Archäologie III.* Leipzig, 1912 (reprinted in Hildesheim, 1966). 199–239 (schools in ancient Israel). **Lang, B.** "Schule und Unterricht im Alten Israel." In *La Sagesse de l'Ancien Testament.* Ed. M. Gilbert. BETL 51. Gembloux and Louvain: 1979. 186–201. ————. "Vor einer Wende im Verständnis des israelitischen Gottesglaubens?" *ThQ* 160 (1980) 53–60. ————. "Jahwe allein!" *Conc* 21 (1985) 30–35. **Lee, J. W.** "The Shema." *BibIll* 14 (1988) 70–72. **Lemaire, A.** "Les inscriptions de Khirbet el-Qôm et l'Ashérah de Yhwh." *RB* 84 (1977) 595–608. ————. *Les écoles et la formation de la Bible dans l'Ancien Israel.* OBO 39. Göttingen: Vandenhoeck & Ruprecht, 1981 (26–30—Kuntilat-Ajrud). ————. "Sagesse et École." *VT* 34 (1984) 270–81). **Levin, C.** *Die Verheissung des neuen Bundes.* FRLANT 137. Göttingen: Vandenhoeck & Ruprecht, 1985. **Lévy, S.** "Le Chema Israel, une prière juive citée dans les Evangiles (Mt 22, 35)." *Rencontre Chrétiens et Juifs* 10 (1976) 296–302. **Loewenstamm, S. E.** "The Address 'Listen' in the Ugaritic Epic and the Bible." In *FS C. H. Gordon* (1980). 123–31. **Lohfink, N.** *Das Hauptgebot* (1963). ————. "Glauben lernennin Israel." *KatBl* 108 (1983) 83–99. ——. *Option for the Poor.* Berkeley: BIBAL Press, 1987. 9. **Lohfink, N.** and **Bergman, J.** "אֶחָד." *TDOT* 1. Grand Rapids: Eerdmans, 1974. 193–201. **Luciani, F.** "Le aggiunte finali nella versione Greca di Deut 6, 6; 16, 8." *RivB* 33 (1985) 81–98. **Maier, M. P.** *Göttliche Pädagogik—Israels Geschichte mit JHWH in deuteronomistischer Sicht. Literaturwissenschaftliche und theologische Untersuchung zu Dtn 11, 1–9.* Munich: Ludwig-Mazimilians-Universität, 1989. **Martin-Achard, R.** "Note sur une confession de foi inspirée du 'shemaᶜ' d'Israel." *ETR* 60 (1985) 255–58. **Mayer, R.** "Monotheistische Strömungen in der altorientalischen Umwelt Israels." *MThZ* 8 (1957) 97–113. **McBride, S. D.** "The Yoke of the Kingdom: An Exposition of Deut. 6:4–5." *Int* 27 (1973) 273–306. **McCarter, P. K.** "Aspects of the Religion of the Israelite Monarchy." In *FS F. M. Cross* (1987). 137–55. **McCarthy, D. J.** "Notes on the Love of God in Deuteronomy and the Father-Son Relationship between Yahweh and Israel." *CBQ* 27 (1965) 144–47. **McKay, J. W.** "Man's Love for God in Deuteronomy and the Father/Teacher—Son/Pupil Relationship." *VT* 22 (1972) 426–35. **Meek, T. J.** "Monotheism and the Religion of Israel." *JBL* 61 (1942) 21–43. **Meshel, Z.** "Kuntilat-ᶜAjrud: An Israelite Site on the Sinai Border." *Qadmoniot* 9 (1976) 119–24. ————. "Did Yahweh have a Consort? The New Religious Inscriptions from the Sinai." *BARev* 5 (1979) 24–35. **Meshel, Z.** and **Meyers, C.** "The Name of God in the Wilderness of Zin." *BA* 39 (1976) 6–10. **Mettinger, T. N. D.** *Solomonic State Officials.* ConB OT 5. Lund: Gleerup, 1971. 140–57. **Millard, A. R.** "An Assessment of the Evidence for Writing in Ancient Israel." In *Biblical Archaeology Today: Proceedings of the International Congress on Biblical Archaeology in Jerusalem, April 1984.* Jerusalem: Israel Exploration Society, 1985. 301–12. **Miller, P. D.** "Apotropaic Imagery in Proverbs 6:20–22." *JNES* 29 (1970) 129–130. ————. "God and the Gods." *Affirmation* 1/5 (Richmond, VA, 1973) 37–62 (57). ————. "The Most Important Word: The Yoke of the Kingdom." *The Iliff Review* 41 (1984) 17–29. ————. "The Human Sabbath: A Study in Deuteronomic Theology." *PSB* 6 (1985) 81–97 (82). **Mittmann, S.** "Die Grabinschrift des Sängers Uriahu." *ZDPV* 97 (1981) 139–52. **Miyoshi, M.** "Das jüdische Gebet Šemaᶜ und die Abfolge der Traditionsstücke in Luke 10–13." In *AJBI* 7 (1981). 70–123. **Moberly, R. W. L.** "Yahweh Is One: The Translation of the Shema." In VTSup 41. Leiden: Brill, 1990. 209–15. **Moor, J. D. de.** "The Crisis of Polytheism in Late Bronze Ugarit." In *Crises and Perspectives.* OTS 24.

Leiden: Brill, 1986. 1–20. **Moran, W. L.** "The Ancient Near Eastern Background of the Love of God in Deuteronomy." *CBQ* 25 (1963) 77–87. **Naveh, J.** "Graffiti and Dedications." *BASOR* 235 (1979) 27–30. **Naville, E.** "Egyptian Writings in the Foundations-Walls and the Age of the Book of Deuteronomy." *PSBA* 29 (1907) 232–42. **Neumann, P. K.** *Hört das Wort Jahwäs. Ein Beitrag zur Komposition alttestamentlicher Schriften.* Schriften zur Stiftung Europa-Colleg 30. Hamburg: Fundament Verlag Sasse, 1975. 59–61. **Nielsen, E.** "'Weil Jahwe unser Gott ein Jahwe ist' (Dtn 6, 4f.)." In *FS W. Zimmerli* (1977). 288–301 [=*Law, History and Tradition* (1983) 106–18]. **O'Connor, M.** "The Poetic Inscription from Khirbet el-Qom." *VT* 37 (1987) 224–30. **Olivier, J. P. J.** "Schools and Wisdom Literature." *JNSL* 4 (1975) 49–60. **Perlitt, L.** *Bundestheologie* (1970). 78–82. **Perles, F.** "Was bedeutet אחד יהוה Dt 6, 4?" *OLZ* 11 (1908) 537–38. **Pesch, R.** "Jesus und das hauptgebot." In *FS R. Schnackenburg* (1989). 99–109. **Peter, M.** "Dtn 6, 4—ein monotheistischer Text?" *BZ* n.s. 24 (1980) 252–62. **Porton, G. G.** *Understanding Rabbinic Midrash: Texts and Commentary.* New Jersey: Ktav, 1985. **Puech, E.** "Les écoles dans l'Israel préexlique: Données épigraphiques." VTSup 40. Leiden: Brill, 1988. 189–203. **Reit, S. C.** "Ibn Ezra on Psalm i 1–2." *VT* 34 (1984) 232–36. **Reuter, H.-R.** "Erinnerungszeichen: Predigt über 5. Mose 6, 4–9 am 24.6.84 in der Versöhnungskirche Heidelberg-Ziegelhausen." In *FS L. Steiger.* Ed. G. and E. Stegemann. BDBAT 5. Heidelberg, 1985. 569–78. **Riesner, R.** *Jesus als Lehrer: Eine Untersuchung zum Ursprung der Evangelien-Überlieferung.* WUNT 2, 7. Tübingen, 1981. **Riessler, P.** "Schulunterricht im Alten Testament." *ThQ* 91 (1909) 606–07. **Rössler, E.** *Jahwe und die Götter im Pentateuch und im Deuteronomistischen Geschichtswerk.* Diss., Bonn, 1966. **Rose, M.** *Der Ausschliesslichkeitsanspruch Jahwes* (1975). ——. "Yahweh in Israel—Qaus in Edom?" *JSOT* 2 (1977) 28–34. ——. *Jahwe: Zum Streit um den alttestamentlichen Gottesnamen.* Zürich: Evangelischer Verlag, 1978. **Rowley, H. H.** "Mose und der Monotheismus." *ZAW* 69 (1957) 1–21. **Saebø, M.** "'Kein anderer Name': Sieben Thesen zur christologischen Ausschliesslichkeitsforderung aus dem Horizont des alttestamentlichen Gottesglaubens." *KD* 22 (1976) 181–90. **Schedl, C.** "Die Mezûza-Texte in den Höhlen von Qumrân." In *FS G. Molin* (1983). 291–305. **Schmidt, W. H.** *Das Erste Gebot. Seine Bedeutung für das Alte Testament.* TEH 165. Munich, 1969. **Schmökel, H.** *Jahwe und die Fremdgötter.* Breslau, 1934. **Schneider, H.** "Der Dekalog in den Phylakterien von Qumran." *BZ* 3 (1959) 18–30. **Schultz, S. J.** *The Gospel of Moses.* Chicago: Moody Press, 1978. **Seitz, G.** *Studien zum Deuteronomium* (1971). 70–79. **Simon, U.** *L'Education et l'Instruction des Enfants chez les Anciens Juifs.* Nîmes, 1879. **Snaith, N. H.** "The Advent of Monotheism in Israel." In ALUOS 5 (1963/65). 100–13. **Speiser, E. A.** "'Coming' and 'Going' at the City Gate." *BASOR* 144 (1956) 20–23. ——. "TWTPT." *JQR* 48 (1957/58) 208–17. **Stern, J. B.** "Jesus' Citation of Deut 6:5 and Lev 19:18 in the Light of Jewish Tradition." *CBQ* 28 (1966) 312–16. **Suzuki, Y.** "Deut. 6:4–5: Perspectives as a Statement of Nationalism and of Identity of Confession." In AJBI 9 (1983). 45–52. **Swift, F. H.** *Education in Ancient Israel from Earliest Times to 70 A.D.* Chicago-London: Open Court Pub. Co., 1919. **Thompson, J. A.** "Israel's Lovers." *VT* 27 (1977) 475–81. **Tigay, J. E.** "On the Meaning of T(W)TPT." *JBL* 101 (1982) 321–31. **Tov, E.** "The Nature and Background of Harmonizations in Biblical Manuscripts." *JSOT* 31 (1985) 3–29. **Tsevat, M.** "Alalakhiana." *HUCA* 29 (1958) 109–36. **Ussishkin, D.** "The Date of the Judaean Shrine at Arad." *IEJ* 38 (1988) 142–57. **Vermes, G.** "Pre-Mishnaic Jewish Worship and the Phylacteries from the Dead Sea." *VT* 9 (1959) 65–72. **Voeltzel, R.** *L'Enfant et son Éducation dans la Bible.* Le Point Théologique 6. Paris: Beauchesne, 1973. 11–55. **Walle, R.** "'Love Yahweh Your God with All Your Heart': the Deuteronomist's Understanding of Love." *Jeevadhara* 13 (1983) 122–29. **Walsh, M. F.** "Shema Yisrael: Reflections on Dt 6, 4–9." *TBT* 90 (1977) 1220–25. **Warner, S.** "The Alphabet: An Innovation and Its Diffusion." *VT* 30 (1980) 81–90. **Weinfeld, M.** "Instructions for Temple Visitors in the Bible and in Ancient Egypt." In *Egyptological Studies.* Ed. S. Israelit-Groll. Jerusalem: Magnes Press, 1982. 224–50. ——. "Kuntillet ʿAjrud Inscriptions and Their Significance." *Studi Epigrafici e Linguistici* 1 (1984) 121–30. **Wiéner, C.** *Recherches sur l'Amour pour Dieu dans l'Ancient Testament: Étude d'une Racine.* Paris, 1957. **Willoughby, B. E.** "A Heartfelt Love: An Exegesis of Deuteronomy 6, 4–19." *ResQ* 20 (1977) 73–87. **Wilson, G. H.**

"'The Words of the Wise': The Intent and Significance of Qohelet 12:9–14." *JBL* 103 (1984) 175–92. **Winter, G.** "Die Liebe zu Gott im Alten Testament." ZAW 9 (1889) 211–46. **Wiseman, D. J.** "A New Text of the Babylonian Poem of the Righteous Sufferer." *AnSt* 30 (1980) 101–17. **Zevit, Z.** "The Khirbet el-Qôm Inscription Mentioning a Goddess." *BASOR* 255 (1984) 39–47. **Zimmerli, W.** "Das Gottesrecht bei den Propheten Amos, Hosea und Jesaja." In *FS C. Westermann* (1980). 216–35 (228).

## Translation and Prosodic Analysis

6:4–9   [(4+5):5] [5:(4+5)]

| | | | |
|---|---|---|---|
| 4 | **HEAR** [a] / **O Israel** // | 7 | 2 |
| | **YHWH (is) our God / YHWH alone** [a] // | 16 | 2_ |
| 5 | *And you shall love / (him) / (that is) YHWH your God //* | 16 | 3 |
| | *With all your heart and with all your soul-life /* | 14 | 1 |
| | *and with all your might //* | 9 | 1_ |
| 6 | *And they shall be / these words* (דברים) / | 16 | 2 |
| | *which I command you / TODAY /* | 15 | 2 |
| | *upon your heart /* | 6 | 1_ |
| 7 | *And you shall teach them diligently to your children /* | 10 | 1 |
| | *and you shall speak* (ודברת) */ of them //* | 7 | 2 |
| | *When you sit in* [a]*your house* [a] / *and* [b] *when you go by the way /* | 18 | 2_ |
| | *And* [c] *when you lie down / and when you get up //* | 13 | 2 |
| 8 | *And you shall bind them as a sign / upon your hand(s)* [a] // | 14 | 2_ |
| | *And they shall be as frontlets / between your eyes //* | 18 | 2 |
| 9 | *And you* [a] *shall write them / on the doorposts of your house* [b]/ | 16 | 2 |
| | *and on* [c] *your gates //* ס | 7 | 1_ |

## Notes

4.a. LXX adds a sentence before the *shema*[c]. In MT the final letters of the first and last words of v 4 are enlarged, perhaps to call attention to the importance of this passage or to warn that the reading must be precise.

7.a-a. SP and LXX read בבית (LXX[L] reads pl); cf. 11:19 below.

7.b. SP omits *waw*-conj; cf. 11:19 below.

7.c. The *waw*-conj is omitted in a few Heb. Mss, SP, and Vg; cf. 11:19 below. Prosodic analysis supports MT.

8.a. LXX reads pl ידיך.

9.a. LXX reads 2nd masc pl וּכְתַבְתָּם for MT וּכְתַבְתָּֽם.

9.b. SP, LXX, and Syr read pl בביתיך.

9.c. One Heb. Ms (V[Ken 69]) omits the prep.

## Form/Structure/Setting

The boundaries of this rhetorical unit are clearly marked off, with the opening שְׁמַע יִשְׂרָאֵל and the switch to the 1st c pl suffix in אֱלֹהֵינוּ marking the beginning (v 4), and the *s*[e]*tûmā*[ʾ] paragraph marker indicating the end at v 9. The rhythmic subunits follow the received verse divisions until we reach the occurrence of הַיּוֹם, "today," in v 6. The phrase that follows serves to separate v 6 from what follows, from a rhythmic perspective, and divides the whole into two similar subunits.

Known in Jewish tradition as the *Shemaʿ*, Deut 6:4–9 contains what Driver has called "the fundamental truth of Israel's religion" and "the fundamental duty founded upon it" (ICC [1895] 89). The fundamental truth has to do with the "oneness" of God (v 4), which will ultimately be spelled out in the doctrine of monotheism. The fundamental duty is the response of love which God requires of us (v 5). As Craigie has noted (NICOT [1976] 168), both of these themes are taken up in the NT teaching of Jesus (Mark 12:29–30; cf. Matt 22:37; Luke 10:27). In vv 6–9 the relationship of these two themes to the community is spelled out. "These words" (i.e., the book of Deuteronomy) are to be known by every adult member of the community, and they are to be taught diligently to their children. Nothing is more important to the future of God's people than the communication of "these words."

### Comment

**4** The phrase *Hear, O Israel* was used in 5:1 to open the chapter containing the Decalogue. Earlier in 4:1 the phrase was used, along with ועתה, *and now*. Together the three terms ועתה ישראל שמע make up important structural signals in the first part of the Inner Frame of Deut 4–11. On the use of these words in Deut, see N. Lohfink, *Das Hauptgebot* (1963) 65–68, and his book *Höre, Israel! Auslegung von Texten aus dem Buch Deuteronomium* (1965) 54–71. In 4:1 the phrase opens "The Great Peroration" (Deut 4–11), and specifically the key section 4:1–40; in 5:1 שמע ישראל opens the chapter containing the Decalogue; in 6:4 שמע ישראל opens the major section of 6:4–7:11; and in 9:1 the same phrase opens the parallel structure of 9:1–12 within the larger concentric structural design of Deut 4–11. In 10:12 the phrase ועתה ישראל is used to open the final major section of the first part of the Inner Frame in Deut 10:12–11:25. The term ועתה alone is used in 26:10, after the historical prologue (26:1–9) in the presentation of the *first fruits* at the Feast of Tabernacles, and once again in 31:19 to introduce the great "Song of Moses" (32:1–43), which was to be taught to the children of Israel.

The six words of v 4 have been translated in numerous ways, each of which may have a measure of truth in the poetic form of the present text. C. H. Gordon has suggested, "Yahweh is our God, Yahweh is 'One'" (*JNES* 29 [1970] 198). The late M. Dahood translated the whole verse as follows: "Obey, Israel, Yahweh. Yahweh our God is the Unique" (*RSP* I [1972] 361). S. D. McBride rendered it: "Our God is Yahweh, Yahweh alone!" (*Int* 27 [1973] 274).

**5** In some respects it can be argued that the whole book of Deuteronomy is simply a commentary on this one verse: *You shall love Yahweh your God with all your heart, and with all your soul-life, and with all your might.* The command to love is central because it concerns renewal of the covenant with God which demands obedience. That obedience is possible only when it is a response of love to the God who brought the people out of Egypt and was now about to bring them in to their promised land. In short, it is the historical events that make up the Exodus-Conquest that provide the motivation for a covenant relationship between God and his people.

ואהבת את יהוה אלהיך, *you shall love Yahweh your God*—as W. Moran has noted, the command to love belongs to the treaty language of the ancient Near East (*CBQ*

25 [1963] 144–47). It is also characteristic of the father/son metaphor used elsewhere in the book of Deuteronomy. It should be noted, however, that the language of loving God is not drawn directly from treaty terminology as such (see J. W. McKay, "Man's Love for God in Deuteronomy," *VT* 22 (1972) 426–35). The command to love God was based on the precedent of God's prior love, as shown in the specific events of the Exodus and Conquest, and, a larger context, in God's very choice of this people from the time of Abraham.

בכל לבבך ובכל נפשך ובכל מאדך, *with all your heart and with all your soul-life, and with all your might.* The people are called to love God with their whole being (cf. also 4:9, 29; 10:12). Though the Heb. word לבב means "heart," it is not the physical organ as such in this context but rather what we would call the mind. The pairing of לבב, "heart," and נפש, "soul-life," suggests that a distinction of some sort is being made between mental and emotional energy and activity. In terms of modern depth psychology, we would say that our love for God is to embrace the whole of our mind, both conscious and unconscious. Self-discipline is required, in that we are to love God with all our might (מאד) as well. (On the translation of these key words in the LXX and NT, see Keil and Delitzsch, *The Pentateuch* [Grand Rapids: Eerdmans, 1956] III, 322–25). The all-encompassing love for God will find its expression in joyful obedience to the commandments of God, which is the focus of that which follows.

**6** The phrase הדברים האלה (v 6), "these words," recalls the opening words of Deuteronomy (1:1). The commandments are to be *upon your heart*; that is, the people are to meditate upon them to the point that the law is internalized, exactly as Jeremiah saw so clearly when he spoke of a *"new covenant"* in which Yahweh declares that "I will put my law within them, and I will write it upon their hearts" (Jer 31:31–33). Obedience is not to be a matter of formal legalism, but rather a response out of deep understanding. By reflecting on God's words (6:1), and by knowing the path of life set forth through the commandments, the people would discover for themselves the way in which God's love for them was shown.

**7–9** Having understood these commandments in depth, they were then responsible to *teach them diligently to [their] children* (v 7; cf. 4:9). The commandments were to be the focus of constant discussion inside and outside the home. In short, they were to permeate every sphere of human life. The injunctions of vv 8–9 led in turn to specific practices which, at times, caused people to lose sight of the remarkable vision of an "internalized covenant" suggested in vv 5–7: namely, phylacteries (טטפת) and mezuzoth (מזוזות). Whether or not the words here were intended in a metaphorical sense, they came to be taken literally in subsequent Jewish history. The frontlet, or phylactery, came into use as a small container for a parchment containing certain biblical verses. Though the actual texts vary slightly, the standard texts used were Exod 13:1–10, 11–16; Deut 6:4–9; 11:13–21; and sometimes the Decalogue. A number of such frontlets have been found among the discoveries in the region of the Dead Sea since 1947 (see DJD II [1961] 83–84; DJD III [1962] 149–57). The mezuzah also came into use as a small box containing parchment, one of which was discovered at Qumran containing the text of Deut 10:12–11:21 (see DJD III [1962] 158–61). Any traveler to modern Israel is familiar with the various forms of mezuzoth on the doorposts of each hotel room. A beautiful silver one greets me each time I enter my study. Whether understood literally or metaphorically, vv 8–9 show that the individual person, his home, and his community (שעריך, "your gates") were to be distinguished as the focus of obedience to the commandments as a response of love for God.

### Explanation

The words of the *Shema* in Deut 6:4 have both practical and theological implications. The people of ancient Israel had already discovered the practical significance when they sang: "Who is like you, O Yahweh, among the gods?" (Exod 15:11), for they knew the response. There were no other gods like Yahweh! In the experience of the Exodus from Egypt, the children of Israel discovered the uniqueness of their God, for the "gods" of Egypt could do nothing to stop Yahweh's people in their departure. The experience of the living presence of their God in history was what created them as a people.

It was a relatively short step from the practical knowledge to theological conclusions. The word אחד in the text of the *Shema* speaks not only of the *uniqueness*, but also the *unity* of God. The doctrine of monotheism is implicit in this brief creedal statement.

There is a striking contrast to the presentation of God in Deuteronomy over against that of Mesopotamian religious thought, where multiplicity of gods in turn led to great tension in human life. Though a person might carry out his religious duties with care, he or she could not be guaranteed any security, for if there was strife among the gods, that would radically affect human life. Note in particular the example of the flood account in the Gilgamesh Epic, where the flood seems to be a result of Enlil's whim. It was only through the goodness of Enki that Utnapishtim was warned and escaped from the deluge. Though a given god might promise much to the individual person, a more powerful god might still bring disaster. The resulting tension often led to pessimism in religious thought. Yahweh was not only first among the gods, as perhaps Baal in Canaan, or Amon-Re in Egypt, or Marduk in Babylon. Yahweh was the one and only God who imposed on his people the charge to love him as he had already loved them.

The focus on teaching your children "these words" diligently within the context of the family—at all conceivable times and places—illustrates once again the pedagogical purpose of the book of Deuteronomy. The content of this book was the primary curriculum in an ongoing program of religious education in ancient Israel. The use of phylacteries and mezuzoth were essentially pedagogical tools, designed to keep the great summary statements of the "Words of Yahweh" central in the experience of each individual member of the covenant community.

### Bibliography for Deut 6:10–15

**Baltzer, K.** *The Covenant Formulary* (1971). 20–21. **Benjamin, D. C.** *Deuteronomy and City Life* (1983). **Berg, W.** "Die Eifersucht Gottes—ein problematischer Zug des alttestamentlichen Gottesbildes?" *BZ* n.s. 23 (1979) 197–211. **Braulik, G.** "Das Deuteronomium und die Geburt des Monotheismus." In *Gott, der Einzige* (1985). 115–59 [=SBAB 2 (1988) 257–300]. **Brongers, H. A.** "Der Eifer des Herrn Zebaoth." *VT* 13 (1963) 269–84. **Brunner, A.** "Der eifersüchtige Gott." *StZ* 148 (1950–51) 401–10. **Caloz, M.** "Exode XIII, 3–16 et son rapport au Deutéronome." *RB* 75 (1968) 5–62 (43–51). **Earwood, G. C.** *El-Kanna: A Theology of In-*

*tolerance*. Diss., Southern Baptist Theological Seminary, 1980. **Giesen, G.** *Die Wurzel* שבע (1981). 178–80, 274–75. **Gottfriedsen, C.** *Die Fruchtbarkeit von Israels Land.* Europäische Hochschulschriften 23. Frankfurt: Peter Lang, 1985. **Hammer, R.** "Section 38 of Sifre Deuteronomy: An Example of the Use of Independent Sources to Create a Literary Unit." *HUCA* 50 (1979) 165–78. **Hempel, J.** "Zur Septuaginta-Vorlage im Dt. Eine Entgegnung auf [J. Ziegler] *ZAW* 1960, 237ff." *ZAW* 73 (1961) 87–96 (94). **Kuechler, F.** "Der Gedanke des Eifers Jahwes im Alten Testament." *ZAW* 28 (1908) 42–52. **Miller, P. D.** "Psalm 127: The House that YAHWEH Builds." *JSOT* 22 (1982) 119–32 (121–22). **Renaud, B.** *Je Suis un Dieu Jaloux. Étude d'un Théme Biblique.* Paris: du Cerf, 1963. **Tigay, J. H.** *You Shall Have No Other Gods: Israelite Religion in the Light of Hebrew Inscriptions.* HSS 31. Atlanta: Scholars Press, 1986 (176–77).

### Translation and Prosodic Analysis

6:10–15   [(8:7:8:8):(7:8)]

| | | |
|---|---|---|
| [10] *And it shall be /* | 5 | 1 |
| *when YHWH your God / brings you / into the land /* | 21 | 3 |
| *Which he promised to your fathers /* | 10 | 1 |
| *to Abraham / to Isaac* \|[a] *and to Jacob /* | 16 | 3_ |
| *To give to you // cities / great and goodly /* | 19 | 3 |
| *which you did not build //* | 9 | 1 |
| [11] *[And][a] houses / full of good things / which you did not fill /* | 20 | 3_ |
| *And[b] cisterns hewn out / which you did not hew /* | 20 | 2 |
| *Vineyards and olive trees / which you did not plant //* | 20 | 2 |
| *And you shall eat* \[c] *and you shall be sated //* | 12 | 1 |
| [12] *Take heed[a] / lest you forget / YHWH[b] //* | 13 | 3_ |
| *Who brought you out / from the land of Egypt /* | 15 | 2 |
| *from the house of bondage //* | 8 | 1 |
| [13] *(it is) YHWH your God /* | 9 | 1 |
| *You shall fear (him) / and him you shall serve[a] //* | 13 | 2 |
| *and by his name / you shall swear //* | 11 | 2_ |
| | | |
| [14] You[a] shall not go / after / other gods // | 21 | 3 |
| Of the gods / of the peoples / who are / round about you // | 22 | 4_ |
| [15] For (he is) a jealous God / YHWH *your God* \[a] *in your midst //* | 19 | 2 |
| *Lest it be kindled[b] / the anger of YHWH your God / against you /* | 16 | 3 |
| *And he destroy you / from off / the face of the ground //* ס | 19 | 3_ |

### Notes

10.a. Adding disj *ṭipḥāʾ* because of the misplaced *ʾatnāḥ* in MT.

11.a. Omitting *waw*-conj with one Heb. Ms, SP, LXX°, and Vg.

11.b. SP, LXX, and Vg omit *waw*-conj. Prosodic analysis supports MT.

11.c. See note 1:1.c.

12.a. Tg[J] reads 2nd masc pl.

12.b. A number of Heb. Mss, SP, LXX, and Syr add אלהיך. Prosodic analysis supports MT.

13.a. A few Heb. Ms and LXX add ובו תדבק. Prosodic analysis favors MT.

14.a. Cairo geniza fragments and LXX witnesses add *waw*-conj, which is possible in terms of mora-count.

15.a. See note 1:1.c.
15.b. SP reads יחר instead of יחרה of MT.

## Form/Structure/Setting

Within the MT the limits of this rhetorical unit are set off by the *sᵉtûmâ* paragraph markers at beginning and end. The *Numeruswechsel* in vv 14 and 15 serves to divide the unit into two parts, which, once again, are arranged in a concentric rhythmic pattern:

vv 10–13    When you enter the land, remember to fear Yahweh. [8:7:8:8]
vv 14–15    Remain faithful to Yahweh, for he is a jealous God. [7:8]

The poetic quality of these lines is discussed by Craigie, who scans vv 10b–11 and comments on the Hebrew equivalent to rhyme here, in that each of the five successive lines end in *-tā* (NICOT [1976] 173).

## Comment

**10–11** These verses anticipate the entry into the promised land, with explicit reference to fulfillment of the promise made to the *fathers* Abraham, Isaac, and Jacob. In five successive poetic lines the bounty of the land is described in detail. The people will receive cities, houses, cisterns, vineyards, and olive trees, which they will take from the former inhabitants of the land.

**12** The temptation would be for the people to *forget Yahweh,* once they had settled in the land. The poetic form of the brief reflection on the goodness of the land in vv 10–11 evokes a feeling of pleasure and satisfaction, which is interrupted sharply by the imperative השמר לך, "take heed." The comforts of the good land may lull the people into forgetfulness. They are to remember that it is *Yahweh who brought you out from the land of Egypt, from the house of bondage.*

**13** On what it means to *fear Yahweh* see 10:12–13 below (cf. 4:10; 5:29; 6:2). The term תעבד, "you shall serve," stands in sharp contrast to the "house of bondage" (עבדים) in Egypt, since both words come from the same Heb. root. The nature of the "service" depends on the nature of the master one is called to serve. If the master is Pharaoh in Egypt, the service is tantamount to slavery. But if it is Yahweh, the God of love, that same service becomes worship. The nation of ancient Israel was established by the power of God who liberated his people from oppression. Because of that fact, the people were commanded to continue to serve their Lord. On the significance of this verse to Jesus in the NT, see Matt 4:10; Luke 4:8.

*And by his name you shall swear*—the context suggests that the oath here is to Yahweh as Lord of the covenant. The people are to commit themselves solemnly to obedience and love of their God, which is the essence of true worship. On the relationship of this command to Matt 5:34, see R. V. G. Tasker, *The Gospel according to Matthew* (Tyndale NT Commentaries [1961] 66–67). On subsequent debates within the Christian communities on issues raised here, see E. G. Kraeling (*The Old Testament Since the Reformation* [New York: Harper, 1955] 27), who discusses the differences between Calvin and the Anabaptists.

**14–15** On *other gods* see the *Comment* on the first commandment (5:7). The temptation to follow other gods became a central issue whenever the people forgot Yahweh (v 12), their liberator. As an act of unfaithfulness, such action would certainly arouse God's anger, since it is tantamount to returning to Egypt (cf. 17:16). On Yahweh as *a jealous God* see also 4:24. To follow another god or suzerain is to violate the first commandment (5:6–7), and thereby to reject the grace of God celebrated in the Exodus-Conquest (see *Excursus*: "Holy War as Celebrated Event in Ancient Israel").

## Explanation

One of the great tragedies of events in modern Israel, since the war of independence in 1948, is the tendancy on the part of some to see Deut 6:10–11 as legitimation for the taking of the property of Palestinians who were displaced in that conflict. The language used here is poetry, as Craigie and others have noted. To take it literally as a way to justify selfish actions is to miss the point of the passage. The focus is on the grace of God who has shown his love for his people by delivering them from oppression. They, in turn, are to show love to God by acting in the same manner: to make sure that justice, love, and mercy become a way of life (cf. Deut 10:12–13; Mic 6:8). To "walk in [God's] ways" (10:12) is to show mercy to those who are oppressed, particularly when, for whatever reasons, we become the oppressor.

It is all too easy "to forget YHWH" who delivered us "from the house of bondage," and to serve "other gods": the gods of money, power, and prestige. When we take the bounty of his gifts for granted and enjoy them at the expense of others, we are on dangerous ground, for God is "a jealous God" (v 15). He will not tolerate our serving another master, however legitimate our actions may be in our own eyes.

## Bibliography for Deut 6:16–25

**Anbar, M.** "Genesis 15: A Conflation of Two Deuteronomic Narratives." *JBL* 101 (1982) 39–55 (44). **Bee, R. E.** "A Study of Deuteronomy Based on Statistical Properties of the Text." *VT* 29 (1979) 1–22 (5, 18–20). **Bissoli, C.** "'Quando tuo figlio ti domanderà . . . , tu gli risponderai': a proposito dell'educazione dei figli nella Bibbia." *ParVi* 28 (1983) 363–72. **Braulik, G.** "Gesetz als Evangelium. Rechtfertigung und Begnadigung nach der deuteronomischen Tora." *ZTK* 79 (1982) 127–60 (137–40, 144–46) [=SBAB 2 (1988) 123–60]. **Cazelles, H.** "De l'idologie royale." In *FS T. H. Gaster* (1973). 59–73 (65). **Childs, B. S.** "A Study of the Formula 'Until this Day.'" *JBL* 82 (1963) 279–92. ————. "The Etiological Tale Re-Examined." *VT* 24 (1974) 387–97. **Conrad, J.** *Die Junge Generation in Alten Testament. Möglichkeiten und Grundzüge einer Beurteilung.* AVTRW 47. Stuttgart: Calwer Verlag, 1970. **Diakonoff, I. M.** "Agrarian Conditions in Middle Assyria." In *Ancient Mesopotamia: Socio-Economic History.* Moscow: Nauka, 1969. 204–34. **Fabry, H.-J.** "Gott im Gespräch zwischen den Generationen: Überlegungen zur 'Kinderfrage' im Alten Testament." *KatBl* 107 (1982) 754–60. ————. "Spuren des Pentateuchredaktors in Jos 4, 21ff: Anmerkungen zur Deuteronomiums-Rezeption." In *Das Deut* (1985). 351–56. **Falk, Z. W.** "The Deeds of Manumission of Elephantine." *JJS* 3 (1954) 114–17. **Fishbane, M.** "Teaching and Transmission." In *Text and Texture: Close Readings of Selected Biblical Texts.* New York: Schocken Books, 1979. 79–83. **Gerhardsson, B.** *The Testing of God's Son (Matt 4:1–11 & Par): An Analysis of an Early Christian Midrash.* ConB NT 2. Lund: Gleerup, 1966. 28–31. **Giesen, G.** *Die Wurzel* שבע (1981). 278–79. **Greenberg, M.** "Some Postulates of Biblical Criminal Law." In *FS Y. Kaufmann* (1960). 21–25 (11). **Helck, W.** "Die soziale Schichtung des Ägyptischen Volkes im 3. und 2. Jahrtausend v. Chr." *JESHO* 2 (1959) 1–36. **Hermisson, H.-J.** "Gottes Freiheit—

Spielraum des Menschen." *ZTK* 82 (1985) 129–52. **Hossfeld, F.-L.** "Die alttestamentliche Familie vor Gott." In *Freude am Gottesdienst: Aspekte ursprünglicher Liturgie.* Ed. J. Schreiner. Stuttgart: Katholische Bibelwerk, 1983. 217–28. **Humbert, P.** "Dieu fait sortir." *ThZ* 18 (1962) 357–61, 433–36. **Jepsen, A.** *"Sedeq* und *ṣĕdāqāh* im Alten Testament." In *FS Hertzberg* (1965). 78–89. **Krašovec, J.** *La Justice (Sdq) de Dieu dans la Bible Hébraïque et l'Interprétation Juive et Chrétienne.* OBO 76. Freiburg/Göttingen: Vandenhoeck & Ruprecht, 1988. 182–84. **Lehming, S.** "Massa und Meriba." *ZAW* 73 (1961) 71–77. **Lemaire, A.** *Les écoles et la formation de la Bible dans l'Ancien Israel.* OBO 39. Göttingen: Vandenhoeck & Ruprecht, 1981. 57. **Lohfink, N.** *Höre Israel* (1965). 68–69. ————. *Das Hauptgebot* (1963). 113–24. ————. *Option for the Poor.* Berkeley: BIBAL Press, 1987. 44–45. **Loza, J.** "Les catéchès étiologiques dans l'Ancien Testament." *RB* 78 (1971) 481–500. **Moran, W. L.** "Review of E. R. Dalglish, *Psalm Fifty-One in the Light of Ancient Near Eastern Patternism.*" *Bib* 45 (1964) 111–13. **Nielsen, E.** *Oral Traditon.* SBT 11. London, 1954. 58–60. **Otto, E.** *Das Mazzotfest in Gilgal.* BWANT 107. Stuttgart: Kohlhammer, 1975. 131–32. ————. "Erwägungen zum überlieferungsgeschichtlichen Ursprung und 'Sitz im Leben' des jahwistischen Plagenzyklus." *VT* 26 (1976) 3–27 (22–23). **Pax, E.** "'Als Gerechte werden wir dastehen, wenn wir dieses Gesetz treulich erfüllen' (Dt 6, 25)." *Conc* 3 (1967) 807–12. **Perlitt, L.** "Der Vater im Alten Testament." In *Das Vaterbild in Mythos und Geschichte.* Ed. H. Tellenbach. Stuttgart: Kohlhammer, 1976. 50–101 (69–71). **Rad, G. von.** "'Gerechtigkeit' und 'Leben' in der Kultsprache der Psalmen." In *FS A. Bertholet* (1950). 418–37 [=GesStAT ³1965, 225–47]. **Rüterswörden, U.** *Die Beamten der isrealitischen Königszeit.* BWANT 117. Stuttgart: Kohlhammer, 1985. 10. **Soggin, J. A.** "Cultic-Aetiological Legends and Catechesis in the Hexateuch." In *Old Testament and Oriental Studies.* Rome: Biblical Institute Press, 1975. 72–77 [ET from Ger., *VT* 10 (1960) 341–47]. **Swetnam, J.** "Some Observations on the Background of *ṣādiq* in Jeremias 23, 5a." *Bib* 46 (1965) 29–40. **Weinfeld, M.** *Deuteronomy and Deuteronomic School* (1972). 34–35. **Zeitlin, S.** "Some Reflections on the Text of the Pentateuch." *JQR* 51 (1960/61) 321–31 (324).

### Translation and Prosodic Analysis

6:16–25   [5:5] [5:8] [(6:5:5:6):8:5:(5:5)]

| | | | |
|---|---|---|---|
| 16 | You shall not put him to the test / YHWH / your God // | ⌈ 16 | 3 |
| | as you tested (him) / at Massah // | ⌊ 11 | 2_ |
| 17 | You shall be exceedingly careful to keep (them) / | 8 | 1 |
| | The commandments / of YHWH your God // | ⌈ 13 | 2 |
| | [and][a] his testimonies and his statutes / | | 10 ⌉ 1 |
| | which *he commanded you* // | ⌊ 5 ⌋ 1_ |

| | | | |
|---|---|---|---|
| 18 | *And you shall do / what is right and good /* | 15 | 2 |
| | *In the eyes of YHWH* [a] *// that / it might go well with you /* | 16 | 3_ |
| | *And you shall go in / and you shall possess / the good land /* | 23 | 3 |
| | *Which YHWH promised / to your fathers //* | 13 | 2 |
| 19 | *By thrusting out all your enemies* \\[a] *from before you //* | ⌈ 16 | 1 |
| | *just as / YHWH said //* ס | ⌊ 8 | 2_ |

| | | | |
|---|---|---|---|
| 20 | *<And it will be>*[a] */ when your son asks you / in time to come /* | ⌈ 17 | 3 |
| | *Saying / "What are these testimonies / and*[b] *these statutes /* | ⌊ 16 | 3_ |
| | *And these ordinances / which he commanded /* | ⌈ 12 ⌉ 2 |
| | *YHWH our*[c] *God / (to you)*[d]*?" //* | ⌊ 12 ⌋ 2 |
| 21 | *And you shall say to your son /* | 8 | 1_ |

| | | |
|---|---|---|
| *"Servants / we were to Pharaoh* [a] *in Egypt //* | ⌈ 20 | 2 |
| *And YHWH brought us out / from Egypt / with a strong hand //* | ⌊ 24 | 3_ |
| [22] *And YHWH gave (us) /* | 7 | 1 |
| *signs and wonders / great and grievous /* [a] *in Egypt /* | ⌈ 25 | 3 |
| *Against Pharaoh and all his house / before our eyes //* | ⌊ 19 | 2_ |
| [23] *And us / he brought out from there //* | 14 | 2 |
| *That / he might bring us in /* | 13 | 2_ |
| *To give us / the land /* | 13 | 2 |
| *Which he swore* [a] */ to our fathers //* | 12 | 2_ |
| [24] *And YHWH commanded us / to do /* | 14 | 2 |
| *all these statutes /* | 9 | 1 |
| *To fear / YHWH our God //* | 15 | 2_ |
| *For our good / ALWAYS* [a] */ that he might preserve us alive /* | ⌈ 21 | 3 |
| *As at THIS DAY //* | ⌈ 6⌉ | 1 |
| [25] *indeed,* [a] *it will be \\* [b] *righteousness for us //* | ⌊ 12⌋ | 1 |
| *If we are careful to do / all this commandment /* | ⌈ 18 | 2 |
| *Before / YHWH our God / as he has commanded us" //* ס | ⌊ 21 | 3_ |

## Notes

17.a. Omitting *waw*-conj to achieve closer balance in terms of mora-count. Note that the *waw* does not appear in either of the other two occurrences of the term העדת in Deuteronomy, both of which appear together with the phrase והחקים והמשפטים (Deut 4:45 and 6:20).

18.a. SP, Syr, and LXX add אלהיך. Prosodic analysis supports MT.

19.a. See note 1:1.c.

20.a. Adding והיה with one Heb. Ms, SP, and LXX.

20.b. A few Heb. Mss and SP omit *waw*-conj.

20.c. A Cairo geniza fragment reads 2nd sg; LXX^min and Old Latin read 2nd masc pl. MT is retained as the more difficult reading to explain.

20.d. LXX^min and Vg read 1 c pl.

21.a. See note 1:1.c.

22.a. MT has *dargā'* with *pāseq* here, which would normally not be counted as a disj accent in the system followed in this analysis. The sequence of *'azlā'* followed by *dargā'*, however, is sometimes read as a disj.

23.a. One Heb. Ms and SP add יהוה; a number of LXX witnesses apparently added יהוה אלהינו. Prosodic analysis supports MT.

24.a. ALWAYS (for כל הימים) appears in capitals as part of the list of temporal markers throughout the Hebrew text of Deut; see note 1:9.a.

25.a. Reading the *waw*-conj as emphatic. Prosodic analysis suggests that the expression "as at this day" (כהיום הזה) belongs with this clause.

25.b. See note 1:1.c.

## Form/Structure/Setting

The boundaries of the three major prosodic subunits in Deut 6:16–25 are clearly marked within the MT: by the *Numeruswechsel* in vv 16 and 17 and by the *setûmā'* paragraph markers at the end of vv 19 and 25. The boundary between vv 20–22 and 23–25 is more subtle. The *Numeruswechsel* at the end of v 20 seems to mark the center, or rhythmic turning point, of the /6:5:5:6/ unit, which is closely connected with what follows, namely the continuation of what the people are to say in response to the question posed by their children in time to come. The disjunctive *waw* at the beginning of v 23 signals the beginning of another unit which, from a rhythmic perspective, is set over against vv 16–17 in the larger concentric structure.

| A | Be careful to keep the commandments (vv 16–17) | [5:5] |
| | B    Do what is right and good "in the eyes of Yahweh" (vv 18–19) | [5:8] |
| | B'    Tell your children of the Exodus from Egypt (vv 20–22) | [6:5:5:6] |
| A' | God will preserve us if we keep his commandments (vv 23–25) | [8:5:(5:5)] |

Repetition of the verb שׁמר, "keep" or "observe," together with terms מצות and מצוה, "commandment(s)," in vv 17 and 25 ties together the first and fourth of the above rhythmic subunits, forming an envelope around the larger unit as a whole. The two center subunits are framed by repetition of the term "eyes," with בעיני יהוה (v 18) set over against לעינינו (v 22).

Deut 20–25 are in the form of a child's question followed by the father's answer (vv 21–25), which may be the remnant of an ancient creed, perhaps related to that of 26:5–9. Craigie has outlined the content of vv 21–24 as follows (NICOT [1976] 175):

INTRODUCTION
    1. *The previous situation*: vassals of the Egptian pharaoh (v 21)
THE REVELATION OF GOD IN HISTORY
    2. *The experience of God*: the deliverance of the Exodus (v 21)
    3. *The judgment of God*: God's dealing with Egypt (v 22)
    4. *The purpose of God*: to grant his people the promised land (v 23)
THE REVELATION OF THE WORD OF GOD
    5. *The word of God*: the giving of the law (v 24)
    6. *The conditions given*: obedience and reverence (v 24)

The outline suggests that the verses are indeed "a condensation of the principal elements of the faith of the Israelites" (Craigie, 175), patterned along the lines of the familiar vassal treaties of the ancient Near East.

The posing of a religious question, which is in turn answered in quasi-creedal form, suggests a worship setting somewhat parallel to the beginning of the Passover seder meal, which also begins with a question on the lips of the youngest child present: "Why is this night different from all others?" The nature of the question asked here implies a family setting, the kind envisioned by proper observance of the fifth commandment (see *Comment* on 5:16). Even though the one who poses the question was not actually present at the initial making of the covenant, the child is asking about the commandments which "Yahweh our God" has commanded (v 20). It is the question of a youth within the context of a covenant community, who is learning to understand the full significance of the commandments so far as daily life is concerned.

## Comment

**16** As a place name, the term בְּמַסָּה means literally "in the (place of) testing." Three of the seven lexical items in this verse involve the Heb. root נסה, "to test." On the incident at Massah, see Exod 17:1–7 and Deut 9:22. On that occasion the people of Israel rebelled against Moses and Yahweh by not trusting God when they were thirsty in their journey through the wilderness. This incident out of their past became a paradigmatic warning for all time. In Matt 4:7 (cf. Luke 4:12) Jesus made use of this same verse in refuting Satan during his period of testing in the wilderness.

**17** שָׁמוֹר תִּשְׁמְרוּן, *be exceedingly careful to keep* (the commandments)—for a discussion of the uses of שָׁמַר and עשׂה in Deuteronomy, see N. Lohfink, *Das Hauptgebot* (1963) 68–70. Rather than testing Yahweh, the people are to diligently keep his commandments.

Two of the three occurrences of עֵדֹת, "testimonies," in Deuteronomy appear in this passage, in vv 17 and 20. The term is probably related to Akkadian *adē*, a term for a vassal treaty (see D. J. Wiseman, *The Vassal-Treaties of Esarhaddon* [London: British School of Archaeology in Iraq, 1958] 81). It is possible that עדת may have been the original term for the whole of the laws in the covenant tradition in ancient Israel (see N. Lohfink, "*ᶜd(w)t* in Deuteronomium und in den Königsbüchern," BZ [forthcoming]). For a discussion of all the terms for "law" in Deuteronomy, see G. Braulik, "Die Ausdrücke für 'Gesetz' im Buch Deuteronomium," *Bib* 51 (1970) 39–66 (=SBAB 2 [1988] 11–38).

**18–19** The terms הַיָּשָׁר and הַטּוֹב appear only twice in Deut, in similar contexts but in reverse order: v 18 הַיָּשָׁר וְהַטּוֹב and 12:28 הַטּוֹב וְהַיָּשָׁר. Both appear with the verbs עשׂה and the phrases לְמַעַן יִיטַב לָךְ and בְּעֵינֵי יהוה (also in reverse order). On the phrase הָאָרֶץ הַטֹּבָה, "the good land," see Deut 8:7–9.

**20–25** The content of vv 20–24 contains the essence of covenant theology in ancient Israel. The continuity of that covenant depends on the transmission of the relationship to each new generation; hence the catechizing style. The actions and words of Yahweh, on the one hand, reveal his concern and purpose for his people. The relationship imposes the responsibility on God's people to honor and obey Him, in order that they might continue to experience his presence in history and continue to hear his words. The result of such action on the part of the people is stated clearly in v 15, *it will be righteousness for us*. In this context צְדָקָה, "righteousness," means a right personal relationship with the covenant God (cf. Gen 15:6), which will lead to right conduct. The answer to the child's question thus ultimately focuses attention on the proper relationship of a person to God and the fruit of that relationship in daily life.

## Explanation

The continuity of faith within the context of a religious community depends on the observance of that faith within individual families. Though it is probable that parents carried a greater responsibility in general for the education of their children in ancient Israel than is the case today, the principle remains true. If parents cannot embody their faith and inculcate it responsibly to their children, the very existence of that faith community is in jeopardy.

## Bibliography for Deut 7:1–11

**Altmann, P.** *Erwählungstheologie und Universalismus im Alten Testament.* BZAW 92. Berlin: Töpelmann, 1964. **Anbar, M.** "Le châtiment du crime de sacrilège d'après la Bible et un text hèpatoscopique paléo-babylonien." *RA* 68 (1974) 172–73. ————. "Genesis 15 a

Conflation of Two Deuteronomic Narratives." *JBL* 101 (1982) 39–55 (53–54). **Angerstorfer, A.** "Aserah als 'consort of Jahwe' oder Asirtah?" *BN* 17 (1982) 7–16. **Bach, R.** "Die Erwählung Israels in der Wüste." *TLZ* 78 (1953) 687. **Bächli, O.** "Die Erwählung des Geringen im Alten Testament." *ThZ* 22 (1966) 385–95. **Beck, P.** "The Drawings from Horvat Teiman (Kuntillet ʿAjrud)." *Tel Aviv* 9 (1982) 3–68. **Begg, C.** "The Significance of the *Numeruswechsel* in Deuteronomy." *ETL* 55 (1979) 116–24 (123). **Braulik, G.** "Das Deuteronomium und die Geburt des Monotheismus." In *Gott, der Einzige* (1985). 115–59 [=SBAB 2 (1988) 257–300]. **Brueggemann, W.** "Old Testament as a Particular Conversation: Adjudication of Israel's Socio-Theological Alternatives." *TD* 32 (1985) 303–25 (315). **Canby, J.** "The Stelenreihen at Assur, Tell Halaf and *Maṣṣēbôt*." *Iraq* 38 (1976) 113–28. **Caspari, W.** "Beweggründe der Erwählung nach dem Alten Testament." *NKZ* 32 (1921) 202–15 (209–11). **Clements, R. E.** "Deuteronomy and the Jerusalem Cult Tradition." *VT* 15 (1965) 300–12 (305–7). **Cody, A.** "When is the chosen people called a *Gōy*?" *VT* 14 (1964) 1–6 (4). **Coppens, J.** "La doctrine biblique sur l'amour de Dieu et du prochain." *ETL* 40 (1964) 252–99 (256). **Craigie, P. C.** "Some Further Notes on the Song of Deborah." *VT* 22 (1972) 349–53 (350—Perizites). **Crump, W.** "Deuteronomy 7: A Covenant Sermon." *RevQ* 17 (1974) 222–35. **Dahl, N. A.** "Election and the People of God: Some Comments." *LuthQ* 21 (1969) 430–36. **Dahood, M.** "Hebrew-Ugaritic Lexicography III." *Bib* 46 (1965) 313. ———. "Hebrew-Ugaritic Lexicography VII." *Bib* 50 (1969) 341. **Dever, W. G.** "Asherah, Consort of Yahweh? New Evidence from Kuntillet ʿAjrud." *BASOR* 255 (1984) 21–37. **Dobbie, R.** "Deuteronomy and the Prophetic Attitude to Sacrifice." *SJT* 12 (1959) 68–82 (81). **Dohmen, C.** " פֶּסֶל-פָּסִיל: Zwei Nominalbildungen von פסל?" *BN* 16 (1981) 11–12. **Dommershausen, W.** "Heiligkeit, ein alttestamentliches Sozialprinzip?" *ThQ* 148 (1968) 153–66 (157). **Ehrlich, E. L.** "Die Erwählung Israels." In *FS G. Molin* (1983). 73–88. **Emerton, J. A.** "New Light on Israelite Religion: The Implications of the Inscriptions of Kuntillet ʿAjrud." *ZAW* 94 (1982) 2–20 (13–18). **Fishbane, M.** "Torah and Tradition." In *Tradition and Theology in the Old Testament*. Ed. D. A. Knight. Philadelphia: Fortress, 1977. 279–80. **Floss, J. P.** *Jahwe dienen—Göttern dienen.* BBB 45 (1975). 287–88. **Fohrer, G.** "Israels Haltung gegenüber den Kanaanäern und anderen Völkern." In *Studien zu Alttestamentlichen Texten und Themen 1966–1972.* Ed. G. Fohrer. BZAW 155. Berlin: de Gruyter, 1981. 108–14 (111–12) [=*JSS* 13 (1968) 64–75]. **Fox, M. V.** "Jeremiah 2:2 and the 'Desert Ideal.'" *CBQ* 35 (1973) 441–50. **Galling, K.** *Die Erwählungstraditionen in Israel.* BZAW 48. Berlin: Töpelmann, 1928. **García López, F.** "Election-Vocation d'Israel et de Jérémie: Deutéronome VII et Jérémie I." *VT* 35 (1985) 1–12. **Gese, H.** "The Structure of the Decalogue." In *Fourth World Congress of Jewish Studies, Papers.* Jerusalem, 1967. I, 155–59 (156–57). **Gibson, J. C. L.** "Observations on Some Important Ethnic Terms in the Pentateuch." *JNES* 20 (1961) 217–38. **Giesen, G.** *Die Wurzel* שבע *(1981)*. 286–89, 305. **Gilula, M.** "To Yahweh Shomron and His Asherah." *Shnaton* 3 (1978/79) 129–37 (Heb.). **Glueck, N.** *Ḥesed in the Bible.* Tr. A. Gottschalk. Ed. E. L. Epstein. Cincinatti: Hebrew Union College Press, 1967. **Görg, M.** "Hiwwiter im 13. Jahrhunder v. Chr." *UF* 8 (1976) 53–55. ———. "Dor, die Teukrer und die Girgasiter." *BN* 28 (1985) 7–14. **Golebiewski, M.** "L'alliance éternelle en Is 54–55 en comparaison avec d'autres textes prophétiques." *ColT* 50 (1980) 89–102. **Golka, F. W.** "Schwierigkeiten bei der Datierung des Fremdgötterverbots." *VT* 28 (1978) 352–54 (354). **Good, R. M.** *The Sheep of His Pasture: A Study of the Hebrew Noun ʿam(m) and Its Semitic Cognates.* HSM 29. Chico: Scholars Press, 1983. **Graesser, C. F.** "Standing Stones in Ancient Palestine." *BA* 35 (1972) 34–63. **Greenberg, M.** "Hebrew *segullā*: Akkadian *sikiltu*." *JAOS* 71 (1951) 172–74. **Grintz, Y. M.** "The Josianic Reforms and the Book of Deuteronomy." In *Môṣāʾē Dôrōt [Studies in Early Biblical Ethnology and History].* Tel Aviv, 1969. 227–33. **Gröndahl, F.** *Die Personennamen der Texte aus Ugarit.* Studia Pohl 1. Rome: Biblical Institute Press, 1967. (332—Girgashites). **Gutmann, J.** "Deuteronomy: Religious Reformation or Iconoclastic Revolution?" In *Image and the Word.* Ed. J. Gutmann (1977). 5–25. **Helfmeyer, F. J.** "Segen und Erwählung." *BZ* 18 (1974) 208–23. **Heltzer, M.** "Mortgage of Land Property and Freeing from It in Ugarit." *JESHO* 19 (1976) 89–95. **Hermisson, H.-J.** "Zur Erwählung Israels: Alttestamentliche Gedanken zum Amt der Gemeinde." In *FS G. Krause* (1982). 37–66. **Hesse, F.** "Erwägungen zur religionsgeschichtlichen und theologischen Bedeutung der Erwählungsgewissheit Israels." In *FS T. C. Vriezen* (1966). 125–37. **Hestrin, R.** "The Lachish Ewer and the ʾAsherah." *IEJ* 37 (1987) 212–23. *HOTTP* I, 278. **Hulst, A. R.** "Besprechung von: Th. C. Vriezen, *Die Erwählung Israels nach dem Alten Testament.* ATANT 24. Zürich: Zwingli, 1953." *BO* 19 (1962) 59–62. **Ibáñez Arana, A.** "El deuteronomismo de los marcos, en el libro de los Jueces." In *FS J. Alonso Díaz* (1984). **Ishida, T.** "The Structure and Historical Implications of the Lists of Pre-Israelite Nations." *Bib* 60 (1979) 461–90. **Jenni, E.** "Faktitiv und Kausativ von ʾbd ʿzugrunde gehen.'" In *FS W. Baumgartner* (1967). 143–57. **Kamp, K. A.** and **Yoffee, N.** "Ethnicity in Ancient Western Asia During the Early Second Millennium B.C.: Archaeological Assessments and Ethnoarchaeological Prospectives." *BASOR* 237 (1980) 85–104. **Keel, O.** *Monotheismus im Alten Testament und Seiner Umwelt.* BB 14. Freiburg/Schweiz, 1980 (168–72—Kuntilat-Ajrud). **Kippenberg, H. G.** *Religion und Klassenbildung im antiken Judäa.* StUNT 14. Göttingen: Vandenhoeck & Ruprecht, 1978 (2nd ed., 71). **Kleinig, J. W.** "'On Eagles' Wing': An Exegetical Study of Exodus 19, 2–8." *LTJ* 21 (1987) 18–27. **Koch, K.** "Zur Geschichte der Erwählungsvorstellung in Israel." *ZAW* 67 (1955) 205–26. **Koschel, A.** *"Volk Gottes" in der deuteronomistischen Paränese. Untersuchungen zum Begriffsfeld "Volk Gottes" in Dt 7, 1–11.* Diss., Münster, 1969. **Kraus, H. J.** "Das heilige Volk. Zur alttestamentliche Bezeichnung ʿam qodeš" In *FS A. de Quervain* (1966). 50–61. **Lang, B.** "Persönliche Gott und Ortsgott." In *FS H. Brunner* (1983). 271–301 (273). **Langlamet, F.** "Israël et 'l'habitant du pays'." *RB* 76 (1969) 321–50, 481–507. **Lemaire, A.** "Les inscriptions de Khirbet el-Qôm et l'Ashérah de Yhwh." *RB* 84 (1977) 595–608. ———. *Les écoles et la formation de la Bible dans l'Ancien Israel.* OBO 39. Göttingen: Vandenhoeck & Ruprecht, 1981. 26–30. **Lipiński, E.** "The Goddess Atirat in Ancient Arabia, in Babylon, and in Ugarit." *OLP* 3 (1972) 101–19. ———. "The Syro-Palestinian Iconography of Woman and Goddesses." *IEJ* 36 (1986) 87–96. **Lohfink, N.** *Das Hauptgebot* (1963). 172–88. **Losier, M. A.** "Witness in Israel of the Hebrew Scriptures in the Context of the Ancient Near East." *Diss Abstr* 33 (1972/73) 6441. **Manteufel, T.** "7th Sunday after Epiphany." *CJ* 10 (1984) 23–24. **Marin, F.** "Exégesis y alcance teológico de Ex 19, 5." In *FS J. Alonso Díaz* (1984). 47–54. **McCarter, P. K., Jr.** "Aspects of the Religion of the Israelite Monarchy." *FS F. M. Cross* (1987). 143–49. **Meshel, Z.** "Kuntilat-ʿAjrud: An Israelite Site on the Sinai Border." *Qadmoniot* 9 (1976) 119–24. ———. *Kuntillet ʿAjrud: A Religious Centre from the Time of the Judaen Monarchy on the Border of Sinai.* The Israel Museum, Catalogue No. 175. Jerusalem, 1978. *BAR* 5 (1979) 24–35. ———. "Did Yahweh have a Consort? The New Religious Inscriptions from the Sinai." *BARev* 5 (1979) 24–35. **Meshel, Z.** and **Meyers, C.** "The Name of God in the Wilderness of Zin." *BA* 39 (1976) 6–10. **Miller, P. D.** "Syntax and Theology in Genesis XII 31." *VT* 34 (1984) 472–76. ———. "Aspects of the Religion of Ugarit." In *FS F. M. Cross* (1987). 53–66 (55–59). **Moran, W. L.** "A Kingdom of Priests." In *The Bible in Current Catholic Thought: Gruenthaner Memorial Volume.* Ed. J. L. McKenzie. St. Mary's Theology Studies 1. New York: Herder and Herder, 1962. 7–20. **Mosis, R.** "Ex 19, 5b.6a: Syntaktischer Aufbau und lexikalische Semantik." *BZ* n.s. 22 (1978) 1–25. **Naveh, J.** "Graffiti and Dedications." *BASOR* 235 (1979) 27–30. **Nelson, R. D.** "Josiah in the Book of Joshua." *JBL* 100 (1981) 531–40 (539). **North, R.** "The Hivites." *Bib* 54 (1973) 43–46. **Otto, E.** *Das Mazzotfest in Gilgal.* BWANT 107. Stuttgart, 1975. 224–38. **Patrick, D.** "I and Thou in the Covenant Code." *SBLSASP.* Ed. P. Achtemeier. Missoula: Scholars, 1978. 71–86. **Perlitt, L.** *Bundestheologie im Alten Testament.* WMANT 36. Neukirhen-Vluyn, 1969. 55–77, 168–75. **Rendtorff, R.** "Die Erwählung Israels als Thema der Deuteronomischen Theologie." In *FS H. W. Wolff* (1981). 75–86. **Rivard, R.** "Pour une relecture d'Ex 19 et 20: analyse sémiotique d'Ex 19, 1–8." *ScEs* 33 (1981) 335–56. **Rose, M.** *Der Ausschliesslichkeitsanspruch Jahwes* (1975). **Roux, J. H. le.** "A Holy Nation Was Elected (The Election Theology of Exodus 19:5–6)." *OTWSA* 25/26 (1982/83) 59–78. **Rowley, H. H.** *The Biblical Doctrine of Election.* London: Lutterworth, 1950. **Ruprecht, E.** "Exodus 24, 9–11 als Beispiel lebendiger Erzähltradition aus der Zeit des babylonischen Exils." In *FS C. Westermann* (1986). 138–73 (141). **Schäfer-Lichtenberger, C.** "Das gibeonitische Bündnis

im Lichte deuteronomischer Kriegsgebote." *BN* 34 (1986) 58–81. **Scharbert, J.**
"Formgeschichte und Exegese von Ex 34, 6f. und seiner Parallelen." *Bib* 38 (1957) 130–50.
————. "ŠLM im Alten Testament." In *Um das Prinzip der Vergeltung in Religion und Recht des Alten Testaments.* Ed. K. Koch. WF 125. Darmstadt: Wiss. Buchgesellschaft, 1972. 300–24
(316–17, 322). **Schmidt, W. H.** "'Volk Gottes'—Aspekte des Alten Testaments." *Glaube und Lernen* 2 (1987) 19–32. **Schmitt, G.** *Du sollst keinen Frieden schliessen mit den Bowohnern des Landes.* BWANT 91. Stuttgart, 1970. 13–24, 131–44. **Seebass, H.** "Erwählung." In TRE X,
184–97. ————. "Noch einmal *bḥr* im alttestamentlichen Schrifttum." *ZAW* 90 (1978) 105–
6. **Seitz, G.** *Studien zum Deuteronomium* (1971). 77–79. **Shafer, B.** "The Root *bḥr* in the Hebrew Bible." *ZAW* 89 (1977) 20–42. **Siegel, S.** "Election and the People of God: a Jewish Perspective." *LQ* 21 (1969) 437–50. **Snaith, N. H.** *The Distinctive Ideas of the Old Testament.* New York: Schocken Books, 1964. 94–130. **Stoebe, H. J.** "Die Bedeutung des Wortes *ḥäsäd* im Alten Testament." *VT* 2 (1952) 244–54 (250). **Tigay, J. H.** *You shall have no other gods: Israelite Religion in the Light of Hebrew Inscriptions.* HSST 31. Atlanta: Scholars, 1986. 173–74.
**Toombs, L. E.** "Love and Justice in Deuteronomy." *Int* 19 (1965) 399–411. **Tromp, N. J.**
*Harmonie van Contrasten: Beschouwingen over Exodus 34, 6–7.* Utrecht, 1980. **Uffenheimer, B.**
"The Semantics of *segullâ*." *BethM* 22 (1977) 427–34 (Heb., Eng. summary). **Weinfeld, M.**
" 'A Holy People' and 'A Great Nation': The Spiritual as Distinct from the Political Charge."
*Molad* 22 (1964) 262–69 (Heb.). ————. "The Covenant of Grant in the Old Testament and in the Ancient Near East." *JAOS* 90 (1970) 184–203. ————. 'Bond and Grace':
Covenantal Expressions in the Bible and in the Ancient World—A Common Heritage."
*Leš* 36 (1971/72) 85–105 (Heb., Eng. summary). **Wildberger, H.** *Jahwes Eigentumsvolk.*
ATANT 37. Zürich: Theologischer Verlag, 1960. **Wiseman, D. J.** "'Is It Peace?': Covenant and Diplomacy." *VT* 32 (1982) 311–26 (314). **Zimmerli, W.** "'Heiligkeit' nach dem sogenannten Heiligkeitsgesetz." *VT* 30 (1980) 493–512.

## *Translation and Prosodic Analysis*

7:1–10  [(5:3):(5+4):(4:6):(4:5) [7:7:6] [5:4:(6:4)] [(5+4):(3:5)]
7:11  [3:3]

| | | |
|---|---|---|
| 1 | *When he brings you / YHWH your God / into the land /* | ⌈ 20 ⌉ 3 |
| | *which you are coming thither / to possess it //* | ⌊ 14 ⌋ 2 |
| | *And he clears away many nations / from before you /* | ⌈ 15 ⌉ 2 |
| | *the Hittites and the Girgashites and the Amorites /* | ⌊ 19 ⌋ 1_ |
| | *And the Canaanites and the Perizzites /* | ⌈ 13 ⌉ 1 |
| | *and the Hivites / and the Jebusites /* | ⌊ 12 ⌋ 2 |
| | *Seven nations / greater and mightier* \[a] *than you //* | 19  2 |
| 2 | *And he gives them / YHWH your God / over to you /* | ⌈ 19 ⌉ 3 |
| | *and you smite them //* | ⌊ 6 ⌋ 1_ |
| | *You must utterly destroy* \[a] *them /* | ⌈ 12 ⌉ 1 |
| | *You shall not make with them / a covenant /* | ⌊ 11 ⌋ 2 |
| | *And you shall not show mercy to them //* | 8  1_ |
| 3 | *And*[a] *you shall not make marriages / with them //* | ⌈ 9 ⌉ 2 |
| | *Your daughter / you shall not give to his son /* | ⌈ 10 ⌉ 2 |
| | *And his daughter / you shall not take for your son //* | ⌊ 11 ⌋ 2_ |
| 4 | *For he will turn away your son / from (following) me /* | ⌈ 15 ⌉ 2 |
| | *And they*[a] *will serve / other gods //* | ⌊ 16 ⌋ 2_ |
| | *And the anger of YHWH will be kindled / against you /* | ⌈ 12 ⌉ 2 |
| | *and he will destroy you* \[b] *quickly //* | ⌊ 8 ⌋ 1 |
| 5 | *For thus you shall deal*[a] */ with them /* | ⌊ 12 ⌋ 2_ |

Their altars you shall break down /
  and their pillars / you shall dash in pieces //
And their Asherim / you shall hew down /
  and their idols / you shall burn with fire //
⁶ For a holy people / *you (are)* / *to YHWH* / *your God* //
  *you*ᵃ / *he has chosen* / *YHWH your God* /
  *To be to him* / *a treasured people* / *out of all* / *the peoples* /
  *that (are)* / *on the face of the earth* // ס

| | | |
|---|---:|---:|
| | 12 | 1 |
| | 15 | 2 |
| | 13 | 2 |
| | 16 | 2_ |
| | 19 | 4 |
| | 13 | 3_ |
| | 19 | 4 |
| | 13 | 2_ |

⁷ It is not because you were more numerous / than other peoples /
  (That) YHWH set his love / upon you / and he chose you //
  For you (were) the fewest / of all the peoples //
⁸ Indeedᵃ it is because of YHWH's love / for you /
  And his keeping of the oath / which he swore /
    to your fathers /
  (That) YHWH brought / you (out) / with a strong hand //
  *And he has redeemed you* / *from the house of bondage* /
  *From the hand* / *of Pharaoh king of Egypt* //

| | | |
|---|---:|---:|
| | 14 | 2 |
| | 15 | 3_ |
| | 13 | 2 |
| | 12 | 2_ |
| | 17 | 2 |
| | 7 | 1 |
| | 17 | 3_ |
| | 12 | 2 |
| | 11 | 2_ |

⁹ *And you shall know* / *that YHWH your God* / *he (is) the God* //
  *the God* / *(who is) faithful* /
  *Who keeps covenant and steadfast love* / *with those who love him* /
  *And who keep his commandments*ᵃ / *to a thousand generations* //
¹⁰ *And who requites those who hate him* / *to*ᵃ *their faces* /
  *by destroying them* //
  *He*ᵇ *will not* / *be slack* / *with him who hates him* /
  *to his face* / *he will requite him* //

| | | |
|---|---:|---:|
| | 25 | 3 |
| | 9 | 2 |
| | 18 | 2 |
| | 17 | 2_ |
| | 17 | 2 |
| | 7 | 1 |
| | 12 | 3 |
| | 12 | 2_ |

¹¹ *And you shall keep* /
  *the commandment* / *and*ᵃ *the statutes and the ordinances* /
  *which I am commanding you* / *TODAY* / *to do them* //

| | | |
|---|---:|---:|
| | 6 | 1 |
| | 19 | 2 |
| | 20 | 3_ |

## Notes

1.a. See note 1:1c.

2.a. Disj *paštā*ʾ is replaced with a conj accent to achieve closer balance in mora-count over against v 8. See note 1:1.c.

3.a. Two Heb. Mss omit *waw*-conj, which is possible in terms of mora-count.

4.a. Two Heb. Mss, LXX, and Vg read 3rd masc sg form ועבד.

4.b. See note 1:1.c.

5.a. SP and Old Latin read 2nd masc sg.

6.a. A few Heb. Mss, Cairo geniza fragments, SP, LXX, and Syr read ובך. Prosodic analysis tends to favor MT.

8.a. On the various rhetorical uses of the particle כי, see J. Muilenberg, "The Linguistic and Rhetorical Usages of the Particle כי in the Old Testament," *HUCA* 32 (1961) 135–60.

9.a. Reading the plural form with Qere, numerous Heb. Mss, Cairo geniza fragments, LXX, Syr, Vg, and Tgᴶ.

10.a. SP reads על.

10.b. Numerous Heb. Mss, LXX, Vg, and Tgᴶ read ולא, which is possible in terms of mora-count.

11.a. A few Heb. Mss and SP omit *waw*-conj; cf. 5:31; 6:1.

*Form/Structure/Setting*

In terms of prosodic structure, 7:1–10 is in four parts, the boundaries of which are clearly marked, except for the very end. Deut 7:11 stands outside this structure as a summary of the larger structure of 6:4–7:11 as a whole. The first section, vv 1–5a, may be divided into two parts, on the basis of content and comparison with the last two units, vv 7–8 and 9–10. The concentric prosodic structure of 7:1–10 may then be outlined as follows:

| | | | |
|---|---|---|---|
| A | When Yahweh defeats the "seven enemies" in the land, (vv 1–2a) | | [8:(5:4)] |
| | B | You must utterly destroy them (vv 2b–5a) | [(4:6):(4:5)] |
| | | C  Destroy their religous paraphernalia, for you are holy (v 5b–6) | [7:7:6] |
| | B' | Yahweh redeemed you because he loves you (vv 7–8) | [5:4:(6:4)] |
| A' | Yahweh is faithful in both blessing and punishment (vv 9–10) | | [(5:4):8] |

From a prosodic perspective vv 1–2a are set over against vv 9–10 as parallel structures. In vv 1–2a the focus is on Yahweh's "Holy War" against the seven traditional enemies of Israel, whereas vv 9–10 present the character of the covenant God who is faithful to those who keep his commandments and will destroy those who "hate" him.

In the second prosodic subunit (vv 2b–5a), the people are commanded to utterly destroy the enemies in the land, so as not to be enticed to serve other gods. In the corresponding structure (vv 7–8), the focus is on the reason God chose Israel. He chose them because of his love for them and the promise he had sworn to their fathers. It was purely a matter of grace.

In the central prosodic subunit (vv 5b–6), the *Numeruswechsel* is used to mark the center, or turning point, of the larger structure. The people are commanded to remove all the places of worship of other gods in the land, for they are a holy people whom Yahweh has chosen.

In the larger prosodic structure of 7:1–10 as a whole, the first half tends to be negative in tone: when Yahweh defeats their enemies, Israel is commanded to destroy them utterly, including their places of worship (vv 1–5). At the midpoint of the prosodic structure the tone shifts: to Israel's status as "a treasured people" chosen by Yahweh (v 6), whom he has redeemed from bondage in Egypt (vv 7–8), and to whom he will remain faithful—so long as they observe his commandments (vv 9–10).

*Comment*

**1–4** When the Israelites conquered their new land, they were instructed to destroy the previous inhabitants. They were not to enter into any treaty with them, either political or marital. Failure to carry out this injunction would lead to compromise and eventual disaster, because of the temptation to *serve other gods* (v 4). The inhabitants whom the Israelites were instructed to destroy consisted of *seven nations* (v 1), which are probably traditional in nature (see the *Excursus:* "Holy War as Celebrated Event in Ancient Israel"). Some of these peoples have been identified, though caution should be exercised in matters of detail. These are traditional folk, who constitute paradigmatic enemies within the context of cultic celebration. For detailed discussion of parallel texts on the *seven nations* see S. R. Driver (ICC [1895] 97) and G. T. Manley (*The Book of the Law* [Grand Rapids: Eerdmans, 1957] 62–63).

*The Hittites,* properly speaking, were from Anatolia. From an early date there were Hittite migrants who settled in Palestine (e.g., Ephron, in the vicinity of Hebron according to Gen 23). Little is known of *the Girgashites,* though they are mentioned elsewhere (Gen 10:16; Josh 3:10; 24:11; 1 Chr 1:14). The name is also attested in Ugaritic texts (see F Gröndahl, *Die Personennamen der Texte aus Ugarit* [1967] 332; C. Gordon, *UT* [1965] 381). *The Amorites and the Canaanites* in this context are probably to be identified with specific groups settled in Palestine, though the terms have a much wider sphere of reference (see J. C. L. Gibson, "Observations on Some Important Ethnic Terms in the Pentateuch," *JNES* 20 [1961] 217–38). The Amorites in Deuteronomic tradition appear to be located in the Judean hill country and the Canaanites further west, toward the coastland (cf. Josh 5:1; 11:3). *The Perizzites* appear to have been a people living in the central hill country in northern Palestine (cf. Josh 11:3). *The Hivites* seem to have been located in the vicinity of the Lebanon mountains in northern Palestine (Judg 3:3). *The Jebusites* were located in Jerusalem and its vicinity and were not conquered until the time of David. These *seven nations* constituted the enemy, *which were greater and mightier than* the people of Israel (v 1). Their numbers and strength were of little consequence since this was Yahweh's "Holy War"; he would hand them over, and the people of Israel were to *smite them* and *utterly destroy them* (v 2).

בְּרִית, "covenant" or "treaty" (v 2)—the word gives a clue as to the reason for the harsh policy of war in this context. The Israelites were bound by their בְּרִית with Yahweh, which was both a religious and political bond. To make a treaty with other peoples would indicate a lack of faithfulness on the part of the Israelites to their God.

*And you shall not make marriages with them* (v 3)—this prohibition probably refers to making of political treaties by means of marriage, since there are numerous instances of people in ancient Israel marrying foreign women. In Deut 21:10–14 regulations are laid down for a Hebrew who desires to marry a foreign woman taken as a prisoner in war. Moses himself was married to a foreigner (Exod 2:21), as was David and other leaders in ancient Israel. To forge political alliances by means of marriage would be an indication of compromise that would lead to disruption of covenant fidelity to Yahweh. Witness Solomon's foreign wives and the pagan practices that subsequently found their way even into the Temple in Jerusalem (cf. 1 Kgs 11:1–8; 2 Kgs 21:1–9).

There are ambiguities in the Heb. of v 4. The subject *he* probably refers to the foreign father-in-law of v 3. The use of the first person pronoun *me* appears to be a relapse on Moses' part into the use of God's words to him. The pronoun *they* refers to sons and daughters involved in the mixed marriages.

5 פְּסִילִים . . . אֲשֵׁרִים . . . מַצֵּבוֹת . . . מִזְבְּחוֹת, *"altars," "pillars," "Asherim," "idols"*—the paraphernalia of worship among the foreign peoples in the land was to be totally destroyed, so as to remove all temptations to follow pagan religious practices. For a fuller discussion of this religious equipment, see *Comment* on 12:3 and 16:21–22.

6 עַם קָדוֹשׁ, "holy people"—Israel was a holy people in that they were set apart

or cut off from other peoples and pagan religious practices. Their holiness is not an indication of merit, but simply God's grace: God chose them *to be to him a treasured people* (עַם סְגֻלָּה), a term which describes their special relationship (cf. Deut 14:2; 26:18). The Akk cognate *sikiltu* appears in a treaty seal from Alalah, which describes the king as a "treasured possession" of his god (see J. A. Thompson, *The Ancient Near Eastern Treaties and the OT* [London: Tyndale Press, 1964] 35). Israel's status as a *holy people* is no ground for pride, but rather imposes on them added responsibility to be worthy of their calling.

**7–8** Though numerical strength was part of the blessing and covenant promise from the time of Abraham (cf. Gen 15:5; 17:2), Israel was a small people in the context of other Near Eastern nations. God chose them not because of any inherent superiority, but because he loved them. It was a matter of grace. From the time of Abraham, God established a covenant with his people and charted their course of history: liberating them from slavery in Egypt (v 8) and bringing them to the plains of Moab and imminent fulfillment of those ancient covenant promises. God's love is a matter of experiential knowledge, not philosophical or theological speculation.

**9–11** הָאֵל הַנֶּאֱמָן, "the God who is faithful"—God maintains his *covenant and steadfast love* to those *who keep his commandments, to a thousand generations*. In sharp contrast, those *who hate him* (שֹׂנְאָיו) will see God's speedy judgment. On the basis of God's election and continued love for them, the people are commanded to *keep the commandment, and the statutes and the ordinances* of God, that is, the whole of the law which Moses is about to delineate in detail.

## Explanation

Holiness is one of the most difficult concepts to express in human language. Rudolf Otto found it necessary to turn to Latin to find terminology to describe what he called *The Idea of the Holy* (New York: Oxford UP, 1950). The theologians of ancient Israel chose stories, rather than abstract technical terminology, to convey the mystery and demands of Yahweh's holiness. For the most part these stories were shaped in terms of specific cultic activity which focused on the figure of Yahweh as Divine Warrior.

Military imagery has frequently been utilized in various religious traditions to explore the divine mystery, and even to structure the community of faith (witness the Salvation Army and the Jesuits, both of which are organized along military lines). Unfortunately, the horrors of modern warfare, as captured in the news media of today's world, make it increasingly difficult for the average person to find ultimate meaning in military images. Moreover, the preoccupation with history in modern society exacerbates the problem. We tend to take the statements of the biblical text literally and often lose sight of the profound theological mystery that Israel's theologians clothed in military imagery.

The command to "utterly destroy them" (7:2), without showing any mercy, is simply more than most people today can handle. Such language suggests fanaticism and intolerance. What we need to remember is that this language belongs to the sphere of "Holy War as celebrated event" in ancient Israel (see *Excursus*) and is to be read poetically. The absolute destruction of evil is a way of expressing the meaning of holiness in relation to God himself.

The matter of mixed marriages (7:3–4) shares to a large measure the same linguistic world as that of "Holy War." It is a graphic portrayal of what holiness means so far as the people of Yahweh are concerned. They are the "family property" of Yahweh and, as such, they share in Yahweh's holiness. The problem comes when this imagery is applied literally, in specific situations, as was the case in the time of Ezra and Nehemiah (cf. Ezra 9:1–15; Neh 13:3, 23–30). There is an important principle here, but there are also practical problems as well. Fundamentalists, past and present, have wrought great mischief with this command.

Israel's theologians were well aware of the moral questions raised by a literal reading of the commands prohibiting mixed marriages. On the one hand, they could affirm the fact that it was the failure on Israel's part to observe the demands of holiness that led to their destruction and exile. On the other hand, stories like that of Ruth make it clear that there are exceptions to the rule of exclusivity on the part of Yahweh's people that speak more loudly than the fundamentalist reading of this text in Deut 7:3–4. Sometimes the people of Yahweh are in fact the very ones a superficial reading of texts like this seem to exclude (see D. Christensen, "A New Israel: The Righteous from among All Nations," in *FS R. K. Harrison* [1988] 251–59).

The other side of holiness, so far as God is concerned, is the grace of God. The people of God are chosen not because of any merit they have but because God loves them (7:7). When that love is returned in terms of obedience to "his commandments," God is faithful to maintain his "steadfast love" (7:9). At the same time God is holy, and he will not tolerate a people who fail to love him by keeping his commandments (7:10–11).

# When You Obey, You Will Be Blessed (7:12-26)

*Bibliography for Deut 7:12-26*

**Crump, W.** "Deuteronomy 7: A Covenant Sermon." *RevQ* 17 (1974) 222–35. **Floss, J. P.** *Jahwe Dienen—Göttern Dienen. Terminologische, Literarische und Semantische Untersuchung einer Theologischen Aussage zum Gottesverhältnis im Alten Testament.* BBB 45. Köln, 1975. 287–306. **García López, F.** "'Un peuple consacré': Analyse critique de Deutéronome VII." *VT* 32 (1982) 438–63. ————. "Election-Vocation d'Israel et de Jérémie: Deutéronome VII et Jérémie I." *VT* 35 (1985) 1–12. **Halbe, J.** *Das Privilegrecht Jahwes Ex 34,10–26.* FRLANT 114. Göttingen: Vandenhoeck & Ruprecht, 1975. 256–69. **Hestrin, R.** "The Lachish Ewer and the 'Asherah." *IEJ* 37 (1987) 212–23. **Langlamet, F.** "Israël et 'l'habitant du pays.'" *RB* 76 (1969) 321–50, 481–507. **Lipiński, E.** "The Syro-Palestinian Iconography of Woman and Goddesses." *IEJ* 36 (1986) 87–96. **Lohfink, N.** *Das Hauptgebot* (1963). 172–88. **Otto, E.** *Das Mazzotfest in Gilgal.* BWANT 107. Stuttgart: Kohlhammer, 1970. 25, 203–38. **Perlitt, L.** *Bundestheologie* (1970). 55–77. **Schmitt, G.** *Du sollst keinen Frieden schliessen mit den Bewohnern des Landes. Die Wegweisung gegen die Kanaanäer in Israels Geschichte und Geschichtsschreibung.* BWANT 91. Stuttgart, 1970. 13–24; 131–44. **Seitz, G.** *Studien zum Deuteronomium* (1971). 77–79. **Weimar, P.** and **Zenger, E.** *Exodus—Geschichten und Geschichte zur Befreiung Israels.* SBS 75. Stuttgart: Katholische Bibelwerk, 1975. 57–62. **Welch, A. C.** "The Purpose of Deuteronomy. . . " *ExpTim* 42 (1930/31) 409. **Wilms, F. E.** "Das Jahwistische Bundesbuch in Ex 34." *BZ* 16 (1972) 24–53.

As was noted above in the discussion of the structure of 6:4–7:11, the central section in 7:12–8:20 is framed by the repetition of the words עקב (לא) תשמעון a phrase which appears nowhere else in the Bible. It was suggested there that the term עקב in this context may well be a pun on the word יעקב, "Jacob" (= Israel), in relation to the repetition of the more familiar phrase שמע ישראל in 6:4 and 9:1.

It would appear that chaps. 7 and 8 in Deuteronomy are so closely connected in terms of content that they may be presented as a single rhetorical unit, with 8:1 at its center. On the other hand, careful prosodic analysis suggests that there is wisdom in retaining the division of the text into separate chapters as in the MT, with chap. 7 focusing on the positive aspect of deuteronomic theology and chap. 8 on the negative.

Deuteronomy 7:12–26 may be analyzed in two parts, the first of which (7:12–16) displays a familiar chiastic design in both content and rhythmic structure:

| | | |
|---|---|---|
| A | Yahweh will keep his covenant with you (7:12–13a) | [6:8] |
| B | Yahweh will bless you and multiply you (7:13b–d) | [9] |
| B' | You shall be blessed above all peoples (7:14–15a) | [9] |
| A' | Yahweh will curse those who hate you (7:15b–16) | [8:6] |

The larger structure in 7:12–26, however, does not seem to be constructed in a concentric design of this sort. Rather, the content seems to display a linear arrangement which flows quite naturally across the chapter division. The reflection on "Holy War" which continues in 7:17–26 may be outlined as follows:

Do not be afraid of "these nations" (vv 17–18)
Remember what Yahweh did in Egypt (vv 19–20)
Do not fear for Yahweh will remove them (vv 21–22)
Yahweh will destroy them before you (vv 23–24)

The following section in 8:1–18 may be outlined in concentric fashion as follows:

A    Be careful to observe all the law (8:1)
  B      Remember how God humbled you to test you (8:2–6)
    C      Yahweh is bringing you into a good land (8:7–10)
    C'     Take heed not to forget God's commandments (8:11)
  B'     God humbled you to test you (8:12–17)
A'   Remember Yahweh so as to establish his covenant (8:18)

Except for the very center of this structure in vv 7–11, the design is carefully worked out in terms of length and internal prosodic structure between the parallel elements.

An alternate reading, which combines vv 17–20 into a single prosodic unit, and perhaps vv 22b–26 as well, is presented below.

### Bibliography for Deut 7:12–16

**Crump, W.** "Deuteronomy 7: A Covenant Sermon." *RevQ* 17 (1974) 222–35. **Delcor, M.** "Astartè et la fécondité des troupaux en Deut. 7, 13 et parallèles." *UF* 6 (1974) 7–14. **Esh, S.** "Variant Readings in Medieval Hebrew Commentaries: R. Samuel Ben Meir (Rashbam)." *Textus* 5 (1966) 84–92. Fisher, L. *RSP* I, 305. **Floss, J. P.** *Jahwe dienen—Göttern dienen.* BBB 45 (1975). 287–306. **Giesen, G.** *Die Wurzel* שבע (1981). 312–13. **García López, F.** "'Un peuple consacré': Analyse critique de Deutéronome VII." *VT* 32 (1982) 438–63. **Gottfriedsen, C.** *Die Fruchtbarkeit von Israels Land.* Europäische Hochschulschriften 23. Frankfurt: Peter Lang, 1985. **Halbe, J.** *Das Privilegrecht Jahwes Ex 34,10–26.* FRLANT 114 (1975). 256–69. **Held, M.** "Rhetorical Questions in Ugaritic and Biblical Hebrew." *EI* 9 (1969) 71–79 (72, n. 13). **Jamme, A.** "South Arabian Inscriptions." *ANET*, 507. **Kselman, J. S.** "The abcb Pattern: Further Examples." *VT* 32 (1982) 224–29. **Langlamet, F.** Israël et 'l'habitant du pays'." *RB* 76 (1969) 321–50, 481–507. **Lohfink, N.** "'Ich bin Jahwe, dein Arzt' (Ex 15,26). Gott, Gesellschaft und menschliche Gesundheit in einer nachexilischen Pentateuchbearbeitung (Ex 15, 25b. 26)." In *Ich Will Euer Gott Werden Beispiele Biblischen Redens von Gott.* Ed. N. Lohfink et al. SBS 100. Stuttgart: Katholisches Bibelwerk, 1981. 11–73. **Marti-Ibanez, R.** (ed.). *A Pictorial History of Medicine.* 1965. 33–51, 283–84 (bibliog). **Meir, S. B.** "Variant Readings in Mediaeval Hebrew Commentaries." *Textus* 5 (1966) 84–92. **Miller, P. D.** "Studies in Hebrew Word Patterns." *HTR* 73 (1980) 79–89. **Perlitt, L.** *Bundestheologie* (1970). 55–77. **Schmitt, G.** *Du sollst keinen Frieden schliessen mit den Bewohnern des Landes.* BWANT 91 (1970). 131–43. **Seitz, G.** *Studien zum Deuteronomium* (1971). 77–79. **Seybold, K.** *Das Gebet der Kranken im Alten Testament.* BWANT 99. Stuttgart: Kohlhammer, 1973. 17–29; 39–55; 169. **Weimar, P.** and **Zenger, E.** *Exodus— Geschichten und Geschichte zur Befreiung Israels.* SBS 75. Stuttgart: Katholisches Bibelwerk, 1975. 57–62. **Welch, A. C.** "The Purpose of Deuteronomy." *ExpTim* 42 (1930/31) 409–12. **Wilms, F. E.** *Das jahwistische Bundesbuch in Exodus 34.* StANT 32. Munich, 1973.

### Translation and Prosodic Analysis

7:12–16    [(6:8):(5+4):(5+4):8:6]

| | | |
|---|---|---|
| $^{12}$And it will be / | 5 | 1 |
| because you obey / these / legal instructions / | ⌈ 20 | 3 |
| and you keep and do / them // | ⌊ 13 | 2_ |

| | | |
|---|---|---|
| (That) YHWH *your God will keep* / *with you* / | 13 | 2 |
| *the covenant* / *and the steadfast love* / | 10 | 2 |
| *which he promised* / *to your fathers* // | 10 | 2 |
| <sup>13</sup> *And he will love you* / | 5 | 1 |
| *And he will bless you* / | 6 | 1_ |
| *And he will multiply you* // | 4 | 1 |
| *and he will bless the fruit of your womb*<sup>a</sup> | 11 | 0 |
| *and the fruit of your ground* / | 10 | 1 |
| *Your grain* <sup>b</sup>/ *and*<sup>c</sup> *your wine and your oil* / | 18 | 2 |
| *the offspring of your cattle* / | 7 | 1_ |
| *And the young of your flock* / *upon* \<sup>d</sup> *the ground* / | 16 | 2 |
| *Which he* <sup>e</sup> *swore to your fathers* / *to give to you* // | 15 | 2_ |
| <sup>14</sup> *You shall be blessed* / *above all peoples* // | 14 | 2 |
| *There shall not be among you* / *a barren male or female* / | 15 | 2 |
| *or among your cattle* // | 6 | 1 |
| <sup>15</sup> *And YHWH will take away* / *from you* / *all sickness* // | 15 | 3 |
| *And all the evil diseases* <sup>a</sup> *of Egypt* / | 14 | 1_ |
| *Which you knew* / *he will not* \<sup>b</sup> *afflict them* / *upon you* / | 16 | 3 |
| *but he will put them* / *upon all who hate you* // | 13 | 2 |
| <sup>16</sup> *And you shall consume all the peoples* / | 13 | 1 |
| *which YHWH your God* / *is giving to you* / | 16 | 2_ |
| *Your eye shall not pity* / *them* // | 14 | 2 |
| *And you shall not serve* / *their gods* / | 14 | 2 |
| *for that would be a snare* / *to you* // ס | 10 | 2_ |

### Notes

13.a. There is no disj accent here in MT. The accentual-stress unit in this instance is unusually long, with a mora-count of 21. Comparison with the corresponding rhythmic element in v 14 below supports MT and illustrates the flexibility of the system. A given accentual stress unit within MT varies from 1 to 21 morae.

13.b. A few Heb. Mss and SP read דגניך.

13.c. A few Heb. Mss, SP and some LXX witnesses omit *waw*-conj.

13.d. Disj *y<sup>e</sup>tîb* is read as conj *mahpāk* to achieve closer rhythmic balance over against v 14. The two accents are identical in form and easily confused under monosyllabic prep and particles.

13.e. Two Heb. Mss, SP, and LXX add יהוה.

15.a. Numerous Heb. Mss and Cairo geniza fragment read מדוה.

15.b. See note 13.d. above. It is not always easy to determine which of the two accents is intended, particularly here and in v 22 below with לא.

### Form/Structure/Setting

The boundaries of this rhythmic unit are clearly marked off in MT by the *p<sup>e</sup>tûhā*' and *s<sup>e</sup>tûmā*' paragraph markers after vv 11 and 26, and by the *Numeruswechsel* in v 12. The internal structure of the unit may be outlined as follows:

| | | | |
|---|---|---|---|
| A | | Yahweh will keep his covenant with you (vv 12–13a) | [6:8] |
| | B | Yahweh will bless you and multiply you (vv 13b–d) | [5+4] |
| | B' | You shall be blessed above all peoples (vv 14–15a) | [5+4] |
| A' | | Yahweh will curse those who hate you (vv 15b–16) | [8:6] |

The larger unit 7:12–8:20 stands at the center of the concentric structural design of the first half of the Outer Frame of Deuteronomy, i.e., chaps. 4–11. Its content highlights what is often presented as the essence of Deuteronomic theology, namely: If you keep the covenant, God will bless you; and if you break the covenant, you will experience the covenant curses.

## Comment

**12**    The phrase עקב תשמעון, "because you obey," together with עקב לא תשמעון, "because you would not obey," in 8:20, forms an inclusion around the larger structure of 7:12–8:20. The phrase appears nowhere else in the Hebrew Bible. The term המשפטים, "legal instructions," appears in Deuteronomy independent of החקים, "statutes," only here and in the "Blessing of Moses", "33:10, 21). To indicate the uniqueness of the occurrence of המשפטים here, it is rendered "legal instructions" rather than the usual "ordinances," when it occurs together with related legal terms. It would appear that the term here includes the "law" in its entirety, that is the whole of את־המצוה ואת־החקים ואת־המשפטים in 7:11. On the meaning of משפט see H. W. Hertzberg (Die Entwicklung des Begriffes *mišpaṭ* im Alten Testament," ZAW 41 (1923) 13–21; and J. van der Ploeg, "*Šapaṭ* et *mišpaṭ*," in *OTS* 2 (1943) 144–55.

**13**    If the people of Israel obey the commandments of Yahweh, they will continue to experience his love and blessing, which is here described in traditional language of fertility. There would be many children (*the fruit of your womb*) to make the original promise to Abraham a reality (Gen 15:5). The ground would produce *grain, new wine*, and (olive) *oil* in abundance; these three items constitute the principal food products in Palestine. Their cattle and sheep would also produce *offspring* in abundance. On the term שגר, "offspring," see C. Gordon, *UT* (1965) 488 (19.2384).

**14–15**    The people will also experience the blessing of good health, *Yahweh will take away from you all sickness.* The *evil diseases of Egypt* probably include elephantiasis, boils, and afflictions of the eyes and bowels which were commonplace. For a description of sickness and medicine in ancient Egypt, see F. Marti-Ibanez, ed., *A Pictorial History of Medicine* (1965) 33–51 (with bibliography 283–84). The Israelites would be free from such illness, but not their enemies.

**16**    The section concludes with reference to military success, which recalls the content of 7:1–10. The blessings described will be experienced only after the people *consume all the peoples, which Yahweh your God is giving to you.* Israel's military action was to be without compassion, so as to remove all temptation to *serve their gods.* The *snare* (מוקש) would be the violation of the first commandment (5:6–7).

## Explanation

One of the great dangers so far as the concept of covenant blessings is concerned is that of oversimplification. We cannot manipulate God to our own ends, for that would be a violation of the third commandment.

It is true that obedience to God's covenant stipulations carries with it the promise of blessing. At the same time it must be remembered that we live in an imperfect world, in which the principle of sin and evil is operative. Members of the covenant community are not immune to the tragedies of human existence, however completely they may observe God's commandments. Those who drafted the Deuteronomic History struggled with this reality in their attempts to deal with the death of Josiah and the failure of the deuteronomic reform he initiated to avert his own death and the subsequent fall of Judah and destruction of the Temple in Jerusalem at the hands of Nebuchadnezzar. In that instance it was the sin of Manasseh that was singled out as being so great that even the obedience of Josiah could not undo it (2 Kgs 21).

The individual member of the community of faith does not exist in a vacuum. Though our obedience to God's commandments carries with it the promise of God's abundant blessing (7:13–15), we must remember that sin and disobedience within the larger community of which we are part effects us as well. God's ways are not our ways. We do not have the privilege of seeing the total picture through the eyes of God. We must keep God's commandments because it is the right thing to do, not for ulterior reasons based on expected reward for our good behavior.

### Bibliography for Deut 7:17–26

**Borowski, O.** "The Identity of the Biblical *ṣirʿâ*." In *FS D. N. Freedman* (1983). 315–19. **Doron, P.** "Motive Clauses in the Law of Deuteronomy: Their Forms, Functions and Contents." In *HAR* 2 (1978). 61–77 (67–68). **Eybers, I. H.** "Some Examples of Hyperbole in Biblical Hebrew." *Semitics* 1 (1970) 38–49. **Fabry, H.-J.** "'Gedenken' im Alten Testament." In *FS J. Plöger* (1983). 177–87. **Greenberg, M.** "Some Postulates of Biblical Criminal Law." In *FS Y. Kaufmann* (1960). 23–24. **Herrmann, W.** "Jahwes Triumph über Mot." *UF* 11 (1979–80) 371–77 (372). **Humbert, P.** "Le substantif *toʿeba* et le verbe *tʿb* dans l'AT." *ZAW* 72 (1960) 217–37 (223–24). **Jackson, B. S.** *Essays in Jewish and Comparative Legal History.* SJLA 10. Leiden: Brill, 1975. 204, 215. **Jenni, E.** "Faktitiv und Kausativ von ʿbd 'zugrunde gehen'." In *FS W. Baumgartner* (1967). 143–57. **Malamat, A.** "Israelite Conduct of War in the Conquest of Canaan according to the Biblical Tradition." In *Symposia 75th Anniversary of AASOR.* Ed. F. M. Cross. Cambridge: ASOR, 1979. 35–55. **Merendino, R. P.** *Das deuteronomische Gesetz* (1969). 225–32. **Neufeld, E.** "Insects as Warfare Agents in the Ancient Near East (Ex 23:28; Deut 7:20; Josh 24:12; Isa 7:18–20)." *Or* 49 (1980) 30–57. **Riese, G.** *Die alttestamentlichen Zitate im Römerbrief.* Diss., Munich, 1977. 140. **Weinfeld, M.** "The Origin of the Humanism in Deuteronomy." *JBL* 80 (1961) 241–47 (246–47). **Yadin, Y.** "The Transition from a Semi-Nomadic to a Sedentary Society in the Twelfth Century B.C.E." In *Symposia Celebrating 75th Anniversary of ASOR.* Ed. F. M. Cross. Cambridge: AASOR, 1979. 57–68. **Yahuda, A. S.** *The Language of the Pentateuch in Its Relation to Egyptian.* London: Oxford UP, 1933. 66, 75, 81, 95. **Zenger, E.** "Funktion und Sinn der ältesten Herausfthrungsformel." *ZDMG* Suppl 1 (1969) 334–42 (335).

### Translation and Prosodic Analysis

7:17–26    [(7:7):4:(5+4):7] [5:4:4] [7:(5+4):(4:7):7]

| | | |
|---|---|---|
| [17] *Indeed,*[a] *you may say / in your heart /* | 11 | 2 |
| *"Greater / are these nations / than I //* | 17 | 3 |
| *How*[b] *can I / dispossess them?" //* | 14 | 2 |
| [18] *You shall not be afraid / of them //* | 9 | 2 |
| *you shall take care to remember / what YHWH your God / did /* | 23 | 3 |
| *to pharaoh / and to all Egypt //* | 12 | 2 |

| | | |
|---|---|---|
| <sup>19</sup> *The great trials / which your eyes saw /* | 21 | 2 |
| *The signs and the wonders / and the mighty hand /* | <u>22</u> | 2_ |
| *And the outstretched arm /* | ⌐ 12 | 1 |
| *by which he brought you out / YHWH your God //* | ∟ 16 | 2 |
| *so will he do / YHWH your God* | 13 | 2 |
| *To all the peoples / of whom you are afraid* \ª *before them //* | ⌐ 21 | 2 |
| <sup>20</sup> *And moreover / (there is) the "hornet" /* | ∟ 7 | 2_ |
| *He will send (it) / YHWH your God / upon them //* | 13 | 3 |
| *Until they are destroyed / the ones who are left /* | 11 | 2 |
| *Yea,* ª *those who hide themselves / from before you //* | <u>12</u> | 2_ |
| | | |
| <sup>21</sup> *You shall not be in dread* \ª *of them //* | ⌐ 11 | 1 |
| *for YHWH your God / is in your midst /* | ⌐ 14 ⌐ | 2 |
| *a God who is great / and terrible //* | ∟ 11 ∟ | 2_ |
| <sup>22</sup> *YHWH your God will clear away / these* ª *nations /* | ⌐ 23 | 2 |
| *from before you* ᵇ / *little by little //* | ∟ 10 | 2_ |
| *You must not / make an end to them quickly /* | 13 | 2 |
| *Lest they grow too numerous for you / the wild beasts //* | <u>14</u> | 2_ |
| | | |
| <sup>23</sup> *And he will give them / YHWH your God / over to you //* | 19 | 3 |
| *and he will confuse them /* | 5 | 1 |
| *with a great confusion / until / they are destroyed //* | 7 | 3_ |
| <sup>24</sup> *And he will give their kings / into your hand<s>* ª / | ⌐ 13 | 2 |
| *and you will make their name perish* ᵇ / | ∟ 10 | 1 |
| *from under / heaven //* | 9 | 2 |
| *Not a person will be able to stand / against you* ᶜ / | ⌐ 13 | 2 |
| *until you have destroyed / them //* | ∟ 10 | 2_ |
| | | |
| <sup>25</sup> The graven images of their gods / you shall burn with fire // | ⌐ 19 | 2 |
| You shall not covet the silver and gold on them / | ⌐ 16 ⌐ | 1 |
| and take (it) for yourselves / | ∟ 7 ∟ | 1_ |
| Lest / you are ensnared by it / | ⌐ 8 | 2 |
| for an abomination / to YHWH your God / it is // | ∟ 16 ∟ | 3 |
| <sup>26</sup> And you shall not bring an abomination / into your house / | ∟ 18 | 2_ |
| Or you will become accursed / like it / | 16 | 2 |
| you shall utterly /ªdetest it / | 9 | 2 |
| And you shall utterly /ª abhor it/ | ⌐ 10 | 2 |
| for it is an accursed ᵇ thing // פ | ∟ 7 | 1_ |

## Notes

17.a. On the range of rhetorical meaning for the particle כֹּ see J. Muilenberg, "The Linguistic and Rhetorical Usages of the Particle כֹּ in the Old Testament," *HUCA* 32 (1961) 135–60.

17.b. DSS reads אֵיך.

19.a. Deleting the *waw*-conj with a few Heb. Mss, SP, LXX, Syr, and Tg.

20.a. Reading the *waw*-conj as emphatic.

21.a. See note 1:1.c..

22.a. Reading הָאֵלֶּה with one Heb. Ms and SP; cf. note 4:42.b.

22.b. SP reads מלפניך.

24.a. Reading בידיך with a few Heb. Mss, Cairo geniza fragment, Syr, and Vg.

24.b. SP reads ואבדת.
24.c. One Heb. Ms and SP read לפניך.
26.a. The sequences of *dargā᾽* plus *pāseq* and *mêrekā᾽* plus *pāseq* are not normally read as disj, since the addition of the *pāseq* in such contexts appears to be have been a secondary development in the Masoretic tradition. Both are read here as disj accents to achieve rhythmic balance over against v 17.
26.b. *BHS* introduced an error here, reading הרם for חרם in the 1972 fasicle edition. The error is corrected in the Editio minor of 1984.

## Form/Structure/Setting

Though the boundaries of 7:17–26 as a whole are clearly marked within MT by *setûmā᾽* and *petûhā᾽* paragraph markers at the end of vv 16 and 26, the internal structure is less clear. On the basis of the prosodic analysis, it may be outlined as follows:

Fear not; remember what happened in Egypt (vv 17–20)        [(7:7):4:(5+4):7]
Do not fear for Yahweh will (help you) remove them, (vv 21–22a)        [5:4:4]
    but do not remove them too quickly (v 22b)
Yahweh will confound them that you may destroy them (vv 23–24).        [7:(5+4)]
Do not be ensnared by their gods (vv 25–26)        [(4:7):7]

With the exception of the *Numeruswechsel* in v 25, there are no rhetorical markers, as such, to divide the larger unit of 7:17–26 into rhythmic subunits. The flow of thought moves directly from one part to the next. Nonetheless, the concentric rhythmic structure reflects the orderly arrangement of the content as well.

The rhythmic center of the unit (vv 21–22a), with its command not to be "in dread of them," forms an inclusion with the beginning, "You shall not be afraid of them" (v 18). The recital in vv 19–20 of what "God did to pharaoh and to all Egypt" to illustrate what he will also do to "these nations" is set over against vv 23–24, which also focuses on Yahweh's "Holy War" against Israel's enemies (see *Excursus:* "Holy War as Celebrated Event in Ancient Israel").

## Comment

**17–20** The subject is once again that of warfare, which the people of Israel are about to wage against *these nations* in the promised land. The danger is that they will reflect more on the strength of their enemy (v 17) than the strength of their God, as revealed in the events of the Exodus from Egypt (vv 18–19). In another military encounter, this same negative mental attitude had already led to defeat (Deut 1:27–18). Moses urges them *to remember what Yahweh your God did to pharaoh and to all Egypt* (v 18). The remedy for fear is memory of actual experience. The marvelous events of the Exodus journey from Egypt through the wilderness will be repeated, when the people place their trust in the strength of their God. In the past the people had been chased from the battlefield "just as the bees do" (1:44). The reverse would now be the case when God sends *the "hornet"* (הצרעה) upon their enemies, *until they are destroyed,* even *those who hide themselves* (v 20). The word "hornet" is in quotation marks to suggest that it may well be a metaphor for the concept of "panic," or something of the sort (see L. Köhler in *ZAW* 44 [1926] 15; and his later suggestion of the translation "depression, discouragement" in KB, 817).

**21–22** The people are told לא תערץ מפניהם, "not to be in dread of them," for Yahweh their God *is great and terrible* (v 21); he will fight for them, for this is Yahweh's war. He *will clear away these nations from before you, little by little* (v 22). Though the initial conquest would be sudden, the actual process of settlement would be gradual. The enemy was not to be removed completely, lest *wild beasts grow too numerous* in the land (v 22). The term חית השׂדה means literally "beasts of the field," but "field" here has the sense of countryside. The reference is not to domestic animals. The danger is that rapid removal of the inhabitants would result in the land returning to a primitive state of natural anarchy.

**23–24** This is Yahweh's war, for it is he who will *confuse them with a great confusion* (והמם מהומה גדלה) *until they are destroyed* (v 23). Their destruction will be complete, *not a person will be able to stand against you until you have destroyed them* all (v 24). The kings, and memory of them, would be lost in the forgetfulness of human history.

**25–26** The religious paraphernalia of the Canaanites is to be destroyed utterly, lest it become a snare to the people of Israel. Even the precious metals from which their images were made are to be discarded as תועבת יהוה, "an abomination to Yahweh" (v 25). A. S. Yahuda has argued that the noun תועבה is borrowed from Egyptian (see *The Language of the Pentateuch in its Relation to Egyptian.* [Oxford UP, 1933.] 75, 95). See also G. A. Cooke (*A Text–book of North-Semitic Inscriptions* [Oxford: Clarendon Press, 1903] 29) for a cognate usage in a Phoenician inscription on an Egyptian-style sarcophagus from Sidon: "an abomination *(tᶜbt)* of Ashtart."

### Explanation

Deut 7:17–26 is transitional in nature, continuing the discussion of the "Holy War" the people are about to wage in the promised land, which was the focus of 7:12–16, and setting the stage for the grand summary of deuteronomic theology contained in 8:1–20. The people are urged not to be concerned with the strength of their enemy (7:17–18) but rather to recall the mighty acts of God in their behalf during the Exodus from Egypt. On an earlier occasion it was failure to trust Yahweh that led to defeat (cf. Deut 1:27–28). Moses urges them this time not to fear.

The remedy for fear is memory. This is why each generation is called to experience the Exodus from Egypt anew in cultic drama each year in the festival of Passover. The mighty acts of God are not to be seen as mere actions in history, accomplished once and for all time at particular moments in the past. The Exodus from Egypt is a paradigm. It is to be the personal reality of each member of the community, part of their own experience (see D. Christensen, ed., *Experiencing the Exodus* [BIBAL Press, 1988]). When this becomes a reality, the individual has the inner resources to indeed "remember what Yahweh your God did to pharaoh and to all Egypt" (7:18) and to trust God to do it again (cf. Hab 3:2).

The strong language of the concluding verses (7:25–26) bear witness once again to the demands of holiness in our relation to God. We must shun the very appearance of evil. Even the precious metals used to make "graven images of their gods," however valuable they may be in themselves, are to be abhorred and discarded as "an accursed thing" (v 26). The story of the golden calf that Aaron made at Mount Sinai stands as a powerful reminder of this reality (see Exod 32).

# *When You Disobey, You Will Perish (8:1–20)*

*Bibliography for Deut 8:1–20*

**Aharoni, Y.** "Three Hebrew Ostraca from Arad." *BASOR* 197 (1970) 16–42 (25). **Begg, C.** "Bread, Wine and Strong Drink, Dtn 29:5a." *Bijdragen* 41 (1980) 266–75. **Bellefontaine, E.** "Deuteronomy 21,18–21: Reviewing the Case of the Rebellious Son." *JSOT* 13 (1979) 13–31 (25). **Bimson, J. J.** "King Solomon's Mines": A Re-assessment of Finds in the Araba." *TynBul* 32 (1981) 123–49. **Blair, E. P.** "An Appeal to Remembrance: The Memory Motif in Deuteronomy." *Int* 15 (1961) 41–47. **Blau, J.** "Zum Hebräisch der Übersetzer des alten Testament." *VT* 6 (1956) 97–99. **Blenkinsopp, J.** "Are There Traces of the Gibeonite Covenant in Deuteronomy?" *CBQ* 28 (1966) 207–19 (209). **Bodenheimer, F. S.** "The Manna of Sinai." *BA* 10 (1047) 2–6. **Brunner, H.** "Was aus dem Munde Gottes geht." *VT* 8 (1958) 428–29. **Buis, P.** "Comment au septième siècle envisagait-on l'avenir de l'Alliance? Étude de Lv 26, 3–45." In *Questions Disputées d'Ancien Testament. Méthode et Théolgie.* Ed. C. Brekelmans. BETL 33. Leuven, 1974. 136. ———. "Les conflicts entre Moïse et Israel dans Exode et nombres." *VT* 28 (1978) 257–70. **Cazelles, H.** Jérémie et le Deutéronome." *RSR* 38 (1951/52) 5–36 (11–12). ———. "La rupture de la *berît* selon les Prophetes." *JJS* 33 (1982) 133–44 (140). **Cogswell, J.** "Lest We Forget: A Sermon (Dt 8,11.14)." *Int* 15 (1961) 32–40. **Coppens, J.** "Les traditions relatives à la manne dans Exode XVI." *EstEcl* 34 (1960) 473–89. **Davies, G. I.** "The Wilderness Itineraries: A Comparative Study." *TynBul* 25 (1974) 46–81 (12). **Dion, P. E.** "Sennacherib's Expedition to Palestine." *EglT* 20 (1989) 5–25. **Eybers, I. H.** "Some Examples of Hyperbole in Biblical Hebrew." *Semitics* 1 (1970) 38–49. **Fensham, F. C.** "An Ancient Tradition of the Fertility of Palestine." *PEQ* 98 (1966) 166–67. ———. "Father and Son as Terminology for Treaty and Covenant." In *FS W. F. Albright* (1971). 121–35 (129). **Friedman, R. E.** "From Egypt to Egypt." In *FS F. M. Cross* (1981). 184–85. **Gammie, J. G.** "The Theology of Retribution in the Book of Deuteronomy." *CBQ* 32 (1970) 1–12 (10–11). **Garcia Lopéz, F.** "Yahvé, fuente última de vida: análisis de Dt 8." *Bib* 62 (1981) 21–54. **Gerhardsson, B.** *The Testing of God's Son (Matt 4:11 & Parallels).* ConB NT 2. Lund: Gleerup, 1966. 27–28. **Giesen, G.** *Die Wurzel* שבע (1981). 280–81, 292–94. **Gottfriedsen, C.** *Die Fruchtbarkeit von Israels Land.* Europäischen Hochschulschriften 23. Frankfurt: Peter Lang, 1985. **Gottstein, M. H.** "Afterthought and the Syntax of Relative Clauses in Biblical Hebrew." *JBL* 68 (1949) 35–47 (39). **Greenberg, M.** "נסה in Exod 20:20 and the Purpose of the Sinaitic Theophanie." *JBL* 79 (1960) 173–76. **Halévy, J.** "Recherches biblique: le Deutéronome." *RSEHA* 7 (1899) 326. **Jenni, E.** "Faktitiv und Kausativ von ʿbd 'zugrunde gehen'." In *FS W. Baumgartner* (1967). 143–57. **Koch, D.-A.** *Die Schrift als Zeuge zur Evangeliums.* Tübingen: Mohr, 1986. 185–86. **Leeuwen, R. C. van.** "What Comes Out of God's Mouth: Theological Wordplay in Deuteronomy 8." *CBQ* 47 (1985) 55–57. **Levenson, J. D.** "Some Unnoticed Connotations in Jeremiah 20:9." *CBQ* 46 (1984) 223–25. **Lohfink, N.** *Das Hauptgebot* (1963). 125–26, 192, 194–95, 266. ———. "'Ich bin Jahwe dein Arzt'

(Ex 15, 26). Gott, Gesellschaft und menschliche Gesundheit in einer nachexilischen Pentateuchbearbeitung (Ex 15,25b.26)." In *"Ich will euer Gott werden." Beispiele biblischen Redens von Gott.* SBS 100. Stuttgart: Katholisches Bibelwerk, 1981. 11–73 [=SBAB 4 (1988). 91–155]. **Maiberger, P.** *Das Manna: Eine literarische, etymologische und naturkundliche Untersuchung.* ÄgAT 6. Wiesbaden: Otto Harrassowitz, 1983. **Malina, B. J.** *The Palestinian Manna Tradition: The Manna Tradition in the Palestinian Targums and Its Relationship to the New Testament Writings.* Leiden, 1968. **Mallau, H. H.** *Die theologische Bedeutung der Wüste im Alten Testament.* Diss., Kiel, 1963. **McCarthy, D. J.** "Notes on the Love of God in Deuteronomy and the Father-Son Relationship between Yahweh and Israel." *CBQ* 27 (1965) 144–47. **Perlitt, L.** "Wovon der Mensch lebt (Dtn 8, 3b)." In *FS H. W. Wolff* (1981). 403–26. **Petuchowski, J. J.** "Not by Bread Alone." *Judaism* 7 (1958) 229–34. **Raabe, P.** "3rd Sunday after Pentecost." *CJ* 10 (1984) 102–03. **Rowley, H. H.** "The Prophet Jeremiah and the Book of Deuteronomy." In *From Moses to Qumran* (1963). 187–208. **Ruppert, L.** "Das Motiv der Versuchung durch Gott in vordeuteronomischer Tradition." *VT* 22 (1972). 55–63. **Schmocker, H. K.** "'. . . dass der Mensch nicht vom Brot allein lebt. . . ' Thesen zu Dt 8, 3." *Int Dial Z* 6 (1973) 101–02. **Seebass, H.** "Landverheissungen an die Väter." *EvT* 37 (1977) 210–229 (222). **Seitz, G.** *Studien zum Deuteronomium* (1971). 79–81. **Soden, W. von.** "Kleine Beiträge zum Ugaritischen und Hebräischen." In *FS W. Baumgartner* (1967). 291–300 (297–300—ḥallāmîš). **Speiser, E. A.** "The *muškênum.*" *Or* 27 (1958) 19–28. **Stegner, W. R.** "Wilderness and Testing in the Scrolls and in Mt 4,1–11." *BR* 12 (1967) 18–27. **Talmon, S.** "The 'Desert Motif' in the Bible and in Qumran Literature." In *Biblical Motifs: Origins and Transformations.* Ed. A. Altmann. Cambridge, MA: Harvard UP, 1966. 31–63. **Taylor, A. B.** "Decisions in the Desert: The Temptation of Jesus in the Light of Deuteronomy." *Int* 14 (1960) 300–309. **Weinfeld, M.** *Deuteronomy and the Deuteronomic School* (1972). 316. **Wildberger, H.** "Die Rede des Rabsake vor Jerusalem." *TZ* 35 (1979) 35–47 [=*Jahwe und sein Volk* TB 66. Munich, 1979. 285–97]. **Willis, J. T.** "Man Does Not Live by Bread Alone." *ResQ* 16 (1973) 141–49. **Wiseman, D. J.** "Flying Serpents?" *TynBul* 23 (1972) 108–10 (Dt 8:15). **Wright, S.** *"Rock" in the Mosaic Traditions.* Diss., Southern Baptist Theological Seminary, 1984.

### Translation and Prosodic Analysis

8:1     [5:5]
8:2–17     [6:6:(7+6):6:7:4] [(4:4):6:4:4:6:(4:4)] [4:7:6:(7+6):6:6)]
8:18     [5:5]
8:19–20     [(4:4):4:(4:4)]

| | | |
|---|---|---|
| 8:1   *All the commandment / which I command you / TODAY /* | 20 | 2 |
| *you shall be careful to do // that you may live /* | 14 | 3_ |
| *And you may multiply / and come in /* | 10 | 2 |
| *and you may possess the land /* | 10 | 1 |
| *which YHWH swore / to your fathers //* | 14 | 2_ |
| | | |
| 2   *And you shall remember all the way /* | 10 | 1 |
| *which he led you / YHWH your God /* | 16 | 2 |
| *these / forty years / in the wilderness //* | 14 | 3_ |
| *That he might humble you / by testing you /* | 14 | 2 |
| *to know / what [a] is in your heart /* | 13 | 2 |
| *whether you would keep his commandments [b] / or not //* | 12 | 2_ |
| 3   *And he humbled you /* | 5 | 1 |
| *And he let you hunger /* | 5 | 1 |

| | | |
|---|---|---|
| *And he fed you manna / which you did not know /* | 20 | 2 |
| *and your fathers / did not know //* | 13 | 2 |
| *that he might make you know /* | 8 | 1 |
| *That / not by bread alone / do humans live /* | 20 | 3 |
| *but / by all that proceeds from the mouth of YHWH /* | 13 | 2 |
| *do humans live //* | 8 | 1 |
| [4] *Your clothing / did not \*[a] *wear out / upon you /* | 18 | 3 |
| *and your foot* [b] *\*[c] *did not swell // these / forty years //* | 22 | 3 |
| [5] *Know then / in your heart //* | 12 | 2 |
| *that / as a man disciplines / his son /* | 15 | 3 |
| *YHWH your God / disciplines you* [a] *//* | 13 | 2 |
| [6] *So keep / the commandments \*[a] *of YHWH your God //* | 18 | 2 |
| *By walking in his ways / and by fearing him //* | 18 | 2 |
| | | |
| [7] *For / YHWH (is) your God /* | 10 | 2 |
| *Who is bringing you / into a good land* [a] *//* | 12 | 2 |
| *A land / (with) brooks of water /* | 9 | 2 |
| *of fountains / and springs /* | 12 | 2 |
| *Flowing forth in valleys \*[b] *and hills //* | 15 | 1 |
| [8] *a land of wheat / and barley /* | 11 | 2 |
| *And* [a] *vines and* [a] *fig trees \*[b] *and pomegranates //* | 14 | 1 |
| *a land of olive trees / and honey //* | 11 | 2 |
| [9] *A land / which is without \*[a] *scarcity /* | 12 | 2 |
| *you will eat in it bread /* | 7 | 1 |
| *<and>*[b] *you will lack nothing \*[c] *in it //* | 9 | 1 |
| *A land / whose stones are iron /* | 12 | 2 |
| *and out of whose hills / you can dig copper //* | 17 | 2 |
| [10] *And you shall eat /* | 6 | 1 |
| *And you shall be sated /* | 7 | 1 |
| *And you shall bless / YHWH your God /* | 17 | 2 |
| *Upon*[a] *the good land / which he has given you //* | 18 | 2 |
| | | |
| [11] *Take heed / lest you forget / YHWH your God //* | 18 | 3 |
| *by not keeping his commandments /* | 12 | 1 |
| *And his ordinances and his statutes /* | 13 | 1 |
| *which / I command you / TODAY //* | 15 | 3 |
| | | |
| [12] *Lest when you have eaten / and you are sated //* | 10 | 2 |
| *and goodly houses / you have built /* | 12 | 2 |
| *And you live (in them) //* | 8 | 1 |
| [13] *and when your herds and your flocks / multiply* [a] */* | 15 | 2 |
| *And your silver and gold / is multiplied //* | 12 | 2 |
| *and all that you have / is multiplied //* | 10 | 2 |
| [14] *And it be lifted up \*[a] *your heart //* | 8 | 1 |
| *and you forget / YHWH your God /* | 15 | 2 |
| *Who brought you out / of the land of Egypt //* | 14 | 2 |
| *from the house of bondage //* | 8 | 1 |

| | | |
|---|---|---|
| ¹⁵ *Who led you / through the wilderness /* | 11 | 2 |
| *The great and terrible (place) /* | <u>11</u> | 1 |
| *(With its) fiery* \ᵃ *serpents / and* ᵇ *scorpions /* | 12 | 2 |
| *And thirsty ground / where there is no water //* | <u>13</u> | 2_ |
| *Who brought you / water / out of the flinty / rock //* | ⌈ 18 | 4 |
| ¹⁶   *who fed you manna / in the wilderness /* | ⌊ 13 | 2_ |
| *Which your fathers / did not know //* | 14 | 2 |
| *that he might humble you / and that he might test you /* | ⌈ 17 | 2 |
| *to do you good / in the end //* | ⌊ <u>14</u> | 2_ |
| ¹⁷ *But you may say / in your heart //* | 12 | 2 |
| *"My power / and the might of my hand /* | 12 | 2 |
| *has gotten me / this wealth" //* | <u>12</u> | 2_ |
| | | |
| ¹⁸ *And you shall remember / YHWH your God /* | ⌈ 15 | 2 |
| *that (it is) he / who gives to you / power /* | ⌊ 14 | 3_ |
| *To get wealth //* | 7 | 1 |
| *in order* ᵃ *to establish* \ᵇ *his covenant /* | ⌈ 13 | 2 |
| *which he swore to your fathers / as at THIS DAY //* Đ | ⌊ <u>15</u> | 2_ |
| | | |
| ¹⁹ *And it shall be / if you indeed forget / YHWH your God /* | ⌈ 22 | 3 |
| *and you go /* | ⌊ 6 | 1_ |
| *After / other gods /* | ⌈ 14 | 2 |
| *and you serve them / and you bow down before them //* | ⌊ 15 | 2_ |
| *I solemnly warn you / TODAY /* | ⌈ 13 | 2 |
| *that you shall surely* \ᵃ *perish //* | ⌈ 12 ⌉ | 1 |
| ²⁰   *like the nations /* | ⌊ <u>5</u> ⌋ | 1_ |
| *Which YHWH / makes to perish*ᵃ *before you /* | ⌈ 14 | 2 |
| *so / shall you perish //* | ⌊ 8 | 2_ |
| *Because / you would not obey / the voice /* | ⌈ 12 | 3 |
| *of YHWH your God //*  Đ | ⌊ <u>9</u> | 1_ |

## Notes

2.a. The term אֲשֶׁר is omitted on one Heb. Ms and SP. Prosodic analysis supports MT.

2.b. Reading Qere מִצְוֹתָיו with numerous Heb. Mss, Cairo geniza fragment, SP, LXX, Syr, Vg, and TgᴶJ.

4.a. Reading conj *mahpāk* rather than disj *yᵉtîb*. The symbols for the two accents are identical and the position of the accent here in *BHS* is somewhat ambiguous.

4.b. SP and Syr read pl וְרַגְלֶיךָ, which is possible in terms of mora-count.

4.c. See note 1:1.c.

5.a. The reason for the *dagesh* in final *kaph* here is not clear.

6.a. See note 1:1.c.

7.a. One Heb. Ms, DSS, SP, and LXX add וּרְחָבָה, perhaps from Exod 3:8. Prosodic analysis supports MT.

7.b. See note 1:1.c.

8.a. SP and LXX omit *waw*-conj. Prosodic analysis favors MT.

8.b. See note 1:1.c..

9.a. See note 4.a. above.

9.b. Adding *waw*-conj with one Heb. Ms, LXX, and Syr.

9.c. See note 1:1.c.

10.a. A few Heb. Mss and SP read אֶל.

13.a. Reading יְרֻבּוּן with SP.

14.a. See note 1:1.c..

15.a. The disj accent *mᵉhuppāk lᵉgarmeh* is characteristic of the three poetic books and is not nor-mally found in Deuteronomy. The *pāseq* is here taken as secondary and the accent read as conj.

15.b. The *waw*-conj is omitted in SP, which reads עקרב שָׂרוּף.

18.a. DSS, SP, and LXX add *waw*-conj. Prosodic analysis supports MT.

18.b. The sequence of *'azlā'* plus *dargā'* is here read as disj.

18.c. SP and LXX^L add לאברהם ליצחק וליעקב, perhaps from 9:5 below. Prosodic analysis supports MT.

19.a. See note 1:1.c.

20.a. SP reads piel ptcp מאבד, which is possible from a prosodic perspective, but does not alter the meaning.

### Form/Structure/Setting

As was the case with Deut 7:12–16, this section is predominantly in the 2nd masc sg, so far as the *Numeruswechsel* is concerned, and has minimal rhetorical markers to indicate internal structure. Three sections are clearly marked: v 1, vv 2–18, and vv 19–20. The *Numeruswechsel* in vv 1 and 2 marks the boundaries of the opening subunit and the center, or rhythmic turning point, of the final subunit in vv 19–20. The *pᵉtûḥā'* paragraph marker marks the boundary between vv 18 and 19. Rhythmic boundaries within vv 1–18 may be determined from prosodic analysis as follows:

| | | |
|---|---|---|
| A | Be careful to observe all the law (v 1) | [5:5] |
| B | Remember how God humbled you to test you (v 2–6) | [6:6:(7+6):6:7:4] |
| C | Yahweh is bringing you into a good land (v 7–10) | [(4:4):6:4:4::6] |
| C' | Take heed not to forget God's commandments (v 11) | [4:4] |
| B' | God humbled you to test you (vv 12–17) | [4:7:6:(7+6):6:6] |
| A' | Remember Yahweh so as to establish his covenant (v 18) | [5:5] |

From a prosodic perspective, vv 19–20 are independent of the concentric rhythmic structure of vv 1–18, since these verses are separated by the *pᵉtûḥā'* paragraph marker and appear to be a summary of the larger section 7:12–8:18 as a whole. The inclusion marked by the parallel phrases עקב תשמעון in 7:12 and עקב לא תשמעון in 8:20 supports this conclusion. The concluding /(4:4):4:(4:4)/ prosodic unit in 8:19–20 may be summarized as follows: If you forget Yahweh, you will perish.

The "A" elements in the above outline balance each other in content and re-peated language as well as rhythmic structure: v 1 mentions the land "which Yahweh swore to your fathers," whereas v 18 makes reference to God's covenant "which he swore to your fathers." The only difference is the 2nd masc pl form לאבתיכם in v 1 and 2nd masc sg לאבתיך in v 18. Both verses also contain the inf abs לעשות, "to do." The way "to establish [Yahweh's] covenant" with his people (v 18) is to observe "all the commandment" which Yahweh has commanded (v 1).

The "B" elements, vv 2–6 and 12–17, have much in common in both language and content. Both make reference to a journey through "the wilderness" (במדבר) (vv 2, 15, and 16) using the same verbal root הליכך (v 2) and המוליכך (v 15). Both mention (ה)מן "mannah" (vv 3 and 16); both use the word לבב, "heart," twice (vv 2, 5, 14, and 17); and both repeat the verbal root ידע, "to know" (vv 3 [3 times], 5, and 16). The most striking repetition is that of an entire clause, למען ענתך לנסתך (v 2), which appears in slightly augmented form in v 16 as למען ענתך ולמען נסתך, "that he might humble you and that he might test you." These two sections (vv 2–6 and 12–17) are of identical rhythmic structure, in terms of accentual stress units, but in reverse order. They also are of approximately the same length in terms of mora-count: 287 and 271 respectively.

The central rhythmic subunit (vv 7–11) is perfectly symmetrical in terms of rhythmic structure: scanning /8:6:8:6:8/ in accentual-stress units, though the two parts are of unequal length. Most of this rhythmic subunit consists of a remarkable "hymn-like poem" (so Craigie, NICOT [1976] 186), the "Song of the Good Land."

Craigie has called attention to the presence of two double themes in Deuteronomy 8:1–20, which emphasize the call to obedience: (a) "remember/forget"; and (b) "wilderness/promised land." He outlined the structure of the chapter as follows (NICOT [1976] 184):

| | |
|---|---|
| vv 2–6 | *remember* the *wilderness* and God's presence there |
| vv 7–10 | God will bring his people into the *promised land* |
| vv 11–16 | beware of *forgetting* God in the promised land |
| | beware of *forgetting* God who was present in the *wilderness* |
| vv 17–20 | beware of presumption: *remember* God, the source of strength |
| | do not *forget* God and follow other gods |
| | *forgetfulness* leads to disasters |

The act of *remembering* provides the motivation for obedience to the covenant law, for it brings to consciousness the reality and faithfulness of God.

Lohfink has traced a palistrophic arrangement in the repetition of specific words and phrases in 8:1–19, which supports the conclusions reached independently here (see *Das Hauptgebot* [1963] 189–99). His summary outline of the repetition of key words (195) is reproduced here:

| | |
|---|---|
| v 1 | כל־המצוה אשר אנכי מצוך היום תשמרון |
| v 1 | אשר־נשבע . . . לאבתיכם |
| v 2 | וזכרת את . . . |
| vv 2d–3 | הליך . . . במדבר . . . ויאכלך את־המן אשר לא |
| | ידעון אבתיך . . . |
| v 10 | אכל / שבע / הטבה |
| v 11 | פן־תשכח את־יהוה אלהיך . . . שמר מצותיו . . . |
| | אשר אנכי מצוך היום |
| v 12 | אכל / שבע / טובים |
| vv 15–16 | המוליך במדבר . . . המאכלך מן . . . אשר לא־ידעון אבתיך |
| v 18 | וזכרת את־ |
| v 18 | אשר־נשבע לאבתיך |
| v 19 | אם־שכח תשכח את־יהוה אלהיך . . . היום |

The repetition of the temporal marker היום at the outer boundaries and center of this structure is of particular interest, as is the repetition of the roots זכר (vv 2 and 18) and both אכל and שבע along with טוב in vv 10 and 12. This chapter is indeed a tightly constructed literary work of art.

## Comment

**1–6** The term כָּל־הַמִּצְוָה, "all the commandment," is used independent of the several other key words for "law" in Deuteronomy, here and in 6:25; 11:8, 22; 15:5; 19:9; and 27:1 (cf. 30:11; 31:5). It is to be taken in a collective sense, the whole of the law as delivered by Moses on this occasion. The people are to *remember all the way* in which Yahweh led them in the wilderness of times past. Those *forty years* were a time of testing, *to know what was in your heart* (v 2). The term לְבָב, "heart," is often rendered mind. Here it refers to the inner attitude of the people.

The term (הַ)מָּן, "[the] manna," appears only twice in Deut, here and in v 16 below (cf. Exod 16:14, 31; Num 11:8). As N. Sarna has noted (*Exploring Exodus* [New York: Schocken Books, 1986] 117), there is no known substance that corresponds in all details to the biblical description. Two types of homopterans, or sucking insects, are known to infest the hardy tamarisk bushes in the semiarid desert regions of the Sinai peninsula: the *Trabutina mannipara E.* in the upper elevations and the *Nojacoccus serpentinus G.* in the lowlands. These scale insects suck the sap of the tamarisk and excrete the surplus onto the twigs in the form of tiny globules that soon crystallize and fall to the ground. The substance is sweet, sticky, and edible, but it must be collected quickly, before the heat rises and the ants get to it. Chemical analysis reveals that this "manna" is a combination of three basic sugars with pectin. The quantity produced is conditioned by the winter rainfall, but under the best of conditions, the annual yield would not exceed 600 pounds for the whole of the Sinai peninsula. Moreover, the phenomenon usually begins in early June and lasts no more than six weeks.

The manna of the biblical account is not to be explained so simply. When the people were hungry, God fed them manna, and this provision was simply a miracle, designed to teach them a fundamental principle of their existence as the covenant people of God. The basic source of life was God and הַדְּבָרִים, "the words of God," to his people, namely *all that proceeds from the mouth of Yahweh* (v 3). This principle did not mean that the people were to expect at all times such miraculous provision of food. Normal circumstances demand normal provisions. But, when the command of God comes, it must be obeyed. Physical limitations are not sufficient excuse, for "God's commandments are God's enablements," as my Sunday school teacher was wont to say years ago. The principle expressed here was also employed by Jesus in his period of testing in the wilderness. When he refused to turn the stones into bread, he did so with this very passage in mind (cf. Matt 4:1–4; Luke 4:1–4).

The miracle of the manna is underscored by the fact that their c*lothing did not wear out . . . and your foot did not swell these forty years* (v 4). God provided not only food, but clothing and physical strength as well. These lessons in the wilderness taught the people about the nature of God's dealings with them, *that as a man disciplines his son, [so] Yahweh your God disciplines you* (v 5). This disciplinary action on the part of God is prompted by love and the desire to see his children grow from adolescence to maturity.

**7–10** "The Song of the Good Land"—G. von Rad has suggested that these verses are perhaps quoted from a hymn-like poem extolling the beauties of the land (OTL [1966] 72). M. Weinfeld has noted that the historical prologue of political treaties in the ancient Near East often contains what he calls a land grant, which is sometimes followed by a description of the land with details somewhat similar to those described here (*Deuteronomic School* [1972] 71–72). The song begins with a description of the bountiful supply of waters, *a land with brooks of water, of fountains and springs, flowing forth in valleys and hills* (v 7), which stands in sharp contrast to the barren wilderness experienced in vv 2–6 (and vv 15–16 below). The land described is also rich in crops, *a land of wheat and barley, and vines and fig trees, and pomegranates, a land of olive trees and honey* (v 8), all these being symbols of the staples of the good life in the ancient Near East, which, in this case, are known in abundance—*you will lack nothing in it* (v 9). There is also an abundance of mineral deposits including *iron* and *copper*, which can be mined from the hills (v 9). Copper and iron were mined, for the most part, in the region from the Dead Sea to the Gulf of Aqaba, in the so-called Arabah (see *Comment* on 1:7). It would appear that the land described here is not just that of the "West Bank" and the hill country of Samaria and Judea, of modern terminology. Here we find a much larger conception of the promised land, as outlined earlier in 1:7–8. When God brings his people into the good land, *you shall eat, and you shall be sated* (v 10). In this new prosperity they are to remember the source of their bounty, and *bless Yahweh your God upon the good land which he has given you* (v 10).

**11–16** The danger of forgetting God is the theme here. The essence of forgetfulness is *not keeping his commandments, and his ordinances and his statutes* (v 11). The danger is real and constant. When we *have eaten and are sated* and have built ourselves comfortable homes (v 12), and experience material blessings (v 13) in abundance, the human condition is to *forget* (v 14). We tend to see those good things as the product of our own efforts and abilities. As the people of Israel experienced prosperity in their newly acquired land, it was easy to remember how hard they had fought for it, and how much they deserved it after so much hardship in the wilderness. At the same time, it was also easy to forget that the land was a gift from God, and that any military success they had experienced was only because of God's presence in their midst.

This subunit concludes with a list of four gracious actions on the part of God in behalf of his people in times past, each of which is something that might be forgotten in their future prosperity. In the first place, the people are told not to forget the one *who brought you out of the land of Egypt, from the house of bondage* (v 14b). In the Exodus from Egypt the people were liberated from physical oppression and became a covenant community, "a holy nation" (Exod 19:6). Freedom from Egypt was significant in so far as it formed the basis of a new allegiance to God within that faith community. Any belief in self-sufficient freedom and independence is dangerous, for it causes us to forget our commitment to trust in God and to depend on him.

The second gracious action which might be forgotten is that God *led you through the wilderness, the great and terrible place, with its fiery serpents and scorpions* (v 15). Besides being their liberator, God was their leader through a time of great testing in the wilderness. The significance of the term שָׂרָף, "fiery," in relation to נָחָשׁ, "serpent(s)," is not clear. The reference may be to the burning inflammation that results from snakebite, as G. A. Smith has suggested (*Deuteronomy* [1918] 122). On the other hand, the meaning may simply be "venomous serpent," with *fiery* referring to the nature of the venom, as H. Cazelles (*Le Deutéronomie* [Paris: du Cerf, 1958] 54) and D. J. Wiseman ("Flying Serpents?" *TynBul* 23 [1972] 108-10) have argued.

The third thing about God's gracious actions in their behalf, which was not to be forgotten, was the fact that he *brought . . . water out of the flinty rock* (v 15b). As their leader through the barren wilderness, God provided water for his people (cf. Exod 17:1–6; Num 20:11; Ps 78:15–20; 114:8). On the subsequent tradition of a "wandering well" in ancient Judaism, see Jo Milgrom, "Moses Sweetens the 'Bitter Waters' of the 'Portable Well': An Interpretation of a Panel at Dura-Europas Synagogue," in *Experiencing the Exodus from Egypt*, ed. D. Christensen (Berkeley: BIBAL Press, 1988) 81–87. The final gracious act which is not to be forgotten is that God *fed you manna in the wilderness* (v 16a; see *Comment* above on v 3). This fact, along with each of the other descriptions of God contains a reminder that there was a purpose in God's disciplining and testing. It was *that he might humble you and that he might test you to do you good in the end* (v 16b). The people face the danger that when they come to experience the good for which God was preparing them, they might also forget the very actions on the part of God that made the blessings possible.

**17** From a structural point of view, this verse functions as a bridge between vv 10–16 and 18. The presumptuous action of saying *in your heart* echoes the content of v 14 and *your heart* being lifted up. At the same time, the repetition of the words כֹּחַ, "power," and חַיִל, "wealth," in v 18 ties the two sections together. From a prosodic perspective, v 17 belongs primarily with vv 10–16, and v 18 is set over against v 1.

**18–20** For a member of the covenant community to speak of *my power* and the *might of my hand* (v 17) is presumptuous and dangerous. It is Yahweh *who gives you power to get wealth* (v 18). God grants this power and wealth for a purpose, *in order to establish his covenant, which he swore to your fathers* (v 18). This chapter began with the command to keep carefully *all the commandment* in order *that you may live* (v 1). It ends with the warning that *you shall surely perish* (v 19), if you continue in such presumptuous behaviour. When Yahweh and his gracious acts in your behalf are no longer central, it becomes easy to *go after other gods and serve them and bow down before them* (v 19). To do this is to violate the first commandment (5:6–7), with dire consequences.

G. von Rad has argued that vv 19–20 are not original, because the warning against going after other gods does not really fit in with the theme (OTL [1966] 73). The significance of these two verses, however, must be seen against the context of the book of Deuteronomy as a whole, as Craigie has argued, for a central theme in the book is the demand for covenant loyalty (NICOT [1976] 189). This covenant fidelity is always contrasted with the dangers and consequences of unfaithfulness to the covenant. In short, these last two verses serve to tie together the themes of chap. 8 with the overall themes of the book as a whole.

## Explanation

One of the most difficult lessons to learn in spiritual matters is the complete dependence on the word of God and God's ability and faithfulness to provide our essential needs. Jesus spoke to this issue in the Sermon on the Mount (cf.

Matt 5:25–33). It is the rediscovery of this principle time and again that made the "vow of poverty" such a central aspect of the monastic tradition in Christianity. We know that we must work to provide the essentials of human existence, but in that very labor we often forget that it is God who makes provision for human life. It is when material blessings abound that we are most tempted to say in our hearts: *My power and the might of my hand has gotten me this wealth* (7:17). We must constantly be reminded that it is God *who gives to [us] power to get wealth in order to establish his covenant* with us (7:18).

Israel was not in fact a free nation, even though her newly found prosperity in the promised land led her to delusions of freedom. The first chapter of the book of Jonah explores, at least in part, the same issue. Jonah thought he was free to flee from the presence of Yahweh (Jonah 1:3). The lesson he eventually learned, however shortlived that insight turned out to be, was that true freedom is found only within the covenant restraints as delineated in God's commandments. The freedom from Egypt was significant only in that it formed the basis for a new allegiance, the allegiance to God within the context of the covenant relationship between God and his people.

There is constant danger of forgetting God and the need to find new ways to "remember" his mighty acts in times past. Christians as well as Jews need to find ways to own the great festival traditions of ancient Israel in our own time. These traditions are not the private property of any single religious community. They constitute the paradigm that enables the individual at any time or in any place to experience the redemptive grace of God and to make that experience both a living reality and the basis of their collective memory in time to come.

# "Hear, O Israel, You Are About to Cross the Jordan" (9:1–29)

The previous section (7:12–8:20) focused primarily on the contrast between memory and forgetfulness. A living memory of the gracious redemptive acts of God in times past would be useful in sustaining a living relationship with God, whereas forgetfulness would undermine the very covenant on which that relationship was based. In this chapter the emphasis shifts markedly to focus on the stubbornness of Israel, in the sense of her perversity and continued rebellion. The theme serves as a warning. If they are to continue to experience God's blessing in the land, they must learn to yield and turn from their stubborn ways. The scene is set with a brief description of anticipated conquest in the promised land, in which Israel will fight nations greater than they (vv 1–3). Moses then stresses the fact that the coming conquest has nothing to do with any merit on the part of the people of Israel; it is not because of their righteousness, but because of the wickedness of the nations they are to dispossess (vv 4–6). Verse 7 presents a summary of what follows: Israel has provoked God to anger since the day the people departed from Egypt. That perversity is then spelled out in detail, particularly in reference to the incident of the golden calf at Mount Sinai/Horeb (vv 8–21). That was but the most significant rebellion, as vv 22–24 make clear. The chapter concludes with the recollection of Moses on Mount Sinai pleading in behalf of the rebellious people (vv 25–29).

In the larger structure of the first part of the Inner Frame (chaps. 4–11), this chapter is set over against 6:4–7:11, the great commandment to love God by keeping his commandments and to be a holy people. Holiness and perfidy are thus set in sharp contrast. The use of contrast as a principle of structural organization is somewhat parallel to Deut 1:19–3:11, the central section of the first part of the Inner Frame (chaps. 4–11), where Israel's "Unholy War" (1:19–2:1) was set over against Yahweh's "Holy War" (2:26–3:11), with the recollection of the "March of Conquest" (2:2–25) in between. The recollection of events associated with Mount Sinai/Horeb here are similar to themes developed in Deut 1–3. The choice of Horeb is probably dictated by its central importance in the experience of nascent Israel. If there was ever a time when the people should have been faithful to their covenant God, it was during the events which actually produced that covenant. But even "at Horeb you provoked Yahweh to anger" (9:8). The people's behavior at that time was such that God almost destroyed them; thus, there was no way they could argue that the gift of the land was the reward for righteous behavior on their part.

## Bibliography for Deut 9–10 (11)

**Aberbach, M.** and **Smolar, L.** "Aaron, Jeroboam and Golden Calves." *JBL* 86 (1967) 129–40. **Airoldi, N.** "La funzione giuridica dei cosidetti 'racconti storici' del IIo discorso di Mosè al popolo (Dt 5. 9s)." *Aug* 13 (1973) 75–92 (80–81). **Almiñana Lloret, V. J.** "El pecado en el Deuteronomio." *EstBib* 29 (1970) 267–85. **Aurelius, E.** *Der Fürbitter Israels. Eine Studie zum*

*Mosebild im Alten Testament.* Ed. T. N. D. Mettinger and M. Y. Ottosson. ConB OT 27. Stockholm: Almqvist, 1988. **Bailey, L. R.** "The Golden Calf." *HUCA* 42 (1971) 97–115. **Balentine, S. E.** "Prayer in the Wilderness: In Pursuit of Divine Justice." In *HAR* 9 (1985). 53–74. **Begg, C.** "The Tables and the Lawbook." *VT* 33 (1983) 96–97. ————. "The Function of Josh 7, 1–8, 29 in the Deuteronomistic History." *Bib* 67 (1986) 320–34 (326–27). **Beyerlin, W.** *Origins and History of the Oldest Sinaitic Traditions* (1965). **Brichto, C.** "The Worship of the Golden Calf: A Literary Analysis of the Fable on Idolatry." *HUCA* 54 (1983) 1–44. **Childs, B. S.** "The Etiological Tale Re–examined." *VT* 24 (1974) 387–97 (396). **Coats, G. W.** "The Golden Calf in Psalm 22." *HBT* 9 (1987) 1–12. **Dummermuth, F.** "Zur deuteronomischen Kulttheologie." *ZAW* 70 (1958) 59–98 (88). **Gammie, J. G.** "The Theology of Retribution in the Book of Deuteronomy." *CBQ* 32 (1970) 1–12. **Garcia Lopéz, F.** "En los umbrales de la tierra prometida. Análisis de Dt. 9, 1–7; 10, 12–11, 17." *Salm* 28 (1981) 37–64. **Giesen, G.** *Die Wurzel* עשב (1981). 262–63. **Ginsberg, L. H.** *The Israelian Heritage of Judaism.* TSJTSA 24. New York, 1982. chap. 8. **Hahn, J.** *Das "Goldene Kalb." Die Jahweverehrung bei Stierbildern in der Geshcichte Israels.* Europäische Hochschulschriften 23, 154. Frankfurt: Peter Lang, 1981 ($^2$1987). **Hossfeld, F.-L.** *Der Dekalog.* OBO 45. 1982. 147–61. **Hvidberg-Hansen, O.** "Die Vernichtung des goldenen Kalbes und der ugaritische Ernteritus: Der rituelle Hintergrund für Exod. 32, 20 und andere alttestamentliche Berichte über die Vernichtung von Götterbildern." *AcOr* 33 (1971) 5–46. **Kaunfer, A. H.** "Aaron and the Golden Calf: Biblical Tradition and Midrashic Interpretation." *ConsJud* 41 (1988) 87–94. **Kooij, A. van der.** "Zur Exegese von II Reg 17, 2." *ZAW* 96 (1984) 109–12. **Lambert, C.** *The Golden Calf: A Critical and Historical Study of Chapter 32 of the Book of Exodus.* Diss., Paris III, 1982 (French). **Lewy, J.** "The Story of the Golden Calf Reanalysed." *VT* 9 (1959) 318–22. **Lohfink, N.** *Das Hauptgebot* (1963). 207–18. ————. "Review of Baltzer, *Bundesformular.*" *Schol* 36 (1961) 419–23 (423). **Loza, J.** "Exode XXXII et la Rédaction JE." *VT* 23 (1973) 31–55. **Minkner, K.** "Die Einwirkungen des Bürgerschaftsrechts auf Leben und Religion Altisraels." *ThVers* 11 (1979) 21–32 (29). **Motzki, H.** "Ein Beitrag zum Problem des Stierkultes in der Religionsgeschichte Israels. *VT* 25 (1975) 470–85. **Noth, M.** "Zur Anfertigung des 'Goldenen Kalbes'." *VT* 9 (1959) 419–22. **Peckham, B.** "The Composition of Deut 9:1–10:11." In *FS* D. M. Stanley (1975a). 3–59. **Sassan, J. M.** "The Worship of the Golden Calf." In *FS* C. H. Gordon (1973). 151–59. **Seitz, G.** *Studien zum Deuteronomium* (1971). 51–65. **Snaith, N. H.** "Again the Golden Calf: Shades of Hosea." *ExpTim* 91 (1979) 19–20. **Street, R. A.** "The Calf: A Cultic Symbol of Jahwism." Diss., Univ. of Michigan, 1973. **Thiel, W.** "Altorientalische und israelitisch–jüdische Religion." In JLH, 28 (1984). 166–91 (187). **Valentin, H.** *Aaron: Eine Studie zur vorpriesterschriftlichen Aaron-Überlieferung.* OBO 18. Freiburg/Schweiz: Universitätsverlag, 1978. **Vermeylen, J.** "L'affaire du veau d'or (Ex 32–34): une cle pour la 'question deuteronomiste'." *ZAW* 97 (1985) 1–23. **Weimar, P.** "Das Goldene Kalb. Redaktionskritische Erwägungen zu Ex 32." *BN* 38/39 (1987) 117–60. **Wyatt, N.** "The Hollow Crown: Ambivalent Elements in West Semitic Royal Ideology." *UF* 18 (1986) 421–36.

### Bibliography for Deut 9:1–7

**Amran, D. W.** *The Jewish Law of Divorce according to Bible and Talmud.* New York: Hermon Press, 1969. 1–31 (27). **Anbar, M.** "Genesis 15: A Conflation of Two Deuteronomic Narratives." *JBL* 101 (1982) 39–55 (48). **Aurelius, E.** *Der Fürbitter Israels* (1988). **Boer, P. A. H. de.** "Some Observations on Deuteronomy vi 4 and 5." In *FS* J. P. M. van der Ploeg (1982). 45–52. **Braulik, G.** "Gesetz als Evangelium. Rechtfertigung und Begnadigung nach der deuteronomischen Tora." *ZTK* 79 (1982) 127–60 (146–51) [=SBAB 2 (1988) 123–60]. **Cazelles, H.** "La Rupture de la Berît selon les Prophetes." *JJS* 33 (1982) 133–44 (140). **Craigie, P. C.** "Yahweh is a Man of Wars." *SJT* 22 (1969) 183–88. **Furlani, G.** "Le guerre quali giudizi di dio presso i babilonesi e assiril." In *Miscellanea Giovanni Galbiati.* Milan, 1951. III, 39–47. **Garcia Lopéz, F.** "Analyse littéraire de Dt V–XI." *RB* 84 (1977) 481–522; 85 (1978) 5–49. ————. "En los umbrales de la tierra prometida. Análisis de Dt. 9, 1–7; 10, 12–11, 17." *Salm* 28 (1981) 37–64. **Geus, C. de.** "The Profile of an Israelite City." *BA* 49 (1986) 224–27. **Giesen, G.** *Die Wurzel* שבע (1981). *HOTTP* I, 278. **Jenni, E.** "Faktitiv und Kausativ von ʿbd 'zugrunde gehen'." In *FS W. Baumgartner* (1967). 143–57. **Koch, D.-A.** *Die Schrift als Zeuge zur Evangeliums.* Tübingen: Möhr, 1986. **Köckert, M.** "Das nahe Wort: Zum entscheidenden Wandel des Gesetzesverständnis im Alten Testament." *ThPh* 60 (1985) 496–519. **Langlamet, F.** *Gilgal et les Récits de la traversée du Jourdain (Jos III–IV).* CahRB 11. Paris, 1969. 107–8, 142–43. **Lohfink, N.** *Das Hauptgebot* (1963). 201–2. ———. "Die Wandlung des Bundesbegriffes im Buch Deuteronomium." In *FS K. Rahner* (1964). 423–44 (436–37). **Miller, P. D.** "Fire in the Mythology of Canaan and Israel." *CBQ* 27 (1965) 256–61. **Neumann, P. K.** *Hört das Wort Jahwäs* (1975). 59–61. **Riese, G.** *Die alttestamentlichen Zitate in Römerbrief.* Diss., Munich, 1977. 245, 247, 432. **Seebass, H.** "Landverheissungen an die Väter." *EvT* 37 (1977) 210–29 (222).

## Translation and Prosodic Analysis

9:1–7   [7:5:(5+4)] [5:(5:4):(4:4):(4:5):5] [(5+4):5:7]

| | | |
|---|---:|---:|
| 1 **Hear, O Israel** / *you are about to cross TODAY* / *the Jordan* / | 22 | 3 |
| *to go in* / | 4 | 1 |
| *To dispossess nations* / *greater and mightier* / *than you*[a] // | 22 | 3_ |
| *Cities* / *great and fortified* / *up to heaven* // | 22 | 3 |
| 2 *A people great <and numerous>*[a] *and tall* / | ⌈13 | 1 |
| *the children of the Anakim* // | ⌊8 | 1_ |
| *Whom you know* / *and of whom you have heard* (*it said*) / | ⌈17 | 2 |
| *"Who can stand* / *before* / *the children of Anak?"* // | ⌊15 | 3 |
| 3 *Know therefore TODAY* / *that YHWH your God* / | ⌈18 | 2 |
| *he is the One crossing over before you* / | ⌊13 | 2_ |
| | | |
| *A consuming fire* / (*is*) *he* |[a] *he will destroy them* / | 14 | 3 |
| *And he himself will subdue them* / *before you* // | 13 | 2_ |
| *And you shall drive them out and make them perish*[b] / *quickly*[c] / | ⌈15 | 2 |
| *just as* / *YHWH spoke* (דבר) / *to you* // | ⌊10 | 3_ |
| 4 *Do not say in your heart* / | 10 | 1 |
| *after YHWH your God has thrust them out* /[a] | ⌈16 | 1 |
| *from before you*[b] / *saying* / | ⌊10 | 2_ |
| *"(It is) because of my righteousness* / | ⌈6 | 1 |
| (*that*) *YHWH brought me in* / *to possess* / *this land"* // | ⌊22 | 3_ |
| *Whereas it is because of the wickedness* / *of these nations* / | ⌈14 | 2 |
| *that YHWH* / *is driving them out before you* // | ⌊14 | 2_ |
| 5 (*It is*) *not because of your righteousness* / | ⌈8⌉ | 1 |
| *or the uprightness of your heart* / | 11⌟ | 1 |
| (*that*) *you are coming* / *to possess their land* // | ⌊13 | 2_ |
| *But* / *because of the wickedness* / *of these nations* / | ⌈14 | 3 |
| *YHWH* [a]*your God*[a] / *is driving them out from before you* / | ⌊19 | 2_ |
| *And that* \[b] *he may establish the word* (הדבר) / | ⌈14 | 1 |
| *which YHWH*[c] *swore* / | ⌊7 | 1 |
| *To your fathers* / *to Abraham to Isaac* / *and to Jacob* // | 22 | 3_ |

6  *Know (therefore) /*                                                      6⌐  1
     *that / (it is) not \ᵃ because of your righteousness /*            10⌐  2
     *(that) YHWH your God / is giving you /*                              14    2_
   *This / good land \ᵇ to possess it / /*                                 18    2
     *for a stiff-necked people / you are / /ᶜ*                          13    2_
7  *Remember / andᵃ do not forget / how you provoked /*               14    3
   *YHWH your God to anger / in the wilderness / /*                     13    2_
   *From the day / when youᵇ came out / from the land of Egypt /*   19    3
     *until you came /*                                                         5     1
   to this place / you have been rebellious / against YHWH / /       19    3_

### Notes

1.a. LXX reads 2nd masc pl. The reason for the *dagesh* in the final *kaph* here is not clear (cf. note 8:5.a.).

2.a. Adding וְרָם with LXX to achieve closer balance in terms of mora-count (cf. 1:28; 2:10, 21).

3.a. Adding a disj accent here to achieve closer rhythmic balance in accentual-stress units over against v 5c below. Note that the identical phrase אֵשׁ אֹכְלָה הוּא appears also in 4:24, where it receives two disj accents in the same manner.

3.b. SP reads וְאִבַּדְתָּם.

3.c. The term מַהֵר is omitted in LXXᴮ. Prosodic analysis supports MT.

4.a. Though the sequence of *mêrᵉkāʾ* plus *pāsēq* with אֹתָם is not among the normal options for disj accents in the so-called twenty-one books, it is here read as disj.

4.b. One Heb. Ms and SP read מִפָּנֶיךָ; cf. Deut 7:22.

5.a-a. LXX omits אֱלֹהֶיךָ. Prosodic analysis supports MT.

5.b. A conj accent is read in place of disj *gereš* here to achieve closer rhythmic balance over against v 3b above.

5.c. The term יהוה is omitted in two Heb. Mss, SP, LXX, and Syr. Prosodic analysis supports MT.

6.a. Reading a *mahpāk* here rather than *yᵉtîb*. The location of the accent is ambiguous in *BHS*, and the two accents are identical in form.

6.b. See note 1:1.c.

6.c. *BHS* and *BHK* both add extra space between vv 6 and 7.

7.a. One Heb. Ms, SP, Syr, and Vg add *waw*-conj. Prosodic analysis favors MT.

7.b. SP, LXX, and Syr read 2nd masc pl.

### Form/Structure/Setting

The boundaries of this rhythmic unit (vv 1–8) are marked by the *pᵉtûḥāʾ* paragraph marker between chaps. 8 and 9, along with the rhetorical phrase שְׁמַע יִשְׂרָאֵל, "Hear, O Israel," (cf. 4:1 and 6:4), on the one hand, and the *Numeruswechsel* in v 8, on the other. The internal structural detail is much more difficult to determine, particularly because of the extra space between vv 7 and 8 in both *BHS* and *BHK*. At first glance, this suggests that the rhythmic unit is in fact vv 1–7. Moreover, the content of v 8 is a summary of what follows in vv 9–29. Nonetheless, careful prosodic analysis suggests that the *Numeruswechsel* in v 8 is to be trusted as a more accurate determinant of the latter boundary. The resultant internal structure may be outlined as follows:

You are about to dispossess nations greater than you (vv 1–3a)     [7:5:9]
Yahweh is doing this because of their wickedness (vv 3b–5)          [5:9:8:9:5]
For you are a stiff-necked people (vv 6–8)                                   [9:5:7]

The concentric rhythmic pattern here is not carried over into the content of the respective subunits in the manner of most of the larger rhetorical units.

The opening /7:5:9/ subunit is framed by chiastic repetition of terms in vv 1 and 3a, as follows: עבר היום // היום . . . העבר. On the one hand, it is the people of Israel who are about to "cross over today" the Jordan River; on the other hand, it is Yahweh who is "today crossing over" before them. The temporal marker היום, "today," appears again in v 8, along with the *Numeruswechsel*, to mark the end of the unit and its correspondence with vv 1–3a.

The /4:4/ rhythmic subunit in v 4b stands at the very center of the structure of vv 3b–5 and summarizes the content of the whole: Israel is possessing the promised land not because of their righteousness but because of the wickedness of the nations whom Yahweh is driving out. Repetition of the root דבר in vv 3b and 5b functions as a frame of sorts around this subunit. On the one hand, Yahweh is "driving out" the nations just as he said (דבר) he would (v 3b); on the other, Yahweh "is driving them out from before you" to confirm his "word" (הדבר), which "he swore" (נשבע) to the fathers of old (v 5b). Once again key words appear in chiastic order, לפניך והורשתם // מורישם מפניך, to form a rhetorical frame around the subunit in vv 3b–5.

*Comment*

1–3   The opening verses pick up themes already discussed elsewhere in Deuteronomy, particularly in 1:28; 2:18; 4:24, 38; 5:1; 6:4; 7:1, 15, 21–24. The people are ready to cross over the Jordan to conquer the promised land. *Today* here probably means the immediate future rather than the same day. Beyond the river are powerful nations in fortified cities, including the בני ענקים, "the Anakim," who were legendary giants (cf. LXX which renders the term γιγάντων). Sharp contrast is made between the strength of the Canaanites and the power of God, *the One crossing over before* his people (v 3). Yahweh their God is described as *a consuming fire* who will *destroy them* and *subdue them before* his people. Though strong emphasis is given to God's action in the coming military encounter, the people are not to be mere bystanders. It is they who are commanded to *drive them out and to make them perish quickly* (v 3). The people are called to participate in the work of God. This point leads rather quickly to a necessary warning for the people not to draw the wrong conclusions from that participation.

4   The human condition is such that we tend to legitimate God's gracious acts in our behalf as our just reward. The people are warned not to *say in your heart* that this has happened בצדקתי, *because of my righteousness* (v 4). On the relatively uncommon use of the prep ב with the nuance "because of," see T. L. Fenton, "Ugaritica-Biblica," *UF* 1 (1969), 64, n. 4; and *IBHS*, 11.2.5e.29, p. 198. The reason for God's action against the Canaanites was to be found, at least in part, *because of the wickedness of these nations* (v 4). God is the God of all nations, at least in his sovereignty, and hence the expelling of the Canaanites from the land is an act of judgment on the part of a just God.

5–6   These two verses expand the discussion of Israel's presumption regarding God's blessing. Both verses begin with the phrase *it is not because of your righteousness*. The repetition of the reference to *the wickedness of these nations* seems, at first glance, to merely restate what was already expressed in v 4. There is an important addition, however, for God's act of dispossession was in order to *establish the word which Yahweh swore to your fathers* (v 5). In short, the action of God is the fulfillment of an ancient promise to Abraham, which incidentally also made reference to the "iniquity of the Amorites" (Gen 15:16). The gift of God's land was an act of judgment by God on the Canaanites (v 4), as well as an act out of God's faithfulness to the covenant promise in times past (v 5). A third reason is given to emphasize that the gift of the land should not be regarded as a reward for righteousness on the part of the people of Israel. As a matter of fact, they were not righteous at all. To the contrary, the people were reminded that they were indeed *a stiff-necked people* (v 6). If the gift of the land were contingent on the righteousness of the people, it would never be received. It was a gift, graciously given, not a reward. Nonetheless, as will be emphasized in what follows, continued possession of the gift of the land is contingent on obedience. Disobedience of the covenant will lead to forfeiture of the land.

7   The emphatic call to *remember* is reminiscent of the theme of chap. 8, but here it is prompted by a different context. If the people were foolish enough to claim that the gift of the land was a result of their own righteousness, they are surely suffering a case of amnesia. They are reminded explicitly of the long history of their stubbornness and rebellion, which began the very *day when you came out from the land of Egypt* until the present moment on the plains of Moab (v 7b).

## Explanation

In situations of material prosperity we are tempted to take personal credit for our wealth, as was noted above in reference to Deut 7:17–18. That danger is expanded here in terms of the concept of righteousness. In this context "righteousness" means our right relationship with God and the divine favor and protection that relationship brings. For Israel to speak of "my righteousness" (9:4) was to claim ownership and control of God's free gift. Such presumption on Israel's part was a direct assault on God's grace and a profound forgetting of the Great Commandment in 6:5. It is also a forgetting of their own history.

## Bibliography for Deut 9:8–29

**Ap-Thomas, D. R.** "Notes on Some Terms Relating to Prayer." *VT* 6 (1956) 225–41. **Barth, C.** "Moses, Knecht Gottes." In *FS K. Barth* (1966). 68–81 (75, n. 51). **Begg, C. T.** "The Destruction of the Calf (Exod 32, 20/Deut 9, 21)." In *Das Deut* (1985). 208–51. **Bellefontaine, E.** "Deuteronomy 21:18–21: Reviewing the Case of the Rebellious Son." *JSOT* 13 (1979) 13–31 (25). **Carroll, R. P.** "Rebellion and Dissent in Ancient Israelite Society." *ZAW* 89 (1977) 176–204. **Cazelles, H.** "Jérémie et la Deutéronome." *RSR* 38 (1951/52) 5–36 (12). ————. "La Rupture de la Berît selon les Prophetes." *JJS* 33 (1982) 133–44 (136). **Couroyer, B.** "'Avoir la nuque raide': Ne pas incliner l'oreille." *RB* 88 (1981) 216–25. **Daube, D.** "The Culture of Deuteronomy." *Orita* 3 (1969) 27–52 (51). **Driver, G. R.** "Colloquialisms in the Old Testament." In *Mélanges Marcel Cohen*. Paris/ Den Haag: Mouton, 1970. 232–39 (235). **Dummermuth, F.** "Zur deuteronomischen Kulttheologie." *ZAW* 70 (1958) 59–98 (85–88). **Fensham, F. C.** "The Burning of the Golden Calf and Ugarit." *IEJ* 16 (1966) 191–93. **Foresti, F.** "Composizione e redazione deuteronomistica in Ex 15, 1–18." *Lat* 48 (1982) 56. **Friedman, R. E.** "From Egypt to Egypt: Dtr¹ and Dtr²." In *FS F. M. Cross* (1981). 167–92 (172). **Greenberg, M.** "Moses' Intercessory Prayer (Exod. 32:11–13; 31–32; Deut. 9:26–29)." In *Ecumenical Institute Tantur Yearbook*

*1977/78.* 221–35. **Ha, J.** *Genesis 15: A Theological Compendium of Pentateuchal History.* Ed. O. Kaiser. BZAW 181. Berlin: de Gruyter, 1989. **Halkin, A. S.** "The Scholia to Numbers and Deuteronomy in the Samaritan-Arabic Pentateuch." *JQR* 34 (1943/44) 41–59. **Hesse, F.** *Die Fürbitte im Alten Testament.* Diss., Erlangen, 1949. *HOTTP* I, 279. **Huffmon, H. B.** "The Treaty Background of Hebrew *Yādaʿ. BASOR* 181 (1966) 31–37. **Huffmon, H. B.** and **Parker, S. B.** "A Further Note on the Treaty Background of Hebrew *Yādaʿ.*" *BASOR* 181 (1966) 31–37 (36–37). **Johansson, N.** *Parakletoi: Vorstellungen von Fürsprechern für die Menschen vor Gott in der alttestamentlichen Religion, im Spätjudentum und Urchristentum.* Diss., Lund, 1940. **Lloret, V. J. A.** "El pecado en el Deuteronomio." *EstBib* 29 (1970) 267–85. **Loewenstamm, S. E.** "The Making and Destruction of the Golden Calf." *Bib* 48 (1967) 481–90. **Lohfink, N.** *Das Hauptgebot* (1963). 218, n. 36. ———. "Dtn 12, 1 und Gen 15, 18: Das dem Samen Abrahams geschenkte Land als der Geltungsbereich der deuteronomischen Gesetze." In *FS J. Scharbert* (1989). 183–210 (188). **Niehaus, J.** "*Paʿ am ʾehāt* and the Israelite Conquest." *VT* 30 (1980) 236–38. **Rendsburg, G. A.** "The Egyptian Sun-God Ra in the Pentateuch." *Hen* 10 (1988) 3–15. **Roscher, W. H.** *Die Zahl 40 im Glauben, Brauch und Schriften der Semiten.* Leipzig: Teubner, 1909. 106. **Rüterswörden, U.** "Beiträge zur Vernichtungssymbolik." *BN* 2 (1977) 16–22. **Scharbert, J.** "Die Fürbitte im Alten Testament." In *FS A. Hofmann* (1984). 91–109. **Schmitt, H.-C.** "Redaktion des Pentateuch im Geiste der Prophetie." *VT* 32 (1982) 170–89. **Seitz, C. R.** "The Prophet Moses and the Canonical Shape of Jeremiah." *ZAW* 101 (1989) 3–27. **Seitz, G.** *Studien zum Deuteronomium* (1971). 54–57. **Seters, J. Van.** "Confessional Reformulations in the Exilic Period." *VT* 22 (1972) 448–59. **Talmon, S.** "Polemics and Apology in Biblical Historiography: 2 Kings 17, 24–41." In *The Creation of Sacred Literature: Composition and Redaction of the Biblical Text.* Ed. R. E. Friedman. UCPNES 22. Berkeley: Univ. of California, 1981. 57–68 (65). **Valentin, H.** *Aaron* (1978). **Vanhoye, A.** "Longue marche ou accès tout proche? Le contexte biblique de Hébreux 3, 7–4, 11." *Bib* 49 (1968) 9–26. **Virgulin, S.** "La fede nel libro dell'Esodo." *Lat* 48 (1982) 35–40. **Vorländer, H.** *Die Entstehungszeit des Jehowistischen Geschichtswerkes.* Frankfurt: Peter Lang, 1978. **Wall, R.** "The Finger of God: Deuteronomy 9:10 and Luke 11:20." *TS* 33 (1987) 144–50.

### Translation and Prosodic Analysis

9:8–21   [4:(5:7):8:4:8:4:(4:5)] [5:4:6] [8:5:4] [(5:5):4:4:(5:5)] [(4:5):8]
9:22–24   [6:(5+4):(5:4)]
9:25–29   [4:8:4:8:7:(5:4)]

| | | |
|---|---|---|
| [8] Indeed,[a] at Horeb you provoked / YHWH to anger // | 14 | 2 |
| And he was angry [YHWH \][b] with you / so as to destroy you // | 13 | 2_ |
| [9] When I went up the mountain / to receive / the stone tablets / | ⌐26 | 3 |
| the tablets of the covenant / which YHWH cut \[a] with you // | └20 | 2_ |
| I remained on the mountain / forty days / and forty nights / | ⌐25 | 3 |
| bread / I did not eat / and water / I did not drink // | └21 | 4_ |
| [10] And YHWH gave / to me / the two / stone tablets / | 24 | 4 |
| Written / by the finger of God // | ⌐13 | 2 |
| and on them / were all[a] the words (הדברים) / | └12 | 2_ |
| Which YHWH spoke (דבר) with you[b] / ᶜon the mountainᶜ / | 15 | 2 |
| [d]From the midst of the fire[d] / ᵉon the day of assemblyᵉ // | 15 | 2_ |
| [11] And it was / at the end / of forty days \[a] and forty nights // | 23 | 3 |
| (that) YHWH gave / to me / | 9 | 2 |
| The two / [b]stone tablets[b] / the tablets of the covenant // | 22 | 3_ |

| | | |
|---|---|---|
| <sup>12</sup> And YHWH said / to me / | 10 | 2 |
| "Arise (and) go down quickly / from here / | <u>9</u> | 2_ |
| For / your people have acted corruptly / | ⌐7 | 2 |
| whom you brought out / from Egypt // | └13 | 2_ |
| They have turned aside quickly / from the way / | 11 | 2 |
| which I commanded them / | ⌐8 | 1 |
| they have made for themselves / a molten image!"ᵃ // | └<u>12</u> | 2_ |
| | | |
| <sup>13</sup> And YHWH said / to me (saying) // | 14 | 2 |
| "I have seen / this ˡᵃ people / | <u>13</u> | 3_ |
| And behold a stiff-necked people / it (is) // | 13 | 2 |
| <sup>14</sup> Let me alone! / and I will destroy them / | <u>12</u> | 2_ |
| And I will blot out their name / from under \ᵃ heaven // | 16 | 2 |
| And I will make / of you / | 7 | 2 |
| a nation mightierᵇ and more numerous / than they" // | <u>15</u> | 2_ |
| | | |
| <sup>15</sup> So I turned / and I went down / from the mountain / | ⌐16 | 3 |
| And the mountain \ᵃ was burning with fire // | 13⌐ | 1 |
| and the two / tablets of the covenant / | 13⌐ | 2 |
| were in / my two hands // | └8⌐ | 2_ |
| <sup>16</sup> And I looked / and behold you had sinned / | ⌐13⌐ | 2 |
| against YHWH your God / | 10⌐ | 1 |
| you had made yourselves / a molten image [/ calf]ᵃ // | 12⌐ | 2_ |
| You had turned aside [quickly]ᵇ / from the way / | 6⌐ | 2 |
| which YHWH had commanded / you // | └10⌐ | 2_ |
| | | |
| <sup>17</sup> So I took hold / of the two tablets / | ⌐13 | 2 |
| and I cast them / out of / my two hands // | └17 | 3_ |
| And I shattered them / before your eyes // | ⌐13 | 2 |
| <sup>18</sup> And I lay prostrate ˡᵃ before YHWH / | 11⌐ | 2 |
| as (I did) the first time / | └<u>7</u>⌐ | 1_ |
| Forty days / and forty nights / bread / I did not eat / | 24 | 4 |
| And water / I did not drink // | ⌐12 | 2 |
| because of all your sinᵇ / which you sinned / | └<u>11</u> | 2_ |
| By doing the evil / in the eyes of YHWHᶜ \ᵈ to provoke him // | ⌐21 | 2 |
| <sup>19</sup> for I was afraid / of the anger / | └14 | 2 |
| and hot displeasure / | 6 | 1_ |
| Which YHWH bore / against you \ᵃ to destroy you // | ⌐18 | 2 |
| and YHWH hearkened / to me / that time also // | └<u>16</u> | 3_ |
| | | |
| <sup>20</sup> But with Aaron / he was angry [ ]ᵃ (enough) to destroy him // | ⌐16 | 2 |
| so I prayed / for Aaron also \ᵇ at THAT TIME // | └20 | 2 |
| <sup>21</sup> And your sinful thingᵃ / the calf which you had made / | ⌐17 | 2 |
| I took it / and I burned it / with fire / | └<u>18</u> | 3_ |
| And I crushed it / thoroughly / | ⌐17 | 2 |
| until it was as fine \ᵇ as dust // | └9 | 2 |
| And I threw / the dust of it / into the river / | ⌐15 | 3 |
| the one descending out of the mountain //ᶜ | └<u>10</u> | 1_ |

<sup>22</sup> At Taberah also / and at Massah /     14   2  
    and at Kibroth- / hattavah //     11   2  
    You were provoking / YHWH to anger //     <u>13</u>   2_  
<sup>23</sup> And when YHWH sent / you / from Kadesh-barnea \ᵃ saying /     24   3  
    "Go up / and possess the land /     13   2  
    Which I have given \ᵇ you" //     10   1  
    but you rebelled / against the mouth of YHWH / your God /     <u>16</u>   3_  
    And you did not / believe / him /     9   3  
    and you did not obey / his voice //     11   2  
<sup>24</sup> You have been rebellious / against YHWH //     11   2  
    from the day / (that) Iᵃ knew you //ᵇ     8   2_  

<sup>25</sup> So I lay prostrate / before YHWH /     11   2  
    for forty days / and forty nights /     20   2_  
    (The time) that I lay prostrate //     8   1  
    because YHWH said / (that he wanted) to destroy you //     14   2  
<sup>26</sup> And I prayed to YHWH /     <u>10</u>   1_  
    And I said / "O Lord, YHWH /     13   2  
    Do not destroy your people / and your family property /     <u>14</u>   2_  
    Whom you have redeemed / through your greatness //     11   2  
    Whom you have brought out from Egypt /     11   1  
    ᵃwith <your> mighty handᵃ //     <u>11</u>   1_  
<sup>27</sup> Remember / your servants / Abraham, Isaac \ᵃ and Jacobᵇ //     25   3  
    Do notᶜ regard / the stubbornness / of this people /     14   3  
    orᵈ their wickedness / or their sin //     <u>12</u>   2_  
<sup>28</sup> Lest they say / <those dwelling in>ᵃ the land /     16   2  
    from which you broughtᵇ us out from there /     13   1  
    'Because YHWH was notᶜ \ᶜ able / to bring themᵈ /     17   2  
    into the land / which he promised (דבר) them //     <u>13</u>   2_  
    And because he hated them /     12   1  
    he has brought them out / to slay them in the wilderness' //     16   2  
<sup>29</sup> Indeed they are your people / and your family property //     13   2_  
    Whom you brought outᵃ / by your great power ᵇ /     17   2  
    and by your outstretched / arm" // פ     <u>13</u>   2_  

## Notes

8.a. Reading the *waw* as emphatic.  
8.b. Deleting יהוה with LXX, which includes a disj accent.  
9.a. See note 1:1.c.  
10.a. Reading כל in place of ככל with one Heb. Ms, LXX, Syr, and Vg.  
10.b. SP reads אליכם with 10:4.  
10.c-c. Omitted in some LXX witnesses.  
10.d-d. Omitted in LXXᴮ and other LXX witnesses; has asterisk in Origen's Hexapla.  
10.e-e. Omitted in LXXᴬ and other LXX witnesses; cf. 10:4 below.  
11.a. See note 1:1.c.  
11.b-b. Omitted in SP.  
12.a. Two Heb. Mss and SP add עגל with v 16 (cf. Exod 32:8). Prosodic analysis favors MT.  
13.a. Adding a disj accent to achieve closer rhythmic balance in accentual-stress units over against v 23 below. According to prosodic analysis there should have been an ᵓ*atnāḥ* under הזה, which would require a *tiphāᵓ* before it under העם.

14.a. See note 1:1.c.

14.b. A few Heb. Mss and LXX (except for Origen's Hexapla) add גדול. Prosodic analysis supports MT.

15.a. See note 1:1.c.

16.a. Deleting עגל, and its disj accent, with LXX^B and other lesser LXX witnesses; cf. v 12 above.

16.b. Omitting מהר, and its disj accent, with a few Heb. Mss, SP^Mss, LXX^B, and other Greek witnesses (cf. Origen's Hexapla).

18.a. Reading a disj accent in place of *ṭelîšāʾ parvum* to achieve closer rhythmic balance in vv 18–19, which scan /5:5:4:4:5:5/ and constitute the center of the larger rhythmic structure embracing 9:8–29.

18.b. Some Heb. Mss, SP, LXX, Syr, Vg, and Tg^J read חטאתיכם; cf. v 21 below.

18.c. Some Heb. Mss add אלהיך; LXX adds אלהיכם.

18.d. See note 1:1.c.

19.a. See note 1:1.c.

20.a. Omitting יהוה מאד, and two disj accents, with LXX^B to achieve closer rhythmic balance over against v 16 above.

20.b. See note 1:1.c.

21.a. SP reads pl מַשְאתיכם.

21.b. See note 1:1.c.

21.c. *BHS* and *BHK* leave extra space between vv 21 and 22.

23.a. Reading a conj accent in place of *paśṭāʾ* to achieve a closer rhythmic balance over against v 13 above.

23.b. See note 1:1.c.

24.a. SP and LXX read 3rd masc sg suff דעתו.

24.b. Both *BHS* and *BHK* add extra space between vv 24 and 25.

26.a-a. Reading בידך החזקה with SP and LXX (except for Origin's Hexapla); cf. 3:24 and 11:2.

27.a. See note 1:1.c.

27.b. LXX (except for Origen's Hexapla) add οἷς ὤμοσας κατὰ σεαυτοῦ. Prosodic analysis supports MT.

27.c. Some LXX witnesses and Tg^J add *waw*-conj. Prosodic analysis favors MT.

27.d. Some Heb. Mss, some LXX witnesses, and Tg^J omit *waw*-conj.

28.a. Adding ישבי with LXX (οἱ κατοικοῦντες); SP adds עם for עמי with 28:10.

28.b. DSS reads יוצאן (ו).

28.c. Three Heb. Mss and SP read מבלתי, from Num 14:16. The disj *paśṭāʾ* here is read as a conj accent to achieve closer balance over against v 9 in the larger rhythmic structure of vv 8–29.

28.d. SP reads להביא אתם.

29.a. SP and LXX add ממצרים. Prosodic analysis supports MT.

29.b. LXX^B adds ובידך החזקה from Exod 32:11 (cf. note 26.a-a. above).

## *Form/Structure/Setting*

The outer boundaries of the complex rhythmic unit in vv 8–29 are clearly marked by the *Numeruswechsel* in v 8 and the *petûḥāʾ* paragraph marker at the end of v 29. Within the larger structure, however, the boundaries of the subunits are not marked in MT, except for extra space after vv 21 and 24 in *BHS* and *BHK*. On the basis of careful prosodic analysis, the structure of the whole may be outlined as follows:

| | | | | | |
|---|---|---|---|---|---|
| A | | | While I was on Horeb you acted corruptly (vv 8–12) | | [4:5:7:12:12:4:5] |
| | B | | God decided to destroy his stiff-necked people (vv 13–14) | | [9:6] |
| | | C | I went down and saw the calf you had made (vv 15–16) | | [8:5:4] |
| | | | D | I broke the tablets and went up on Horeb (vv 17–19) | [10:4:4:10] |
| | | C' | I crushed the calf you had made (vv 20–21) | | [4:5:8] |
| | B' | | This was not your first rebellion (vv 22–24) | | [6:9:5:4] |
| A' | | | I argued on your behalf on Mount Horeb (vv 25–29) | | [12:12:7:5:4] |

The concentric nature of the structure is indicated by the repetition of the phrase "forty days and forty nights" (twice in section "A" [vv 8–12], once in the central section "D" [vv 17–19], and again in "A' " [vv 25–29]; and of the term לוחת, "tablets," (particularly in the repetition of the phrase "the two stone tablets" [vv 10, 11] and the phrase "the tablets of the covenant" [vv 9, 11], both of which are echoed in the reference to "the two tablets" in v 17, which ties the opening rhythmic unit [vv 8–12] to the center section [vv 17–19]). The description of Moses "prostrate before Yahweh" (v 18), which is repeated in v 25, serves to tie the center section to the concluding rhythmic subunit in vv 25–29. The location of Moses on the mountain is limited to these three subunits within the larger structure. The content of Moses' prayer in vv 26–29 is framed by repetition of the key phrase עמך ונחלתך, "your people and your family property."

The "C" sections are closely connected in terms of the repeated reference to the "molten image" (v 16), or "the calf" (v 21), which Aaron had made for the people. The fact that the reference to Moses crushing the image, burning it, and throwing it into the river (v 21) seems to be misplaced is easily explained in terms of the concentric structure. Moses went back up the mountain, where he spent another "forty days and forty nights" fasting (v 18). In vv 25–29 Moses is also clearly on the mountain, interceding with God in the people's behalf, during those same "forty days and forty nights" (v 25). The reason for placing the destruction of the calf between these two sections, even though it must have actually preceded Moses' second ascent of the mountain, is to form a structural balance with the parallel reference to this infamous object of worship in vv 15–16, within the larger rhythmic structure of the whole.

It should be noted that the rhythmic pairing of subunits in the above outline is not always exact. The final /4:5/ element in v 12 of "A" (vv 8–12) has its counterpart as the final /5:4/ element in "B' " (vv 22–24), which suggests that vv 8–14 ("A" and "B") and vv 22–29 ("B' " and "A' ") may, in fact, be single subunits, or at least more closely connected structurely than other adjacent subunits in the larger structure.

### Comment

**8–12** The recollection of events at Mount Sinai/Horeb is significant because the renewal of the covenant on the plains of Moab, for which Moses is preparing the people (cf. *Comment* on Deut 27–30), is itself a renewal of the very commitment made by the people of Israel at that time. The relevance of the specific historical recollection is all too clear. If the people had been guilty of provoking the anger of God in the very midst of those awe-inspiring events of times past, the danger of rebellion in the present and future was obvious. At Horeb Moses *went up the mountain to receive . . . the tablets of the covenant* (v 9). There he fasted *forty days and forty nights* and received *the two stone tablets, written by the finger of God*, which contained *all the words* of the covenant (vv 9–10). While Moses was on the mountain, the people had already *turned aside quickly from the way* God had commanded and had *made for themselves a molten image* (vv 11–12).

לוחת האבנים, "the stone tablets" (vv 9–11)—see *Comment* on 4:13.

On the symbolic use of the term ארבעים, "forty" (vv 9, 11), in Semitic thought, see W. H. Roscher, *Die Zahl 40 im Glauben, Brauch und Schriften der Semiten* (Leipzig:

Teubner, 1909). The completeness of Moses' fast here, in its total abstinence from food and drink, emphasizes his total dependence on God.

כל הדברים, "all the words" (v 10), echoes the opening words and title of the book of Deuteronomy, אלה הדברים, and calls specific attention to עשרת הדברים, "the ten words" (see 4:13; 10:4), which are called הדברים האלה in 5:22 where they are also said to written "upon two stone tablets."

מסכה, "molten image"—the term appears also in 9:16 and 27:15. In the present context it is clearly the "golden calf" of Exod 32:4, 8.

**13–14** The phrase עם קשה ערף, "stiff-necked people" (v 13), appeared earlier in v 6. In the first instance it was on the lips of Moses, but here it is the speech of Yahweh himself, whose patience is exhausted. God threatens to destroy the people utterly, to blot out all memory of them—and to start over again, from Moses alone (v 14).

**15–17** Moses *went down from the mountain*, which was still *burning with fire* (cf. *Comment* on 4:11–13 on the language of theophany), with the *two tablets of the covenant* in his hands (v 15). When he saw what was going on among the people below who *had turned aside from the way Yahweh had commanded*, he *shattered* the tablets (vv 16–17).

**18–20** This section constitutes a brief interlude before the narrative proper resumes in v 21. Moses went up the mountain again, where he *lay prostrate before Yahweh* another *forty days and forty nights* (v 18). Yahweh's anger with the people, and with Aaron in particular, was intense, and so Moses *prayed* for them (vv 19–20).

**21** The interrupted narrative resumes. Moses took *the calf* (העגל) and *crushed it thoroughly* and *threw the dust of it into the river*. In the parallel account in Exod 32:20, Moses then "made the people of Israel drink it." Construction of the molten calf was a blatant violation of the first or second commandment (see 5:7–10). The seriousness of the crime helps to explain the violence of Moses' reaction portrayed in v 17 above. The shattering of the tablets was not a simple act of anger, but a symbolic portrayal of what the people had already done to the covenant which God had granted them. At the very moment God gave the people the covenant tablets, they already had broken the conditions of the covenant and had potentially rendered it null and void.

העגל, "the (golden calf)," may have been a simple lapse into idolatry, or it may have been an attempt to make a physical symbol to represent the presence of Yahweh, perhaps as a footstool of God. In ancient Near Eastern iconography, the gods were often portrayed astride a bull (see J. B. Pritchard, ed., *ANEP*, plate 140) or a leopard (see the familiar portrayal of "King Tut" in T. E. S. Edwards, *Treasures of Tutankhamun* [New York: Ballantine Books, 1976] plate 21 [cat. no. 38]). The cognate word ʿgl appears in Ugar several times in association with deities: in describing Anat's yearning for Baal (*CTA* 6.II.7, 28); and in the description of Mot as the "calf of El" (*CTA* 3.III.41, following the reading of C. Gordon, *UT*, 255). For arguments in favor of an Egyptian background to the bull or calf-cult, see K. A. Kitchen, *New Bible Dictionary* [London: Inter-varsity, 1962] 179–80.

**22–24** These verses present still further examples of the stubbornness and rebellion of the people of Israel. The incident of Mount Sinai/Horeb was but one of several Moses could have drawn from in his arguments to emphasize the fact that the gift of the land could never be considered a reward for the righteousness of the people. *At Taberah* the people complained of their misfortunes and were saved from God's wrath only by the intercession of Moses (Num 11:1–3). *At Massah* they thirsted for water and murmured against Moses and put Yahweh to the test, which occasioned the incident when Moses brought water forth from the rock (Exod 17:1–7). *At Kibroth-hattavah* (lit., "graves of desire/lust") the people again incurred God's anger in the incident of the quails, which God had supplied them (Num 11:31–35). *At Kadesh-barnea* they were again disobedient to God's command (see Deut 1:19–40 and *Comment*). This particular instance was of special relevance in that the people now faced essentially the same command as that given at Kadesh-barnea. Keil and Delitzsh have suggested that, since the examples given here are not in chronological order, the sequence moves from the lesser to the more serious forms of rebellion. The long history of Israel's stubborn rebellion against God underscores the fact that they would not be standing in the plains of Moab to renew their covenant but for the grace of God.

**25–29** The prayer of Moses on behalf of the people of Israel resumes what began in v 18. In fact it could be argued that what lies between vv 18 and 25 is secondary and was so marked by the redactor in what C. Kuhl called "resumptive repetition" (see "Die 'Wiederaufnahme'—ein literarkritishches Princip?" *ZAW* 64 [1952] 1–11). It is more likely that the apparently disjointed nature of the text here, and with respect to the destruction of the calf-image in vv 16 and 21, is to be explained in terms of the concentric structural design of the passage as a whole (see discussion above under *Form/ Structure/ Setting*).

אֲדֹנָי יְהוִה, "Lord Yahweh"—this title is used only twice in Deuteronomy, both times as the introduction to prayer (cf. 3:24), "and may indicate the relationship between Moses and God on which the petition was based, namely the recognition of God's Lordship and sovereign power," as Craigie has noted (NICOT [1976] 197).

נַחֲלָתֶךָ, "Your family property" (vv 26, 29)—see discussion of this term in *Comment* on 4:21. The term is here used as a rhetorical envelope around the prayer of vv 26–29. In Deut 4 it stands at the very center of the larger rhythmic structure of 4:1–40 and is obviously a key concept within Deuteronomic theology.

Moses is requesting forgiveness on the basis of God's own act of liberation in the Exodus from Egypt (v 26). There was a divine purpose in the Exodus, and Moses is arguing that that purpose should not be abrogated by the people's unfaithfulness. The second point in Moses' argument goes back even further in time than the Exodus, to the promises given to *Your servants Abraham, Isaac, and Jacob* (v 27). As Craigie has noted, it is interesting to note the contrasting manner in which Moses uses history and memory in this prayer and his address to the people. "To the people, Moses recalls that history which shows their unfaithfulness, and on this basis he calls them to obedience and faithfulness. In prayer to God, Moses recalls the long history of God's covenant faithfulness and seeks God's forgiveness for the people on the basis of God's nature, not the people's worthiness" (NICOT [1976] 197). The third point in Moses' argument is more subtle, as he raises the question of the honor of Yahweh in the eyes of the Egyptians (v 28). If the people perish in the wilderness, the Egyptians will interpret this in terms of God's inability to keep his promise, and his "hate" for his people. The prayer concludes with repetition of the words וְנַחֲלָתֶךָ and הַגָּדֹל (cf. בְּגָדְלְךָ) and parallel descriptions of the Exodus from v 26: *whom you have redeemed through your greatness;*

*whom you have brought out from Egypt,* which in v 29 becomes *whom you brought out by your great power and by your outstretched arm.*

### Explanation

The witness of Israel's perfidy in times past, which was raised in 9:1–7, goes back to the very beginning. "Indeed at Horeb you provoked Yahweh to anger" (9:8). For a fuller treatment of the rebellion in question, see Exod 32–34, which presents in detail the apostasy of the people in worshiping the golden calf while Moses was still on the sacred mountain and their subsequent punishment followed by the renewal of the covenant and Yahweh's promise to remain with his people by means of his angel, his presence, and his name. In spite of Yahweh's abiding presence with them the perfidy continued "at Taberah also and at Massah and at Kibroth-hattavah" (9:22) where "you rebelled against the mouth of Yahweh your God and you did not believe him and you did not obey his voice" (9:23).

On these earlier occasions Moses stood in the gap as mediator between God and the people of Israel. The prayer of Moses in 9:26–29 expresses his theology, namely that the justice of God must be balanced against the mercy of God. It is to God's mercy that he directs his appeal in behalf of the people. At the same time, the prayer expresses boldness in its successful efforts to dissuade God from his wrathful decision, however just it may be.

# "At That Time Yahweh Spoke the Ten Words" (10:1–7)

Unlike its counterpart in the larger structural design of the first part of the Inner Frame (Deut 4–11), this section is a brief transitional bridge to other materials. Its counterpart in the concentric structural pattern of chaps. 4–11 is 4:44–6:3, which contains the Ten Commandments. At the structural center of 10:1–7 stands a specific reference to the "ten words, which Yahweh spoke to you on the mountain, from the midst of the fire on the day of assembly" (v 4). In many respects the unit forms a fitting conclusion to the example of Horeb used in Deut 9, which in that context focused on Israel's rebellion. The opening verses here describe the preparation for and the second giving of the Decalogue to Moses on Mount Sinai/Horeb, followed by the depositing of the stone tablets in the wooden ark (vv 1–5). The section concludes with comments on further travels of the Israelites and the death of Aaron (vv 6–7).

## Bibliography

**Abba, R.** "Priests and Levites in Deuteronomy." *VT* 27 (1977) 257–67 (258–59). **Abramson, S.** "Biblical Explanations Based on Medieval Exegesis." *BMik* 32 (1986/87) 355–57 (Heb.). **Begg, C. T.** "The Tables (Deut x) and the Lawbook (Deut xxxi)." *VT* 33 (1983) 96–97. **Beyerlin, W.** *Origins* (1965). 110, 114. **Brongers, H. A.** "Einige Aspekte der gegenwärtigen Lage der Ladeforschung." *NedTTs* 25 (1971) 6–27. **Bruston, C.** "Le Deutéronome primitif et ce qu'il suppose." *RThQR* 5 (1896) 247–57 (251). **Budde, K.** "Imageless Worship in Antiquity." *ExpTim* 9 (1897/98) 396–99 (398–99). **Cazelles, H.** "Les origines du Décalogue." *EI* 9 (1969) 14–19. **Clements, R. E.** "Deuteronomy and the Jerusalem Cult Tradition." *VT* 15 (1965) 301–3. **Cody, A.** *A History of Old Testament Priesthood.* AnBib 35. Rome: Pontifical Biblical Institute, 1969. 138, n. 27. **Davies, G. I.** "The Significance of Deuteronomy 1:2 for the Location of Mount Horeb." *PEQ* 111 (1979) 87–101 (88). ————. "The Wilderness Itineraries and the Composition of the Pentateuch." *VT* 33 (1983) 1–13 (8). **Dummermuth, F.** "Zut deuteronomischen Kulttheologie." *ZAW* 70 (1958) 59–98 (89). **Dus, J.** "Die Herabfahrung Jahwes auf die Lade und Entziehung der Feuerwolke." *VT* 19 (1969) 290–311. ————. "Zur bewegten Geschichte der israelitischen Lade." *Annali* 41 (1981) 351–83. **Faiman, D.** "The Route of the Exodus." *DD* 14 (1985) 209–19. **Fohrer, G.** "Die alttestamentliche Ladeerzählung." *JNSL* 1 (1971) 21–31. **Fretheim, T. E.** "The Ark in Deuteronomy." *CBQ* 30 (1968) 1–14. **Gutmann, J.** "The History of the Ark." *ZAW* 83 (1971) 22–30. ————. "Deuteronomy: Religious Reformation or Iconoclastic Revolution?" In *Image and the Word.* Ed. J. Gutmann (1977). 5–25. **Haag, H.** "Das 'Buch des Bundes' (Ex 24, 7)." In *FS K. H. Schelkle* (1973). 22–30 (25). **Halévy, J.** "Recherches biblique: le Deutéronome." *RSEHA* 7 (1899) 316, 326–27. **Haran, M.** "The Disappearance of the Ark." *IEJ* 13 (1963) 46–58. **Holstein, J. A.** "Max Weber and Biblical Scholarship." *HUCA* 46 (1975) 159–79 (175). **Hulst, A. R.** *Old Testament Translation Problems.* Leiden: Brill, 1960. 14. **Kumaki, F. K.** "The Deuteronomistic Theology of the Temple—as Crystallized in 2 Sam 7, 1 Kings 8." In AJBI 7 (1981). 16–52. **Lemche, N. P.** "Israel in the Period of the Judges: The Tribal League in Recent Research." *ST* 38 (1984) 1–28. **Lewis, J.** "Ark and the Tent." *RevExp* 74 (1977) 537–48. **Loretz, O.** "Die steinernen Gesetzestafeln in der Lade." *UF* 9 (1977) 159–61. **Manley, G. T.** "A Problem in Deuteronomy." *EvQ* 27 (1955) 201–4. **Nielsen, E.** "Some

Reflections on the History of the Ark." Congress volume 1959. VTSup 7. Leiden: Brill, 1960. 60–74 (61ff) [=*Law, History and Tradition* (1983) 59–70] **Noth, M.** "Der Wallfahrtsweg zum Sinai." *PJ* 36 (1940) 5–28 [=*AbLA* I (1971) 55–74 (67, n. 40)] **Phillips, A.** *Ancient Israel's Criminal Law: A New Approach to the Decalogue.* Oxford: Blackwell, 1970. 6. **Robert, P. de.** "Arche et guerre sainte." *ETR* 56 (1981) 51–53. **Thiel, W.** "Altorientalische und israelitisch-jüdische Religion." In JLH 28 (1984). 166–91 (187). **Valentin, H.** *Aaron* (1978). 41–45. **Vaux, R. de.** "Arche d'alliance et tente de reunion." In *A la rencontre de Dieu: A. Gelin.* Ed. M. Jourjon et al. (1961). 55–70.

### Translation and Prosodic Analysis

10:1–7  [5:(5:4)]  [(4:4):(5:5):(4:4)]  [(4:5):5]

| | | | |
|---|---|---|---|
| 1 | AT THAT TIME / YHWH said to me / "Hew for *yourself* / | 20 | 3 |
| | *Two stone tablets / like the first (ones) /* | 20 | 2_ |
| | *And come up to me \ª on the mountain //* | ⌐12 ¬ | 1 |
| | *and make for yourself \ª a wooden ark //* | 13 ⌐ | 1 |
| 2 | *And I will write / on the tablets / the words (הדברים) /* | └17 | 3_ |
| | *That were / on the first tablets \ª which you broke //* | ⌐26 | 2 |
| | *And you shall put them / in the ark" //* | └16 | 2_ |
| 3 | So I made an ark / of acacia wood / | ⌐13 | 2 |
| | and I hewed / two stone tablets / | └17 | 2_ |
| | Like the first (ones) // and I went up on the mountain / | ⌐17 | 2 |
| | with the two tablets / in my hand // | └14 | 2_ |
| 4 | And he wrote on the tablets / as at the first writing / | ⌐20 | 2 |
| | the /ª TEN WORDS (הדברים) / | └11 | 2 |
| | which YHWH spoke (דבר) to you[b] |[c] | 11 | 1_ |
| | On the mountain / from the midst of the fire / | ⌐11 ¬ | 2 |
| | [d]on the DAY OF ASSEMBLY[d] // | 8 ⌐ | 1 |
| | and YHWH gave them / to me // | └11 | 2_ |
| 5 | And I turned / and I went down \ª from the mountain / | ⌐16 | 2 |
| | and I put / the tablets / | └12 | 2 |
| | into the ark \ᵇ which I had made // | ⌐14 | 1 |
| | and there they are / as he commanded me / (namely) YHWH //[c] | └16 | 3_ |
| **6** | **And the children of Israel / journeyed /** | ⌐15 | 2 |
| | **ªfrom Beeroth Bene-yaakan / to Moserahª //** | └19 | 2_ |
| | **ᵇThere Aaron diedᵇ / and he was buried there /** | ⌐18 | 2 |
| | **and Eleazar his son / ministered as priest / in his stead //** | └16 | 3_ |
| **7** | **From there they journeyedª / to Gudgodah //** | 13 | 2 |
| | **ᵇAnd from Gudgodah to Yotbathahᵇ /** | 13 | 1 |
| | **a land / with brooks of water //[c]** | 9 | 2_ |

### Notes

1.a. See note 1:1.c.
2.a. See note 1:1.c.
4.a. Reading disj *yᵉtib.*

4.b. A few Heb. Mss and SP read עמכם (cf. 5:4 and 9:10).

4.c. Reading a disj accent, perhaps *t*ᵉ*bîr* with 5:4, in place of conj *mêᵉkāʾ* in MT and 9:10.

4.d-d. Omitted in Cairo geniza fragment and LXX (cf. 9:10). Prosodic analysis favors MT.

5.a. Reading a conj accent in place of *paštāʾ* before *zāqēf parvum* to achieve closer rhythmic balance over against v 3.

5.b. See note 1:1.c.

5.c. *BHS* and *BHK* leave extra space here.

6.a-a. SP reads ממסרות ויחנו בבני יעקן with Num 33:31.

6.b-b. Reading וי01מת שם אהרן with SP to achieve closer balance in terms of mora-count.

7.a. SP adds ויחנו. Prosodic analysis supports MT.

7.b-b. SP reads משם נסעו ויחנו ביטבתה.

7.c. There is extra space between vv 7 and 8 in both *BHS* and *BHK.*

## Form/ Structure/ Setting

The boundaries of the rhythmic subunits in 10:1–7 are clearly marked in MT with the *p*ᵉ*tûḥāʾ* paragraph marker between 9:29 and 10:1, the *Numeruswechsel* at the beginning of v 1 and end of v 2, and extra space between both vv 5 and 6 and vv 7 and 8. In terms of the larger structural design of the first half of the Inner Frame (Deut 4–11), this section is set over against 4:44–6:3, which contains the Decalogue. In 10:4, the center of this rhythmic unit, there is explicit reference to the "ten words" (i.e., the Decalogue). The content of 10:1–7 may be outlined as follows:

| | | | |
|---|---|---|---|
| A | Moses is told to prepare new stone tablets and an ark (vv 1–2) | | [5:5:4] |
| | B | Moses prepared the objects and went up the mountain (v 3) | [4:4] |
| | | C   God wrote the "ten words" on the tablets (v 4a) | [5] |
| | | C'   God gave them to Moses on the mountain (v 4b) | [5] |
| | B' | Moses went down and put the tablets in the ark (v 5) | [4:4] |
| A' | The people journeyed on as far as Yotbathah (vv 6–7) | | [4:5:5] |

The concentric rhythmic structural design matches the content as well, except for the "A" subunits. The opening subunit in vv 1–2 contains Yahweh's command to Moses, which in turn is carried out in vv 3–5. The concentric structural design of vv 3–5 is carefully worked out. In v 3 Moses makes an ark, hews out new stone tablets, and ascends the mountain with the two tablets in his hand. In the parallel unit of v 5 Moses descends from the mountain and puts the tablets in the ark. Between this spatial chiasm stands two parallel subunits in which God first writes the "ten words" on the tablets (v 4a) and then gives the tablets to Moses, from out of "the midst of the fire on the day of assembly" (v 4b). The concluding subunit in vv 6–7 moves on to other matters outlining the journey from Beeroth as far as Yotbathah, during which Aaron died and was buried.

It is interesting to note that the ark of the covenant is mentioned four times in Deut 10:1–5, whereas the "two stone tablets" are mentioned seven times in a carefully structured manner, as follows:

| | | | |
|---|---|---|---|
| A | "two stone tablets like the first ones" (10:1) | | |
| | B | "I will write on the tablets the words" (את הדברים) (10:2) | |
| | | C | "on the first tablets which you broke" (10:2) |
| | | | D   "two stone tablets like the first ones" (10:3) |
| | | C' | "on the tablets as at the first writing" (10:4) |
| | B' | "He wrote . . . the ten words" (את עשרת הדברים) (10:4) | |
| A' | "I put the tablets into the ark which I had made" (10:5) | | |

G. Braulik has shown numerous examples of the arranging of key words and concepts in Deuteronomy into groups of seven ("Die Funktion von Siebenergruppierungen im Endtext des Deuteronomiums." In *FS N. Füglister* [1991]. 37–50. That is apparently one of the conventions with which the author of the book is consciously working.

## Comment

**1–2** *At that time*—the temporal marker here refers to the time of Moses' prayer of intercession for the people of Israel (9:25–29). It is clear that the request of Moses was granted, for after the prayer he was instructed to make specific preparations for a renewal of the covenant. The substance of the historical recollection here reflects the content of Exod 34:1–4, with significant changes in matters of detail. On the relationship between vv 1–5 here and the narratives in Exodus, see S. R. Driver, ICC (1895) 117–18. Moses was commanded to *hew . . . two stone tablets, like the first ones* (v 1), which he had shattered (9:17). He was also to make *a wooden ark* to contain the covenant tablets.

**3–5** Moses prepared the stone tablets (v 3), but it was Yahweh who actually wrote the *ten words* upon them (v 4). The ark was constructed from עצי שטים, "acacia wood." According to Num 33:49, the Israelites had pitched camp near Abel-shittim ("meadow/grove of acacia trees"). On the nature of the wood, see G. A. Smith, *Deuteronomy* (1918) 132–33. It is a hard wood which was also used in the carpentry of Egypt; see J. R. Harris, ed., *The Legacy of Egypt*, 2nd ed. (Oxford: Clarendon Press, 1971) 94. Since the ark contained tablets of the covenant, it was parallel in function to the religious shrines of the ancient Near East which housed international treaties (cf. A. Phillips, *Ancient Israel's Criminal Law* [1970] 6).

עשרת הדברים, "the ten words" (v 4), are the Ten Commandments (see the *Comment* on 4:13 and 5:1–22). The phrase עשרת הדברים appears only twice in Deuteronomy, here in v 4 and in 4:13. The giving of the Ten Commandments a second time to Moses involved more than merely making a copy to replace the one that was shattered. The breaking of the tablets symbolized the breaking of the covenant relationship itself, and thus the second writing of the law and the presentation of the tablets to Moses is itself a renewal of the covenant in response to his intercessory prayer. The language used is once again that of theophany: *Yahweh spoke to you on the mountain from the midst of the fire on the day of assembly* (v 4; cf. 4:11–13). Moses then *went down from the mountain* and *put the tablets into the ark*, which he had made (v 5).

**6–7** These verses appear to be an extract from a travel itinerary similar to that in Num 33, as Craigie has noted (NICOT [1976] 200), and are here taken as a continuation of the series of such Travel Notices already observed in the Outer Frame of Deut 1–3 (see 1:6b–8 and *Excursus*: "Travel Notices in the Outer Frame"); hence the boldface type in the translation. *Beeroth Bene-yaakan* is the full form of Bene-ya'akan of Num 33:31. *Moserah* ("chastisement") is given the plural form Moseroth in Num 33:31. *Gudgodah* appears as Hor-haggidgad in Num 33:2. *Yotbathah* is the only term which is identical in both places, which suggests that there is no direct relationship between the two texts in Deuteronomy and Numbers. The actual location of these places is problematic. Beeroth Bene-yaakan and Moserah are not identified with any certainty; the former, however, may be related to the family or tribe of Akan in Gen 36:27. Gudgodah has been located in the vicinity of Wadi Ḥadaḥid by D. Baly, *Geographical Companion to the Bible* (New York: McGraw-Hill, 1963) 174.

*There Aaron died* (v 6)—this reference is to 9:20 and more generally to Aaron's role in the golden calf incident of 9:16–21. At that point, God was angry with Aaron "enough to destroy him" (9:20). Moses' prayer for Aaron was answered, as the reference here indicates. Aaron did not die at Horeb at the time of the incident in question but lived on and died at Moserah, which was presumably in the vicinity of Mount Hor (see Num 20:27–28). In one sense, then, as Craigie has noted, "10:6 is parallel in function to 10:1–5, in that both passages indicate that Moses' intercession, described in chap. 9, was answered by the Lord" (NICOT [1976] 200). The prosodic analysis presented above supports that conclusion.

## Explanation

The renewal of the covenant relationship at Horeb following the incident with the golden calf illustrates the graciousness of God who has made possible the very survival of the people of Israel throughout their long journey in the wilderness. The ark of the covenant is the visible symbol of God's presence, and a constant reminder of the covenant obligations which are based on the contents of the two stone tablets within that container. The death of Aaron sets the stage for the death of his brother Moses as well, and the beginning of a new era in the life of God's chosen people.

# "At That Time Yahweh Set Apart The Tribe of Levi" (10:8–11)

Like its counterpart in 4:41–43 in the overall architectural design of Deut 4–11, this section is a brief transitional unit that sets the stage for the summation of deuteronomic theology in the final section, Deut 10:12–11:25. It is the use of the verb בדל, "to divide, set apart," that ties the two sections together. On the one hand, Moses "set apart [יבדיל] three cities in the vicinity of the Jordan in the east" (4:41); while, on the other, "Yahweh set apart [הבדיל] the tribe of Levi" (10:8). Of the five occurrences of the root בדל in the hiphil in Deuteronomy, four have to do with either the cities of refuge (4:41; 19:2, 7) or the tribe of Levi (10:8).

## Bibliography

**Abba, R.** "Priests and Levites in Deuteronomy." *VT* 27 (1977) 257–67. **Bruston, C.** "Deutéronome primitif et ce qu'il suppose." *RThQR* 5 (1896) 247–57 (252). **Childs, B. S.** "A Study of the Formula 'Until this Day.'" *JBL* 82 (1963) 280. **Dahan, G.** "Les interprétations juives dans les commentaires du pentateuque de Pierre le Chantre." In *FS B. Smalley* (1985). 131–55. **Emerton, J. A.** "Priests and Levites in Deuteronomy." *VT* 12 (1962) 129–38 (132). **Fowler, M. D.** "The Meaning of *lipnê YHWH* in the Old Testament." *ZAW* 99 (1987) 384–90 (389). **Haag, H.** "Das 'Buch des Bundes' (Ex 24,7). "In *FS K. H. Schelkle* (1973). 22–30. **Halévy, J.** "Recherches biblique: le Deutéronome." *RSEHA* 7 (1899) 327–28. **Haran, M.** "Priestertum, Tempeldienst und Gebet." In *Das Land Israel in Biblischer Zeit.* Ed. G. Strecker (1983). 141–53 (142). **Hempel, J.** "Zur Septuaginta-Vorlage im Dt. Eine Entgegnung auf [J. Ziegler,] *ZAW* 1960, 237ff." *ZAW* 73 (1961) 87–96 (95). **Horst, F.** "Zwei Begriffe für Eigentum (Besitz)." In *FS W. Rudolph* (1961) 1315–56 (143). **Kuschke, A.** "Arm und reich im Alten Testament." *ZAW* 57 (1939) 31–57 (42). **Niehaus, J.** *"Pa‘am ʾeḥat* and the Israelite Conquest." *VT* 30 (1980) 236–38. **Sirard, L.** "Sacrifices et Rites sanglants dans l'Ancien Testament." *ScEccl* 15 (1963) 173–97 (183). **Stoebe, H. J.** "Raub und Beute." In *FS W. Baumgartner.* VTSup 16, (1967). 340–54. **Ziegler, J.** "Zur Septuaginta-Vorlage im Deuteronomium." *ZAW* 72 (1960) 237–62 (261).

## Translation and Prosodic Analysis

10:8–11    [5:4:4:5] [(5+4):5:4]

| | | |
|---|---|---|
| 8 At THAT TIME / | 7 | 1 |
| YHWH set apart / the tribe of Levi / | 15 | 2 |
| to carry / the ark of the covenant of YHWH // | 14 | 2_ |
| To stand[a] before YHWH / to minister to him[b] / | 15 | 2 |
| and to bless his name / to THIS DAY // | 15 | 2_ |
| 9 Therefore / there is for Levi / | 14 | 2 |
| no portion or family property / with his brothers // | 12 | 2_ |
| YHWH / he is his family property / | 11 | 2 |
| as [a]YHWH *your God*[a] / *spoke* (דבר) / *to him* // | 15 | 3_ |

<sup>10</sup> *And as for me / I stayed on the mountain / [    ]*<sup>a</sup>          16    2
    *forty days / and forty / nights //*                          16    3
    *And YHWH hearkened / to me / also / on that occasion /*       <u>16</u>    4_
    *YHWH was not willing* \\<sup>b</sup> *to destroy you*<sup>c</sup> *//*    14    1
<sup>11</sup>    *and YHWH said to me /*                           9    1
    *"Arise / go on your journey / before the people*<sup>a</sup> *//*    <u>14</u>    3_
    *(That) they may go in / and (that) they may possess the land /*    19    2
    *Which I swore to their fathers*<sup>b</sup> */ to give to them" //* פ    <u>19</u>    2_

### Notes

8.a. Some Heb. Mss, DSS, SP, Syr, and Vg add *waw*-conj, which is possible in terms of mora-count.
8.b. LXX (except for Lucianic traditon) reads לְשָׁרֵת; cf. 18:5.
9.a.–a. Omitted in one Heb. Ms and LXX (except for Lucianic tradition). Prosodic analysis supports MT.
10.a. Omitting the phrase כימים הראשנים with LXX to achieve closer rhythmic balance in terms of both accentual-stress units and mora-count.
10.b. See note 1:1.c.
10.c. LXX reads 2nd pl suff השחיתכם.
11.a. One Heb. Ms, SP, and LXX add הזה. Prosodic analysis supports MT.
11.b. Some Heb. Mss and SP, read לאבותם; DSS reads לאבותיהמה.

### Form/Structure/Setting

In terms of the larger structural design of the first half of the Inner Frame (Deut 4–11), 10:8–11 is set over against 4:41–43, which is also a brief transitional unit. Both passages begin with the hiph of the root בדל, *divide* or *separate*, which occurs only three times in Deut (4:41; 10:8; 29:20). In 4:41 the term is the impf יבדיל, with Moses as subject, who "set apart three cities," whereas in 10:8 (and 29:20) it is the pf הבדיל, with Yahweh as subject, "who set apart the tribe of Levi." In terms of prosodic structure, 10:8–11 is in two parts, the boundaries of which are clearly marked in MT. The two parts are separated by the occurrence of the *Numeruswechsel* at the end of v 9, and the end of the unit is marked with the *pᵉtûḥâ* paragraph marker after v 11. The internal structure of the unit may be outlined as follows:

| | |
|---|---|
| Yahweh set apart the tribe of Levi to minister to him (v 8) | [5:4] |
| Levi has no family property other than Yahweh (v 9) | [4:5] |
| Yahweh heard my prayer and spared you (v 10) | [4:5] |
| Yahweh recommissioned Moses to lead the people (v 11) | [5:4] |

The concentric rhythmical structure is not carried through in the content of the unit as a whole. There is repetition of the temporal marker "at that time" in vv 8 and 10, of "Levi" at the beginning of both vv 8 and 9, and of the key theological term נחלה, which appears in successive lines within v 9.

### Comment

**8–9** For further discussion of the Levites, see 18:1–8 below. Two functions of the Levites are indicated here: 1) *to carry the ark of the covenant of Yahweh;* and

2) *to stand before Yahweh to minister to him and to bless his name* (v 8). On the *ark of the covenant* as a container for the Ten Commandments, see Deut 10:1–5. Responsibility for the ark clearly meant responsibility for its contents. The Levites were also responsible for formal worship in ancient Israel—namely the offering of sacrifices and all matters pertaining to the sanctuary in which the ark of the covenant was kept. The phrase *to this day* indicates that the ancient duties assigned to the Levites still applied in the present. On v 9 see Deut 18:1–5, "the law of the Levites." The Levites were not assigned a share of the promised land, like the other eleven tribes. Theirs was the noblest inheritance of all, for Yahweh himself is declared to be Levi's *family property* (נחלה). The Levites in ancient Israel lived by participating directly in what was presented to Yahweh. Though they lacked physical security in terms of personal property, they had the privilege and honor of serving Yahweh in behalf of the people as a whole. The final remark that Yahweh *spoke* (דבר) *to him* (i.e., to Levi) is perhaps a subtle reminder that *these words* (הדברים; i.e., the book of Deuteronomy) were "in the hands of the Levites."

**10–11** The concluding part of this transitional section emphasizes the fact that Moses' prayer was answered. The people had not been destroyed, and thus the covenant relationship between God and his people was still intact. Attention then shifts from the past, and Moses' intercession in behalf of the people on Mount Horeb, to the present and the future (v 11). On the phrase *Arise! Go on your journey* . . . (קוּם לך) see the *Comment* under 10:12–13, and the discussion of that phrase in the book of Jonah in particular. The command indicates that God will continue to be with his people. He has not forgotten the ancient covenant promise— namely, *the land which I swore to their fathers to give to them.* God's grace had brought them to the plains of Moab. That grace will see them through to the journey's end, provided the people remain faithful to God's requirements, which will now take center stage in the book of Deuteronomy.

# "And Now, O Israel, What Does Yahweh Ask of You?" (10:12–11:32)

In the larger structural design of the Inner Frame (Deut 4–11), 10:12–11:25 is set over against 4:1–40, which begins with the same phrase "And now, O Israel" (4:1; 10:12). The focus of the earlier section was on Israel as Yahweh's "family property" and the land as Israel's "family property" (נחלה; 4:20–21). The same idea is picked up here, in different language, at the very outset. The command to "fear Yahweh your God" (v 12) is grounded in the fact that he has chosen Israel "above all peoples" (10:15) and that he has already fulfilled the promise to Abraham to make his descendants "as the stars of the heavens for multitude" (10:22). The center of this section focuses on Israel's "family property," the promised land, which was the second aspect of meaning in the term נחלה in the center of chap. 4 (vv 20 and 21).

A 10:12–22 God's requirement of Israel: Fear Yahweh
 B 11:1–9 Love God and remember what he did for you in the wilderness
  C 11:10–12 The promised land—a land which Yahweh cares for
 B' 11:13–21 Love God and serve him with all your heart
A' 11:22–25 If you love God, you will possess the land

### Bibliography for Deut 10:12–11:25

**Begg, C.** "The Tables (Deut. x) and the Lawbook (Deut. xxxi)." *VT* 33 (1983) 96–96. **Boissonard, R.** and **Vouga, F.** "Pour une éthique de la propriété." *BCPE* 32 (1980) 4–47. **Garcia Lopéz, F.** *Un Dios, un pueblo, una tierra, una ley. Análisis de crítica literaria, de la forma y del género, de la composición y redacción de Dt 6, 4–9, 7; 10, 12–11, 25.* Diss., Pontifical Biblical Institute (Rome), 1977. **Horowitz, H. L.** "The Sh³ma." *Judaism* 24 (1975) 476–81. **Lohfink, N.** *Das Hauptgebot* (1963). 219–31. **Shafer, B.** "The Root *bḥr* in Pre-Exilic Concepts of Chosenness in the Hebrew Bible." *ZAW* 89 (1977) 20–42. (26–27).

### Bibliography for Deut 10:12–22

**Alt, A.** "Gedanken über das Königtum Jahwes" (1945). In *KlSchr* (1953). I, 345–57. **Amusin, J. D.** "Die Gerim in der sozialen Legislatur des Alten Testaments." *Klio* 63 (1981) 15–23. **Astour, M.** "Les étrangers a Ugarit et le statut juridique des Habiru." *RA* 53 (1959) 70–76. **Aymard, A.** "Les etrangers dans les cités grecques aux temps classiques." In *L'Etranger, Premiere Partie Recueils de la Societe Jean Bodin.* Brussels, 1958. IX, 119–39. **Bertholet, A.** *Die Stellung der Israeliten und Juden zu den Fremden.* Leipzig, 1896. 173. **Bianchi, E.** "Das Alte Testament und die Nichtgewürdigten der Gesellschafat." *Conc* 15 (1979) 624–29. **Bordreuil, P.** "Textes alphabétiques inédits de Ras Shamra. Nouveaux textes alphabétiques de Ras Ibn Hani." *AAAS* 29/30 (1979/80) 11–15 (11, 13). **Braulik, G.** "Das Deuteronomium und die Geburt des Monotheismus." In *Gott, der Einzige* (1985). 115–59 [=SBAB 2 (1988) 257–300]. **Bückers, H.** *Die biblische Lehre vom Eigentum.* Bonn: Barramäus-vereins, 1947. 23–46. **Cardascia, G.** "Le statut de l'etranger dans la Mesopotamie ancienne." In *L'Étranger Premiere Partie, Recueils de la Societé Jean Bodin.* Brussels, 1958. IX, 105–17. **Cazelles, H.** "Jérémie et le Deutéronome." *RSR* 38 (1951/52) 5–36 (13). **Couroyer, B.** "'Avoir la nuque raide': Ne pas incliner l'oreille." *RB* 88 (1981) 216–25. **Crüsemann, F.** "Fremdenliebe und Identitätssicherung. Zum Verständnis der 'Fremden-Gesetze' im Alten Testament." *WD* N.S. 19 (1987) 11–24. **Dahan, G.** "Les interprétations juives dans les commentaires du pentateuque de Pierre le Chantre." In *FS B. Smalley* (1985). 131–55. **Dahood, M.** *Psalms III.* AB 17A. Garden City: Doubleday, 1970. 142. **Dandamayev, M.** "Aliens and the Community in Babylonia in the 6th–5th Centuries B.C." *RSJB* 41 (1983) 133–45. **Degner, G. W.** "23rd Sunday after Pentecost." *CTQ* 47 (1983) 169–70. **Doron, P.** "Motive Clauses in the Law of Deuteronomy: Their Forms, Functions and Contents." *HAR 2* (1978) 61–77 (63). **Eissfeldt, O.** "Jahwe als König" (1928). In *KlSchr* (1962). I, 172–93. **Fensham, F. C.** "Widow, Orphan and the Poor in Ancient Near Eastern Legal and Wisdom Literature." *JNES* 21 (1962) 129–39. ————. "Notes on Keret in CTA 14:90–103a." *JNSL* 8 (1980) 35–47. **Fichtner, J.** "Der Begriff des 'Nächsten' im Alten Testament mit einem Ausblick auf Spätjudentum und Neues Testament." In *Gottes Weisheit: Gesammelte Studien zum Alten Testament.* Ed. K. D. Fricke. AzTh 2/3. Stuttgart, 1965. 88–114 (102). **Fishbane, M.** "The Biblical ʾôt." *Shnaton* 1 (1975) 213–34; x–xi (Eng. summary). **Fitzmyer, J. A.** "The Aramaic Letter of King Adon to the Egyptian Pharaoh." *Bib* 46 (1965) 41–55 (55). **Foresti, F.** "Composizione e radazione deuteronomistica in Ex 15,1–18." *Lat* 48 (1982) 41–69 (47). **Galling, K.** "Eschmunazar und der Herr der Könige." *ZDPV* 79 (1963) 140–51. **Giesen, G.** *Die Wurzel* שבע (1981). 180–82. **Gowan, D. E.** "Prophets, Deuteronomy and the Syncretistic Cult in Israel." In *Transitions in Biblical Scholarship.* Ed. J. C. Rylaarsdam. Chicago-London, 1968. 93–112. **Greenberg, M.** "Mankind: Israel and the Nations in the Hebraic Heritage." In *No Man is Alien: Essays on the Unity of Mankind.* Ed. R. J. Nelson. Leiden: Brill, 1971. 15–40 (24–26). **Gruber, M. I.** "The Many Faces of Hebrew *nśʾ pnym* 'Lift up the Face.'" *ZAW* 95 (1983) 252–60 (258). **Gunn, B.** "The Religion of the Poor in Ancient Egypt." *JEA* 3 (1916) 81–94. **Halévy, J.** "Recherches biblique: le Deutéronome." *RSEHA* 7 (1899) 316. **Hammond, N. G. L.** "Land Tenure in Attica and Solon's Seisachtheia." *JHS* 81 (1961) 76–98. **Havice, H. K.** "The Concern for the Widow and the Fatherless in the Ancient Near East: A Case Study in Old Testament Ethics." Diss., Yale Univ., 1978. **Helck, W.** "Die Ägypter und die Fremden." *Saeculum* 15 (1964) 103–14. **Heller, J.** "Die Entmythisierung des ugartisichen Pantheons im Alten Testament." *TLZ* 101 (1976) 1–10. **Herrmann, S.** "Grenzen der Toleranz im Alten Testament: Die Bücher Deuteronomium, Jermia und Hiob." In *Glaube und Toleranz.* Ed. T. Rendtorff. Gütersloh, 1982. 180–90 (184–85). **Hoppe, L.** "Deuteronomy and the Poor." *TBT* 24 (1986) 371–75. **Johnson, A. R.** *Sacral Kinship in Ancient Israel.* Cardiff: Univ. of Wales Press, ²1967. 4–11 (משׁפט). **Krapf, T.** "Traditionsgeschichtliches zum deuteronomischen Fremdling-Waise-Witwe-Gebot." *VT* 34 (1984) 87–91. **Lebrun, R.** *Pauvres et démunis dans la sociéte Hittite.* Ed. E. Laroche. Hethitica 4. Leuven: Peeters, 1981. 109–15. **Liagre Böhl, F. M. T. de.** "De Zonnegod als de Beschermer der Nooddruftigen." In *Opera Minora.* Groningen-Djakarta: J. B. Wolters, 1953. 188–206. **Limet, H.** "L'etranger dans la societe sumerienne." In *Bayerische Akademie der Wissenschaften: XVII Rencontre Assyriologique Internationale, München 29. Juni bis 3. Juli 1970.* Ed. D. O. Edzard. Munich: Verlag der Bayerischen Akaemie der Wissenschaften, 1972. 123–38. **Lindsay, L.** "The Babylonian Kings and Edom 605–550 B.C." *PEQ* 108 (1976) 23–39. **Lohfink, N.** *Das Hauptgebot* (1963). 223 (n. 14), 229. **Loretz, O.** "Die prophetische Kritik des Rentenkapitalismus. Grundlagen-Probleme der Prophetenforschung." *UF* 7 (1975) 271–78. ————. "Vom Baal-Epitheton *adn* zu Adonis und Adonaj." *UF* 12 (1980) 287–92. **Meier, W.** " '. . . Fremdlinge, die aus Israel gekommen waren . . . ': Eine Notiz in 2 Chronik 30, 25f. aus der Sicht der Ausgrabungen im jüdischen Viertel der Altstadt von Jerusalem." *BN* 15 (1981) 40–43. **Mettinger, T. N. D.** "Fighting the Powers of Chaos and Hell: Towards the Biblical Portrait of God." *ST* 39 (1985) 21–38 (34). **Miller, P. D.** "Studies in Hebrew Word Patterns." *HTR* 73 (1980) 79–89. ————. "Israel as Host to Strangers." In *Today's Immigrants and Refugees: A Christian Understanding.* Washington: National Conference of Catholic Bishops, 1988. 1–18. **Oden, R. A.** "Baʿal Šāmēm and ʾEl." *CBQ* 39 (1977) 457–73. **Okeke, J.** *The Concept of LB/LBB "Heart" in Jer. 31:33: A Case Study in the Message and Theology of the Jeremiah Tradition, Compared with* *the Occurrences of the Same Word in Deut. 10:12–18.* Diss., Lutheran School of Theology at Chicago, 1983. **Patterson, R. D.** "The Widow, the Orphan, and the Poor in the Old Testament and the Extra-Biblical Literature." *BSac* 130/519 (1973) 223–34. **Pirenne, J.** "Le statut de l'etranger dans l'ancienne Egypte." In *L'Etranger, Premiere Partie Recueils de la Société Jean Bodin.* Brussels, 1958. 93–103. **Pons, J.** "La référence au séjour en Egypte et à la sortie d'Egypte dans les codes de loi de l'Ancien Testament." *ETR* 63 (1988) 169–82. **Rose, M.** *Der Ausschliesslichkeitsanspruch Jahwes* (1975). **Rücker, H.** "Warum wird ᵓāhāb (lieben) im Alten Testament selten zur Bezeichnung für die Nächstenliebe gebraucht?" In *Dein Wort Beachten: Alttestamentliche Aufsätze.* Ed. J. Reindl and G. Hentschel. Leipzig: St. Benno-Verlag, 1981. 9–15 (13). **Ruppert, L.** "Der Umgang mit den Volksangehörigen und mit den Fremden im alttestamentlichen Gottesvolk." In *Und wer ist mein Nächster? Reflektionen über Nächsten-, Bruder- und Feindesliebe.* Ed. J. Horstmann. Dokumentationen 5. Schwerte: Katholische Akademie, 1982. 1–36. **Sanmartín, J.** "Semantisches über UG.ADN." *UF* 9 (1977) 269–72. **Scaria, K. J.** "Social Justice in the Old Testament." *Biblebhashyam* 4 (1978) 163–92 (176–78). **Schäfer, G.** *"'König der Könige—Lied der Lieder.'" Studien zum paronomastischen Intensitätsgenitiv.* Abh. d. Heidelberger Akad. d. Wissenschaften—Philosophisch-historische Klasse 1972. w.Abh.; Heidelberg, 1974. **Schmidt, K. L.** "Israels Stellung zu den Fremdlingen und Beisassen und Israels Wissen um seine Fremdling- und Beisassenschaft." *Jud* 1 (1945) 269–96. **Schmidt, W.** *Königtum Gottes in Ugarit und Israel: Zur Herkunft der Königsprädikation Jahwes.* BZAW 80. Berlin, 1961. **Schultz, S.J.** *Deuteronomy: The Gospel of Love.* Chicago: Moody, 1971. **Spina, F. A.** *The Concept of Social Rage in the Old Testament and the Ancient Near East.* Diss., Univ. of Michigan, 1977. 190–225. **Stadelman, L. I. J.** *The Hebrew Conception of the World.* AnBib 39. Rome, 1970. **Stamm, J. J.** "Fremde, Flüchtlinge und ihr Schutz im Alten Israel und in seiner Umwelt." In *Der Flüchtling in der Weltgeschichte.* Ed. A. Mercier. Bern/Frankfurt: Lang, 1974. 31–66. **Szlechter, E.** "Le statut juridique de la veuve dans la mésopotamie ancienne." In *Deutscher Orientalistentag vom a. bis 5. Oktober 1972 in Lübeck, Vorträge.* Ed. B. Voigt. ZDMG Supplementa 2. Wiesbaden: Steiner, 1974. 45–61. **Tillesse, G. M. de.** "Sections 'Tu' et Sections 'Vous' dans le Deutéronome." *VT* 12 (1962) 29–87 (37). **Toombs, L. E.** "Love and Justice in Deuteronomy." *Int* 19 (1965) 399–411. **Wanke, G.** "Zu Grundlagen und Absicht prophetischer Sozialkritik." KD 18 (1972) 2–17. **Weiler, I.** "Zum Schicksal der Witwen und Waisen bei den Völkern der Alten Welt." *Saeculum* 31 (1981) 157–93. **Weinfeld, M.** "Jeremiah and the Spritual Metamorphosis of Israel." *ZAW* 88 (1976) 17–56. ——————. "Social and Cultic Institutions in the Priestly Source against Their Ancient Near Eastern Background." *Proceedings of the Eighth World Congress of Jewish Studies: Bible Studies and Hebrew Language.* Jerusalem: World Union of Jewish Studies, 1982. 95–129 (n. 80).

### Translation and Prosodic Analysis

10:12–22   [(5:4):(5:6)] [(6:8):6] [6:8:6] [(6:5):(4:5)]

| | | |
|---|---|---|
| [12] **And now / O Israel /** | 9 | 2 |
| *what does / YHWH your God / ask* \ᵃ *of you? //* | 19 | 3 |
| *But to fear / YHWH your God /* | 16 | 2 |
| *<and>*ᵇ *to walk* \ᶜ *in all his ways /* | 12 | 2_ |
| *And to love him / and to serve / YHWH your God /* | 24 | 3 |
| *with all your heart / and with all your soul-life //* | 14 | 2_ |
| [13] *<Yea>*ᵃ *to keep / the commandments of YHWH* ᵇ / *and his statutes /* | 18 | 3 |
| *Which / I command you* \ᶜ *TODAY //* | 15 | 2 |
| *that it might be well* \ᵈ *with you //* | 5 | 1_ |

| | | |
|---|---|---|
| ¹⁴ *Behold / to YHWH your God / belong the heavens /* | ⌐16 | 3 |
| *And the heaven of heavens //* | ⌐10 ⌐ | 1 |
| *the earth / and all that is in it //* | ∟11 ⌡ | 2_ |
| ¹⁵ *Yet*ᵃ *upon your fathers / YHWH set his heart /* | 13 | 2 |
| *To love them //* | ⌐ 9 ⌐ | 1 |
| *and he chose / their descendants after them /* | 12 ⌡ | 2 |
| *(Namely) you / above all peoples / as* AT THIS DAY *//* | ∟<u>15</u> | 3_ |
| ¹⁶ So circumcise / the / foreskinᵃ of your hearts // | 12 | 3 |
| And your necks / stiffen / no longer / | <u>11</u> | 3_ |
| | | |
| ¹⁷ For / YHWH your God / he / is God of gods / | 25 | 4 |
| And Lordᵃ \ᵇ of lords // | ⌐11 | 1 |
| he is the great God <and>ᶜ the mighty One / | ∟<u>14</u> | 1_ |
| The terrible One / who / is not partial / | 17 | 3 |
| and who takes / no bribe // | 8 | 2 |
| ¹⁸ He does / justice for the fatherless / and the widow // | <u>16</u> | 3_ |
| And he loves the sojourner / giving him \ᵃ food and clothing // | 18 | 3 |
| ¹⁹ so love the sojourner // | 8 | 1 |
| For you were sojourners / in the land of Egypt // | <u>17</u> | 2_ |
| | | |
| ²⁰ YHWH *your God / you shall fear / him*ᵃ *you shall serve //* | ⌐21 | 3 |
| *and to him you shall cleave*ᵇ */* | ⌐ 7 ⌐ | 1 |
| *and by his name / you shall swear //* | ∟11 ⌡ | 2_ |
| ²¹ *He is your praise /* | 8 | 1 |
| *and he is your God // who has done for you /* | ⌐17 | 2 |
| *these*ᵃ */ great and terrible (deeds) /* | ∟<u>21</u> | 2_ |
| *Which* ᵇ*your eyes* \ᶜ *have seen*ᵇ *//* | ⌐10 | 1 |
| ²² *with seventy persons / your fathers went down / to Egypt //* | ∟20 | 3 |
| AND NOW/ *YHWH your God / has made you /* | ⌐15 | 3 |
| *as the stars of the heavens / for multitude //* | ∟<u>15</u> | 2_ |

## Notes

12.a. See note 1:1.c.

12.b. Adding *waw*-conj with 2 Heb. Mss, LXX, Syr, and Vg; cf. 11:22; 19:9; 30:16.

12.c. Replacing conj *mahpāk* with disj *ṭiphā'* to achieve rhythmic balance over against vv 21–22. Prosodic analysis suggests that the *'atnāḥ* or *sillûq* should be relocated to the term דרכיו, which requires a *ṭiphā'* before it.

13.a. Adding *waw*-conj with SP, Syr, and Vg.

13.b. DSS, SP, LXX, and Syr add אלהיך. Prosodic analysis supports MT.

13.c. See 1:1.c.

13.d. The *ṭiphā'* is relocated to replace *'atnāḥ* under היום; see note 12.c. above.

15.a. DSS reads על כן.

16.a. Craigie reads pl. here with DSS. Prosodic analysis supports MT.

17.a. Reading ואדון with SP and Syr to achieve closer balance in terms of mora-count.

17.b. See note 1:1.c.

17.c. Adding *waw*-conj with one Heb. Ms, DSS, SP, LXX, Syr, and Vg.

18.a. See 1:1.c.

20.a. A number of Heb. Mss, DSS, LXX, Syr, and Vg add *waw*-conj; cf. 6:13. Prosodic analysis favors MT.

20.b. DSS reads תקרב.

21.a. הָאֵלֶּה is omitted in DSS and Syr. Prosodic analysis supports MT.
21.b-b. DSS reads בעיניכם.
21.c. See note 1-1.c.

## Form/Structure/Setting

In terms of rhetorical markers, 10:12–22 is divided in MT into three parts, the boundaries of which are marked by the *petûḥāʾ* paragraph marker before v 12, the chapter division after v 22, and the *Numeruswechsel* in vv 15, 17, and 20. The repetition of the temporal marker ועתה in vv 12 and 22 serves as an envelope around the passage as a whole. This term appears only six times in Deuteronomy, two of which are in this passage (see *Comment* at 4:1; cf. 5:25; 26:10; 31:19). Careful prosodic analysis reveals a further boundary between vv 13 and 14. The resultant structure may be outlined as follows:

| | | | |
|---|---|---|---|
| A | The "Great Commandment"—fear YHWH your God (vv 12–13) | | [5:4:5:6] |
| | B | YHWH owns all but he has chosen you (vv 14–16) | [6:8:6] |
| | B' | YHWH is "God of gods" but he loves the sojourner (vv 17–19) | [6:8:6] |
| A' | Fear YHWH for he is your God (vv 20–22) | | [6:5:4:5] |

The concentric design of the rhythmic structure carries over in terms of content and the repetition of specific words. Besides the repetition of ועתה as a structural frame at the beginning of "A" (vv 12–13) and the end of "A' " (vv 20–22), both units specifically command the people "to fear Yahweh your God" and "to serve" him (vv 12, 20). The "B" sections are also parallel in their description of "Yahweh your God" as unique in power and position, who also loves his chosen people. The final section (vv 20–22) contains repetitions of words from sections "B" and "B' " as well, in its reference to "your fathers" (vv 15 and 22) and the terms הגדול and הנורא in relation to God (v 17) and his deeds (v 21).

## Comment

**12–13** The opening words of v 12 are among the most familiar in the Hebrew Bible, partly because of their use in Mic 6:8—"what does Yahweh require of you but to do justice, and to love kindness, and to walk humbly with your God?"

ליראה את־יהוה, "to fear Yahweh"—see *Comment* at 6:2 for further literature. The "fear of the Lord" is a dominant theme in the so-called wisdom literature, particularly the book of Proverbs (cf. Prov 1:7—"The fear of the Lord is the beginning of knowledge"). Careful prosodic analysis suggests that the term is in fact defined here, by means of poetic parallelism: *to fear Yahweh* is *to walk in all his ways*. This phrase is in turn explained by the following rhythmic unit: *to fear God* is *to love him and to serve Yahweh your God with all your heart and with all your soul-life*, in short, with your whole being (v 12).

The requirements of God, as expressed here, are reminiscent of language from Near Eastern political treaties, as Weinfeld has noted (*Deuteronomy and the Deuteronomic School* [1972] 83–84). At the same time, as Craigie has shown, "The requirements may be seen as a positive sermon on the negatively stated first commandment: 'You shall not have other gods besides me'" (NICOT [1976] 204). The requirements summarized in 10:12–13 spell out the positive nature of total commitment to the one God. Another way of exploring the profundity of this passage is to see it as a sermon on the "Great Commandment" (Deut 6:5), as Craigie has also suggested *(ibid.)*. In terms of the prosodic analysis presented here, the command *to love him* stands at the very center of the rhythmnic unit. It is also the central one among the five vocatives used in 10:12–13—*to fear, to walk, to love, to serve,* and *to keep.*

**14–15**   Craigie has noted the "poetic character" of these verses and has drawn attention to a cogent parallel passage in Ps 8:3–4, where God as creator and owner of the entire cosmos nonetheless has *set his heart upon your fathers to love them.* Similar language about *the heavens and the heaven of heavens* is employed in Solomon's dedicatory prayer for the temple at Jerusalem in 1 Kgs 8:27, where the transcendence of God is emphasized. God is contained neither within the physical world nor even within the cosmic heaven of Near Eastern mythology. Against the background of God's universal sovereignty over heaven and earth stands the election of his people: *He chose their descendants after them, namely you above all peoples* (v 15). Events of the distant past are linked to the present moment on the plains of Moab *(as at this day).* It is on the basis of God's prior covenant love that Moses commands the love of God on the part of the people (v 12).

**16**   God's covenant with the patriarchs of old was marked by the sign of the covenant, namely circumcision (cf. Gen 17:9–12). It is not the outward physical sign of the covenant that is important in the matter of covenant renewal, however, but the inner attitude of the heart. To love God requires a proper attitude, which involves decision and specific action—like circumcision. To circumcise the heart is to take an attitude toward God which is the opposite of being stiff-necked or stubborn. On the theme of Israel's stubbornness, see also Deut 9. The prophet Jeremiah makes metaphorical use of circumcision in a similar manner in Jer 4:4, which is but one of a number of such metaphors he employed to emphasize his message.

**17–19**   This hymnlike passage stresses God's transcendent greatness (v 17), and his impartial character, particularly as extended to the powerless (v 18). On the phrases *God of gods and Lord of lords* as superlative constructions, see GKC § 133i (and n. 2, p. 431). The meaning implies the kingship of God in an absolute sense. The statement here may well be the ultimate source of the phrase "Lord of lords and King of kings" in Rev 17:14, as Craigie has noted (NICOT [1976] 205, n. 7). The "Kingship of God" expressed here is cosmic and universal in nature, as opposed to the historically specific implications of the parallel passage in Exod 15:18. The awesome transcendent God, whose nature is beyond comprehension, has revealed himself as *the great God and the mighty One, the terrible One who is not partial.* On the term הַגִּבֹּר, "the mighty One," see also Exod 15:3 where both SP and Syr present Yahweh as a warrior or "mighty man"—a "man of war" (in MT).

The God of the Exodus from Egypt *is not partial and . . . takes no bribe* (v 17). In Deut 1:17 human judges were to possess this same quality. The same theme is taken up in the NT by Peter (Acts 10:34) and Paul (Gal 2:6). God requires wholehearted commitment of his human followers, from which all proper behavior stems. God sees what is in the heart, and he cannot be persuaded or bribed into reducing his requirements in any way. God's impartiality is illustrated in terms of his *justice for the fatherless and the widow* and the fact that *he loves the sojourner giving him food and clothing* (v 18). In short, God is particularly concerned for those whose social and economic status make them most vulnerable in human affairs. On *the sojourner,* or "resident alien," see the *Comment* on Deut 1:16. More detailed legislation concerning orphans, widows, and sojourners is found in Deut 24:17–22. Here the people are reminded of the fact that they *were sojourners in the land of Egypt* as "resident aliens" (v 19). Having been recipients of God's merciful love and care as aliens in Egypt, they are to express similar love and concern for aliens in their midst as well.

**20–22**    The concluding strophe of 10:12–22 repeats the theme of the opening strophe in vv 12–13—the command *to fear Yahweh your God.* The use of the verb דבק, employed here to describe the desired relationship of the people to their God, is used elsewhere of the relationship between a man and his wife (see Gen 2:24).

G. A. Smith has noted that the meaning of the words *He is your praise* (v 21) may either be that God is the object of Israel's praise (cf. Ps 109:1) or that God's deeds for his people are the basis on which others praise Israel (*Deuteronomy* [1918] 142–43). The worship of God is an essential part of the basic requirements of God's people, as stated above in 10:12–13, for in worship the people give an outward expression of their relationship of love to God.

On the descent of *seventy persons* into Egypt, who subsequently become as numerous *as the stars of the heavens for multitude,* see Gen 46:27, Exod 1:5, and Deut 1:10 (and 26:5). Though much of the ancient covenant promise to the fathers was now fulfilled, a vital aspect yet remained: namely, the gift of the land (Gen 17:8). The people are reminded of God's basic requirements of them so that they may live to experience fulfillment of all of God's promise to them through their fathers.

## *Explanation*

Deut 10:12–22 begins and ends with the command *to fear Yahweh your God* (vv 12 and 20). What does this mean? To most people today fear is not a positive emotion. Nonetheless, a little work with a concordance quickly reveals that fear is often presented within the Bible in a positive light, at least in relation to God. "The fear of Yahweh is the beginning of wisdom" (Prov 1:7, 9:10). "The fear of Yahweh leads to life; and the one who has it rests satisfied; and will not be visited by harm" (Prov 19:23).

The issue is actually not as complex as it first appears. The nature of fear is dependent on the object of that fear. When we fear someone, or something, which we know is evil and powerful, and perhaps "out to get us," then our reaction is all too familiar. It either causes us to tense up, perhaps even paralyzing us, or it causes the adrenaline to flow such that we are sometimes capable of remarkable feats of strength for mere survival. But what happens when you fear someone whom you know has your best interests at heart? When you fear someone who loves you, such as God himself, that very fear somehow becomes altogether different. It becomes reverence, a feeling of awe in the presence of divine love and power. It makes us want to surrender our will to God's will—"to walk in all his ways and to love him and to serve Yahweh your God with all your heart and with all your soul-life" (Deut 10:12). This kind of "fear" casts out fear of the negative kind.

An interesting commentary on the meaning of the phrase "to fear Yahweh" is found in the book of Jonah where the reluctant prophet insists that he is a Hebrew and that he "fear[s] Yahweh, the God of heaven, who made the sea and the dry land" (Jonah 1:9). A close look at Jonah's actions in the story will show what it means to "fear God"—it is exactly the opposite of everything Jonah did! Jonah fled "from the presence of Yahweh" (Jonah 1:3), whereas, "to fear Yahweh" is "to walk in his ways" (Deut 10:12). Jonah eventually obeyed Yahweh and went to Nineveh, but it was anything but an instance of a person serving Yahweh with all their heart and soul-life. It is interesting to note that Deut 10:11 contains the phrase קוּם לֵךְ, "arise, go (on your journey)." That phrase appears only eight other times in the entire Hebrew Bible, two of which are in the book of Jonah, where it is the opening words of God's call to the prophet to serve him in Nineveh (Jonah 1:2; 3:2). It would appear, that among other things, the book of Jonah is a "midrash" of sorts on Deut 10:11-12. Jonah is a curious reversal of the figure of Moses. Both "prophets" (cf. Deut 18:18; 34:10-12) receive the same call: "Arise and go on your journey [לֵךְ קוּם] before the people" (Deut 10:11). Jonah's actions are a parody, of sorts, on the meaning of the command "to fear Yahweh your God," which, in essence, is summarized in the familiar words of v 13—namely, "to keep the commandments of Yahweh and his statutes which I command you today."

As the people of Israel prepare to enter the promised land, Moses gives them two explicit instructions: they are to "circumcise the foreskin of [their] hearts" (10:16) and they are to "love the sojourner" (10:19). These two commands point to the primary responsibilities: complete love for God and love for one's neighbor. Together these two responsibilities constitute the essence of what God requires of us, as Jesus saw so clearly in his response to the Pharisee who asked him "which is the great commandment in the law?" (Matt 22:36). Jesus quoted the "Great Commandment" in Deut 6:5 as "the great and first commandment" and then added a second commandment: "You shall love your neighbor as yourself" (Matt 22:38-39). The people of Israel were to love others because God has loved them. The vertical relationship toward God is a prerequisite for the horizontal involvement with other human beings. God loves the stranger, the widow, and the orphan, and, therefore, his people, if they truly love God, must also be concerned for justice and righteousness in relation to their neighbors. In short, God's people are to be known for their concern for those whose social and economic position expose them to exploitation and oppression. This is the "humanism" which is so characteristic of the book of Deuteronomy. What Moses legislated for the people of Israel is not legalism, or ritual, or external minutiae of religious observance, or even a creed. What Moses emphasized was simply a vital relationship with God which is worked out in terms of specific responsibilities toward our neighbors.

### Bibliography for Deut 11:1-9

**Ahuis, F.** *Autorität im Umbruch: Ein formgeschtlicher Beitrag zur Klärung der literaischen Schichtung und der zeitgeschichtlichen Bezüge von Num 16 und 17.* CThM A,13. Stuttgart: Calwer Verlag, 1983. 57. **Avishur, Y.** "Expressions of the Type *byn ydym* in the Bible and Semitic Languages." *UF* 12 (1980) 125–33. **Bowman, J.** "The Exegesis of the Pentateuch among the Samaritans and among the Rabbis." *OTS* 8 (1950). 220–62 (250–51). **Carroll, R. P.** "Rebellion and Dissent in Ancient Israelite Society." *ZAW* 89 (1977) 176–204. **Childs, B. S.** "Deuteronomic Formulae of the Exodus Traditions." In *FS W. Baumgartner.* VTSup 16. Leiden: Brill, 1967. 30–39 (35–36). **Foresti, F.** "Composizione e radazione deuteronomistica in Ex 15, 1–18." *Lat* 48 (1982) 41–69 (65). **Fritz, V.** *Israel in der Wüste. Traditionsgeschichtliche Untersuchung der Wüstenüberlieferung des Jahwisten.* MThSt 7. Marburg, 1970. **Giesen, G.** *Die Wurzel* שבע (1981). 281–82. **Halévy, J.** "Recherches biblique: le Deutéronome." *RSEHA* 7 (1899) 328–29. **Jenni, E.** "Faktitiv und Kausativ von ʿbd 'zurgrunde gehen'." In *FS W. Baumgartner* (1967). 143–57. **Liver, J.** "Korah, Dathan and Abiram." ScrHier 8. Jerusalem: Magnes Press, 1961. 189–217. **Milgrom, J.** "Korah's Rebellion: A Study in Redaction." In *FS H. Cazelles* (1981; Paris). 135–46. **Sanmartín Ascaso, J.** *Las Guerras de Josué: Estudio de Semiótica Narrativa.* Institución San Jerónimo 14. Valencia, 1982. 57. **Scharbert, J.** "Das 'Schilfwunder' in den Texten des Alten Testaments." In *FS H. Cazelles.* AOAT 212 (1981). 395–417. **Seitz, G.** *Studien zum Deuteronomium* (1971). 85. **Vorländer, H.** *Die Entstehungszeit des jehowistischen Geshcichtswerkes.* Frankfurt: P. Lang, 1978. **Weiss, R.** "La Main du Seigneur sera contre vous et contre vos Pères." *RB* 83 (1976) 51–54. Zenger, E. "Tradition und Interpretation in Exodus xv 1–21." Congress volume 1980. Ed. J. A. Emerton. VTSup 32. Leiden: Brill, 1981. 452–83 (466).

## Translation and Prosodic Analysis

11:1–9   [6:5] [6:5:(4+5)] [(4:4):(4+5):5:] [6:(5:6)]

| | | |
|---|---:|---:|
| 1  So love / YHWH your God // and keep his charge / | 26 | 3 |
| And[a] his statutes and his ordinances / | ⌐ 13 | 1 |
| and his commandments / ALWAYS // | ∟ 13 | 2_ |
| | | |
| 2  And you shall know / TODAY / | ⌐ 7 | 2 |
| that / (it is) not with your children / who have not known / | ∟ 18 | 3_ |
| And who have not seen / the discipline \[a] of YHWH your God // | ⌐ 22 | 2 |
| his greatness / | ∟ 4 | 1 |
| <And>[b] his mighty hand / and[c] his outstretched / arm // | 25 | 3_ |
| 3  And[a] his signs / and his deeds / | 14 | 2 |
| which he did in the midst of Egypt // | 13 | 1 |
| To Pharaoh [b]king of Egypt[b] / and to all his land // | 15 | 2_ |
| 4  And what he did to the army of Egypt / | ⌐ 13 | 1 |
| to their horses and chariots / when he made (it) surge / | ∟ 16 | 2 |
| the waters of Yam Suf / | 6 | 1_ |
| (Flooding) over them / as they pursued \[a] after you[b] // | ⌐ 15 | 2 |
| and (how) YHWH destroyed them / to / THIS DAY // | ∟ 15 | 3_ |
| | | |
| 5  And what he did / | ⌐ 7 | 1 |
| to you \[a] in the wilderness // | 7 | 1 |
| until you came / to this place / | ∟ 3 | 2 |
| 6  And what he did / | 7 | 1 |
| to Dathan and Abiram / the sons of Eliab / son of Reuben / | 26 | 3_ |
| When the earth opened / its mouth / | ⌐ 16 | 2 |
| and it swallowed them[a] \|[b] and their houses / | ∟ 13 | 2 |
| And their tents // and every living thing / | ⌐ 14 | 2 |
| that followed after them / in the midst / of all[c] Israel // | ∟ 16 | 3_ |
| 7  For your eyes / have seen / | 13 | 2 |
| All the great / work of YHWH // | 14 | 2 |
| which he did[a] //[b] | 6 | 1_ |

8 So you shall keep / all [ ]ᵃ that / *I command you*ᵇ / *TODAY* //        21    3
  That you may be strong / and go in / and possess the land /              22    3_
  Which you / are crossingᶜ there / to possess it //                    ⌐ 17    3
9 And that you may ᵃextend (your) daysᵃ / on the ground /             └  22    2_
  Which YHWH swore to your fathers / to give to themᵇ /              ⌐ 21    2
  and to their descendantsᵇ //                                           5    1
  a land / flowing with milk / and honey // ס                      └ <u>14</u>    3_

## Notes

1.a. The *waw*-conj is omitted in one Heb. Ms and SP (cf. Jos 22:3). Prosodic analysis favors MT.

2.a. See note 1:1.c.

2.b. Adding *waw*-conj with a number of Heb. Mss, DSS, Cairo Geniza fragments, SP, LXX, Syr, TgJ, and Vg.

2.c. SP reads וזרעו זאת, which is possible from a prosodic perspective.

3.a. A few Heb. Mss, DSS, SP, and Vg omit *waw*-conj. Prosodic analysis favors MT.

3.b-b. The phrase is omitted in SP and some LXX witnesses.

4.a. See note 1:1.c.

4.b. A number of Mss in both Heb. and Tg read 3rd pl suffix.

5.a. See note 1:1.c.

6.a. SP adds לקרח אשר האדם כל ואת. Prosodic analysis supports MT.

6.b. Replacing *mêrᵉkā'* with disj *ṭiphā'* since the *'atnāḥ* appears to be misplaced in MT.

6.c. כל is omitted in one Heb. Ms, Vg, and one LXX witness.

7.a. LXX adds (ἐν) ὑμῖν (ἡμῖν) σήμερον. Prosodic analysis supports MT.

7.b. *BHS* and *BHK* insert extra space here. Prosodic analysis supports the presence of a strophic boundary here.

8.a. Omitting המצוה with one Heb. Ms.

8.b. One Heb. Ms, DSS, SP, Syr, TgJ, Vg, and some LXX witnesses read 2nd pl suff here. The change to 2nd sg in MT may mark the strophic boundary (see *Excursus* on the *Numeruswechsel* above).

8.c. DSS, SP, and Vg read באים. Prosodic analysis favors MT.

9.a-a. DSS reads ירבו ימיכם, which is possible from a prosodic perspective.

9.b. SP has a shorter text, reading לזרעם for ולזרעם להם of MT.

## Form/Structure/Setting

The boundaries of the four strophic units in this section are clearly marked, with the *Numeruswechsel* in vv 2 and 8 and the use of the temporal markers כל־הימים at the end of v 1 and (הזה) היום at the beginning of v 2 and the end of v 4. The opening verse serves as a summary statement of the previous section (10:12–22) in that the people are commanded to "love Yahweh your God" by keeping "his statutes and his ordinances and his commandments always." The strophic unit in vv 2–4 continues with a reminder of Yahweh's redemptive act in delivering them from Egypt, which is framed by repetition of היום. That was Yahweh's "Holy War" within history (see *Excursus* on "Holy War as Celebrated Event").

The second strophic unit (vv 5–7) is framed by repetition of the phrase אשר עשה, a phrase which also appears in vv 3 and 4 of the opening strophe and is repeated at the beginning of v 6 as well. Yahweh's actions were directed against Pharaoh and his army, on the one hand (vv 3–4), and against enemies from within the ranks of the people of Israel themselves in the wilderness—namely Dathan and Abiram (vv 5–6). The concluding verse of the second strophe makes summary reference to "all the great work [מעשה] of Yahweh which he did [עשה]."

The beginning of the third strophic unit is marked by the *Numeruswechsel* in v 8 and the *sᵉtûmā'* paragraph marker at the end of v 9. The opening reference here to "all the commandment that I command you" looks back to 11:1 and the summary of the Great Commandment to "love Yahweh your God" (cf. Deut 6:4–9). Continued blessing in the promised land is dependent on the faithfulness of the people in keeping God's commandments.

## Comment

**1** Though the commandment to *keep his charge* (מִשְׁמַרְתּוֹ) looks back to both 10:12 and 6:5, the word מִשְׁמַרְתּוֹ itself appears only here in Deuteronomy (see Driver, ICC [1895] 127) and functions as a summary term for the laws contained within the book. Those laws pertain to all time: כָּל־הַיָּמִים.

**2–4** The Exodus events are presented as *the discipline of Yahweh your God*, which consists of Yahweh's *greatness, his mighty hand and his outstretched arm, and his signs and his deeds* (see also 4:34). In short, the discipline of God consists of religious education, in which God taught his people through gracious acts in their behalf and by acts of judgment. For further uses of the verb יסר, "to discipline," see Deut 4:36; 8:5; 21:18; and 22:18. The language of vv 3b–4 is similar to that of the "Song of the Sea" in Exod 15:1–6. The events of that great deliverance are here attributed to God directly in the manner of "Holy War," and not to the military strength or expertise of the Israelites. It should be noted that the term רכב in v 4 means "chariot" and not "rider." Cavalry was not employed in Egypt until a later date (see W. F. Albright, *Archaeology and the Religion of Israel* [²1946], 213, n. 25).

**5–7** The Exodus from Egypt, as the first of the lessons from history, was a positive experience in Israel's education. The lessons in the wilderness broadened their education (cf. 8:2–15), for there they experienced chastisement and rebuke as well as miraculous provisions. For a more detailed account of the affair with *Dathan and Abiram . . . when the earth opened its mouth and it swallowed them and their houses and their tents* (v 6) see Num 16. The Exodus was the beginning of new life for the people of Israel, but the rebellion in the wilderness led to the death of many of them and almost to the destruction of the entire community (see Num 16:45). The lessons of the past *which your eyes have seen* (v 7) stress both the grace and judgment of God. The people are to remember *all the great work of Yahweh which he did.*

**8–9** In a refrain which opens each subunit in chap. 11 the people are urged once again to keep all of God's commandments, but now the focus shifts from the lessons of past history to anticipation of the future in the promised land. That future blessing is dependent on their continued faithfulness to God's commandments.

## Explanation

The discipline of God is to be understood pedagogically. God teaches by both gracious acts done in our behalf and through acts of judgment. Positive examples of God's discipline of his people Israel include the events of the Exodus from Egypt, namely what God did in their behalf "to pharaoh king of Egypt and to all his land and what he did to the army of Egypt" (11:3–4). Negative examples include the destruction of Dathan and Abiram from the midst of Israel in the wilderness trek toward the promised land (11:5–6). In his address Moses makes the common experience of the past a present reality for his hearers: "it is not with your children who have not known and have not seen" these things (11:2). The divine education which they had received since the departure from Egypt up to the present was by way of preparation for the events still lying ahead of them. The younger people who had not actually experienced the events in question are to know them as well and to learn from "the discipline of Yahweh your God" (11:2).

### Bibliography for Deut 11:10–12

**Brentjes, R.** "Studien zum Bewässerungsackerbau des Vorderen Orients." *Altorientalische Forschungen* 1 (1974) 43–54. **Carmichael, C. M.** "A Common Element in Five Supposedly Disparate Laws." *VT* 29 (1979) 129–42 (128). **Englert, D. M. C.** "Bowdlerizing in the Old Testament." In *FS J. M. Myers* (1974). 141–43. **Eslinger, L.** "Watering Egypt (Deuteronomy xi 10–11)." *VT* 37 (1987) 85–90. **Gilead, C.** "The Vegetable Garden in the Bible." *BMik* 32 (1986/87) 121–23 (Heb.). **Gottfriedsen, C.** *Die Fruchtbarkeit von Israels Land.* Europäische Hochschulschriften 23. Frankfurt: Peter Lang, 1985. **Gross, W.** "Das nicht substantivierte Partizip als Prädikat im Relativsatz hebräischer Prosa." *JNSL* 4 (1974) 23–47 (41). **Hammer, R.** "Section 38 of Sifre Deuteronomy: An Example of the Use of Independent Sources to Create a Literary Unit." *HUCA* 50 (1979) 165–78. *HOTTP* I, 279. **Lohfink, N.** *Höre Israel! Auslegung von Texten aus dem Buch Deuteronomium.* Welt der Bibel 18. Düsseldorf, 1965. 51–52. **Naville, E.** "Deuteronomy 11:10." *JRAS* (1926) 306–8. **Nicol, G. G.** "Watering Egypt (Deuteronomy xi 10–11) Again." *VT* 38 (1988) 347–48. **Vischer, W.** "Foi et technique (Méditation biblìque sur Dt 11, 10–15." *RHPR* 44 (1964) 102–9.

### Translation and Prosodic Analysis

11:10–12    [(4:4):(4:4)] [4:3:3:4]

| | | |
|---|---:|---:|
| ¹⁰ For the land / which *you*ᵃ /ᵇ *are entering there* / *to possess it* / | 21 | 4 |
| *It is* / *not like the land of Egypt* / | 10 | 2 |
| ᶜ*from which* / you have gone out ᶜ // | 11 | 2_ |
| Where you sowed / your seed / | 8 | 2 |
| and *you watered it with your foot* ᵈ / *like a vegetable garden* // | 16 | 2 |
| ¹¹ ᵃ*Indeed (such is) the land* / | 6 | 1 |
| which ᵇyou / are going overᵇ there / to possess itᵃ / | 16 | 3_ |
| | | |
| (It) is a land of hills / and valleys // | 13 | 2 |
| (Which) drinks water / by the rain from heaven // | 12 | 2 |
| ¹² A landᵃ / which YHWH *your God* / *cares for* // | 20 | 3_ |
| *Always* / *the eyes of YHWH your God* / *are on it* / | 18 | 3 |
| *From the beginning*ᵇ / *of [the]*ᶜ *year* / | 10 | 2 |
| *to the* / *end of (the)*ᶜ *year* // ם | 10 | 2_ |

### Notes

10.a. DSS, SP, Syr, and some LXX witnesses read 2nd pl as in v 11 below.

10.b. Reading the sequence of ʾ*azlā*ʾ followed by *mahpāk* as disj.

10.c-c. The phrase is missing in some Heb. Mss, perhaps due to homoioarchton.

10.d. SP and some LXX witnesses read pl. MT is to be preferred as the *lectio difficilior* ("more difficult reading"). The term "foot" here is probably a euphemism for penis (see *Comment* below).

11.a-a. Omitted in Vg. Prosodic analysis supports MT.

11.b-b. LXX εἰσπορεύῃ may be reading Heb. אתה בא.

12.a. Tg and some Mss of both SP and Syr read הארץ, which is possible from a prosodic point of view.

12.b. Some Heb. Mss and SP read מראשית.

12.c. Omitting the article with a few Heb. Mss and DSS in the first instance. SP, Syr, and Tg add the article at the end of the verse.

### Form/Structure/Setting

Somewhat analogous to the situation in 1:6b–8, 11:10–12 consists of two short strophes. Vv 10–11a are framed by repetition of the phrase "the land which you are entering [going over there] to possess it." The boundary between the two units is marked by the *Numeruswechsel* at the beginning of v 11. The second strophe consists of two parts, the first of which (vv 11b–12a) is likewise framed, this time by repetition of the term ארץ without the article. The *Numeruswechsel* in v 12 marks the approaching boundary of the pericope as a whole. The final rhythmic unit in v 12b is introduced by the temporal marker תמיד, "always"—that is, "from the beginning of the year to the end of the year."

### Comment

**10–12** The fourfold repetition here of the term ארץ in relation to the promised land is reminiscent of the sevenfold repetition of the same term in the "Song of the Good Land" in 8:7–10. It is interesting to note that the term ארץ is used seven times in the larger pericope of 11:1–12 in reference to the promised land. As G. Braulik has noted in a recent study, key terms frequently appear in Deuteronomy in groups of seven (see "Die Funktion von Siebenergruppierungen im Eudtext des Deuteronomium." In *FS N. Fuglister* [1919] 37–50).

In the parallel passage in Num 16:12–14, Dathan and Abiram claimed that Moses had brought the people "out of a land flowing with milk and honey," that is, Egypt! Perhaps to counter the language in the description of that rebellion, Moses here compares and contrasts Egypt with the promised land: *it is not like the land of Egypt from which you have gone out* (v 10). In Egypt the land had to be irrigated to produce crops, but the land which Yahweh is giving them *drinks water by the rain from heaven* (v 11).

The reference to watering the land by foot has been interpreted in terms of some practice of foot-dug channels through which irrigation waters flowed, as Naville has argued insisting that "the true sense of the expression is to be found in the Egyptian language" (JRAS [1926] 307). The Egyptian word *uar* with the same determinative of the foot has various meanings. Where the word foot is followed by the determinative of water, Renouf translates "canal" and Budge "stream." In short, Egypt was watered with running water. The reference here may also have referred to the *shaduf,* though that was normally operated by hand (see P. Montet, *Egypt and the Bible* [1968] 83–84). The water-wheel *(saqqieh),* which could be operated by foot, was probably not introduced in Egypt until a later point in time. It is more likely, however, that the phrase "watering with the foot" is a form of bowdlerizing as D. M. C. Englert has suggested and meant simply "to urinate" (see *FS J. M. Myers* [1974] 142). L. Eslinger (*VT* 37 [1987] 88) notes that the phrase מימי רגלים ("waters of the feet") appears in similar fashion as the

Qere reading in 2 Kgs 18:27 (= Isa 36:12), in reference to the inhabitants of Jerusalem being forced to eat their own excrement and drink their own urine (שֵׁינֵיהֶם, which is translated "their own piss" in KJV). In his response to Eslinger, G. G. Nicol has seen the significance of the terminology here when he stated (*VT* 38 [1988] 347):

> The comparison is not focused on the means of irrigating the land, but on the land itself. In "the land of Egypt from which you have come," the Israelites possessed little they could call their own, so little, in fact, that a man could well have irrigated all the land he possessed simply by urinating on it. In marked contrast, the land in prospect is "a land of mountains and valleys watered by the rains of heaven."

### Bibliography for Deut 11:13–21

**Arden-Close, C. F.** "The Rainfall of Palestine." *PEQ* 73 (1941) 122–28. **Bee, R. E.** "A Study of Deuteronomy Based on Statistical Properties of the Text." *VT* 29 (1979) 1–22 (5). **Cassuto, U.** "The Second Chapter of the Book of Hosea." In *Biblical and Oriental Studies I: Bible.* Jerusalem: Magnes, 1973. 101–40 (127, 133). **Couroyer, B.** "La tablette du coeur." *RB* 90 (1983) 416–34. **Daniel, D. P.** "Homiletical Helps on LW Series W: Old Testament Readings." *CJ* 13 (1987) 160–77. Finkelstein, L. "An Old Baraita on Deuteronomy." *EI* 10 (1971) 218–20 (Heb., Eng. summary). **Fischer, G.** and **Lohfink, N.** "'Diese Worte sollst du summen': Dtn 6, 7 *weḏibbarta bam*—ein verlorener Schüssel zur meditativen Kultur in Israel." *ThPh* 62 (1987) 59–72. **Floss, J. P.** "Verbfunktionen der Basis HYY." BN 30 (1986) 35–101 (60). **Giesen, G.** *Die Wurzel* שׁבע (1981). 282–83. **Görg, M.** "Ein weiters Beispiel hebraisierter Nominal bildung." *Hen* 3 (1981) 336–39. **Goldin, J.** "Not by Means of an Angel and Not by Means of a Messenger." SHR 14 [=*FS E. R. Goodenough* (1968)]. Leiden: Brill, 1969. 412–24. **Haran, M.** "Priestertum, Tempeldienst und Gebet." In *Das Land in Biblischer Zeit.* Ed. G. Strecker (1983). 141–53 (147). *HOTTP* I, 280. **Keel, O.** "Zeichen der Verbundenheit. Zur Vorgeschichte und Bedeutung der Forderungen von Deuteronomium 6,8f und Par." In *FS. D. Barthélemy* (1981). 159–240. **Meek, T. J.** "Old Testament Notes." *JBL* 67 (1948) 233–39 (235–36). **Miyoshi, M.** "Das jüdische Gebet Šemaᶜ und die Abfolge der Traditionsstücke in Lk 10–13." In AJBI 7 (1981). 70–123. **Ruprecht, E.** "Exodus 24, 9–11 als Beispiel lebendiger Erzähltradition aus der Zeit des babylonischen Exils." In *FS C. Westermann* (1980). 138–73 (160). **Sanmartin Ascaso, J.** *Las guerras de Josué* (1982). 57–58. **Schneider, H.** "Der Dekalog in den Phylakterien von Qumran." *BZ* 3 (1959) 18–30. **Seitz, G.** *Studien zum Deuteronomium* (1971). 87–88.

### Translation and Prosodic Analysis

11:13–21   [(6:5):6:5] [6:(5:5):6] [5:6] [6:5]

| | | |
|---|---:|---:|
| [13] And it shall be / | 5 | 1 |
| if you indeed obey / my [a] commandments / | 15 | 2 |
| which I / command you / TODAY / | 16 | 3 |
| To love / YHWH your God / | 15 | 2 |
| and [b] to serve him / with all your heart / | 10 | 2 |
| and with all your soul-life // | 7 | 1 |
| [14] I [a] will give rain for your [b] land / | 11 | 1 |
| in its season / the early rain and the later rain // | 12 | 2 |

| | | |
|---|---|---|
| (That) *you<sup>c</sup> may gather in your grain /* | ⌐ 10 | 1 |
| *and <sup>d</sup> your wine / and your oil //* | ∟ 13 | 2_ |
| <sup>15</sup> *And I<sup>a</sup> will give / grass in your fields /* | 14 | 2 |
| *for your cattle /* | 4 | 1 |
| *and you<sup>b</sup> shall eat / and you<sup>b</sup> shall be sated //* | <u>13</u> | 2_ |
| | | |
| <sup>16</sup> Take heed / lest your<sup>a</sup> heart / be deceived // | 16 | 3 |
| And you turn aside / and you serve / other gods / | <u>17</u> | 3_ |
| And you bow down \<sup>b</sup> before them // | ⌐ 10 ⌐ | 1 |
| <sup>17</sup> And the anger of YHWH be kindled / against you / | ⌊ 12 ⌋ | 2 |
| And he shut up the heavens / so that there is no rain / | ∟ 19 | 2_ |
| And the earth / yields \<sup>a</sup> no fruit // | ⌐ 19 | 2 |
| And you perish quickly / | ⌊ 9 ⌐ | 2 |
| from off / the good land / | ∟ <u>13</u> ⌋ | 1_ |
| Which YHWH / is giving to you // | 12 | 2 |
| <sup>18</sup> So you shall lay up / these my words (דברי) / | 11 | 2 |
| In your heart / and in your soul-life // | <u>10</u> | 2_ |
| | | |
| And you shall bind them as a sign / upon your hand<s><sup>a</sup> / | ⌐ 16 | 2 |
| And they shall be as frontlets / between your eyes // | ⌊ 19 ⌐ | 2 |
| <sup>19</sup>     and you shall teach them / | ∟ 8 ⌋ | 1_ |
| To your children / speaking (לדבר) of them // | ⌐ 11 ⌐ | 2 |
| *when you are sitting in your<sup>a</sup> house /* | ⌊ 9 ⌋ | 1 |
| *and<sup>b</sup> when you are walking by the way /* | ⌊ 9 ⌋ | 1 |
| *And<sup>c</sup> when you lie down / and when you get up //* | ∟ <u>13</u> ⌋ | 2_ |
| | | |
| <sup>20</sup> *And you<sup>a</sup> shall write them /* | ⌐ 6 | 1 |
| *upon the doorposts of your house<s><sup>b</sup> /* | ∟ 11 | 1 |
| *and upon your<sup>c</sup> gates //* | ⌐ 7 | 1 |
| <sup>21</sup> *That* your days may be multiplied / | ∟ 10 | 1 |
| And the days of your children / upon \<sup>a</sup> the land / | <u>16</u> | 2_ |
| Which YHWH swore / to your fathers / | 14 | 2 |
| to give to them / | 7 | 1 |
| As long as the heavens / are above the earth // ס | 15 | 2_ |

## Notes

13.a. Most LXX witnesses read 3rd sg suffix, "his commandments."

13.b. Some Mss of both Heb. and LXX omit *waw*-conj, which is possible from a prosodic point of view.

14.a. SP, most LXX witnesses, and Vg read ונתן (cf. note 15.a. below). A *mezuzah* text from Qumran which quotes this passage adds further weight to this reading (see DJD 3, 161).

14.b. One Heb. Ms, SP, and LXX read 2nd sg suff.

14.c. Vg reads 2nd pl suff.

14.d. The *waw*-conj is omitted in a few Heb. Mss.

15.a. SP and most LXX witnesses read ונתן (cf. note 14.a. above). Some LXX witnesses read και δώσεις = וְנָתַתָּ. The term is omitted in Vg and Cairo geniza fragments.

15.b. Vg reads 2nd pl.

16.a. Most LXX witnesses read 2nd sg.

16.b. See note 1:1.c.

17.a. See note 1:1.c.

18.a. SP, some LXX Mss, old Latin, Syr, and Vg read יֵדיכם. Prosodic analysis supports MT.

19.a. A few Heb. Mss read בביתך; Cairo geniza fragments read בבאתיך; SP and most LXX witnesses read בְּבֵיתָ (cf. 6:7).

19.b. Omitting waw-conj with SP.

19.c. Waw-conj is omitted in some Heb. Mss and SP.

20.a. LXX, Syr, and Tgᴶ read 2nd pl.

20.b. SP, LXX, Syr, and Tgᴶ read ביתיך (cf. 6:9).

20.c. Most LXX witnesses read 2nd pl suff.

21.a. Reading conj mahpāk.

## Form/Structure/Setting

The boundaries of the strophic units in 11:13–21 are marked with the *s͓tûmā'* paragraph markers at the beginning and end, the *Numeruswechsel* in vv 15 and 19, at the end of strophes one and three, and the words דברי אלה, "these my words" in v 18a, which are reminiscent of the opening words of the book of Deuteronomy, אלה הדברים. The opening strophe (vv 13–15) begins with the word והיה, which stands as a coda outside the carefully balanced rhythmic structure of what follows. The following phrase is introduced by repetition of the key verb שמע, here with the meaning "to obey," followed by the familiar reference to "commandments" (מצות), which calls attention back to the beginning of previous prosodic units in 10:13, 11:1, and 11:8. The requirement of obedience, love, and service is here stated in the form of a conditional sentence. If the condition is met (v 13), Yahweh will bless them with prosperity in the land he is giving them (v 14).

The second strophe (vv 16–19) is introduced with the key verb שמר, "take heed." If the people turn to other gods, Yahweh will remove his provisions and cause them to "*perish quickly from off the good land*" (v 17). The term דברי, "my words," forms an inclusion with the words מצותי, "my commandments," in v 13. It is interesting to note the similarity in prosodic structure between the first two strophes in terms of both mora-count (145//148) and distribution of syntactic accentual stress units: [6:5:6:5] over against [6:5:5:6].

The third and fourth strophes (vv 18b–19 and 20–21) are also of equal length in terms of mora count (85//86) and together make up a similar prosodic unit to the first two strophes in terms of the distribution of syntactic accentual stress units, namely [5:6:6:5]. Strophe three (vv 18b–19) opens with the verb קשר, "to bind," and concerns the use of phylacteries, whereas strophe four (vv 20–21) begins with the verb כתב, "to write," and deals with specific texts which are to be placed "upon the doorposts [*mezuzoth*] of your houses." These "commandments" (v 13) constitute God's "words" (v 18a), which are to be kept central as a teaching device for the children. The promise of prosperity in the land if the commandments are kept as long "as the heavens are above the earth" (v 21) forms an inclusion with the similar promise of prosperity in strophe one (vv 13–14).

## Comment

**13–15** In the larger structural design of 10:12–11:25, the command *to love Yahweh your God and to serve him with all your soul and with all your soul-life* (v 13) stands in parallel with the same command in 10:12 and 10:20, which in turn echo the Great Commandment of 6:5. For stylistic reasons Moses uses the 1st sg of direct quotation of the words of God at the beginning of each of the verses here. The mixing of 1st and 3rd person forms is somewhat comparable to that of 1:8 above. The fact that such usage is unexpected is illustrated by frequent emendation in the early versions and the quotation of this passage found in a *mezuzah* text from Qumran (see DJD 3, 161).

*The early rain and the later rain* (v 14) refers to the beginning and end of the rainy season in Palestine, which extends approximately from October to April. God promised to provide seasonal rain, and prosperity in crops and livestock, so long as the people live according to his commandments.

**16–17** T. J. Meek (*JBL* 67 [1948] 235–6) argued that the verb פתה means "to be open," for which he finds support in the LXX. The alternate translation he proposed is: "Take care lest you become so open-minded that . . . " If the Israelites turn to the Canaanite god Baal/Hadad as the giver of rain, God will *shut up the heavens so that there is no rain* and the people will *perish quickly from off the good land* (v 17), which Yahweh has given them.

**18–21** The command to *lay up these my words in your heart* functions as a bridge forming an inclusion with the command in v 13 *to love Yahweh your God . . . with all your heart*, on the one hand, and introducing the specific *words* of God, on the other hand, which are to be written on phylacteries (vv 18b–19) and *the doorposts of your houses* (vv 20–21). The content of vv 18–21 is summary in nature and is discussed in detail above in parallel passages: v 18 in 6:8; v 19 in 4:9–10 and 6:7; v 20 in 6:9; and v 21 in 4:40 and 6:2.

### Explanation

The basic requirement of obedience, love, and service appears here in the form of a condition. If the people are faithful, they will receive provision and prosperity in the promised land, the fertility of which is spelled out in some detail (11:14–15). The previous illustration in 11:9–12 had contrasted the past with the future. The focus here is entirely on the future. The reference to the danger of apostasy in 11:16 is introduced so that the Israelites will be careful to recognize Yahweh as the giver of rain and not the Canaanite god Baal/Hadad. If they fail to do so, God will "shut up the heavens so that there is no rain and the earth yields no fruit" (11:17).

The substance of 11:18–21 is essentially repetition of material presented earlier in Deut 4–6. It is a restatement of the essential features of the basic commandments of the covenant, which sets the stage for the detailed recitation of the law in Deut 12–26.

### Bibliography for Deut 11:22–25

**Anbar, M.** "Genesis 15: A Conflation of Two Deuteronomic Narratives." *JBL* 101 (1982) 39–55 (51–52). **Coppens, J.** "La doctrine biblique sur l'amour de Dieu et du prochain." *ETL* 40 (1964) 252–99 (269). **Diepold, P.** *Israels Land.* BWANT 95. Stuttgart, 1972. 31–32. **Doron, P.** "Motive Clauses in the Law of Deuteronomy: Their Forms, Functions and Contents." In *HAR* 2 (1978). 61–77 (66). *HOTTP* I, 280. **Lohfink, N.** "Dtn 12, 1 und Gen 15, 18: Das dem Samen Abrahams geschenkte Land als der Geltungsbereich der deuteronomischen Gesetze." In *FS J. Scharbert* (1989). 183–210 (204–7). **Lubetski, M.** "New Light on Old Seas."

*JQR* 68 (1977) 65–77. **Nelson, R. D.** "Josiah in the Book of Joshua." *JBL* 100 (1981) 531–40. **Weinfeld, M.** "Zion and Jerusalem as Religious and Political Capital." In *The Poet and the Historian.* Ed. R. E. Friedman. HSS 26. Chico: Scholars, 1983. 75–115 (98–99). **Wiener, H. M.** "Zur Deuteronomiumfrage." *MGWJ* 72 (1928) 24–48.

### Translation and Prosodic Analysis

11:22–25    [(6:5):6:6:(5:6)]

| | | |
|---|---|---|
| [22] For if you will be careful to keep / all this commandment / | 19 | 2 |
| which I / command you[a] / <TODAY>[b] / | 16 | 3 |
| to do it // | 6 | 1_ |
| To love / YHWH your[c] God / | 15 | 2 |
| <and>[d] to walk |[d] in all his way / and to cleave to him // | _21_ | 3_ |
| [23] YHWH will drive out / all these nations / | 20 | 2 |
| from before you[a] // | 5 | 1 |
| And you will dispossess nations / | 8 | 1 |
| greater and mightier / than you[a] // | _13_ | 2_ |
| [24] Every place / on which the sole of our foot treads / | 15 | 2 |
| on it / shall be yours // | 8 | 2 |
| From the wilderness and the Lebanon / | 12 | 1 |
| from[a] the River,[b] the river Euphrates / | _11_ | 1_ |
| Yea, as far as the western sea / it shall be / your territory // | 17 | 3 |
| [25] No man shall be able to stand \[a] against [b] you // | 12 ] | 1 |
| (for) the fear of you and the dread of you / | 10 ⌐ | 1_ |
| YHWH your God / will put (it) / upon the whole land / | 22 | 3 |
| on which you shall tread / as / he said (דבר) to you // ס | _16_ | 3_ |

### Notes

22.a. LXX[B] reads 2nd sg.

22.b. Adding היום with some Heb. Mss, SP, LXX (including Origen), and Syr.

22.c. Most LXX witnesses read τὸν θεὸν ἡμῶν.

22.d. Adding *waw*-conj with Cairo geniza fragments, LXX[B], Syr, and Vg. An additional disj accent is read to form a closer rhythmic balance over against vv 24d–25.

23.a. SP reads 2nd sg suff.

24.a. A few Heb. Mss, SP, LXX, and Syr add *waw*-conj.

24.b. A few Heb. Mss, Cairo geniza fragments, LXX, Vg, and Tg[J] add הגדול.

25.a. See note 1:1.c.

25.b. SP reads לפניכם.

### Form/Structure/Setting

In both content and rhythmic structure 11:22–25 is closely connected with 11:13–21. The basic [11:11] rhythmic pattern, which is repeated three times in vv 13–21, is here used as a frame into which a [6:6] unit (vv 23–24c) is inserted. The parallels in length of the subunits here, in terms of mora-count, are striking: 77 + (46 + 46) + 77 morae respectively. The content of the whole may be outlined as follows:

| A | Condition: If you keep "this commandment" (11:22) | [6:5] |
|---|---|---|
| B | Yahweh will dispossess "these nations from before you" (11:23) | [6] |
| B' | Every place you tread shall be yours (11:24a–c) | [6] |
| A' | Result: The whole of this land is yours (11:24d–25). | [5:6] |

## Comment

**22–25** The opening verse once again repeats the basic requirement of obedience and love which is found at the outset of the previous subunits in 10:12–13; 11:1; and 11:13 (see also Deut 6:1). The summary nature of the content continues, in reference to the following parallel passages where the language is discussed in detail: v 23 in 4:38 and 9:1; v 24 in 1:7–8; and v 25 in 2:25 and 7:23–24.

הים האחרון, "the western sea"—M. Lubetski argues that the Targum views this sea as legendary rather than actual (*JQR* 68 [1977] 72. See also his doctoral dissertation, *Maritime Horizons of the Jews in the Talmudic Period* [New York Univ., 1976] 152–61). But even though it is considered a mythological sea, it has a geographical location. It is to the west, "indeed to the far west of Israel" (*JQR* 68 [1977] 73). See Deut 34:2, where the phrase is rendered "the hinder or last sea" in the Targum, which suggests that it is beyond the Mediterranean (i.e., the western half of the Mediterranean or perhaps the Atlantic Ocean).

## Bibliography for Deut 11:26–32

**Brichto, H. C.** *The Problem of 'Curse' in the Hebrew Bible.* JBLMonSer 13. Philadelphia: Society of Biblical Literature and Exegesis, 1963. 183. **Dexinger, F.** "Das Garizimgebot in Dekalog der Samaritaner." In *FS W. Kornfeld* (1977). 111–33 (126–29). **Eerdmans, B. D.** *Deuteronomy.* Ed. D. C. Simpson. London: Griffin & Co., 1927. 77–84 (78). **Eissfeldt, O.** "Gilgal oder Sichem (Dtn 11, 29–32; 27, 11–13; 27, 1–8; Jos 8, 30–35). In *KlSchr* (1973). V, 165–73. **Gemser, B.** *Be῾ēber hajjardēn:* In Jordan's Borderland." *VT* 2 (1952) 349–55 (350). *HOTTP* I, 281. **Jacob ben Aaron.** "Mount Gerizim: The One True Sanctuary." *BSac* 64 (1907) 489–518 (496–97). **Kuenen, H. H.** "Bijdragen tot de critiek van Pentateuch en Jozua. V: De godsdienstige vergadering bij Ebal en Garizim (Deut. XI: 29, 30; XXVII; Joz VIII: 30–35)." *TT* 12 (1887) 297–323. **Lohfink, N.** *Das Hauptgebot* (1963). 233–34. L'Hour, J. "L'alliance de Sichem." *RB* 69 (1962) 5–36, 161–84 (166–68). **Nyberg, H. S.** "Studien zum Religionskampf im Alten Testament." *ARW* 35 (1938) 329–87 (367). **Rothstein, W.** *Juden und Samaritaner.* BWAT 3. Leipzig: J. C. Hinrichs, 1908. **Schmidt, W.** "Zum Baumbestand des Garizim." *ZDPV* 78 (1962) 89–90. **Seebass, H.** "Garizim und Ebal als Symbole von Segen und Fluch." *Bib* 63 (1982) 22–131. **Tigay, J. H.** "Conflation as a Redactional Technique." In *Empirical Models for Biblical Criticism.* Ed. J. H. Tigay. Philadelphia: Pennsylvania UP, 1985. 53–89. **Wächter, L.** "Das Baumheiligtum bei Sichem." *FolOr* 17 (1976) 71–86 (75).

## Translation and Prosodic Analysis

11:26–32   [(7:6:6):7] [(6:4:4):6] [4:(4:6)]

| | | |
|---|---|---|
| [26] *See!* [a] / | 3 | 1 |
| I / *am setting before* you / TODAY // | 17 | 3 |
| a blessing / and a curse // | ⌈ 11 | 2 |
| [27]    (as for) the blessing // | ⌊ 7 | 1 ⌋ |

|                                                                          |      |     |
|--------------------------------------------------------------------------|------|-----|
| (It is) for those who obey /                                             | 7 ⌐  | 1   |
| the commandments / of YHWH your God /                                    | 13 ⌐ | 2   |
| which I / am commanding you / TODAY //                                   | 16 ⌐ | 3_  |
| 28 And the curse / (it is) if you do not / obey /                        | 14   | 3   |
| the commandments / of YHWH your God /                                    | 13 ⌐ | 2   |
| and you turn aside from the way /                                        | 7 ⌐  | 1_  |
| Which I / am commanding you / TODAY //                                   | 16   | 3   |
| to go / after /                                                          | 8    | 2   |
| other gods / whom you have not known // ס                               | 17   | 2_  |
|                                                                          |      |     |
| 29 And it shall be /                                                     | 5    | 1   |
| when *YHWH your God* / *brings you* / *into the land* /                  | 21 ⌐ | 3   |
| *which you are about to enter there* / *to possess it* //                | 14 ⌐ | 2_  |
| *Then you shall set the blessing* / *on Mount Gerizim*ᵃ /               | 20 ⌐ | 2   |
| *and the curse* / *on Mount Ebal* //                                     | 14 ⌐ | 2_  |
| 30 *Are they*ᵃ *not* / *in the vicinity of the Jordan* /                | 14 ⌐ | 2   |
| *beyond* \ᵇ *the "Western Road"* / *in the land of the Canaanites* /    | 21 ⌐ | 2_  |
| *Who live* / *in the Arabah* /                                           | 12   | 2   |
| *opposite* / *Gilgal* /                                                  | 6    | 2   |
| *Beside* / *the oaks*ᶜ *of Moreh*ᵈ ? //                                 | 12   | 2_  |
|                                                                          |      |     |
| 31 For you / are about to cross over the Jordan /                        | 14   | 2   |
| To go in / to possess the land /                                         | 14   | 2_  |
| Which YHWH your God / is giving you //                                   | 18 ⌐ | 2   |
| and you shall possess itᵃ / and you shall live in it //                 | 14 ⌐ | 2_  |
| 32 And you shall be careful to do /                                      | 8    | 1   |
| allᵃ the statutes / and the judgments //                                | 15 ⌐ | 2   |
| which I / am giving you / TODAY //ᵇ                                      | 19 ⌐ | 3_  |

## Notes

26.a. The term ראה is missing in two Heb. Mss. Prosodic analysis suggests that it lies outside the rhythmic structure in terms of mora-count, since the next three lines scan 35+35+34 morae without it. Tgᴶ and two Syr Mss read 2nd pl form, but all parallel usages in Deuteronomy within MT are in the sg.

29.a. Reading גריזים with SP. Note that there is no *dagesh* in the *zayin* here or in 27:12. The term is counted five morae.

30.a. SP reads הלוא הם. Prosodic analysis favors MT.

30.b. Reading the conj accent *mahpāk.*

30.c. Reading אלון with LXX, Syr, *a′σ′θ′* and SPᵂ; cf. Gen 12:6.

30.d. One Heb. Ms and SP read מורא; Syr and Tg read ממרא; SP adds מול שכם.

31.a. LXX adds כל־הימים from Deut 4:40.

32.a. The כל may be omitted as secondary, to improve the rhythmic balance here in terms of mora-count.

32.b. Though there is no pᵉtûḥāʾ paragraph marker in *BHS* or *BHK,* the boundary between chaps. 11 and 12 clearly marks a major division in the structure of Deuteronomy.

## Form/Structure/Setting

In terms of prosodic structure, this closing unit in the first half of the Inner Frame (Deut 4–11) is in three parts, the boundaries of which are clearly marked in MT—by the *setumaᵓ* paragraph marker after v 28 and the *Numeruswechsel* in vv 29 and 31. The content of this section is summary in nature and may be outlined as follows:

| | |
|---|---|
| The blessing and the curse are before you (vv 26–28) | [7:6:6:7] |
| Set the blessing on Gerizim and the curse on Ebal (v 29–30) | [6:4:4:6] |
| When you enter the land, observe the commandments (vv 31–32) | [4:4:6] |

Though one could argue that the first and last of these subunits form a fitting balance to each other in terms of content, it is difficult to see a concentric design in the content of this brief unit. Threefold repetition of the temporal marker היום serves to divide vv 26–28 into two parts, both of which are concluded by the clause "which I am commanding you today" (vv 27 and 28). It is also possible to interpret the opening term of this unit ראה as an instance of the *Numeruswechsel,* since the 2nd sg form is followed almost immediately by the 2nd pl suff on לפניכם. It should be noted, however, that this term seems to lie outside the prosodic structure here and is omitted in some significant textual witnesses.

The *Numeruswechsel* at the beginning and end of the second subunit mark off vv 29–30 as the center of the larger structure of vv 26–32 as a whole. The content clearly anticipates the beginning of the second half of the Inner Frame in Deut 27:1–8, which depicts the covenant ceremony at Shechem. That ceremony features blessings delivered by six of the tribal groups from Mount Gerizim (27:11–14) and an elaborate list of curses delivered from Mount Ebal (27:15–26) by representatives from the other six tribal groups. The presentation of covenant blessings and curses continues in chap. 28.

The final two verses in this section of the Inner Frame (Deut 4–11) restate the central theme of Deut as a whole: when you "cross over the Jordan to go in to possess the land, . . . be careful to do all the statutes and judgments which I am giving you today."

## Comment

**26–28** For a discussion of the usages of the term ראה in Deuteronomy, see the *Comment* on 1:8 and the *Excursus:* "Travel Notices in the Outer Frame of Deuteronomy." The focus here is clearly on the "present" with three occurrences of the term היום, *today.* The people are reminded that their future existence in the land depends on their response to God's commandments, which will result in either *blessing* or *curse.* For more detailed discussion of the covenant blessings and curses within the context of the ceremony of covenant renewal on the plains of Moab, see Deut 28. Once again it becomes clear how the commandments are much more than a mere body of legislation but, rather, a way of life. One disobeys God's commandments by *turn[ing] aside from the way,* that is, by *go[ing] after other gods* (v 28). In the detailed exposition of the law, which follows in Deut 12–26, Moses is not so much a jurist as he is a spokesman for God, one who knows in his heart what God requires of his people, if they are to know the fullness of life he desires for them. The covenant relationship is the only way for the people of Israel to experience a lasting relationship with the covenant God.

**29–30** The focus here shifts to the future, *when Yahweh your God brings you into the land which you are about to enter*, and the regular renewal of the covenant at Shechem (v 29). For a discussion of the relation of this passage, and its context, to Deut 27 and Josh 8:30–35, see O. Eissfeldt, "Gilgal and Shechem" (in *FS G. H. Davies* [1970] 90–101), though his attempts to separate the layers of tradition as it relates to these two places is problematic. The location of Mount Gerizim and Mount Ebal is specified in v 30 as across the Jordan and beyond the "Western Road" (literally, the Hebrew reads "the road of the setting of the sun"), which probably indicates the road up the Jordan Valley from Jericho to Bethshan, as Craigie has suggested (NICOT [1976] 213). The Arabah is the great rift valley, extending from the Sea of Galilee in the north to the Gulf of Aqaba in the south. Here the region of the Jordan Valley going north from the Dead Sea is in view. The location of Gilgal is problematic, since the most explicit statement within the so-called deuteronomic tradition places it "on the east border of [the territory of] Jericho" (Josh 4:19), the site of the "battle camp" from which early Israel launched the Conquest. Here it seems to be in the vicinity of Shechem, in light of the specific reference to *the oaks of Moreh* (cf. Gen 12:6 for Abraham's association with this place). One way to explain the apparent shifting of the location of Gilgal within the traditions of ancient Israel is to note its centrality within the worship of pre-monarchic Israel (see *Excursus:* "Holy War as Celebrated Event in Ancient Israel"). For a brief, but excellent, survey of the relevant textual evidence (with bibliography), see W. H. Brownlee's article on "Gilgal" in *ISBE* 2 (1982) 470–72. See also my article on "The March of Conquest in Isaiah X 27c–34," *VT* 26 (1976) 385–99. An original cultic march probably went from the vicinity of Shechem to Jericho, and back, perhaps by way of Wadi Farah as reflected in this text. Later the route seems to have been up the so-called Taiba pass, from behind the ruins of "Old Testament Jericho," to Ai and Bethel and then on to Shiloh. Still later, the route was apparently changed to make its final destination that of Jerusalem, which is what Isaiah had in mind. For a map of the "Route of the Conquest" see D. Christensen, *Prophecy and War in Ancient Israel* (Berkeley: BIBAL Press, 1989), 148.

**31–32** This summary statement of the "crossing over" of the Jordan *to possess the land which Yahweh your God is giving you* (v 31) probably reflects the traditions of "Holy War as Celebrated Event" (see *Excursus*). The Exodus-Conquest constitutes Israel's primary epic story. The way to *live in* the promised land is to *be careful to do all the statutes and the judgments which I am giving you today* (v 32). The two go together. The memory of Yahweh's "Holy War" of the Exodus-Conquest tradition should be sufficient motivation to ensure covenant fidelity on the part of Yahweh's people.

### Explanation

Deut 11:26–32 functions as both the conclusion to the first half of the Inner Frame (chaps. 4–11) and the introduction to the second half of the Inner Frame (chaps. 27–30). In the latter role this section is closely tied to Deut 27–28 in terms of literary structure, as Craigie has noted (NICOT [1976] 212). That framework may be outlined as follows:

A       Blessing and curse in *present* covenant renewal (11:26–28)
  B         Blessing and curse in *future* covenant renewal (11:29–32)
  B'        Blessing and curse in *future* covenant renewal (27:1–26)
A'      Blessing and curse in *present* covenant renewal (28:1–29:1)

In short, Deut 11:26–32 is carefully worked out in terms of literary structure to form a concentric framework around the specific legislation contained in the Central Core (chaps. 12–26), to which we now turn our full attention. What is of primary importance is the simple fact that the deuteronomic blessing and curse are contingent upon obedience to the covenant legislation both in the present and in the future, so far as God's people are concerned.

It is important to note that the commandments to follow were not to be taken as simply a body of legislation but as a way of life. Thus to disobey the commandments is to "turn aside from the way" (11:28). Moses is not presented so much as a great jurist or giver of the law, but as a pastor/teacher. His task is to see that the people under his charge experience the good life, in all its fullness, that constitutes the potential for each member of the community within the context of the covenant relationship with their God.